# THE SPORTS ILLUSTRATED

# 1993

# PRO & COLLEGE FOOTBALL ALMANAC

**By The Editors Of Sports Illustrated**

## LITTLE, BROWN AND COMPANY

Boston • Toronto • London

*Sports Illustrated 1993 Pro & College Football Almanac* was produced by
Bishop Books of New York City.

Back cover photography credits:
top (O.J. Simpson): Neil Leifer
middle (Red Grange): UPI/Bettmann Newsphotos
bottom (Troy Aikman): John W. McDonough

COM

Published simultaneously in Canada by
Little, Brown & Company (Canada) Limited

PRINTED IN THE UNITED STATES OF AMERICA

In compiling the *Sports Illustrated 1993 Pro and College Football Almanac*, the editors would like to thank the media relations offices of the following organizations for their assistance in providing information and materials relating to their organizations: Canadian Football League; National Football League; National Collegiate Athletic Association.

The following sources were consulted in gathering information:

**Pro Football:** *The Official 1992 National Football League Record & Fact Book*, The National Football League, 1992; *The Official National Football League Encyclopedia*, New American Library, 1990; *The Sporting News Football Guide*, The Sporting News Publishing Co., 1992; *The Sporting News Football Register*, The Sporting News Publishing Co., 1992; *The Sporting News Complete Super Bowl Book*, The Sporting News Publishing Co., 1992; *The Sports Encyclopedia: Pro Football*, by David S. Neft and Richard M. Cohen, St. Martin's Press, 1988; *Pro Football Hall of Fame All-Time Greats*, by Don R. Smith, Gallery Books, 1988; *The Encyclopedia of Football*, by Roger Treat, A. S. Barnes and Co., 1979; *The Super Bowl: Celebrating a Quarter Century of America's Greatest Game*, Simon and Schuster, 1990; *NFL Top 40: The Greatest Pro Football Games of All Time*, by Shelby Strother, Viking/Penguin Inc., 1988.

**College Football:** *1992 NCAA Football*, The National Collegiate Athletic Association, 1992; *Who's Who in Football*, by Ronald L. Mendell and Timothy B. Phares, Arlington House, 1974; *Biographical Dictionary of American Sports: Football*, edited by David L. Porter, Greenwood Press, 1987.

# CONTENTS

**CRUNCH TIME**
*Super Bowl
Sunday was hardly
super for Kenneth
Davis and the
Buffalo Bills, who
were stopped
52–17 by Ken
Norton and
the Dallas
Cowboys.*

JOHN BIEVER

**Jan 1, 1992**—Washington and Miami conclude perfect 12–0 seasons as the Huskies defeat Michigan 34–14 in the Rose Bowl and the Hurricanes blank Nebraska 22–0 in the Orange Bowl. The two share the national championship when the Associated Press media poll ranks Miami No. 1 and Washington No. 2, and the USA Today/CNN coaches poll reverses that order.

**Jan 16**—Bill Walsh, who coached Stanford to a 17–7 record during the 1977–1978 seasons and then led the 49ers to three Super Bowl titles in the 1980s, announces that he will return to Stanford as head coach with a five-year contract reportedly worth $350,000 a year.

**Jan 21**—Heisman Trophy winner Desmond Howard announces that he will pass up his final year of eligibility at Michigan and turn pro.

**Jan 31**—Washington defensive tackle Steve Emtman announces he will forego his final year of eligibility and enter the NFL draft.

**Aug 26**—The season opens at the Disneyland Pigskin Classic with seventh-ranked Texas A&M spoiling Stanford coach Bill Walsh's return to the college sidelines, 10–7, on a fourth quarter field goal. The next day, the campaign begins in the East with N.C. State upsetting Iowa, 24–14, in the Kickoff Classic at Giants Stadium.

**Aug 28**—Former sports agent Lloyd Bloom pleads guilty to a mail fraud charge related to his practice of secretly signing college players to pro contracts, and is sentenced to five years probation and 500 hours of community service.

**Sep 5**—Former Nebraska rb Scott Baldwin, under psychiatric care after his January attack on a Lincoln woman, is shot in the chest and paralyzed during a fight with Omaha police.

**Emtman opted for the greener pro pastures.**

**Sep 5**—Adjusting to an interrupted practice schedule and a change in training site due to Hurricane Andrew, the University of Miami Hurricanes, whose nickname comes from a tragedy of the school's early days, wins its opener, 24–7 at Iowa, behind Gino Torretta's 433 passing yards.

**Sep 10**—Sophomore Marshall Faulk rambles for 299 yards and three touchdowns to lead San Diego State to a 45–38 win over Brigham Young. The previous week he gained 220 yards in a 31–31 tie with USC.

**Sep 12**—For the first time in 23 meetings dating back to 1887, Michigan and Notre Dame play to a tie as the Irish botch their last possession and the clock runs out with the score at 17 apiece.

**Sep 12**—Charlie Ward quarterbacks Florida State to a 24–20 victory over Clemson before 83,500 in tiny Clemson, South Carolina in a battle for Atlantic Coast Conference supremacy.

**Sep 19**—The Washington Huskies defeat the Nebraska Cornhuskers 29–14 in an early meeting of national powers. In another PAC-10-Big Eight matchup, Southern California scores 20 fourth quarter points and downs Oklahoma 20–10.

**Sep 19**—Tennessee shocks fourth-ranked Florida 31–14 in Knoxville without coach Johnny Majors, who is recuperating from heart surgery. Majors returns the following week to lead the Vols over Cincinnati, 40–0, and to a 4–0 record.

**Sep 19**—In a game *Sports Illustrated* tabs as the year's most exciting, Texas A&I defeats Portland State 44–43. Portland State leads 21–0 in the first quarter and 43–30 in the fourth, but Texas A&I completes the winning six-yard touchdown pass with 54 seconds to play. The game ends with Texas A&I intercepting Portland State quarterback John Charles's pass in the end zone.

**Sep 26**—David Palmer comes back from a three-game suspension for drunken driving offenses and leads Alabama to their 14th consecutive win, 13–0 over Louisiana Tech. Palmer's 63-yard punt return for a touchdown in the fourth quarter breaks open the tight game.

**Oct 3**—It's déjà vu when, for the second straight year, a Florida State kicker misses wide right in the final minute against Miami and the Hurricanes prevail, this time by 19–16. Miami won 8–7 the previous week as 27-point underdog Arizona saw its upset bid sail, you guessed it, wide right with a 51-yard field goal attempt on the game's final play.

**Oct 10**—Tennessee falls from the unbeaten ranks when Arkansas' Todd Wright kicks a 41-yard field goal with two seconds remaining to give the 2–4 Razorbacks a 25–24 victory over the top-five Volunteers, who fall to 5–1.

**Oct 11**—On the strength of their second straight three-point victory against a top five team, 17–14 over Penn State, the Miami Hurricanes regain the top spot in the *USA Today/CNN* poll by one point over Washington. *The Associated Press* poll reverses the order, the vote going to the Huskies, also by a single point.

**Oct 17**—Unbeaten Alabama collects its 17th consecutive victory, 17–10, over Tennessee, to take a two-game lead in the West division of the newly realigned SEC. The Tide is 7–0.

**Oct 17**—Trailing 47–21 after 40 straight points by Iowa State, 25th-ranked Kansas makes the greatest comeback in school history behind quarterback Chip Hilleary's second-half heroics to win 50–47. The victory was the first for Kansas at Iowa State since 1981 and spoiled an impressive display by the Iowa State offense, which gained 516 yards against Kansas's heralded defense.

**Oct 18**—For the first time in 51 years, and the second time since the poll started in 1936, two teams, Miami and Washington, tie for No. 1 in the Associated Press poll, each receiving 1,517 points from a nationwide panel of sports writers and broadcasters.

**Oct 24**—Washington State, which had turned heads by running its record to 6–0, loses its first game of the year, 31–21, to USC—a team it has not beaten on the road in 36 years.

**Oct 24**—The Michigan Wolverines play their 1,000th game since their opener on May 30, 1879 against Racine, and the result is a 63–13 trouncing of Minnesota for their 728th victory in 113 seasons. The following week Syracuse plays its 1,000th game, becoming the fourth Division I-A college team, along with Navy and Rutgers, to reach the milestone in its 41–10 pasting of Pittsburgh.

**Oct 31**—Coach Bobby Bowden of Florida State notches his 150th victory at Florida State as his Seminoles, in their first season in the conference, wrap up the ACC title with a 13–3 victory over Virginia.

**Oct 31**—Navy sinks, 28–7, to Notre Dame for their 29th consecutive defeat to the Irish, while 14th-ranked Penn State loses for the third time in its last four outings, 30–17, to Brigham Young. Nebraska wins 52–7 over Colorado, with whom they shared the No. 8 ranking in the AP poll. The loss ends Colorado's 25-game Big Eight unbeaten streak.

AL TIELEMANS

**Bowden racked up his 150th victory at FSU.**

**Nov 5**—The University of Washington suspends Husky quarterback Billy Joe Hobert for the upcoming game against Arizona after learning that Hobert received $50,000 in loans from a friend's father-in-law the previous spring.

**Nov 7**—After losing its quarterback two days before, Washington loses its unbeaten status, its No. 1 rating and, as becomes clear later, its shot at a national championship, in a 16–3 defeat to Arizona at Tucson. Arizona has knocked off Stanford and Washington and come within a point of Miami. Stanford prevents Southern California from moving into a tie with Washington for first in the PAC-10 with a 23–9 home victory.

**Nov 7**—Ninth ranked Boston College brings its 7-0-1 record to Notre Dame for its first test of the season on the national stage and suffers its third worst defeat in school history, 54–7.

**Nov 10**—Quarterback Billy Joe Hobert is declared ineligible to play intercollegiate athletics by the University of Washington after athletic director Barbara Hedges says an investigation determined that the $50,000 in no-interest loans he received from the father-in-law of a friend were improper. The school is later absolved of responsibility in the matter.

**Nov 14**—San Diego State's Marshall Faulk runs for 300 yards and four touchdowns, breaking out of a four game slump as his team defeats Hawaii 52–28 to delay the 24th-ranked Rainbows' clinching of the Western Athletic Conference title.

JOHN BIEVER

**Sherwin Williams' TD helped the Tide to the title.**

**Nov 14**—The Crimson Tide of Alabama rolls to its 20th consecutive victory with a 30–21 defeat of Mississippi State and clinches a spot in the inaugural Southeastern Conference championship game.

**Nov 21**—Columbia University wins its second in a row, 34–28, over Brown, for its first two-game winning streak since 1978.

**Nov 23**—Ron Dickerson becomes the only current African-American head football coach in Division I-A when Temple University signs him to a five-year contract. The former defensive coordinator at Clemson, Dickerson has his work cut out for him as the Owls have had eight losing seasons in the last 10, including a 1–10 mark this year.

**Nov 25**—On the eve of his team's annual "bragging rights" showdown with Alabama, Auburn coach Pat Dye resigns, citing poor health and a pending NCAA investigation into his program. Dye's tenure at Auburn included four Southeastern Conference titles but ended with nine charges of rules violations by the NCAA. The next day the Tigers are shut out by Alabama for the first time since 1975, gaining only 20 yards rushing in a 17–0 defeat.

**Nov 28**—The Miami Hurricanes conclude their second consecutive undefeated regular season and their fourth in the last seven years with a 63–17 rout of San Diego State.

**Dec 5**—On the strength of Antonio Langham's 26-yard interception return for a touchdown with 3:25 remaining, Alabama wins the Southeastern Conference championship game 28–21 over Florida, to post a 12–0 regular season record and set up a showdown with 11–0, No.1-ranked Miami in the Sugar Bowl.

**Dec 10**—Alabama coach Gene Stallings, who played for Bear Bryant at Texas A&M and was on his staff at Alabama, wins the Bear Bryant award as the college football coach of the year.

**Dec 11**—Johnny Majors returns to the head coaching post at Pittsburgh, where he guided teams to three bowl appearances and one national championship from 1973–1976. In November, he learned he'd be ousted after the season from the head coaching position he'd held for 16 years at his alma mater, Tennessee, where he had gone 63-23-5 since 1985.

**Dec 12**—Miami quarterback Gino Torretta wins the 58th Heisman Trophy as the nation's top college football player. Sophomore running back Marshall Faulk of San Diego State finishes second and Georgia junior Garrison Hearst, also a running back, is third.

**Dec 12**—Jacksonville (AL) State takes the NCAA Division II title with a 17–13 victory over Pittsburg State. Wisconsin-LaCrosse wins the Amos Alonzo Stagg Bowl for the Division III Championship with a 16–12 win over Washington & Jefferson.

**Dec 14**—Earle Bruce, dismissed Nov. 23 as coach at Colorado State, reaches a contract settlement with the school that will pay him an estimated $110,000 in salary and benefits. The university detailed charges against Bruce of mental and physical abuse of players and NCAA violations after the community rallied around him.

**Dec 19**—Playing at their home stadium in Huntington, WV, Marshall University overcomes an impressive rally by Youngstown State to win the Division I-AA national championship game by a 31–28 score. Youngstown State comes back from a 28–0 deficit to tie the game late in the fourth quarter, but Marshall wins it on Willy Merrick's 22-yard field goal with 10 seconds left.

**Jan 1, 1993**—Stanford secures its first 10-victory season in 52 years, beating Penn State 24–3 in the Blockbuster Bowl. In the Cotton Bowl, Notre Dame crushes unbeaten Texas A&M, 28–3, spoiling the Aggies national championship hopes. Michigan avenges last season's Rose Bowl defeat with a 38–31 win over Washington, and Florida State wins 27–14 over Nebraska in the Orange Bowl. Syracuse takes an exciting 26–22 win from Colorado in the Fiesta Bowl.

**Jan 1**—Alabama stuns Miami with 14 third quarter points in the Sugar Bowl on the way to a lopsided 34–13 victory, ending the Hurricanes' 29-game winning streak and completing a perfect 13–0–0 season to capture its first national title since 1979.

**Dec 26, 1991**—After 23 seasons, 12 playoff appearances, and four Super Bowl victories, Chuck Noll resigns as head coach of the Pittsburgh Steelers. He is replaced on Jan. 21 by 34-year-old Bill Cowher, former defensive coordinator for the Kansas City Chiefs.

**Dec 27**—The Cincinnati Bengals hire 32-year-old David Shula, making him the youngest head coach in NFL history and establishing, along with Miami Dolphin coach Don Shula, the first-ever father-son pair of head coaches in the league.

**Jan 10, 1992**—Stanford's Dennis Green becomes the NFL's second African-American head coach when he is hired by the Minnesota Vikings to replace the retiring Jerry Burns, the Minnesota coach since 1986.

**Jan 12**—Buffalo beats Denver 10–7 in the AFC Championship to advance to the Super Bowl against Washington, a 41–10 winner over Detroit in the NFC title game.

**Jan 25**—Two longtime rebels, L.A. Raider managing general partner Al Davis and tight end John Mackey, are voted into the Pro Football Hall of Fame along with defensive back Lem Barney and running back John Riggins.

**Jan 26**—The Washington Redskins, led by quarterback and game MVP Mark Rypien, defeat the Buffalo Bills 37–24 in Super Bowl XXVI, played at the Hubert H. Humphrey Metrodome in Minneapolis.

**Sanders was named the MVP in the NFC.**

DAMIAN STROHMEYER

**Feb 2**—Jerry Rice's 12-yard TD reeption of a Chris Miller pass with 4:04 to play gives the NFC a 21–15 triumph over the AFC in the Pro Bowl.

**Feb 24**—In polling of NFL players conducted by *USA Today,* Detroit Lions running back Barry Sanders and Buffalo Bills running back Thurman Thomas are voted NFC and AFC most valuable players, respectively.

**Mar 18**—Ending a five-year "experiment," NFL owners fail to vote in sufficient numbers to retain instant replay as an officiating tool.

**Mar 30**—The New Orleans Saints match the Detroit Lions' three-year, $5.475 million contract offer, retaining Pat Swilling's services and making him the highest paid defensive player in NFL history.

**Apr 26**—The Indianapolis Colts kick off the 57th NFL draft by claiming defensive lineman Steve Emtman and linebacker Quentin Coryatt with the first two picks.

**May 3**—Indianapolis Colts defensive end Shane Curry is shot in the head and killed by a 15-year-old assailant following a traffic dispute in a Cincinnati parking lot.

**May 29**—The Minnesota Vikings release running back Herschel Walker.

**June 6**—In Montreal, the Sacramento Surge overcome the Orlando Thunder 21–17 in the second World Bowl, championship of the World League of American Football.

**June 16**—With jury selection complete, eight players' antitrust suit challenging the NFL's limited free-agency system goes to trial in Minneapolis.

**June 22**—The Philadelphia Eagles sign veteran running back Herschel Walker.

**June 23**—Detroit Lions offensive lineman Eric Andolsek, 25, is killed by a runaway truck while doing yardwork at his home in Thibodaux, LA.

**June 25**—Philadelphia all-pro defensive lineman Jerome Brown, 27, is killed in a one-car accident in his hometown of Brooksville, FL.

**July 6**—Placekicker Pat Leahy, the third highest scorer in NFL history, retires after 18 years with the New York Jets. His is the longest tenure of any placekicker with one club.

**Aug 28**—The Miami Dolphins and the New England Patriots, in response to the devastation wreaked by Hurricane Andrew, reschedule their September 6 season opener at Miami's Joe Robbie Stadium to their October 18 open date.

JOHN W. MCDONOUGH

**Lofton leaped ahead of Largent on the career list.**

**Sep 6**—Buffalo receiver James Lofton's sixth catch of the day in the Bill's 40–7 season-opening rout of the Rams moves him past Steve Largent and into the top spot on the NFL career receiving-yardage list.

**Sep 6**—Paying tribute before the game to Jerome Brown, the defensive tackle killed in an automobile accident on June 25th, the Philadelphia Eagles open the season with a 15–13 win over New Orleans. Newly-acquired running back Herschel Walker gains 114 yards on 26 carries.

**Sep 10**—A Minneapolis jury finds the NFL's plan B free agency plan too restrictive and in violation of federal anti-trust laws.

**Sep 10**—Deion Sanders reverses field and signs a $2 million one-year contract with the Atlanta Falcons. Three days later he returns a kickoff 99 yards for a touchdown.

**Sep 13**—The Bills outscore the 49ers 34–31 in a game that features 1,086 yards of offense and, for the first time in NFL history, no punts.

**Sep 17**—NFL owners decide to shelve the World League.

**Sep 20**—Under rookie head coach Bill Cowher, the Pittsburgh Steelers jump out to a surprising 3–0 start, defeating San Diego 23–6 for their third victory.

**Sep 24**—In the aftermath of the Sept. 10 verdict that the NFL's limited free agency is illegal, federal judge David Doty declares four players who had not signed 1992 contracts to be unrestricted free agents for five days. In the designated period Keith Jackson signs with the Miami Dolphins, Garin Veris signs with the San Francisco 49ers, Webster Slaughter signs with the Houston Oilers, and the Detroit Lions release D.J. Dozier, who continues to play baseball for the New York Mets.

**Sep 27**—The Tampa Bay Buccaneers stop a two-year, 15-game road losing streak with a 27–23 victory at Detroit. A 14-yard bootleg screen pass from Vinny Testaverde to tight end Ron Hall with 49 seconds left provides the winning score. Houston shuts out San Diego 27–0 to send the Chargers to their fourth straight defeat after Shawn Jefferson, a former Oiler playing for San Diego, had guaranteed a Chargers victory. San Francisco edges New Orleans 16–10 as Eric Davis's end zone interception with ten seconds left clinches the victory.

**Sep 28**—The Los Angeles Raiders suffer a 27–7 Monday night defeat to the Kansas City Chiefs and drop to 0–4. Dating to the previous December, they've lost eight consecutive games, their worst losing streak since 1964.

**Oct 4**—Miami Dolphins safety Louis Oliver intercepts three passes and returns one an NFL record-tying 103 yards for a touchdown in Miami's 37–10 victory over the Buffalo Bills in a pivotal AFC East matchup.

**Oct 4**—John Elway conducts the 30th game-winning fourth quarter drive of his ten-year career, capping it with a 12-yard touchdown pass to Vance Johnson with 38 seconds left to give Denver a 20–19 win over Kansas City. The following week, Elway leads his 31st fourth quarter comeback in the Broncos' 27–21 win over Houston.

**Oct 5**—Herschel Walker runs for 86 yards and two touchdowns against his former team in Philadelphia's 31–7 plastering of Dallas in a battle of NFC East unbeatens.

**Oct 12**—Washington receiver Art Monk's seventh catch of the night, the 820th of his career, moves him past former Seattle star Steve Largent to the top of the NFL career reception list as the Redskins defeat the Broncos 34–3.

**Oct 18**—Dallas defeats Kansas City 17–10, while Washington edges Philadelphia 16–12, and the Cowboys are alone at the top of the NFC East for the first time since 1986.

**Oct 18**—Dan Marino throws four touchdown passes for the 17th time in his career, tying Johnny Unitas's NFL record as the Dolphins beat the New England Patriots 38–17 and remain undefeated at 6–0.

**Oct 25**—Steve Emtman, the Indianapolis Colts defensive end and the first pick in the 1992 draft, intercepts Miami's Dan Marino on fourth down at the Colts' 10-yard line with 17 seconds to play and runs 90 yards for a touchdown to clinch a 31–20 win over the Dolphins, the league's last remaining unbeaten team.

**Nov 1**—The Pittsburgh Steelers improve to 6–2 and complete a regular-season sweep over the Houston Oilers as Al Del Greco's 39-yard field goal attempt with six seconds remaining misses wide left and the Steelers cling to a 21–20 lead. The 1–6 Phoenix Cardinals upset the San Francisco 49ers 24–14 in Sun Devil Stadium, the site of their 23-point comeback win over the 49ers in 1988. The San Diego Chargers win their fourth straight, 26–0 over the Colts, after dropping four to start the year.

**Nov 8**—All-Pro N.Y. Giants linebacker Lawrence Taylor ruptures his Achilles' tendon during a 27–7 home victory over Green Bay and declares that his career is over. By Monday, however, Taylor moderates this statement, saying he hasn't decided whether or not to retire.

**Nov 15**—Hit after a five-yard scramble that sets up a game-winning score, Houston quarterback Warren Moon breaks his left arm and is lost to his team for five games. It is the third consecutive

week that Moon is injured and replaced by backup Cody Carlson.

**Nov 15**—Steve Young throws an eight-yard touchdown pass to tight end Brent Jones with 46 seconds remaining to lift the 49ers to a 21–20 victory against the New Orleans Saints and a sweep of the season series against the Saints.

**Nov 16**—Buffalo recovers from a 14–3 deficit to defeat Miami 26–20 at Joe Robbie Stadium and even the season series between the AFC East rivals. The win gives them the division lead by one game over the Dolphins.

**Nov 23**—The injury-plagued defending champion Washington Redskins drop to 6–5 with a 20–3 defeat at New Orleans. It is their third loss in the past four games and the fifth consecutive week in which they've failed to score an offensive touchdown in the first half.

**Nov 27**—Citing the advice of "a million doctors" in the wake of, by his count, the ninth concussion of his career, suffered on Nov. 8 against Denver, N.Y. Jets wide receiver Al Toon announces his retirement after eight seasons in the league.

**Nov 29**—New York Jets defensive lineman Dennis Byrd fractures his fifth vertebra in a full-speed collision with teammate Scott Mersereau. The injury leaves him partially paralyzed. Already this season almost 500 NFL players have been hurt seriously enough to miss at least one game.

**Nov 29**—Led by quarterback and game-MVP Doug Flutie's 480 passing yards, the Calgary Stampeders win the Canadian Football League's Grey Cup, 24–10, over the Winnipeg Blue Bombers, in the Toronto SkyDome.

**Nov 29**—Pittsburgh's Barry Foster breaks Franco Harris's club records for yards rushing and yards from scrimmage in a season when he rushes for

**Taylor was carted off the field after his injury.**

JOHN GRIESHOP

102 yards in the Steelers 21–9 victory against Cincinnati. It is his ninth 100-yard game of the year, two more than the previous franchise record, also set by Harris.

**Dec 6**—San Francisco wide receiver Jerry Rice sets a career mark for touchdown receptions, besting Steve Largent with his 101st scoring catch—a 12-yarder from Steve Young in the fourth quarter of a 27–3 drowning of the Miami Dolphins.

**Dec 6**—Dedicating the game to defensive lineman Dennis Byrd who suffered a broken neck in the previous week's game, the New York Jets defeat the heavily-favored Buffalo Bills, 24–17 in Buffalo. The victory stops the Jets 10-game losing streak against the Bills dating to 1987.

**Dec 20**—With a 36–14 triumph over the Raiders in Los Angeles, the San Diego Chargers (10–5) become the first team in league history to make the playoffs after starting 0–4.

**Dec 27**—The Buffalo Bills lose quarterback Jim Kelly, the AFC East title and critical home-field advantage through the playoffs in their last regular-season game, a 27–3 loss to Houston in the Astrodome.

**Dec 27**—Emmitt Smith gains 131 yards in the Dallas Cowboys' 27–14 win against Chicago to become the ninth player to win consecutive NFL rushing titles, besting Pittsburgh's Barry Foster by 23 yards. His 1,713 yards break Tony Dorsett's club record of 1,646, set in 1981. The Cowboys' 13 wins are a franchise regular season record. By contrast, the Bears' 5–11 record makes this their worst full season since 1973. The game would be

**Frank Reich led the greatest NFL comeback ever.**

NADIA BOROWSKI/THE ORANGE COUNTY REGISTER

the last for two great Bears: veteran linebacker Mike Singletary, who retired after playing 12 years for Chicago, and Mike Ditka, who will be relieved of his duties nine days later after 11 stormy seasons as the Chicago coach.

**Dec 27**—Sterling Sharpe makes six catches to bring his season total to an NFL-record 108, two more than the previous record set by Art Monk. Unfortunately for the Green Bay faithful, the Packers lose the game, 27–7 to the Minnesota Vikings, and are eliminated from playoff contention.

**Dec 28**—After leading Denver to three Super Bowl appearances in 12 years, Broncos coach Dan Reeves is dismissed. Wade Phillips is hired on Jan. 25 to fill the vacancy. Reeves is tabbed Jan. 26 by the N.Y. Giants to succeed Ray Handley, who is let go on Dec. 30.

**Jan 3, 1993**—In the greatest comeback in NFL history, the Buffalo Bills recover from a seemingly insurmountable 35–3 third quarter deficit to snatch a dramatic 41–38 overtime victory from the Houston Oilers in the AFC wild-card playoff game.

**Jan 5**—Chicago favorite Mike Ditka is dismissed as head coach by the Bears after a 5–11 season. Dallas Cowboy defensive coordinator Dave Wannstedt becomes his successor on Jan. 19.

**Jan 10**—In divisional playoffs, the 49ers beat the Redskins 20–13, and the Bills down Pittsburgh 24–3.

**Jan 11**—Miami shuts out San Diego 31–0, and Dallas blitzes Philadelphia 34–10 to complete the final four.

**Jan 17**—The Buffalo Bills defeat the Miami Dolphins 29–10 in Joe Robbie Stadium to win their third straight AFC championship, and the Dallas Cowboys surprise the San Francisco 49ers at Candlestick Park by a 30–20 score to reach the Super Bowl just three years after going a woeful 1–15.

**Jan 21**—Bill Parcells accepts the head coaching job at New England, filling the space created by Dick MacPherson's dismissal on Jan. 8.

**Jan 31**—The Dallas Cowboys send the Buffalo Bills to a record-setting third consecutive Super Bowl loss with a 52–17 shellacking in Super Bowl XXVII in Pasadena. Cowboy quarterback Troy Aikman throws for 273 yards and four touchdowns and is named the game's MVP.

# Pro Football

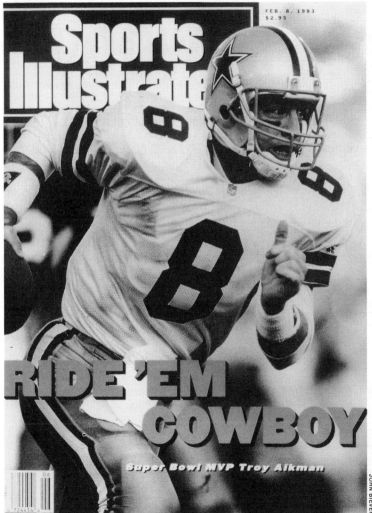

FEB. 8, 1993
$2.95

Sports
Illustrated

RIDE 'EM
COWBOY

Super Bowl MVP Troy Aikman

JOHN BIEVER

# The Year of the Cowboy

*After a four-year ascent, the rebuilt Cowboys are on top of the NFL and looking to stay awhile*   |   by PETER KING

FROM THE START, JIMMY JOHNSON knew he would win. He knew after the Cowboys' 1–15 season in 1989. "We're going to build it the right way here, and we'll win. I'm sure of it," he said after that season. He knew after the Cowboys' 7–9 season in 1990, after which he said, "We're going to be good. Big-time good. There's no doubt about it." He knew after the Cowboys' 11–5 playoff season of 1991—everyone could feel it happening—and of course he knew on that beautiful Sunday evening in Pasadena in early 1993, when the rest of the world found out why Johnson never truly despaired in some of those dark early days he and Jerry Jones spent building the Dallas Cowboys back to prominence.

They were damned good.

Football is football, Johnson knew.

Whether it be building college football's dominant team at the University of Miami or pro football's best with the Cowboys, he differed with many prominent football minds who thought great teams had to be huge and bulky and imposing. Johnson thought the best football on any level was played by fast and quick and intimidating men. Speedy guys. Tough guys. Brawling guys. They might give up 20 pounds to their adversaries, but they would fight like pit bulls to win. And they just loved football, the kind they played in the 1992 postseason, the kind that culminated in a 52–17 Super Bowl XXVII rout of Buffalo. It was the toughest of the three straight Super Bowl losses for erudite Buffalo coach Marv Levy and his Bills, and that's because the Cowboys were the toughest of the three Super Bowl teams that had pounded them.

Yes, Johnson, with Jones's money, built a team of speed and quickness and relentlessness with a franchise quarterback in Troy Aikman and a franchise runner in Emmitt Smith and a franchise pass rusher in Charles Haley leading the way. If pure power football—Giant football, Redskin football—was going to beat Johnson, fine. He had given it his best shot, doing it his way. But power football couldn't beat the Cowboys. Nor could anyone's finesse football. And it might not for a long time.

"We have players," Johnson said, emphasizing *players* in his Texas twang. "You know, while Marv Levy is over there reading about Truman, [defensive tackle] Jimmie Jones is on his bed, belly-laughing at Fred and Barney on the Flintstones."

Dallas did not corner the market on players in 1992, although the Cowboys did have rushing titlist Smith (1,713 yards) and a quarterback, Aikman, who emerged from a superb postseason (eight touchdowns, no interceptions, a 126.4 rating) as one of the game's very best. The 1992 season certainly will go down as the year of the Cowboy, but this wasn't a one-story season.

You want stories? Pick one. Green Bay, for instance. New coach Mike Holmgren turned a bunch of guys with 3–13 talent into 9–7, on-the-playoff-brink overachievers. The best new aerial combination in the game helped, with 23-year-old quarterback Brett Favre throwing darts to wideout Sterling Sharpe, who set an alltime NFL record with 108 catches. The Vikings won the NFC Central with another rookie coach,

**The Cowboy win was sweet vindication for Dallas architects Johnson (left) and Jones.**

AL TIELEMANS

Dennis Green, who somehow juggled the worst quarterback situation in the conference and piloted the team to an 11–5 finish. The 49ers (14–2) and Saints (12–4) were again the class of the West. Again the Saints found a way to lose the big ones—jittery quarterback Bobby Hebert, fired after the season, over and over again disappointed the football-starved Louisianans—and fellow disappointment Philadelphia got blown out of the playoffs by the upstart Cowboys in the East.

In the AFC the stunning story happened in Pittsburgh, where rookie coach Bill Cowher energized the dormant Steeler fans. You kept waiting for the Steelers to fall to earth, but they never did until January, winning homefield advantage through the playoffs and losing to the Bills at Three Rivers Stadium. The Chargers started 0–4

# A Fresh Start?

Chuck Schmidt looked flustered. Here was Schmidt, the CEO of the Detroit Lions, at the 1993 National Football League owners' meetings in California, dying to make anyone with a bit more bulk than the hotel janitor the highest-paid offensive lineman in NFL history. And no one, apparently, wanted his money in the new era of NFL free-agency. "We've got to get some linemen," he said, sounding determined to make up for the loss of two starting guards—Mike Utley, paralyzed in 1991, and Eric Andolsek, run over by a truck in 1992. But beefy Houston tackle Don Maggs signed with Denver before Schmidt could get his paws on him. Guard Houston Hoover of Atlanta defected to Cleveland, jilting the Lions too. The big hurt came when Miami guard Harry Galbreath picked Green Bay over Detroit, even though the Lions offered more money.

Join the frenzy, Chuck. In the first year of unencumbered free-agency in the 74-year history of the league, offensive linemen became the glamour players. Just glance at the chart below to see what happened to the list of the ten highest-paid linemen before and after the advent of free-agency on March 1, 1993.

Interesting dynamic at work here. Not only did Lachey move from 1 to 8 in the salary standings in six weeks, but the Lions, in their desperation, had to vastly overpay for three marginal NFL linemen—Fralic, Richards, and former Kansac City guard David Lutz, who signed for $1.2 million a year for two years. "I'm afraid," said Jets general manager Dick Steinberg, "that we might be getting into an era where we're paying incredible money for .220-hitting shortstops and 4–10 pitchers."

So why did the Lions, and so many others, go out and pay filet-mignon prices for Salisbury-steak players? "There's more of a value on offensive linemen than any of us in the league ever thought there was," said Denver director of football

| BEFORE FREE AGENCY | | | AFTER ONE FREE-AGENCY SEASON | | |
|---|---|---|---|---|---|
| | Player, Club | Avg. Salary | | Player, Club | Avg. Salary |
| 1. | Jim Lachey, Wash. | $1.35m | 1. | Will Wolford, Ind. | $2.55m |
| 2. | Bob Whitfield, Atl. | $1.25m | 2. | Kirk Lowdermilk, Ind. | $2.00m |
| 3. | Jay Hilgenberg, Cle. | $1.051m | 3. | Bill Fralic, Det. | $1.80m |
| 4. | Mike Munchak, Hou. | $1.05m | 4. | Harry Swayne, SD | $1.80m |
| 5. | Jackie Slater, Rams | $1.05m | 5. | Dave Richards, Det. | $1.70m |
| 6. | Tony Mandarich, GB | $1.03m | 6. | Harry Galbreath, GB | $1.52m |
| 7. | Mike Kenn, Atl. | $1.025m | 7. | Brian Habib, Den. | $1.40m |
| 8. | Ray Roberts, Sea | $1.006m | 8. | Gerald Perry, Raiders | $1.35m |
| 9. | Bruce Matthews, Hou. | $1.00m | | Jim Lachey, Wash. | $1.35m |
| 10. | Leon Searcy, Pitt. | $1.00m | 10. | Houston Hoover, Cle. | $1.25m |
| | | | | Bob Whitfield, Atl. | $1.25m |

but won 11 of their last 12; 11–5 San Diego lost on a flooded Miami field in a second-round playoff game but made believers of the up-for-grabs AFC West. And the Bills. The poor, pathetic Bills. They struggled into the playoffs, losing in the regular season to Indianapolis and the Jets, then falling behind 35–3 in the playoffs to Houston. They won in overtime, 41–38, in the greatest football comeback ever. "I can feel it," defensive end Bruce Smith said. "This is our year."

Unfortunately for the Bills, though, the Cowboys could feel it too, and the result was a joke of a Super Bowl. "The ultimate embarrassment," linebacker Darryl Talley said before slinking off into the off-season. The Dallas defense just outquicked and outfoxed anything Buffalo's offense tried. It didn't hurt that Aikman played the

operations Bob Ferguson. "We're seeing how important it is to build a solid core of big, strong, smart and tenacious guys to set the tone for your offense."

The Broncos seemed to be the clever ones in the talent chase for linemen. "We had a plan," said Ferguson, "to overpay, get the guys we wanted, and get out of the market." Whew. Overpay? Admittedly? That's right, and it was a wise move. The Broncos judged Maggs the top tackle and Habib the top guard of the unrestricted free-agent class, and so Ferguson went to coach Wade Phillips and owner Pat Bowlen to see if he could go all-out to sign them. Phillips said he trusted Ferguson, and Bowlen handed him the checkbook.

Neither Maggs, a plodder Houston wasn't too sorry to lose, nor Habib, a first-year starter for the Vikings in 1992, had ever been a Pro Bowler. But Denver didn't have much of a choice. The Broncos' line allowed 52 sacks in 1992—only four teams gave up more—and everyone knows they're going nowhere unless John Elway has time to make things happen. After his visit to Denver, Maggs planned to make several trips to visit other prospective new teams. So what did Ferguson do? Offer Maggs, and then Habib, more money than they dreamed they'd be making, and not let them get out of town without agreeing to a contract. That done, the pressure now lands squarely on the front-office of the Broncos

for the players to perform like the million-dollar ballplayers they have become. "This is definitely not a system for the timid," Ferguson said.

"Now comes the hard part," said Kirk Lowdermilk, the new center of the Colts. He's never made the Pro Bowl, but he's making twice as much as the previously highest-paid center of all-time, Bruce Matthews of Houston. "Now it's time to justify the money and expectations."

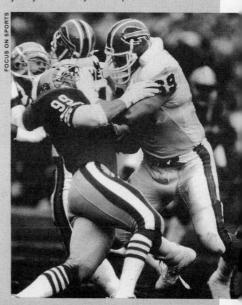

FOCUS ON SPORTS

**Former Bill Will Wolford will have to justify his status as the NFL's highest paid lineman.**

BILL FRAKES

**After flirting with free agency, Smith (108 yards in the Super Bowl) stayed in Dallas.**

greatest game of his life—22 of 30, 273 yards, 73% completion rate, four touchdowns, no interceptions. After a player plays a game like that, and indeed after a player plays a postseason like Aikman's, what doubt can there be that he is one of the premier players in the game?

In the rush to crown Dallas the team of the '90s, America's sporting press forgot something, though. It's a new game. No longer can general manager George Young build an offensive line for a decade with the Giants, like he tried to do in the mid-'80s. No longer can the Redskins keep a Monk–Sanders–Clark triumvirate intact to catch passes for eight or 10 years. "We're building more for the short term than we ever have before,'' says Jets GM Dick Steinberg, "because we don't know what tomorrow will bring." With the advent of true free agency a month after Dallas put on its crown, we can't assume that the Troy Aikman–Emmitt Smith–Michael Irvin–Erik

Williams–Charles Haley–Russell Maryland nucleus (and friends) will stay intact the way it would have in past eras.

Every great football team will have to deal with this now. As free agency showed, teams aren't building for the next six to eight years with a solid core of players. They're building for two to four years, signing aging veterans who can contribute a couple of quality seasons. And here's the critical factor: Beginning in 1994, each team will almost certainly be limited to a uniform salary cap on the amount they can spend on players, probably about $31 million. So the free-spending clubs like San Francisco and Washington will have to be relative tightwads now.

As you might expect, the Cowboys aren't daunted by the new freedom and salary restrictions. When there were rumors that Smith, the NFL's leading rusher in 1992, would be signed by another team for about $4 million a year, Johnson was asked if the Cowboys, who retained the right to match any offer to Smith, would match any contract that came down the pike. "If teams are trying to put our feet to the fire and force us to screw up our structure, they can forget it," Johnson said. "If anybody offers Emmitt that kind of money, they'd better be prepared to eat it."

"We'll figure out how to deal with free agency, like we've figured a way to deal with everything else that comes up," owner Jones said.

If they do, they'll be the team of the '90s. But who will be their competition for that title if they don't? In order, here's who will challenge Dallas as the team of the decade:

1. The 49ers. They were coming off an NFL-best 14–2 regular season in 1992, but a couple of signs early in 1993 showed they would have trouble with the looming salary cap. San Francisco, still with 1992 NFL MVP quarterback Steve Young left to sign, already lost two salary fights with great defensive players before the off-season was very old. The 49ers will have problems paying all their great players and having enough money left to pay the average guys you need to win titles. Raiders owner Al Davis said that he was stunned the 49ers allowed free-agent defensive tackle Pierce Holt—San Francisco's best defensive player—to jump to Atlanta for a guaranteed $2.5 million a year. The 49ers gambled that they could lure Reggie White for a nonguaranteed, more expensive deal and lost. This is still a great team, but a great team won't stay great for long without a continuing infusion of great players.

2. The Redskins. They were only 9–7 in 1992 to begin with, with a quarterback (Mark Rypien) who looked awful, a receiving corps (Monk–Sanders–Clark) getting old and a backfield need-

ing new talent. And then Joe Gibbs retired abruptly in March, Clark flew off to Phoenix as a free agent and the Redskins failed to land White because their offer was $3 million less than Green Bay. Now they face the same problems most teams face. Their quarterback is fallible. They have two segments of their team—receivers, offensive line—getting quite threadbare. And they can't spend Jack Kent Cooke's money like they once did to reel in a Jason Buck here, a Jumpy Geathers there. This isn't exactly a fortress that Richie Petitbon is inheriting entering the mid-'90s.

3. The Packers. Shocked to see them up this high? Don't be. Money was the primary reason that prime free-agent White chose the Packers after his March 1993

**Young was the league's top-rated passer and MVP in 1993.**

PETER READ MILLER

quest for a new team, but he saw things happening here. "I love the quarterback," White said in the middle of his free-agency fling. "I think he's the best young quarterback playing today." Favre came to Green Bay for a first-round pick from Atlanta before the 1992 draft, and all he did in '92 was nearly lead the Pack to the playoffs by being the sixth-rated NFL quarterback. That's better than Dan Marino, Jim Kelly or John Elway. He has Sharpe, a 28-year-

**According to White, his new teammate is "the best young quarterback playing today."**

JOHN BIEVER

old speedster in his prime, as his main target. The Packers beefed up their offensive line with the signing of guard Harry Galbreath and their backfield by acquiring running back John Stephens from New England. And they have the best one-two architectural punch in the NFL: G.M. Ron Wolf, who has a blank checkbook and lots of football savvy, and Holmgren, whom players respect and play hard for.

4. The Bills. Kelly's mortal. The defense will dissolve slowly through free agency, as we saw with Shane Conlan's defection to the Rams and Bruce Smith's possible defection in 1994. And the players are getting unhappy. Wouldn't you, after getting slapped in the face three straight Januaries? One more thing: G.M. Bill Polian, fired by owner Ralph Wilson, and assistant G.M. Bob Ferguson, who left for Denver, will be big losses.

5. Everybody else. The Eagles are dismantling and readying a Dallas-like run of draft choices to try to get them back on top. It's impossible to declare them serious contenders until we see who they pick in the next two drafts. The Dolphins are too myopic and not tough enough defensively; unfortunately, Dan Marino can't rush the passer. The Giants? Nah. Any team claiming to be serious about White and then contacting his agents 11 days into the free-agency period is serious all right—seriously fragmented at the top. Houston, even with Buddy Ryan, doesn't have the character. The Chargers? Now there's a bright young team. But can Stan Humphries be a prime-time quarterback, and can the defense suddenly stop aging?

One April day in 1993, almost three months after the Super Bowl, Johnson sat back in his office and mused about the near future. "No player will be more important than the team," Johnson vowed. "Free agency is going to test us on that. But I've got faith that we're going to win again, and win big."

Champions talk that way. Expect Johnson to keep talking just like that through the decade.

# FOR THE RECORD · 1992 - 1993

## 1992 NFL Final Standings

### American Football Conference

#### EASTERN DIVISION

|  | W | L | T | Pct | Pts | OP |
|---|---|---|---|---|---|---|
| Miami | 11 | 5 | 0 | .688 | 340 | 281 |
| †Buffalo | 11 | 5 | 0 | .688 | 381 | 283 |
| Indianapolis | 9 | 7 | 0 | .563 | 216 | 302 |
| NY Jets | 4 | 12 | 0 | .250 | 220 | 315 |
| New England | 2 | 14 | 0 | .125 | 205 | 363 |

#### CENTRAL DIVISION

|  | W | L | T | Pct | Pts | OP |
|---|---|---|---|---|---|---|
| Pittsburgh | 11 | 5 | 0 | .688 | 299 | 225 |
| †Houston | 10 | 6 | 0 | .625 | 352 | 258 |
| Cleveland | 7 | 9 | 0 | .438 | 272 | 275 |
| Cincinnati | 5 | 11 | 0 | .313 | 274 | 364 |

#### WESTERN DIVISION

|  | W | L | T | Pct | Pts | OP |
|---|---|---|---|---|---|---|
| San Diego | 11 | 5 | 0 | .688 | 335 | 241 |
| †Kansas City | 10 | 6 | 0 | .625 | 348 | 282 |
| Denver | 8 | 8 | 0 | .500 | 262 | 329 |
| LA Raiders | 7 | 9 | 0 | .438 | 249 | 281 |
| Seattle | 2 | 14 | 0 | .125 | 140 | 312 |

† Wild Card team.

### National Football Conference

#### EASTERN DIVISION

|  | W | L | T | Pct | Pts | OP |
|---|---|---|---|---|---|---|
| Dallas | 13 | 3 | 0 | .813 | 409 | 243 |
| †Philadelphia | 11 | 5 | 0 | .688 | 354 | 245 |
| †Washington | 9 | 7 | 0 | .563 | 300 | 255 |
| NY Giants | 6 | 10 | 0 | .375 | 306 | 367 |
| Phoenix | 4 | 12 | 0 | .250 | 243 | 332 |

#### CENTRAL DIVISION

|  | W | L | T | Pct | Pts | OP |
|---|---|---|---|---|---|---|
| Minnesota | 11 | 5 | 0 | .688 | 374 | 249 |
| Green Bay | 9 | 7 | 0 | .563 | 276 | 296 |
| Tampa Bay | 5 | 11 | 0 | .313 | 267 | 365 |
| Chicago | 5 | 11 | 0 | .313 | 295 | 361 |
| Detroit | 5 | 11 | 0 | .313 | 273 | 332 |

#### WESTERN DIVISION

|  | W | L | T | Pct | Pts | OP |
|---|---|---|---|---|---|---|
| San Francisco | 14 | 2 | 0 | .875 | 431 | 236 |
| †New Orleans | 12 | 4 | 0 | .750 | 330 | 202 |
| Atlanta | 6 | 10 | 0 | .375 | 327 | 414 |
| LA Rams | 6 | 10 | 0 | .375 | 313 | 383 |

## 1993 NFL Playoffs

| AFC FIRST ROUND | AFC DIVISIONAL PLAYOFF | AFC CHAMPIONSHIP | NFC CHAMPIONSHIP | NFC DIVISIONAL PLAYOFF | NFC FIRST ROUND |
|---|---|---|---|---|---|

**SUPER BOWL XXVI**
January 26, 1993

Houston 38
Buffalo 41

Buffalo 24

Buffalo 29

Pittsburgh 3

San Francisco 20

San Francisco 20

Washington 13

Washington 24
Minnesota 7

**DALLAS 52**
**Buffalo 17**

Kansas City 0
San Diego 17

San Diego 0

Miami 10

Miami 31

Philadelphia 10

Dallas 30

Dallas 34

Philadelphia 36
New Orleans 20

## AFC Wild Card Games

| | | | | | |
|---|---|---|---|---|---|
| Houston | 7 | 21 | 7 | 3 | 0—38 |
| Buffalo | 3 | 0 | 28 | 7 | 3—41 |

### FIRST QUARTER

Houston: Jeffires 3 pass from Moon (Del Greco kick), 9:09. Drive: 80 yards, 14 plays.
Buffalo: FG Christie 36, 13:36. Drive: 38 yards, 10 plays.

### SECOND QUARTER

Houston: Slaughter 7 pass from Moon (Del Greco kick), 6:01. Drive: 80 yards, 12 plays.
Houston: Duncan 26 pass from Moon (Del Greco kick), 10:51. Drive: 67 yards, 5 plays.
Houston: Jeffires 27 pass from Moon (Del Greco kick), 14:46. Drive: 67 yards, 8 plays.

### THIRD QUARTER

Houston: McDowell 58 interception return (Del Greco kick), 1:41.
Buffalo: Davis 1 run (Christie kick), 6:08. Drive: 50 yards, 10 plays.
Buffalo: Beebe 38 pass from Reich (Christie kick), 7:04. Drive: 52 yards, 4 plays.
Buffalo: Reed 26 pass from Reich (Christie kick), 10:39. Drive: 59 yards, 4 plays.
Buffalo: Reed 18 pass from Reich (Christie kick), 13:00. Drive: 23 yards, 4 plays.

### FOURTH QUARTER

Buffalo: Reed 17 pass from Reich (Christie kick), 11:52. Drive: 74 yards, 7 plays.
Houston: FG Del Greco 26, 14:48. Drive: 63 yards, 12 plays.

### OVERTIME

Buffalo: FG Christie 32, 3:06.

A: 75,141; T: 3:25.

| | | | | |
|---|---|---|---|---|
| Kansas City | 0 | 0 | 0 | 0— 0 |
| San Diego | 0 | 0 | 10 | 7—17 |

### THIRD QUARTER

San Diego: Butts 54 run (Carney kick), 9:07. Drive: 74 yards, 4 plays.
San Diego: FG Carney 34, 11:27. Drive: 9 yards, 4 plays.

### FOURTH QUARTER

San Diego: Hendrickson 5 run (Carney kick), 10:03. Drive: 90 yards, 10 plays.

A: 58,278; T: 3:05.

## NFC Wild Card Games

| | | | | |
|---|---|---|---|---|
| Washington | 3 | 14 | 7 | 0—24 |
| Minnesota | 7 | 0 | 0 | 0 —7 |

### FIRST QUARTER

Minnesota: Allen 1 run (Reveiz kick), 4:55. Drive: 79 yards, 9 plays.
Washington: FG Lohmiller 44, 14:07. Drive: 6 yards, 4 plays.

### SECOND QUARTER

Washington: Byner 3 run (Lohmiller kick), 5:37. Drive: 33 yards, 6 plays.
Mitchell 8 run (Lohmiller kick), 13:04. Drive: 86 yards, 10 plays.

### THIRD QUARTER

Washington: Clark 24 pass from Rypien (Lohmiller kick), 14:43. Drive: 71 yards, 10 plays.

A: 57,353; T: 2:47.

| | | | | |
|---|---|---|---|---|
| Philadelphia | 7 | 0 | 3 | 26—36 |
| New Orleans | 7 | 10 | 3 | 0—20 |

### FIRST QUARTER

New Orleans: Hayward 1 run (Andersen kick), 5:40. Drive: 73 yards, 8 plays.
Philadelphia: Barnett 57 pass from Cunningham (Ruzek kick), 11:38. Drive: 80 yards, 4 plays.

### SECOND QUARTER

New Orleans: FG Andersen 35, 6:42. Drive: 71 yards, 13 plays.
New Orleans: Early 7 pass from Hebert (Andersen kick), 10:46. Drive: 53 yards, 4 plays.

### THIRD QUARTER

New Orleans: FG Andersen 42, 8:32. Drive: 44 yards, 5 plays.
Philadelphia: FG Ruzek 40, 13:59. Drive: 39 yards, 9 plays.

### FOURTH QUARTER

Philadelphia: Barnett 35 pass from Cunningham (Ruzek kick), 4:23. Drive: 64 yards, 9 plays.
Philadelphia: Sherman 6 run (Ruzek kick), 8:12. Drive: 26 yards, 5 plays.
Philadelphia: Safety, White tackled Hebert in end zone, 9:24.
Philadelphia: FG Ruzek 39, 12:24. Drive: 40 yards, 11 plays.
Philadelphia: Allen 18 interception return (Ruzek kick), 12:43.

A: 68,893; T: 3:02.

## AFC Divisional Games

| Buffalo | 0 | 7 | 7 | 10—24 |
|---|---|---|---|---|
| Pittsburgh | 3 | 0 | 0 | 0— 3 |

### FIRST QUARTER

Pittsburgh: FG Anderson 38, 7:46. Drive: 33 yards, 9 plays.

### SECOND QUARTER

Buffalo: Frerotte 1 pass from Reich (Christie kick), 13:04. Drive: 59 yards, 9 plays.

### THIRD QUARTER

Buffalo: Lofton 17 pass from Reich (Christie kick), 11:00. Drive: 80 yards, 13 plays.

### FOURTH QUARTER

Buffalo: FG Christie 43, 4:47. Drive: 44 yards, 10 plays.
Buffalo: Gardner 1 run (Christie kick), 13:04. Drive: 86 yards, 8 plays.

A: 64,991; T: 2:58.

| San Diego | 0 | 0 | 0 | 0— 0 |
|---|---|---|---|---|
| Miami | 0 | 21 | 0 | 10—31 |

### SECOND QUARTER

Miami: Paige 1 pass from Marino (Stoyanovich kick), 8:30. Drive: 48 yards, 9 plays.
Miami: K. Jackson 9 pass from Marino, (Stoyanovich kick), 13:14. Drive: 37 yards, 2 plays.
Miami: K. Jackson 30 pass from Marino (Stoyanovich kick), 14:33. Drive: 42 yards, 4 plays.

### FOURTH QUARTER

Miami: FG Stoyanovich 22, :57. Drive: 60 yards, 12 plays.
Miami: Craver 25 run (Stoyanovich kick), 6:41. Drive: 53 yards, 6 plays.

A: 71,224; T: 3:00.

## NFC Divisional Games

| Washington | 3 | 0 | 3 | 7—13 |
|---|---|---|---|---|
| San Francisco | 7 | 10 | 0 | 3—20 |

### FIRST QUARTER

San Francisco: Taylor 5 pass from Young (Cofer kick), 3:12. Drive: 83 yards, 6 plays.
Washington: FG Lohmiller 19, 10:34. Drive: 61 yards, 10 plays.

### SECOND QUARTER

San Francisco: FG Cofer 23, 2:52. Drive: 76 yards, 13 plays.
San Francisco: Jones pass 16 from Young (Cofer kick), 14:36. Drive: 35 yards, 5 plays.

### THIRD QUARTER

Washington: FG Lohmiller 32, 12:37. Drive: 71 yards, 14 plays.

### FOURTH QUARTER

Washington: Rypien 1 run (Lohmiller kick), :24. Drive: 15 yards, 3 plays.
San Francisco: FG Cofer 33, 12:38. Drive: 59 yards, 14 plays.

A: 64,991; T: 2:58.

| Philadelphia | 3 | 0 | 0 | 7—10 |
|---|---|---|---|---|
| Dallas | 7 | 10 | 10 | 7—34 |

### FIRST QUARTER

Philadelphia: FG Ruzek 32, 7:15. Drive: 56 yards, 12 plays.
Dallas: Tennell 1 pass from Aikman (Elliott kick), 13:02. Drive: 46 yards, 10 plays.

### SECOND QUARTER

Dallas: Novacek 6 pass from Aikman (Elliott kick), 14:13. Drive: 67 yards, 5 plays.
Dallas: FG Elliott 20, 15:00. Drive: 27 yards, 6 plays.

### THIRD QUARTER

Dallas: E. Smith 23 run (Elliott kick), 3:44. Drive: 70 yards, 6 plays.
Dallas: FG Elliott 43, 11:43. Drive: 26 yards, 7 plays.

### FOURTH QUARTER

Dallas: Gainer 1 run (Elliott kick), 11:41. Drive: 80 yards, 13 plays.
Philadelphia: C. Williams 18 pass from Cunningham (Ruzek kick), 14:10. Drive: 70 yards, 8 plays.

A: 63,721; T: 2:52.

## AFC Championship

| Buffalo | 3 | 10 | 10 | 6—29 |
|---------|---|----|----|------|
| Miami | 3 | 0 | 0 | 7—10 |

### FIRST QUARTER

Buffalo: FG Christie 21, 9:17. Drive: 43 yards, 6 plays.
Miami: FG Stoyanovich 51, 13:03. Drive: 39 yards, 7 plays.

### SECOND QUARTER

Buffalo: Thomas 17 pass from Kelly (Christie kick), :40. Drive: 64 yards, 7 plays.
Buffalo: FG Christie 33, 2:59. Drive: 2 yards, 4 plays.

### THIRD QUARTER

Buffalo: Davis 2 run (Christie kick), 1:58. Drive: 24 yards, 5 plays.
Buffalo: FG Christie 21, 11:33. Drive: 67 yards, 15 plays.

### FOURTH QUARTER

Buffalo: FG Christie 31, :04. Drive: 39 yards, 5 plays.
Miami: Duper 15 pass from Marino, (Stoyanovich kick), 7:28. Drive: 62 yards, 7 plays.
Buffalo: FG Christie 38, 12:23. Drive: 23 yards, 7 plays.

A: 72,703; T: 2:57.

## NFC Championship

| Dallas | 3 | 7 | 7 | 13—30 |
|--------|---|---|---|-------|
| San Francisco | 7 | 3 | 3 | 7—20 |

### FIRST QUARTER

Dallas: FG Elliott 20, 8:20. Drive: 20 yards, 5 plays.
San Francisco: Young 1 run (Cofer kick), 11:11. Drive: 48 yards, 8 plays.

### SECOND QUARTER

Dallas: E. Smith 5 run (Elliott kick), 9:55. Drive: 39 yards, 7 plays.
San Francisco: FG Cofer 28, 13:41. Drive: 65 yards, 10 plays.

### THIRD QUARTER

Dallas: Johnston 4 run (Elliott kick), 4:15. Drive: 78 yards, 8 plays.
San Francisco: FG Cofer 42, 8:35. Drive: 66 yards, 7 plays.

### FOURTH QUARTER

Dallas: E. Smith 16 pass from Aikman (Elliott kick), 2:35. Drive: 79 yards, 14 plays.
San Francisco: Rice 5 pass from Young (Cofer kick), 10:38. Drive: 93 yards, 9 plays.
Dallas: K. Martin 6 pass from Aikman (kick failed), 11:17. Drive: 79 yards, 4 plays.

A: 64,920; T: 2:56.

# Super Bowl Box Score

| Buffalo | 7 | 3 | 7 | 0—17 |
|---------|---|---|---|------|
| Dallas | 14 | 14 | 3 | 21—52 |

### FIRST QUARTER

Buffalo: Thomas 2 run (Christie kick), 5:00. Drive: 16 yards, 4 plays. Key plays: Tasker block of Saxon's punt from Cowboys' 16 rolls out of bounds for no gain; Tolbert's sack of Kelly on 3rd and 3 nullified by defensive holding call, giving Bills first down at Cowboys' 5. Buffalo 7, Dallas 0.
Dallas: Novacek 23 pass from Aikman (Elliott kick), 13:24. Drive: 47 yards, 6 plays. Key plays: Washington interception of Kelly's pass and 13 return to Bills' 47; Aikman 20 pass to Irvin. Dallas 7, Buffalo 7.
Dallas: J. Jones 2 fumble return (Elliott kick), 13:39. Key play: Haley 8-yard sack of Kelly forces fumble recovered by J. Jones. Dallas 14, Buffalo 7.

### SECOND QUARTER

Buffalo: FG Christie 21, 11:36. Drive: 82 yards, 12 plays. Key plays: Reich, on first play after replacing injured Kelly, 7 pass to Metzelaars on 3rd and 3; Reich 38 pass to Reed. Dallas 14, Buffalo 10.
Dallas: Irvin 19 pass from Aikman (Elliott kick), 13:08. Drive: 72 yards, 5 plays. Key plays: Aikman 9 pass to Novacek; E. Smith 38 run. Dallas 21, Buffalo 10.
Dallas: Irvin 18 pass from Aikman (Elliott kick), 13:24. Drive: 18 yards, 1 play. Key play: Thomas fumble on screen pass forced by Lett and recovered by J. Jones at Bills' 18. Dallas 28, Buffalo 10.

### THIRD QUARTER

Dallas: FG Elliott 20, 6:39. Drive: 77 yards, 12 plays. Key plays: E. Smith 11 run; Irvin 25 and 12 passes from Aikman. Dallas 31, Buffalo 10.
Buffalo: Beebe 40 pass from Reich (Christie kick), 15:00. Drive: 61 yards, 5 plays Key plays: K. Davis 12 run; Reed 13 pass from Reich. Dallas 31, Buffalo 17.

### FOURTH QUARTER

Dallas: Harper 45 pass from Aikman (Elliott kick), 4:56. Drive: 56 yards, 2 plays. Key play: E. Smith 11 run. Dallas 38, Buffalo 17.
Dallas: E. Smith 10 run (Elliott kick), 8:12. Drive: 8 yards, 3 plays. Key play: Everett 22 interception return to Bills' 8. Dallas 45, Buffalo 17.
Dallas: Norton 9 fumble return (Elliott kick), 7:29. Dallas 52, Buffalo 17.

A: 98,374; T: 3:23.

## Team Statistics

| | Buffalo | Dallas |
|---|---|---|
| FIRST DOWNS | 22 | 20 |
| Rushing | 7 | 9 |
| Passing | 11 | 11 |
| Penalty | 4 | 0 |
| THIRD DOWN EFF. | 5–11 | 5–11 |
| FOURTH DOWN EFF | 0–2 | 0–1 |
| TOTAL NET YARDS | 362 | 408 |
| Total plays | 71 | 60 |
| Avg gain | 5.1 | 6.8 |
| NET YARDS RUSHING | 108 | 137 |
| Rushes | 29 | 29 |
| Avg per rush | 3.7 | 4.7 |
| NET YARDS PASSING | 254 | 271 |
| Completed-Att. | 22–38 | 22–30 |
| Yards per pass | 6.0 | 8.7 |
| Sacked-yards lost | 0–0 | 5-46 |
| Had intercepted | 4 | 0 |
| PUNTS-Avg. | 3–45.3 | 4–32.8 |
| TOTAL RETURN YARDS | 90 | 149 |
| Punt returns | 1–0 | 3–35 |
| Kickoff returns | 4–90 | 4–79 |
| Interceptions | 0–0 | 4–35 |
| PENALTIES-Yds | 4–30 | 8-53 |
| FUMBLES-Lost | 8–5 | 4–2 |
| TIME OF POSSESSION | 28:48 | 31:12 |

## Passing

### BUFFALO

| | Comp | Att | Yds | Int | TD |
|---|---|---|---|---|---|
| Kelly | 4 | 7 | 82 | 2 | 0 |
| Reich | 18 | 31 | 194 | 2 | 1 |

### DALLAS

| | Comp | Att | Yds | Int | TD |
|---|---|---|---|---|---|
| Aikman | 22 | 30 | 273 | 0 | 4 |
| Beuerlein | 0 | 0 | 0 | 0 | 0 |

## Rushing

### BUFFALO

| | No. | Yds | Lg | TD |
|---|---|---|---|---|
| K. Davis | 15 | 86 | 14 | 0 |
| Thomas | 11 | 19 | 9 | 1 |
| Gardner | 1 | 3 | 3 | 0 |
| Reich | 2 | 0 | 0 | 0 |

### DALLAS

| | No. | Yds | Lg | TD |
|---|---|---|---|---|
| E. Smith | 22 | 108 | 38 | 1 |
| Aikman | 3 | 28 | 19 | 0 |
| Gainer | 2 | 1 | 1 | 0 |
| Johnston | 1 | 0 | 0 | 0 |
| Beuerlein | 1 | 0 | 0 | 0 |

## Receiving

### BUFFALO

| | No. | Yds | Lg | TD |
|---|---|---|---|---|
| Reed | 8 | 152 | 40 | 0 |
| Thomas | 4 | 10 | 7 | 0 |
| K. Davis | 3 | 16 | 13 | 0 |
| Beebe | 2 | 50 | 40 | 1 |
| Tasker | 2 | 30 | 16 | 0 |
| Metzelaars | 2 | 12 | 7 | 0 |
| McKeller | 1 | 6 | 6 | 0 |

### DALLAS

| | No. | Yds | Lg | TD |
|---|---|---|---|---|
| Novacek | 7 | 72 | 23 | 1 |
| Irvin | 6 | 114 | 25 | 2 |
| E. Smith | 6 | 27 | 18 | 0 |
| Johnston | 2 | 15 | 8 | 0 |
| Harper | 1 | 45 | 45 | 1 |

## Defense

### BUFFALO

| | Tck | Ast | Int | Sack |
|---|---|---|---|---|
| Bennett | 8 | 1 | 0 | 1 |
| Talley | 6 | 0 | 0 | 0 |
| Patton | 6 | 0 | 0 | 0 |
| B. Smith | 5 | 0 | 0 | 0 |
| Odomes | 4 | 0 | 0 | 0 |
| Conlon | 3 | 5 | 0 | 0 |
| Jones | 3 | 2 | 0 | 0 |
| Williams | 3 | 2 | 0 | 0 |
| Derby | 3 | 0 | 0 | 0 |
| Wright | 3 | 0 | 0 | 0 |
| Pike | 3 | 0 | 0 | 0 |
| Kelso | 2 | 2 | 0 | 0 |
| Hanson | 2 | 1 | 0 | 0 |
| Hale | 2 | 0 | 0 | 0 |
| Maddox | 1 | 0 | 0 | 0 |
| K. Davis | 1 | 0 | 0 | 0 |
| Beebe | 1 | 0 | 0 | 0 |
| Metzelaars | 1 | 0 | 0 | 0 |
| Tasker | 0 | 1 | 0 | 0 |
| Goganious | 0 | 1 | 0 | 0 |
| Awalt | 0 | 0 | 0 | 0 |
| Hicks | 0 | 0 | 0 | 0 |

### DALLAS

| | Tck | Ast | Int | Sack |
|---|---|---|---|---|
| Norton | 8 | 1 | 0 | 0 |
| Haley | 5 | 0 | 0 | 1 |
| Washington | 4 | 2 | 1 | 0 |
| Edwards | 4 | 2 | 0 | 0 |
| Maryland | 4 | 2 | 0 | 0 |
| Woodson | 4 | 0 | 0 | 0 |
| Lett | 3 | 0 | 0 | 1 |
| Everett | 3 | 0 | 2 | 1 |
| Holmes | 3 | 0 | 0 | 0 |
| Casillas | 2 | 3 | 0 | 0 |
| Jeffcoat | 2 | 0 | 0 | 1 |
| Brown | 2 | 0 | 1 | 0 |
| J. Williams | 1 | 0 | 0 | 0 |
| Jones | 1 | 0 | 0 | 0 |
| Thomas | 1 | 0 | 0 | 0 |
| Ritcher | 1 | 0 | 0 | 0 |
| Lofton | 1 | 0 | 0 | 0 |

# 1992 Associated Press All-NFL Team

## OFFENSE

| | |
|---|---|
| Sterling Sharpe, Green Bay | Wide Receiver |
| Jerry Rice, San Francisco | Wide Receiver |
| Jay Novacek, Dallas | Tight End |
| Harris Barton, San Francisco | Tackle |
| Richmond Webb, Miami | Tackle |
| Randall McDaniel, Minnesota | Guard |
| Steve Wisniewski, LA Raiders | Guard |
| Bruce Matthews, Houston | Center |
| Steve Young, San Francisco | Quarterback |
| Emmitt Smith, Dallas | Running Back |
| Barry Foster, Pittsburgh | Running Back |

## DEFENSE

| | |
|---|---|
| Clyde Simmons, Philadelphia | Defensive End |
| Chris Doleman, Minnesota | Defensive End |
| Cortez Kennedy, Seattle | Defensive Tackle |
| Ray Childress, Houston | Nose Tackle |
| Pat Swilling, New Orleans | Outside Linebacker |
| Wilbur Marshall, Washington | Outside Linebacker |
| Junior Seau, San Diego | Inside Linebacker |
| Al Smith, Houston | Inside Linebacker |
| Rod Woodson, Pittsburgh | Cornerback |
| Audray McMillian, Minnesota | Cornerback |
| Steve Atwater, Denver | Safety |
| Henry Jones, Buffalo | Safety |

## SPECIALISTS

| | |
|---|---|
| Pete Stoyanovich, Miami | Kicker |
| Rich Camarillo, Phoenix | Punter |
| Deion Sanders, Atlanta | Kick Returner |

# 1992 AFC Team-by-Team Results

| BUFFALO BILLS (11-5) | | | CINCINNATI BENGALS (5-11) | | | CLEVELAND BROWNS (7-9) | | |
|---|---|---|---|---|---|---|---|---|
| 40 | LA RAMS | 7 | 21 | at Seattle | 3 | 3 | at Indianapolis | 14 |
| 34 | at San Francisco | 31 | 24 | LA RAIDERS (OT) | 21 | 23 | MIAMI | 27 |
| 38 | INDIANAPOLIS | 0 | 23 | at Green Bay | 24 | 28 | at LA Raiders | 16?? |
| 41 | at New England | 7 | 7 | MINNESOTA | 42 | 0 | DENVER | 12 |
| 10 | MIAMI | 37 | | OPEN DATE | | | OPEN DATE | |
| 3 | at LA Raiders | 20 | 24 | HOUSTON | 38 | 17 | PITTSBURGH | 9 |
| | OPEN DATE | | 0 | at Pittsburgh | 20 | 17 | GREEN BAY | 6 |
| 24 | at NY Jets | 20 | 10 | at Houston | 26 | 19 | at New England | 17 |
| 16 | NEW ENGLAND | 7 | 30 | CLEVELAND | 10 | 10 | at Cincinnati | 30 |
| 28 | PITTSBURGH | 20 | 31 | at Chicago (OT) | 28 | 24 | at Houston | 14 |
| 26 | at Miami | 20 | 14 | at NY Jets | 17 | 13 | SAN DIEGO | 14 |
| 41 | ATLANTA | 14 | 13 | DETROIT | 19 | 13 | at Minnesota | 17 |
| 13 | at Indianapolis (OT) | 16 | 9 | PITTSBURGH | 21 | 27 | CHICAGO | 14 |
| 17 | NY JETS | 24 | 21 | at Cleveland | 37 | 31 | CINCINNATI | 21 |
| 27 | DENVER | 17 | 10 | at San Diego | 27 | 14 | at Detroit | 24 |
| 20 | at New Orleans | 16 | 20 | NEW ENGLAND | 10 | 14 | HOUSTON | 17 |
| 3 | at Houston | 27 | 17 | INDIANAPOLIS | 21 | 13 | at Pittsburgh | 23 |
| 381 | | 283 | 274 | | 364 | 272 | | 275 |

## DENVER BRONCOS (8-8)

| | | |
|---|---|---|
| 17 | LA RAIDERS | 13 |
| 21 | SAN DIEGO | 13 |
| 0 | at Philadelphia | 30 |
| 12 | at Cleveland | 0 |
| 20 | KANSAS CITY | 19 |
| 3 | at Washington | 34 |
| 27 | HOUSTON | 21 |
| 21 | at San Diego | 24 |
| | OPEN DATE | |
| 27 | NY JETS | 16 |
| 27 | NY GIANTS | 13 |
| 0 | at LA Raiders | 24 |
| 13 | at Seattle (OT) | 16 |
| 27 | DALLAS | 31 |
| 17 | at Buffalo | 27 |
| 10 | SEATTLE | 6 |
| 20 | at Kansas City | 42 |
| 262 | | 329 |

## HOUSTON OILERS (10-6)

| | | |
|---|---|---|
| 24 | PITTSBURGH | 29 |
| 20 | at Indianapolis | 10 |
| 23 | KANSAS CITY (OT) | 20 |
| 27 | SAN DIEGO | 0 |
| | OPEN DATE | |
| 38 | at Cincinnati | 24 |
| 21 | at Denver | 27 |
| 26 | CINCINNATI | 10 |
| 20 | at Pittsburgh | 21 |
| 14 | CLEVELAND | 24 |
| 17 | at Minnesota | 13 |
| 16 | at Miami | 19 |
| 24 | at Detroit | 21 |
| 24 | CHICAGO | 7 |
| 14 | GREEN BAY | 16 |
| 17 | at Cleveland | 14 |
| 27 | BUFFALO | 3 |
| 352 | | 258 |

## INDIANAPOLIS COLTS (9-7)

| | | |
|---|---|---|
| 14 | CLEVELAND | 3 |
| 10 | HOUSTON | 20 |
| 0 | at Buffalo | 38 |
| | OPEN DATE | |
| 24 | at Tampa Bay | 14 |
| 6 | NY JETS (OT) | 3 |
| 14 | SAN DIEGO | 34 |
| 31 | at Miami | 20 |
| 0 | at San Diego | 26 |
| 0 | MIAMI | 28 |
| 34 | NEW ENGLAND (OT) | 37 |
| 14 | at Pittsburgh | 30 |
| 16 | BUFFALO (OT) | 13 |
| 6 | at New England | 0 |
| 10 | at NY Jets | 6 |
| 16 | PHOENIX | 13 |
| 21 | at Cincinnati | 17 |
| 216 | | 302 |

## KANSAS CITY CHIEFS (10-6)

| | | |
|---|---|---|
| 24 | at San Diego | 10 |
| 26 | SEATTLE | 7 |
| 20 | at Houston (OT) | 23 |
| 27 | LA RAIDERS | 7 |
| 19 | at Denver | 20 |
| 24 | PHILADELPHIA | 17 |
| 10 | at Dallas | 17 |
| 3 | PITTSBURGH | 27 |
| | OPEN DATE | |
| 16 | SAN DIEGO | 14 |
| 35 | WASHINGTON | 16 |
| 24 | at Seattle | 14 |
| 23 | at NY Jets | 7 |
| 7 | at LA Raiders | 28 |
| 27 | NEW ENGLAND | 20 |
| 21 | at NY Giants | 35 |
| 42 | DENVER | 20 |
| 348 | | 282 |

## LOS ANGELES RAIDERS (7-9)

| | | |
|---|---|---|
| 13 | at Denver | 17 |
| 21 | at Cincinnati (OT) | 24 |
| 16 | CLEVELAND | 28 |
| 7 | at Kansas City | 27 |
| 13 | NY GIANTS | 10 |
| 20 | BUFFALO | 3 |
| 19 | at Seattle | 0 |
| 13 | DALLAS | 28 |
| | OPEN DATE | |
| 10 | at Philadelphia | 31 |
| 20 | SEATTLE | 3 |
| 24 | DENVER | 0 |
| 3 | at San Diego | 27 |
| 28 | KANSAS CITY | 7 |
| 7 | at Miami | 20 |
| 14 | SAN DIEGO | 36 |
| 21 | at Washington | 20 |
| 249 | | 281 |

## MIAMI DOLPHINS (11-5)

| | | |
|---|---|---|
| | OPEN DATE | |
| 27 | at Cleveland | 23 |
| 26 | LA RAMS | 10 |
| 19 | at Seattle | 17 |
| 37 | at Buffalo | 10 |
| 21 | ATLANTA | 17 |
| 38 | NEW ENGLAND | 17 |
| 20 | INDIANAPOLIS | 31 |
| 14 | at NY Jets | 26 |
| 28 | at Indianapolis | 0 |
| 20 | BUFFALO | 26 |
| 19 | HOUSTON | 16 |
| 13 | at New Orleans | 24 |
| 3 | at San Francisco | 27 |
| 20 | LA RAIDERS | 7 |
| 19 | NY JETS | 17 |
| 16 | at New England (OT) | 13 |
| 340 | | 281 |

## NEW ENGLAND PATRIOTS (2-14)

| | | |
|---|---|---|
| | OPEN DATE | |
| 0 | at LA Rams | 14 |
| 6 | SEATTLE | 10 |
| 7 | BUFFALO | 41 |
| 21 | at NY Jets | 30 |
| 12 | SAN FRANCISCO | 24 |
| 17 | at Miami | 38 |
| 17 | CLEVELAND | 19 |
| 7 | at Buffalo | 16 |
| 14 | NEW ORLEANS | 31 |
| 37 | at Indianapolis (OT) | 34 |
| 24 | NY JETS | 3 |
| 0 | at Atlanta | 34 |
| 0 | INDIANAPOLIS | 6 |
| 20 | at Kansas City | 27 |
| 10 | at Cincinnati | 20 |
| 13 | MIAMI (OT) | 16 |
| 205 | | 363 |

## NEW YORK JETS (4-12)

| | | |
|---|---|---|
| 17 | at Atlanta | 20 |
| 10 | at Pittsburgh | 27 |
| 14 | SAN FRANCISCO | 31 |
| 10 | at LA Rams | 18 |
| 30 | NEW ENGLAND | 21 |
| 3 | at Indianapolis (OT) | 6 |
| | OPEN DATE | |
| 20 | BUFFALO | 24 |
| 26 | MIAMI | 14 |
| 16 | at Denver | 27 |
| 17 | CINCINNATI | 14 |
| 3 | at New England | 24 |
| 7 | KANSAS CITY | 23 |
| 24 | at Buffalo | 17 |
| 6 | INDIANAPOLIS | 10 |
| 17 | at Miami | 19 |
| 0 | NEW ORLEANS | 20 |
| 220 | | 315 |

## PITTSBURGH STEELERS (11-5)

| | | |
|---|---|---|
| 29 | at Houston | 24 |
| 27 | NY JETS | 10 |
| 23 | at San Diego | 6 |
| 3 | at Green Bay | 17 |
| | OPEN DATE | |
| 9 | at Cleveland | 17 |
| 20 | CINCINNATI | 0 |
| 27 | at Kansas City | 3 |
| 21 | HOUSTON | 20 |
| 20 | at Buffalo | 28 |
| 17 | DETROIT | 14 |
| 30 | INDIANAPOLIS | 14 |
| 21 | at Cincinnati | 9 |
| 20 | SEATTLE | 14 |
| 6 | at Chicago | 30 |
| 3 | MINNESOTA | 6 |
| 23 | CLEVELAND | 13 |
| 299 | | 225 |

### SAN DIEGO CHARGERS (11-5)

| | | |
|---:|---|---:|
| 10 | KANSAS CITY | 24 |
| 13 | at Denver | 21 |
| 6 | PITTSBURGH | 23 |
| 0 | at Houston | 27 |
| 17 | SEATTLE | 6 |
| | OPEN DATE | |
| 34 | at Indianapolis | 14 |
| 24 | DENVER | 21 |
| 26 | Indianapolis | 0 |
| 14 | at Kansas City | 16 |
| 14 | at Cleveland | 13 |
| 29 | TAMPA BAY | 14 |
| 27 | LA RAIDERS | 3 |
| 27 | at Phoenix | 21 |
| 27 | CINCINNATI | 10 |
| 36 | at LA Raiders | 14 |
| 31 | at Seattle | 14 |
| **335** | | **241** |

### SEATTLE SEAHAWKS (2-14)

| | | |
|---:|---|---:|
| 3 | CINCINNATI | 21 |
| 7 | at Kansas City | 26 |
| 10 | at New England | 6 |
| 17 | MIAMI | 19 |
| 6 | at San Diego | 17 |
| 0 | at Dallas | 27 |
| 0 | LA RAIDERS | 19 |
| 10 | at NY Giants | 23 |
| | OPEN DATE | |
| 3 | WASHINGTON· | 16 |
| 3 | at LA Raiders | 20 |
| 14 | KANSAS CITY | 24 |
| 16 | DENVER (OT) | 13 |
| 14 | at Pittsburgh | 20 |
| 17 | PHILADELPHIA (OT) | 20 |
| 6 | at Denver | 10 |
| 14 | SAN DIEGO | 31 |
| **140** | | **312** |

### ATLANTA FALCONS (6-10)

| | | |
|---:|---|---:|
| 20 | NY JETS | 17 |
| 17 | at Washington | 24 |
| 7 | NEW ORLEANS | 10 |
| 31 | at Chicago | 41 |
| 24 | GREEN BAY | 10 |
| 17 | at Miami | 21 |
| 17 | at San Francisco | 56 |
| | OPEN DATE | |
| 30 | LA RAMS | 28 |
| 3 | SAN FRANCISCO | 41 |
| 20 | PHOENIX | 17 |
| 14 | at Buffalo | 41 |
| 34 | NEW ENGLAND | 0 |
| 14 | at New Orleans | 22 |
| 35 | at Tampa Bay | 7 |
| 17 | DALLAS | 41 |
| 27 | at LA Rams | 38 |
| **327** | | **414** |

### CHICAGO BEARS (5-11)

| | | |
|---:|---|---:|
| 27 | DETROIT | 24 |
| 6 | at New Orleans | 28 |
| 14 | NY GIANTS | 27 |
| 41 | ATLANTA | 31 |
| 20 | at Minnesota | 21 |
| | OPEN DATE | |
| 31 | TAMPA BAY | 14 |
| 30 | at Green Bay | 10 |
| 10 | MINNESOTA | 38 |
| 28 | CINCINNATI (OT) | 31 |
| 17 | at Tampa Bay | 20 |
| 3 | GREEN BAY | 17 |
| 14 | at Cleveland | 27 |
| 7 | at Houston | 24 |
| 30 | PITTSBURGH | 6 |
| 3 | at Detroit | 16 |
| 14 | at Dallas | 27 |
| **295** | | **361** |

### DALLAS COWBOYS (13-3)

| | | |
|---:|---|---:|
| 23 | WASHINGTON | 10 |
| 34 | at NY Giants | 28 |
| 31 | PHOENIX | 20 |
| | OPEN DATE | |
| 7 | at Philadelphia | 31 |
| 27 | SEATTLE | 0 |
| 17 | KANSAS CITY | 10 |
| 28 | at LA Raiders | 13 |
| 20 | PHILADELPHIA | 10 |
| 37 | at Detroit | 3 |
| 23 | LA RAMS | 27 |
| 16 | at Phoenix | 10 |
| 30 | NY GIANTS | 3 |
| 31 | at Denver | 27 |
| 17 | at Washington | 20 |
| 41 | at Atlanta | 17 |
| 27 | CHICAGO | 14 |
| **409** | | **243** |

### DETROIT LIONS (5-11)

| | | |
|---:|---|---:|
| 24 | at Chicago | 27 |
| 31 | MINNESOTA | 17 |
| 10 | at Washington | 13 |
| 23 | TAMPA BAY | 27 |
| 7 | NEW ORLEANS | 13 |
| | OPEN DATE | |
| 14 | at Minnesota | 31 |
| 38 | at Tampa Bay | 7 |
| 13 | GREEN BAY | 27 |
| 3 | DALLAS | 37 |
| 14 | at Pittsburgh | 17 |
| 19 | at Cincinnati | 13 |
| 21 | HOUSTON | 24 |
| 10 | at Green Bay* | 38 |
| 24 | CLEVELAND | 14 |
| 16 | CHICAGO | 3 |
| 6 | at San Francisco | 24 |
| **273** | | **332** |

### GREEN BAY PACKERS (9-7)

| | | |
|---:|---|---:|
| 20 | MINNESOTA (OT) | 23 |
| 3 | at Tampa Bay | 31 |
| 24 | CINCINNATI | 23 |
| 17 | PITTSBURGH | 3 |
| 10 | at Atlanta | 24 |
| | OPEN DATE | |
| 6 | at Cleveland | 17 |
| 10 | CHICAGO | 30 |
| 27 | at Detroit | 13 |
| 7 | at NY Giants | 27 |
| 27 | PHILADELPHIA* | 24 |
| 17 | at Chicago | 3 |
| 19 | TAMPA BAY* | 14 |
| 38 | DETROIT* | 10 |
| 16 | at Houston | 14 |
| 28 | LA RAMS | 13 |
| 7 | at Minnesota | 27 |
| **276** | | **296** |

### LOS ANGELES RAMS (6-10)

| | | |
|---:|---|---:|
| 7 | at Buffalo | 40 |
| 14 | NEW ENGLAND | 0 |
| 10 | at Miami | 26 |
| 18 | NY JETS | 10 |
| 24 | at San Francisco | 27 |
| 10 | at New Orleans | 13 |
| 38 | NY GIANTS | 17 |
| | OPEN DATE | |
| 28 | at Atlanta | 30 |
| 14 | PHOENIX | 20 |
| 27 | at Dallas | 23 |
| 10 | SAN FRANCISCO | 27 |
| 17 | MINNESOTA | 31 |
| 31 | at Tampa Bay | 27 |
| 14 | NEW ORLEANS | 37 |
| 13 | at Green Bay | 28 |
| 38 | ATLANTA | 27 |
| **313** | | **383** |

### MINNESOTA VIKINGS (11-5)

| | | |
|---|---|---|
| 23 | at Green Bay (OT) | 20 |
| 17 | at Detroit | 31 |
| 26 | TAMPA BAY | 20 |
| 42 | at Cincinnati | 7 |
| 21 | CHICAGO | 20 |
| | OPEN DATE | |
| 31 | DETROIT | 14 |
| 13 | WASHINGTON | 15 |
| 38 | at Chicago | 10 |
| 35 | at Tampa Bay | 7 |
| 13 | HOUSTON | 17 |
| 17 | CLEVELAND | 13 |
| 31 | at LA Rams | 17 |
| 17 | at Philadelphia | 28 |
| 17 | SAN FRANCISCO | 20 |
| 6 | at Pittsburgh | 3 |
| 27 | GREEN BAY | 7 |
| 374 | | 249 |

### NEW ORLEANS SAINTS (12-4)

| | | |
|---|---|---|
| 13 | at Philadelphia | 15 |
| 28 | CHICAGO | 6 |
| 10 | at Atlanta | 7 |
| 10 | SAN FRANCISCO | 16 |
| 13 | at Detroit | 7 |
| 13 | LA RAMS | 10 |
| 30 | at Phoenix | 21 |
| | OPEN DATE | |
| 23 | TAMPA BAY | 21 |
| 31 | at New England | 14 |
| 20 | at San Francisco | 21 |
| 20 | WASHINGTON | 3 |
| 24 | MIAMI | 13 |
| 22 | ATLANTA | 14 |
| 37 | at LA Rams | 14 |
| 16 | BUFFALO | 20 |
| 20 | at NY Jets | 0 |
| 330 | | 202 |

### NEW YORK GIANTS (6-10)

| | | |
|---|---|---|
| 14 | SAN FRANCISCO | 31 |
| 28 | DALLAS | 34 |
| 27 | at Chicago | 14 |
| | OPEN DATE | |
| 10 | at LA Raiders | 13 |
| 31 | PHOENIX | 21 |
| 17 | at LA Rams | 38 |
| 23 | SEATTLE | 10 |
| 24 | at Washington | 7 |
| 27 | GREEN BAY | 7 |
| 13 | at Denver | 27 |
| 34 | PHILADELPHIA | 47 |
| 3 | at Dallas | 30 |
| 10 | WASHINGTON | 28 |
| 0 | at Phoenix | 19 |
| 35 | KANSAS CITY | 21 |
| 10 | at Philadelphia | 20 |
| 306 | | 367 |

### PHILADELPHIA EAGLES (11-5)

| | | |
|---|---|---|
| 15 | NEW ORLEANS | 13 |
| 31 | at Phoenix | 14 |
| 30 | DENVER | 0 |
| | OPEN DATE | |
| 31 | DALLAS | 7 |
| 17 | at Kansas City | 24 |
| 12 | at Washington | 16 |
| 7 | PHOENIX | 3 |
| 10 | at Dallas | 20 |
| 31 | LA RAIDERS | 10 |
| 24 | vs Green Bay | 27 |
| 47 | at NY Giants | 34 |
| 14 | at San Francisco | 20 |
| 28 | MINNESOTA | 17 |
| 20 | at Seattle (OT) | 17 |
| 17 | WASHINGTON | 13 |
| 20 | NY GIANTS | 10 |
| 354 | | 245 |

### PHOENIX CARDINALS (4-12)

| | | |
|---|---|---|
| 7 | at Tampa Bay | 23 |
| 14 | PHILADELPHIA | 31 |
| 20 | at Dallas | 31 |
| | OPEN DATE | |
| 27 | WASHINGTON | 24 |
| 21 | at NY Giants | 31 |
| 21 | NEW ORLEANS | 30 |
| 3 | at Philadelphia | 7 |
| 24 | SAN FRANCISCO | 14 |
| 20 | at LA Rams | 14 |
| 17 | at Atlanta | 20 |
| 10 | DALLAS | 16 |
| 3 | at Washington | 31 |
| 21 | SAN DIEGO | 27 |
| 19 | NY GIANTS | 0 |
| 13 | at Indianapolis | 16 |
| 3 | TAMPA BAY | 7 |
| 243 | | 332 |

### SAN FRANCISCO 49ERS (14-2)

| | | |
|---|---|---|
| 31 | at NY Giants | 14 |
| 31 | BUFFALO | 34 |
| 31 | at NY Jets | 14 |
| 16 | at New Orleans | 10 |
| 27 | LA RAMS | 24 |
| 24 | at New England | 12 |
| 56 | ATLANTA | 17 |
| | OPEN DATE | |
| 14 | at Phoenix | 24 |
| 41 | at Atlanta | 3 |
| 21 | NEW ORLEANS | 20 |
| 27 | at LA Rams | 10 |
| 20 | PHILADELPHIA | 14 |
| 27 | MIAMI | 3 |
| 20 | at Minnesota | 17 |
| 21 | TAMPA BAY | 14 |
| 24 | DETROIT | 6 |
| 431 | | 236 |

### TAMPA BAY BUCCANEERS (5-11)

| | | |
|---|---|---|
| 23 | PHOENIX | 7 |
| 31 | GREEN BAY | 3 |
| 20 | at Minnesota | 26 |
| 27 | at Detroit | 23 |
| 14 | INDIANAPOLIS | 24 |
| | OPEN DATE | |
| 14 | at Chicago | 31 |
| 7 | DETROIT | 38 |
| 21 | at New Orleans | 23 |
| 7 | MINNESOTA | 35 |
| 20 | CHICAGO | 17 |
| 14 | at San Diego | 29 |
| 14 | vs Green Bay | 19 |
| 27 | LA RAMS | 31 |
| 7 | ATLANTA | 35 |
| 14 | at San Francisco | 21 |
| 7 | at Phoenix | 3 |
| 267 | | 365 |

### WASHINGTON REDSKINS (9-7)

| | | |
|---|---|---|
| 10 | at Dallas | 23 |
| 24 | ATLANTA | 17 |
| 13 | DETROIT | 10 |
| | OPEN DATE | |
| 24 | at Phoenix | 27 |
| 34 | DENVER | 3 |
| 16 | PHILADELPHIA | 12 |
| 15 | at Minnesota | 13 |
| 7 | NY GIANTS | 24 |
| 16 | at Seattle | 3 |
| 16 | at Kansas City | 35 |
| 3 | at New Orleans | 20 |
| 41 | PHOENIX | 3 |
| 28 | at NY Giants | 10 |
| 20 | DALLAS | 17 |
| 13 | at Philadelphia | 17 |
| 20 | LA RAIDERS | 20 |
| 300 | | 255 |

## American Football Conference
### Scoring

| TOUCHDOWNS | TD | Rush | Rec | Ret | Pts | KICKING | PAT | FG | Lg | Pts |
|---|---|---|---|---|---|---|---|---|---|---|
| Thomas. Buff | 12 | 9 | 3 | 0 | 72 | Stoyanovich, Mia | 34/36 | 30/37 | 53 | 124 |
| Foster, Pitt | 11 | 11 | 0 | 0 | 66 | Christie, Buff | 43/44 | 24/30 | 54 | 115 |
| Givins, Hou | 10 | 0 | 10 | 0 | 60 | Anderson, Pitt | 29/31 | 28/36 | 49 | 113 |
| Culver, Ind | 9 | 7 | 2 | 0 | 54 | Carney, SD | 35/35 | 26/32 | 50 | 113 |
| Jeffires, Hou | 9 | 0 | 9 | 0 | 54 | Lowery, KC | 39/39 | 22/24 | 52 | 105 |
| Fenner, Cin | 8 | 7 | 1 | 0 | 48 | Del Greco, Hou | 41/41 | 21/27 | 54 | 104 |
| Jackson, Den | 8 | 0 | 8 | 0 | 48 | Stover, Cle | 29/30 | 21/29 | 51 | 92 |
| Miller, SD | 8 | 0 | 7 | 1 | 48 | Breech, Cin | 31/31 | 19/27 | 48 | 88 |
| White, Hou | 8 | 7 | 1 | 0 | 48 | Treadwell, Den | 28/28 | 20/24 | 46 | 88 |
| Brown, Rai | 7 | 0 | 7 | 0 | 42 | Jaeger, Rai | 28/28 | 15/26 | 54 | 73 |

### Passing

| | Att | Comp | Pct Comp | Yds | Avg Gain | TD | Pct TD | Int | Pct Int | Lg | Rating Pts |
|---|---|---|---|---|---|---|---|---|---|---|---|
| Moon, Hou | 346 | 224 | 64.7 | 2521 | 7.29 | 18 | 5.2 | 12 | 3.5 | 72 | 89.3 |
| Marino, Mia | 554 | 330 | 59.6 | 4116 | 7.43 | 24 | 4.3 | 16 | 2.9 | t62 | 85.1 |
| O'Donnell, Pitt | 313 | 185 | 59.1 | 2283 | 7.29 | 13 | 4.2 | 9 | 2.9 | 51 | 83.6 |
| Kelly, Buff | 462 | 269 | 58.2 | 3457 | 7.48 | 23 | 5.0 | 19 | 4.1 | t65 | 81.2 |
| Carlson, Hou | 227 | 149 | 65.6 | 1710 | 7.53 | 9 | 4.0 | 11 | 4.8 | 65 | 81.2 |
| Krieg, KC | 413 | 230 | 55.7 | 3115 | 7.54 | 15 | 3.6 | 12 | 2.9 | t77 | 79.9 |
| Humphries, SD | 454 | 263 | 57.9 | 3356 | 7.39 | 16 | 3.5 | 18 | 4.0 | t67 | 76.4 |
| Elway, Den | 316 | 174 | 55.1 | 2242 | 7.09 | 10 | 3.2 | 17 | 5.4 | t80 | 65.7 |
| Schroeder, Rai | 253 | 123 | 48.6 | 1476 | 5.83 | 11 | 4.3 | 11 | 4.3 | 53 | 63.3 |
| George, Ind | 306 | 167 | 54.6 | 1963 | 6.42 | 7 | 2.3 | 15 | 4.9 | t57 | 61.5 |

### Pass Receiving

| RECEPTIONS | No. | Yds | Avg | Lg | TD | YARDS | Yds | No. | Avg | Lg | TD |
|---|---|---|---|---|---|---|---|---|---|---|---|
| Jeffires, Hou | 90 | 913 | 10.1 | 47 | 9 | Miller, SD | 1060 | 72 | 14.7 | t67 | 7 |
| Duncan, Hou | 82 | 954 | 11.6 | 72 | 1 | Duncan, Hou | 954 | 82 | 11.6 | 72 | 1 |
| Harmon, SD | 79 | 914 | 11.6 | 55 | 1 | Harmon, SD | 914 | 79 | 11.6 | 55 | 1 |
| Williams, Sea | 74 | 556 | 7.5 | 27 | 2 | Jeffires, Hou | 913 | 90 | 10.1 | 47 | 9 |
| Miller, SD | 72 | 1060 | 14.7 | t67 | 7 | Reed, Buff | 913 | 65 | 14.0 | 51 | 3 |
| Givins, Hou | 67 | 787 | 11.7 | 45 | 10 | Langhorne, Ind | 811 | 65 | 12.5 | 34 | 1 |
| Reed, Buff | 65 | 913 | 14.0 | 51 | 3 | Hester, Ind | 792 | 52 | 15.2 | 81 | 1 |
| Langhorne,.Ind | 65 | 811 | 12.5 | 34 | 1 | Fryar, NE | 791 | 55 | 14.4 | t54 | 4 |
| Thomas, Buff | 58 | 626 | 10.8 | 43 | 3 | Givins, Hou | 787 | 67 | 11.7 | 41 | 10 |
| Burkett, NYJ | 57 | 724 | 11.2 | t37 | 1 | Lofton, Buff | 786 | 51 | 15.4 | 50 | 6 |

### Rushing

| | Att | Yds | Avg | Lg | TD | Total Yards from Scrimmage | Total | Rush | Rec |
|---|---|---|---|---|---|---|---|---|---|
| Foster, Pitt | 390 | 1690 | 4.3 | 69 | 11 | Thomas, Buff | 2113 | 1487 | 626 |
| Thomas, Buff | 312 | 1487 | 4.8 | 44 | 9 | Foster, Pitt | 2034 | 1690 | 344 |
| White, Hou | 265 | 1226 | 4.6 | 44 | 7 | White, Hou | 1867 | 1226 | 641 |
| Green, Cin | 265 | 1170 | 4.4 | 53 | 2 | Green, Cin | 1384 | 1170 | 214 |
| Warren, Sea | 223 | 1017 | 4.6 | 52 | 3 | Warren, Sea | 1151 | 1017 | 134 |
| Higgs, Mia | 256 | 915 | 3.6 | 23 | 7 | Harmon, SD | 1149 | 235 | 914 |
| Butts, SD | 218 | 809 | 3.7 | 22 | 4 | Johnson, Ind | 1109 | 592 | 517 |
| Dickerson, Rai | 187 | 729 | 3.9 | t40 | 2 | Miller, SD | 1059 | -1 | 1060 |
| Baxter, NYJ | 152 | 698 | 4.6 | 30 | 6 | Higgs, Mia | 1057 | 915 | 142 |
| Green, Den | 161 | 648 | 4.0 | t67 | 2 | Humphrey, Mia | 978 | 471 | 507 |

### Interceptions

| | No. | Yds | Lg | TD | Sacks | |
|---|---|---|---|---|---|---|
| Jones, Buff | 8 | 263 | t82 | 2 | O'Neal, SD | 17.0 |
| Robinson, Sea | 7 | 126 | 49 | 0 | Fletcher, Den | 16.0 |
| Carter, KC | 7 | 65 | t36 | 1 | N. Smith, KC | 14.5 |
| Kelso, Buff | 7 | 21 | 13 | 0 | Thomas, KC | 14.5 |
| Carrington, SD | 6 | 152 | 69 | 1 | Cox, Mia | 14.0 |
| Brim, NYJ | 6 | 139 | t77 | 1 | Kennedy, Sea | 14.0 |
| Perry, Pitt | 6 | 69 | 34 | 0 | B. Smith, Buff | 14.0 |
| Washington, NYJ | 6 | 59 | t23 | 1 | Childress, Hou | 13.0 |
| Prior, Ind | 6 | 44 | 19 | 0 | A. Smith, Rai | 13.0 |
| Gray, Hou | 6 | 24 | 22 | 0 | | |

## American Football Conference (Cont.)

### Punting

| | No. | Yds | Avg | Net Avg | TB | In 20 | Lg | Blk | Ret | Ret Yds |
|---|---|---|---|---|---|---|---|---|---|---|
| Montgomery, Hou | 53 | 2487 | 46.9 | 37.3 | 9 | 14 | 66 | 2 | 31 | 255 |
| Stark, Ind | 83 | 3716 | 44.8 | 39.3 | 7 | 22 | 64 | 0 | 45 | 313 |
| Tuten, Sea | 108 | 4760 | 44.1 | 38.7 | 8 | 29 | 65 | 0 | 56 | 416 |
| Barker, KC | 75 | 3245 | 43.3 | 35.3 | 13 | 16 | 65 | 1 | 35 | 300 |
| Royals, Pitt | 73 | 3119 | 42.7 | 35.6 | 9 | 22 | 58 | 1 | 39 | 308 |

### Punt Returns

| | No. | Yds | Avg | Lg | TD |
|---|---|---|---|---|---|
| Woodson, Pitt | 32 | 364 | 11.4 | t80 | 1 |
| Verdin, Ind | 24 | 268 | 11.2 | t84 | 2 |
| Marshall, Den | 33 | 349 | 10.6 | 47 | 0 |
| Carter, KC | 38 | 398 | 10.5 | t86 | 2 |
| Brown, Rai | 37 | 383 | 10.4 | 40 | 0 |

### Kickoff Returns

| | No. | Yds | Avg | Lg | TD |
|---|---|---|---|---|---|
| Vaughn, NE | 20 | 564 | 28.2 | t100 | 1 |
| Baldwin, Cle | 30 | 675 | 22.5 | 47 | 0 |
| Montgomery, Den | 21 | 466 | 22.2 | 64 | 0 |
| Verdin, Ind | 39 | 815 | 20.9 | 42 | 0 |
| Ball, Cin | 20 | 411 | 20.6 | 48 | 1 |

## National Football Conference

### Scoring

| TOUCHDOWNS | TD | Rush | Rec | Ret | Pts | KICKING | PAT | FG | Lg | Pts |
|---|---|---|---|---|---|---|---|---|---|---|
| E. Smith, Dall | 19 | 18 | 1 | 0 | 114 | Andersen, NO | 33/34 | 29/34 | 52 | 120 |
| Allen, Minn | 15 | 13 | 2 | 0 | 90 | Lohmiller, Wash | 30/30 | 30/40 | 53 | 120 |
| Hampton, NYG | 14 | 14 | 0 | 0 | 84 | Elliott, Dall | 47/48 | 24/35 | 53 | 119 |
| Sharpe, GB | 13 | 0 | 13 | 0 | 78 | Cofer, SF | 53/54 | 18/27 | 46 | 107 |
| Anderson, Chi | 11 | 5 | 6 | 0 | 66 | Reveiz, Minn | 45/45 | 19/25 | 52 | 102 |
| Rice, SF | 11 | 1 | 10 | 0 | 66 | Jacke, GB | 30/30 | 22/29 | 53 | 96 |
| Rison, Atl | 11 | 0 | 11 | 0 | 66 | Hanson, Det | 30/30 | 22/29 | 52 | 93 |
| Watters, SF | 11 | 9 | 2 | 0 | 66 | Johnson, Atl | 39/39 | 18/22 | 54 | 93 |
| Gary, Rams | 10 | 7 | 3 | 0 | 60 | Butler, Chi | 34/34 | 19/26 | 50 | 91 |
| Haynes, Atl | 10 | 0 | 10 | 0 | 60 | Ruzek, Phi | 40/44 | 16/25 | 50 | 88 |
| Sanders, Det | 10 | 9 | 1 | 0 | 60 | Zendejas, Rams | 38/38 | 15/20 | 49 | 83 |

### Passing

| | Att | Comp | Pct Comp | Yds | Avg Gain | TD | Pct TD | Int | Pct Int | Lg | Rating Pts |
|---|---|---|---|---|---|---|---|---|---|---|---|
| Young, SF | 402 | 268 | 66.7 | 3465 | 8.62 | 25 | 6.2 | 7 | 1.7 | t80 | 107.0 |
| Miller, Atl | 253 | 152 | 60.1 | 1739 | 6.87 | 15 | 5.9 | 6 | 2.4 | t89 | 90.7 |
| Aikman, Dall | 473 | 302 | 63.8 | 3445 | 7.28 | 23 | 4.9 | 14 | 3.0 | t87 | 89.5 |
| Cunningham, Phi | 384 | 233 | 60.7 | 2775 | 7.23 | 19 | 4.9 | 11 | 2.9 | t75 | 87.3 |
| Favre, GB | 471 | 302 | 64.1 | 3227 | 6.85 | 18 | 3.8 | 13 | 2.8 | t76 | 85.3 |
| Hebert, NO | 422 | 249 | 59.0 | 3287 | 7.79 | 19 | 4.5 | 16 | 3.8 | t72 | 82.9 |
| Everett, Rams | 475 | 281 | 59.2 | 3323 | 7.00 | 22 | 4.6 | 18 | 3.8 | t67 | 80.2 |
| Chandler, Pho | 413 | 245 | 59.3 | 2832 | 6.86 | 15 | 3.6 | 15 | 3.6 | t72 | 77.1 |
| Harbaugh, Chi | 358 | 202 | 56.4 | 2486 | 6.94 | 13 | 3.6 | 12 | 3.4 | t83 | 76.2 |
| Testaverde, TB | 358 | 206 | 57.5 | 2554 | 7.13 | 14 | 3.9 | 16 | 4.5 | t81 | 74.2 |

### Pass Receiving

| RECEPTIONS | No. | Yds | Avg | Lg | TD | YARDS | Yds | No. | Avg | Lg | TD |
|---|---|---|---|---|---|---|---|---|---|---|---|
| Sharpe, GB | 108 | 1461 | 13.5 | t76 | 13 | Sharpe, GB | 1461 | 108 | 13.5 | t76 | 13 |
| Rison, Atl | 93 | 1121 | 12.1 | t71 | 11 | Irvin, Dall | 1396 | 78 | 17.9 | t87 | 7 |
| Rice, SF | 84 | 1201 | 14.3 | t80 | 10 | Rice, SF | 1201 | 84 | 14.3 | t80 | 10 |
| Irvin, Dall | 78 | 1396 | 17.9 | t87 | 7 | Rison, Atl | 1121 | 93 | 12.1 | t71 | 11 |
| Pritchard, Atl | 77 | 827 | 10.7 | t38 | 5 | Barnett, Phil | 1083 | 67 | 16.2 | t71 | 6 |
| Perriman, Det | 69 | 810 | 11.7 | t40 | 4 | E. Martin, NO | 1041 | 68 | 15.3 | t52 | 5 |
| E. Martin, NO | 68 | 1041 | 15.3 | t52 | 5 | Moore, Det | 966 | 51 | 18.9 | t77 | 4 |
| Novacek, Dall | 68 | 630 | 9.3 | 34 | 6 | Clark, Wash | 912 | 64 | 14.3 | 47 | 5 |
| Barnett, Phil | 67 | 1083 | 16.2 | t71 | 6 | R. Hill, Pho | 861 | 58 | 14.8 | 49 | 3 |
| Clark, Wash | 64 | 912 | 14.3 | 47 | 5 | Pritchard, Atl | 827 | 77 | 10.7 | t38 | 5 |

## National Football Conference (Cont.)

### Rushing

| | Att | Yds | Avg | Lg | TD |
|---|---|---|---|---|---|
| E. Smith, Dall | 373 | 1713 | 4.6 | t68 | 18 |
| B. Sanders, Det | 312 | 1352 | 4.3 | t55 | 9 |
| Allen, Minn | 266 | 1201 | 4.5 | 51 | 13 |
| Cobb, TB | 310 | 1171 | 3.8 | 25 | 9 |
| Hampton, NYG | 257 | 1141 | 4.4 | t63 | 14 |
| Gary, LA Rams | 279 | 1125 | 4.0 | 63 | 7 |
| Walker, Phil | 267 | 1070 | 4.0 | 38 | 8 |
| Watters, SF | 206 | 1013 | 4.9 | 43 | 9 |
| Byner, Wash | 262 | 998 | 3.8 | 23 | 6 |
| Johnson, Phoe | 178 | 734 | 4.1 | t42 | 6 |

### Total Yards from Scrimmage

| | Total | Rush | Rec |
|---|---|---|---|
| E. Smith, Dall | 2048 | 1713 | 335 |
| Allen, Minn | 1679 | 1201 | 478 |
| Sanders, Det | 1577 | 1352 | 225 |
| Sharpe, GB | 1469 | 8 | 1461 |
| Gary, LA Rams | 1418 | 1125 | 293 |
| Watters, SF | 1418 | 1013 | 405 |
| Irvin, Dall | 1387 | -9 | 1396 |
| Hampton, NYG | 1356 | 1141 | 215 |
| Walker, Phil | 1348 | 1070 | 278 |
| Byner, Wash | 1336 | 998 | 338 |

### Interceptions

| | No. | Yds | Lg | TD |
|---|---|---|---|---|
| McMillian, Minn | 8 | 157 | t51 | 2 |
| Woolford, Chi | 7 | 67 | 32 | 0 |
| Edwards, Wash | 6 | 157 | t53 | 1 |
| Cook, NO | 6 | 90 | t48 | 1 |

Note: Four players tied with five.

### Sacks

| | |
|---|---|
| Simmons, Phil | 19.0 |
| Harris, SF | 17.0 |
| Martin, NO | 15.5 |
| Doleman, Minn | 14.5 |
| White, Phil | 14.0 |
| Bennett, GB | 13.5 |
| Jackson, NO | 13.5 |
| Randle, Minn | 11.5 |

### Punting

| | No. | Yds | Avg | Net Avg | TB | In 20 | Lg | Blk | Ret | Ret Yds |
|---|---|---|---|---|---|---|---|---|---|---|
| Newsome, Minn | 72 | 3243 | 45.0 | 35.7 | 15 | 19 | 84 | 1 | 34 | 339 |
| Barnhardt, NO | 67 | 2947 | 44.0 | 37.7 | 10 | 19 | 62 | 0 | 31 | 218 |
| Arnold, Det | 65 | 2846 | 43.8 | 34.7 | 10 | 12 | 71 | 1 | 30 | 356 |
| Landeta, NY Giants | 53 | 2317 | 43.7 | 31.5 | 9 | 13 | 71 | 2 | 30 | 406 |
| Saxon, Dall | 61 | 2620 | 43.0 | 33.5 | 9 | 19 | 58 | 0 | 34 | 397 |

### Punt Returns

| | No. | Yds | Avg | Lg | TD |
|---|---|---|---|---|---|
| Bailey, Pho | 20 | 263 | 13.2 | 65 | 0 |
| Martin, Dall | 42 | 532 | 12.7 | t79 | 2 |
| Sikahema, Phil | 40 | 503 | 12.6 | t87 | 1 |
| Parker, Minn | 33 | 336 | 10.2 | 42 | 0 |
| Buckley, GB | 21 | 211 | 10.0 | t58 | 1 |

### Kickoff Returns

| | No. | Yds | Avg | Lg | TD |
|---|---|---|---|---|---|
| Sanders, Atl | 40 | 1067 | 26.7 | t99 | 2 |
| Bailey, Pho | 28 | 690 | 24.6 | 63 | 0 |
| Gray, Det | 42 | 1006 | 24.0 | t89 | 1 |
| Meggett, NYG | 20 | 455 | 22.8 | t92 | 1 |
| Lewis, Chi | 23 | 511 | 22.2 | t97 | 1 |

## Anthonia Who?

Do the 49ers have a bottomless pool of talent? Sure seems that way. Lose Joe Montana, plug in Steve Young. Lose John Taylor, plug in Mike Sherrard. Lose Ricky Watters, plug in Anthonia Wayne Lee. That's Amp Lee, for short. In fact, it's the league's shortest name.

But Lee was long on ability in a 20–17 win at Minnesota in December, rushing 23 times for 134 yards and scoring twice. The 49ers drafted Watters and Lee in the second round of the 1991 and '92 drafts, respectively, in the hope that one of them would develop into a long-term replacement for departed multipurpose back Roger Craig. Both might fit the bill.

Watters looked like a franchise back for the first three months of the season, but then he suffered a deep shoulder bruise against the Eagles on Nov. 29. In stepped Lee. "Several times this year I completely forgot to pick up my paycheck because I didn't feel I had done anything," says Lee. "It was like Wednesday or Thursday before I went to get it." Players are paid after games on Sunday, and after the Minmnesota game Lee picked up his check on time. No back in the league had a better day than he did.

## AFC Total Offense

| | Total Yds | Yds Rush | Yds Pass | Time of Poss | Avg Pts/Game |
|---|---|---|---|---|---|
| Buffalo | 5893 | 2436 | 3457 | 28:10 | 23.8 |
| Houston | 5655 | 1626 | 4029 | 31:09 | 22 |
| Miami | 5500 | 1525 | 3975 | 30:30 | 21.3 |
| San Diego | 5221 | 1875 | 3346 | 32:02 | 20.9 |
| Pittsburgh | 4906 | 2156 | 2750 | 32:05 | 18.7 |
| Cleveland | 4492 | 1607 | 2885 | 30:13 | 17 |
| NY Jets | 4431 | 1752 | 2679 | 30:24 | 13.8 |
| Denver | 4430 | 1500 | 2930 | 28:14 | 16.4 |
| LA Raiders | 4384 | 1794 | 2590 | 29:06 | 15.6 |
| Indianapolis | 4368 | 1102 | 3266 | 28:17 | 13.5 |
| Kansas City | 4324 | 1532 | 2792 | 29:37 | 21.8 |
| Cincinnati | 3919 | 1976 | 1943 | 27:06 | 17.1 |
| New England | 3584 | 1550 | 2034 | 28:28 | 12.8 |
| Seattle | 3374 | 1596 | 1778 | 29:01 | 8.8 |

## AFC Total Defense

| | Opp Total Yds | Opp Yds Rush | Opp Yds Pass | Avg PA/Game |
|---|---|---|---|---|
| Houston | 4211 | 1634 | 2577 | 16.1 |
| San Diego | 4227 | 1395 | 2832 | 15.1 |
| Kansas City | 4324 | 1787 | 2537 | 17.6 |
| LA Raiders | 4516 | 1683 | 2833 | 17.6 |
| Miami | 4583 | 1600 | 2983 | 17.6 |
| Seattle | 4583 | 1922 | 2661 | 19.5 |
| Buffalo | 4604 | 1395 | 3209 | 17.7 |
| Pittsburgh | 4658 | 1841 | 2817 | 14.1 |
| Cleveland | 4757 | 1605 | 3152 | 17.2 |
| NY Jets | 4880 | 1919 | 2961 | 19.7 |
| New England | 5048 | 1951 | 3097 | 22.7 |
| Indianapolis | 5074 | 2174 | 2900 | 18.9 |
| Denver | 5083 | 1963 | 3120 | 20.6 |
| Cincinnati | 5333 | 2007 | 3326 | 22.8 |

## NFC Total Offense

| | Total Yds | Yds Rush | Yds Pass | Time of Poss | Avg Pts/Game |
|---|---|---|---|---|---|
| San Francisco | 6195 | 2315 | 3880 | 32:19 | 26.9 |
| Dallas | 5606 | 2121 | 3485 | | 25.6 |
| Philadelphia | 4980 | 2388 | 2592 | 31:47 | 22.1 |
| Chicago | 4941 | 1871 | 3070 | 29:15 | 18.4 |
| Atlanta | 4905 | 1270 | 3635 | 28:36 | 20.4 |
| Minnesota | 4899 | 2030 | 2869 | 29:18 | 23.4 |
| Washington | 4890 | 1727 | 3163 | 31:04 | 18.8 |
| LA Rams | 4877 | 1659 | 3218 | 28:31 | 19.6 |
| New Orleans | 4806 | 1628 | 3178 | 31:10 | 20.6 |
| Green Bay | 4786 | 1556 | 3230 | 32:30 | 17.3 |
| Tampa Bay | 4771 | 1706 | 3065 | 29:15 | 16.7 |
| Phoenix | 4577 | 1491 | 3086 | 31:02 | 15.2 |
| Detroit | 4440 | 1644 | 2796 | 27:36 | 17.1 |
| NY Giants | 4412 | 2077 | 2335 | 29:22 | 19.1 |

## NFC Total Defense

| | Opp Total Yds | Opp Yds Rush | Opp Yds Pass | Avg PA/Game |
|---|---|---|---|---|
| Dallas | 3933 | 1244 | 2689 | 15.2 |
| New Orleans | 4075 | 1605 | 2470 | 12.6 |
| Philadelphia | 4402 | 1481 | 2921 | 15.3 |
| Washington | 4438 | 1696 | 2742 | 15.9 |
| Minnesota | 4515 | 1733 | 2782 | 15.6 |
| San Francisco | 4787 | 1418 | 3369 | 14.8 |
| Chicago | 4952 | 1948 | 3004 | 22.6 |
| NY Giants | 5043 | 2012 | 3031 | 22.9 |
| Detroit | 5058 | 1841 | 3217 | 20.8 |
| Green Bay | 5098 | 1821 | 3277 | 18.5 |
| Phoenix | 5126 | 1635 | 3491 | 20.8 |
| Tampa Bay | 5185 | 1675 | 3510 | 22.8 |
| LA Rams | 5524 | 2231 | 3293 | 23.9 |
| Atlanta | 5549 | 2294 | 3255 | 25.9 |

## Takeaways/Giveaways

### AFC

| | Takeaways Int | Fum | Total | Giveaways Int | Fum | Total | Net Diff |
|---|---|---|---|---|---|---|---|
| Kansas City | 24 | 15 | 39 | 12 | 9 | 21 | 18 |
| Pittsburgh | 22 | 21 | 43 | 14 | 18 | 32 | 11 |
| Cincinnati | 16 | 17 | 33 | 17 | 10 | 27 | 6 |
| Cleveland | 13 | 20 | 33 | 16 | 12 | 28 | 5 |
| San Diego | 25 | 11 | 36 | 21 | 12 | 33 | 3 |
| NY Jets | 21 | 18 | 39 | 24 | 15 | 39 | 0 |
| Miami | 18 | 14 | 32 | 17 | 17 | 34 | -2 |
| Indianapolis | 20 | 15 | 35 | 26 | 11 | 37 | -2 |
| Buffalo | 23 | 12 | 35 | 21 | 17 | 38 | -3 |
| Houston | 20 | 11 | 31 | 23 | 12 | 35 | -4 |
| Seattle | 20 | 12 | 32 | 23 | 18 | 41 | -9 |
| Denver | 15 | 16 | 31 | 29 | 15 | 44 | -13 |
| New England | 14 | 15 | 29 | 19 | 26 | 45 | -16 |
| LA Raiders | 12 | 7 | 19 | 23 | 15 | 38 | -19 |

### NFC

| | Takeaways Int | Fum | Total | Giveaways Int | Fum | Total | Net Diff |
|---|---|---|---|---|---|---|---|
| Minnesota | 28 | 14 | 42 | 15 | 17 | 32 | 10 |
| Washington | 23 | 11 | 34 | 17 | 7 | 24 | 10 |
| New Orleans | 18 | 20 | 38 | 16 | 13 | 29 | 9 |
| Philadelphia | 24 | 13 | 37 | 13 | 15 | 28 | 9 |
| San Francisco | 17 | 12 | 29 | 9 | 13 | 22 | 7 |
| Dallas | 17 | 14 | 31 | 15 | 9 | 24 | 7 |
| Tampa Bay | 20 | 13 | 33 | 20 | 9 | 29 | 4 |
| NY Giants | 14 | 12 | 26 | 10 | 13 | 23 | 3 |
| Green Bay | 15 | 19 | 34 | 15 | 21 | 36 | -2 |
| LA Rams | 18 | 15 | 33 | 20 | 17 | 37 | -4 |
| Detroit | 21 | 11 | 32 | 21 | 15 | 36 | -4 |
| Chicago | 14 | 16 | 30 | 24 | 10 | 34 | -4 |
| Atlanta | 11 | 12 | 23 | 15 | 14 | 29 | -6 |
| Phoenix | 16 | 12 | 28 | 24 | 18 | 42 | -14 |

## THEY SAID IT

*Bruce Coslet, New York Jet coach, on the NFL's new free agency system: "It's like recruiting for college, only the money's on the table instead of under it."*

## Conference Rankings

### American Football Conference

| | Offense | | | Defense | | |
|---|---|---|---|---|---|---|
| | Total | Rush | Pass | Total | Rush | Pass |
| Buffalo | 1 | 1 | 3 | 7 | 1T | 13 |
| Cincinnati | 12 | 3 | 13 | 14 | 13 | 14 |
| Cleveland | 6 | 8 | 7 | 9 | 4 | 12 |
| Denver | 8 | 13 | 6 | 13 | 12 | 11 |
| Houston | 2 | 7 | 1 | 1 | 5 | 2 |
| Indianapolis | 10 | 14 | 5 | 12 | 14 | 7 |
| Kansas City | 11 | 11 | 8 | 3 | 7 | 1 |
| LA Raiders | 9 | 5 | 11 | 4 | 6 | 6 |
| Miami | 3 | 12 | 2 | 5T | 3 | 9 |
| New England | 13 | 10 | 12 | 11 | 11 | 10 |
| NY Jets | 7 | 6 | 10 | 10 | 9 | 8 |
| Pittsburgh | 5 | 2 | 9 | 8 | 8 | 4 |
| San Diego | 4 | 4 | 4 | 2 | 1T | 5 |
| Seattle | 14 | 9 | 14 | 5T | 10 | 3 |

### National Football Conference

| | Offense | | | Defense | | |
|---|---|---|---|---|---|---|
| | Total | Rush | Pass | Total | Rush | Pass |
| Atlanta | 5 | 14 | 2 | 14 | 14 | 9 |
| Chicago | 4 | 6 | 9 | 7 | 11 | 6 |
| Dallas | 2 | 3 | 3 | 1 | 1 | 2 |
| Detroit | 13 | 10 | 12 | 9 | 10 | 8 |
| Green Bay | 10 | 12 | 4 | 10 | 9 | 10 |
| LA Rams | 8 | 9 | 5 | 13 | 13 | 11 |
| Minnesota | 6 | 5 | 11 | 5 | 8 | 4 |
| New Orleans | 9 | 11 | 6 | 2 | 4 | 1 |
| NY Giants | 14 | 4 | 14 | 8 | 12 | 7 |
| Philadelphia | 3 | 1 | 13 | 3 | 3 | 5 |
| Phoenix | 12 | 13 | 8 | 11 | 5 | 13 |
| San Francisco | 1 | 2 | 1 | 6 | 2 | 12 |
| Tampa Bay | 11 | 8 | 10 | 12 | 6 | 14 |
| Washington | 7 | 7 | 7 | 4 | 7 | 3 |

# 1992 AFC Team-by-Team Statistical Leaders

## Buffalo Bills

| SCORING | TD Rush | Rec | Ret | PAT | FG | S | Pts |
|---|---|---|---|---|---|---|---|
| Christie | 0 | 0 | 0 | 43/44 | 24/30 | 0 | 115 |
| Thomas | 9 | 3 | 0 | 0/0 | 0/0 | 0 | 72 |
| K. Davis | 6 | 0 | 0 | 0/0 | 0/0 | 0 | 36 |
| Lofton | 0 | 6 | 0 | 0/0 | 0/0 | 0 | 36 |
| Metzelaars | 0 | 6 | 0 | 0/0 | 0/0 | 0 | 36 |

| RUSHING | No. | Yds | Avg | Lg | TD |
|---|---|---|---|---|---|
| Thomas | 312 | 1487 | 4.8 | 44 | 9 |
| K. Davis | 139 | 613 | 4.4 | t64 | 6 |
| Gardner | 40 | 166 | 4.2 | 19 | 2 |
| Reed | 8 | 65 | 8.1 | 24 | 0 |
| Kelly | 31 | 53 | 1.7 | 10 | 1 |

| PASSING | Att | Comp | Pct Comp | Yds | Avg Gain | TD | Int | Rating Pts |
|---|---|---|---|---|---|---|---|---|
| Kelly | 462 | 269 | 58.2 | 3457 | 7.48 | 23 | 19 | 81.2 |
| Reich | 47 | 24 | 51.1 | 221 | 4.70 | 0 | 2 | 46.5 |

| RECEIVING | No. | Yds | Avg | Lg | TD |
|---|---|---|---|---|---|
| Reed | 65 | 913 | 14.0 | 51 | 3 |
| Thomas | 58 | 626 | 10.8 | 43 | 3 |
| Lofton | 51 | 786 | 15.4 | 50 | 6 |
| Beebe | 33 | 554 | 16.8 | t65 | 2 |
| Metzelaars | 30 | 298 | 9.9 | t53 | 6 |

**INTERCEPTIONS:** Jones, 8

| PUNTING | No. | Yds | Avg | Net Avg | TB | In 20 | Lg | Blk |
|---|---|---|---|---|---|---|---|---|
| Mohr | 60 | 2531 | 42.2 | 36.8 | 7 | 13 | 61 | 0 |

**SACKS:** Smith, 14.0

## Cincinnati Bengals

| SCORING | TD Rush | Rec | Ret | PAT | FG | S | Pts |
|---|---|---|---|---|---|---|---|
| Breech | 0 | 0 | 0 | 31/31 | 19/27 | 0 | 88 |
| Fenner | 7 | 1 | 0 | 0/0 | 0/0 | 0 | 48 |
| Ball | 2 | 2 | 0 | 0/0 | 0/0 | 0 | 24 |
| Query | 0 | 3 | 0 | 0/0 | 0/0 | 0 | 18 |
| McGee | 0 | 3 | 0 | 0/0 | 0/0 | 0 | 18 |

| RUSHING | No. | Yds | Avg | Lg | TD |
|---|---|---|---|---|---|
| Green | 265 | 1170 | 4.4 | 53 | 2 |
| Fenner | 112 | 500 | 4.5 | t35 | 7 |
| Hollas | 20 | 109 | 5.5 | 24 | 0 |
| Esiason | 21 | 66 | 3.1 | 15 | 0 |
| Ball | 16 | 55 | 3.4 | 17 | 2 |

| PASSING | Att | Comp | Pct Comp | Yds | Avg Gain | TD | Int | Rating Pts |
|---|---|---|---|---|---|---|---|---|
| Esiason | 278 | 144 | 51.8 | 1407 | 5.06 | 11 | 15 | 57.0 |
| Klingler | 98 | 47 | 48.0 | 530 | 5.41 | 3 | 2 | 66.3 |
| Hollas | 58 | 35 | 60.3 | 335 | 5.78 | 2 | 0 | 87.9 |

| RECEIVING | No. | Yds | Avg | Lg | TD |
|---|---|---|---|---|---|
| Green | 41 | 214 | 5.2 | 19 | 0 |
| McGee | 35 | 408 | 11.7 | 36 | 3 |
| Pickens | 26 | 326 | 12.5 | 38 | 1 |
| Holman | 26 | 266 | 10.2 | t26 | 2 |
| Rembert | 19 | 219 | 11.5 | 27 | 0 |

**INTERCEPTIONS:** D. Williams, 4

| PUNTING | No. | Yds | Avg | Net Avg | TB | In 15 | Lg | Blk |
|---|---|---|---|---|---|---|---|---|
| Johnson | 76 | 3196 | 42.1 | 35.9 | 9 | 15 | 64 | 0 |

**SACKS:** A. Williams, 10.0

**End Zone**

For years Ron Dixon has fired a cannon on the sideline whenever the San Diego Chargers have scored a touchdown, field goal or safety in a home game. That was a busy job in the Dan Fouts era; Dixon fired the cannon 16 times at one game. But, after the Chargers went 0–3 to start the 1992 season, the club told Dixon he could fire when the team was introduced before the game. Even so, he shot the thing only six times in the Chargers' first two home games last year—two introductions, three field goals and one touchdown. "I am the Maytag repairman," he says.

## Cleveland Browns

### SCORING

| | Rush | TD Rec | Ret | PAT | FG | S | Pts |
|---|---|---|---|---|---|---|---|
| Stover | 0 | 0 | 0 | 29/30 | 21/29 | 0 | 92 |
| Metcalf | 1 | 5 | 1 | 0/0 | 0/0 | 0 | 42 |
| M. Jackson | 0 | 7 | 0 | 0/0 | 0/0 | 0 | 42 |
| Mack | 6 | 0 | 0 | 0/0 | 0/0 | 0 | 36 |

### RUSHING

| | No. | Yds | Avg | Lg | TD |
|---|---|---|---|---|---|
| Mack | 169 | 543 | 3.2 | 37 | 6 |
| Vardell | 99 | 369 | 3.7 | 35 | 0 |
| Metcalf | 73 | 301 | 4.1 | 31 | 1 |
| Hoard | 54 | 236 | 4.4 | 37 | 0 |
| Tomczak | 24 | 39 | 1.6 | 16 | 0 |
| Baldwin | 10 | 31 | 3.1 | 11 | 0 |

### PASSING

| | Att | Comp | Pct Comp | Yds | Avg Gain | TD | Int | Rating Pts |
|---|---|---|---|---|---|---|---|---|
| Tomczak | 211 | 120 | 56.9 | 1693 | 8.02 | 7 | 7 | 80.1 |
| Kosar | 155 | 103 | 66.5 | 1160 | 7.48 | 8 | 7 | 87.0 |

### RECEIVING

| | No. | Yds | Avg | Lg | TD |
|---|---|---|---|---|---|
| M. Jackson | 47 | 755 | 16.1 | t69 | 7 |
| Metcalf | 47 | 614 | 13.1 | t69 | 5 |
| Hoard | 26 | 310 | 11.9 | t46 | 1 |
| Tillman | 25 | 498 | 19.9 | 52 | 0 |
| Bavaro | 25 | 315 | 12.6 | 39 | 2 |

**INTERCEPTIONS:** Newsome and Walls, 3

### PUNTING

| | No. | Yds | Avg | Net Avg | TB | In 20 | Lg | Blk |
|---|---|---|---|---|---|---|---|---|
| Hansen | 74 | 3083 | 41.7 | 36.1 | 7 | 28 | 73 | 1 |

**SACKS:** Burnett and Matthews, 9

## Houston Oilers

### SCORING

| | Rush | TD Rec | Ret | PAT | FG | S | Pts |
|---|---|---|---|---|---|---|---|
| Del Greco | 0 | 0 | 0 | 41/41 | 21/27 | 0 | 104 |
| Givins | 0 | 10 | 0 | 0/0 | 0/0 | 0 | 60 |
| Jeffires | 0 | 9 | 0 | 0/0 | 0/0 | 0 | 54 |
| White | 7 | 1 | 0 | 0/0 | 0/0 | 0 | 48 |
| Slaughter | 0 | 4 | 0 | 0/0 | 0/0 | 0 | 24 |

### RUSHING

| | No. | Yds | Avg | Lg | TD |
|---|---|---|---|---|---|
| White | 265 | 1226 | 4.6 | 44 | 7 |
| Moon | 27 | 147 | 5.4 | 23 | 1 |
| G. Brown | 19 | 87 | 4.6 | 26 | 1 |
| Carlson | 27 | 77 | 2.9 | 13 | 1 |

### PASSING

| | Att | Comp | Pct Comp | Yds | Avg Gain | TD | Int | Rating Pts |
|---|---|---|---|---|---|---|---|---|
| Moon | 346 | 224 | 64.7 | 2521 | 7.29 | 18 | 12 | 89.3 |
| Carlson | 227 | 149 | 65.6 | 1710 | 7.53 | 9 | 11 | 81.2 |

### RECEIVING

| | No. | Yds | Avg | Lg | TD |
|---|---|---|---|---|---|
| Jeffires | 90 | 913 | 10.1 | 47 | 9 |
| Duncan | 82 | 954 | 11.6 | 72 | 1 |
| Givins | 67 | 787 | 11.7 | 41 | 10 |
| White | 57 | 641 | 11.2 | t69 | 1 |
| Slaughter | 39 | 486 | 12.5 | t36 | 4 |

**INTERCEPTIONS:** Gray, 6

### PUNTING

| | No. | Yds | Avg | Net Avg | TB | In 20 | Lg | Blk |
|---|---|---|---|---|---|---|---|---|
| Gr. Montgomery | 53 | 2487 | 46.9 | 37.3 | 9 | 14 | 66 | 2 |

**SACKS:** Childress, 13.0

## Denver Broncos

### SCORING

| | Rush | TD Rec | Ret | PAT | FG | S | Pts |
|---|---|---|---|---|---|---|---|
| Treadwell | 0 | 0 | 0 | 28/28 | 20/24 | 0 | 88 |
| Jackson | 0 | 8 | 0 | 0/0 | 0/0 | 0 | 48 |
| Lewis | 4 | 0 | 0 | 0/0 | 0/0 | 0 | 24 |
| Rivers | 3 | 1 | 0 | 0/0 | 0/0 | 0 | 24 |

Four tied with 12.

### RUSHING

| | No. | Yds | Avg | Lg | TD |
|---|---|---|---|---|---|
| Green | 161 | 648 | 4.0 | t67 | 2 |
| Rivers | 74 | 282 | 3.8 | 48 | 3 |
| Lewis | 73 | 268 | 3.7 | 22 | 4 |
| Elway | 34 | 94 | 2.8 | 9 | 2 |
| S. Smith | 23 | 94 | 4.1 | 15 | 0 |

### PASSING

| | Att | Comp | Pct Comp | Yds | Avg Gain | TD | Int | Rating Pts |
|---|---|---|---|---|---|---|---|---|
| Elway | 316 | 174 | 55.1 | 2242 | 7.09 | 10 | 17 | 65.7 |
| Maddox | 121 | 66 | 54.5 | 757 | 6.26 | 5 | 9 | 56.4 |
| Moore | 34 | 17 | 50.0 | 232 | 6.82 | 0 | 3 | 35.4 |

### RECEIVING

| | No. | Yds | Avg | Lg | TD |
|---|---|---|---|---|---|
| Sharpe | 53 | 640 | 12.1 | 56 | 2 |
| Jackson | 48 | 745 | 15.5 | t51 | 8 |
| Rivers | 45 | 449 | 10.0 | 37 | 1 |
| Marshall | 26 | 493 | 19.0 | t80 | 1 |
| V. Johnson | 24 | 294 | 12.3 | 40 | 2 |

**INTERCEPTIONS:** D. Smith and Henderson, 4

### PUNTING

| | No. | Yds | Avg | Net Avg | TB | In 20 | Lg | Blk |
|---|---|---|---|---|---|---|---|---|
| Horan | 37 | 1681 | 45.4 | 40.2 | 1 | 7 | 62 | 1 |
| Parker | 12 | 491 | 40.9 | 31.9 | 1 | 1 | 61 | 0 |

**SACKS:** Fletcher, 16.0

## Indianapolis Colts

### SCORING

| | Rush | TD Rec | Ret | PAT | FG | S | Pts |
|---|---|---|---|---|---|---|---|
| Biasucci | 0 | 0 | 0 | 24/24 | 16/29 | 0 | 72 |
| Culver | 7 | 2 | 0 | 0/0 | 0/0 | 0 | 54 |
| Cash | 0 | 3 | 0 | 0/0 | 0/0 | 0 | 18 |
| Johnson | 0 | 3 | 0 | 0/0 | 0/0 | 0 | 18 |
| Verdin | 0 | 0 | 2 | 0/0 | 0/0 | 0 | 12 |

Seven tied with 6.

### RUSHING

| | No. | Yds | Avg | Lg | TD |
|---|---|---|---|---|---|
| Johnson | 178 | 592 | 3.3 | 19 | 0 |
| Culver | 121 | 321 | 2.7 | t36 | 7 |
| Clark | 40 | 134 | 3.4 | 13 | 0 |
| George | 14 | 26 | 1.9 | 13 | 1 |

### PASSING

| | Att | Comp | Pct Comp | Yds | Avg Gain | TD | Int | Rating Pts |
|---|---|---|---|---|---|---|---|---|
| George | 306 | 167 | 54.6 | 1963 | 6.42 | 7 | 15 | 61.5 |
| Trudeau | 181 | 105 | 58.0 | 1271 | 7.02 | 4 | 8 | 68.6 |
| Tupa | 33 | 17 | 51.5 | 156 | 4.73 | 1 | 2 | 49.6 |
| Herrmann | 24 | 15 | 62.5 | 177 | 7.38 | 1 | 1 | 81.4 |

### RECEIVING

| | No. | Yds | Avg | Lg | TD |
|---|---|---|---|---|---|
| Langhorne | 65 | 811 | 12.5 | 34 | 1 |
| Hester | 52 | 792 | 15.2 | 81 | 1 |
| Johnson | 49 | 517 | 10.6 | t57 | 3 |
| Brooks | 44 | 468 | 10.6 | 26 | 1 |
| Cash | 43 | 521 | 12.1 | 41 | 3 |

**INTERCEPTIONS:** Prior, 6

### PUNTING

| | No. | Yds | Avg | Net Avg | TB | In 20 | Lg | Blk |
|---|---|---|---|---|---|---|---|---|
| Stark | 83 | 3716 | 44.8 | 39.3 | 7 | 22 | 64 | 0 |

**SACKS:** Banks, 9.0

## Kansas City Chiefs

| SCORING | Rush | TD Rec | Ret | PAT | FG | S | Pts |
|---|---|---|---|---|---|---|---|
| Lowery | 0 | 0 | 0 | 39/39 | 22/24 | 0 | 105 |
| Okoye | 6 | 0 | 0 | 0/0 | 0/0 | 0 | 36 |
| Barnett | 0 | 4 | 0 | 0/0 | 0/0 | 0 | 24 |
| Word | 4 | 0 | 0 | 0/0 | 0/0 | 0 | 24 |
| Four tied with 18. | | | | | | | |

| RUSHING | No. | Yds | Avg | Lg | TD |
|---|---|---|---|---|---|
| Word | 163 | 607 | 3.7 | t44 | 4 |
| Okoye | 144 | 448 | 3.1 | 22 | 6 |
| Williams | 78 | 262 | 3.4 | 11 | 1 |
| McNair | 21 | 124 | 5.9 | 30 | 1 |
| Krieg | 37 | 74 | 2.0 | 17 | 2 |

| PASSING | Att | Comp | Pct Comp | Yds | Avg Gain | TD | Int | Rating Pts |
|---|---|---|---|---|---|---|---|---|
| Krieg | 413 | 230 | 55.7 | 3115 | 7.54 | 15 | 12 | 79.9 |

| RECEIVING | No. | Yds | Avg | Lg | TD |
|---|---|---|---|---|---|
| McNair | 44 | 380 | 8.6 | 36 | 1 |
| Birden | 42 | 644 | 15.3 | t72 | 3 |
| Davis | 36 | 756 | 21.0 | t74 | 3 |
| Barnett | 24 | 442 | 18.4 | t77 | 1 |
| F. Jones | 18 | 265 | 14.7 | 56 | 0 |

**INTERCEPTIONS:** Carter, 7

| PUNTING | No. | Yds | Avg | Net Avg | In TB | 20 | Lg | Blk |
|---|---|---|---|---|---|---|---|---|
| Barker | 75 | 3245 | 43.3 | 35.3 | 13 | 16 | 65 | 1 |
| Lowery | 4 | 141 | 35.3 | 32.8 | 0 | 0 | 39 | 0 |
| Sullivan | 6 | 247 | 41.2 | 38.2 | 0 | 2 | 59 | 0 |

**SACKS:** N. Smith, 14.5

## Miami Dolphins

| SCORING | Rush | TD Rec | Ret | PAT | FG | S | Pts |
|---|---|---|---|---|---|---|---|
| Stoyanovich | 0 | 0 | 0 | 34/36 | 30/37 | 0 | 124 |
| Duper | 0 | 7 | 0 | 0/0 | 0/0 | 0 | 42 |
| Higgs | 7 | 0 | 0 | 0/0 | 0/0 | 0 | 42 |
| K. Jackson | 0 | 5 | 0 | 0/0 | 0/0 | 0 | 30 |

| RUSHING | No. | Yds | Avg | Lg | TD |
|---|---|---|---|---|---|
| Higgs | 256 | 915 | 3.6 | 23 | 7 |
| Humphrey | 102 | 471 | 4.6 | 21 | 1 |
| Marino | 20 | 66 | 3.3 | 12 | 0 |
| Parmalee | 6 | 38 | 6.3 | 20 | 0 |
| Paige | 7 | 11 | 1.6 | 6 | 1 |

| PASSING | Att | Comp | Pct Comp | Yds | Avg Gain | TD | Int | Rating Pts |
|---|---|---|---|---|---|---|---|---|
| Marino | 554 | 330 | 59.6 | 4116 | 7.43 | 24 | 16 | 85.1 |
| Mitchell | 8 | 2 | 25.0 | 32 | 4.00 | 0 | 1 | 4.2 |
| Martin | 1 | 0 | 0 | 0.0 | 0.0 | 0 | 0 | 39.6 |

| RECEIVING | No. | Yds | Avg | Lg | TD |
|---|---|---|---|---|---|
| Humphrey | 54 | 507 | 9.4 | 26 | 1 |
| K. Jackson | 48 | 594 | 12.4 | 42 | 5 |
| Paige | 48 | 399 | 8.3 | 30 | 1 |
| Duper | 44 | 762 | 17.3 | t62 | 7 |
| Clayton | 43 | 619 | 14.4 | t44 | 3 |
| Martin | 33 | 319 | 16.8 | t55 | 2 |

**INTERCEPTIONS:** Oliver, 5

| PUNTING | No. | Yds | Avg | Net Avg | In TB | 20 | Lg | Blk |
|---|---|---|---|---|---|---|---|---|
| Roby | 35 | 1443 | 41.2 | 34.3 | 3 | 11 | 60 | 0 |
| Stoyanovich | 2 | 90 | 45.0 | 45.0 | 0 | 0 | 48 | 0 |

**SACKS:** Cox, 14.0

## Los Angeles Raiders

| SCORING | Rush | TD Rec | Ret | PAT | FG | S | Pts |
|---|---|---|---|---|---|---|---|
| Jaeger | 0 | 0 | 0 | 28/28 | 15/26 | 0 | 73 |
| Brown | 0 | 7 | 0 | 0/0 | 0/0 | 0 | 42 |
| Gault | 0 | 4 | 0 | 0/0 | 0/0 | 0 | 24 |
| Dickerson | 2 | 1 | 0 | 0/0 | 0/0 | 0 | 18 |
| Allen | 2 | 1 | 0 | 0/0 | 0/0 | 0 | 18 |
| N. Bell | 3 | 0 | 0 | 0/0 | 0/0 | 0 | 18 |

| RUSHING | No. | Yds | Avg | Lg | TD |
|---|---|---|---|---|---|
| Dickerson | 187 | 729 | 3.9 | t40 | 2 |
| N. Bell | 81 | 366 | 4.5 | 21 | 3 |
| Allen | 67 | 301 | 4.5 | 21 | 2 |
| Schroeder | 28 | 160 | 5.7 | 19 | 0 |
| S. Smith | 44 | 129 | 2.9 | 15 | 0 |

| PASSING | Att | Comp | Pct Comp | Yds | Avg Gain | TD | Int | Rating Pts |
|---|---|---|---|---|---|---|---|---|
| Schroeder | 253 | 123 | 48.6 | 1476 | 5.83 | 11 | 11 | 63.3 |
| Marinovich | 165 | 123 | 49.1 | 1102 | 6.68 | 5 | 9 | 58.2 |
| Evans | 53 | 29 | 54.7 | 372 | 7.02 | 4 | 3 | 78.5 |

| RECEIVING | No. | Yds | Avg | Lg | TD |
|---|---|---|---|---|---|
| Brown | 49 | 693 | 14.1 | t68 | 7 |
| Horton | 33 | 409 | 12.4 | 30 | 2 |
| Allen | 28 | 277 | 9.9 | 40 | 1 |
| S. Smith | 28 | 217 | 7.8 | 19 | 1 |
| Gault | 27 | 508 | 18.8 | 53 | 4 |

**INTERCEPTIONS:** McDaniel, 4

| PUNTING | No. | Yds | Avg | Net Avg | In TB | 20 | Lg | Blk |
|---|---|---|---|---|---|---|---|---|
| Gossett | 77 | 3255 | 42.3 | 36.5 | 3 | 17 | 56 | 0 |

**SACKS:** A. Smith, 13.0

## New England Patriots

| SCORING | Rush | TD Rec | Ret | PAT | FG | S | Pts |
|---|---|---|---|---|---|---|---|
| Baumann | 0 | 0 | 0 | 22/24 | 11/17 | 0 | 55 |
| Fryar | 0 | 4 | 0 | 0/0 | 0/0 | 0 | 24 |
| Coates | | 3 | 0 | 0/0 | 0/0 | 0 | 18 |
| Six tied with 12. | | | | | | | |

| RUSHING | No. | Yds | Avg | Lg | TD |
|---|---|---|---|---|---|
| Vaughn | 113 | 451 | 4.0 | 36 | 1 |
| Russell | 123 | 390 | 3.2 | 23 | 2 |
| Stephens | 75 | 277 | 3.7 | 19 | 2 |
| Lockwood | 35 | 162 | 4.6 | 23 | 0 |
| Millen | 17 | 108 | 6.4 | 26 | 1 |

| PASSING | Att | Comp | Pct Comp | Yds | Avg Gain | TD | Int | Rating Pts |
|---|---|---|---|---|---|---|---|---|
| Millen | 203 | 124 | 61.1 | 1203 | 5.93 | 8 | 10 | 70.3 |
| Zolak | 100 | 52 | 52.0 | 561 | 5.61 | 2 | 4 | 58.8 |
| Hodson | 91 | 50 | 54.9 | 496 | 5.45 | 2 | 2 | 68.8 |
| Carlson | 49 | 18 | 36.7 | 232 | 4.73 | 1 | 3 | 33.7 |

| RECEIVING | No. | Yds | Avg | Lg | TD |
|---|---|---|---|---|---|
| Fryar | 55 | 791 | 14.4 | t54 | 4 |
| Cook | 52 | 413 | 7.9 | 27 | 2 |
| McMurtry | 35 | 424 | 12.1 | t65 | 1 |
| Timpson | 26 | 315 | 12.1 | 25 | 1 |
| Stephens | 21 | 161 | 7.7 | 32 | 0 |

**INTERCEPTIONS:** Hurst and Henderson, 3

| PUNTING | No. | Yds | Avg | Net Avg | In TB | 20 | Lg | Blk |
|---|---|---|---|---|---|---|---|---|
| McCarthy | 103 | 4212 | 40.9 | 35.4 | 4 | 18 | 61 | 0 |

**SACKS:** Tippett, 7

## New York Jets

### SCORING

| SCORING | Rush | TD Rec | Ret | PAT | FG | S | Pts |
|---|---|---|---|---|---|---|---|
| Blanchard | 0 | 0 | 0 | 17/17 | 16/22 | 0 | 65 |
| Baxter | 6 | 0 | 0 | 0/0 | 0/0 | 0 | 36 |
| Moore | 0 | 4 | 0 | 0/0 | 0/0 | 0 | 24 |
| Mathis | 1 | 3 | 0 | 0/0 | 0/0 | 0 | 24 |
| Staurovsky | 0 | 0 | 0 | 6/6 | 3/8 | 0 | 15 |

### RUSHING

| RUSHING | No. | Yds | Avg | Lg | TD |
|---|---|---|---|---|---|
| Baxter | 152 | 698 | 4.6 | 30 | 6 |
| Thomas | 97 | 440 | 4.5 | 19 | 0 |
| Chaffey | 27 | 186 | 6.9 | 32 | 1 |
| McNeil | 43 | 170 | 4.0 | 18 | 0 |
| Hector | 24 | 67 | 2.8 | 14 | 0 |

### PASSING

| PASSING | Att | Comp | Pct Comp | Yds | Avg Gain | TD | Int | Rating Pts |
|---|---|---|---|---|---|---|---|---|
| Nagle | 387 | 192 | 49.6 | 2280 | 5.89 | 7 | 17 | 55.7 |
| O'Brien | 98 | 55 | 56.1 | 642 | 6.55 | 5 | 6 | 67.6 |
| Blake | 9 | 4 | 44.4 | 40 | 4.44 | 0 | 1 | 18.1 |

### RECEIVING

| RECEIVING | No. | Yds | Avg | Lg | TD |
|---|---|---|---|---|---|
| Burkett | 57 | 724 | 12.7 | t37 | 1 |
| Moore | 50 | 726 | 14.5 | t48 | 4 |
| Toon | 31 | 311 | 10.0 | 32 | 2 |
| Mathis | 22 | 316 | 14.4 | t55 | 3 |
| Boyer | 19 | 149 | 7.8 | 23 | 0 |

**INTERCEPTIONS:** Brim and Washington, 6

| PUNTING | No. | Yds | Avg | Net Avg | TB | In 20 | Lg | Blk |
|---|---|---|---|---|---|---|---|---|
| Aguiar | 73 | 2993 | 41.0 | 37.6 | 3 | 22 | 65 | 0 |

**SACKS:** Washington, 8.5

## Pittsburgh Steelers

### SCORING

| SCORING | Rush | TD Rec | Ret | PAT | FG | S | Pts |
|---|---|---|---|---|---|---|---|
| Anderson | 0 | 0 | 0 | 29/31 | 28/36 | 0 | 113 |
| Foster | 11 | 0 | 0 | 0/0 | 0/0 | 0 | 66 |
| Cooper | 0 | 3 | 0 | 0/0 | 0/0 | 0 | 18 |
| Mills | 0 | 3 | 0 | 0/0 | 0/0 | 0 | 18 |
| Stone | 0 | 3 | 0 | 0/0 | 0/0 | 0 | 18 |

### RUSHING

| RUSHING | No. | Yds | Avg | Lg | TD |
|---|---|---|---|---|---|
| Foster | 390 | 1690 | 4.3 | 69 | 11 |
| Thompson | 35 | 157 | 4.5 | 25 | 1 |
| Hoge | 41 | 150 | 3.7 | 15 | 0 |
| Stone | 12 | 118 | 9.8 | 30 | 0 |
| Mills | 1 | 20 | 20.0 | 20 | 0 |

### PASSING

| PASSING | Att | Comp | Pct Comp | Yds | Avg Gain | TD | Int | Rating Pts |
|---|---|---|---|---|---|---|---|---|
| O'Donnell | 313 | 185 | 59.1 | 2283 | 7.29 | 13 | 9 | 83.6 |
| Brister | 116 | 63 | 54.3 | 719 | 6.20 | 2 | 5 | 61.0 |
| Foster | 1 | 0 | 0.0 | 0 | 0 | 0 | 0 | 39.6 |
| Royals | 1 | 1 | 100.0 | 44 | 44.0 | 0 | 0 | 118.8 |

### RECEIVING

| RECEIVING | No. | Yds | Avg | Lg | TD |
|---|---|---|---|---|---|
| Graham | 49 | 711 | 14.5 | 51 | 1 |
| Foster | 36 | 344 | 9.6 | 42 | 0 |
| Stone | 34 | 501 | 14.7 | 49 | 3 |
| Mills | 30 | 383 | 12.8 | 22 | 3 |

**INTERCEPTIONS:** Perry, 6

| PUNTING | No. | Yds | Avg | Net Avg | TB | In 20 | Lg | Blk |
|---|---|---|---|---|---|---|---|---|
| Royals | 73 | 3119 | 42.7 | 35.6 | 9 | 22 | 58 | 1 |

**SACKS:** Lloyd, 6.5

## San Diego Chargers

### SCORING

| SCORING | Rush | TD Rec | Ret | PAT | FG | S | Pts |
|---|---|---|---|---|---|---|---|
| Carney | 0 | 0 | 0 | 35/35 | 26/32 | 0 | 113 |
| Miller | 0 | 7 | 1 | 0/0 | 0/0 | 0 | 48 |
| Lewis | 0 | 4 | 0 | 0/0 | 0/0 | 0 | 24 |
| Humphries | 4 | 0 | 0 | 0/0 | 0/0 | 0 | 24 |
| Bernstine | 4 | 0 | 0 | 0/0 | 0/0 | 0 | 24 |
| Harmon | 3 | 1 | 0 | 0/0 | 0/0 | 0 | 24 |
| Butts | 4 | 0 | 0 | 0/0 | 0/0 | 0 | 24 |

### RUSHING

| RUSHING | No. | Yds | Avg | Lg | TD |
|---|---|---|---|---|---|
| Butts | 218 | 809 | 3.7 | 22 | 4 |
| Bernstine | 106 | 499 | 4.7 | t25 | 4 |
| Bieniemy | 74 | 264 | 3.6 | 21 | 3 |
| Harmon | 55 | 235 | 4.3 | 33 | 3 |
| Humphries | 28 | 79 | 2.8 | 25 | 4 |

### PASSING

| PASSING | Att | Comp | Pct Comp | Yds | Avg Gain | TD | Int | Rating Pts |
|---|---|---|---|---|---|---|---|---|
| Humphries | 454 | 263 | 57.9 | 3356 | 7.39 | 16 | 18 | 76.4 |
| Gagliano | 42 | 19 | 45.2 | 258 | 6.14 | 0 | 3 | 35.6 |

### RECEIVING

| RECEIVING | No. | Yds | Avg | Lg | TD |
|---|---|---|---|---|---|
| Harmon | 79 | 914 | 11.6 | 55 | 1 |
| A. Miller | 72 | 1060 | 14.7 | t67 | 7 |
| Lewis | 34 | 580 | 17.1 | 62 | 4 |
| Walker | 34 | 393 | 11.6 | 59 | 2 |
| Jefferson | 29 | 377 | 13.0 | 51 | 2 |

**INTERCEPTIONS:** Carrington, 6

| PUNTING | No. | Yds | Avg | Net Avg | TB | In 20 | Lg | Blk |
|---|---|---|---|---|---|---|---|---|
| Kidd | 68 | 2899 | 42.6 | 36.4 | 9 | 22 | 65 | 0 |

**SACKS:** O'Neal, 17

## Seattle Seahawks

### SCORING

| SCORING | Rush | TD Rec | Ret | PAT | FG | S | Pts |
|---|---|---|---|---|---|---|---|
| Kasay | 0 | 0 | 0 | 14/14 | 14/22 | 0 | 56 |
| Williams | 1 | 2 | 0 | 0/0 | 0/0 | 0 | 18 |
| Kane | 0 | 3 | 0 | 0/0 | 0/0 | 0 | 18 |
| Warren | 3 | 0 | 0 | 0/0 | 0/0 | 0 | 18 |

### RUSHING

| RUSHING | No. | Yds | Avg | Lg | TD |
|---|---|---|---|---|---|
| Warren | 223 | 1017 | 4.6 | 52 | 3 |
| Williams | 114 | 339 | 3.0 | 14 | 1 |
| Gelbaugh | 16 | 79 | 4.9 | 22 | 0 |
| Mayes | 28 | 74 | 2.6 | 14 | 0 |

### PASSING

| PASSING | Att | Comp | Pct Comp | Yds | Avg Gain | TD | Int | Rating Pts |
|---|---|---|---|---|---|---|---|---|
| Gelbaugh | 255 | 121 | 47.5 | 1307 | 5.13 | 6 | 11 | 52.9 |
| Stouffer | 190 | 92 | 48.4 | 900 | 4.74 | 3 | 9 | 47.7 |
| McGwire | 30 | 17 | 56.7 | 116 | 3.87 | 0 | 3 | 25.8 |
| Tuten | 1 | 0 | 0.0 | 0 | 0.0 | 0 | 0 | 39.6 |

### RECEIVING

| RECEIVING | No. | Yds | Avg | Lg | TD |
|---|---|---|---|---|---|
| Williams | 74 | 556 | 7.5 | 27 | 2 |
| Kane | 27 | 369 | 13.7 | 31 | 3 |
| J. Jones | 21 | 190 | 9.0 | 30 | 0 |
| L. Clark | 20 | 290 | 14.5 | 33 | 1 |

**INTERCEPTIONS:** Robinson, 7

| PUNTING | No. | Yds | Avg | Net Avg | TB | In 20 | Lg | Blk |
|---|---|---|---|---|---|---|---|---|
| Tuten | 108 | 4760 | 44.1 | 38.7 | 8 | 29 | 65 | 0 |

**SACKS:** Kennedy, 14.0

# 1992 NFC Team-by-Team Statistical Leaders

## Atlanta Falcons

### SCORING

| | | TD | | | | | |
|---|---|---|---|---|---|---|---|
| | Rush | Rec | Ret | PAT | FG | S | Pts |
| N. Johnson | 0 | 0 | 0 | 39/39 | 18/22 | 0 | 93 |
| Rison | 0 | 11 | 0 | 0/0 | 0/0 | 0 | 66 |
| Haynes | 0 | 10 | 0 | 0/0 | 0/0 | 0 | 60 |
| Pritchard | 0 | 5 | 0 | 0/0 | 0/0 | 0 | 30 |

Two tied with 18.

### RUSHING

| | No. | Yds | Avg | Lg | TD |
|---|---|---|---|---|---|
| Broussard | 84 | 363 | 4.3 | 27 | 1 |
| T. Smith | 87 | 329 | 3.8 | 32 | 2 |
| K. Jones | 79 | 278 | 3.5 | 26 | 0 |
| Miller | 23 | 89 | 3.9 | 16 | 0 |
| Pegram | 21 | 89 | 4.2 | 15 | 0 |

### PASSING

| | Att | Comp | Pct Comp | Yds | Avg Gain | TD | Int | Rating Pts |
|---|---|---|---|---|---|---|---|---|
| Miller | 253 | 152 | 60.1 | 1739 | 6.87 | 15 | 6 | 90.7 |
| Wilson | 163 | 111 | 68.1 | 1368 | 8.39 | 13 | 4 | 110.2 |
| Tolliver | 131 | 73 | 55.7 | 787 | 6.01 | 5 | 5 | 70.4 |

### RECEIVING

| | No. | Yds | Avg | Lg | TD |
|---|---|---|---|---|---|
| Rison | 93 | 1121 | 12.1 | t71 | 11 |
| Pritchard | 77 | 827 | 10.7 | t38 | 5 |
| Hill | 60 | 623 | 10.4 | 43 | 3 |
| Haynes | 48 | 808 | 16.8 | t89 | 10 |
| T. Jones | 14 | 138 | 9.9 | 24 | 1 |

INTERCEPTIONS: Sanders 3

### PUNTING

| | No. | Yds | Avg | Net Avg | TB | In 20 | Lg | Blk |
|---|---|---|---|---|---|---|---|---|
| Fulhage | 68 | 2818 | 41.4 | 33.0 | 3 | 11 | 56 | 1 |
| Johnson | 1 | 37 | 37 | 37.0 | 0 | 1 | 37 | 0 |

SACKS: Conner, 7.0

## Dallas Cowboys

### SCORING

| | | TD | | | | | |
|---|---|---|---|---|---|---|---|
| | Rush | Rec | Ret | PAT | FG | S | Pts |
| Elliott | 0 | 0 | 0 | 47/48 | 24/35 | 0 | 119 |
| E. Smith | 18 | 1 | 0 | 0/0 | 0/0 | 0 | 114 |
| Irvin | 0 | 7 | 0 | 0/0 | 0/0 | 0 | 42 |
| Novacek | 0 | 6 | 0 | 0/0 | 0/0 | 0 | 36 |
| Martin | 0 | 3 | 2 | 0/0 | 0/0 | 0 | 30 |

### RUSHING

| | No. | Yds | Avg | Lg | TD |
|---|---|---|---|---|---|
| E. Smith | 373 | 1713 | 4.6 | t68 | 18 |
| Richards | 49 | 176 | 3.6 | 15 | 1 |
| Aikman | 37 | 105 | 2.8 | 19 | 1 |
| Johnston | 17 | 61 | 3.6 | 14 | 0 |
| Agee | 16 | 54 | 3.4 | 10 | 0 |

### PASSING

| | Att | Comp | Pct Comp | Yds | Avg Gain | TD | Int | Rating Pts |
|---|---|---|---|---|---|---|---|---|
| Aikman | 473 | 302 | 63.8 | 3445 | 7.28 | 23 | 14 | 89.5 |
| Beuerlein | 18 | 12 | 66.7 | 152 | 8.44 | 0 | 1 | 69.7 |

### RECEIVING

| | No. | Yds | Avg | Lg | TD |
|---|---|---|---|---|---|
| Irvin | 78 | 1396 | 17.9 | t87 | 7 |
| Novacek | 68 | 630 | 9.3 | 34 | 6 |
| E. Smith | 59 | 335 | 5.7 | t26 | 1 |
| Harper | 35 | 562 | 16.1 | 52 | 4 |

INTERCEPTIONS: Washington and Gant, 3

### PUNTING

| | No. | Yds | Avg | Net Avg | TB | In 20 | Lg | Blk |
|---|---|---|---|---|---|---|---|---|
| Saxon | 61 | 2620 | 43.0 | 33.5 | 9 | 19 | 58 | 0 |

SACKS: Jeffcoat, 10.5

## Chicago Bears

### SCORING

| | | TD | | | | | |
|---|---|---|---|---|---|---|---|
| | Rush | Rec | Ret | PAT | FG | S | Pts |
| Butler | 0 | 0 | 0 | 34/34 | 19/26 | 0 | 91 |
| Anderson | 5 | 6 | 0 | 0/0 | 0/0 | 0 | 66 |
| Muster | 3 | 2 | 0 | 0/0 | 0/0 | 0 | 30 |
| Lewis | 4 | 0 | 1 | 0/0 | 0/0 | 0 | 30 |
| Waddle | 0 | 4 | 0 | 0/0 | 0/0 | 0 | 24 |

Three tied with 12.

### RUSHING

| | No. | Yds | Avg | Lg | TD |
|---|---|---|---|---|---|
| Anderson | 156 | 582 | 3.7 | t49 | 5 |
| Muster | 98 | 414 | 4.2 | 35 | 3 |
| Lewis | 90 | 382 | 4.2 | 33 | 4 |
| Harbaugh | 47 | 272 | 5.8 | 17 | 1 |
| Green | 23 | 107 | 4.7 | 18 | 2 |

### PASSING

| | Att | Comp | Pct Comp | Yds | Avg Gain | TD | Int | Rating Pts |
|---|---|---|---|---|---|---|---|---|
| Harbaugh | 358 | 202 | 56.4 | 2486 | 6.94 | 13 | 12 | 76.2 |
| Willis | 92 | 54 | 58.7 | 716 | 7.78 | 4 | 8 | 61.7 |
| Furrer | 25 | 9 | 36.0 | 89 | 3.56 | 0 | 3 | 7.3 |

### RECEIVING

| | No. | Yds | Avg | Lg | TD |
|---|---|---|---|---|---|
| Davis | 54 | 734 | 13.6 | 40 | 2 |
| Waddle | 46 | 674 | 14.7 | t68 | 4 |
| Anderson | 42 | 399 | 9.5 | t30 | 6 |
| Muster | 34 | 389 | 11.4 | t44 | 2 |
| Jennings | 23 | 264 | 11.5 | 23 | 1 |

INTERCEPTIONS: Woolford, 7

### PUNTING

| | No. | Yds | Avg | Net Avg | TB | In 20 | Lg | Blk |
|---|---|---|---|---|---|---|---|---|
| Gardocki | 79 | 3393 | 42.9 | 36.2 | 9 | 19 | 61 | 0 |

SACKS: McMichael, 10.5

## Detroit Lions

### SCORING

| | | TD | | | | | |
|---|---|---|---|---|---|---|---|
| | Rush | Rec | Ret | PAT | FG | S | Pts |
| Hanson | 0 | 0 | 0 | 30/30 | 21/26 | 0 | 93 |
| B. Sanders | 9 | 1 | 0 | 0/0 | 0/0 | 0 | 60 |
| Green | 0 | 5 | 0 | 0/0 | 0/0 | 0 | 30 |
| Perriman | 0 | 4 | 0 | 0/0 | 0/0 | 0 | 24 |
| Moore | 0 | 4 | 0 | 0/0 | 0/0 | 0 | 24 |

### RUSHING

| | No. | Yds | Avg | Lg | TD |
|---|---|---|---|---|---|
| B. Sanders | 312 | 1352 | 4.3 | t55 | 9 |
| Ware | 20 | 124 | 6.2 | 32 | 0 |
| Peete | 21 | 83 | 4.0 | 12 | 0 |
| Stradford | 12 | 41 | 3.4 | 11 | 0 |

### PASSING

| | Att | Comp | Pct Comp | Yds | Avg Gain | TD | Int | Rating Pts |
|---|---|---|---|---|---|---|---|---|
| Peete | 213 | 123 | 57.7 | 1702 | 7.99 | 9 | 9 | 80.0 |
| Kramer | 106 | 58 | 54.7 | 771 | 7.27 | 4 | 8 | 59.1 |
| Ware | 86 | 50 | 58.1 | 677 | 7.87 | 3 | 4 | 75.6 |

### RECEIVING

| | No. | Yds | Avg | Lg | TD |
|---|---|---|---|---|---|
| Perriman | 69 | 810 | 11.7 | t40 | 4 |
| Moore | 51 | 966 | 18.9 | t77 | 4 |
| Green | 33 | 586 | 17.8 | t73 | 5 |
| B. Sanders | 29 | 225 | 7.8 | 48 | 1 |
| Farr | 15 | 115 | 7.7 | 14 | 0 |

INTERCEPTIONS: Crockett, White, Scott, Jenkins, 6

### PUNTING

| | No. | Yds | Avg | Net Avg | TB | In 20 | Lg | Blk |
|---|---|---|---|---|---|---|---|---|
| Arnold | 65 | 2846 | 43.8 | 34.7 | 10 | 12 | 71 | 1 |

SACKS: Scroggins, 7.5

## Green Bay Packers

| SCORING | Rush | TD Rec | Ret | PAT | FG | S | Pts |
|---|---|---|---|---|---|---|---|
| Jacke | 0 | 0 | 0 | 30/30 | 22/29 | 0 | 96 |
| Sharpe | 0 | 13 | 0 | 0/0 | 0/0 | 0 | 78 |
| Sydney | 2 | 1 | 0 | 0/0 | 0/0 | 0 | 18 |
| Thompson | 2 | 1 | 0 | 0/0 | 0/0 | 0 | 18 |

Three tied with 12.

| RUSHING | No. | Yds | Avg | Lg | TD |
|---|---|---|---|---|---|
| Workman | 159 | 631 | 4.0 | 44 | 2 |
| Thompson | 76 | 255 | 3.4 | 33 | 2 |
| Bennett | 61 | 214 | 3.5 | 18 | 0 |
| Favre | 47 | 198 | 4.2 | 19 | 1 |
| Sydney | 51 | 163 | 3.2 | 19 | 2 |

| PASSING | Att | Comp | Pct Comp | Yds | Avg Gain | TD | Int | Rating Pts |
|---|---|---|---|---|---|---|---|---|
| Favre | 471 | 302 | 64.1 | 3227 | 6.85 | 18 | 13 | 85.3 |
| Majkowski | 55 | 38 | 69.1 | 271 | 4.93 | 2 | 2 | 77.2 |

| RECEIVING | No. | Yds | Avg | Lg | TD |
|---|---|---|---|---|---|
| Sharpe | 108 | 1461 | 13.5 | t76 | 13 |
| Harris | 55 | 595 | 10.8 | 40 | 2 |
| Sydney | 49 | 384 | 7.8 | 20 | 1 |
| Workman | 47 | 290 | 6.2 | 21 | 0 |

**INTERCEPTIONS:** Cecil, 4

| PUNTING | No. | Yds | Avg | Net Avg | TB | In 20 | Lg | Blk |
|---|---|---|---|---|---|---|---|---|
| McJulien | 36 | 1386 | 38.5 | 30.2 | 4 | 8 | 67 | 2 |
| Wagner | 30 | 1222 | 40.7 | 35.0 | 5 | 10 | 52 | 0 |

**SACKS:** Bennett, 13.5

## Minnesota Vikings

| SCORING | Rush | TD Rec | Ret | PAT | FG | S | Pts |
|---|---|---|---|---|---|---|---|
| Reveiz | 0 | 0 | 0 | 45/45 | 19/25 | 0 | 102 |
| Allen | 13 | 2 | 0 | 0/0 | 0/0 | 0 | 90 |
| C. Carter | 0 | 6 | 0 | 0/0 | 0/0 | 0 | 36 |
| Craig | 4 | 0 | 0 | 0/0 | 0/0 | 0 | 24 |
| Jones | 0 | 4 | 0 | 0/0 | 0/0 | 0 | 24 |

| RUSHING | No. | Yds | Avg | Lg | TD |
|---|---|---|---|---|---|
| Allen | 266 | 1201 | 4.5 | 51 | 13 |
| Craig | 105 | 416 | 4.0 | 21 | 4 |
| Gannon | 45 | 187 | 4.2 | 14 | 0 |
| Henderson | 44 | 150 | 3.4 | 12 | 1 |

| PASSING | Att | Comp | Pct Comp | Yds | Avg Gain | TD | Int | Rating Pts |
|---|---|---|---|---|---|---|---|---|
| Gannon | 279 | 159 | 57.0 | 1905 | 6.83 | 12 | 13 | 72.9 |
| Salisbury | 175 | 97 | 55.4 | 1203 | 6.87 | 5 | 2 | 81.7 |

| RECEIVING | No. | Yds | Avg | Lg | TD |
|---|---|---|---|---|---|
| C. Carter | 53 | 681 | 12.8 | 44 | 6 |
| Allen | 49 | 478 | 9.8 | t36 | 2 |
| A. Carter | 41 | 580 | 14.1 | 54 | 2 |
| Jordan | 28 | 394 | 14.1 | t60 | 2 |
| Jones | 22 | 308 | 14.0 | t43 | 4 |

**INTERCEPTIONS:** McMillian, 8

| PUNTING | No. | Yds | Avg | Net Avg | TB | In 20 | Lg | Blk |
|---|---|---|---|---|---|---|---|---|
| Newsome | 72 | 3243 | 45.0 | 35.7 | 15 | 19 | 84 | 1 |

**SACKS:** Doleman, 14.5

## Los Angeles Rams

| SCORING | Rush | TD Rec | Ret | PAT | FG | S | Pts |
|---|---|---|---|---|---|---|---|
| Zendejas | 0 | 0 | 0 | 38/38 | 15/20 | 0 | 83 |
| Gary | 7 | 3 | 0 | 0/0 | 0/0 | 0 | 60 |
| Anderson | 0 | 7 | 0 | 0/0 | 0/0 | 0 | 42 |
| Lang | 5 | 1 | 0 | 0/0 | 0/0 | 0 | 36 |

Three tied with 18.

| RUSHING | No. | Yds | Avg | Lg | TD |
|---|---|---|---|---|---|
| Gary | 279 | 1125 | 4.0 | 63 | 7 |
| Lang | 33 | 203 | 6.2 | 71 | 5 |
| Everett | 32 | 133 | 4.2 | 22 | 0 |
| Delpino | 32 | 115 | 3.6 | 31 | 0 |

| PASSING | Att | Comp | Pct Comp | Yds | Avg Gain | TD | Int | Rating Pts |
|---|---|---|---|---|---|---|---|---|
| Everett | 475 | 281 | 59.2 | 3323 | 7.00 | 22 | 18 | 80.2 |
| Pagel | 20 | 8 | 40.0 | 99 | 4.95 | 1 | 2 | 33.1 |

| RECEIVING | No. | Yds | Avg | Lg | TD |
|---|---|---|---|---|---|
| Gary | 52 | 293 | 5.6 | 22 | 3 |
| Ellard | 47 | 727 | 15.5 | t33 | 3 |
| Anderson | 38 | 17.3 | 17.3 | 51 | 7 |
| Price | 34 | 324 | 9.5 | 25 | 2 |
| Chadwick | 29 | 362 | 12.5 | t27 | 3 |

**INTERCEPTIONS:** Henley and Newman, 3

| PUNTING | No. | Yds | Avg | Net Avg | TB | In 20 | Lg | Blk |
|---|---|---|---|---|---|---|---|---|
| Bracken | 76 | 3122 | 41.1 | 33.2 | 4 | 20 | 59 | 0 |

**SACKS:** Greene, 10.0

## New Orleans Saints

| SCORING | Rush | TD Rec | Ret | PAT | FG | S | Pts |
|---|---|---|---|---|---|---|---|
| Andersen | 0 | 0 | 0 | 33/34 | 29/34 | 0 | 120 |
| Hilliard | 3 | 4 | 0 | 0/0 | 0/0 | 0 | 42 |
| E. Martin | 0 | 5 | 0 | 0/0 | 0/0 | 0 | 30 |
| Early | 0 | 5 | 0 | 0/0 | 0/0 | 0 | 30 |

Three tied with 18.

| RUSHING | No. | Yds | Avg | Lg | TD |
|---|---|---|---|---|---|
| Dunbar | 154 | 565 | 3.7 | 25 | 3 |
| Hilliard | 115 | 445 | 3.9 | 22 | 3 |
| Heyward | 104 | 416 | 4.0 | 23 | 3 |
| McAfee | 39 | 114 | 2.9 | 19 | 1 |
| Hebert | 32 | 95 | 3.0 | 18 | 0 |

| PASSING | Att | Comp | Pct Comp | Yds | Avg Gain | TD | Int | Rating Pts |
|---|---|---|---|---|---|---|---|---|
| Hebert | 422 | 249 | 59.0 | 3287 | 7.79 | 19 | 16 | 82.9 |
| M. Buck | 4 | 2 | 50.0 | 10 | 2.50 | 0 | 0 | 56.3 |

| RECEIVING | No. | Yds | Avg | Lg | TD |
|---|---|---|---|---|---|
| E. Martin | 68 | 1041 | 15.3 | t52 | 5 |
| Hilliard | 48 | 465 | 9.7 | 41 | 4 |
| Early | 30 | 566 | 18.9 | t59 | 5 |
| Small | 23 | 278 | 12.1 | 33 | 3 |
| Heyward | 19 | 159 | 8.4 | 21 | 0 |

**INTERCEPTIONS:** Cook, 6

| PUNTING | No. | Yds | Avg | Net Avg | TB | In 20 | Lg | Blk |
|---|---|---|---|---|---|---|---|---|
| Barnhardt | 67 | 2947 | 44.0 | 37.7 | 10 | 19 | 62 | 0 |

**SACKS:** Martin, 15.5

## New York Giants

| SCORING | Rush | TD Rec | Ret | PAT | FG | S | Pts |
|---|---|---|---|---|---|---|---|
| Hampton | 14 | 0 | 0 | 0/0 | 0/0 | 0 | 84 |
| Bahr | 0 | 0 | 0 | 29/29 | 16/21 | 0 | 77 |
| Willis | 0 | 0 | 0 | 27/27 | 10/16 | 0 | 57 |
| McCaffrey | 0 | 5 | 0 | 0/0 | 0/0 | 0 | 30 |
| Bunch | 3 | 1 | 0 | 0/0 | 0/0 | 0 | 24 |

| RUSHING | No. | Yds | Avg | Lg | TD |
|---|---|---|---|---|---|
| Hampton | 257 | 1141 | 4.4 | t63 | 14 |
| Bunch | 104 | 501 | 4.8 | 37 | 3 |
| Hostetler | 34 | 172 | 5.1 | 27 | 3 |
| Meggett | 32 | 167 | 5.2 | 30 | 0 |

| PASSING | Att | Comp | Pct Comp | Yds | Av Gain | TD | Int | Rating Pts |
|---|---|---|---|---|---|---|---|---|
| Hostetler | 192 | 103 | 53.6 | 1225 | 6.38 | 8 | 3 | 80.8 |
| Simms | 137 | 83 | 60.6 | 912 | 6.66 | 5 | 3 | 83.3 |
| Graham | 97 | 42 | 43.3 | 470 | 4.85 | 1 | 4 | 44.6 |
| Brown | 7 | 4 | 57.1 | 21 | 3.00 | 0 | 0 | 62.2 |

| RECEIVING | No. | Yds | Avg | Lg | TD |
|---|---|---|---|---|---|
| McCaffrey | 49 | 610 | 12.4 | 44 | 5 |
| Meggett | 38 | 229 | 6.0 | 24 | 2 |
| Hampton | 28 | 215 | 7.7 | 31 | 0 |
| Ingram | 27 | 408 | 15.1 | 34 | 1 |
| Cross | 27 | 357 | 13.2 | 29 | 2 |

**INTERCEPTIONS:** Jackson, 4

| PUNTING | No. | Yds | Avg | Net Avg | TB | In 20 | Lg | Blk |
|---|---|---|---|---|---|---|---|---|
| Landeta | 53 | 2317 | 43.7 | 31.5 | 9 | 13 | 71 | 2 |
| Prokop | 32 | 1184 | 37.0 | 28.9 | 0 | 2 | 56 | 0 |
| Rodriguez | 46 | 1907 | 37.0 | 34.5 | 4 | 9 | 55 | 1 |

**SACKS:** Taylor, 5.0

## Philadelphia Eagles

| SCORING | Rush | TD Rec | Ret | PAT | FG | S | Pts |
|---|---|---|---|---|---|---|---|
| Ruzek | 0 | 0 | 0 | 40/44 | 16/25 | 0 | 88 |
| Walker | 8 | 2 | 0 | 0/0 | 0/0 | 0 | 60 |
| Barnett | 0 | 6 | 0 | 0/0 | 0/0 | 0 | 36 |
| Sherman | 5 | 1 | 0 | 0/0 | 0/0 | 0 | 36 |
| Cunningham | 5 | 0 | 0 | 0/0 | 0/0 | 0 | 30 |

| RUSHING | No. | Yds | Avg | Lg | TD |
|---|---|---|---|---|---|
| Walker | 267 | 1070 | 4.0 | 38 | 8 |
| Sherman | 112 | 583 | 5.2 | 34 | 5 |
| Cunningham | 87 | 549 | 6.3 | 30 | 5 |
| Byars | 41 | 176 | 4.3 | 23 | 1 |

| PASSING | Att | Comp | Pct Comp | Yds | Avg Gain | TD | Int | Rating Pts |
|---|---|---|---|---|---|---|---|---|
| Cunningham | 384 | 233 | 60.7 | 2775 | 7.23 | 19 | 11 | 87.3 |
| McMahon | 43 | 22 | 51.2 | 279 | 6.49 | 1 | 2 | 60.1 |

| RECEIVING | No. | Yds | Avg | Lg | TD |
|---|---|---|---|---|---|
| Barnett | 67 | 1083 | 16.2 | t71 | 6 |
| Byars | 56 | 502 | 9.0 | 46 | 2 |
| Williams | 42 | 598 | 14.2 | t49 | 7 |
| Walker | 38 | 278 | 7.3 | 41 | 2 |

**INTERCEPTIONS:** Allen, Joyner and Evans, 4

| PUNTING | No. | Yds | Avg | Net Avg | TB | In 20 | Lg | Blk |
|---|---|---|---|---|---|---|---|---|
| Feagles | 82 | 3459 | 42.2 | 36.9 | 7 | 26 | 68 | 0 |

**SACKS:** Simmons, 19.0

## Phoenix Cardinals

| SCORING | Rush | TD Rec | Ret | PAT | FG | S | Pts |
|---|---|---|---|---|---|---|---|
| G. Davis | 0 | 0 | 0 | 28/28 | 13/26 | 0 | 67 |
| Johnson | 6 | 0 | 0 | 0/0 | 0/0 | 0 | 36 |
| E. Jones | 0 | 4 | 0 | 0/0 | 0/0 | 0 | 24 |

Three tied with 18.

| RUSHING | No. | Yds | Avg | Lg | TD |
|---|---|---|---|---|---|
| Johnson | 178 | 734 | 4.1 | t42 | 6 |
| Bailey | 52 | 233 | 4.5 | 15 | 1 |
| Brown | 68 | 194 | 2.9 | 13 | 2 |
| Chandler | 36 | 149 | 4.1 | 18 | 1 |
| Centers | 37 | 139 | 3.8 | 28 | 0 |

| PASSING | Att | Comp | Pct Comp | Yds | Avg Gain | TD | Int | Rating Pts |
|---|---|---|---|---|---|---|---|---|
| Chandler | 413 | 245 | 59.3 | 2832 | 6.86 | 15 | 15 | 77.1 |
| Rosenbach | 92 | 49 | 53.3 | 483 | 5.25 | 0 | 6 | 41.2 |
| Sacca | 11 | 4 | 36.4 | 29 | 2.64 | 0 | 2 | 5.3 |

| RECEIVING | No. | Yds | Avg | Lg | TD |
|---|---|---|---|---|---|
| Proehl | 60 | 744 | 12.4 | t63 | 3 |
| R. Hill | 58 | 861 | 14.8 | 49 | 3 |
| Centers | 50 | 417 | 8.3 | 26 | 2 |
| E. Jones | 38 | 559 | 14.7 | t72 | 4 |
| Bailey | 33 | 331 | 10.0 | 34 | 1 |

**INTERCEPTIONS:** Massey, 5

| PUNTING | No. | Yds | Avg | Net Avg | TB | In 20 | Lg | Blk |
|---|---|---|---|---|---|---|---|---|
| Camarillo | 54 | 2317 | 42.9 | 39.6 | 2 | 23 | 73 | 0 |
| Davis | 4 | 167 | 41.8 | 36.8 | 1 | 0 | 52 | 0 |

**SACKS:** Harvey and M. Jones, 9.0

## San Francisco 49ers

| SCORING | Rush | TD Rec | Ret | PAT | FG | S | Pts |
|---|---|---|---|---|---|---|---|
| Cofer | 0 | 0 | 0 | 53/54 | 18/27 | 0 | 107 |
| Rice | 1 | 10 | 0 | 0/0 | 0/0 | 0 | 66 |
| Watters | 9 | 2 | 0 | 0/0 | 0/0 | 0 | 66 |
| Rathman | 5 | 4 | 0 | 0/0 | 0/0 | 0 | 54 |

Three tied with 24.

| RUSHING | No. | Yds | Avg | Lg | TD |
|---|---|---|---|---|---|
| Watters | 206 | 1013 | 4.9 | 43 | 9 |
| Young | 76 | 537 | 7.1 | t39 | 4 |
| Lee | 91 | 362 | 4.0 | 43 | 2 |
| Rathman | 57 | 194 | 3.4 | 17 | 5 |

| PASSING | Att | Comp | Pct Comp | Yds | Avg Gain | TD | Int | Rating Pts |
|---|---|---|---|---|---|---|---|---|
| Young | 402 | 268 | 66.7 | 3465 | 8.62 | 25 | 7 | 107.0 |
| Bono | 56 | 36 | 64.3 | 463 | 8.27 | 2 | 2 | 87.1 |
| Montana | 21 | 15 | 71.4 | 126 | 6.00 | 2 | 0 | 118.4 |

| RECEIVING | No. | Yds | Avg | Lg | TD |
|---|---|---|---|---|---|
| Rice | 84 | 1201 | 14.3 | t80 | 10 |
| Jones | 45 | 628 | 14.0 | 43 | 4 |
| Rathman | 44 | 343 | 7.8 | t27 | 4 |
| Watters | 43 | 405 | 9.4 | 35 | 2 |
| Sherrard | 38 | 607 | 16.0 | 56 | 0 |

**INTERCEPTIONS:** Griffin, 5

| PUNTING | No. | Yds | Avg | Net Avg | TB | In 20 | Lg | Blk |
|---|---|---|---|---|---|---|---|---|
| Prokop | 40 | 1541 | 38.5 | 34.6 | 1 | 8 | 58 | 0 |

**SACKS:** Roberts and Haley, 7.0

## Tampa Bay Buccaneers

| SCORING | Rush | Rec | Ret | PAT | FG | S | Pts |
|---|---|---|---|---|---|---|---|
| Cobb | 9 | 0 | 0 | 0/0 | 0/0 | 0 | 54 |
| Stryzinski | 0 | 0 | 0 | 13/13 | 5/9 | 0 | 42 |
| Carrier | 0 | 4 | 0 | 0/0 | 0/0 | 0 | 24 |
| Hall | 0 | 4 | 0 | 0/0 | 0/0 | 0 | 24 |

| RUSHING | No. | Yds | Avg | Lg | TD |
|---|---|---|---|---|---|
| Cobb | 310 | 1171 | 3.8 | 25 | 9 |
| Testaverde | 36 | 197 | 5.5 | 18 | 2 |
| Anderson | 55 | 194 | 3.5 | 18 | 1 |
| McDowell | 14 | 81 | 5.8 | 23 | 0 |

| PASSING | Att | Comp | Pct Comp | Yds | Avg Gain | TD | Int | Rating Pts |
|---|---|---|---|---|---|---|---|---|
| Testaverde | 358 | 206 | 57.5 | 2554 | 7.13 | 14 | 16 | 74.2 |
| DeBerg | 125 | 76 | 60.8 | 710 | 5.68 | 3 | 4 | 71.1 |
| Erickson | 26 | 15 | 57.7 | 121 | 4.65 | 0 | 0 | 69.6 |

| RECEIVING | No. | Yds | Avg | Lg | TD |
|---|---|---|---|---|---|
| Dawsey | 60 | 776 | 12.9 | 41 | 1 |
| Carrier | 56 | 692 | 12.4 | 40 | 4 |
| Ro. Hall | 39 | 351 | 9.0 | 32 | 4 |
| Anderson | 34 | 284 | 8.4 | 34 | 0 |
| McDowell | 27 | 258 | 9.6 | t51 | 2 |

**INTERCEPTIONS:** Carter, Fullington and Mack, 3

| PUNTING | No. | Yds | Avg | Net Avg | TB | In 20 | Lg | Blk |
|---|---|---|---|---|---|---|---|---|
| Stryzinski | 74 | 3015 | 40.7 | 36.2 | 11 | 15 | 57 | 0 |

**SACKS:** Dotson, 10.0

## Washington Redskins

| SCORING | Rush | Rec | Ret | PAT | FG | S | Pts |
|---|---|---|---|---|---|---|---|
| Lohmiller | 0 | 0 | 0 | 30/30 | 30/40 | 0 | 120 |
| Byner | 6 | 1 | 0 | 0/0 | 0/0 | 0 | 42 |
| Clark | 0 | 5 | 0 | 0/0 | 0/0 | 0 | 30 |
| Three tied with 18. | | | | | | | |

| RUSHING | No. | Yds | Avg | Lg | TD |
|---|---|---|---|---|---|
| Byner | 262 | 998 | 3.8 | 23 | 6 |
| Ervins | 151 | 495 | 3.3 | 25 | 2 |
| Mitchell | 6 | 70 | 11.7 | 33 | 0 |
| Rypien | 36 | 50 | 1.4 | 11 | 2 |

| PASSING | Att | Comp | Pct Comp | Yds | Avg Gain | TD | Int | Rating Pts |
|---|---|---|---|---|---|---|---|---|
| Rypien | 479 | 269 | 56.2 | 3282 | 6.85 | 13 | 17 | 71.7 |
| Byner | 3 | 1 | 33.3 | 41 | 13.67 | 1 | 0 | 121.5 |
| Conklin | 2 | 2 | 100.00 | 16 | 8.00 | 1 | 0 | 139.6 |

| RECEIVING | No. | Yds | Avg | Lg | TD |
|---|---|---|---|---|---|
| Clark | 64 | 912 | 14.3 | 47 | 5 |
| Clark | 70 | 1340 | 19.1 | t82 | 10 |
| Sanders | 51 | 707 | 13.9 | t62 | 3 |
| Monk | 46 | 644 | 14.0 | t49 | 3 |
| Byner | 39 | 338 | 8.7 | 29 | 1 |

**INTERCEPTIONS:** Edwards, 6

| PUNTING | No. | Yds | Avg | Net Avg | TB | In 20 | Lg | Blk |
|---|---|---|---|---|---|---|---|---|
| Goodburn | 64 | 2555 | 39.9 | 32.7 | 5 | 17 | 66 | 1 |

**SACKS:** Johnson and Marshall, 6.0

### Question of Substance

The indictments in January 1993 of New York Giant guard Eric Moore and Tampa Bay Buccaneer defensive end Mark Duckens on federal charges that they possessed and intended to distribute anabolic steroids and human growth hormone (HGH) focus new attention on the use of these bodybuilding substances in the NFL. Moore and Duckens pleaded not guilty, but Drug Enforcement Administration officials in Atlanta, where the indictments were handed down, said that large quantities of steroids and HGH were seized from the pair and that arrests of other NFL players were possible.

The NFL tried to characterize the indictments as an aberration, claiming that it has administered 18,000 tests for steroids over the last three years, with no more than five positives. But HGH can't be detected through testing, and players can beat steroid tests with masking agents or by getting off the drugs in time. Also, there is reason to question the league's testing procedures. "I had one player call me who was frantic," says Tony Fitton, a convicted steroid trafficker who now advises athletes on steroid alternatives. "He had a test that week, and he had used Winstrol V [an anabolic steroid]. He turned out negative. It makes you wonder about the validity of the testing."

The difficulty of combating the use of performance-enhancing drugs in sports was underscored by an estimate by Prince Alexandre de Merode, president of the International Olympic Committee's medical commission, that while only five of the 10,274 athletes at the Barcelona Olympics tested positive, 10% of the participants in the Games use steroids or other performance-enhancing substances. De Merode's 10% figure—and even that may be low—would mean that the IOC is catching barely one of every 200 drug users. There's no reason to think the NFL is doing much better.

First four rounds of the 58th annual NFL Draft held April 25-26 in New York City.

| First Round | | | Second Round | | |
|---|---|---|---|---|---|
| **Team** | **Selection** | **Position** | **Team** | **Selection** | **Position** |
| 1. .......New England | Drew Bledsoe, Washington St | QB | 30. ......Seattle | Carlton Gray, UCLA | DB |
| 2. .......Seattle | Rick Mirer, Notre Dame | QB | 31. ......New England | Chris Slade, Virginia | DE |
| 3. .......Phoenix* | Garrison Hearst, Georgia | RB | 32. ......Phoenix | Ben Coleman, Wake Forest | T |
| 4. .......NY Jets† | Marvin Jones, Miami | LB | 33. ......Detroit* | Ryan McNeil, Miami | DB |
| 5. .......Cincinnati | John Copeland, Alabama | DT | 34. ......Tampa Bay | Demetrius DuBose, Notre Dame | LB |
| 6. .......Tampa Bay | Eric Curry, Alabama | DE | 35. ......Chicago | Carl Simpson, Florida State | DT |
| 7. .......Chicago | Curtis Conway, Southern Cal | WR | 36. ......NY Jets† | Coleman Rudolph, Georgia Tech | DE |
| 8. .......New Orleans# | Willie Roaf, Louisiana Tech | OT | 37. ......Cincinnati | Tony McGee, Michigan | TE |
| 9. .......Atlanta | Lincoln Kennedy, Washington | OT | 38. ......Atlanta | Roger Harper, Ohio State | DB |
| 10. ......LA Rams | Jerome Bettis, Notre Dame | RB | 39. ......LA Rams | Troy Drayton, Penn State | TE |
| 11. ......Denver‡ | Dan Williams, Toledo | DE | 40. ......NY Giants | Michael Strahan, Texas Southern | DE |
| 12. ......LA Raiders | Patrick Bates, Texas A & M | DB | 41. ......San Diego# | Natrone Means, North Carolina | RB |
| 13. ......Houston** | Brad Hopkins, Illinois | OG | 42. ......Cleveland | Dan Footman, Florida State | DE |
| 14.    Cleveland†† | Steve Everitt, Michigan | C | 43. ......Denver | Glyn Milburn, Stanford | RB |
| 15. ......Green Bay | Wayne Simmons, Clemson | LB | 44. ......Pittsburgh‡ | Chad Brown, Colorado | LB |
| 16. ......Indianpolis | Sean Dawkins, California | WR | 45. ......Washington | Reggie Brooks, Notre Dame | RB |
| 17. ......Washington | Tom Carter, Notre Dame | DB | 46. ......Dallas** | Kevin Williams, Miami | WR |
| 18. ......Phoenix## | Ernest Dye, South Carolina | OT | 47. ......Houston†† | Micheal Barrow, Miami | LB |
| 19. ......Philadelphia‡‡ | Lester Holmes, Jackson State | OT | 48. ......San Francisco## | Adrian Hardy, NW Louisiana | DB |
| 20. ......New Orleans*** | Irv Smith, Notre Dame | TE | 49. ......Indianapolis‡‡ | Roosevelt Potts, NE Louisiana | RB |
| 21. ......Minnesota | Robert Smith, Ohio State | RB | 50. ......Philadelphia | Victor Bailey, Missouri | WR |
| 22. ......San Diego | Darrien Gordon, Stanford | DB | 51. ......New England*** | Todd Rucci, Penn State | T |
| 23. ......Pittsburgh | Deon Figures, Colorado | DB | 52. ......Minnesota | Qadry Ismail, Syracuse | WR |
| 24. ......Philadelphia | Leonard Renfroe, Colorado | DE | 53. ......New Orleans | Reggie Freeman, Florida State | LB |
| 25. ......Miami | O.J. McDuffie, Penn State | WR | 54. ......Dallas††† | Darrin Smith, Miami | LB |
| 26. ......San Francisco††† | Dana Stubblefield, Kansas | DE | 55. ......Buffalo | John Parella, Nebraska | DT |
| 27. ......San Francisco | Todd Kelly, Tennessee | DE | 56. .....LA Raiders### | Passed | |
| 28. ......Buffalo | Thomas Smith, North Carolina | DB | 56. ......New England | Vincent Brisby, NE Louisiana | WR |
| 29. ......Green Bay### | George Teague, Alabama | DB | | | |

*From NY Jets †From Phoenix #From Detroit ‡From Cleveland **From Philadelphia. ††From Denver ##From Kansas City through San Francisco. ‡‡From Houston. ***From Phoenix through San Francisco †††From New Orleans ###From Dallas.

*From NY Jets †From Detroit #From LA Raiders through San Francisco ‡From Indianapolis **From Green Bay ††Kansas City exercised in supplemental draft ##From San Diego ‡‡From Pittsburgh ***From Miami †††From San Francisco through Green Bay ###From Dallas through San Francisco.

## Third Round

| Team | Selection | Position |
|---|---|---|
| 57. ......Minnesota* | John Gerak, Penn State | OL |
| 58. ......LA Raiders† | Billy Joe Hobert, Washington | QB |
| 59. ......Cincinnati# | Steve Tovar, Ohio State | LB |
| 60. ......Tampa Bay‡ | Lamar Thomas, Miami | WR |
| 61. ......Chicago | Chris Gedney, Syracuse | TE |
| 62. ......Detroit | Antonio London, Alabama | LB |
| 63. ......Cincinnati | Ty Parten, Arizona | DL |
| 64. ......San Diego** | Joe Cocozzo, Michigan | G |
| 65. ......Indianapolis†† | Ray Buchanan, Louisville | DB |
| 66. ......NY Giants | Marcus Buckley, Texas A & M | LB |
| 67. ......Atlanta | Harold Alexander, Appalachian St | P |
| 68. ......Detroit## | Mike Compton, West Virginia | C |
| 69. ......Denver‡‡ | Rondell Jones, North Carolina | DB |
| 70. ......Denver | Jason Elam, Hawaii | K |
| 71. ......Washington | Rick Hamilton, Central Florida | LB |
| 72. ......LA Raiders*** | James Trapp, Clemson | DB |
| 73. ......Indianapolis | Russell White, California | RB |
| 74. ......Kansas City | Will Shields, Nebraska | G |
| 75. ......Philadelphia††† | Derrick Frazier, Texas A & M | DB |
| 76. ......Pittsburgh | Andre Hastings, Georgia | WR |
| 77. Philadelphia | Mike Reid, North Carolina St | DB |
| 78. ......Miami | Terry Kirby, Virginia | RB |
| 79. ......Minnesota | Gilbert Brown, Kansas | DT |
| 80. ......Washington### | Ed Bunn, UTEP | P |
| 81. ......Green Bay‡‡‡ | Earl Dotson, Texas A & I | DT |
| 82. ......Tampa Bay**** | John Lynch, Stanford | DB |
| 83. ......Cleveland†††† | Michael Caldwell, Midd Tenn St | LB |
| 84. ......Dallas | Mike Middleton, Indiana | DB |

## Fourth Round

| Team | Selection | Position |
|---|---|---|
| 85. ......Seattle | Dean Wells, Kentucky | LB |
| 86. ......New England | Kevin Johnson, Texas Southern | DT |
| 87. ......Phoenix | Ronald Moore, Pittsburg (KS) St | RB |
| 88. ......NY Jets | David Ware, Virginia | OT |
| 89. ......New Orleans* | Lorenzo Neal, Fresno State | RB |
| 90. ......Cincinnati | Marcello Simmons, Southern Methodist | DB |
| 91. ......Tampa Bay | Rudy Harris, Clemson | RB |
| 92. ......Indianapolis† | Derwin Gray, Brigham Young | DB |
| 93. ......NY Giants | Greg Bishop, Pacific | OT |
| 94. ......Dallas# | Derrick Lassic, Alabama | RB |
| 95. ......San Diego‡ | Ray Lee Johnson, Arkansas | DE |
| 96. ......Dallas** | Ron Stone, Boston College | OT |
| 97. ......Chicago†† | Todd Perry, Kentucky | G |
| 98. ......Denver | Jeff Robinson, Idaho | DE |
| 99. ......San Diego## | Lewis Bush, Washington St | LB |
| 100. ......Chicago‡‡ | Myron Baker, Louisiana Tech | LB |
| 101. ....Washington | Sterling Palmer, Brigham Young | DE |
| 102. ....Houston | Travis Hannah, Southern Cal | WR |
| 103. ....Kansas City | Jaime Fields, Washington | LB |
| 104. ....Tampa Bay*** | Horace Copeland, Miami | WR |
| 105. ....Miami | Ronnie Bradford, Colorado | DB |
| 106. ....Minnesota | Ashley Sheppard, Clemson | LB |
| 107. ....Indianapolis††† | Devon McDonald, Notre Dame | LB |
| 108. ....Pittsburgh | Kevin Henry, Mississippi St | DE |
| 109. ....New Orleans | Derek Brown, Nebraska | RB |
| 110. ....New England### | Corwin Brown, Michigan | DB |
| 111. ....Buffalo | Russell Copeland, Memphis St | WR |
| 112. ....Chicago‡‡‡ | Albert Fontenot, Baylor | DE |

*From Seattle †From Dallas through San Francisco. #From NTY Jets ‡From Phoenix **From Tampa Bay ††From LA Rams. ##From Cleveland. ‡‡From LA Raiders. ***From Green Bay †††From Houston ###From San Diego ‡‡‡From New Orleans through San Francisco and LA Raiders. ****From San Francisco through San Diego. ††††From Buffalo through Atlanta and Denver.

*From Detroit †From Chicago #From Atlanta through Green Bay ‡From LA Rams **From LA Raiders ††From Cleveland ##From Green Bay through New England ‡‡From Indianapolis ***From Philadelphia through San Diego ††† From San Diego through Pittsburgh ###From San Francisco through San Diego ‡‡‡From Dallas through Green Bay.

## American Football Conference

### Buffalo

| Rd. | No. | Selection | Position |
|---|---|---|---|
| 1 | 28 | Thomas Smith, North Carolina | DB |
| 2 | 55 | John Parrella, Nebraska | DT |
| 4 | 111 | Russell Copeland, Memphis St | WR |
| 5 | 136 | Mike Devlin, Iowa | C |
| 5 | 139 | Sebastian Savage, NC State | DB |
| 6 | 167 | Corbin Lacina, Augustana (S.D.) | OT |
| 7 | 195 | Willie Harris, Mississippi St | WR |
| 8 | 223 | Chris Luneberg, West Chester (PA) | OT |

### Denver

| Rd. | No. | Selection | Position |
|---|---|---|---|
| 1 | 11 | Dan Williams, Toledo | DE |
| 2 | 43 | Glyn Milburn, Stanford | RB |
| 3 | 69 | Rondell Jones, North Carolina | DB |
| 3 | 70 | Jason Elam, Hawaii | K |
| 4 | 98 | Jeff Robinson, Idaho | DE |
| 5 | 126 | Kevin Williams, UCLA | RB |
| 6 | 154 | Melvin Bonner, Baylor | WR |
| 7 | 169 | Clarence Williams, Washington St | TE |
| 7 | 182 | Antonio Kimbrough, Jackson St | WR |
| 8 | 210 | Brian Stablein, Ohio State | WR |

### Cincinnati

| Rd. | No. | Selection | Position |
|---|---|---|---|
| 1 | 5 | John Copeland, Alabama | DE |
| 2 | 37 | Tony McGee, Michigan | TE |
| 3 | 59 | Steve Tovar, Ohio State | LB |
| 3 | 63 | Ty Parten, Arizona | DL |
| 4 | 90 | Marcello Simmons, SMU | DB |
| 5 | 117 | Forey Duckett, Nevada | DB |
| 6 | 148 | Tom Scott, East Carolina | OT |
| 7 | 175 | Lance Gunn, Texas | DB |
| 8 | 202 | Doug Pelfry, Kentucky | K |

### Houston

| Rd. | No. | Selection | Position |
|---|---|---|---|
| 1 | 13 | Brad Hopkins, Illinois | G |
| 2 | 47 | Micheal Barrow, Miami | LB |
| 4 | 102 | Travis Hannah, Southern Cal | WR |
| 5 | 131 | John Henry Mills, Wake Forest | TE |
| 6 | 158 | Chuck Bradley, Kentucky | OT |
| 7 | 187 | Patrick Robinson, Tennessee St | WR |
| 8 | 214 | Blaine Bishop, Ball St | DB |

### Cleveland

| Rd. | No. | Selection | Position |
|---|---|---|---|
| 1 | 14 | Steve Everitt, Michigan | C |
| 2 | 42 | Dan Footman, Florida St | DE |
| 3 | 83 | Michael Caldwell, Middle Tenn St | LB |
| 5 | 124 | Herman Arvie, Grambling | OT |
| 6 | 153 | Rich McKenzie, Penn State | LB |
| 7 | 180 | Travis Hill, Nebraska | LB |

## American Football Conference *(Cont.)*

### Indianapolis

| Rd. | No. | Selection | Position |
|-----|-----|-----------|----------|
| 1 | 16 | Sean Dawkins, California | WR |
| 2 | 49 | Roosevelt Potts, NE Louisiana | RB |
| 3 | 65 | Ray Buchannan, Louisville | DB |
| 4 | 92 | Derwin Gray, Brigham Young | DB |
| 4 | 107 | Devon McDonald, Notre Dame | LB |
| 6 | 157 | Carlos Etheredge, Miami | TE |
| 7 | 184 | Lance Lewis, Nebraska | RB |
| 8 | 211 | Marquise Thomas, Mississippi | LB |

### Miami

| Rd. | No. | Selection | Position |
|-----|-----|-----------|----------|
| 1 | 25 | O.J. McDuffie, Penn State | WR |
| 3 | 78 | Terry Kirby, Virginia | RB |
| 4 | 105 | Ronnie Bradford, Colorado | DB |
| 5 | 132 | Chris Gray, Auburn | G |
| 6 | 164 | Robert O'Neal, Clemson | DB |
| 7 | 191 | David Merritt, NC State | LB |
| 8 | 218 | Dwayne Gordon, New Hampshire | LB |

### Kansas City

| Rd. | No. | Selection | Position |
|-----|-----|-----------|----------|
| 3 | 74 | Will Shields, Nebraska | DB |
| 4 | 103 | Jaime Fields, Washington | LB |
| 5 | 130 | Lindsay Knapp, Notre Dame | G |
| 6 | 159 | Darius Turner, Washington | RB |
| 7 | 186 | Darian Hughes, Iowa | WR |

### New England

| Rd. | No. | Selection | Position |
|-----|-----|-----------|----------|
| 1 | 1 | Drew Bledsoe, Washington St | QB |
| 2 | 31 | Chris Slade, Virginia | DE |
| 2 | 51 | Todd Rucci, Penn State | OT |
| 2 | 56 | Vincent Brisby, NE Louisiana | WR |
| 4 | 86 | Kevin Johnson, Texas Southern | DT |
| 4 | 110 | Corwin Brown, Michigan | DB |
| 5 | 113 | Scott Sisson, Georgia Tech | K |
| 5 | 138 | Richard Griffith, Arizona | TE |
| 6 | 142 | Lawrence Hatch, Florida | DB |
| 8 | 198 | Troy Brown, Marshall | KR |

### LA Raiders

| Rd. | No. | Selection | Position |
|-----|-----|-----------|----------|
| 1 | 12 | Patrick Bates, Texas A & M | DB |
| 3 | 58 | Billy Joe Hobert, Washington | QB |
| 3 | 72 | James Trapp, Clemson | DB |
| 5 | 125 | Orlanda Truitt, Mississippi St | WR |
| 7 | 181 | Greg Biekert, Colorado | LB |
| 8 | 208 | Greg Robinson, NE Louisiana | RB |

## American Football Conference *(Cont.)*

### NY Jets

| Rd. | No. | Selection | Position |
|---|---|---|---|
| 1 | 4 | Marvin Jones, Florida St | LB |
| 2 | 36 | Coleman Rudolph, Georgia Tech | DE |
| 4 | 88 | David Ware, Virginia | OT |
| 5 | 115 | Fred Baxter, Auburn | TE |
| 5 | 120 | Adrian Murrell, West Virginia | RB |
| 5 | 129 | Kenny Shedd, Northern Iowa | WR |
| 6 | 144 | Richie Anderson, Penn State | RB |
| 7 | 171 | Alec Millen, Georgia | OT |
| 8 | 200 | Craig Hentrich, Notre Dame | K |

### San Diego

| Rd. | No. | Selection | Position |
|---|---|---|---|
| 1 | 22 | Darrien Gordon, Stanford | DB |
| 2 | 41 | Natrone Means, North Carolina | RB |
| 3 | 64 | Joe Cocozzo, Michigan | G |
| 4 | 95 | Ray Lee Johnson, Arkansas | DE |
| 4 | 95 | Lewis Bush, Washington St | LB |
| 5 | 134 | Walter Dunson, Middle Tenn St | WR |
| 6 | 161 | Eric Castle, Oregon | DB |
| 7 | 188 | Doug Miller, South Dakota St | LB |
| 8 | 222 | Trent Green, Indiana | QB |

### Pittsburgh

| Rd. | No. | Selection | Position |
|---|---|---|---|
| 1 | 23 | Deon Figures, Colorado | DB |
| 2 | 44 | Chad Brown, Colorado | LB |
| 3 | 76 | Andre Hastings, Georgia | WR |
| 4 | 108 | Kevin Henry, Mississippi St | DE |
| 5 | 135 | Lonnie Palelei, UNLV | G |
| 5 | 140 | Mark Woodard, Mississippi | LB |
| 6 | 162 | Willie Williams, Western Carolina | DB |
| 7 | 185 | Jeff Zgonina, Purdue | DT |
| 7 | 189 | Craig Keith, Lenoir-Rhyne (N.C.) | TE |
| 8 | 216 | Alex Van Pelt, Pittsburgh | QB |

### Seattle

| Rd. | No. | Selection | Position |
|---|---|---|---|
| 1 | 2 | Rick Mirer, Notre Dame | QB |
| 2 | 30 | Carlton Gray, UCLA | DB |
| 4 | 85 | Dean Wells, Kentucky | LB |
| 5 | 114 | Terrence Warren, Hampton (VA) | WR |
| 7 | 170 | Michael McCrary, Wake Forest | DE |
| 8 | 197 | Jeff Blackshear, NE Louisiana | G |
| 8 | 204 | Antonio Edwards, Valdosta (GA) St | DE |

## THEY SAID IT

*Sammy Lilly, out-of-work NFL cornerback who had just interviewed for a job at a nuclear power plant in Georgia, after getting a call to play for the Los Angeles Rams: "I'm thrilled about this. I'm glowing right now."*

## National Football Conference

### Atlanta

| Rd. | No. | Selection | Position |
|---|---|---|---|
| 1 | 9 | Lincoln Kennedy, Washington | OT |
| 2 | 38 | Roger Harper, Ohio State | DB |
| 3 | 67 | Harold Alexander, Appalachian St | P |
| 5 | 121 | Roger George, Stanford | LB |
| 6 | 151 | Mitch Lyons, Michigan St | TE |
| 7 | 178 | Darnell Walker, Oklahoma | DB |
| 8 | 205 | Shannon Baker, Florida St | WR |

### Dallas

| Rd. | No. | Selection | Position |
|---|---|---|---|
| 2 | 46 | Kevin Williams, Miami | WR |
| 2 | 54 | Darrin Smith, Miami | LB |
| 3 | 84 | Mike Middleton, Indiana | DB |
| 4 | 94 | Derrick Lassic, Alabama | RB |
| 4 | 96 | Ron Stone, Boston College | OT |
| 6 | 168 | Barry Minter, Tulsa | LB |
| 7 | 196 | Brock Marion, Nebraska | DB |
| 7 | 203 | Dave Thomas, Tennessee | DB |
| 8 | 213 | Reggie Givens, Penn State | DB |

### Chicago

| Rd. | No. | Selection | Position |
|---|---|---|---|
| 1 | 7 | Curtis Conway, Southern Cal | WR |
| 2 | 35 | Carl Simpson, Florida St | DT |
| 3 | 61 | Chris Gedney, Syracuse | TE |
| 4 | 97 | Todd Perry, Kentucky | G |
| 4 | 100 | Myron Baker, Louisiana Tech | LB |
| 4 | 112 | Albert Fontenot, Baylor | DE |
| 6 | 146 | Dave Hoffman, Washington | LB |
| 7 | 173 | Keshon Johnson, Arizona | CB |

### Detroit

| Rd. | No. | Selection | Position |
|---|---|---|---|
| 2 | 33 | Ryan McNeil, Miami | DB |
| 3 | 62 | Antonio London, Alabama | LB |
| 3 | 68 | Mike Compton, West Virginia | C |
| 6 | 147 | Gregg Jeffries, Virginia | DB |
| 7 | 174 | Ty Hallock, Michigan State | LB |
| 8 | 201 | Kevin Minniefield, Arizona St | DB |

### Green Bay

| Rd. | No. | Selection | Position |
|---|---|---|---|
| 1 | 15 | Wayne Simmons, Clemson | LB |
| 1 | 29 | George Teague, Alabama | DB |
| 3 | 81 | Earl Dotson, Texas A & I | OT |
| 5 | 118 | Mark Brunell, Washington | QB |
| 5 | 119 | James Willis, Auburn | LB |
| 6 | 141 | Doug Evans, Louisiana Tech | DB |
| 6 | 152 | Paul Hutchins, Western Michigan | OT |
| 6 | 156 | Tim Watson, Howard | DB |
| 7 | 183 | Robert Kuberski, Navy | DE |

## National Football Conference *(Cont.)*

### LA Rams

| Rd. | No. | Selection | Position |
|---|---|---|---|
| 1 | 10 | Jerome Bettis, Notre Dame | RB |
| 2 | 39 | Troy Drayton, Penn State | TE |
| 3 | 73 | Russell White, California | RB |
| 5 | 122 | Sean LaChapelle, UCLS | WR |
| 5 | 127 | Chuck Belin, Wisconsin | G |
| 6 | 149 | Deral Boykin, Louisville | DB |
| 7 | 179 | Brad Fitchell, Eastern Illinois | C |
| 8 | 206 | Jeff Buffaloe, Memphis State | P |
| 8 | 209 | Maa Tanuvasa, Hawaii | DT |

### New Orleans

| Rd. | No. | Selection | Position |
|---|---|---|---|
| 1 | 8 | Willie Roaf, Louisiana Tech | OT |
| 1 | 20 | Irv Smith, Notre Dame | TE |
| 2 | 53 | Reggie Freeman, Florida State | LB |
| 4 | 89 | Lorenzo Neal, Fresno State | RB |
| 4 | 109 | Derek Brown, Nebraska | RB |
| 5 | 137 | Tyron Hughes, Nebraska | DB |
| 6 | 165 | Ronnie Dixon, Cincinnati | NT |
| 7 | 193 | Othello Henderson, UCLA | DB |
| 8 | 221 | Jon Kirksey, Sacramento St | NT |

### Minnesota

| Rd. | No. | Selection | Position |
|---|---|---|---|
| 1 | 21 | Robert Smith, Ohio State | RB |
| 2 | 52 | Qadry Ismail, Syracuse | WR |
| 3 | 57 | John Gerak, Penn State | OL |
| 3 | 79 | Gilbert Brown, Kansas | DT |
| 4 | 106 | Ashley Sheppard, Clemson | LB |
| 5 | 133 | Everett Lindsay, Mississippi | OT |
| 7 | 192 | Gino Torretta, Miami | QB |

### NY Giants

| Rd. | No. | Selection | Position |
|---|---|---|---|
| 2 | 40 | Michael Strahan, Texas Southern | DE |
| 3 | 66 | Marcus Buckley, Texas A & M | LB |
| 4 | 93 | Greg Bishop, Pacific | OT |
| 5 | 123 | Tommy Thigpen, North Carolina | LB |
| 6 | 150 | Scott Davis, Iowa | G |
| 7 | 177 | Todd Peterson, Georgia | K |
| 8 | 207 | Jessie Armstead, Miami | LB |

### Rah

Last season's firing of New England Patriot coach Dick MacPherson by CEO Sam Jankovich and the subsequent resignation of Jankovich, both developments following the buyout of co-owner Francis Murray by owner James Orthwein, the ouster of vice-president Joe Mendes and the resignation of p.r. man Pat Hanlon, had Boston scribes trying to scope out the team's new chain of command. As best anyone could figure, the top person in the organization behind Orthwein, who, for his part, had been trying to sell his sinking ship of a team, was then Lisa Coles, the director of the Pats' cheerleader corps.

## National Football Conference *(Cont.)*

### Philadelphia

| Rd. | No. | Selection | Position |
|---|---|---|---|
| 1 | 19 | Lester Holmes, Jackson St | T |
| 1 | 24 | Leonard Renfro, Colorado | DT |
| 2 | 50 | Victor Bailey, Missouri | WR |
| 3 | 75 | Derrick Frazier, Texas A & M | DB |
| 3 | 77 | Mike Reid, NC State | DB |
| 6 | 163 | Derrick Oden, Alabama | LB |
| 7 | 190 | Joey Mickey, Oklahoma | TE |
| 8 | 217 | Doug Skene, Michigan | OT |

### Phoenix

| Rd. | No. | Selection | Position |
|---|---|---|---|
| 1 | 3 | Garrison Hearst, Georgia | RB |
| 1 | 18 | Ernest Dye, South Carolina | T |
| 2 | 32 | Ben Coleman, Wake Forest | T |
| 4 | 87 | Ronald Moore, Pittsburg (KS) St | RB |
| 6 | 143 | Brett Wallerstadt, Arizona St | LB |
| 7 | 172 | Will White, Florida | DB |
| 8 | 199 | Chad Brown, Mississippi | DE |
| 8 | 215 | Steve Anderson, Grambling | WR |

### San Francisco

| Rd. | No. | Selection | Position |
|---|---|---|---|
| 1 | 26 | Dana Stubblefield, Kansas | DT |
| 1 | 27 | Todd Kelly, Tennessee | DE |
| 2 | 48 | Adrian Hardy, NW Louisiana | DB |
| 5 | 116 | Artie Smith, Louisiana Tech | DT |
| 6 | 166 | Chris Dalman, Stanford | C |
| 7 | 194 | Troy Wilson, Pittsburg (KS) St | LB |
| 8 | 219 | Elvis Grbac, Michigan | QB |

### Tampa Bay

| Rd. | No. | Selection | Position |
|---|---|---|---|
| 1 | 6 | Eric Curry, Alabama | DE |
| 2 | 34 | Demetrius DuBose, Notre Dame | LB |
| 3 | 60 | Lamar Thomas, Miami | WR |
| 3 | 82 | John Lynch, Stanford | DB |
| 4 | 91 | Rudy Harris, Clemson | RB |
| 4 | 104 | Horace Copeland, Miami | WR |
| 6 | 145 | Chidi Ahanotu, California | DT |
| 7 | 176 | Tyree Davis, Central Arkansas | WR |
| 8 | 220 | Darrick Branch, Hawaii | WR |
| 8 | 224 | Daron Alcorn, Auburn | K |

### Washington

| Rd. | No. | Selection | Position |
|---|---|---|---|
| 1 | 17 | Tom Carter, Notre Dame | DB |
| 2 | 45 | Reggie Brooks, Notre Dame | RB |
| 3 | 71 | Rick Hamilton, Central Florida | LB |
| 3 | 80 | Ed Bunn, UTEP | P |
| 4 | 101 | Sterling Palmer, Florida State | DE |
| 5 | 128 | Greg Huntington, Penn State | C |
| 6 | 155 | Darryl Morrison, Arizona | DB |
| 6 | 160 | Frank Wycheck, Maryland | TE |
| 8 | 212 | Lamont Hollinquest, Southern Cal | LB |

# 1992 World League of American Football

## Final Standings

### EUROPEAN DIVISION

| | W | L | T | Pct | Pts/ Tm | Pts/ Opp |
|---|---|---|---|---|---|---|
| Barcelona | 5 | 5 | 0 | .500 | 104 | 161 |
| Frankfurt | 3 | 7 | 0 | .300 | 150 | 257 |
| London | 2 | 7 | 1 | .250 | 178 | 203 |

### NORTH AMERICAN/EAST DIVISION

| | W | L | T | Pct | Pts/ Tm | Pts/ Opp |
|---|---|---|---|---|---|---|
| Orlando | 8 | 2 | 0 | .800 | 247 | 127 |
| NY/NJ | 6 | 4 | 0 | .600 | 284 | 188 |
| Montreal | 2 | 8 | 0 | .200 | 175 | 274 |
| Ohio | 1 | 9 | 0 | .100 | 132 | 230 |

### NORTH AMERICAN/WEST DIVISION

| | W | L | T | Pct | Pts/ Tm | Pts/ Opp |
|---|---|---|---|---|---|---|
| Sacramento | 8 | 2 | 0 | .800 | 250 | 152 |
| Birmingham | 7 | 2 | 1 | .750 | 192 | 165 |
| San Antonio | 7 | 3 | 0 | .700 | 195 | 150 |

## Playoff Results

### SEMIFINALS

Orlando 45, Birmingham 7
Sacramento 17, Barcelona 15

## 1992 World Bowl

June 6, 1992 at Olympic Stadium, Montreal

| | | | | | |
|---|---|---|---|---|---|
| Sacramento | 0 | 6 | 0 | 15— | 21 |
| Orlando | 7 | 10 | 0 | 0— | 17 |

### FIRST QUARTER

Orlando: Ford 10 pass from Mitchell (Bennett kick), 11:27

### SECOND QUARTER

Sacramento: FG Blanchard 32, 5:16
Orlando: FG Bennett (Bennett kick), 8:12
Orlando: FG Bennett 20, 14:06
Sacramento: FG Blanchard 24, 14:59

### FOURTH QUARTER

Sacramento: Green 12 pass from Archer (Stock pass from Archer), 3:33
Sacramento: Brown 2 pass from Archer (Blanchard kick), 9:16

A: 43,789.

## WLAF Individual Leaders

### PASSING

| | Att | Comp | Pct Comp | Yds | Avg Gain | TD | Pct TD | Int | Pct Int | Lg | Rating Pts |
|---|---|---|---|---|---|---|---|---|---|---|---|
| Archer, Sacramento | 317 | 194 | 61.2 | 2964 | 9.35 | 23 | 7.3 | 7 | 2.2 | t80 | 107.0 |
| Slack, NY/NJ | 215 | 140 | 65.1 | 1898 | 8.83 | 12 | 5.6 | 7 | 3.3 | 68 | 98.2 |
| Proctor, Montreal | 193 | 113 | 58.5 | 1478 | 7.66 | 8 | 4.1 | 5 | 2.6 | 61 | 85.8 |
| Perez, Frankfurt | 147 | 86 | 58.5 | 985 | 6.70 | 6 | 4.1 | 5 | 3.4 | 46 | 78.2 |
| Johnson, San Antonio | 257 | 144 | 56.0 | 1760 | 6.85 | 8 | 3.1 | 6 | 2.3 | 63 | 78.0 |

### RECEIVING

| RECEPTIONS | No. | Yds | Avg | Lg | TD | YARDS | Yds | No. | Avg | Lg | TD |
|---|---|---|---|---|---|---|---|---|---|---|---|
| W. Wilson, Ohio | 65 | 776 | 11.9 | 52 | 2 | Brown, Sacramento | 1011 | 48 | 21.1 | t80 | 12 |
| Bouyer, Birmingham | 57 | 706 | 12.4 | 50 | 0 | Ford, London | 833 | 45 | 18.5 | 55 | 6 |
| Johnson, Orlando | 56 | 687 | 12.3 | 41 | 5 | W. Wilson, Ohio | 776 | 65 | 11.9 | 52 | 2 |
| Garrett, London | 55 | 509 | 9.3 | 35 | 1 | Bouyer, Birmingham | 706 | 57 | 12.4 | 50 | 0 |
| T. Woods, Barcelona | 51 | 546 | 10.7 | t86 | 1 | Johnson, Orlando | 687 | 56 | 12.3 | 41 | 5 |

### RUSHING

| | Att | Yds | Avg | Lg | TD |
|---|---|---|---|---|---|
| Brown, San Antonio | 166 | 767 | 4.6 | 54 | 7 |
| Rasul, Ohio | 136 | 572 | 4.2 | 36 | 4 |
| Clack, Orlando | 117 | 517 | 4.4 | 23 | 6 |
| Pringle, Sacramento | 152 | 507 | 3.3 | 22 | 6 |
| J. Alexander, London | 125 | 501 | 4.0 | 20 | 1 |

## Other Statistical Leaders

| | | |
|---|---|---|
| Points (TDs) | Brown, Sacramento | 72 |
| Points (Kicking) | Doyle, Birmingham | 64 |
| Yards from Scrimmage | Brown, Sacramento | 1011 |
| Interceptions | Jones, Barcelona | 9 |
| Sacks | Lockett, London | 14.0 |
| Punting Avg. | Sullivan, San Antonio | 41.6 |
| Punt Return Avg. | D. Smith, NY/NJ | 12.5 |
| Kickoff Return Avg. | Burbage, NY/NJ | 26.9 |

# 1992 Canadian Football League

## EASTERN DIVISION

| | W | L | T | Pts | Pct | PF | PA |
|---|---|---|---|---|---|---|---|
| Winnipeg | 11 | 7 | 0 | 22 | .611 | 507 | 499 |
| Hamilton | 11 | 7 | 0 | 22 | .611 | 536 | 514 |
| Ottawa | 9 | 9 | 0 | 18 | .500 | 484 | 439 |
| Toronto | 6 | 12 | 0 | 12 | .333 | 469 | 523 |

## WESTERN DIVISION

| | W | L | T | Pts | Pct | PF | PA |
|---|---|---|---|---|---|---|---|
| Calgary | 13 | 5 | 0 | 26 | .722 | 507 | 430 |
| Edmonton | 10 | 8 | 0 | 20 | .556 | 552 | 515 |
| Saskatchewan | 9 | 9 | 0 | 18 | .500 | 505 | 545 |
| B.C. | 3 | 15 | 0 | 6 | .167 | 472 | 667 |

## Regular Season Statistical Leaders

| | | |
|---|---|---|
| Points (TDs) | Volpe, British Columbia | 90 |
| | Sandusky, Edmonton | 90 |
| Points (Kicking) | McLoughlin, Calgary | 208 |
| Yards (Rushing) | Richardson, Winnipeg | 1153 |
| Yards (Passing) | Austin, Saskatchewan | 6225 |
| Yards (Receiving) | Pitts, Calgary | 1591 |
| Receptions | Pitts, Calgary | 103 |

## 1992 Playoff Results

### DIVISION SEMIFINALS

Eastern: HAMILTON 29, Ottawa 28
Western: EDMONTON 22, Saskatchewan 20

### FINALS

Eastern: WINNIPEG 59, Hamilton 11
Western: CALGARY 23, Edmonton 22

## 1992 Grey Cup Championship

Nov. 24, 1992, at Winnipeg

| | | | | |
|---|---|---|---|---|
| Calgary Stampeders | 11 | 6 | 0 | 7—24 |
| Winnipeg Blue Bombers | 0 | 0 | 0 | 10—10 |

A: 45,863

## Thanks, Al

At last March's NFL's annual meeting in Palm Desert, Calif., somebody asked L.A. Raider owner Al Davis about the remarkable resurgence of the Dallas Cowboys. Davis, who fancies himself the fount of football wisdom, correctly noted that soon after the Cowboys were sold in 1989, the team's new owner asked him for advice. "Call [Dallas owner] Jerry Jones and ask him who he copied and who he visited," Davis implored. We did just that, and Jones said, "I'm sending Al a Super Bowl ring—not for his advice but for the trades he gave us."

As Davis may be somewhat less eager to acknowledge, the Cowboys have picked his pocket as well as his brain. Trades with L.A. have given Jones's team its starting fullback Daryl Johnston (acquired in 1989, through a five-draft-pick swap with the Raiders); starting guard John Gesek (in 1990 for a '91 seventh-round choice); and backup quarterback Steve Beuerlein (in '91 for the '92 fourth-round pick).

## THEY SAID IT

*Jay Leno, talk-show host, after the Houston Oilers squandered a 35–3 lead to lose to the Buffalo Bills in the NFL playoffs: "No other team in history has blown a lead that large—except for the Republicans, of course."*

## The Super Bowl

### Results

| | Date | Winner (Share) | Loser (Share) | Score | Site (Attendance) |
|---|---|---|---|---|---|
| I | 1-15-67 | Green Bay ($15,000) | Kansas City ($7,500) | 35-10 | Los Angeles (61,946) |
| II | 1-14-68 | Green Bay ($15,000) | Oakland ($7,500) | 33-14 | Miami (75,546) |
| III | 1-12-69 | NY Jets ($15,000) | Baltimore ($7,500) | 16-7 | Miami (75,389) |
| IV | 1-11-70 | Kansas City ($15,000) | Minnesota ($7,500) | 23-7 | New Orleans (80,562) |
| V | 1-17-71 | Baltimore ($15,000) | Dallas ($7,500) | 16-13 | Miami (79,204) |
| VI | 1-16-72 | Dallas ($15,000) | Miami ($7,500) | 24-3 | New Orleans (81,023) |
| VII | 1-14-73 | Miami ($15,000) | Washington ($7,500) | 14-7 | Los Angeles (90,182) |
| VIII | 1-13-74 | Miami ($15,000) | Minnesota ($7,500) | 24-7 | Houston (71,882) |
| IX | 1-12-75 | Pittsburgh ($15,000) | Minnesota ($7,500) | 16-6 | New Orleans (80,997) |
| X | 1-18-76 | Pittsburgh ($15,000) | Dallas ($7,500) | 21-17 | Miami (80,187) |
| XI | 1-9-77 | Oakland ($15,000) | Minnesota ($7,500) | 32-14 | Pasadena (103,438) |
| XII | 1-15-78 | Dallas ($18,000) | Denver ($9,000) | 27-10 | New Orleans (75,583) |
| XIII | 1-21-79 | Pittsburgh ($18,000) | Dallas ($9,000) | 35-31 | Miami (79,484) |
| XIV | 1-20-80 | Pittsburgh ($18,000) | Los Angeles ($9,000) | 31-19 | Pasadena (103,985) |
| XV | 1-25-81 | Oakland ($18,000) | Philadelphia ($9,000) | 27-10 | New Orleans (76,135) |
| XVI | 1-24-82 | San Francisco ($18,000) | Cincinnati ($9,000) | 26-21 | Pontiac (81,270) |
| XVII | 1-30-83 | Washington ($36,000) | Miami ($18,000) | 27-17 | Pasadena (103,667) |
| XVIII | 1-22-84 | LA Raiders ($36,000) | Washington ($18,000) | 38-9 | Tampa (72,920) |
| XIX | 1-20-85 | San Francisco ($36,000) | Miami ($18,000) | 38-16 | Stanford (84,059) |
| XX | 1-26-86 | Chicago ($36,000) | New England ($18,000) | 46-10 | New Orleans (73,818) |
| XXI | 1-25-87 | NY Giants ($36,000) | Denver ($18,000) | 39-20 | Pasadena (101,063) |
| XXII | 1-31-88 | Washington ($36,000) | Denver ($18,000) | 42-10 | San Diego (73,302) |
| XXIII | 1-22-89 | San Francisco ($36,000) | Cincinnati ($18,000) | 20-16 | Miami (75,129) |
| XXIV | 1-28-90 | San Francisco ($36,000) | Denver ($18,000) | 55-10 | New Orleans (72,919) |
| XXV | 1-27-91 | NY Giants ($36,000) | Buffalo ($18,000) | 20-19 | Tampa (73,813) |
| XXVI | 1-26-92 | Washington ($36,000) | Buffalo ($18,000) | 37-24 | Minneapolis (63,130) |
| XXVII | 1-31-93 | Dallas ($36,000) | Buffalo ($18,000) | 52-17 | Pasadena (98,374) |

### Most Valuable Players

| | | Position |
|---|---|---|
| I | Bart Starr, GB | QB |
| II | Bart Starr, GB | QB |
| III | Joe Namath, NY Jets | QB |
| IV | Len Dawson, KC | QB |
| V | Chuck Howley, Dall | LB |
| VI | Roger Staubach, Dall | QB |
| VII | Jake Scott, Mia | S |
| VIII | Larry Csonka, Mia | RB |
| IX | Franco Harris, Pitt | RB |
| X | Lynn Swann, Pitt | WR |
| XI | Fred Biletnikoff, Oak | WR |
| XII | Randy White, Dall | DT |
| | Harvey Martin, Dall | DE |
| XIII | Terry Bradshaw, Pitt | QB |
| XIV | Terry Bradshaw, Pitt | QB |
| XV | Jim Plunkett, Oak | QB |
| XVI | Joe Montana, SF | QB |
| XVII | John Riggins, Wash | RB |
| XVIII | Marcus Allen, LA Raiders | RB |
| XIX | Joe Montana, SF | QB |
| XX | Richard Dent, Chi | DE |
| XXI | Phil Simms, NY Giants | QB |
| XXII | Doug Williams, Wash | QB |
| XXIII | Jerry Rice, SF | WR |
| XXIV | Joe Montana, SF | QB |
| XXV | Ottis Anderson, NY Giants | RB |
| XXVI | Mark Rypien, Washington | QB |
| XXVII | Troy Aikman, Dallas | QB |

### Composite Standings

| | W | L | Pct | Pts | Opp Pts |
|---|---|---|---|---|---|
| Pittsburgh Steelers | 4 | 0 | 1.000 | 103 | 73 |
| San Francisco 49ers | 4 | 0 | 1.000 | 139 | 63 |
| Green Bay Packers | 2 | 0 | 1.000 | 68 | 24 |
| NY Giants | 2 | 0 | 1.000 | 59 | 39 |
| Chicago Bears | 1 | 0 | 1.000 | 46 | 10 |
| NY Jets | 1 | 0 | 1.000 | 16 | 7 |
| Oakland/LA Raiders | 3 | 1 | .750 | 111 | 66 |
| Washington Redskins | 3 | 2 | .600 | 122 | 103 |
| Baltimore Colts | 1 | 1 | .500 | 23 | 29 |
| Dallas Cowboys | 3 | 3 | .500 | 164 | 102 |
| Kansas City Chiefs | 1 | 1 | .500 | 33 | 42 |
| Miami Dolphins | 2 | 3 | .400 | 74 | 103 |
| LA Rams | 0 | 1 | .000 | 19 | 31 |
| New England Patriots | 0 | 1 | .000 | 10 | 46 |
| Philadelphia Eagles | 0 | 1 | .000 | 10 | 27 |
| Cincinnati Bengals | 0 | 2 | .000 | 37 | 46 |
| Buffalo Bills | 0 | 3 | .000 | 60 | 109 |
| Denver Broncos | 0 | 4 | .000 | 50 | 163 |
| Minnesota Vikings | 0 | 4 | .000 | 34 | 95 |

## THEY SAID IT

*Troy Aikman, Dallas Cowboy quarterback, on his reaction to being named one of People's 50 Most Beautiful People: "I thought, Well, they don't know that many people."*

## Career Leaders

### Passing

| | GP | Att | Comp | Pct Comp | Yds | Avg Gain | TD | Pct TD | Int | Pct Int | Lg | Rating Pts |
|---|---|---|---|---|---|---|---|---|---|---|---|---|
| Joe Montana, SF | 4 | 122 | 83 | 68.0 | 1142 | 9.36 | 11 | 9.0 | 0 | 0.0 | 44 | 127.8 |
| Jim Plunkett, Raiders | 2 | 46 | 29 | 63.0 | 433 | 9.41 | 4 | 8.7 | 0 | 0.0 | t80 | 122.8 |
| Terry Bradshaw, Pitt | 4 | 84 | 49 | 58.3 | 932 | 11.10 | 9 | 10.7 | 4 | 4.8 | t75 | 112.8 |
| Bart Starr, GB | 2 | 47 | 29 | 61.7 | 452 | 9.62 | 3 | 6.4 | 1 | 2.1 | t62 | 106.0 |
| Roger Staubach, Dall | 4 | 98 | 61 | 62.2 | 734 | 7.49 | 8 | 8.2 | 4 | 4.1 | t45 | 95.4 |
| Len Dawson, KC | 2 | 44 | 28 | 63.6 | 353 | 8.02 | 2 | 4.5 | 2 | 4.5 | t46 | 84.8 |
| Bob Griese, Mia | 3 | 41 | 26 | 63.4 | 295 | 7.20 | 1 | 2.4 | 2 | 4.9 | t28 | 72.7 |
| Dan Marino, Mia | 1 | 50 | 29 | 58.0 | 318 | 6.36 | 1 | 2.0 | 2 | 4.0 | 30 | 66.9 |
| Joe Theismann, Wash | 2 | 58 | 31 | 53.4 | 386 | 6.66 | 2 | 3.4 | 4 | 6.9 | 60 | 57.1 |
| Jim Kelly, Buff | 3 | 95 | 50 | 52.6 | 569 | 5.99 | 2 | 2.1 | 6 | 6.3 | 61 | 51.6 |
| John Elway, Den | 3 | 101 | 46 | 45.5 | 669 | 6.62 | 2 | 1.9 | 6 | 5.9 | t56 | 49.5 |

Note: Minimum 40 attempts.

### Rushing

| | GP | Yds | Att | Avg | Lg | TD |
|---|---|---|---|---|---|---|
| Franco Harris, Pitt | 4 | 354 | 101 | 3.5 | 25 | 4 |
| Larry Csonka, Mia | 3 | 297 | 57 | 5.2 | 9 | 2 |
| John Riggins, Wash | 2 | 230 | 64 | 3.6 | 43 | 2 |
| Timmy Smith, Wash | 1 | 204 | 22 | 9.3 | 58 | 2 |
| Roger Craig, SF | 3 | 198 | 52 | 3.8 | 18 | 2 |
| Marcus Allen, LA Raiders | 1 | 191 | 20 | 9.6 | t74 | 2 |
| Thurman Thomas, Buff | 3 | 167 | 36 | 4.6 | 31 | 3 |
| Tony Dorsett, Dall | 2 | 162 | 31 | 5.2 | 29 | 1 |
| Mark van Eeghen, Oak | 2 | 148 | 36 | 4.1 | 11 | 0 |
| Rocky Bleier, Pitt | 4 | 144 | 44 | 3.3 | 18 | 0 |

### Receiving

| | GP | No. | Yds | Avg | Lg | TD |
|---|---|---|---|---|---|---|
| Andre Reed, Buff | 3 | 21 | 248 | 11.8 | 40 | 0 |
| Roger Craig, SF | 3 | 20 | 212 | 10.6 | 40 | 2 |
| Jerry Rice, SF | 2 | 18 | 363 | 20.2 | 44 | 4 |
| Lynn Swann, Pitt | 4 | 16 | 364 | 22.8 | t64 | 3 |
| Chuck Foreman, Minn | 3 | 15 | 139 | 9.3 | 26 | 0 |
| Cliff Branch, Raiders | 3 | 14 | 181 | 12.9 | 50 | 3 |
| Preston Pearson, Balt-Pitt-Dall | 5 | 12 | 105 | 8.8 | 14 | 0 |
| John Stallworth, Pitt | 4 | 11 | 268 | 24.4 | t75 | 3 |
| Dan Ross, Cin | 1 | 11 | 104 | 9.5 | 16 | 2 |
| Gary Clark, Wash | 2 | 10 | 169 | 16.9 | 34 | 2 |

## Single-Game Leaders

### Scoring

| | Pts |
|---|---|
| Roger Craig: XIX, San Francisco vs Miami (1 R, 2 P) | 18 |
| Jerry Rice: XXIV, San Francisco vs Denver (3 P) | 18 |
| Don Chandler: II, Green Bay vs Oakland (3 PAT, 4 FG) | 15 |

### Rushing Yards

| | Yds |
|---|---|
| Timmy Smith: XXII, Washington vs Denver | 204 |
| Marcus Allen: XVIII, LA Raiders vs Washington | 191 |
| John Riggins: XVII, Washington vs Miami | 166 |
| Franco Harris: IX, Pittsburgh vs Minnesota | 158 |
| Larry Csonka: VIII, Miami vs Minnesota | 145 |
| Clarence Davis: XI, Oakland vs Minnesota | 137 |
| Thurman Thomas: XXV, Buffalo vs NY Giants | 135 |
| Matt Snell: III, NY Jets vs Baltimore | 121 |

### Receptions

| | No. |
|---|---|
| Dan Ross: XVI, Cincinnati vs San Francisco | 11 |
| Jerry Rice: XXIII, San Francisco vs Cincinnati | 11 |
| Tony Nathan: XIX, Miami vs San Francisco | 10 |
| Ricky Sanders: XXII, Washington vs Denver | 9 |
| George Sauer: III, NY Jets vs Baltimore | 8 |
| Roger Craig: XXIII, San Francisco vs Cincinnati | 8 |
| Andre Reed: XXV, Buffalo vs NY Giants | 8 |
| Andre Reed: XXVII, Buffalo vs Dallas | 8 |

### Touchdown Passes

| | No. |
|---|---|
| Joe Montana: XXIV, San Francisco vs Denver | 5 |
| Terry Bradshaw: XIII, Pittsburgh vs Dallas | 4 |
| Doug Williams: XXII, Washington vs Denver | 4 |
| Troy Aikman: XXVII, Dallas vs Buffalo | 4 |
| Roger Staubach: XIII, Dallas vs Pittsburgh | 3 |
| Jim Plunkett: XV, Oakland vs Philadelphia | 3 |
| Joe Montana: XIX, San Francisco vs Miami | 3 |
| Phil Simms: XXI, NY Giants vs Denver | 3 |

### Receiving Yards

| | Yds |
|---|---|
| Jerry Rice: XXIII, San Francisco vs Cincinnati | 215 |
| Ricky Sanders: XXII, Washington vs Denver | 193 |
| Lynn Swann: X, Pittsburgh vs Dallas | 161 |
| Andre Reed: XXVII, Buffalo vs Dallas | 152 |
| Jerry Rice: XXIV, San Francisco vs Denver | 148 |
| Max McGee: I, Green Bay vs Kansas City | 138 |
| George Sauer: III, NY Jets vs Baltimore | 133 |

### Passing Yards

| | Yds |
|---|---|
| Joe Montana: XXIII, San Francisco vs Cincinnati | 357 |
| Doug Williams: XXII, Washington vs Denver | 340 |
| Joe Montana: XIX, San Francisco vs Miami | 331 |
| Terry Bradshaw: XIII, Pittsburgh vs Dallas | 318 |
| Dan Marino: XIX, Miami vs San Francisco | 318 |
| Terry Bradshaw: XIV, Pittsburgh vs LA Rams | 309 |
| John Elway: XXI, Denver vs NY Giants | 304 |
| Ken Anderson: XVI, Cincinnati vs San Francisco | 300 |

## 1933

| New York Giants | 0 | 7 | 7 | 7—21 |
|---|---|---|---|---|
| Chicago Bears | 3 | 3 | 10 | 7—23 |

### FIRST QUARTER

Chicago: FG Manders 16.

### SECOND QUARTER

Chicago: FG Manders 40.
New York: Badgro 29 pass from Newman (Strong kick).

### THIRD QUARTER

Chicago: FG Manders 28.
New York: Krause 1 run (Strong kick).
Chicago: Karr 8 pass from Nagurski (Manders kick).

### FOURTH QUARTER

New York: Strong 8 pass from Newman (Strong kick).
Chicago: Karr 19 lateral from Hewitt (Brumbaugh kick).

A: 26,000.

**Recap:** The first official championship game proved auspicious for the NFL as the Bears and Giants staged an exciting contest that featured six lead changes and an assortment of quirky and dramatic plays. In the end it was the Bears who emerged triumphant as Bronko Nagurski dumped a short pass to Bill Hewitt, who lateraled to Bill Karr, who dashed to the end zone with the game-winning touchdown.

## 1934

| Chicago Bears | 0 | 10 | 3 | 0—13 |
|---|---|---|---|---|
| New York Giants | 3 | 0 | 0 | 27—30 |

### FIRST QUARTER

New York: FG Strong 38.

### SECOND QUARTER

Chicago: Nagurski 1 run (Manders kick).
Chicago: FG Manders 17.

### THIRD QUARTER

Chicago: FG Manders 22.

### FOURTH QUARTER

New York: Frankian 28 pass from Danowski (Strong kick).
New York: Strong 42 run (Strong kick).
New York: Strong 11 run (kick failed).
New York: Danowski 9 run (Molenda kick).

A: 35,059.

**Recap:** Played at the ice-covered Polo Grounds in 9° F. weather, this title matchup became known as the Sneaker game because New York coach Steve Owen procured basketball shoes for his squad at halftime. With their newfound traction, the Giants charged back with four fourth-quarter touchdowns to defeat the mighty Bears, who had won their previous 33 straight games, including a pair of victories over the Giants that season.

## 1935

| New York Giants | 0 | 0 | 7 | 0 —7 |
|---|---|---|---|---|
| Detroit Lions | 13 | 0 | 0 | 13—26 |

### FIRST QUARTER

Detroit: Gutowsky 5 run (Presnell kick).
Detroit: Clark 40 run (kick failed).

### THIRD QUARTER

New York: Strong 42 pass from Danowski (Strong kick).

### FOURTH QUARTER

Detroit: Caddel 4 run (kick failed).
Detroit: Parker 4 run (Clark kick).

A: 15,000.

**Recap:** Detroit set the tone of this contest early, scoring on its first two possessions. Ace Gutowsky bulled over from the two, capping the opening drive, then Earl (Dutch) Clark put the Giants 13 down when he rambled 40 yards to paydirt following New York's fruitless first series. The Giants made comeback steps in the third quarter as Ken Strong took an Ed Danowski pass at the 30, blazed to the end zone, then kicked the extra point, making it 13–7. But that would be New York's last score as the Lions' defense blocked a punt and stole a Danowski pass, setting up two fourth-quarter scores.

## 1936

| Green Bay Packers | 7 | 0 | 7 | 7—21 |
|---|---|---|---|---|
| Boston Redskins | 0 | 6 | 0 | 0— 6 |

### FIRST QUARTER

Green Bay: Hutson 50 pass from Herber (Smith kick).

### SECOND QUARTER

Boston: Rentner 2 run (kick failed).

### THIRD QUARTER

Green Bay: Gantenbein 5 pass from Herber (Smith kick).

### FOURTH QUARTER

Green Bay: Monnett 3 run (Smith kick).

A: 29,545.

**Recap:** The Polo Grounds were in great condition for the 1936 title game, as was the Green Bay offense. Capitalizing on a Boston fumble of the opening kickoff, Arnie Herber tossed a 43-yard touchdown to Don Hutson. Pug Rentner got the Redskins back into it with a one-yard scoring run, but that would be all for Boston as Green Bay struck twice more. Herber went deep again, to Johnny (Blood) McNally, for 52 yards to set up the second touchdown, and a blocked punt set up the third and final score.

# NFL Playoff History (Cont.)

## 1937

**Washington Redskins......7  0  7  14—28**
**Chicago Bears .................7  7  7   0—21**

### FIRST QUARTER

Washington: Battles 7 run (Smith kick).
Chicago: Manders 10 run (Manders kick).

### SECOND QUARTER

Chicago: Manders 37 pass from Masterson (Manders kick).

### THIRD QUARTER

Washington: Millner 40 pass from Baugh (Smith kick).
Chicago: Manske 3 pass from Masterson (Manders kick).

### FOURTH QUARTER

Washington: Millner 78 pass from Baugh (Smith kick).
Washington: Justice 35 pass from Baugh (Smith kick).

A: 15,870.

**Recap:** A hot rookie named Sammy Baugh scorched the Bears on their ice-covered Chicago turf. It was not the last time he would frustrate Chicago. The Bears led 14–7 at the half and 21–14 after three quarters before Baugh took over in the fourth, hooking up with Wayne Millner for a 78-yard touchdown pass and then finding Ed Justice for 35 yards and the championship-winning score. The rookie also led the league in passing that year.

## 1938

**Green Bay Packers..........0  14  3   0—17**
**New York Giants..............9   7  7   0—23**

### FIRST QUARTER

New York: FG Cuff 13.
New York: Leemans 6 run (kick failed).

### SECOND QUARTER

Green Bay: Mulleneaux 40 pass from Herber.
New York: Barnard 21 pass from Danowski (Cuff kick).
Green Bay: Hinkle 1 run (Engebretsen kick).

### THIRD QUARTER

Green Bay: FG Engebretsen 15.
New York: Soar 23 pass from Danowski (Cuff kick).

A: 48,120.

**Recap:** With attendance up 15% over the previous season and a record 48,120 on hand in New York for the championship game, the league was flourishing in 1938. The huge crowd was not disappointed as the Giants and the Packers served up a rugged thriller. New York rallied to take their second title since 1933, on a 23-yard Ed Danowski-to-Hank Soar touchdown pass. Their defense was instrumental in the victory as well, blocking two punts in the first quarter—each leading to scores by the offense—and shutting out the Packers in the fourth quarter.

## 1939

**New York Giants...............0  0   0   0— 0**
**Green Bay Packers..........7  0  10  10—27**

### FIRST QUARTER

Green Bay: Gantenbein 7 pass from Herber (Engebretsen kick).

### THIRD QUARTER

Green Bay: FG Engebretsen 23.
Green Bay: Laws 31 pass from Isbell (Engebretsen kick).

### FOURTH QUARTER

Green Bay: FG Smith 42.
Green Bay: Jankowski 1 run (Smith kick).

A: 32,279.

**Recap:** There was a 35-mph wind blowing during the 1939 championship game in Milwaukee, but it didn't bother the Packers, who extracted sweet revenge from the Giants, the team that defeated them the previous year for the NFL title. Milt Gantenbein caught a seven-yard Arnie Herber pass in the end zone during the first quarter, and Paul Engebretsen converted, making the score 7–0, Packers. In the second half Green Bay was dominant, putting 20 points on the board and the defensive clamps on the Giants, as well as completing a nifty double reverse to set up their final score.

## 1940

**Chicago Bears................21  7  26  19—73**
**Washington Redskins .....0  0   0   0— 0**

### FIRST QUARTER

Chicago: Osmanski 68 run (Manders kick).
Chicago: Luckman 1 run (Snyder kick).
Chicago: Maniaci 42 run (Martinovich kick).

### SECOND QUARTER

Chicago: Kavanaugh 30 pass from Luckman (Snyder kick).

### THIRD QUARTER

Chicago: Pool 15 int return (Plasman kick).
Chicago: Nolting 23 run (kick failed).
Chicago: McAfee 34 int return (Stydahar kick).
Chicago: Turner 21 int return (kick blocked).

### FOURTH QUARTER

Chicago: Clark 44 run (kick failed).
Chicago: Famiglietti 2 run (Maniaci pass from Sherman PAT).
Chicago: Clark 1 run (pass failed).

A: 36,034.

**Recap:** Down 7–0, the Redskins failed to score after a promising early drive. Asked what the score might have been had his team tied it, quarterback Sam Baugh replied, "Seventy-three to seven."

## 1941

| New York Giants | 6 | 0 | 3 | 0— 9 |
|---|---|---|---|---|
| Chicago Bears | 3 | 6 | 14 | 14—37 |

### FIRST QUARTER

Chicago: FG Snyder 14.
New York: Franck 31 pass from Leemans (kick blocked).

### SECOND QUARTER

Chicago: FG Snyder 39.
Chicago: FG Snyder 37.

### THIRD QUARTER

New York: FG Cuff 16.
Chicago: Standlee 2 run (Snyder kick).
Chicago: Standlee 7 run (Maniaci kick).

### FOURTH QUARTER

Chicago: McAfee 5 run (Artoe kick).
Chicago: Kavanaugh 42 fum return (McLean kick).

A: 13,341.

**Recap:** Played only two weeks after Pearl Harbor, this second consecutive championship for a great Chicago team was sparsely attended. The Giants were tied with the Bears early in the third quarter but couldn't keep pace as Chicago exploded for 28 second-half points on their way to a 37–9 rout. Norm Standlee ran for two scores in the third period, and George McAfee added one in the fourth. Ken Kavanaugh finished the scoring with a 42-yard fumble return.

## 1942

| Chicago Bears | 0 | 6 | 0 | 0— 6 |
|---|---|---|---|---|
| Washington Redskins | 0 | 7 | 7 | 0—14 |

### SECOND QUARTER

Chicago: Artoe 52 fum return (PAT failed).
Washington: Moore 39 pass from Baugh (Masterson kick).

### THIRD QUARTER

Washington: Farkas 1 run (Masterson kick).

A: 36,006.

**Recap:** Legendary passers Sammy Baugh and Sid Luckman squared off after leading their respective teams through their best regular-season records to date. The Redskins had gone 10–1 with Baugh, and Luckman and the Bears were a perfect 11–0. Washington's Andy Farkas rushed 10 times during a 12-play third-quarter drive, diving across from the one with the score that held up for the victory as the Redskins' defense shut out the Bears in the fourth quarter.

## THEY SAID IT

*Howie Long, Oakland Raider defensive end, on Tommie Maddox, rookie quarterback for the Denver Broncos, who was making his first NFL start against the Raiders: "He looked like my paperboy. I was going to give him a tip."*

## Renaissance Man

Since his days as an All-America defensive end and English major at Syracuse in the mid-1980s, Tim Green of the Falcons has successfully balanced two passions—football and writing. A first-round draft pick by Atlanta in 1986, Green spent his first four years as a pro fighting through injuries and position changes. But in 1990 he was moved back to end, and he has become the most dependable performer on the Falcon defensive front, despite being small (6'2'', 245 pounds) for his position.

Green has made remarkable progress in his off-field endeavors as well. He has completed an as-yet-unpublished novel, *Ruffians*, which is an account of what pro football is really like; he does occasional commentary on life in the NFL for National Public Radio; and he writes a weekly column for the *Syracuse Herald-Journal* on his experiences as a pro. He writes whenever the mood strikes him, sometimes working on his laptop computer during flights to road games.

Green has also completed two years of law school at Syracuse, and he would like to be a trial lawyer when his football career is over. "I love reading and writing," Green says. "I've always enjoyed doing more than one thing at one time. I'd consider it a great compliment to be known as a Rensaissance man, because I've always wanted to develop the mind and the body and the spirit at the same time."

## 1943

| | | | | |
|---|---|---|---|---|
| Washington Redskins | 0 | 7 | 7 | 7—21 |
| Chicago Bears | 0 | 14 | 13 | 14—41 |

### SECOND QUARTER

Washington: Farkas 1 run (Masterson kick).
Chicago: Clark 31 pass from Luckman (Snyder kick).
Chicago: Nagurski 3 run (Snyder kick).

### THIRD QUARTER

Chicago: Magnani 36 pass from Luckman (Snyder kick).
Chicago: Magnani 66 pass from Luckman (kick failed).
Washington: Farkas 17 pass from Baugh (Masterson kick).

### FOURTH QUARTER

Chicago: Benton 29 pass from Luckman (Snyder kick).
Chicago: Clark 16 pass from Luckman (Snyder kick).
Washington: Aguirre 25 pass from Baugh (Aguirre kick).

A: 34,320.

**Recap:** The NFL ranks had been depleted by World War II, but Washington still had Sammy Baugh, and the Chicago Bears retained Sid Luckman. Each put on a season-long aerial show that maintained wartime fan interest and propelled his team to the title game. But the championship matchup proved anticlimactic as Luckman threw five touchdown passes, including a 66-yard strike to Dante Magnani, and Bronko Nagurski came out of retirement to score for the Bears, who romped to an easy win over their nemeses.

## 1944

| | | | | |
|---|---|---|---|---|
| Green Bay Packers | 0 | 14 | 0 | 0—14 |
| New York Giants | 0 | 0 | 0 | 7— 7 |

### SECOND QUARTER

Green Bay: Fritsch 1 run (Hutson kick).
Green Bay: Fritsch 26 pass from Comp (Hutson kick).

### FOURTH QUARTER

New York: Cuff 1 run (Strong kick).

A: 46,016.

**Recap:** The Packers brought their 8–2 record to New York on Dec. 17 to face the 8-1-1 Giants for the title. Ted Fritsch provided all the offense they needed, scoring twice in the second quarter. He punched in from the two and later caught a 26-yard pass from Irv Comp to put the Packers ahead by two touchdowns. Ward Cuff scored on the first play of the fourth quarter to bring New York within seven points, but the Packer defense shut down the Giant offense the rest of the way for the victory.

## 1945

| | | | | |
|---|---|---|---|---|
| Washington Redskins | 0 | 7 | 7 | 0—14 |
| Cleveland Rams | 2 | 7 | 6 | 0—15 |

### FIRST QUARTER

Cleveland: Safety. Baugh pass blown into goalpost.

### SECOND QUARTER

Washington: Bagarus 38 pass from Filchock (Aguirre kick).
Cleveland: Benton 37 pass from Waterfield (Waterfield kick).

### THIRD QUARTER

Cleveland: Gillette 53 pass from Waterfield (kick failed).
Washington: Seymour 8 pass from Filchock (Aguirre kick).

A: 32,178.

**Recap:** On a December day so cold the Redskin band saw its instruments freeze up, the 9–1 Cleveland Rams took the melody out of Washington's would-be title tune. A windblown Sammy Baugh pass resulted in an early safety that would prove to be the winning margin. Bob Waterfield's 53-yard scoring pass to Jim Gillette gave the Rams a 15–7 lead in the third quarter before Frank Filchock's eight-yard pass to Bob Seymour brought the Redskins to within a point. Washington then missed two field goal attempts in the scoreless final session.

## 1946

| | | | | |
|---|---|---|---|---|
| Chicago Bears | 14 | 0 | 0 | 10—24 |
| New York Giants | 7 | 0 | 7 | 0—14 |

### FIRST QUARTER

Chicago: Kavanaugh 21 pass from Luckman (Maznicki kick).
Chicago: Magnani 19 int return (Magnani kick).
New York: Liebel 38 pass from Filchock (Strong kick).

### THIRD QUARTER

New York: Filipowicz 5 pass from Filchock (Strong kick).

### FOURTH QUARTER

Chicago: Luckman 19 run (Maznicki kick).
Chicago: FG Maznicki 26.

A: 58,346.

**Recap:** Sid Luckman responded to championship pressure once again, passing for a touchdown in the first quarter, then fooling the Giants on a brilliantly executed 19-yard bootleg for the game-winning score in the fourth. The Giants, playing at home, had rallied from 14 points down earlier in the game but were unable to come back again.

## 1947

| Philadelphia Eagles | 0 | 7 | 7 | 7—21 |
|---|---|---|---|---|
| Chicago Cardinals | 7 | 7 | 7 | 7—28 |

### FIRST QUARTER
Chicago: Trippi 44 run (Harder kick).

### SECOND QUARTER
Chicago: Angsman 70 run (Harder kick).
Philadelphia: McHugh 70 pass from Thompson (Patton PAT).

### THIRD QUARTER
Chicago: Trippi 75 punt return (Harder kick).
Philadelphia: Van Buren 1 run (Patton PAT).

### FOURTH QUARTER
Chicago: Angsman 70 run (Harder kick).
Philadelphia: Craft 1 run (Patton PAT).

A: 30,759.

**Recap:** Philadelphia coach Earle (Greasy) Neale's new eight-man line, a well-lubed defensive machine all season, suddenly froze up on the chilly day of the title game. Playing at home the Eagles were slow to adjust to the quick-opener, a play the Cardinal offense used to burn them for three scores, two of them on 70-yard dashes by Elmer Angsman, the third on a 44-yard run by Charlie Trippi. Trippi also returned a punt 75 yards for a touchdown in the 28–21 Chicago victory.

## 1948

| Chicago Cardinals | 0 | 0 | 0 | 0—0 |
|---|---|---|---|---|
| Philadelphia Eagles | 0 | 0 | 0 | 7—7 |

### FOURTH QUARTER
Philadelphia: Van Buren 5 run (Patton kick).

A: 36,309.

**Recap:** This rematch of the previous year's championship game took place during one of the worst winter storms in Philadelphia history. The field was covered with snow before the opening kickoff, and blizzard conditions prevailed throughout the game, severely hindering both offenses. Perhaps the most impressive performance was turned in by referee Ronald Gibbs and his crew, who had to officiate without line markers. After three scoreless quarters of futility, Cardinal quarterback Ray Mallouf fumbled on his team's 17-yard line in the fourth quarter, and Philadelphia's Frank Kilroy pounced on the loose ball. The Eagles quickly capitalized on the mistake as Steve Van Buren secured the win with a five-yard dive into the arctic end zone.

## 1949

| Philadelphia Eagles | 0 | 7 | 7 | 0—14 |
|---|---|---|---|---|
| Los Angeles Rams | 0 | 0 | 0 | 0— 0 |

### SECOND QUARTER
Philadelphia: Pihos 31 pass from Thompson (Patton kick).

### THIRD QUARTER
Philadelphia: Skladany 2 blocked punt return (Patton kick).

A: 27,980.

**Recap:** The defending champion Eagles were appearing in their third consecutive NFL title game and their second straight in which the elements were a major factor—despite the shift in site to Southern California. The skies poured rain instead of snow this year, making for treacherous footing. Midway through the second quarter the Eagles broke through the muck as quarterback Tommy Thompson connected with end Pete Pihos on a 31-yard scoring pass. Philadelphia increased its lead late in the third quarter when Ram quarterback Bob Waterfield slipped while punting from his own five-yard line. Ed Skladany blocked the kick, recovered the loose ball and scored.

## 1950

| Los Angeles Rams | 14 | 0 | 14 | 0—28 |
|---|---|---|---|---|
| Cleveland Browns | 7 | 6 | 7 | 10—30 |

### FIRST QUARTER
Los Angeles: Davis 82 pass from Waterfield (Waterfield kick).
Cleveland: Jones 32 pass from Graham (Groza kick).
Los Angeles: Hoerner 3 run (Waterfield kick).

### SECOND QUARTER
Cleveland: Lavelli 35 pass from Graham (kick failed).

### THIRD QUARTER
Cleveland: Lavelli 39 pass from Graham (Groza kick).
Los Angeles: Hoerner 1 run (Waterfield kick).
Los Angeles: Brink 6 fum return (Waterfield kick).

### FOURTH QUARTER
Cleveland: Bumgardner 14 pass from Graham (Groza kick).
Cleveland: FG Groza 16.

A: 29,751.

**Recap:** In their first year in the NFL after winning four consecutive titles in the All-America Football Conference, the Browns took the title in a thrilling fight to the finish with the Rams. The lead changed hands four times, and the outcome was in doubt until a late interception set up Lou Groza's game-winning 16-yard field goal with 28 seconds left on the clock.

## 1951

| Cleveland Browns | 0 | 10 | 0 | 7—17 |
|---|---|---|---|---|
| Los Angeles Rams | 0 | 7 | 7 | 10—24 |

### SECOND QUARTER
Los Angeles: Hoerner 1 run (Waterfield kick).
Cleveland: FG Groza 52.
Cleveland: Jones 17 pass from Graham (Groza kick).

### THIRD QUARTER
Los Angeles: Towler 1 run (Waterfield kick).

### FOURTH QUARTER
Los Angeles: FG Waterfield 17.
Cleveland: Carpenter 2 run (Groza kick).
Los Angeles: Fears 73 pass from Van Brocklin (Waterfield kick).

A: 57,522.

**Recap:** The Los Angeles Rams finally won a title game after two straight championship defeats, sending the Cleveland Browns, winners of one NFL and four AAFC titles in the previous five years, to unaccustomed defeat. In a seesaw battle that included a championship-record 52-yard field goal by Cleveland's Lou Groza, the Browns drew even in the fourth quarter on a two-yard plunge by Ken Carpenter. But the Rams roared back on a 73-yard touchdown strike from Norm Van Brocklin to Tom Fears to secure the win.

## 1952

| Detroit Lions | 0 | 7 | 7 | 3—17 |
|---|---|---|---|---|
| Cleveland Browns | 0 | 0 | 7 | 0— 7 |

### SECOND QUARTER
Detroit: Layne 2 run (Harder kick).

### THIRD QUARTER
Detroit: Walker 67 run (Harder kick).
Cleveland: Jagade 7 run (Groza kick).

### FOURTH QUARTER
Detroit: FG Harder 36.

A: 50,934.

**Recap:** The Browns made their third trip to the NFL title game in as many seasons as a league member but lost to the Detroit Lions and their sturdy defense. Setting the tone early, the teams held each other scoreless through the first 15 minutes. In the second period Lion quarterback Bobby Layne took his team from midfield to the Cleveland two-yard line, then plunged over for the touchdown himself. Doak Walker exploded for a 67-yard touchdown romp in the third quarter to put the Lions ahead 14–0. Harry Jagade brought the Browns closer with a seven-yard touchdown run, and Cleveland threatened after that, driving as close as the Lions' five, but couldn't crack the Detroit defense. The Lions later recovered a Brown fumble to set up the final Detroit score, a 36-yard field goal by Pat Harder.

## Minority Report

The disparity between the number of blacks playing sports and the far smaller number employed in coaching and front-office jobs is drawing the ire of civil rights leaders, some of whom met in January in New York with officials of major league baseball, the NBA, the NFL and their players' associations, and discussed a possible boycott by black athletes. Hiring practices in sports have also been assailed by Jesse Jackson, who is forming a Rainbow Commission on Fairness in Athletics, dedicated to getting more blacks and other minorities into the broadcast booth as well as into front-office jobs.

In singling out sports, the civil rights leaders can point to the number of qualified blacks, former players and otherwise, who are routinely passed over in favor of whites for head coaching or managing jobs. Surprisingly, given the uproar over Cincinnati Red owner Marge Schott's racist utterances, the sport that has made the greatest strides in this area is baseball. Thirty-one percent of baseball players are members of minorities, and with the offseason hirings of Don Baylor by the Colorado Rockies, Tony Perez by the Reds and Dusty Baker by the San Francisco Giants, 21% (six of 28) of the managers were too as of opening day. By contrast, in the NFL 64% of the players but only 7% (two of 28) of the head coaches are minorities, and in the NBA the disparity is even more glaring: 75% of the players and 11% (three of 27) of the coaches are minorities.

Blacks in high-level front-office positions are even rarer than black coaches and managers. It is especially discouraging that in the supposedly enlightened NBA, the percentage of coaches who are black has declined from a high of 27 in the mid 1970s to the current 11, and that most blacks in front-office jobs perform glad-handing roles as community-relations officers. All this helps explain why Jackson wrote Chicago Bear president Michael McCaskey last January urging him to hire Bear assistant coach Johnny Roland, who is black, to succeed the fired Mike Ditka as Chicago's head coach. In the end, the Bears hired Dallas offensive coordinator Dave Wannstedt, who is white. Though Wannstedt clearly is qualified, the Bears have nonetheless fumbled a golden opportunity to advance the cause of equality.

## 1953

| Cleveland Browns | 0 | 3 | 7 | 6—16 |
|---|---|---|---|---|
| Detroit Lions | 7 | 3 | 0 | 7—17 |

### FIRST QUARTER
Detroit: Walker 1 run (Walker kick).

### SECOND QUARTER
Cleveland: FG Groza 13.
Detroit: FG Walker 23.

### THIRD QUARTER
Cleveland: Jagade 9 run (Groza kick).

### FOURTH QUARTER
Cleveland: FG Groza 15.
Cleveland: FG Groza 43.
Detroit: Doran 33 pass from Layne (Walker kick).

A: 54,577.

**Recap:** The Lions were seeking a second straight NFL title at home against their victims of the previous year, the Browns. The 54,577 in attendance were not disappointed as Detroit came from behind in the final minutes to win a 17–16 nail-biter. Bobby Layne engineered the game-winning drive, firing a 33-yard scoring strike to Jim Doran. Doak Walker provided the winning margin with his extra point, and Carl Karilivacz picked off Otto Graham's first pass after the kickoff to seal the victory.

## 1954

| Detroit Lions | 3 | 7 | 0 | 0—10 |
|---|---|---|---|---|
| Cleveland Browns | 14 | 21 | 14 | 7—56 |

### FIRST QUARTER
Detroit: FG Walker 36.
Cleveland: Renfro 35 pass from Graham (Groza kick).
Cleveland: Brewster 8 pass from Graham (Groza kick).

### SECOND QUARTER
Cleveland: Graham 1 run (Groza kick).
Cleveland: Graham 5 run (Groza kick).
Cleveland: Renfro 31 pass from Graham (Groza kick).
Detroit: Bowman 5 run (Walker kick).

### THIRD QUARTER
Cleveland: Graham 1 run (Groza kick).
Cleveland: Morrison 12 run (Groza kick).

### FOURTH QUARTER
Cleveland: Hanulak 12 run (Groza kick).

A: 43,827.

**Recap:** The Browns avenged their one-point loss in the 1953 championship game by rolling over the Lions on the strength of an outstanding performance by Otto Graham, who threw for three touchdowns and ran for three more.

## 1955

| Cleveland Browns | 3 | 14 | 14 | 7—38 |
|---|---|---|---|---|
| Los Angeles Rams | 0 | 7 | 0 | 7—14 |

### FIRST QUARTER
Cleveland: FG Groza 26.

### SECOND QUARTER
Cleveland: Paul 65 int return (Groza kick).
Los Angeles: Quinlan 67 pass from Van Brocklin (Richter kick).
Cleveland: Lavelli 50 pass from Graham (Groza kick).

### THIRD QUARTER
Cleveland: Graham 15 run (Groza kick).
Cleveland: Graham 1 run (Groza kick).

### FOURTH QUARTER
Cleveland: Renfro 35 pass from Graham (Groza kick).
Los Angeles: Waller 4 run (Richter kick).

A: 85,693.

**Recap:** Los Angeles played host to future Hall of Famer Otto Graham and the fearsome Cleveland Browns in what would be Graham's last game. The Rams were no match for number 14 and the rest of Paul Brown's squad, as Graham closed out his career brilliantly, scoring two touchdowns and passing for two more in the 38–14 rout.

## 1956

| Chicago Bears | 0 | 7 | 0 | 0— 7 |
|---|---|---|---|---|
| New York Giants | 13 | 21 | 6 | 7—47 |

### FIRST QUARTER
New York: Triplett 17 run (Agajanian kick).
New York: FG Agajanian 17.
New York: FG Agajanian 43.

### SECOND QUARTER
New York: Webster 3 run (Agajanian kick).
Chicago: Casares 9 run (Blanda kick).
New York: Webster 1 run (Agajanian kick).
New York: Moore recovered blocked punt in end zone (Agajanian kick).

### THIRD QUARTER
New York: Rote 9 pass from Conerly (kick failed).

### FOURTH QUARTER
New York: Gifford 14 pass from Conerly (Agajanian kick).

A: 56,836.

**Recap:** After Mel Triplett bulled 17 yards over the frozen field for their first TD, the Giants never looked back. Ben Agajanian added two field goals, and when Alex Webster pounded three yards into the end zone to start the second quarter, the rout was on.

## 1957

| Cleveland Browns | 0 | 7 | 7 | 0—14 |
|---|---|---|---|---|
| Detroit Lions | 17 | 14 | 14 | 14—59 |

### FIRST QUARTER

Detroit: FG Martin 31.
Detroit: Rote 1 run (Martin kick).
Detroit: Gedman 1 run (Martin kick).

### SECOND QUARTER

Cleveland: Brown 29 run (Groza kick).
Detroit: Junker 26 pass from Rote (Martin kick).
Detroit: Barr 19 int return (Martin kick).

### THIRD QUARTER

Cleveland: Carpenter 5 run (Groza kick).
Detroit: Doran 78 pass from Rote (Martin kick).
Detroit: Junker 23 pass from Rote (Martin kick).

### FOURTH QUARTER

Detroit: Middleton 32 pass from Rote (Martin kick).
Detroit: Cassady 16 pass from Reichow (Martin kick).

A: 55,263.

**Recap:** Detroit finished the regular season tied with San Francisco at 8–4 atop the Western Conference. The Lions rode the momentum of a come-from-behind 31–27 playoff victory over the 49ers into the title game where, without star Bobby Layne, they thoroughly routed the 9-2-1 Browns.

## 1958

| Baltimore Colts | 0 | 14 | 0 | 3 | 6—23 |
|---|---|---|---|---|---|
| New York Giants | 3 | 0 | 7 | 7 | 0—17 |

### FIRST QUARTER

New York: FG Summerall 36.

### SECOND QUARTER

Baltimore: Ameche 2 run (Myhra kick).
Baltimore: Berry 15 pass from Unitas (Myhra kick).

### THIRD QUARTER

New York: Triplett 1 run (Summerall kick).

### FOURTH QUARTER

New York: Gifford 15 pass from Conerly (Summerall kick).
Baltimore: FG Myhra 20.

### OVERTIME

Baltimore: Ameche 1 run (no kick).

A: 64,185.

**Recap:** This classic was the first sudden-death overtime game in NFL championship history. The Giants held a three-point lead late in the fourth quarter, but the Colts charged back as Johnny Unitas marched his team into position for Steve Myhra's game-tying 20-yard field goal with seven seconds left in regulation. In overtime the Giants won the coin toss but were unable to make a first down; Unitas and the Colts answered with the game-winning drive, capped by Alan Ameche's famous one-yard plunge. Seen by a large television audience, pro football had arrived dramatically on the national scene.

## 1959

| New York Giants | 3 | 3 | 3 | 7—16 |
|---|---|---|---|---|
| Baltimore Colts | 7 | 0 | 0 | 24—31 |

### FIRST QUARTER

Baltimore: Moore 59 pass from Unitas (Myhra kick).
New York: FG Summerall 23.

### SECOND QUARTER

New York: FG Summerall 37.

### THIRD QUARTER

New York: FG Summerall 22.

### FOURTH QUARTER

Baltimore: Unitas 4 run (Myrha kick).
Baltimore: Richardson 12 pass from Unitas (Myrha kick).
Baltimore: Sample 42 int return (Myrha kick).
Baltimore: FG Myrha 25.
New York: Schnelker 32 pass from Conerly (Summerall kick).

A: 57,545.

**Recap:** Johnny Unitas and the Colts had too many weapons for the Giants as they won their second straight NFL title in a rematch of the previous year's memorable contest. The Giants stayed close—even led 9–7 in the third quarter—playing superb defense, but the Colts put the game away with 24 fourth-quarter points, including two touchdowns set up by interceptions as the Giants took to the air in desperation.

### Boom-erang

Next fall the NFL will reveal which two cities will receive expansion franchises beginning with the 1995 season. For now, fans in the five contending cities can ponder the possible names of the teams that they hope to be rooting for. The NFL has registered this list of likely names with the U.S. Patent and Trademark Office:
*Baltimore*: Bombers or Cobras.
*Charlotte*: Panthers.
*Jacksonville*: Jaguars or Sharks.
*Memphis*: Bombers, Hound Dogs or Showboats.
*St. Louis*: Archers, Rivermen, Scouts, Stallions or Stokers.
One observation: In light of the terrorist attack on New York's World Trade Center and explosion in London's Financial District in April, one hopes that should Baltimore and/or Memphis join the league, they'll jettison the Bombers.

## 1960

### NFL CHAMPIONSHIP GAME

| | | | | |
|---|---|---|---|---|
| Green Bay Packers | 3 | 3 | 0 | 7—13 |
| Philadelphia Eagles | 0 | 10 | 0 | 7—17 |

#### FIRST QUARTER

Green Bay: FG Hornung 20.

#### SECOND QUARTER

Green Bay: FG Hornung 23.
Philadelphia: McDonald 35 pass from Van Brocklin (Walston kick).
Philadelphia: FG Walston 15.

#### FOURTH QUARTER

Green Bay: McGee 7 pass from Starr (Hornung kick).
Philadelphia: Dean 5 run (Walston kick).

A: 67,325.

**Recap:** Rookie fullback Ted Dean's 58-yard kickoff return early in the fourth quarter set up the Eagles' game-winning touchdown—a five-yard scamper around left end, also by Dean. It was the second time the Eagles had come from behind that day against the Packers of Bart Starr, Paul Hornung and Vince Lombardi. Norm Van Brocklin, an 11-year veteran, quarterbacked his first NFL championship team and threw an early 35-yard touchdown pass for the Eagles' first lead. After Dean's go-ahead score, Starr and the Packers, needing six, drove to the Eagle nine, but time ran out, and Philadelphia had its title.

### AFL CHAMPIONSHIP GAME

| | | | | |
|---|---|---|---|---|
| Los Angeles Chargers | 6 | 3 | 7 | 0—16 |
| Houston Oilers | 0 | 10 | 7 | 7—24 |

#### FIRST QUARTER

Los Angeles: FG Agajanian 38.
Los Angeles: FG Agajanian 22.

#### SECOND QUARTER

Houston: Smith 17 pass from Blanda (Blanda kick).
Houston: FG Blanda 18.
Los Angeles: FG Agajanian 27.

#### THIRD QUARTER

Houston: Groman 7 pass from Blanda (Blanda kick).
Los Angeles: Lowe 2 run (Agajanian kick).

#### FOURTH QUARTER

Houston: Cannon 88 pass from Blanda (Blanda kick).

A: 32,183.

**Recap:** The fourth league to use the name since 1926, the AFL began play with eight franchises. Two of them, Los Angeles and Houston, took 10-4 records into the inaugural title game. Led by the passing and kicking of quarterback George Blanda, the Oilers came charging back from a 9–0 deficit to defeat Los Angeles 24–16. Blanda connected with Billy Cannon on an 88-yard scoring pass for the insurance points, then kicked his third extra point of the game.

## 1961

### NFL CHAMPIONSHIP GAME

| | | | | |
|---|---|---|---|---|
| New York Giants | 0 | 0 | 0 | 0— 0 |
| Green Bay Packers | 0 | 24 | 10 | 3—37 |

#### SECOND QUARTER

Green Bay: Hornung 6 run (Hornung kick).
Green Bay: Dowler 13 pass from Starr (Hornung kick).
Green Bay: R Kramer 14 pass from Starr (Hornung kick).
Green Bay: FG Hornung 17.

#### THIRD QUARTER

Green Bay: FG Hornung 22.
Green Bay: R Kramer 13 pass from Starr (Hornung kick).

#### FOURTH QUARTER

Green Bay: FG Hornung 19.

A: 39,029.

**Recap:** Green Bay tends to be frigid in late December, and December 1961, much to the Giants' dismay, was no exception. Although they had their chances early—Kyle Rote dropped a sure TD pass, and halfback Bob Gaiters overthrew a wide-open Rote in the end zone—the Giants were on ice by halftime as Green Bay cruised to a 24–0 lead. The Pack scored 13 more in the shutout win.

### AFL CHAMPIONSHIP GAME

| | | | | |
|---|---|---|---|---|
| Houston Oilers | 0 | 3 | 7 | 0—10 |
| San Diego Chargers | 0 | 0 | 0 | 3— 3 |

#### SECOND QUARTER

Houston: FG Blanda 46.

#### THIRD QUARTER

Houston: Cannon 35 pass from Blanda (Blanda kick).

#### FOURTH QUARTER

San Diego: FG Blair 12.

A: 29,556.

**Recap:** Relocated a few hours south to San Diego, the Chargers made it back to the championship for a rematch with Houston. Perhaps the offenses of both teams were distracted by visions of sugar plums on this Christmas Eve in San Diego as they committed a total of 17 turnovers, including 10 interceptions. In spite of being picked off five times, George Blanda provided the Oilers with all the offense they needed. He kicked a 46-yard field goal to open the scoring and hit Billy Cannon over the middle for a 35-yard touchdown. The Oiler defense sacked Charger quarterback and future Republican leader Jack Kemp a total of six times and intercepted him with under two minutes to play to seal the victory.

## 1962

### NFL CHAMPIONSHIP GAME

| | | | | |
|---|---|---|---|---|
| **Green Bay Packers** | 3 | 7 | 3 | 3—16 |
| **New York Giants** | 0 | 0 | 7 | 0— 7 |

#### FIRST QUARTER

Green Bay: FG J Kramer 26.

#### SECOND QUARTER

Green Bay: Taylor 7 run (J Kramer kick).

#### THIRD QUARTER

New York: Collier recovered blocked punt in end zone (Chandler kick).
Green Bay: FG J Kramer 29.

#### FOURTH QUARTER

Green Bay: FG J Kramer 30.

A: 64,892.

**Recap:** The Packers brought Green Bay weather with them to New York when they met the Giants in a rematch for the title in Yankee Stadium. There was a 35-mph wind, and the 20° kickoff temperature dropped steadily all afternoon. The Packers triumphed in the fierce defensive struggle that ensued, holding the Giants to just a single touchdown all day. Down 10–7, New York fumbled at its own 40 in the third quarter, and the Packers added two field goals to put the game out of reach.

### AFL CHAMPIONSHIP GAME

| | | | | | | |
|---|---|---|---|---|---|---|
| **Dallas Texans** | 3 | 14 | 0 | 0 | 3—20 |
| **Houston Oilers** | 0 | 0 | 7 | 10 | 0 | 0—17 |

#### FIRST QUARTER

Dallas: FG Brooker 16.

#### SECOND QUARTER

Dallas: Haynes 28 pass from Dawson (Brooker kick).
Dallas: Haynes 2 run (Brooker kick).

#### THIRD QUARTER

Houston: Dewveall 15 pass from Blanda (Blanda kick).

#### FOURTH QUARTER

Houston: FG Blanda 31.
Houston: Tolar 1 run (Blanda kick).

#### SECOND OVERTIME

Dallas: FG Brooker 25.

A: 37,981.

**Recap:** It took 77 minutes, 54 seconds to settle this Texas shoot-out, the longest game to date. Despite a blown 17-point lead and a bungled choice of direction in the overtime coin toss, the Texans managed to pull out the win in double overtime as Jack Spikes made a key third-down reception and a subsequent 19-yard run to put Dallas in position for the winning field goal by Tommy Brooker.

## 1963

### NFL CHAMPIONSHIP GAME

| | | | | |
|---|---|---|---|---|
| **New York Giants** | 7 | 3 | 0 | 0—10 |
| **Chicago Bears** | 7 | 0 | 7 | 0—14 |

#### FIRST QUARTER

New York: Gifford 14 pass from Tittle (Chandler kick).
Chicago: Wade 2 run (Jencks kick).

#### SECOND QUARTER

New York: FG Chandler 13.

#### THIRD QUARTER

Chicago: Wade 1 run (Jencks kick).

A: 45,801.

**Recap:** The Bears' fierce defense won out over the air attack of Y.A. Tittle and the Giants, picking off five Tittle passes and using two of those thefts to set up touchdowns. In the early going, however, Tittle was on target as Frank Gifford caught a 14-yard touchdown pass, and Del Shofner had a Tittle strike bounce off his hands when he was wide open in the end zone. But the Bear defense took over after that, shutting the Giants down and providing the offense with solid field position as Billy Wade scored twice on quarterback sneaks. Tittle twisted his knee in the second quarter, and the Bears intercepted two more passes in the fourth to preserve the 14–10 victory.

### AFL CHAMPIONSHIP GAME

| | | | | |
|---|---|---|---|---|
| **Boston Patriots** | 7 | 3 | 0 | 0—10 |
| **San Diego Chargers** | 21 | 10 | 7 | 13—51 |

#### FIRST QUARTER

San Diego: Rote 2 run (Blair kick).
San Diego: Lincoln 67 run (Blair kick).
Boston: Garron 7 run (Cappelletti kick).
San Diego: Lowe 58 run (Blair kick).

#### SECOND QUARTER

San Diego: FG Blair 11.
Boston: FG Cappelletti 15.
San Diego: Norton 14 pass from Rote (Blair kick).

#### THIRD QUARTER

San Diego: Allworth 48 pass from Rote (Blair kick).

#### FOURTH QUARTER

San Diego: Lincoln 25 pass from Hadl (PAT failed).
San Diego: Hadl 1 run (Blair kick).

A: 30,127.

**Recap:** Boston's defense was as heralded as San Diego's offense, but the irresistible force proved stronger than the immovable object as San Diego's Keith Lincoln rambled 67 yards to a touchdown on the game's second play, and the Chargers never looked back on their way to a 41-point rout.

## 1964

### NFL CHAMPIONSHIP GAME

| | | | | |
|---|---|---|---|---|
| **Baltimore Colts**.............0 | 0 | 0 | 0— | 0 |
| **Cleveland Browns**.........0 | 0 | 17 | 10—27 | |

#### THIRD QUARTER

Cleveland: FG Groza 43.
Cleveland: Collins 18 pass from Ryan (Groza kick).
Cleveland: Collins 42 pass from Ryan (Groza kick).

#### FOURTH QUARTER

Cleveland: FG Groza 9.
Cleveland: Collins 51 pass from Ryan (Groza kick).

A: 79,544.

**Recap:** Johnny Unitas brought his heavily favored Baltimore Colts to Cleveland and met a Brown defense determined to stop his vaunted passing attack. The teams played conservatively through the scoreless first half. Early in the third quarter Baltimore's Tom Gilburg shanked a 29-yard punt, giving the Browns good field position. Lou Groza kicked a 46-yard field goal. On Cleveland's next possession, Jim Brown grabbed a pitch from Frank Ryan and barreled 46 yards downfield. Ryan took the next snap and hit Gary Collins for an 18-yard score. Before the quarter was over Ryan threw again to Collins, for 42 yards and another TD. The conversion made it 17–0, and the Colts were on the ropes. Collins caught a third, 51-yard touchdown pass, Groza booted a second field goal, and the Browns' defense kept the clamps on for the 27–0 knockout.

### AFL CHAMPIONSHIP GAME

| | | | | |
|---|---|---|---|---|
| **San Diego Chargers** .....7 | 0 | 0 | 0— | 7 |
| **Buffalo Bills** .................3 | 10 | 0 | 7—20 | |

#### FIRST QUARTER

San Diego: Kocourek 26 pass from Rote (Lincoln kick).
Buffalo: FG Gogolak 12.

#### SECOND QUARTER

Buffalo: Carlton 4 run (Gogolak kick).
Buffalo: FG Gogolak 17.

#### FOURTH QUARTER

Buffalo: Kemp 1 run (Gogolak kick).

A: 40,242.

**Recap:** The San Diego Chargers, participants in four of the five AFL championships to date, began an auspicious defense of their title by marching 80 yards in four plays for the game's first touchdown. Keith Lincoln galloped 38 yards to set up the scoring play, a 26-yard pass from Tobin Rote to Dave Kocourek. But such offensive success would prove short-lived for the Chargers. The Buffalo defense turned the game around on San Diego's next drive when linebacker Mike Stratton put a hit on Lincoln that broke the back's grip on the ball as well as one of his ribs. With their star out, San Diego couldn't move the ball, and Buffalo's Cookie Gilchrist gained 122 yards against them, fueling the Bills' 20-point effort.

## 1965

### NATIONAL FOOTBALL LEAGUE

| | | | | |
|---|---|---|---|---|
| **Cleveland Browns** ...........9 | 3 | 0 | 0—12 | |
| **Green Bay Packers**..........7 | 6 | 7 | 3—23 | |

#### FIRST QUARTER

Green Bay: Dale 47 pass from Starr (Chandler kick).
Cleveland: Collins 17 pass from Ryan (kick failed).
Cleveland: FG Groza 24.

#### SECOND QUARTER

Green Bay: FG Chandler 15.
Green Bay: FG Chandler 23.
Cleveland: FG Groza 28.

#### THIRD QUARTER

Green Bay: Hornung 13 run (Chandler kick).

#### FOURTH QUARTER

Green Bay: FG Chandler 29.

A: 50,777.

**Recap:** Green Bay's muddy Lambeau Field put ball control at a premium in this game, and the Packers, under coach Vince Lombardi, were well schooled in ball control. They took seven minutes off the clock and put six points on the board with a 90-yard, 11-play drive in the third quarter. Jim Taylor and Paul Hornung followed steamroller blocking on numerous off tackles and power sweeps, with Hornung taking it 13 yards for a 20–12 third-quarter lead.

### AMERICAN FOOTBALL LEAGUE

| | | | | |
|---|---|---|---|---|
| **Buffalo Bills** ......................0 | 14 | 6 | 3 | —23 |
| **San Diego Chargers** .........0 | 0 | 0 | 0— | 0 |

#### SECOND QUARTER

Buffalo: Warlick 18 pass from Kemp (Gogolak kick).
Buffalo: Byrd 74 punt return (Gogolak kick).

#### THIRD QUARTER

Buffalo: FG Gogolak 11.
Buffalo: FG Gogolak 39.

#### FOURTH QUARTER

Buffalo: FG Gogolak 32.

A: 30,361.

**Recap:** The San Diego Chargers returned yet again to the AFL title game and were beaten once more, with feeling, by Buffalo. The Chargers never advanced past the Buffalo 24 in the 23–0 whitewashing. The game looked to be a defensive struggle as the teams were deadlocked 0–0 for nearly two quarters. Future Republican leader Jack Kemp broke the tie with an 18-yard TD pass to Ernie Warlick. Butch Byrd returned the next Charger punt 74 yards down the sideline to give Buffalo a 14–0 edge at halftime. Pete Gogolak added three field goals in the second half, and the Chargers string of scoreless quarters against the Bills—dating back to the previous year's title game—increased to seven.

## 1966

### NATIONAL FOOTBALL LEAGUE

| | | | | |
|---|---|---|---|---|
| Green Bay Packers | 14 | 7 | 7 | 6—34 |
| Dallas Cowboys | 14 | 3 | 3 | 7—27 |

#### FIRST QUARTER

Green Bay: Pitts 17 from Starr (Chandler kick).
Green Bay: Grabowski 18 fum return (Chandler kick).
Dallas: Reeves 3 run (Villanueva kick).
Dallas: Perkins 23 run (Villanueva kick).

#### SECOND QUARTER

Green Bay: Dale 51 pass from Starr (Chandler kick).
Dallas: FG Villanueva 11.

#### THIRD QUARTER

Dallas: FG Villanueva 32.
Green Bay: Dowler 16 pass from Starr (Chandler kick).

#### FOURTH QUARTER

Green Bay: McGee 28 pass from Starr (kick blocked).
Dallas: Clarke 68 pass from Meredith (Villanueva kick).

A: 74,125.

**Recap:** With a trip to Super Bowl I at stake, both teams performed brilliantly. The Pack struck twice early, returning the fumbled kickoff after their first TD for another. Undaunted, the Cowboys tied the score before the quarter ended and battled to the very last.

### AMERICAN FOOTBALL LEAGUE

| | | | | |
|---|---|---|---|---|
| Kansas City Chiefs | 7 | 10 | 0 | 14—31 |
| Buffalo Bills | 7 | 0 | 0 | 0— 7 |

#### FIRST QUARTER

Kansas City: Arbanas 29 pass from Dawson (Mercer kick).
Buffalo: Dubenion 69 pass from Kemp (Lusteg kick).

#### SECOND QUARTER

Kansas City: Taylor 29 pass from Dawson (Mercer kick).
Kansas City: FG Mercer 32.

#### FOURTH QUARTER

Kansas City: Garrett 1 run (Mercer kick).
Kansas City: Garrett 18 run (Mercer kick).

A: 42,080.

**Recap:** The Bills were playing in their third straight AFL championship, but the previous two—victories both—did not offer the opportunity this one did: a chance at the NFL champion and respectability in the first Super Bowl. Buffalo would have traded their wins the two years before for a victory in this one, but it was not to be as the Chiefs solved the Bills' tough defense and won a date with Green Bay at the Coliseum in Los Angeles. An interception and 72-yard return out of the end zone by Johnny Robinson prevented the Bills from tying the game before the half, and the Chiefs pulled away from there.

## Super Bowl I

| | | | | |
|---|---|---|---|---|
| Green Bay Packers | 7 | 7 | 14 | 7—35 |
| Kansas City Chiefs | 0 | 10 | 0 | 0—10 |

#### FIRST QUARTER

Green Bay: McGee 37 pass from Starr (Chandler kick).

#### SECOND QUARTER

Kansas City: McClinton 7 pass from Dawson (Mercer kick.
Green Bay: Taylor 14 run (Chandler kick).
Kansas City: FG Mercer 31.

#### THIRD QUARTER

Green Bay: Pitts 5 run (Chandler kick).
Green Bay: McGee 13 pass from Starr (Chandler kick).

#### FOURTH QUARTER

Green Bay: Pitts 1 run (Chandler kick).

A: 61,946. At Los Angeles.

**Recap:** They had competed for players, fans and television revenues during the past seven years but never in that time had a team from the NFL faced a team from the AFL on the gridiron. The Packers came into the contest as 14-point favorites, representing over 40 years of NFL tradition compared to the mere six the AFL had been in existence. Nonetheless, Green Bay felt the pressure of upholding the NFL's reputation. Frank Gifford later recalled interviewing a shaking Vince Lombardi on the field before kickoff. The Chiefs, for their part, had talked a good game all week. But according to Kansas City linebacker E.J. Holub, there were wet pants and lost lunches in the tunnel leading to the field at game time. The nerves showed in the early, conservative stages of the game. On the third play Green Bay's best receiver, Boyd Dowler, separated his shoulder. His replacement Max McGee had been carousing until 7:30 that morning, thinking he would play only in the unlikely event of an injury to Dowler. Out went Dowler, in came McGee, shaking his aching head and promptly making a one-handed 37-yard touchdown catch. At the half the Chiefs were quite pleased to be down just 14–10. But the second half belonged to the Packer defense and to quarterback Bart Starr. Blitzing on third-and-five, the Packers forced an interception, and Willie Wood returned it to the Chiefs' five, setting up a touchdown that put the Pack up 21–10 and broke the game open. Starr went on to complete eight of 10 passes in the second half for 122 yards. In one stretch he hit McGee three times for 11, 16 and 13 yards, the last a juggling one-handed touchdown reception by the hungover sub. Starr finished with 250 yards passing, completing 16 of 23 attempts, and was named MVP of the game.

## 1967

| NATIONAL FOOTBALL LEAGUE | | | | |
|---|---|---|---|---|
| Dallas Cowboys | 0 | 10 | 0 | 7—17 |
| Green Bay Packers | 7 | 7 | 0 | 7—21 |

### FIRST QUARTER

Green Bay: Dowler 8 pass from Starr (Chandler kick).

### SECOND QUARTER

Green Bay: Dowler 43 pass from Starr (Chandler kick).
Dallas: Andrie 7 fumble return (Villanueva kick).
Dallas: FG Villanueva 21.

### FOURTH QUARTER

Dallas: Rentzel 50 pass from Reeves (Villanueva kick).
Green Bay: Starr 1 run (Chandler kick).

A: 50,861.

**Recap:** This rematch of the previous year's classic is one of football's alltime thrillers. It was 13° below zero with a 15-mph wind, and the Packers, as they had the year before, surged ahead 14–0. But Dallas got back into the game with big plays on defense, eventually taking the lead on the first play of the fourth quarter, a 50-yard halfback pass from Dan Reeves to Lance Rentzel. The Packers trailed 17–14 when they took over on their own 31 with 4:51 left. Starr led a drive to the Dallas one. With no timeouts and 20 seconds to play, Starr chose to sneak across for the win instead of settling for a game-tying field goal.

| AMERICAN FOOTBALL LEAGUE | | | | |
|---|---|---|---|---|
| Houston Oilers | 0 | 0 | 0 | 7— 7 |
| Oakland Raiders | 3 | 14 | 10 | 13—40 |

### FIRST QUARTER

Oakland: FG Blanda 37.

### SECOND QUARTER

Oakland: Dixon 69 run (Blanda kick).
Oakland: Kocourek 17 pass from Lamonica (Blanda kick).

### THIRD QUARTER

Oakland: Lamonica 1 run (Blanda kick).
Oakland: FG Blanda 40.

### FOURTH QUARTER

Oakland: FG Blanda 42.
Houston: Frazier 5 pass from Beathard (Wittenborn kick).
Oakland: FG Blanda 36.
Oakland: Miller 12 pass from Lamonica (Blanda kick).

A:53,330.

**Recap:** After Hewritt Dixon's 69-yard touchdown run around left end, the Raiders seized momentum in the final seconds of the first half with a pass for six more off a faked field goal. The Oilers fumbled the second-half kickoff, setting up Lamonica's one-yard sneak, which made it 24–0 and put the Oilers away.

## Super Bowl II

| | | | | |
|---|---|---|---|---|
| Green Bay Packers | 3 | 13 | 10 | 7—33 |
| Oakland Raiders | 0 | 7 | 0 | 7—14 |

### FIRST QUARTER

Green Bay: FG Chandler 39.

### SECOND QUARTER

Green Bay: FG Chandler 20.
Green Bay: Dowler 62 pass from Starr (Chandler kick).
Oakland: Miller 23 pass from Lamonica (Blanda kick).
Green Bay: FG Chandler 43.

### THIRD QUARTER

Green Bay: Anderson 2 run (Chandler kick).
Green Bay: FG Chandler 31.

### FOURTH QUARTER

Green Bay: Adderly 60 int return (Chandler kick).
Oakland: Miller 23 pass from Lamonica (Blanda kick).

A:75,546. At Miami.

**Recap:** Rumors of Vince Lombardi's impending retirement had been swirling around Green Bay for weeks prior to the Packers' meeting with the Oakland Raiders in Miami. Indeed, the legendary coach seemed to confirm the rumor by calling his troops together and telling them in a cracking voice that he was proud of them before sending them out to the wildly cheering crowd of 75,546 at the Orange Bowl.

Don Chandler kicked two field goals before Bart Starr surprised Oakland by throwing deep on first down, finding Boyd Dowler wide open for 62 yards and a touchdown. Down 13 to the world champs, Oakland did not panic; instead they marched 78-yards to get back in the game, Daryle Lamonica passing 23 yards to Bill Miller for the touchdown. As it had the previous year, the tide turned Green Bay's way in the third quarter. The Packers' second series of the half yielded an 82-yard, 11-play touchdown drive that took 4:41 off the clock. Oakland ran three plays, then punted back to Green Bay. The Packer machine again clicked into action, churning out 37 yards in eight plays to set up Don Chandler's fourth field goal, a 31-yarder. The thrust had eaten up another 4:47, and the Raiders entered the fourth quarter trailing 26–7. Starr took the rest of the afternoon off. The backbreaker came early in the fourth when cornerback Herb Adderly stepped in front of Oakland receiver Fred Biletnikoff and raced 60 yards to the end zone with the interception. The Raiders scored a late touchdown to make the score 33–14 but could get no closer than that as the Packers became champions of the first two Super Bowls. Starr was the MVP in both. As expected, Lombardi retired soon after the game to become general manager of the Packers.

## 1968

### NATIONAL FOOTBALL LEAGUE

| | | | | |
|---|---|---|---|---|
| Baltimore Colts | 0 | 17 | 7 | 10—34 |
| Cleveland Browns | 0 | 0 | 0 | 0— 0 |

#### SECOND QUARTER

Baltimore: FG Michaels 28.
Baltimore: Matte 1 run (Michaels kick).
Baltimore: Matte 12 run (Michaels kick).

#### THIRD QUARTER

Baltimore: Matte 2 run (Michaels kick).

#### FOURTH QUARTER

Baltimore: FG Michaels 10.
Baltimore: Brown 4 run (Michaels kick).

A: 80,628.

**Recap:** Bubba Smith's block of Don Cockroft's 41-yard field goal attempt in the first quarter sent the message early: The Colts would smother the Browns. After a scoreless first quarter, Baltimore put up 17 in the second on the strength of a Mike Curtis interception and the running of Tom Matte and Jerry Hill. Matte scored his third touchdown of the day on a two-yard plunge in the third quarter. The Colts looked virtually unbeatable going into Super Bowl III.

### AMERICAN FOOTBALL LEAGUE

| | | | | |
|---|---|---|---|---|
| Oakland Raiders | 0 | 10 | 3 | 10—23 |
| New York Jets | 10 | 3 | 7 | 7—27 |

#### FIRST QUARTER

New York: Maynard 14 pass from Namath (J. Turner kick).
New York: FG J. Turner 33.

#### SECOND QUARTER

Oakland: Biletnikoff 29 pass from Lamonica (Blanda kick).
New York: FG J. Turner 36.
Oakland: FG Blanda 26.

#### THIRD QUARTER

Oakland: FG Blanda 9.
New York: Lammons 20 pass from Namath (J. Turner kick).

#### FOURTH QUARTER

Oakland: FG Blanda 20.
Oakland: Banaszak 4 run (Blanda kick).
New York: Maynard 6 pass from Namath (J. Turner kick).

A: 62,627.

**Recap:** In an exciting seesaw affair, Namath threw 52 yards to Don Maynard to set up the game-winner, a six-yarder, also to Maynard.

## Super Bowl III

| | | | | |
|---|---|---|---|---|
| New York Jets | 0 | 7 | 6 | 3—16 |
| Baltimore Colts | 0 | 0 | 0 | 7— 7 |

#### SECOND QUARTER

New York: Snell 4 run (J Turner kick).

#### THIRD QUARTER

New York: FG J Turner 32.
New York: FG J Turner 30.

#### FOURTH QUARTER

New York: FG J Turner 9.
Baltimore: Hill 1 run (Michaels kick).

A: 75,377. At Miami.

**Recap:** Joe Namath violated the shibboleth that warns against tempting fate when he approached the podium at an awards banquet in Miami Springs in the week before Super Bowl III and personally guaranteed a Jet victory over Baltimore. This from the quarterback of an underdog team that had 20 veterans of knee surgery, was essentially without the services of veteran Don Maynard and had barely scraped by the Raiders to get to the game; not to mention the roguish league from which they sprang, described by Maynard as a scrap heap because of the number of its players who had been cut from the NFL. But that scrap heap was set to merge with the NFL in the coming years, and this game would prove it worthy, as well as fulfill Namath's brash promise.

The Colts blew huge opportunities early. They marched with their first possession to the New York 19, where they botched two pass plays and Lou Michaels missed a 27-yard field goal attempt. Late in the opening quarter Baltimore recovered a Jet fumble on the New York 12. Earl Morrall hit a wide-open Tom Mitchell in the shoulder pads with a short pass but the ball caromed high in the air, and Jet cornerback Randy Beverly made a rolling interception in the end zone. The Jets took over on their 20 and, powered by Matt Snell's running and Namath's passes, reached the end zone in 12 plays, the last a 4-yard Snell carry. Before the half the Colts would miss another field goal and throw two more interceptions, both inside the Jet 20-yard line. On the first Baltimore play from scrimmage in the third period, Tom Matte fumbled. Jim Turner kicked a 32-yard field goal to put New York ahead 10–0. Turner added another field goal, from 30 yards away, and the quarter ended with the Jets leading 13–0 and driving again. George Sauer, for whom the injured Maynard acted as a decoy, was having a splendid game. Johnny Unitas came off the Colt bench and led one fourth-quarter scoring drive, but time ran out on the Baltimore comeback and Namath left the field, head bowed, index finger raised to the football gods who had smiled upon him that afternoon.

## 1969

**NATIONAL FOOTBALL LEAGUE**

| | | | | |
|---|---|---|---|---|
| Cleveland Browns ...........0 | 0 | 0 | 7— | 7 |
| Minnesota Vikings.........14 | 10 | 3 | 0— | 27 |

### FIRST QUARTER

Minnesota: Kapp 7 run (Cox kick).
Minnesota: Washington 75 pass from Kapp (Cox kick).

### SECOND QUARTER

Minnesota: FG Cox 30.
Minnesota: Osborn 20 run (Cox kick).

### THIRD QUARTER

Minnesota: FG Cox 32.

### FOURTH QUARTER

Cleveland: Collins 3 pass from Nelsen (Cockcroft kick).

A: 46,503.

**Recap:** The Vikings won the NFL championship in only their ninth year of existence, beating the Browns on a typically frigid January afternoon in Minnesota. Cleveland cornerback Erich Barnes slipped while covering Gene Washington, and Joe Kapp fired to the open receiver, who took it 75 yards over the tundra to put the Vikings ahead 14–0. Against a stingy Viking defense things only got worse for the Browns, while the rugged Kapp led the Vikings to 13 more points.

**AMERICAN FOOTBALL LEAGUE**

| | | | | |
|---|---|---|---|---|
| Kansas City Chiefs ...........0 | 7 | 7 | 3— | 17 |
| Oakland Raiders...............7 | 0 | 0 | 0— | 7 |

### FIRST QUARTER

Oakland: Smith 3 run (Blanda kick).

### SECOND QUARTER

Kansas City: Hayes 1 run (Stenerud kick).

### THIRD QUARTER

Kansas City: Holmes 5 run (Stenerud kick).

### FOURTH QUARTER

Kansas City: FG Stenerud 22.

A:53,564.

**Recap:** Oakland took a 7–0 first-quarter lead while Kansas City quarterback Len Dawson threw seven straight incomplete passes. Dawson recovered to connect with Frank Pitts on a 41-yard bomb that tied the game at the half. Oakland quarterback Daryle Lamonica left the game in the second half with an injury to his hand and was replaced by George Blanda, who threw an end zone interception. The Chiefs then rolled from their six to the Raiders' goal line for a 14–7 lead. Lamonica came back in but, clearly hurting, threw three interceptions. The Chiefs, second in the West behind the Raiders but winners over the Eastern champion Jets in the playoffs, were New Orleans bound.

## Super Bowl IV

| | | | | |
|---|---|---|---|---|
| Kansas City Chiefs ........3 | 13 | 7 | 0— | 23 |
| Minnesota Vikings .........0 | 0 | 7 | 0— | 7 |

### FIRST QUARTER

Kansa City: FG Stenerud 48.

### SECOND QUARTER

Kansas City: FG Stenerud 32.
Kansas City: FG Stenerud 25.
Kansas City: Garrett 5 run (Stenerud kick).

### THIRD QUARTER

Minnesota: Osborn 4 run (Cox kick).
Kansas City: Taylor 46 pass from Dawson (Stenerud kick).

A: 80,562. At New Orleans.

**Recap:** Kansas City quarterback Len Dawson had, to put it mildly, a tough week leading up to Super Bowl IV. The prelude to this last game before the AFL-NFL merger was an ultimately unsubstantiated NBC-TV report that the justice department wanted to interrogate Dawson concerning suspected ties to illegal gambling. There was a firestorm of controversy and speculation. Dawson attended a press conference in an attempt to quell the rumors and was assailed with skeptical queries. So much for the game. The quarterback spent a sleepless night Saturday, then walked out and gave what Kansas City coach Hank Stram called one of the greatest clutch performances he'd ever seen. Pretty clutch also was Chief kicker Jan Stenerud, who nailed three threes in the first half, including a 48-yarder on Kansas City's first series. After Stenerud's third boot put the Chiefs ahead 9–0, the Dane kicked off to Minnesota amid gusting winds. The Vikings' Charlie West was there to field the kick but had to dive for the windblown ball, and Kansas City's Remi Prudhomme fell on it at the Minnesota 19. It was a game-breaking play. The Chiefs' Mike Garrett ran for the touchdown past trapped Viking tackle Alan Page, and Kansas City led 16–0. For the second year in a row, the vagabonds from the AFL took a halftime shutout lead. The Chiefs quickly picked up two first downs in the second half and appeared to be moving again, but the drive was killed by a penalty. The Vikings took the ensuing punt and built a drive of their own: 69 yards on 10 plays with Dave Osborn finishing on a four-yard carry. The Vikings were very much alive. Dawson had an answer for them, though, as he took over on his own 18 and guided the Chiefs swiftly down the field. They got a first down on a reverse to receiver Frank Pitts. Two plays later, from the Viking 46, Dawson passed five yards to Otis Taylor, who broke a tackle, tore down the sideline, slipped another defender and ran in for a touchdown. The Chiefs never looked back.

## 1970

### NATIONAL FOOTBALL CONFERENCE

| | | | | |
|---|---|---|---|---|
| **Dallas Cowboys** | 0 | 3 | 14 | 0—17 |
| **San Francisco 49ers** | 3 | 0 | 7 | 0—10 |

**FIRST QUARTER**
San Francisco: FG Gossett 16.

**SECOND QUARTER**
Dallas: FG Clark 21.

**THIRD QUARTER**
Dallas: Thomas 13 run (Clark kick).
Dallas: Garrison 5 pass from Morton (Clark kick).
San Francisco: Witcher 26 pass from Brodie (Gossett kick).

A: 59,364.

**Recap:** The 49ers tried to win it through the air on John Brodie's passing, while the Cowboys, whose quarterback Craig Morton had a sore arm, worked the ground with backs Duane Thomas and Walt Garrison. Brodie's arm failed him twice; Thomas and Garrison collectively ate up 214 yards rushing. Lee Roy Jordan intercepted Brodie in the third quarter, and Thomas rambled 13 yards on the next play for the score. Brodie brought the 49ers back into Dallas territory but was intercepted again. Thomas and Garrison ran Dallas downfield, and Garrison caught a Morton five-yarder to make it 17–3. Dallas's defense did the rest.

### AMERICAN FOOTBALL CONFERENCE

| | | | | |
|---|---|---|---|---|
| **Oakland Raiders** | 0 | 3 | 7 | 7—17 |
| **Baltimore Colts** | 3 | 7 | 10 | 7—27 |

**FIRST QUARTER**
Baltimore: FG O'Brien 16.

**SECOND QUARTER**
Baltimore: Bulaich 2 run (O'Brien kick).
Oakland: FG Blanda 48.

**THIRD QUARTER**
Oakland: Biletnikoff 38 pass from Blanda (Blanda kick).
Baltimore: FG O'Brien 23.
Baltimore: Bulaich 11 run (O'Brien kick).

**FOURTH QUARTER**
Oakland: Wells 15 pass from Blanda (Blanda kick).
Baltimore: Perkins 68 pass from Unitas (O'Brien kick).

A:54,799.

**Recap:** Two of the game's elders met in this battle for the first AFC crown: 43-year-old George Blanda replaced Daryle Lamonica, trailing 10–0 to Johnny Unitas's Colts in the second quarter. Blanda kicked a field goal and passed 38 yards to Fred Biletnikoff to tie it. But Unitas led two drives to net 10 points for the Colts in the third, and the Baltimore defense blunted Blanda, picking him off twice in the end zone.

## Super Bowl V

| | | | | |
|---|---|---|---|---|
| **Baltimore Colts** | 0 | 6 | 0 | 10—16 |
| **Dallas Cowboys** | 3 | 10 | 0 | 0—13 |

**FIRST QUARTER**
Dallas: FG Clark 14.

**SECOND QUARTER**
Dallas: FG Clark 30.
Baltimore: Mackey 75 pass from Unitas (kick blocked).
Dallas: 7 pass from Morton (Clark kick).

**FOURTH QUARTER**
Baltimore: Nowatzke 2 run (O'Brien kick).
Baltimore: FG O'Brien 32.

A: 79,204. At Miami.

**Recap:** The various mishaps and overall ugliness of this contest prompted *Sports Illustrated's* Tex Maule to suggest it be renamed the Blunder Bowl. All told, there were 11 turnovers—three interceptions by the Colts in the final period alone—and 164 yards in penalties. Trailing 13–6 after missing several golden opportunities and losing Unitas to injury, the Colts finally cashed in when safety Rick Volk intercepted Craig Morton in the fourth quarter and raced 30 yards to the Cowboy three. Two plays later fullback Tom Nowatzke slashed in for the tying touchdown. The teams traded fruitless possessions, and then the Cowboys had a horrendous series, which set up Baltimore's dramatic, last-second field goal that won it. They took possession at the Colt 48 with 1:52 to play. The game was theirs to win; overtime seemed the only alternative to a Dallas victory. Then disaster struck, followed by catastrophe. On second-and-11, Morton was sacked and a Cowboy blocker was whistled for holding. In 1970 the NFL rulebook required that the penalty be stepped off from the point of infraction, so the Cowboys lost a total of 24 yards on the play. On the next play Morton's pass to Dan Reeves slipped through the running back's hands and into those of Colt middle linebacker Mike Curtis at the Dallas 41. Curtis took it back 13 yards and Dallas's good fortune was reversed: The Colts had first-and-10 on the Cowboys' 28 with 59 seconds remaining. After a pair of runs by Norm Bulaich produced only three yards, kicker Jim O'Brien entered the game to attempt the game-winning field goal with five seconds remaining. Nicknamed Lassie for his long hair by the Baltimore veterans, the rookie out of Cincinnati had won the job from 13-year veteran Lou Michaels. When Earl Morrall noticed the nervous O'Brien trying to pull blades of grass to test the wind, he was forced to remind the rookie they were on artificial turf. O'Brien then settled down to make the 32-yard kick for the Baltimore win. The Cowboys had enough time for a desperation heave, but it was intercepted.

## 1971

| NATIONAL FOOTBALL CONFERENCE | | | |
|---|---|---|---|
| San Francisco 49ers | 0 | 3 | 0— 3 |
| Dallas Cowboys | 0 | 7 | 0—14 |

### SECOND QUARTER
Dallas: Hill 1 run (Clark kick).
San Francisco: FG Gossett 28.

### FOURTH QUARTER
Dallas: D Thomas 2 run (Clark kick).

A:63,409.

**Recap:** Both teams brought sturdy defenses to Dallas, and defense was the name of the game in this replay of the previous year's conference championship. After a scoreless first quarter Cowboy defensive end George Andrie struck a decisive blow, intercepting John Brodie deep in 49er territory and returning it to the one-yard line. Calvin Hill took it across from there, and Dallas led 7–0. A 28-yard Bruce Gossett field goal before the half made it 7-3. The third quarter saw more defensive dominance as neither team was able to mount a scoring attack. In the fourth Dallas quarterback Roger Staubach started to make things happen with his scrambling, allowing his receivers time to get open, and running for significant yardage himself. Dallas converted four third downs on an 80-yard drive, which ended in Daune Thomas's two-yard end run for a score. Ahead 14–3, the Cowboys defense held the 49ers scoreless the rest of the way.

| AMERICAN FOOTBALL CONFERENCE | | | |
|---|---|---|---|
| Baltimore Colts | 0 | 0 | 0— 0 |
| Miami Dolphins | 7 | 0 | 7—21 |

### FIRST QUARTER
Miami: Warfield 75 pass from Griese (Yepremian kick).

### THIRD QUARTER
Miami: Anderson 62 int return (Yepremian kick).

### FOURTH QUARTER
Miami: Csonka 5 run (Yepremian kick).

A: 76,622.

**Recap:** Miami was coming off an exhausting 27–24 overtime victory against the Chiefs in the longest game ever played. The Colts, meanwhile, had coasted by Cleveland 20–3. But if the Dolphins were drained, they didn't show it. Bob Griese hooked up with Paul Warfield for a 75-yard first quarter TD pass. The Colts were missing backs Tom Matte and Norm Bulaich, so their running game lacked punch. But their defense hung tough to keep the score 7–0 at the half. Unitas went to the air with disastrous results in the third quarter. His bomb to Eddie Hinton was picked off by Dick Anderson, who followed some well-placed blocks 62 yards to the end zone for a 14–0 Miami lead. Griese later went deep again to Warfield to set up a five-yard plunge by Larry Csonka for the final score.

## Super Bowl VI

| Dallas Cowboys | 3 | 7 | 7 | 7—24 |
|---|---|---|---|---|
| Miami Dolphins | 0 | 3 | 0 | 0— 3 |

### FIRST QUARTER
Dallas: FG Clark 9.

### SECOND QUARTER
Dallas: Alworth 7 pass from Staubach (Clark kick).
Miami: FG Yepremian 31.

### THIRD QUARTER
Dallas: D Thomas 3 run (Clark kick).

### FOURTH QUARTER
Dallas: Ditka 7 pass from Staubach (Clark kick).

A: 80,591. At New Orleans.

**Recap:** The Cowboys stalled coming out of the gate for the 1971 season, losing three of their first seven and looking unlikely to return to the Super Bowl, where they felt they had unfinished business, having lost so ignominiously the year before. But after their seventh game, a 23–19 loss at Chicago, coach Tom Landry ditched his platoon system at quarterback and made Roger Staubach his starter, benching Craig Morton. Staubach, with the help of the dominant Dallas Doomsday Defense, led the Cowboys to nine straight victories. By the time they reached New Orleans, Staubach was clicking and the Doomsdayers were more than ready to beach the Dolphins' powerful running combination of Jim Kiick and Larry Csonka. It was Csonka who gave the Cowboys their first break on Miami's second series when he fumbled—for the first time all year—at the Dallas 48. The miscue led to a 9-yard Cowboy field goal by Mike Clark. Griese was sacked for a devastating 29-yard loss at the end of the first period by defensive tackle Bob Lilly, the heart of the Doomsday Defense. Early in the second Miami's Garo Yepremian missed a 49-yard field goal attempt. Dallas soon forged a 76-yard, 10-play scoring march that ended, after taking five minutes off the clock, with Staubach firing seven yards to Lance Alworth in the corner of the end zone. Griese connected with the dangerous Paul Warfield for 23 yards to set up Yepremian's 31-yard boot before the half, and the Dolphins, down only 10–3, felt they were in contention. They had to feel differently after Dallas took the second-half kickoff and drove 71 yards behind the running of Duane Thomas to make it 17–3. Thomas carried four times for 37 yards on the drive, which also featured a 16-yard reverse to the "world's fastest human," Olympian Bob Hayes. Miami's offense accomplished nothing after Thomas's touchdown as Dallas linebacker Chuck Howley intercepted Griese early in the fourth quarter to set up Dallas's final score, a seven-yard catch by veteran Mike Ditka.

## 1972

### NATIONAL FOOTBALL CONFERENCE

**Dallas Cowboys ...............0  3  0  0— 3**
**Washington Redskins ......0  10  0  16—26**

#### SECOND QUARTER

Washington: FG Knight 18.
Washington: Taylor 15 pass from Kilmer (Knight kick).
Dallas: FG Fritsch 35.

#### FOURTH QUARTER

Washington: Taylor 45 pass from Kilmer (Knight kick).
Washington: FG Knight 39.
Washington: FG Knight 46.
Washington: FG Knight 45.

A: 53,129.

**Recap:** Having split their regular season meetings, these Eastern Division archrivals came to the NFC title game for a rubber match. Roger Staubach had returned from injury to lead the Cowboys in a comeback the previous week, but Washington's pass rush proved too much for him this afternoon. Meanwhile the 'Skins Billy Kilmer punished the left side of the Dallas secondary where Charley Waters was adjusting to a switch from safety to cornerback. Charley Taylor beat Waters for a 51-yard catch to set up one score, and later, after Waters left the game with a broken arm, his replacement Mark Washington was also burned by Taylor, on a 45-yard touchdown pass from Kilmer. Kicker Curt Knight added three long field goals in the fourth quarter for the 26–3 final margin.

### AMERICAN FOOTBALL CONFERENCE

**Miami Dolphins ................0  7  7  7—21**
**Pittsburgh Steelers .........7  0  3  7—17**

#### FIRST QUARTER

Pittsburgh: Mullins fum recovery in end zone (Gerela kick).

#### SECOND QUARTER

Miami: Csonka 9 pass from Morrall (Yepremian kick).

#### THIRD QUARTER

Pittsburgh: FG Gerela 14.
Miami: Kiick 2 run (Yepremian kick).

#### FOURTH QUARTER

Miami: Kiick 3 run (Yepremian kick).
Pittsburgh: Young 12 pass from Bradshaw (Gerela kick).

A: 50,845.

**Recap:** The Immaculate Reception and the Immaculate Season. Franco Harris's famous catch allowed the Steelers to reach this game where they faced the 15–0 Dolphins. Terry Bradshaw was knocked out early, and Miami took a 21–10 lead in his absence, with a fake punt and a 52-yard Bob Griese to Paul Warfield pass play doing the damage. Bradshaw came back to lead a fourth-quarter scoring drive but two late interceptions thwarted his attempt to rally his team.

## Super Bowl VII

**Miami Dolphins ..............7  7  0  0—14**
**Washington Redskins ....0  0  0  7— 7**

#### FIRST QUARTER

Miami: Twilley 28 pass from Griese (Yepremian kick).

#### SECOND QUARTER

Miami: Kiick 1 run (Yepremian kick).

#### FOURTH QUARTER

Washington: Bass 49 fum return (Knight kick).

A: 90,192. At Los Angeles.

**Recap:** The mantle of defensive greatness passed from the Doomsday Dallas unit of Super Bowl VI to the Miami Dolphins of Super Bowl VII, who took Tom Landry's remark that he couldn't name any of the Dolphin defenders and made it a nickname, namely, the No-Name Defense. That unit, led by anonymities Nick Buoniconti, Vern Den Herder, Manny Fernandez and Jake Scott, along with offensive stars Bob Griese, Earl Morrall, Larry Csonka and Paul Warfield, had gone 16–0 up to Super Bowl VII. They were motivated, like Dallas before them, by a Super Bowl loss the previous year. It would be a season unequaled before or since. When Bob Griese broke his leg in October, Miami coach Don Shula turned to his old friend Earl Morrall and the 38-year-old backup, who played in Super Bowls III and V, filled in capably, quarterbacking the team to nine victories.

But he was flat in the AFC title game, and Shula decided to return to Griese for the big one. Griese settled back in the saddle, connecting with Howard Twilley for 28 yards and a touchdown in the first quarter. The No-Name Defense controlled the line of scrimmage as well as the secondary, shutting down the Redskins' running game and intercepting Billy Kilmer twice in the first half. The second of those interceptions was returned 32 yards by linebacker Nick Buoniconti to the Washington 27. Griese then passed 19 yards to tight end Jim Mandich, who made a diving catch at the two. Successive one-yard blasts by Jim Kiick put Miami ahead 14–0. In the fourth quarter Washington mounted a 13-play drive to the Dolphin 10-yard line but safety and game-MVP Jake Scott intercepted Kilmer's third-down pass in the end zone and took it back 55 yards. Six plays later Garo Yepremian came on to attempt a 42-yard field goal. When his kick was blocked, the diminutive Cypriot grabbed the ball, rolled right and attempted a pass. The ball rolled off his fingertips right to Washington cornerback Mike Bass, who caught it and rambled 49 yards for a touchdown. Down by only seven points, Washington got the ball back with 1:14 remaining. But while a fearful Yepremian prayed on the sidelines, a pair of tackles for losses by Miami end Bill Stanfill squelched any threat and preserved the perfect 17–0 season for Miami.

## 1973

<table>
<tr><td colspan="6">NATIONAL FOOTBALL CONFERENCE</td></tr>
<tr><td>Minnesota Vikings</td><td>3</td><td>7</td><td>7</td><td>10—27</td></tr>
<tr><td>Dallas Cowboys</td><td>0</td><td>0</td><td>10</td><td>0—10</td></tr>
</table>

### FIRST QUARTER
Minnesota: FG Cox 44.

### SECOND QUARTER
Minnesota: Foreman 5 run (Cox kick).

### THIRD QUARTER
Dallas: Richards 63 punt return (Fritsch kick).
Minnesota: 54 pass from Tarkenton (Cox kick).
Dallas: FG Fritsch 17.

### FOURTH QUARTER
Minnesota: Bryant 63 int return (Cox kick).
Minnesota: FG Cox 34.

A: 60,272.

**Recap:** After 13 years, Minnesota's Fran Tarkenton finally made the playoffs; he did not squander the opportunity. The Vikings took a 10–0 lead, but Dallas answered after the half with Golden Richards's 63-yard punt return for a touchdown. Three plays later, Tarkenton answered by hitting John Gilliam for 54 yards and a 17–7 lead. The fourth period was full of turnovers, the worst a Roger Staubach pass intercepted by Bobby Bryant, who returned it 63 yards to put Minnesota up 24–10. Fred Cox added a field goal to close out the scoring.

<table>
<tr><td colspan="6">AMERICAN FOOTBALL CONFERENCE</td></tr>
<tr><td>Oakland Raiders</td><td>0</td><td>0</td><td>10</td><td>0—10</td></tr>
<tr><td>Miami Dolphins</td><td>7</td><td>7</td><td>3</td><td>10—27</td></tr>
</table>

### FIRST QUARTER
Miami: Csonka 11 run (Yepremian kick).

### SECOND QUARTER
Miami: Csonka 2 run (Yepremian kick).

### THIRD QUARTER
Oakland: FG Blanda 21.
Miami: FG Yepremian 42.
Oakland: Siani 25 pass from Stabler (Blanda kick).

### FOURTH QUARTER
Miami: FG Yepremian 26.
Miami: Csonka 2 run.

A: 75,105.

**Recap:** Using a punishing running attack, Miami rolled over the Raiders and into their third straight Super Bowl. Bob Griese passed just six times, content to hand off to backs Larry Csonka and Mercury Morris. Csonka ran for three TDs, his first from 11 yards out. He bulled over again in the second, and Miami led 14–0. The Raiders made it 17–10 in the third, but Ken Stabler and company were stopped on fourth-and-inches in the final period, and Miami churned downfield for Csonka's third plunge.

## Super Bowl VIII

<table>
<tr><td>Miami Dolphins</td><td>14</td><td>3</td><td>7</td><td>0—24</td></tr>
<tr><td>Minnesota Vikings</td><td>0</td><td>0</td><td>0</td><td>7— 7</td></tr>
</table>

### FIRST QUARTER
Miami: Csonka 5 run (Yepremian kick).
Miami: Kiick 1 run (Yepremian kick).

### SECOND QUARTER
Miami: FG Yepremian 28.

### THIRD QUARTER
Miami: Csonka 2 run (Yepremian kick).

### FOURTH QUARTER
Minnesota: Tarkenton 4 run (Cox kick).

A: 71,882. At Houston.

**Recap:** The first Super Bowl played in a location other than Miami, New Orleans or Los Angeles, this one pitted the Purple People Eaters, Minnesota's heralded defense, against the relentless Miami running attack in Houston's Rice Stadium. Carl Eller, Alan Page, Jim Marshall and Gary Larsen, the Minnesota defensive front four, were in their Purple People Eating prime, and quarterback Fran Tarkenton was eager to shed his "can't win the big one" image, garnered after 12 seasons without a playoff appearance. But the defending world champion Dolphins had a famously nicknamed defense of their own—the increasingly unanonymous No-Name unit, and an inexorable offensive machine powered by the running trio of Jim Kiick, Mercury Morris and Larry Csonka. The methodical Dolphin offense immediately set the tone, marching 62 yards after the opening kickoff on 10 plays—eight of them runs—to take a 7–0 lead as Csonka powered over from the five, carrying two Vikings with him. Minnesota then went three-and-out, and Miami again ran eight times on a 10-play drive for a touchdown. Jim Kiick did the honors this time, scoring his first touchdown of the year on a one-yard carry. Garo Yepremian added a 28-yard field goal in the second quarter. Late in the half Minnesota advanced to the Miami six, where they faced fourth-and-inches, only to have Oscar Reed fumble when hit by Miami linebacker Nick Buoniconti. The Dolphins maintained their 17–0 lead, and the game, it seemed, was firmly in hand. The Vikings went three-and-out to start the second half. Miami returned the punt to the Minnesota 43 and scored in eight plays, Csonka carrying two yards for the touchdown. Yepremian's extra point made it 24–0. Griese, having thrown only seven passes up to that point, didn't throw another all day. Csonka took the MVP award with a Super Bowl record 145 yards rushing, and the Dolphins closed out a near perfect game (no turnovers, one penalty for a measly four yards) to take their second straight title and a place in the NFL pantheon.

## 1974

### NATIONAL FOOTBALL CONFERENCE

| | | | | |
|---|---|---|---|---|
| Los Angeles Rams............ | 0 | 3 | 0 | 7—10 |
| Minnesota Vikings............ | 0 | 7 | 0 | 7—14 |

#### SECOND QUARTER

Minnesota: Lash 29 pass from Tarkenton (Cox kick).
Los Angeles: FG Ray 27.

#### FOURTH QUARTER

Minnesota: Osborn 1 run (Cox kick).
Los Angeles: Jackson 44 pass from Harris (Ray kick).

A: 47,404.

**Recap:** Turnovers told the tale, as the teams committed a total of eight before the gun sounded. Minnesota led 7–3 after Fran Tarkenton's 29-yard touchdown pass to Jim Lash and David Ray's 27-yard field goal. A perfect Viking punt in the third quarter forced the Rams to take possession from their own one where they began an extended drive that, aided by a 73-yard pass from James Harris to Harold Jackson, eventually reached the Minnesota one. But three plays later, a Harris pass was tipped, then intercepted in the end zone by linebacker Wally Hilgenberg, ending the long drive. The Vikings jumped ahead 14–3 in the fourth quarter when Dave Osborn capped an 80-yard drive with a fourth-down, one-yard blast. Harris again threw long to Harold Jackson—for 44 yards and a late TD to make it 14–10—but the Minnesota Purple People Eaters would give up no more, and the Vikings returned to the Super Bowl.

### AMERICAN FOOTBALL CONFERENCE

| | | | | |
|---|---|---|---|---|
| Pittsburgh Steelers ......... | 0 | 3 | 0 | 21—24 |
| Oakland Raiders.............. | 3 | 0 | 7 | 3—13 |

#### FIRST QUARTER

Oakland: FG Blanda 40.

#### SECOND QUARTER

Pittsburgh: FG Gerela 23.

#### THIRD QUARTER

Oakland: Branch 38 pass from Stabler (Blanda kick).

#### FOURTH QUARTER

Pittsburgh: Harris 8 run (Gerela kick).
Pittsburgh: Swann 6 pass from Bradshaw (Gerela kick).
Oakland: FG Blanda 24.
Pittsburgh: Harris 21 run (Gerela kick).

A: 53,515.

**Recap:** The Raiders had ended Miami's reign and, leading Pittsburgh 10–3 entering the fourth quarter, looked set to replace the Dolphins as AFC rep for Super Bowl IX. But the Steelers tied it on Franco Harris's eight-yard carry and took the lead when Jack Ham intercepted Ken Stabler and carried to the nine, setting up a Terry Bradshaw six-yarder to Lynn Swann. Jack Lambert later picked off another Stabler pass to set up Harris's second touchdown run.

## Super Bowl IX

| | | | | |
|---|---|---|---|---|
| Pittsburgh Steelers........ | 0 | 2 | 7 | 7—16 |
| Minnesota Vikings ......... | 0 | 0 | 0 | 6— 6 |

#### SECOND QUARTER

Pittsburgh: Safety. White tackled Tarkenton in end zone.

#### THIRD QUARTER

Pittsburgh: Harris 9 run (Gerela kick).

#### FOURTH QUARTER

Minnesota: T Brown recovered blocked punt in end zone (kick failed).
Pittsburgh: Brown 4 pass from Bradshaw (Gerela kick).

A: 80,997. At New Orleans.

**Recap:** After a phenomenal 1974 draft brought the Steelers Jack Lambert, Mike Webster, Lynn Swann and John Stallworth to complement promising young quarterback Terry Bradshaw, the pieces of the Pittsburgh dynasty were in place, though no one seemed to recognize it at the time. The Vikings entered the game favored and confident of victory in their second straight Super Bowl appearance. They had disposed of St. Louis and Los Angeles on the way, their relentless pass rush playing a critical role. Bradshaw had won his job at midseason and was still raw, as was the Pittsburgh offense in general. The defense, for its part, lined up in a strange formation called Stunt 4–3, instituted only three weeks before the game. The new formation had befuddled opponents in the playoffs, and it stymied the Vikings as well. They didn't advance past their own 35-yard line on their first four possessions. Quarterback Fran Tarkenton had an injured shoulder and was unable to throw effectively as the Vikings averaged just 2.5 yards per offensive play. But the Minnesota defense didn't give up much either, making for a stale contest. After a scoreless first quarter the Steelers notched a safety when Minnesota fumbled at their 10; the ball was kicked back to the end zone where Tarkenton recovered and was touched by Dwight White. The Vikings threatened in the second quarter but Tarkenton was intercepted at the Pittsburgh five-yard line by Mel Blount who caught the ball after receiver John Gilliam was unkindly separated from it by safety Glen (the Blade) Edwards. Turnovers continued to vex the Vikings in the second half as Bill Brown fumbled the opening kickoff, the Steelers recovered and scored in four plays to go ahead 9–0. Minnesota's Matt Blair blocked a punt that Terry Brown recovered for the touchdown that made the score 9–6, but the Vikings didn't threaten again. The Steelers marched 66 yards on the next series with Bradshaw passing four yards to tight end Larry Brown for the final margin.

## 1975

### NATIONAL FOOTBALL CONFERENCE

| | | | | |
|---|---|---|---|---|
| Dallas Cowboys | 7 | 14 | 13 | 3—37 |
| Los Angeles Rams | 0 | 0 | 0 | 7— 7 |

#### FIRST QUARTER
Dallas: P Pearson 18 pass from Staubach (Fritsch kick).

#### SECOND QUARTER
Dallas: Richards 4 pass from Staubach (Fritsch kick).
Dallas: P Pearson 15 pass from Staubach (Fritsch kick).

#### THIRD QUARTER
Dallas: P Pearson 19 pass from Staubach (Fritsch kick).
Dallas: FG Fritsch 40.
Dallas: FG Fritsch 26.

#### FOURTH QUARTER
Los Angeles: Cappelletti 1 run (Dempsey kick).
Dallas: FG Fritsch 26.

A: 84,483.

**Recap:** After scraping by with a last-minute Hail Mary in the previous round, the wildcard Cowboys blew out the favored Rams behind Roger Staubach's four TD passes. Preston Pearson's third scoring catch blew the game open; Toni Fritsch kicked two field goals, and it was 34–0 entering the final period.

### AMERICAN FOOTBALL CONFERENCE

| | | | | |
|---|---|---|---|---|
| Oakland Raiders | 0 | 0 | 0 | 10—10 |
| Pittsburgh Steelers | 0 | 3 | 0 | 13—16 |

#### SECOND QUARTER
Pittsburgh: FG Gerela 36.

#### FOURTH QUARTER
Pittsburgh: Harris 25 run (Gerela kick).
Oakland: Siani 14 pass from Stabler (Blanda kick).
Pittsburgh: Stallworth 20 pass from Bradshaw (kick failed).
Oakland: FG Blanda 41.

A: 49,103.

**Recap:** After three full quarters there was only a single Pittsburgh field goal on the scoreboard, and then, like the flurries that swept the ice-covered field, 20 points blew in during a six-minute span and decided the contest. Franco Harris increased the Pittsburgh lead to 10–0 on a tough 25-yard carry. Oakland's Ken Stabler came right back, hitting Mike Siani with a 14-yard TD pass. Terry Bradshaw had a rejoinder, a 20-yarder to John Stallworth and, after a failed kick, the Steelers led 16–7. Oakland booted a field goal at 14:48 and miraculously recovered the onside kick in time for a last second pass to Cliff Branch. He was stopped at the Pittsburgh 15, and the Steelers advanced to another Super Bowl, frustrating Oakland for the second straight year.

## Super Bowl X

| | | | | |
|---|---|---|---|---|
| Pittsburgh Steelers | 7 | 0 | 0 | 14—21 |
| Dallas Cowboys | 7 | 3 | 0 | 7—17 |

#### FIRST QUARTER
Dallas: D Pearson 29 pass from Staubach (Fritsch kick).
Pittsburgh: Grossman 7 pass from Bradshaw (Gerela kick).

#### SECOND QUARTER
Dallas: FG Fritsch 36.

#### FOURTH QUARTER
Pittsburgh: Safety. Harrison blocked Hoopes's punt through end zone.
Pittsburgh: FG Gerela 36.
Pittsburgh: FG Gerela 18.
Pittsburgh: Swann 64 pass from Bradshaw (kick failed).
Dallas: P Howard 34 pass from Staubach (Fritsch kick).

A: 80,187. At Miami.

**Recap:** The rebuilt Dallas Cowboys were the first wildcard team ever to make the Super Bowl, and they barely made it. They gained confidence, however, in a 37–7 rout of the Rams for the NFC title. The Steelers, on the other hand, never lacked confidence. They were the defending world champions, they had the Steel Curtain defense and a record of 12–2, with 11 straight wins. There was no love lost between the two sides, and they produced the best Super Bowl to date. The Cowboys executed a sly reverse on the opening kickoff with Thomas (Hollywood) Henderson taking the ball from Preston Pearson and running 48 yards to the Pittsburgh 44. Dallas failed to capitalize but got the ball back on a blocked punt, and Staubach immediately zipped a 29-yard pass to Drew Pearson for a 7–0 lead. Minutes later the Steelers tied it on a seven-yard pass from Terry Bradshaw to tight end Randy Grossman. Toni Fritsch kicked a 36-yard field goal to put the Cowboys ahead 10-7 at the half. Early in the fourth quarter Pittsburgh's Reggie Harrison blocked a Dallas punt, and the ball rolled through the end zone for a safety, making it 10–9, Dallas. Pittsburgh took the ensuing free kick and drove for a field goal. Staubach threw an interception on Dallas's next play, leading to yet another Steeler field goal. The Cowboys went three-and-out, and Pittsburgh took over at their own 30. On third down Bradshaw launched a pass just before being knocked unconscious by the Dallas rush. Fifty-nine yards downfield, game-MVP Lynn Swann, himself returning from a concussion, made an acrobatic catch and ran five yards for the touchdown that made it 21–10. Staubach threw a late touchdown and had a last-second chance from the Pittsburgh 38 but was intercepted in the end zone as time ran out.

## 1976

**NATIONAL FOOTBALL CONFERENCE**

| | | | | |
|---|---|---|---|---|
| Los Angeles Rams..........0 | 0 | 13 | 0— | 13 |
| Minnesota Vikings..........7 | 3 | 7 | 7— | 24 |

### FIRST QUARTER
Minnesota: Bryant 90 blocked FG return (Cox kick).

### SECOND QUARTER
Minnesota: FG Cox 25.

### THIRD QUARTER
Minnesota: Foreman 1 run (Cox kick).
Los Angeles: McCutcheon 10 run (kick failed).
Los Angeles: H Jackson 9 pass from Haden (Dempsey kick).

### FOURTH QUARTER
Minnesota: Johnson 12 run (Cox kick).

A: 47,191.

**Recap:** Minnesota reached its third Super Bowl in four years on the strength of some opportunistic special teams play. The first quarter featured a 90-yard return of a blocked field goal attempt by the Vikings' Bobby Bryant. Another block—this one of a punt—set up Minnesota's second score, a 25-yard field goal by Fred Cox. The Rams' late efforts to complete a 17-point rally were crushed by a Bryant interception. Sammy Johnson's 12-yard touchdown run put the game out of reach in the fourth quarter.

**AMERICAN FOOTBALL CONFERENCE**

| | | | | |
|---|---|---|---|---|
| Pittsburgh Steelers .........0 | 7 | 0 | 0— | 7 |
| Oakland Raiders...............3 | 14 | 7 | 0— | 24 |

### FIRST QUARTER
Oakland: FG Mann 30.

### SECOND QUARTER
Oakland: C Davis 1 run (Mann kick).
Pittsburgh: Harrison 3 run (Mansfield kick).
Oakland: Bankston 4 pass from Stabler (Mann kick).

### THIRD QUARTER
Oakland: Banaszak 5 pass from Stabler (Mann kick).

A: 53,739.

**Recap:** With Rocky Bleier and Franco Harris both out of the game due to injuries sustained the previous round against Baltimore, Pittsburgh was forced to install a one-back offense. Coach Chuck Noll had to call every play and the new offense was ineffective; the Steelers were trailing 10–0 before they were able to muster a single first down. They recovered to make the score 10–7 behind Bradshaw's resourceful third-down passing, but Oakland struck just before the half, when Ken Stabler passed four yards to Warren Bankston for a touchdown. Stabler read the Pittsburgh defense all day, adjusting his offense accordingly. He threw five yards to Pete Banaszak for the game's final score, and the defense easily held for the victory.

## Super Bowl XI

| | | | | |
|---|---|---|---|---|
| Oakland Raiders .............0 | 16 | 3 | 13— | 32 |
| Minnesota Vikings .........0 | 0 | 7 | 7— | 14 |

### SECOND QUARTER
Oakland: FG Mann 24.
Oakland: Casper 1 pass from Stabler (Mann kick).
Oakland: Banaszak 1 run (kick failed).

### THIRD QUARTER
Okland: FG Mann 40.
Minnesota: S White 8 pass from Tarkenton (Cox kick).

### FOURTH QUARTER
Oakland: Banaszak 2 run (Mann kick).
Oakland: Brown 75 int return (kick failed).
Minnesota: Voight 13 pass from Lee (Cox kick).

A: 103,438. At Pasadena.

**Recap:** This game pitted two teams with reputations as perennial losers of the Big Game. The Raiders had lost to Green Bay in Super Bowl II and, following that, had appeared in six of the next eight AFL or AFC title games, losing all six. The Vikings had acquired the label of chokers by losing Super Bowls IV, VIII and IX. They never led in any of those games; indeed, they never scored in the first half of a Super Bowl or totaled more than seven points overall. That last mark they would erase with a meaningless late touchdown in Super Bowl XI, but the stain of big-time loser would prove indelible to the Vikings as they lost their fourth Super Bowl by a 32–14 score to the Raiders.

Momentum was in the Vikings' favor when they blocked a first-quarter punt and recovered on the Oakland three-yard line. It shifted back to the Raiders two plays later, however, when Brent McClanahan fumbled and Oakland's Willie Hall recovered. The Raiders drove 90 yards in 12 plays to the Minnesota seven-yard line and Errol Mann kicked a 24-yard field goal to start the second quarter. Minnesota gained six yards in three plays and punted. The Raiders then mounted another time-consuming drive, mixing five running plays with five passes to go 64 yards for a touchdown as the Oakland offensive line, powered by Art Shell and Gene Upshaw, dominated the play in the trenches. After a 25-yard punt return by Neal Colzie, Oakland was in business again. Ken Stabler hit Fred Biletnikoff for 17 yards over the middle, and Pete Banaszak carried it one yard for the score. The kick failed, but Oakland had an imposing 16–0 lead. Mann's 40-yard field goal made it 19–0 in the third quarter. Minnesota used two Oakland penalties to keep a third-quarter drive alive and scored on an eight-yard Fran Tarkenton to Sammy White pass. But any comeback thoughts were snuffed by Willie Hall's interception of a Tarkenton pass early in the fourth quarter, which set up a two-yard plunge by Banaszak to make it 26–7. Oakland hardly needed it, but Willie Brown ran 75 yards with an interception for an insurmountable 25-point lead.

## 1977

**NATIONAL FOOTBALL CONFERENCE**

| | | | | |
|---|---|---|---|---|
| Minnesota Vikings............0 | 6 | 0 | 0— | 6 |
| Dallas Cowboys ...............6 | 10 | 0 | 7— | 23 |

### FIRST QUARTER
Dallas: Richards 32 pass from Staubach (kick failed).

### SECOND QUARTER
Dallas: Newhouse 5 run (Herrera kick).
Minnesota: FG Cox 12.
Minnesota: FG Cox 37.
Dallas: FG Herrera 21.

### FOURTH QUARTER
Dallas: Dorsett 11 run (Herrera kick).

A: 61,968.

**Recap:** The new dawn of the Doomsday Defense, featuring Ed (Too Tall) Jones, Thomas (Hollywood) Henderson and Harvey Martin, carried the Cowboys to Super Bowl XII. In the first quarter Martin forced a fumble which he recovered at the Minnesota 39. Two plays later Roger Staubach faked a screen pass and threw deep to Golden Richards for a touchdown. Danny White faked a punt to set up the Cowboys' second touchdown, a five-yard run by Robert Newhouse. That was more than Dallas would need as the Cowboys defense shut down Chuck Foreman's running attack and disrupted receiver Ahmad Rashad with double coverage all day.

**AMERICAN FOOTBALL CONFERENCE**

| | | | | |
|---|---|---|---|---|
| Oakland Raiders..............3 | 0 | 0 | 14— | 17 |
| Denver Broncos ...............7 | 0 | 7 | 6— | 20 |

### FIRST QUARTER
Oakland: FG Mann 20.
Denver: Moses 74 pass from Morton (Turner kick).

### THIRD QUARTER
Denver: Keyworth 1 run (Turner kick).

### FOURTH QUARTER
Oakland: Casper 7 pass from Stabler (Mann kick).
Denver: Moses 12 pass from Morton (pass failed).
Oakland: Casper 17 pass from Stabler (Mann kick).

A: 75,004.

**Recap:** The defending champion Raiders returned to the playoffs as the wildcard team and faced Denver for the AFC title after winning a 37–31 overtime classic against the Colts. Craig Morton's 74-yard bomb to Haven Moses gave Denver an early 7–3 lead. The Broncos got a break in the third quarter when Rob Lytle's fumble at the two was whistled dead by the officials and Jon Keyworth bulled in on the next play to put them up 14–3. Oakland closed to 14–10 on Dave Casper's seven-yard scoring catch, but Morton threw 12 yards to Moses to make it 20–10. Denver ran out the clock for the win after Casper's second TD of the quarter had closed the gap again.

## Super Bowl XII

| | | | | |
|---|---|---|---|---|
| Dallas Cowboys ...........10 | 3 | 7 | 7— | 27 |
| Denver Broncos .............0 | 0 | 10 | 0— | 10 |

### FIRST QUARTER
Dallas: Dorsett 3 run (Herrera kick).
Dallas: FG Herrera 35.

### SECOND QUARTER
Dallas: FG Herrera 43.

### THIRD QUARTER
Denver: FG Turner 47.
Dallas: Johnson 45 pass from Staubach (Herrera kick).
Denver: Lytle 1 run (Turner kick).

### FOURTH QUARTER
Dallas: Richards 29 pass from Newhouse (Herrera kick).

A: 75,583. At New Orleans.

**Recap:** On the sidelines toward the end of this contest Dallas players squeezed orange drinking cups in their fists for the television cameras, symbolic of what they did to Craig Morton in his orange jersey and to the Orange Crush defense in the 27–10 rout. The Broncos were simply outmanned. Dallas, with diverse weapons on offense and defense, fulfilled expectations in the win against the overachieving Broncos and their hobbled veteran quarterback Morton, a Cowboy teammate of Roger Staubach's in Super Bowl V. The game began sloppily with a bungled double reverse that cost the Cowboys nine yards. On Denver's second series Morton attempted three straight passes, the last of which was intercepted by Randy Hughes at the Denver 25. Dallas scored in five plays, Tony Dorsett taking it three yards off-tackle for the touchdown. Morton was intercepted again on the Broncos' next possession, when his second-down pass over the middle was tipped by Bob Breunig into the hands of cornerback Aaron Kyle, who returned it 19 yards to the Broncos' 35. Dallas settled for three points on Efren Herrera's 35-yard kick. Herrera added another field goal in the second to give Dallas a 13–0 halftime lead. The Cowboys were penalized for having 12 men on the field when the Broncos unsuccessfully faked a punt in the third quarter. Denver's drive continued and resulted in a 47-yard field goal by Jim Turner. Dallas increased its lead to 20–3 on Butch Johnson's diving catch of a 45-yard Staubach pass in the end zone. Rick Upchurch returned the ensuing kickoff 67 yards to set up the Broncos' only TD, a one-yard run by Rob Lytle. Dallas added the final points on a halfback option pass from Robert Newhouse to Golden Richards in the left side of the end zone.

## 1978

### NATIONAL FOOTBALL CONFERENCE

| | | | | |
|---|---|---|---|---|
| **Dallas Cowboys** | 0 | 0 | 7 | 21—28 |
| **Los Angeles Rams** | 0 | 0 | 0 | 0— 0 |

#### THIRD QUARTER
Dallas: Dorsett 5 run (Septien kick).

#### FOURTH QUARTER
Dallas: Laidlaw 4 pass from Staubach (Septien kick).
Dallas: DuPree 11 pass from Staubach (Septien kick).
Dallas: Henderson 68 int return (Septien kick).

A: 71,086.

**Recap:** The Rams had lost three of the previous four NFC title games and were eager to finally break through to the Super Bowl. But it was not to be. The Rams' defense played well, shutting out the Cowboys for two quarters, but the offense stalled, and two interceptions by Dallas safety Charlie Waters against Los Angeles quarterback Pad Haden provided the Cowboys' offense with excellent field position. The first one led to the game's opening score on a five-yard dash by Tony Dorsett in the third period. Dallas got the ball at the Rams' 20 after Waters's next pick, and Roger Staubach passed four yards to Scott Laidlaw to capitalize on the turnover and make the score 14–0. Staubach threw another touchdown, and Thomas Henderson returned an interception 68 yards to finish the rout.

### NATIONAL FOOTBALL CONFERENCE

| | | | | |
|---|---|---|---|---|
| **Houston Oilers** | 0 | 3 | 2 | 0— 5 |
| **Pittsburgh Steelers** | 14 | 17 | 3 | 0—34 |

#### FIRST QUARTER
Pittsburgh: Harris 7 run (Gerela kick).
Pittsburgh: Bleier 15 run (Gerela kick).

#### SECOND QUARTER
Houston: FG Fritsch 19.
Pittsburgh: Swann 29 pass fom Bradshaw (Gerela kick).
Pittsburgh: Stallworth 17 pass from Bradshaw (Gerela kick).
Pittsburgh: FG Gerela 37.

#### THIRD QUARTER
Pittsburgh: FG Gerela 22..
Houston: Safety. Bleier tackled in end zone.

A: 50,725.

**Recap:** Pittsburgh backfield partners Rocky Bleier and Franco Harris each ran for a touchdown in the first quarter and an Oiler field goal made it 14–3 before the Steelers racked up 17 points in 48 seconds to close out the half. Terry Bradshaw hit Lynn Swann with a 29-yard scoring pass, the Oilers fumbled the kickoff, and Bradshaw threw to John Stallworth for another score. Houston then fumbled on its first play from scrimmage, leading to a Pittsburgh field goal and a 31–3 Steeler lead at halftime.

## Super Bowl XIII

| | | | | |
|---|---|---|---|---|
| **Pittsburgh Steelers** | 7 | 14 | 0 | 14—35 |
| **Dallas Cowboys** | 7 | 7 | 3 | 14—31 |

#### FIRST QUARTER
Pittsburgh: Stallworth 28 pass from Bradshaw (Gerela kick).
Dallas: Hill 39 pass from Staubach (Septien kick).

#### SECOND QUARTER
Dallas: Hegman 37 fum recovery return.
Pittsburgh: Stallworth 75 pass from Bradshaw (Gerela kick).
Pittsburgh: Bleier 7 pass from Bradshaw (Gerela kick).

#### THIRD QUARTER
Dallas: FG Septien 27.

#### FOURTH QUARTER
Pittsburgh: Harris 22 run (Gerela kick).
Pittsburgh: Swann 18 pass from Bradshaw (Gerela kick).
Dallas: DuPree 7 pass from Staubach (Septien kick).
Dallas: Johnson 4 pass from Staubach (Septien kick).

A: 79,484. At Miami.

**Recap:** The combatants of Super Bowl X returned for XIII and equaled the excitement of their previous meeting. Dallas was determined to defend its crown, and Pittsburgh—now blessed with a more mature Bradshaw in addition to Lynn Swann and John Stallworth, the dynastic duo—was equally intent on regaining the title they had earned three years before. The Steelers struck first, barely five minutes into the game, when Bradshaw connected with Stallworth for a 28-yard touchdown pass after the Cowboys fumbled a reverse. Roger Staubach answered, throwing 39 yards for a touchdown to Tony Hill. Dallas took the lead when Thomas (Hollywood) Henderson stripped Bradshaw and Mike Hegman returned the fumble 37 yards for a score. Stallworth tied it for Pittsburgh by catching a 10-yard pass from Bradshaw and bolting 65 yards through the middle to the end zone. Pittsburgh got the ball back and took a 21–14 halftime lead on Bradshaw's seven-yard rollout pass to Rocky Bleier. Tight end Jackie Smith dropped a 10-yarder in the third from Staubach that would have tied it, and the Cowboys had to settle for three as the quarter ended with Pittsburgh on top 21–17. A highly disputed interference call gave Pittsburgh 33 yards to sustain their next drive, which ended with Franco Harris running 22 yards for the score. The Cowboys fumbled the subsequent shanked kickoff, and Pittsburgh took over at the Dallas 18. Bradshaw fired to Swann in the back of the end zone on the next play. Staubach cut the lead with two late scoring throws, but the Steelers recovered the Cowboys late onside kick and killed the clock.

## 1979

**NATIONAL FOOTBALL CONFERENCE**

| | | | | |
|---|---|---|---|---|
| **Los Angeles Rams**...........0 | 6 | 0 | 3— | 9 |
| **Tampa Bay Buccaneers**..0 | 0 | 0 | 0— | 0 |

### SECOND QUARTER

Los Angeles: FG Corral 19.
Los Angeles: FG Corral 21.

### FOURTH QUARTER

Los Angeles: FG Corral 23.

A: 72,033.

**Recap:** Having entered the league only two years before as an expansion team, the Tampa Bay Buccaneers captured the fancy of the nation by making it all the way to the NFC title game. But their opponent, the Rams, were also overachievers, getting this far with a 9–7 regular-season record and dim prospects. They shocked Dallas in the first round with the same strong defense that proved itself against the Buccaneers, forcing Tampa Bay quarterback Doug Williams to miss his first eight passes. The Rams' offense, while not dominant, gained steady bits of yardage on the ground, with Cullen Bryant and Wendell Tyler doing the legwork. A pair of Frank Corral field goals in the second quarter gave the Rams a lead; a third from 23 yards out in the fourth put them ahead by nine. With Williams sidelined due to an injured arm, the Buccaneers mounted but one serious threat, which evaporated with an errant fourth-down pass.

**AMERICAN FOOTBALL CONFERENCE**

| | | | | |
|---|---|---|---|---|
| **Houston Oilers**..................7 | 3 | 0 | 3— | 13 |
| **Pittsburgh Steelers**.........3 | 14 | 0 | 10— | 27 |

### FIRST QUARTER

Houston: Perry 75 int return (Fritsch kick).
Pittsburgh: FG Bahr 21.

### SECOND QUARTER

Houston: FG Fritsch 27.
Pittsburgh: Cunningham 16 pass from Bradshaw (Bahr kick).
Pittsburgh: Stallworth 20 pass from Bradshaw (Bahr kick).

### FOURTH QUARTER

Houston: FG Fritsch 23.
Pittsburgh: FG Bahr 39.
Pittsburgh: Bleier 4 run (Bahr kick).

A: 50,475.

**Recap:** Pittsburgh shut down Houston back Earl Campbell to win this rubber match of AFC Central rivals. Houston took a 10–3 lead behind Vernon Perry's 75-yard interception return, but Terry Bradshaw put his mates up 17–10 with scoring throws to Bennie Cunningham and John Stallworth. After the Oilers were forced to settle for three when a Houston catch deep in the end zone was ruled to have been out of bounds, Pittsburgh tacked on 10 points for the final margin of victory.

## Super Bowl XIV

| | | | | |
|---|---|---|---|---|
| **Pittsburgh Steelers**........3 | 7 | 7 | 14— | 31 |
| **Los Angeles Rams** .........7 | 6 | 6 | 0— | 19 |

### FIRST QUARTER

Pittsburgh: FG Bahr 41.
Los Angeles: Bryant 1 run (Corral kick).

### SECOND QUARTER

Pittsburgh: Harris 1 run (Bahr kick).
Los Angeles: FG Corral 31.
Los Angeles: FG Corral 45.

### THIRD QUARTER

Pittsburgh: Swann 47 pass from Bradshaw (Bahr kick).
Los Angeles: Smith 24 pass from McCutcheon (kick failed).

### FOURTH QUARTER

Pittsburgh: Stallworth 73 pass from Bradshaw (Bahr kick).
Pittsburgh: Harris 1 run (Bahr kick).

A: 103,985. At Pasadena.

**Recap:** Perhaps it was the proximity of the site to their home field, or the calming, nothing-to-lose sensation of being 12-point underdogs, or the desire to deny Pittsburgh their fourth Super Bowl ring in the decade; whatever the reason, the Los Angeles Rams did not play like a team just happy to be in the Super Bowl. But they must have felt that way—their 9–7 regular-season record was the worst ever for a Super Bowl contestant, and they had barely made the playoffs. But they had some cagey veterans and, after some early-season difficulties, were peaking at the right time. The Rams were in it to win it and proved as much by answering Pittsburgh's first-quarter field goal with a 45-yard kickoff return and a solid touchdown drive. Frank Corral's two second-quarter field goals gave them a 13–10 halftime lead. They were still ahead, after trading long touchdown passes (Los Angeles's coming on a 24-yard halfback option by Lawrence McCutcheon), when the third quarter came to a close. In fact, their lead would have been even larger had Nolan Cromwell not dropped what would have been an interception for a touchdown. The Rams punted after their first series in the fourth quarter, and then the roof fell in on them. On third-and-eight at the Pittsburgh 27, John Stallworth found himself in rare single coverage over the middle with cornerback Rod Perry; Ram safety Eddie Brown had missed an assignment. Bradshaw threw, Perry just missed and Stallworth made the catch, running untouched into the end zone. Jack Lambert sealed the win by picking off Vince Ferragamo, and another Bradshaw to Stallworth pass set up the final touchdown.

## 1980

| NATIONAL FOOTBALL CONFERENCE | | | | |
|---|---|---|---|---|
| **Dallas Cowboys** ............... | 0 | 7 | 0 | 0— 7 |
| **Philadelphia Eagles** ........ | 7 | 0 | 10 | 3—20 |

### FIRST QUARTER
Philadelphia: Montgomery 42 run (Franklin kick).

### SECOND QUARTER
Dallas: Dorsett 3 run (Septien kick).

### THIRD QUARTER
Philadelphia: FG Franklin 26.
Philadelphia: Harris 9 run (Franklin kick).

### FOURTH QUARTER
Philadelphia: FG Franklin 20.

A: 70,696.

**Recap:** Philadelphia and Dallas had split their regular-season meetings, with the Cowboys winning most recently, but the Eagles clearly dominated this frosty day at Veterans Stadium. Wilbert Montgomery started Philadelphia off on the right foot when he took a handoff on the game's second play and raced 42 yards for a touchdown. After tying it in the second quarter on Tony Dorsett's three-yard carry, Dallas lost two fumbles that led to a field goal and a touchdown for the Eagles. Tony Franklin kicked a fourth-quarter field goal, and Montgomery gained 194 yards, two shy of the playoff record, in the 20–7 triumph.

| AMERICAN FOOTBALL CONFERENCE | | | | |
|---|---|---|---|---|
| **Oakland Raiders** ............ | 21 | 7 | 3 | 3—34 |
| **San Diego Chargers** ........ | 7 | 7 | 10 | 3—27 |

### FIRST QUARTER
Oakland: Chester 65 pass from Plunkett (Bahr kick).
San Diego: Joiner 48 pass from Fouts (Benirschke kick).
Oakland: Plunkett 5 run (Bahr kick).
Oakland: King 21 pass from Plunkett (Bahr kick).

### SECOND QUARTER
Oakland: Van Eeghen 3 run (Bahr kick).
San Diego: Joiner 8 pass from Fouts (Benirschke kick).

### THIRD QUARTER
San Diego: FG Benirschke 26.
San Diego: Muncie 6 run (Benirschke kick).
Oakland: FG Bahr 27.

### FOURTH QUARTER
Oakland: FG Bahr 33.
San Diego: FG Benirschke 27.

A: 52,428.

**Recap:** This high-scoring affair saw San Diego rally from a 28–7 deficit only to be cut short at 28–24 when the Raiders established their running game and ate time while containing Dan Fouts and Co. on defense.

## Super Bowl XV

| | | | | |
|---|---|---|---|---|
| **Oakland Raiders** .......... | 14 | 0 | 10 | 3—27 |
| **Philadelphia Eagles** ....... | 0 | 3 | 0 | 7—10 |

### FIRST QUARTER
Oakland: Branch 2 pass from Plunkett (Bahr kick).
Oakland: King 80 pass from Plunkett (Bahr kick).

### SECOND QUARTER
Philadelphia: FG Franklin 30.

### THIRD QUARTER
Oakland: Branch 29 pass from Plunkett (Bahr kick).
Oakland: FG Bahr 46.

### FOURTH QUARTER
Philadelphia: Krepfle 8 pass from Jaworski (Franklin kick).
Oakland:FG Bahr 35.

A: 76,135. At New Orleans.

**Recap:** In week 12 of the 1980 season the Philadelphia Eagles defeated the Oakland Raiders 10–7 in Philadelphia in a game *Sports Illustrated* suggested might be a Super Bowl preview. The two teams did reach the Big Game, the 11–5 Raiders as the second wildcard ever to make it that far, and the Eagles as 12–4 champions of the NFC East, but the result was vastly different from the week 12 outcome. In that game the Eagles sacked Oakland quarterback Jim Plunkett eight times; in the Super Bowl they got to him just once. The differences didn't end there. Oakland dominated from the outset, intercepting Ron Jaworski on the third play from scrimmage and returning to the Philadelphia 30-yard line. The Raiders scored in seven plays, Plunkett throwing to Cliff Branch in the right side of the end zone. The defenses then held for the better part of the quarter until a scrambling Plunkett threw to Kenny King on the left side and King zipped untouched down the sideline for a Super Bowl–record 80-yard touchdown. The Eagles kicked a field goal and had a chance to get back in the game before halftime with first down at the Oakland 11. But Jaworski threw three straight incompletions, and Tony Franklin's field goal attempt was blocked by Ted Hendricks. Plunkett poured it on in the second half, moving Oakland 76 yards in five plays and capping the drive with a 29-yard toss to Branch for the receiver's second TD. Chris Bahr kicked a 46-yarder, and the Raiders led 24–3 entering the fourth quarter. The Eagles drove for their only touchdown early in the period on an eight-yard toss from Jaworski to Keith Krepfle after a kickoff clipping penalty forced them to start on their own 12-yard line. Bahr's 35-yard field goal completed the scoring. It was a sweet victory for game-MVP Plunkett, who had been waived by the 49ers and then spent two years as a backup to Ken Stabler.

## 1981

### NATIONAL FOOTBALL CONFERENCE

| | | | | |
|---|---|---|---|---|
| Dallas Cowboys | 10 | 7 | 0 | 10—27 |
| San Francisco 49ers | 7 | 7 | 7 | 7—28 |

#### FIRST QUARTER

San Francisco: Solomon 8 pass from Montana (Wersching kick).
Dallas: FG Septien 44.
Dallas: Hill 26 pass from D White (Septien kick).

#### SECOND QUARTER

San Francisco: Clark 20 pass from Montana (Wersching kick).
Dallas: Dorsett 5 run (Septien kick).

#### THIRD QUARTER

San Francisco: Davis 2 run (Wersching kick).

#### FOURTH QUARTER

Dallas: FG Septien 22.
Dallas: Cosbie 21 pass from D White (Septien kick).
San Francisco: Clark 6 pass from Montana (Wersching kick).

A: 60,525.

**Recap:** Forever known as "the Catch," Dwight Clark's leaping six-yard touchdown grab over an outstretched Everson Walls finished a drive that started on the 49er 10 and gave San Francisco a thrilling comeback victory in the game's final minute.

### AMERICAN FOOTBALL CONFERENCE

| | | | | |
|---|---|---|---|---|
| San Diego Chargers | 0 | 7 | 0 | 0— 7 |
| Cincinnati Bengals | 10 | 7 | 3 | 7—27 |

#### FIRST QUARTER

Cincinnati: FG Breech 31.
Cincinnati: M Harris 8 pass from Anderson (Breech kick).

#### SECOND QUARTER

San Diego: Winslow 33 pass from Fouts (Benirschke kick).
Cincinnati: Johnson 1 run (Breech kick).

#### THIRD QUARTER

Cincinnati: FG Breech 38.

#### FOURTH QUARTER

Cincinnati: Bass 3 pass from Anderson (Breech kick).

A: 46,302.

**Recap:** Pete Rozelle considered postponing the game due to the –11° temperature and the 59° below windchill, and the Chargers may have wished he had. After a second-quarter 33-yard Dan Fouts to Kellen Winslow touchdown pass, their offense stalled in the cold. Fouts was intercepted twice deep in Bengal territory and the Chargers hardly threatened thereafter. Cincinnati took a 17–7 lead at the half and added a field goal and a touchdown in the second half.

## Super Bowl XVI

| | | | | |
|---|---|---|---|---|
| San Francisco 49ers | 7 | 13 | 0 | 6—26 |
| Cincinnati Bengals | 0 | 0 | 7 | 14—21 |

#### FIRST QUARTER

San Francisco: Montana 1 run (Wersching kick).

#### SECOND QUARTER

San Francisco: Cooper 11 pass from Montana (Wersching kick).
San Francisco: FG Wersching 22.
San Francisco: FG Wersching 26.

#### THIRD QUARTER

Cincinnati: Anderson 5 run (Breech kick).

#### FOURTH QUARTER

Cincinnati: Ross 4 pass from Anderson (Breech kick).
San Francisco: FG Wersching 40.
San Francisco: FG Wersching 23.
Cincinnati: Ross 3 pass from Anderson (Breech kick).

A: 81,270. At Pontiac, Mich.

**Recap:** Bill Walsh led the San Francisco 49ers from a 6–10 third-place finish in 1980 to a league-leading 13–3 mark and the Super Bowl title in 1981. He did it with a ball-control offensive game plan featuring short, pinpoint passes thrown by Joe Montana, who was in his first full season as a starter. The Bengals had also gone 6–10 in 1980 and finished last in their division.They turned it around in 1981, establishing an AFC-best 12–4 record under coach Forrest Gregg's Lombardi-style, disciplined atmosphere. San Francisco scored on its first possession, an evenly controlled drive of 68 yards on 11 plays that ended with Montana sneaking in for the score from the one. Early in the second quarter the 49ers mounted another impressive drive, beginning at their own eight-yard line and taking 5:29 and 12 plays to cover the distance to the Bengal goal. The touchdown came on an 11-yard pass to Earl Cooper from Montana. Ray Wersching kicked two field goals, and the 49ers appeared to have the game in hand, leading 20–0 at the half. But Cincinnati took the second-half kickoff and drove 83 yards on nine plays for their first score, a five-yard improvised run by quarterback Ken Anderson. The Bengals' comeback was severely thwarted in the third quarter when, after a 49-yard Cris Collinsworth reception, they were denied the end zone on three successive tries from the one. It was an incredible, demoralizing stand by the 49er defense. The Bengals did cut the lead to 20–14 in the fourth quarter on a four-yard pass from Anderson to tight end Dan Ross, but Wersching responded with two field goals to make it 26–14. The Bengals scored a late touchdown, but their onside kick failed and the 49ers ran out the clock for their first Super Bowl victory. They would win three of the next eight with game-MVP Montana at quarterback.

## 1982

### NATIONAL FOOTBALL CONFERENCE

| | | | | |
|---|---|---|---|---|
| **Dallas Cowboys** ...............3 | 0 | 14 | 0— | 17 |
| **Washington Redskins**......7 | 7 | 7 | 10— | 31 |

#### FIRST QUARTER

Dallas: FG Septien 27.
Washington: Brown 19 pass from Theismann (Moseley kick).

#### SECOND QUARTER

Washington: Riggins 1 run (Moseley kick).

#### THIRD QUARTER

Dallas: Pearson 6 pass from Hogeboom (Septien kick).
Washington: Riggins 4 run (Moseley kick).
Dallas: Johnson 23 pass from Hogeboom (Septien kick).

#### FOURTH QUARTER

Washington: FG Moseley 29.
Washington: Grant 10 int return (Moseley kick).

A: 55,045.

**Recap:** With a line nicknamed the Hogs blocking for oxlike back John Riggins, the Redskins plowed through the strike-shortened season and held off the Cowboys in the NFC title game. Two fourth-quarter interceptions turned into 10 points for Washington and killed Dallas's efforts to close a 21–17 deficit.

### AMERICAN FOOTBALL CONFERENCE

| | | | | |
|---|---|---|---|---|
| **New York Jets** ..................0 | 0 | 0 | 0— | 0 |
| **Miami Dolphins**................0 | 0 | 7 | 7— | 14 |

#### THIRD QUARTER

Miami: Bennett 7 run (von Schamann kick).

#### FOURTH QUARTER

Miami: Duhe 35 int return (von Schamann kick).

A: 67,396.

**Recap:** Rain fell steadily the night before and continued throughout the game, turning Miami's uncovered Orange Bowl into a swampy mess. The grounds crew had neglected to use a tarp, claiming they expected the field to drain. The teams struggled in the muck for two quarters without scoring. Jets running back Freeman McNeil couldn't get a foothold, and quarterback Richard Todd had to contend with a slippery ball, the relentless Dolphin pass rush and double coverage on his favorite receiver, Wesley Walker. The Miami offense, quarterbacked by David Woodley, couldn't advance in the Florida swampland either, and, predictably, defense decided the outcome. Early in the third quarter Miami linebacker A.J. Duhe intercepted a pass off the fingertips of the Jets' Mike Augustyniak, and the Dolphins moved 48 yards in seven plays to take a 7–0 lead. Duhe picked off another Todd pass in the fourth quarter and ran 35 yards through the rain for the clinching score.

## Super Bowl XVII

| | | | | |
|---|---|---|---|---|
| **Miami Dolphins** ..............7 | 10 | 0 | 0— | 17 |
| **Washington Redskins** ....0 | 10 | 3 | 14— | 27 |

#### FIRST QUARTER

Miami: Cefalo 76 pass from Woodley (von Schamann kick).

#### SECOND QUARTER

Washington: FG Moseley 31.
Miami: FG von Schamann 20.
Washington: Garrett 4 pass from Theismann (Moseley kick).
Miami: Walker 98 kickoff return (von Schamann).

#### THIRD QUARTER

Washington: FG Moseley 20.

#### FOURTH QUARTER

Washington: Riggins 43 run (Moseley kick).
Washington: Brown 6 pass from Theismann (Moseley kick).

A: 103,667. At Pasadena.

**Recap:** Labor disputes took 57 days out of the regular season and cut it almost in half, down to nine games. The strike also gave birth to a somewhat hokey playoff tournament that included 16 teams, four more than it excluded. Moving through that tournament and into a rematch of Super Bowl VII were the Washington Redskins and the Miami Dolphins. Miami grabbed a 7–0 lead on their second series, when Jimmy Cefalo took advantage of botched coverage and bolted 76 yards with a sideline pass from David Woodley. The teams traded field goals and Miami led 10–3 early in the second quarter. The Redskins tied it with an 11-play, 80-yard drive late in the half. But Miami's Fulton Walker took the ensuing kickoff, started left, cut back behind a block and ran down the middle for a Super Bowl–record 98-yard touchdown return to give the Dolphins a 17–10 lead at the break. Toward the end of the third quarter, Joe Theismann averted disaster by knocking his blocked pass out of the hands of Miami linebacker Kim Bokamper, who was on his way into the end zone to put Miami up by 11. The heads-up play kept Washington close and set the stage for John Riggins's game-breaking, 43-yard touchdown run in the final period. Miami's Don McNeal slipped on the fourth-and-one play while following the tight end in motion, and that split-second delay prevented him from getting a line on Riggins as the big back turned the corner. McNeal lunged, clawing vainly at Riggins, who shed him easily and barreled for the score. Woodley and the Miami offense were again unable to move, and Washington scored again when Theismann hit Charlie Brown with a six-yard TD pass.

## 1983

### NATIONAL FOOTBALL CONFERENCE

| | | | | |
|---|---|---|---|---|
| San Francisco 49ers | 0 | 0 | 0 | 21—21 |
| Washington Redskins | 0 | 7 | 14 | 3—24 |

#### SECOND QUARTER
Washington: Riggins 4 run (Moseley kick).

#### THIRD QUARTER
Washington: Riggins 1 run (Moseley kick).
Washington: Brown 70 pass from Theismann (Moseley kick).

#### FOURTH QUARTER
San Francisco: Wilson 5 pass from Montana (Wersching kick).
San Francisco: Solomon 76 pass from Montana (Wersching kick).
San Francisco: Wilson 12 pass from Montana (Wersching kick).
Washington: FG Moseley 25.

A: 55,363.

**Recap:** RFK Stadium was packed for this matchup of the previous two Super Bowl winners. Washington jumped ahead 21–0 behind the arm of Joe Theismann and the legs of John Riggins. But three Joe Montana touchdown passes, including a 76-yarder to Freddie Solomon, brought the 49ers storming back to tie it with seven minutes left. In the end, though, Montana's heroics weren't enough as a Mark Moseley field goal with 40 seconds remaining won it for the Redskins.

### AMERICAN FOOTBALL CONFERENCE

| | | | | |
|---|---|---|---|---|
| Seattle Seahawks | 0 | 0 | 7 | 7—14 |
| Los Angeles Raiders | 3 | 17 | 7 | 3—30 |

#### FIRST QUARTER
Los Angeles: FG Bahr 20.

#### SECOND QUARTER
Los Angeles: Hawkins 1 run (Bahr kick).
Los Angeles: Hawkins 5 run (Bahr kick).
Los Angeles: FG Bahr 45.

#### THIRD QUARTER
Los Angeles: Allen 3 pass from Plunkett (Bahr kick).
Seattle: Doornink 11 pass from Zorn (N Johnson kick).

#### FOURTH QUARTER
Oakland: FG Bahr 35.
Seattle: Young 9 pass from Zorn (N Johnson kick).

A: 88,734.

**Recap:** The Seahawks, like fellow expansion-team Tampa Bay before them, reached the conference title game in their first playoffs ever. Also like Tampa Bay, they were turned back at the Super Bowl gates, though in far more unkindly fashion than the Bucs had been. The Raiders never let them in the contest, scoring 27 points before Seattle got on the board and intercepting the Seahawks five times during the rout.

## Super Bowl XVIII

| | | | | |
|---|---|---|---|---|
| Los Angeles Raiders | 7 | 14 | 14 | 3—38 |
| Washington Redskins | 0 | 3 | 6 | 0— 9 |

#### FIRST QUARTER
Los Angeles: Jensen recovered blocked punt in end zone (Bahr kick).

#### SECOND QUARTER
Los Angeles: Branch 12 pass from Plunkett (Bahr kick).
Washington: FG Moseley 24.
Los Angeles: Squirek 5 int return (Bahr kick).

#### THIRD QUARTER
Washington: Riggins 1 run (kick blocked).
Los Angeles: Allen 5 run (Bahr kick).
Los Angeles: Allen 74 run (Bahr kick).

#### FOURTH QUARTER
Los Angeles: FG Bahr 21.

A: 72,920. At Tampa.

**Recap:** Led by aggressive hitters like Mike Haynes, Lester Hayes, Howie Long, Lyle Alzado and Matt Millen, the fearsome Los Angeles Raiders defense was the story of Super Bowl XVIII. The defending champion Washington Redskins, who scored an average of 33.8 points per game during their 14–2 regular season, simply could not handle the attacking Raider defense. On the Redskins' first series Joe Theismann threw three passes to Art Monk on the left side, testing Haynes. The cornerback broke up the first one and covered Monk tight on the next two, causing incompletions. The Redskins then suffered a blocked punt at the hands of special-teamer Derrick Jensen, who fell on the ball in the end zone for the Raiders' first score. Los Angeles punter Ray Guy averted disaster early in the second quarter when he made a fabulous leaping catch of an errant snap and managed to get off a 42-yard punt. The Raiders scored on their next series with a 12-yard pass from Jim Plunkett to Cliff Branch. The two had hooked up for a 50-yard gain two plays before. After a Washington field goal, the Raider defense struck again, Jack Squirek intercepting Theismann and running five yards for a touchdown to make the score 21–3 at the half. Washington marched 70 yards and scored on a one-yard run by John Riggins to start the second half, but the Raiders came right back with Marcus Allen's five-yard TD carry. The Redskins went three-and-out twice, were stopped on fourth-and-one by the swarming Raiders, and then game-MVP Allen broke their backs with a 74-yard TD scamper. A fumble-causing sack, an interception by Haynes and a Chris Bahr field goal completed the shellacking.

## 1984

### NATIONAL FOOTBALL CONFERENCE

| | | | | |
|---|---|---|---|---|
| Chicago Bears | 0 | 0 | 0— | 0 |
| San Francisco 49ers | 3 | 3 | 7 | 10—23 |

#### FIRST QUARTER
San Francisco: FG Wersching 21.

#### SECOND QUARTER
San Francisco: FG Wersching 22.

#### THIRD QUARTER
San Francisco: Tyler 9 run (Wersching kick).

#### FOURTH QUARTER
San Francisco: Solomon 10 pass from Montana (Wersching kick).
San Francisco: FG Wersching 34.

A: 61,040.

**Recap:** The Bear's formidable defense carried them to the NFC title game, where they faced a 49er team that had an offense to go with its equally strong defense. Chicago limited Joe Montana's machine to just two field goals in the first half but failed to score at all themselves. The second half saw San Francisco increase their pass rush—they sacked Bear quarterback Steve Fuller nine times all told—while beating the Chicago defense for two touchdowns and a field goal to record the shutout.

### AMERICAN FOOTBALL CONFERENCE

| | | | | |
|---|---|---|---|---|
| Pittsburgh Steelers | 7 | 7 | 7 | 7—28 |
| Miami Dolphins | 7 | 17 | 14 | 7—45 |

#### FIRST QUARTER
Miami: Clayton 40 pass from Marino (von Schamann kick).
Pittsburgh: Erenberg 7 run (Anderson kick).

#### SECOND QUARTER
Miami: FG von Schamann 26.
Pittsburgh: Stallworth 65 pass from Malone (Anderson kick).
Miami: Duper 41 pass from Marino (von Schamann kick).
Miami: Nathan 2 run (von Schamann kick).

#### THIRD QUARTER
Miami: Duper 36 pass from Marino (von Schamann kick).
Pittsburgh: Stallworth 19 pass from Malone (Anderson kick).
Miami: Bennett 1 run (von Schamann kick).

#### FOURTH QUARTER
Miami: Moore 6 pass from Marino (von Schamann kick).
Pittsburgh: Capers 29 pass from Malone (Anderson kick).

A: 76,029.

## Super Bowl XIX

| | | | | |
|---|---|---|---|---|
| San Francisco 49ers | 7 | 21 | 10 | 0—38 |
| Miami Dolphins | 10 | 6 | 0 | 0—16 |

#### FIRST QUARTER
Miami: FG von Schamann 37.
San Francisco: Monroe 33 pass from Montana (Wersching kick).
Miami: Johnson 2 pass from Marino (von Schamann kick).

#### SECOND QUARTER
San Francisco: Craig 8 pass from Montana (Wersching kick).
San Francisco: Montana 6 run (Wersching kick).
San Francisco: Craig 2 run (Wersching kick).
Miami: FG von Schamann 31.
Miami: FG von Schamann 30.

#### THIRD QUARTER
San Francisco: FG Wersching 27.
San Francisco: Craig 16 pass from Montana (Wersching kick).

A: 84,059. At Stanford, Calif.

**Recap:** The Miami Dolphins put on an aerial show in the AFC title game against Pittsburgh with their second-year quarterback Dan Marino passing for 421 yards and four touchdowns. Marino had thrown an NFL-record 48 TD passes, and his receivers Mark Clayton and Mark Duper had torn up the AFC in 1984, the team going 14–2. But the San Francisco 49ers were a more complete unit. They put 10 players in the Pro Bowl, including the entire starting secondary; they had a precision offense led by the great Joe Montana; they posted a 15–1 record; and they blew the Dolphins away in Super Bowl XIX before a partisan Stanford Stadium crowd. The game began well enough for the Dolphins as their opening drive culminated in a field goal. They even answered the 49ers' first touchdown with a lightning drive on five Marino passes to take a 10–7 lead. But that was the last lead the Dolphins would hold, as San Francisco dominated the final three quarters, shredding the notoriously soft Miami defense for 21 points in the second quarter alone. Taking advantage of a weak punt, Joe Montana marched his team 47 yards in four plays to take the lead at 14–10. Miami went three-and-out again, and the 49ers were back in their end zone in six plays, Montana taking six yards for the score. Another shanked Miami punt gave the 49ers the ball at midfield, and they ground up the yardage in nine plays, Roger Craig scoring his second touchdown on a two-yard run. Marino drove his team to a field goal and a fumbled kickoff led to another three Miami points before the half. But the Dolphins were shut out the rest of the way as San Francisco tacked on 10 more before the scoreless fourth quarter.

## 1985

| NATIONAL FOOTBALL CONFERENCE | | | | |
|---|---|---|---|---|
| Los Angeles Rams............ | 0 | 0 | 0— | 0 |
| Chicago Bears ............... | 10 | 0 | 7 | 7—24 |

### FIRST QUARTER

Chicago: McMahon 16 run (Butler kick).
Chicago: FG Butler 34.

### THIRD QUARTER

Chicago: Gault 22 pass from McMahon (Butler kick).

### FOURTH QUARTER

Chicago: Marshall 52 fum recovery return (Butler kick).

A: 63,522.

**Recap:** Both teams were coming off shutout victories, but the Bears cut through the Los Angeles defense on their first series, going 66 yards in five plays to take a 7–0 lead. Jim McMahon scrambled 16 yards for the touchdown, and it would prove all they needed to win. The Chicago defense clamped down, and Kevin Butler kicked a 34-yard field goal on the Bears' next possession. The Rams recovered a fumble at the Chicago 21 late in the half but failed to capitalize, then got steamrolled in the second half. McMahon hit Willie Gault with a 22-yard touchdown pass in the third quarter, and Richard Dent forced a fumble in the final period that Wilber Marshall returned 52 yards for a touchdown.

| AMERICAN FOOTBALL CONFERENCE | | | | |
|---|---|---|---|---|
| New England Patriots ..... | 3 | 14 | 7 | 7—31 |
| Miami Dolphins................ | 0 | 7 | 0 | 7—14 |

### FIRST QUARTER

New England: FG Franklin 23.

### SECOND QUARTER

Miami: Johnson 10 pass from Marino (Reveiz kick).
New England: Collins 4 pass from Eason (Franklin kick).
New England: D Ramsey 1 pass from Eason (Franklin kick).

### THIRD QUARTER

New England: Weathers 2 pass from Eason (Franklin kick).

### FOURTH QUARTER

Miami: Nathan 2 pass from Marino (Reveiz kick).
New England: Tatupu 1 run (Franklin kick).

A: 74,978.

**Recap:** Miami, AFC East champs over the wildcard Patriots, fumbled away a chance to return to the Super Bowl as three Dolphin turnovers resulted in New England scores. On the game's first play, Tony Nathan fumbled, the result being a Patriots field goal. Still, the Dolphins were in the game until Lorenzo Hampton's fumble of the second-half kickoff led to a two-yard TD toss from Tony Eason to Robert Weathers that gave the Pats an insurmountable 17-point lead.

## Super Bowl XX

| | | | | |
|---|---|---|---|---|
| Chicago Bears ............. | 13 | 10 | 21 | 2—46 |
| New England Patriots.... | 3 | 0 | 0 | 7—10 |

### FIRST QUARTER

New England: FG Franklin 36.
Chicago: FG Butler 28.
Chicago: FG Butler 24.
Chicago: Suhey 11 run (Butler kick).

### SECOND QUARTER

Chicago: McMahon 2 run (Butler kick).
Chicago: FG Butler 24.

### THIRD QUARTER

Chicago: McMahon 1 run (Butler kick).
Chicago: Phillips 28 int return (Butler kick).
Chicago: Perry 1 run (Butler kick).

### FOURTH QUARTER

New England: Fryar 8 pass from Grogan (Franklin kick).
Chicago: Safety. Waechter tackled Grogan in end zone.

A: 73,818. At New Orleans.

**Recap:** Riding an unprecedented two consecutive shutouts and a 15–1 record into New Orleans, the Chicago Bears were fully confident of victory and gunning for a third straight shutout. They easily secured the former and if not for an early fumble by their offense and a meaningless late touchdown, would have accomplished the latter. The Bears devastated the wildcard Patriots, putting them in the red for total offensive yardage in the first half at –19. Walter Payton's fumble at the Chicago 19 early on led to a New England field goal, but the Patriots had been unable to move a single yard in three plays before turning to the kicker. Chicago equaled them on their next drive and forced two fumbles before the quarter ended that led to 10 points and a 13–3 lead. Things only got worse after that for the Patriots, who committed six turnovers and trailed by as much as 44–3 in the game. Jim McMahon scored for the Bears on a two-yard run early in the second quarter, and Kevin Butler added a 24-yard field goal to give them a 23–3 halftime lead. They didn't let up, gaining 60 yards on their first play of the second half with a McMahon-to-Willie Gault bomb. That set up McMahon's one-yard touchdown run to make it 30–3. Three plays later it was 37–3, when Reggie Phillips intercepted Steve Grogan and ran 28 yards for a touchdown. Just two plays after that, New England fumbled and Wilber Marshall returned it 13 yards to set up William (the Refrigerator) Perry's one-yard TD smash. The Bears held New England to 123 yards of offense and an average of 2.3 yards per offensive play in the lopsided affair.

## 1986

### NATIONAL FOOTBALL CONFERENCE

| | | | | |
|---|---|---|---|---|
| **Washington Redskins**......0 | 0 | 0 | 0— | 0 |
| **New York Giants**............10 | 7 | 0 | 0— | 17 |

#### FIRST QUARTER

New York: FG Allegre 47.
New York: Manuel 11 pass from Simms (Allegre kick).

#### SECOND QUARTER

New York: Morris 1 run (Allegre kick).

A: 76,633.

**Recap:** The Washington Redskins managed only two first downs in the first half on this gusty day in East Rutherford, NJ. Hindered by both onrushing wind and Giants defenders, quarterback Jay Schroeder struggled. His New York counterpart Phil Simms had the wind at his back as he led his team to 10 first-quarter points, putting Raul Allegre in position to kick a 47-yard field goal and connecting with Lionel Manuel on an 11-yard touchdown pass. Schroeder, with the wind in his favor, completed a 48-yard toss to receiver Art Monk in the second session, but the Redskins failed to capitalize, botching the snap on Jess Atkinson's 51-yard field goal attempt. Simms led another touchdown drive in the second quarter, capping it with a handoff to Joe Morris, who took it over from the one. There was no further scoring as the conservative Giants offense ate up the clock and its defense relinquished nothing.

### AMERICAN FOOTBALL CONFERENCE

| | | | | |
|---|---|---|---|---|
| **Denver Broncos** .........0 | 10 | 3 | 7 | 3—23 |
| **Cleveland Browns**......7 | 3 | 0 | 10 | 0—20 |

#### FIRST QUARTER

Cleveland: Fontenot 3 pass from Kosar (Moseley kick).

#### SECOND QUARTER

Denver: FG Karlis 19.
Denver: Willhite 1 run (Moseley kick).
Cleveland: FG Moseley 29.

#### THIRD QUARTER

Denver: FG Karlis 26.

#### FOURTH QUARTER

Cleveland: Brennan 48 pass from Kosar (Moseley kick).
Denver: M Jackson 5 pass from Elway (Karlis kick).

#### OVERTIME

Denver: FG Karlis 33.

A: 79,915.

**Recap:** Denver stole an overtime victory at Cleveland behind two clutch John Elway drives, the first leading to a Mark Jackson touchdown catch to tie the game in the closing moments of regulation and the second to position Rich Karlis for the 33-yard game-winning field goal in overtime.

## Super Bowl XXI

| | | | | |
|---|---|---|---|---|
| **New York Giants**............7 | 2 | 17 | 13—39 | |
| **Denver Broncos** ...........10 | 0 | 0 | 10—20 | |

#### FIRST QUARTER

Denver: FG Karlis 48.
New York: Mowatt 6 pass from Simms (Allegre kick).
Denver: Elway 4 run (Karlis kick).

#### SECOND QUARTER

New York: Safety. Martin tackled Elway in end zone.

#### THIRD QUARTER

New York: Bavaro 13 pass from Simms (Allegre kick).
New York: FG Allegre 21.
New York: Morris 1 run (Allegre kick).

#### FOURTH QUARTER

New York: McConkey 6 pass from Simms (Allegre kick).
Denver: FG Karlis 28.
New York: Anderson 2 run (kick failed).
Denver: Johnson 47 pass from Elway (Karlis kick).

A: 101,063. At Pasadena.

**Recap:** This game belonged to Phil Simms. The New York Giants' quarterback completed a Super Bowl–record 88% of his passes, threw for three touchdowns and, during a sizzling sequence in the second half, completed 10 consecutive passes.

Coming into the game, Denver's quarterback John Elway had the spotlight for leading his team to a dramatic, come-from-behind overtime victory in the AFC championship against Cleveland. But Elway was a forgotten man after Simms's performance. Symptomatic of an emerging pattern, Denver first seized momentum, then lost it and caved in to lopsided defeat. They led 10–7 after the first quarter on a Rich Karlis field goal and a four-yard quarterback draw. Late in the half Giants defensive end George Martin caught Elway behind the goal line for a safety. After Karlis missed a field goal attempt, the half ended with Denver leading 10–9. New York began the second half with a nine-play, 63-yard touchdown drive to go ahead 16–10. Simms completed five passes along the way, including a 13-yard scoring toss to Mark Bavaro. Behind the running of Joe Morris, the Giants then set up Raul Allegre's 21-yard field goal. The defense stopped Denver on three plays again, and Simms threw a 44-yard flea-flicker pass to Phil McConkey, who was cut down at the one. Morris scored on the next play, and New York led 26–10 entering the final quarter. The Giants put the game away when McConkey caught a six-yard pass from Simms in the end zone after the ball deflected off Bavaro. Elway's 47-yard TD pass to Vance Johnson was too little too late.

## 1987

### NATIONAL FOOTBALL CONFERENCE

| | | | | |
|---|---|---|---|---|
| **Minnesota Vikings**............ | 0 | 7 | 0 | 3—10 |
| **Washington Redskins**...... | 7 | 0 | 3 | 7—17 |

#### FIRST QUARTER

Washington: Bryant 42 pass from Williams (Haji-Sheikh kick).

#### SECOND QUARTER

Minnesota: Lewis 23 pass from Wilson (C Nelson kick).

#### THIRD QUARTER

Washington: FG Haji-Sheikh 28.

#### FOURTH QUARTER

Minnesota: FG C Nelson 18.
Washington: Clark 7 pass from Williams (Haji-Sheikh kick).

A: 55,212.

**Recap:** The upstart Vikings made a bid to become the third wildcard team in history to reach the Super Bowl, but they were denied by a Redskin defense that sacked their quarterback eight times. Down 10–7 in the fourth quarter, Wade Wilson led Minnesota to the Washington one-yard line. But the Vikings were stuffed twice and had to settle for a tying field goal. After the Redskins went up 17–10 in the fourth quarter, Wilson fought back to the enemy six. But his fourth-down pass was dropped at the goal line.

### AMERICAN FOOTBALL CONFERENCE

| | | | | |
|---|---|---|---|---|
| **Cleveland Browns** ............ | 0 | 3 | 21 | 9—33 |
| **Denver Broncos** ............. | 14 | 7 | 10 | 7—38 |

#### FIRST QUARTER

Denver: Nattiel 8 pass from Elway (Karlis kick).
Denver: Sewell 1 run (Karlis kick).

#### SECOND QUARTER

Cleveland: FG Bahr 24.
Denver: Lang 1 run (Karlis kick).

#### THIRD QUARTER

Cleveland: Langhorne 18 pass from Kosar (Bahr kick).
Denver: Jackson 80 pass from Elway (Karlis kick).
Cleveland: Byner 32 pass from Kosar (Bahr kick).
Cleveland: Byner 4 run (Bahr kick).
Denver: FG Karlis 38.

#### FOURTH QUARTER

Cleveland: Slaughter 4 pass from Kosar (Bahr kick).
Denver: Winder 20 pass from Elway (Karlis kick).
Cleveland: Safety. Horan ran out of end zone.

A: 75,993.

**Recap:** This may have topped the overtime classic staged by these same two teams in the previous year's AFC title game. Denver went up 21–3, the Browns tied it late, Denver struck again, and the Browns were set to answer yet again when they fumbled the game away at the Broncos' eight.

## Super Bowl XXII

| | | | | |
|---|---|---|---|---|
| **Washington Redskins** .... | 0 | 35 | 0 | 7—42 |
| **Denver Broncos** ........... | 10 | 0 | 0 | 0—10 |

### FIRST QUARTER

Denver: Nattiel 56 pass from Elway (Karlis kick).
Denver: FG Karlis 24.

### SECOND QUARTER

Washington: Sanders 80 pass from Williams (Haji-Sheikh kick).
Washington: Clark 27 pass from Williams (Haji-Sheikh kick).
Washington: Smith 58 run (Haji-Sheikh kick).
Washington: Sanders 50 pass from Williams (Haji-Sheikh kick).
Washington: Didier 8 pass from Williams (Haji-Sheikh kick).

### FOURTH QUARTER

Washington: Smith 4 run (Haji-Sheikh kick).

A: 73,302. At San Diego.

**Recap:** John Elway returned to the Super Bowl in much the same way he had the year before—by leading his team in a slam-bang shootout victory over Cleveland. And, like the year before, he would be outshined by another, less-heralded quarterback in the big game. Doug Williams began the season as backup to Jay Schroeder and finished it as MVP of the Super Bowl. The first African-American ever to start at quarterback in the Super Bowl, Williams blitzed the Broncos with four touchdown passes in the second quarter alone to lead his team to a 42–10 trouncing. As they had the previous year, the Broncos took an early lead. Elway hurled a 56-yard touchdown to Ricky Nattiel on Denver's first play, just 1:57 into the game, a Super Bowl record. Rich Karlis's added a field goal on his team's next series for a 10–0 lead. On the ensuing kickoff Ricky Sanders fumbled after being hit by Ken Bell at the 16. But after a huge pileup, Washington emerged with the ball, thereby averting a potential 17-point deficit. The teams traded punts and then, on Washington's first play of the second quarter, Doug Williams hung out a pass at midfield for Sanders, who made the catch and raced 80 yards for the touchdown. The play seemed to open the floodgates for the Redskins, who scored touchdowns on their next four series. There was a 27-yard pass to Gary Clark that gave them the lead; a 58-yard TD sprint by rookie Timmy Smith; another bomb to Sanders, this one for 50 yards; and then an eight-yard flip to Clint Didier. By the time the blitz was over, Washington led 35–10 with just over a minute to go in the half. Williams had thrown for 228 yards in the quarter, Smith had rushed for 122. The second half was a formality. Smith rushed for a record 204 yards, breaking one for 32 in the fourth quarter to set up his second touchdown, which completed the scoring.

## 1988

### NATIONAL FOOTBALL CONFERENCE

| | | | | |
|---|---|---|---|---|
| San Francisco 49ers .......7 | 7 | 7 | 7—28 |
| Chicago Bears .................0 | 3 | 0 | 0— 3 |

#### FIRST QUARTER

San Francisco: Rice 61 pass from Montana (Cofer kick).

#### SECOND QUARTER

San Francisco: Rice 27 pass from Montana (Cofer kick).
Chicago: FG Butler 25.

#### THIRD QUARTER

San Francisco: Frank 5 pass from Montana (Cofer kick).

#### FOURTH QUARTER

San Francisco: Rathman 4 run (Cofer kick).

A: 64,830.

**Recap:** San Francisco's offense, especially Joe Montana and Jerry Rice, dominated the Bears on this chilly day in Chicago. Rice was magnificent, beating cornerback Mike Richardson to a short sideline pass in the first quarter and outracing the secondary 61 yards to the end zone. His shoestring 27-yarder in the second quarter gave the 49ers a 14–0 lead. Montana led a 78-yard scoring drive to start the second half, and Tom Rathman added the final blow in the fourth quarter.

### AMERICAN FOOTBALL CONFERENCE

| | | | | |
|---|---|---|---|---|
| Buffalo Bills .....................0 | 10 | 0 | 0—10 |
| Cincinnati Bengals ..........7 | 7 | 0 | 7—21 |

#### FIRST QUARTER

Cincinnati: Woods 1 run (Breech kick).

#### SECOND QUARTER

Buffalo: Reed 9 pass from Kelly (Norwood kick).
Cincinnati: Brooks 10 pass from Esiason (Breech kick).
Buffalo: FG Norwood 39.

#### FOURTH QUARTER

Cincinnati: Woods 1 run (Breech kick).

A: 59,747.

**Recap:** Ickey Woods shuffled for 102 yards on 29 carries, and the Bengals' defense held Buffalo's vaunted offense to 181 total yards as they advanced to the Super Bowl. Woods bulled over from the one to start the scoring. After Buffalo tied it in the second quarter on Andre Reed's nine-yard reception from Jim Kelly, Boomer Esiason replied with a 10-yard scoring strike to the versatile James Brooks. Scott Norwood's 39-yard field goal cut the Bengals' lead to 14–10 at halftime. A fake punt and a Buffalo personal foul sustained a fourth-quarter Cincinnati drive that ended with Woods plunging across from the one to secure the victory.

## Super Bowl XXIII

| | | | | |
|---|---|---|---|---|
| San Francisco 49ers ......3 | 0 | 3 | 14—20 |
| Cincinnati Bengals ........0 | 3 | 10 | 3—16 |

#### FIRST QUARTER

San Francisco: FG Cofer 41.

#### SECOND QUARTER

Cincinnati: FG Breech 34.

#### THIRD QUARTER

Cincinnati: FG Breech 43.
San Francisco: FG Cofer 32.
Cincinnati: Jennings 93 kickoff return (Breech kick).

#### FOURTH QUARTER

San Francisco: Rice 14 pass from Montana (Cofer kick).
Cincinnati: FG Breech 40.
San Francisco: Taylor 10 pass from Montana (Cofer kick).

A: 75,129. At Miami.

**Recap:** Under second-year coach Sam Wyche the 1988 Cincinnati Bengals reversed their 4–11 mark of the previous season, won the AFC Central and reached the championship game. In Miami's brand-new Joe Robbie Stadium, they squared off against Bill Walsh's mighty 49ers—who were seeking their third ring of the decade—in one of the most dramatic Super Bowls to date. Wyche had been on Walsh's staff at San Francisco from 1979 to 1982, so he was well prepared for the 49ers. It showed in the game as his overmatched Bengals stayed with the 49ers until the very end, when Joe Montana added another chapter to his storied career. After a defensive first half that saw three players seriously injured, the score was tied 3–3; it was the first halftime tie in Super Bowl history. Boomer Esiason completed three long passes on a drive to start the second half, but the march stalled, and Jim Breech came in to kick a field goal for a 6–3 lead. Esiason was intercepted on his next series, giving the 49ers the ball at the Cincinnati 23. They were also forced to settle for a field goal before kicking off to Stanford Jennings, who returned the ball 93 yards up the middle to give the Bengals a 13–6 lead. Montana threw back-to-back passes of 31 and 40 yards to Jerry Rice and Roger Craig, bringing the 49ers to the Cincinnati 14. Lewis Billups then dropped a sure interception before Montana hit Rice for the tying score. The Bengals controlled the ball for five minutes after that but came away with only a 40-yard Breech field goal. With 3:20 left, the stage was set for a brilliantly executed drive as Montana completed nine precision strikes on an 11-play, 92-yard march. After a timeout, on second-and-two with 39 seconds left, he fired 10 yards over the middle to John Taylor for the win.

## 1989

### NATIONAL FOOTBALL CONFERENCE

| | | | | |
|---|---|---|---|---|
| Los Angeles Rams | 3 | 0 | 0 | 3 |
| San Francisco 49ers | 0 | 21 | 3 | 6—30 |

#### FIRST QUARTER
Los Angeles: FG Lansford 23.

#### SECOND QUARTER
San Francisco: Jones 20 pass from Montana (Cofer kick).
San Francisco: Craig 1 run (Cofer kick).
San Francisco: Taylor 18 pass from Montana (Cofer kick).

#### THIRD QUARTER
San Francisco: FG Cofer 28.

#### FOURTH QUARTER
San Francisco: FG Cofer 36.
San Francisco: FG Cofer 25.

A: 64,769.

**Recap:** The 49ers reached a second straight Super Bowl behind the brilliant passing of Joe Montana, who threw two touchdowns to break the game open in the second quarter. Montana completed 26 of 30 passes for 262 yards overall in a thorough drubbing of the Rams, who had beaten the 49ers in October and narrowly lost in their second meeting in December.

### AMERICAN FOOTBALL CONFERENCE

| | | | | |
|---|---|---|---|---|
| Cleveland Browns | 0 | 0 | 21 | 0—21 |
| Denver Broncos | 3 | 7 | 14 | 13—37 |

#### FIRST QUARTER
Denver: FG Treadwell 29.

#### SECOND QUARTER
Denver: Young 70 pass from Elway (Treadwell kick).

#### THIRD QUARTER
Cleveland: Brennan 27 pass from Kosar (Bahr kick).
Denver: Mobley 5 pass from Elway (Treadwell kick).
Denver: Winder 7 run (Treadwell kick).
Cleveland: Brennan 10 pass from Kosar (Bahr kick).
Cleveland: Manoa 2 run (Bahr kick).

#### FOURTH QUARTER
Denver: Winder 39 pass from Elway (Treadwell kick).
Denver: FG Treadwell 34.
Denver: FG Treadwell 31.

A: 76,005.

**Recap:** Two of the previous three AFC title games featured these teams in down-to-the-wire thrillers, but John Elway put this one safely away early in the fourth quarter, capping an 80-yard drive with a touchdown pass to Sammy Winder. Bernie Kosar was picked off twice to set up Denver's late field goals.

## Super Bowl XXIV

| | | | | |
|---|---|---|---|---|
| San Francisco 49ers | 13 | 14 | 14 | 14—55 |
| Denver Broncos | 3 | 0 | 7 | 0—10 |

#### FIRST QUARTER
San Francisco: Rice 20 pass from Montana (Cofer kick).
Denver: FG Treadwell 42.
San Francisco: Jones 7 pass from Montana (kick failed).

#### SECOND QUARTER
San Francisco: Rathman 1 run (Cofer kick).
San Francisco: Rice 38 pass from Montana (Cofer kick).

#### THIRD QUARTER
San Francisco: Rice 28 pass from Montana (Cofer kick).
San Francisco: Taylor 35 pass from Montana (Cofer kick).
Denver: Elway 3 run (Treadwell kick).

#### FOURTH QUARTER
San Francisco: Rathman 3 run (Cofer kick).
San Francisco: Craig 1 run (Cofer kick).

A: 72,919. At New Orleans.

**Recap:** In becoming the first team since the Pittsburgh Steelers of the 1970s to win back-to-back titles, the San Francisco 49ers set 18 Super Bowl records, including most points scored and widest margin of victory. Their woeful opponent was the Denver Broncos, who were playing their third Super Bowl in the previous four years. The outcome, never in doubt, established the Broncos as the only team besides the Minnesota Vikings to lose in the Super Bowl four excruciating times. The 49er machine clicked into action immediately, converting its first possession into seven points on 10 plays covering 66 yards. The Denver offense replied with a drive for a 42-yard field goal and then fell silent, not to be heard from again until the 49ers had extended their lead to 41–3. John Elway was sacked four times in the game, threw two interceptions and fumbled once as the 49ers defense overwhelmed him. Joe Montana on the other hand, completed 22 of 29 passes for 292 yards and a Super Bowl–record five touchdowns. His 13 consecutive completions established yet another Super Bowl record. With San Francisco leading 20–3, he threw 38 yards over the middle to Jerry Rice for a touchdown. After a pair of Elway interceptions, he fired TD passes of 28 and 35 yards to Rice and John Taylor, his deadly pair of outside receivers. That made it 41–3, and the 49ers let Elway up for air long enough to guide a five-play, 61-yard scoring drive, the last points Denver would score all afternoon. Montana left the game with 11 minutes to play, his work convincingly done.

## 1990

### NATIONAL FOOTBALL CONFERENCE

| | | | | |
|---|---|---|---|---|
| New York Giants | 3 | 3 | 6 | —15 |
| San Francisco 49ers | 3 | 3 | 7 | 0—13 |

#### FIRST QUARTER

San Francisco: FG Cofer 47.
New York: FG Bahr 28.

#### SECOND QUARTER

New York: FG Bahr 42.
San Francisco: FG Cofer 35.

#### THIRD QUARTER

San Francisco: Taylor 61 pass from Montana (Cofer kick).
New York: FG Bahr 46.

#### FOURTH QUARTER

New York: FG Bahr 38.
New York: FG Bahr 42.

A: 67,325.

**Recap:** The Giants prevented a San Francisco three-peat with a last-second Matt Bahr field goal that allowed them to advance to their second Super Bowl under coach Bill Parcells. Relying on their ferocious defense and a conservative, ball-control offense, they were able to keep the 49ers at bay while scoring just enough points of their own to win. Down 13–9, they faked a punt and recovered a fumble to set up a pair of fourth-quarter Bahr field goals for the win.

### AMERICAN FOOTBALL CONFERENCE

| | | | | |
|---|---|---|---|---|
| Los Angeles Raiders | 3 | 0 | 0 | 0— 3 |
| Buffalo Bills | 21 | 20 | 0 | 10—51 |

#### FIRST QUARTER

Buffalo: Lofton 13 pass from Kelly (Norwood kick).
Los Angeles: FG Jaeger 41.
Buffalo: Thomas 12 run (Norwood kick).
Buffalo: Talley 27 int return (Norwood kick).

#### SECOND QUARTER

Buffalo: K Davis 1 run (kick failed).
Buffalo: K Davis 3 run (Norwood kick).
Buffalo: Lofton 8 pass from Kelly (Norwood kick).

#### FOURTH QUARTER

Buffalo: K Davis 1 run (Norwood kick).
Buffalo: FG Norwood 39.

A: 80,324.

**Recap:** Only the Bears' 73–0 pasting of Washington in 1940 surpasses this one for margin of victory in a league or conference championship game. The Bills responded to Los Angeles's first-quarter field goal with a 41-yard Jim Kelly to James Lofton pass to set up Thurman Thomas's 12-yard touchdown run. Buffalo was nearly flawless from there, scoring on three drives of over 50 yards, returning an interception for a touchdown and thoroughly dominating the Raiders. Reserve running back Kenneth Davis scored three touchdowns.

## Super Bowl XXV

| | | | | |
|---|---|---|---|---|
| New York Giants | 3 | 7 | 7 | 3—20 |
| Buffalo Bills | 3 | 9 | 0 | 7—19 |

#### FIRST QUARTER

New York: FG Bahr 28.
Buffalo: FG Norwood 23.

#### SECOND QUARTER

Buffalo: D Smith 1 run (Norwood kick).
Buffalo: Safety. B Smith tackled Hostetler in end zone.
New York: Baker 14 pass from Hostetler (Bahr kick).

#### THIRD QUARTER

New York: Anderson 1 run (Bahr kick).

#### FOURTH QUARTER

Buffalo: Thomas 31 run (Norwood kick).
New York: FG Bahr 21.

A: 73,813. At Tampa.

**Recap:** The Buffalo Bills had a potent offense, a fact they most recently demonstrated in their 51–3 pounding of Los Angeles for the AFC title. Of course, any offense—however good—has to be on the field to be effective, and the New York Giants did a thorough job of keeping the Buffalo offense on the sidelines. Coach Bill Parcells had stressed ball control all season, and his lessons bore fruit in Super Bowl XXV as his team possessed the ball for 9:29 during a crucial touchdown drive and for 40:33 overall (Super Bowl records both) on the way to a thrilling 20–19 victory. The teams traded short field goals in the first quarter, and then Buffalo mounted an 80-yard, 12-play drive for a touchdown to take a 10–3 lead. Defensive end Bruce Smith added two when he caught Giants quarterback Jeff Hostetler in the end zone for a safety but Hostetler rebounded to make it 12–10 at the half on a 14-yard touchdown pass to Stephen Baker. Then, on the Giants' first series of the second half, there was "the Drive," kept alive by three clutch throws by Hostetler in third down situations. He fired to back Dave Meggett for 11 yards on a third-and-eight and hit receiver Mark Ingram for 14 yards on third-and-13. Ottis Anderson broke a 24-yard run on third-and-one during the series and scored the touchdown from the one to make it 17–12, Giants. The surge effectively ended the third quarter, but to start the fourth, Buffalo's Thurman Thomas ran 31 yards to the end zone to give the Bills a 19–17 edge. New York then drove 74 yards for a field goal, killing over seven minutes and recapturing the lead, then clung in the final seconds as Scott Norwood's 47-yard field goal attempt for Buffalo sailed wide right.

## 1991

**NATIONAL FOOTBALL CONFERENCE**

Detroit Lions ...................0 10 0 0—10
Washington Redskins....10 7 10 14—41

**FIRST QUARTER**

Washington: Riggs 2 run (Lohmiller kick).
Washington: FG Lohmiller 20.

**SECOND QUARTER**

Detroit: Green 18 pass from Kramer (Murray kick).
Washington: Riggs 3 run (Lohmiller kick).
Detroit: FG Murray 30.

**THIRD QUARTER**

Washington: FG Lohmiller 28.
Washington: Clark 45 pass from Rypien (Lohmiller kick).

**FOURTH QUARTER**

Washington: Monk 21 pass from Rypien (Lohmiller kick).
Washington: Green 32 int return (Lohmiller kick).

A: 55,585.

**Recap:** The upstart Detroit Lions suffered two turnovers, which Washington converted into 10 points for an early lead. Mark Rypien hurled second-half scoring tosses of 45 and 21 yards to Gary Clark and Art Monk respectively before an interception return of 32 yards for a touchdown sealed the convincing Redskin victory.

**AMERICAN FOOTBALL CONFERENCE**

Denver Broncos ...............0 0 0 7— 7
Buffalo Bills .....................0 0 7 3—10

**THIRD QUARTER**

Buffalo: Bailey 11 int return (Norwood kick).

**FOURTH QUARTER**

Buffalo: FG Norwood 44.
Denver: Kubiak 3 run (Treadwell kick).

A: 80,272.

**Recap:** The Broncos missed several chances in the first half, and the game turned when John Elway threw a screen pass toward Steve Sewell in the third quarter. Buffalo's Jeff Wright got a hand on it, deflecting it to linebacker Carlton Bailey, who broke Elway's tackle and ran 11 yards to the end zone. Scott Norwood's 44-yard field goal with 4:18 to play proved to be the winning margin, but not before a final scare from Denver. Backup quarterback Gary Kubiak, having announced the week before that he would retire after the season, nearly went out a hero after Elway left the game with a bruised thigh and Denver trailing 10–0 with 2:20 gone in the fourth quarter. Kubiak drove the Broncos 85 yards and scored on a three-yard scramble with 1:28 remaining to make it 10–7. The Broncos recovered an onside kick, and Kubiak zipped a pass to Sewell in Buffalo territory, but the comeback was not to be as Sewell fumbled the ball to Buffalo's Kirby Jackson.

## Super Bowl XXVI

Washington Redskins ....0 17 14 6—37
Buffalo Bills....................0 0 10 14—24

**SECOND QUARTER**

Washington: FG Lohmiller 24.
Washington: Byner 10 pass from Rypien (Lohmiller kick).
Washington: Riggs 1 run (Lohmiller kick).

**THIRD QUARTER**

Washington: Riggs 2 run (Lohmiller kick).
Buffalo: FG Norwood 21.
Buffalo: Thomas 1 run (Norwood kick).
Washington: Clark 30 pass from Rypien (Lohmiller kick).

**FOURTH QUARTER**

Washington: FG Lohmiller 25.
Washington: FG Lohmiller 39.
Buffalo: Metzelaars 2 pass from Kelly (Norwood kick).
Buffalo: Beebe 4 pass from Kelly (Norwood kick).

A: 63,130. At Minneapolis.

**Recap:** Washington Redskin coach Joe Gibbs joined the elite company of Chuck Noll and Bill Walsh as the only men to coach at least three Super Bowl winners when his team sent the Buffalo Bills to their second straight championship defeat, in Super Bowl XXVI. The two teams had the best records in the NFL that year, Buffalo taking the AFC East with a 13–3 mark and Washington going 14–2 en route to the NFC East title. The Redskins dominated from the start, and two Buffalo scores in the final six minutes were all that prevented the final score from reflecting a blowout. Washington advanced inside the Buffalo 20 on each of its first three drives, and though the Redskins netted only three points, their ability to move the ball spoke of things to come. In the second quarter they scored 17 points on a Chip Lohmiller field goal, a 10-yard touchdown pass from Mark Rypien to Earnest Byner and Gerald Riggs's one-yard end zone plunge. Sixteen seconds into the third quarter they increased their lead to 24–0 as Kurt Gouveia picked off a Jim Kelly pass to set up Riggs's second touchdown, this one on a two-yard run. Kelly then completed a 43-yard pass to Don Beebe to get into field position for Scott Norwood, who scored Buffalo's first points on a 21-yard field goal. Midway through the third quarter the Bills capitalized on a muffed punt to drive for a touchdown that made it 24–10. Rypien promptly replied with a 30-yard touchdown pass to Gary Clark, capping an 11-play, 79-yard drive and effectively putting the game away at 31–10. In the final period a Jim Kelly fumble and interception led to a pair of field goals by Lohmiller that raised the score to 37–10. Kelly's two touchdown passes, the second after a recovered onside kick, served only to make the final score respectable.

## Career Leaders

### Scoring

| | Yrs | TD | FG | PAT | Pts |
|---|---|---|---|---|---|
| George Blanda | 26 | 9 | 335 | 943 | 2002 |
| Jan Stenerud | 19 | 0 | 373 | 580 | 1699 |
| Pat Leahy | 18 | 0 | 304 | 558 | 1470 |
| Jim Turner | 16 | 1 | 304 | 521 | 1439 |
| Mark Moseley | 16 | 0 | 300 | 482 | 1382 |
| Jim Bakken | 17 | 0 | 282 | 534 | 1380 |
| Nick Lowery | 14 | 0 | 306 | 449 | 1367 |
| Fred Cox | 15 | 0 | 282 | 519 | 1365 |
| Lou Groza | 17 | 1 | 234 | 641 | 1349 |
| Jim Breech | 14 | 0 | 243 | 517 | 1246 |
| Chris Bahr | 14 | 0 | 241 | 490 | 1213 |
| Matt Bahr | 14 | 0 | 237 | 431 | 1142 |
| Gino Cappelletti | 11 | 42 | 176 | 350 | 1130 |
| Gary Anderson | 11 | 0 | 258 | 356 | 1130 |
| Ray Wersching | 15 | 0 | 222 | 456 | 1122 |
| Eddie Murray | 12 | 0 | 244 | 381 | 1113 |
| Don Cockroft | 13 | 0 | 216 | 432 | 1080 |
| Garo Yepremian | 14 | 0 | 210 | 444 | 1074 |
| Morten Andersen | 11 | 0 | 246 | 347 | 1085 |
| Bruce Gossett | 11 | 0 | 219 | 374 | 1031 |

Cappelletti's total includes four two-point conversions.

### Rushing

| | Yrs | Att | Yds | Avg | Lg | TD |
|---|---|---|---|---|---|---|
| Walter Payton | 13 | 3,838 | 16,726 | 4.4 | 76 | 110 |
| Eric Dickerson | 10 | 2,970 | 13,168 | 4.4 | 85 | 90 |
| Tony Dorsett | 12 | 2,936 | 12,739 | 4.3 | 99 | 77 |
| Jim Brown | 9 | 2,359 | 12,312 | 5.2 | 80 | 106 |
| Franco Harris | 13 | 2,949 | 12,120 | 4.1 | 75 | 91 |
| John Riggins | 14 | 2,916 | 11,352 | 3.9 | 66 | 104 |
| O. J. Simpson | 11 | 2,404 | 11,236 | 4.7 | 94 | 61 |
| Ottis Anderson | 14 | 2,562 | 10,273 | 4.0 | 76 | 81 |
| Earl Campbell | 8 | 2,187 | 9,407 | 4.3 | 81 | 74 |
| Jim Taylor | 10 | 1,941 | 8,597 | 4.4 | 84 | 83 |
| Marcus Allen | 11 | 2,090 | 8,545 | 4.1 | 61 | 79 |
| Joe Perry | 14 | 1,737 | 8,378 | 4.8 | 78 | 53 |
| Gerald Riggs | 10 | 1,989 | 8,188 | 4.2 | 58 | 69 |
| Larry Csonka | 11 | 1,891 | 8,081 | 4.3 | 54 | 64 |
| Freeman McNeil | 12 | 1,798 | 8,074 | 4.5 | 69 | 38 |
| Roger Craig | 10 | 1,953 | 8,070 | 4.1 | 71 | 55 |
| James Brooks | 12 | 1,685 | 7,962 | 4.7 | 65 | 49 |
| Mike Pruitt | 11 | 1,844 | 7,378 | 4.0 | 77 | 51 |
| Leroy Kelly | 10 | 1,727 | 7,274 | 4.2 | 70 | 74 |
| George Rogers | 7 | 1,692 | 7,176 | 4.2 | 79 | 54 |

## Touchdowns

| | Yrs | Rush | Pass Rec | Ret | Total TD |
|---|---|---|---|---|---|
| Jim Brown | 9 | 106 | 20 | 0 | 126 |
| Walter Payton | 13 | 110 | 15 | 0 | 125 |
| John Riggins | 14 | 104 | 12 | 0 | 116 |
| Lenny Moore | 12 | 63 | 48 | 2 | 113 |
| Jerry Rice | 8 | 5 | 103 | 0 | 108 |
| Don Hutson | 11 | 3 | 99 | 3 | 105 |
| Steve Largent | 14 | 1 | 100 | 0 | 101 |
| Franco Harris | 13 | 91 | 9 | 0 | 100 |
| Marcus Allen | 10 | 79 | 18 | 1 | 98 |
| Eric Dickerson | 10 | 90 | 6 | 0 | 96 |

| | Yrs | Rush | Pass Rec | Ret | Total TD |
|---|---|---|---|---|---|
| Jim Taylor | 10 | 83 | 10 | 0 | 93 |
| Tony Dorsett | 12 | 77 | 13 | 1 | 91 |
| Bobby Mitchell | 11 | 18 | 65 | 8 | 91 |
| Leroy Kelly | 10 | 74 | 13 | 3 | 90 |
| Charley Taylor | 13 | 11 | 79 | 0 | 90 |
| Don Maynard | 15 | 0 | 88 | 0 | 88 |
| Lance Alworth | 11 | 2 | 85 | 0 | 87 |
| Paul Warfield | 13 | 1 | 85 | 0 | 86 |
| Ottis Anderson | 13 | 81 | 5 | 0 | 86 |
| Tommy McDonald | 12 | 0 | 84 | 1 | 85 |

## Longest Plays

| RUSHING | Opponent | Year | Yds |
|---|---|---|---|
| Tony Dorsett, Dall | Minn | 1983 | 99 |
| Andy Uram, GB | Chi Cards | 1939 | 97 |
| Bob Gage, Pitt | Chi | 1949 | 97 |
| Jim Spitval, Balt | GB | 1950 | 96 |
| Bob Hoernschemeyer, Det | NY Yanks | 1950 | 96 |

| PASSING | Opponent | Year | Yds |
|---|---|---|---|
| Frank Filchock to Andy Farkas, Washington | Pitt | 1939 | 99 |
| George Izo to Bobby Mitchell, Washington | Cle | 1963 | 99 |
| Karl Sweetan to Pat Studstill, Detroit | Balt | 1966 | 99 |
| Sonny Jurgensen to Gerry Allen, Washington | Chi | 1968 | 99 |
| Jim Plunkett to Cliff Branch, LA Raiders | Wash | 1983 | 99 |
| Ron Jaworski to Mike Quick, Philadelphia | Atl | 1985 | 99 |

| FIELD GOALS | Opponent | Year | Yds |
|---|---|---|---|
| Tom Dempsey, NO | Det | 1970 | 63 |
| Steve Cox, Cle | Cin | 1984 | 60 |
| Morten Andersen, NO | Chi | 1991 | 60 |

| PUNTS | Opponent | Year | Yds |
|---|---|---|---|
| Steve O'Neal, NY Jets | Den | 1969 | 98 |
| Joe Lintzenich, Chi | NY Giants | 1931 | 94 |
| Shawn McCarthy, NE | Buff | 1991 | 93 |
| Randall Cunningham, Phi | NY Giants | 1989 | 91 |

## THEY SAID IT

*Lawrence Taylor, 33-year-old New York Giant linebacker, on aging: "When you get old, everything is hurting. When I get up in the morning, it sounds like I'm making popcorn."*

## Career Leaders (Cont.)

### Combined Yards Gained

| | Yrs | Total | Rush | Rec | Int Ret | Punt Ret | Kickoff Ret | Fum Ret |
|---|---|---|---|---|---|---|---|---|
| Walter Payton | 13 | 21,803 | 16,726 | 4,538 | 0 | 0 | 539 | 0 |
| Tony Dorsett | 12 | 16,326 | 12,739 | 3,554 | 0 | 0 | 0 | 33 |
| Jim Brown | 9 | 15,459 | 12,312 | 2,499 | 0 | 0 | 648 | 0 |
| Eric Dickerson | 10 | 15,262 | 13,168 | 2,079 | 0 | 0 | 0 | 15 |
| James Brooks | 12 | 14,644 | 7,962 | 3,621 | 0 | 565 | 2,762 | 0 |
| Franco Harris | 13 | 14,622 | 12,120 | 2,287 | 0 | 0 | 233 | -18 |
| O.J. Simpson | 11 | 14,368 | 11,236 | 2,142 | 0 | 0 | 990 | 0 |
| James Lofton | 15 | 14,094 | 246 | 13,821 | 0 | 0 | 0 | 27 |
| Bobby Mitchell | 11 | 14,078 | 2,735 | 7,954 | 0 | 699 | 2,690 | 0 |
| John Riggins | 14 | 13,435 | 11,352 | 2,090 | 0 | 0 | 0 | -7 |
| Steve Largent | 14 | 13,396 | 83 | 13,089 | 0 | 68 | 156 | 0 |
| Ottis Anderson | 14 | 13,364 | 10,273 | 3,062 | 0 | 0 | 0 | 29 |
| Greg Pruitt | 12 | 13,262 | 5,672 | 3,069 | 0 | 2,007 | 2,514 | 0 |
| Ollie Matson | 14 | 12,884 | 5,173 | 3,285 | 51 | 595 | 3,746 | 34 |
| Roger Craig | 10 | 12,812 | 8,070 | 4,742 | 0 | 0 | 0 | 0 |
| Marcus Allen | 11 | 12,803 | 8,545 | 4,258 | 0 | 0 | 0 | 0 |
| Tim Brown | 10 | 12,684 | 3,862 | 3,399 | 0 | 639 | 4,781 | 3 |
| Lenny Moore | 12 | 12,451 | 5,174 | 6,039 | 0 | 56 | 1,180 | 2 |
| Don Maynard | 15 | 12,379 | 70 | 11,834 | 0 | 132 | 343 | 0 |
| Charlie Joiner | 18 | 12,367 | 22 | 12,146 | 0 | 0 | 194 | 5 |

### Passing

| | Yrs | Att | Comp | Pct Comp | Yds | Avg Gain | TD | Pct TD | Int | Pct Int | Rating Pts |
|---|---|---|---|---|---|---|---|---|---|---|---|
| Joe Montana | 13 | 4,600 | 2,929 | 63.7 | 35,124 | 7.64 | 244 | 5.3 | 123 | 2.7 | 93.5 |
| Steve Young | 8 | 1,506 | 908 | 60.3 | 11,877 | 7.89 | 76 | 5.0 | 42 | 2.8 | 90.4 |
| Dan Marino | 10 | 5,284 | 3,128 | 59.2 | 39,502 | 7.48 | 290 | 5.5 | 165 | 3.1 | 87.8 |
| Jim Kelly | 7 | 3,024 | 1,824 | 60.3 | 23,031 | 7.62 | 161 | 5.3 | 108 | 3.6 | 86.9 |
| Mark Rypien | 5 | 1,888 | 1,078 | 57.1 | 14,414 | 7.63 | 97 | 5.1 | 65 | 3.4 | 84.3 |
| Roger Staubach | 11 | 2,958 | 1,685 | 57.0 | 22,700 | 7.67 | 153 | 5.2 | 109 | 3.7 | 83.4 |
| Neil Lomax | 8 | 3,153 | 1,817 | 57.6 | 22,771 | 7.22 | 136 | 4.3 | 90 | 2.9 | 82.7 |
| Sonny Jurgensen | 18 | 4,262 | 2,433 | 57.1 | 32,224 | 7.56 | 255 | 6.0 | 189 | 4.4 | 82.6 |
| Len Dawson | 19 | 3,741 | 2,136 | 57.1 | 28,711 | 7.67 | 239 | 6.4 | 183 | 4.9 | 82.6 |
| Dave Krieg | 13 | 3,989 | 2,326 | 58.3 | 29,247 | 7.33 | 210 | 5.3 | 160 | 4.0 | 82.1 |
| Ken Anderson | 16 | 4,475 | 2,654 | 59.3 | 32,838 | 7.34 | 197 | 4.4 | 160 | 3.6 | 81.9 |
| Boomer Esiason | 9 | 3,378 | 1,897 | 56.2 | 25,671 | 7.60 | 174 | 5.2 | 129 | 3.8 | 81.8 |
| Bernie Kosar | 8 | 3,012 | 1,174 | 58.9 | 21,097 | 7.00 | 111 | 3.7 | 78 | 2.6 | 81.8 |
| Danny White | 13 | 2,950 | 1,761 | 59.7 | 21,959 | 7.44 | 155 | 5.3 | 132 | 4.5 | 81.7 |
| Ken O'Brien | 9 | 3,465 | 2,039 | 58.8 | 24,386 | 7.04 | 124 | 3.6 | 95 | 2.7 | 81.0 |
| Warren Moon | 9 | 4,026 | 2,329 | 57.8 | 30,200 | 7.50 | 175 | 4.3 | 145 | 3.6 | 81.0 |
| Bart Starr | 16 | 3,149 | 1,808 | 57.4 | 24,718 | 7.85 | 152 | 4.8 | 138 | 4.4 | 80.5 |
| Fran Tarkenton | 18 | 6,467 | 3,686 | 57.0 | 47,003 | 7.27 | 342 | 5.3 | 266 | 4.1 | 80.4 |
| Dan Fouts | 15 | 5,604 | 3,297 | 58.8 | 43,040 | 7.68 | 254 | 4.5 | 242 | 4.3 | 80.2 |
| Randall Cunningham | 8 | 2,641 | 1,464 | 55.4 | 18,193 | 6.89 | 126 | 4.8 | 82 | 3.1 | 79.9 |

1,500 or more attempts. The passing ratings are based on performance standards established for completion percentage, interception percentage, touchdown percentage, and average gain. Passers are allocated points according to how their marks compare with those standards.

### Receiving

| | Yrs | No. | Yds | Avg | Lg | TD |
|---|---|---|---|---|---|---|
| Art Monk | 13 | 847 | 11,628 | 13.7 | 79 | 63 |
| Steve Largent | 14 | 819 | 13,089 | 16.0 | 74 | 100 |
| Charlie Joiner | 18 | 750 | 12,146 | 16.2 | 87 | 65 |
| James Lofton | 15 | 750 | 13,821 | 18.4 | 80 | 75 |
| Ozzie Newsome? | 13 | 662 | 7,9801 | 12.1 | 74 | 47 |
| Charley Taylor | 13 | 649 | 9,110 | 14.0 | 88 | 79 |
| Don Maynard | 15 | 633 | 11,834 | 18.7 | 87 | 88 |
| Raymond Berry | 13 | 631 | 9,275 | 14.7 | 70 | 68 |
| Jerry Rice | 8 | 610 | 10,273 | 16.8 | 96 | 103 |
| Drew Hill | 13 | 600 | 9,447 | 15.7 | 81 | 60 |
| Harold Carmichael | 14 | 590 | 8,985 | 15.2 | 85 | 79 |
| Fred Biletnikoff | 14 | 589 | 8,974 | 15.2 | 82 | 76 |
| Harold Jackson | 16 | 579 | 10,372 | 17.9 | 79 | 76 |
| Lionel Taylor | 10 | 567 | 7,195 | 12.7 | 80 | 45 |
| Wes Chandler | 11 | 559 | 8,966 | 16.0 | 85 | 56 |
| Stanley Morgan | 14 | 557 | 10,716 | 19.2 | 76 | 72 |
| Roy Green | 14 | 559 | 8,965 | 16.0 | 83. | 66 |
| Mark Clayton | 10 | 550 | 8,643 | 15.7 | 78 | 81 |
| Roger Craig | 10 | 547 | 4,742 | 8.7 | 73 | 16 |
| J.T. Smith | 13 | 544 | 6,974 | 12.8 | 77 | 35 |

### Career Leaders *(Cont.)*

#### Interceptions

| | Yrs | No. | Yds | Avg | Lg | TD |
|---|---|---|---|---|---|---|
| Paul Krause | 16 | 81 | 1185 | 14.6 | 81 | 3 |
| Emlen Tunnell | 14 | 79 | 1282 | 16.2 | 55 | 4 |
| Dick (Night Train) Lane | 14 | 68 | 1207 | 17.8 | 80 | 5 |
| Ken Riley | 15 | 65 | 596 | 9.2 | 66 | 5 |
| Dick LeBeau | 13 | 62 | 762 | 12.3 | 70 | 3 |
| Dave Brown | 16 | 62 | 698 | 11.3 | 90 | 5 |

#### Punting

| | Yrs | No. | Yds | Avg | Lg | Blk |
|---|---|---|---|---|---|---|
| Sammy Baugh | 16 | 338 | 15,245 | 45.1 | 85 | 9 |
| Tommy Davis | 11 | 511 | 22,833 | 44.7 | 82 | 2 |
| Yale Lary | 11 | 503 | 22,279 | 44.3 | 74 | 4 |
| Rohn Stark | 11 | 829 | 36,465 | 44.0 | 72 | 6 |
| Horace Gillom | 7 | 385 | 16,872 | 43.8 | 80 | 5 |

#### Punt Returns

| | Yrs | No. | Yds | Avg | Lg | TD |
|---|---|---|---|---|---|---|
| George McAfee | 8 | 112 | 1431 | 12.8 | 74 | 2 |
| Jack Christiansen | 8 | 85 | 1084 | 12.8 | 89 | 8 |
| Claude Gibson | 5 | 110 | 1381 | 12.6 | 85 | 3 |
| Bill Dudley | 9 | 124 | 1515 | 12.2 | 96 | 3 |
| Rick Upchurch | 9 | 248 | 3008 | 12.1 | 92 | 8 |

#### Kickoff Returns

| | Yrs | No. | Yds | Avg | Lg | TD |
|---|---|---|---|---|---|---|
| Gale Sayers | 7 | 91 | 2781 | 30.6 | 103 | 6 |
| Lynn Chandnois | 7 | 92 | 2720 | 29.6 | 93 | 3 |
| Abe Woodson | 9 | 193 | 5538 | 28.7 | 105 | 5 |
| Claude (Buddy) Young | 6 | 90 | 2514 | 27.9 | 104 | 2 |
| Travis Williams | 5 | 102 | 2801 | 27.5 | 105 | 6 |

### Single-Season Leaders
### Scoring

#### POINTS

| | Year | TD | PAT | FG | Pts |
|---|---|---|---|---|---|
| Paul Hornung, GB | 1960 | 15 | 41 | 15 | 176 |
| Mark Moseley, Wash. | 1983 | 0 | 62 | 33 | 161 |
| Gino Cappelletti, Bos | 1964 | 7 | 38 | 25 | 155 |
| Chip Lohmiller, Wash | 1991 | 0 | 56 | 31 | 149 |
| Gino Cappelletti, Bos | 1961 | 8 | 48 | 17 | 147 |
| Paul Hornung, GB | 1961 | 10 | 41 | 15 | 146 |
| Jim Turner, NY Jets | 1968 | 0 | 43 | 34 | 145 |
| John Riggins, Wash | 1983 | 24 | 0 | 0 | 144 |
| Kevin Butler, Chi | 1985 | 0 | 51 | 31 | 144 |
| Tony Franklin, NE | 1986 | 0 | 44 | 32 | 140 |

Note: Cappelletti's 1964 total includes a two-point conversion.

#### TOUCHDOWNS

| | Year | Rush | Rec | Ret | Total |
|---|---|---|---|---|---|
| John Riggins, Wash | 1983 | 24 | 0 | 0 | 24 |
| O. J. Simpson, Buff | 1975 | 16 | 7 | 0 | 23 |
| Jerry Rice, SF | 1987 | 1 | 22 | 0 | 23 |
| Gale Sayers, Chi | 1965 | 14 | 6 | 2 | 22 |

#### FIELD GOALS

| | Year | Att | No. |
|---|---|---|---|
| Ali Haji-Sheikh, NY Giants | 1983 | 42 | 35 |
| Jim Turner, NY Jets | 1968 | 46 | 34 |
| Chester Marcol, GB | 1972 | 48 | 33 |
| Mark Moseley, Wash | 1983 | 47 | 33 |

### Rushing

#### YARDS GAINED

| | Year | Att | Yds | Avg |
|---|---|---|---|---|
| Eric Dickerson, LA Rams | 1984 | 379 | 2105 | 5.6 |
| O. J. Simpson, Buff | 1973 | 332 | 2003 | 6.0 |
| Earl Campbell, Hou | 1980 | 373 | 1934 | 5.2 |
| Jim Brown, Clev | 1963 | 291 | 1883 | 6.4 |
| Walter Payton, Chi | 1977 | 339 | 1852 | 5.5 |
| Eric Dickerson, LA Rams | 1986 | 404 | 1821 | 4.5 |
| O. J. Simpson, Buff | 1975 | 329 | 1817 | 5.5 |
| Eric Dickerson, LA Rams | 1983 | 390 | 1808 | 4.6 |
| Marcus Allen, LA Raiders | 1985 | 390 | 1759 | 4.6 |
| Gerald Riggs, Atl | 1985 | 397 | 1719 | 4.3 |
| Emmitt Smith, Dall | 1992 | 373 | 1713 | 4.6 |

#### AVERAGE GAIN

| | Year | Avg |
|---|---|---|
| Beattie Feathers, Chi | 1934 | 9.94 |
| Randall Cunningham, Phil | 1990 | 7.98 |
| Steve Young, SF | 1992 | 7.10 |
| Bobby Douglass, Chi | 1972 | 6.87 |
| Dan Towler, LA Rams | 1951 | 6.78 |

#### TOUCHDOWNS

| | Year | No. |
|---|---|---|
| John Riggins, Wash | 1983 | 24 |
| Joe Morris, NY Giants | 1985 | 21 |
| Jim Taylor, GB | 1962 | 19 |
| Earl Campbell, Hou | 1979 | 19 |
| Chuck Muncie, SD | 1981 | 19 |
| Emmitt Smith, Dall | 1992 | 18 |

**An American in Paris**

American football has grown sufficiently popular in France that amateur leagues have begun springing up like chanterelle mushrooms. Marine lieutenant colonel Bob Parnell, who is serving a tour of duty at the U.S. embassy in Paris, coaches in a league in which all the players, except two expatriate Americans per team, are French.

At first Parnell was surprised by the slow pace of the games. There would be a burst of activity, then nothing would happen for a very long time  Just like an NFL game, in other words. Things speeded up considerably, however, when the league passed a rule against smoking in the huddle.

## Single-Season Leaders *(Cont.)*
### Passing

#### YARDS GAINED

| | Year | Att | Comp | Pct | Yds |
|---|---|---|---|---|---|
| Dan Marino, Mia | 1984 | 564 | 362 | 64.2 | 5084 |
| Dan Fouts, SD | 1981 | 609 | 360 | 59.1 | 4802 |
| Dan Marino, Mia | 1986 | 623 | 378 | 60.7 | 4746 |
| Dan Fouts, SD | 1980 | 589 | 348 | 59.1 | 4715 |
| Warren Moon, Hou | 1991 | 655 | 404 | 61.7 | 4690 |
| Warren Moon, Hou | 1990 | 584 | 362 | 62.0 | 4689 |
| Neil Lomax, StL | 1984 | 560 | 345 | 61.6 | 4614 |
| Lynn Dickey, GB | 1983 | 484 | 289 | 59.7 | 4458 |
| Dan Marino, Mia | 1988 | 606 | 354 | 58.4 | 4434 |
| Bill Kenney, KC | 1983 | 603 | 346 | 57.4 | 4348 |
| Don Majkowski, GB | 1989 | 599 | 353 | 58.9 | 4318 |
| Jim Everett, LA Rams | 1989 | 518 | 304 | 58.7 | 4310 |

#### PASS RATING

| | Year | Rat. |
|---|---|---|
| Joe Montana, SF | 1989 | 112.4 |
| Milt Plum, Clev | 1960 | 110.4 |
| Sammy Baugh, Wash | 1945 | 109.9 |
| Dan Marino, Mia | 1984 | 108.9 |
| Steve Young, SF | 1992 | 107.0 |

#### TOUCHDOWNS

| | Year | No. |
|---|---|---|
| Dan Marino, Mia | 1984 | 48 |
| Dan Marino, Mia | 1986 | 44 |
| George Blanda, Hou | 1961 | 36 |
| Y. A. Tittle, NY Giants | 1963 | 36 |

### Receiving

#### RECEPTIONS

| | Year | No. | Yds |
|---|---|---|---|
| Sterling Sharpe, G.B. | 1992 | 108 | 1461 |
| Art Monk, Wash | 1984 | 106 | 1372 |
| Charley Hennigan, Hou | 1964 | 101 | 1546 |
| Lionel Taylor, Den | 1961 | 100 | 1176 |
| Jerry Rice, SF | 1990 | 100 | 1502 |
| Haywood Jeffires, Hou | 1991 | 100 | 1181 |
| Todd Christensen, LA Raiders | 1986 | 95 | 1153 |
| Johnny Morris, Chi | 1964 | 93 | 1200 |
| Al Toon, NY Jets | 1988 | 93 | 1067 |
| Michael Irvin, Dall | 1991 | 93 | 1523 |
| Andre Rison, Atl | 1992 | 93 | 1121 |
| Lionel Taylor, Den | 1960 | 92 | 1235 |
| Todd Christensen, LA Raiders | 1983 | 92 | 1247 |
| Roger Craig, SF | 1985 | 92 | 1016 |

#### YARDS GAINED

| | Year | Yds |
|---|---|---|
| Charley Hennigan, Hou | 1961 | 1746 |
| Lance Alworth, SD | 1965 | 1602 |
| Jerry Rice, SF | 1986 | 1570 |
| Roy Green, StL | 1984 | 1555 |

#### TOUCHDOWNS

| | Year | No. |
|---|---|---|
| Jerry Rice, SF | 1987 | 22 |
| Mark Clayton, Mia | 1984 | 18 |
| Don Hutson, GB | 1942 | 17 |
| Elroy (Crazylegs) Hirsch, LA Rams | 1951 | 17 |
| Bill Groman, Hou | 1961 | 17 |
| Jerry Rice, SF | 1989 | 17 |

### All-Purpose Yards

| | Year | Run | Rec | Ret | Total |
|---|---|---|---|---|---|
| Lionel James, SD | 1985 | 516 | 1027 | 992 | 2535 |
| Terry Metcalf, StL | 1975 | 816 | 378 | 1268 | 2462 |
| Mack Herron, NE | 1974 | 824 | 474 | 1146 | 2444 |
| Gale Sayers, Chi | 1966 | 1231 | 447 | 762 | 2440 |
| Timmy Brown, Phil | 1963 | 841 | 487 | 1100 | 2428 |
| Tim Brown, LA Raiders | 1988 | 50 | 725 | 1542 | 2317 |
| Marcus Allen, LA Raiders | 1985 | 1759 | 555 | -6 | 2308 |
| Timmy Brown, Phil | 1962 | 545 | 849 | 912 | 2306 |
| Gale Sayers, Chi | 1965 | 867 | 507 | 898 | 2272 |
| Eric Dickerson, LA Rams | 1984 | 2105 | 139 | 15 | 2259 |
| O. J. Simpson, Buff | 1975 | 1817 | 426 | 0 | 2243 |

### Punting

| | Year | No. | Yds | Avg |
|---|---|---|---|---|
| Sammy Baugh, Wash | 1940 | 35 | 1799 | 51.4 |
| Yale Lary, Det | 1963 | 35 | 1713 | 48.9 |
| Sammy Baugh, Wash | 1941 | 30 | 1462 | 48.7 |
| Yale Lary, Det | 1961 | 52 | 2516 | 48.4 |
| Sammy Baugh, Wash | 1942 | 37 | 1783 | 48.2 |

### Sacks

| | Year | No. |
|---|---|---|
| Mark Gastineau, NY Jets | 1984 | 22 |
| Reggie White, Phil | 1987 | 21 |
| Chris Doleman, Minn | 1989 | 21 |
| Lawrence Taylor, NY Giants | 1986 | 20.5 |

### Interceptions

| | Year | No. |
|---|---|---|
| Dick (Night Train) Lane, LA Rams | 1952 | 14 |
| Dan Sandifer, Wash | 1948 | 13 |
| Spec Sanders, NY Yanks | 1950 | 13 |
| Lester Hayes, Oak | 1980 | 13 |

### Kickoff Returns

| | Year | Avg |
|---|---|---|
| Travis Williams, GB | 1967 | 41.1 |
| Gale Sayers, Chi | 1967 | 37.7 |
| Ollie Matson, Chi Cardinals | 1958 | 35.5 |
| Jim Duncan, Balt | 1970 | 35.4 |
| Lynn Chandnois, Pitt | 1952 | 35.2 |

### Punt Returns

| | Year | Avg |
|---|---|---|
| Herb Rich, Balt | 1950 | 23.0 |
| Jack Christiansen, Det | 1952 | 21.5 |
| Dick Christy, NY Titans | 1961 | 21.3 |
| Bob Hayes, Dall | 1968 | 20.8 |

## Single-Game Leaders
### Scoring

#### POINTS

| | Date | Pts |
|---|---|---|
| Ernie Nevers, Cards vs Bears | 11-28-29 | 40 |
| Dub Jones, Clev vs Chi Bears | 11-25-51 | 36 |
| Gale Sayers, Chi Bears vs SF | 12-12-65 | 36 |
| Paul Hornung, GB vs Balt | 10-8-61 | 33 |

On Thanksgiving Day, 1929, Nevers scored all the Cardinals' points on six rushing TDs and four PATs. The Cards defeated Red Grange and the Bears, 40-6. Jones and Sayers each rushed for four touchdowns and scored two more on returns in their teams' victories. Hornung scored four touchdowns and kicked 6 PATs and a field goal in a 45-7 win over the Colts.

#### TOUCHDOWNS

| | Date | No. |
|---|---|---|
| Ernie Nevers, Cards vs Bears | 11-28-29 | 6 |
| Dub Jones, Clev vs Chi Bears | 11-25-51 | 6 |
| Gale Sayers, Chi vs SF | 12-12-65 | 6 |
| Bob Shaw, Chi Cards vs Balt | 10-2-50 | 5 |
| Jim Brown, Clev vs Balt | 11-1-59 | 5 |
| Abner Haynes, Dall Texans vs Oak | 11-26-61 | 5 |
| Billy Cannon, Hous vs NY Titans | 12-10-61 | 5 |
| Cookie Gilchrist, Buff vs NY Jets | 12-8-63 | 5 |
| Paul Hornung, GB vs Balt | 12-12-65 | 5 |
| Kellen Winslow, SD vs Oak | 11-22-81 | 5 |
| Jerry Rice, SF vs Atl | 10-14-90 | 5 |

#### FIELD GOALS

| | Date | No. |
|---|---|---|
| Jim Bakken, StL vs Pitt | 9-24-67 | 7 |
| Rich Karlis, Minn vs LA Rams | 11-5-89 | 7 |

Eight players tied with 6 FGs each.

Bakken was 7 for 9, Karlis 7 for 7.

### Rushing

#### YARDS GAINED

| | Date | Yds |
|---|---|---|
| Walter Payton, Chi vs Minn | 11-20-77 | 275 |
| O. J. Simpson, Buff vs Det | 11-25-76 | 273 |
| O. J. Simpson, Buff vs NE | 9-16-73 | 250 |
| Willie Ellison, LA Rams vs NO | 12-5-71 | 247 |
| Cookie Gilchrist, Buff vs NY Jets | 12-8-63 | 243 |

#### CARRIES

| | Date | No. |
|---|---|---|
| Jamie Morris, Wash vs Cin | 12-17-88 | 45 |
| Butch Woolfolk, NY Giants vs Phil | 11-20-83 | 43 |
| James Wilder, TB vs GB | 9-30-84 | 43 |
| James Wilder, TB vs Pitt | 10-30-83 | 42 |
| Franco Harris, Pitt vs Cin | 10-17-76 | 41 |
| Gerald Riggs, Atl vs LA Rams | 11-17-85 | 41 |

#### TOUCHDOWNS

| | Date | No. |
|---|---|---|
| Ernie Nevers, Cards vs Bears | 11-28-29 | 6 |
| Jim Brown, Clev vs Balt | 11-1-59 | 5 |
| Cookie Gilchrist, Buff vs NY Jets | 12-8-63 | 5 |

### Passing

#### YARDS GAINED

| | Date | Yds |
|---|---|---|
| Norm Van Brocklin, LA vs NY Yanks | 9-28-51 | 554 |
| Warren Moon, Hou vs KC | 12-16-90 | 527 |
| Dan Marino, Mia vs NY Jets | 10-23-88 | 521 |
| Phil Simms, NY Giants vs Cin | 10-13-85 | 513 |
| Vince Ferragamo, LA Rams vs Chi | 12-26-82 | 509 |
| Y. A. Tittle, NY Giants vs Wash | 10-28-62 | 505 |

#### COMPLETIONS

| | Date | No. |
|---|---|---|
| Richard Todd, NY Jets vs SF | 9-21-80 | 42 |
| Warren Moon, Hou vs Dall | 11-10-91 | 41 |
| Ken Anderson, Cin vs SD | 12-20-82 | 40 |
| Phil Simms, NY Giants vs Cin | 10-13-85 | 40 |
| Dan Marino, Mia vs Buff | 11-16-86 | 39 |
| Tommy Kramer, Minn vs Clev | 12-14-80 | 38 |
| Tommy Kramer, Minn vs DB | 11-29-81 | 38 |
| Joe Ferguson, Buff vs Mia | 10-9-83 | 38 |

#### TOUCHDOWNS

| | Date | No. |
|---|---|---|
| Sid Luckman, Chi Bears vs NY Giants | 11-14-43 | 7 |
| Adrian Burk, Phil vs Wash | 10-17-54 | 7 |
| George Blanda, Hou vs NY Titans | 11-19-61 | 7 |
| Y. A. Tittle, NY Giants vs Wash | 10-28-62 | 7 |
| Joe Kapp, Minn vs Balt | 9-28-69 | 7 |

## THEY SAID IT

*Linebacker Mike Singletary, on the demise of the Bear defense: "Instead of having a bunch of guys flying to the ball, I go into the huddle and say, 'C'mon! Let's go!' Then I look into their eyes, and I can see it. They're just not with me."*

## Single-Game Leaders *(Cont.)*
### Receiving

**YARDS GAINED**

| | Date | Yds |
|---|---|---|
| Flipper Anderson, LA Rams vs NO | 11-26-89 | 336 |
| Stephone Paige, KC vs SD | 12-22-85 | 309 |
| Jim Benton, Clev vs Det | 11-22-45 | 303 |
| Cloyce Box, Det vs Balt | 12-3-50 | 302 |
| John Taylor, SF vs LA Rams | 12-11-89 | 286 |

**RECEPTIONS**

| | Date | No. |
|---|---|---|
| Tom Fears, LA Rams vs GB | 12-3-50 | 18 |
| Clark Gaines, NY Jets vs SF | 9-21-80 | 17 |
| Sonny Randle, StL vs NY Giants | 11-4-62 | 16 |
| Rickey Young, Minn vs NE | 12-16-79 | 15 |
| William Andrews, Atl vs Pitt | 11-15-81 | 15 |

**TOUCHDOWNS**

| | Date | No. |
|---|---|---|
| Bob Shaw, Chi Cards vs Balt | 10-2-50 | 5 |
| Kellen Winslow, SD vs Oak | 11-22-81 | 5 |
| Jerry Rice, SF vs Atl | 10-14-90 | 5 |

### All-Purpose Yards

| | Date | Yds |
|---|---|---|
| Billy Cannon, Hou vs NY Titans | 12-10-61 | 373 |
| Lionel James, SD vs LA Raiders | 11-10-85 | 345 |
| Timmy Brown, Phil vs StL | 12-16-62 | 341 |
| Gale Sayers, Chi vs Minn | 12-18-66 | 339 |
| Gale Sayers, Chi vs SF | 12-12-65 | 336 |

# Annual NFL Individual Statistical Leaders

## Rushing

| Year | Player, Team | Att. | Yards | Avg. | TD | Year | Player, Team | Att. | Yards | Avg. | TD |
|---|---|---|---|---|---|---|---|---|---|---|---|
| 1932 | Cliff Battles, Bos | 148 | 576 | 3.9 | 3 | 1961 | Jim Brown, Clev, NFL | 305 | 1408 | 4.6 | 8 |
| 1933 | Jim Musick, Bos | 173 | 809 | 4.7 | 5 | | Billy Cannon, Hou, AFL | 200 | 948 | 4.7 | 6 |
| 1934 | Beattie Feathers, Chicago Bears | 101 | 1004 | 9.9 | 8 | 1962 | Jim Taylor, GB, NFL | 272 | 1474 | 5.4 | 19 |
| 1935 | Doug Russell, Chicago Cards | 140 | 499 | 3.6 | 0 | | Cookie Gilchrist, Buff, AFL | 214 | 1096 | 5.1 | 13 |
| 1936 | Alphonse Leemans, NY | 206 | 830 | 4.0 | 2 | 1963 | Jim Brown, Clev, NFL | 291 | 1863 | 6.4 | 12 |
| 1937 | Cliff Battles, Wash | 216 | 874 | 4.0 | 5 | | Clem Daniels, Oak, AFL | 215 | 1099 | 5.1 | 3 |
| 1938 | Byron White, Pitt | 152 | 567 | 3.7 | 4 | 1964 | Jim Brown, Clev, NFL | 280 | 1446 | 5.2 | 7 |
| 1939 | Bill Osmanski, Chi | 121 | 699 | 5.8 | 7 | | Cookie Gilchrist, Buff, AFL | 230 | 981 | 4.3 | 6 |
| 1940 | Byron White, Det | 146 | 514 | 3.5 | 5 | 1965 | Jim Brown, Clev, NFL | 289 | 1544 | 5.3 | 17 |
| 1941 | Clarence Manders, Bklyn | 111 | 486 | 4.4 | 5 | | Paul Lowe, SD, AFL | 222 | 1121 | 5.0 | 7 |
| 1942 | Bill Dudley, Pitt | 162 | 696 | 4.3 | 5 | 1966 | Jim Nance, Bos, AFL | 299 | 1458 | 4.9 | 11 |
| 1943 | Bill Paschal, NY | 147 | 572 | 3.9 | 10 | | Gale Sayers, Chi, NFL | 229 | 1231 | 5.4 | 8 |
| 1944 | Bill Paschal, NY | 196 | 737 | 3.8 | 9 | 1967 | Jim Nance, Bos, AFL | 269 | 1216 | 4.5 | 7 |
| 1945 | Steve Van Buren, Phil | 143 | 832 | 5.8 | 15 | | Leroy Kelly, Clev, NFL | 235 | 1205 | 5.1 | 11 |
| 1946 | Bill Dudley, Pitt | 146 | 604 | 4.1 | 3 | 1968 | Leroy Kelly, Clev, NFL | 248 | 1239 | 5.0 | 16 |
| 1947 | Steve Van Buren, Phil | 217 | 1008 | 4.6 | 13 | | Paul Robinson, Cinn, AFL | 238 | 1023 | 4.3 | 8 |
| 1948 | Steve Van Buren, Phil | 201 | 945 | 4.7 | 10 | 1969 | Gale Sayers, Chi, NFL | 236 | 1032 | 4.4 | 8 |
| 1949 | Steve Van Buren, Phil | 263 | 1146 | 4.4 | 11 | | Dickie Post, SD, AFL | 182 | 873 | 4.8 | 6 |
| 1950 | Marion Motley, Clev | 140 | 810 | 5.8 | 3 | 1970 | Larry Brown, Wash, NFC | 237 | 1125 | 4.7 | 5 |
| 1951 | Eddie Price, NY | 271 | 971 | 3.6 | 7 | | Floyd Little, Den, AFC | 209 | 901 | 4.3 | 3 |
| 1952 | Dan Towler, LA | 156 | 894 | 5.7 | 10 | 1971 | Floyd Little, Den, AFC | 284 | 1133 | 4.0 | 6 |
| 1953 | Joe Perry, SF | 192 | 1018 | 5.3 | 10 | | John Brockington, GB, NFC | 216 | 1105 | 5.1 | 4 |
| 1954 | Joe Perry, SF | 173 | 1049 | 6.1 | 8 | 1972 | O.J. Simpson, Buff, AFC | 292 | 1251 | 4.3 | 6 |
| 1955 | Alan Ameche, Balt | 213 | 961 | 4.5 | 9 | | Larry Brown, Wash, NFC | 285 | 1216 | 4.3 | 8 |
| 1956 | Rick Casares, Chicago Bears | 234 | 1126 | 4.8 | 12 | 1973 | O.J. Simpson, Buff, AFC | 332 | 2003 | 6.0 | 12 |
| 1957 | Jim Brown, Clev | 202 | 942 | 4.7 | 9 | | John Brockington, GB, NFC | 265 | 1144 | 4.3 | 3 |
| 1958 | Jim Brown, Clev | 257 | 1527 | 5.9 | 17 | | | | | | |
| 1959 | Jim Brown, Clev | 290 | 1329 | 4.6 | 14 | | | | | | |
| 1960 | Jim Brown, Clev, NFL | 215 | 1257 | 5.8 | 9 | | | | | | |
| | Abner Haynes, Dall Texans, AFL | 156 | 875 | 5.6 | 9 | | | | | | |

## Rushing (Cont.)

| Year | Player, Team | Att. | Yards | Avg. | TD |
|------|--------------|------|-------|------|-----|
| 1974 | Otis Armstrong, Den, AFC | 263 | 1407 | 5.3 | 9 |
|      | Lawrence McCutcheon, LA Rams, NFC | 236 | 1109 | 4.7 | 3 |
| 1975 | O.J. Simpson, Buff, AFC | 329 | 1817 | 5.5 | 16 |
|      | Jim Otis, StL, NFC | 269 | 1076 | 4.0 | 5 |
| 1976 | O.J. Simpson, Buff, AFC | 290 | 1503 | 5.2 | 8 |
|      | Walter Payton, Chi, NFC | 311 | 1390 | 4.5 | 13 |
| 1977 | Walter Payton, Chi, NFC | 339 | 1852 | 5.5 | 14 |
|      | Mark van Eeghen, Oak, AFC | 324 | 1273 | 3.9 | 7 |
| 1978 | Earl Campbell, Hou, AFC | 302 | 1450 | 4.8 | 13 |
|      | Walter Payton, Chi, NFC | 333 | 1395 | 4.2 | 11 |
| 1979 | Earl Campbell, Hou, AFC | 368 | 1697 | 4.6 | 19 |
|      | Walter Payton, Chi, NFC | 369 | 1610 | 4.4 | 14 |
| 1980 | Earl Campbell, Hou, AFC | 373 | 1934 | 5.2 | 13 |
|      | Walter Payton, Chi, NFC | 317 | 1460 | 4.6 | 6 |
| 1981 | George Rogers, NO, NFC | 378 | 1674 | 4.4 | 13 |
|      | Earl Campbell, Hou, AFC | 361 | 1376 | 3.8 | 10 |
| 1982 | Freeman McNeil, NY Jets, AFC | 151 | 786 | 5.2 | 6 |
|      | Tony Dorsett, Dall, NFC | 177 | 745 | 4.2 | 5 |
| 1983 | Eric Dickerson, LA Rams, NFC | 390 | 1808 | 4.6 | 18 |
|      | Curt Warner, Sea, AFC | 335 | 1449 | 4.3 | 13 |
| 1984 | Eric Dickerson, LA Rams, NFC | 379 | 2105 | 5.6 | 14 |
|      | Earnest Jackson, SD, AFC | 296 | 1179 | 4.0 | 8 |
| 1985 | Marcus Allen, LA Raiders, AFC | 380 | 1759 | 4.6 | 11 |
|      | Gerald Riggs, Atl, NFC | 397 | 1719 | 4.3 | 10 |
| 1986 | Eric Dickerson, LA Rams, NFC | 404 | 1821 | 4.5 | 11 |
|      | Curt Warner, Sea, AFC | 319 | 1481 | 4.6 | 13 |
| 1987 | Charles White, LA Rams, NFC | 324 | 1374 | 4.2 | 11 |
|      | Eric Dickerson, Ind, AFC | 223 | 1011 | 4.5 | 5 |
| 1988 | Eric Dickerson, Ind, AFC | 388 | 1659 | 4.3 | 14 |
|      | Herschel Walker, Dall, NFC | 361 | 1514 | 4.2 | 5 |
| 1989 | Christian Okoye, KC, AFC | 370 | 1480 | 4.0 | 12 |
|      | Barry Sanders, Det, NFC | 280 | 1470 | 5.3 | 14 |
| 1990 | Barry Sanders, Det, NFC | 255 | 1304 | 5.1 | 13 |
|      | Thurman Thomas, Buff, AFC | 271 | 1297 | 4.8 | 11 |
| 1991 | Emmitt Smith, Dall, NFC | 365 | 1563 | 4.3 | 12 |
|      | Thurman Thomas, Buff, AFC | 288 | 1407 | 4.9 | 7 |
| 1992 | Emmitt Smith, Dall, NFC | 373 | 1713 | 4.6 | 18 |
|      | Barry Foster, Pitt, AFC | 390 | 1690 | 4.3 | 11 |

## Passing

| Year | Player, Team | Att. | Comp | Yards | TD | Int |
|------|--------------|------|------|-------|-----|-----|
| 1932 | Arnie Herber, GB | 101 | 37 | 639 | 9 | 9 |
| 1933 | Harry Newman, NY | 136 | 53 | 973 | 11 | 17 |
| 1934 | Arnie Herber, GB | 115 | 42 | 799 | 8 | 12 |
| 1935 | Ed Danowski, NY | 113 | 57 | 794 | 10 | 9 |
| 1936 | Arnie Herber, GB | 173 | 77 | 1239 | 11 | 13 |
| 1937 | Sammy Baugh, Wash | 171 | 81 | 1127 | 8 | 14 |
| 1938 | Ed Danowski, NY | 129 | 70 | 848 | 7 | 8 |
| 1939 | Parker Hall, Clev | 208 | 106 | 1227 | 9 | 13 |
| 1940 | Sammy Baugh, Wash | 177 | 111 | 1367 | 12 | 10 |
| 1941 | Cecil Isbell, GB | 206 | 117 | 1479 | 15 | 11 |
| 1942 | Cecil Isbell, GB | 268 | 146 | 2021 | 24 | 14 |
| 1943 | Sammy Baugh, Wash | 239 | 133 | 1754 | 23 | 19 |
| 1944 | Frank Filchock, Wash | 147 | 84 | 1139 | 13 | 9 |
| 1945 | Sammy Baugh, Wash | 182 | 128 | 1669 | 11 | 4 |
|      | Sid Luckman, Chi | 217 | 117 | 1725 | 14 | 10 |
| 1946 | Bob Waterfield, LA | 251 | 127 | 1747 | 18 | 17 |
| 1947 | Sammy Baugh, Wash | 354 | 210 | 2938 | 25 | 15 |
| 1948 | Tommy Thompson, Phi | 246 | 141 | 1965 | 25 | 11 |
| 1949 | Sammy Baugh, Wash | 255 | 145 | 1903 | 18 | 14 |
| 1950 | Norm Van Brocklin, LA | 233 | 127 | 2061 | 18 | 14 |
| 1951 | Bob Waterfield, LA | 176 | 88 | 1566 | 13 | 10 |
| 1952 | Norm Van Brocklin, LA | 205 | 113 | 1736 | 14 | 17 |
| 1953 | Otto Graham, Clev | 258 | 167 | 2722 | 11 | 9 |
| 1954 | Norm Van Brocklin, LA | 260 | 139 | 2637 | 13 | 21 |
| 1955 | Otto Graham, Clev | 185 | 98 | 1721 | 15 | 8 |
| 1956 | Ed Brown, Chi | 168 | 96 | 1667 | 11 | 12 |
| 1957 | Tommy O'Connell, Clev | 110 | 63 | 1229 | 9 | 8 |
| 1958 | Eddie LeBaron, Wash | 145 | 79 | 1365 | 11 | 10 |
| 1959 | Charlie Conerly, NY | 194 | 113 | 1706 | 14 | 4 |
| 1960 | Milt Plum, Clev, NFL | 250 | 151 | 2297 | 21 | 5 |
|      | Jack Kemp, LA, AFL | 406 | 211 | 3018 | 20 | 25 |
| 1961 | George Blanda, Hou, AFL | 362 | 187 | 3330 | 36 | 22 |
|      | Milt Plum, Clev, NFL | 302 | 177 | 2416 | 18 | 10 |
| 1962 | Len Dawson, Dall, AFL | 310 | 189 | 2759 | 29 | 17 |
|      | Bart Starr, GB, NFL | 285 | 178 | 2438 | 12 | 9 |
| 1963 | Y.A. Tittle, NY, NFL | 367 | 221 | 3145 | 36 | 14 |
|      | Tobin Rote, SD, AFL | 286 | 170 | 2510 | 20 | 17 |
| 1964 | Len Dawson, KC, AFL | 354 | 199 | 2879 | 30 | 18 |
|      | Bart Starr, GB, NFL | 272 | 163 | 2144 | 15 | 4 |
| 1965 | Rudy Bukich, Chi, NFL | 312 | 176 | 2641 | 20 | 9 |
|      | John Hadl, SD, AFL | 348 | 174 | 2798 | 20 | 21 |
| 1966 | Bart Starr, GB, NFL | 251 | 156 | 2257 | 14 | 3 |
|      | Len Dawson, KC, AFL | 284 | 159 | 2527 | 26 | 10 |
| 1967 | Sonny Jurgensen, Wash, NFL | 508 | 288 | 3747 | 31 | 16 |
|      | Daryle Lamonica, Oakland, AFL | 425 | 220 | 3228 | 30 | 20 |
| 1968 | Len Dawson, KC, AFL | 224 | 131 | 2109 | 17 | 9 |
|      | Earl Morrall, Balt, NFL | 317 | 182 | 2909 | 26 | 17 |
| 1969 | Sonny Jurgensen, Wash, NFL | 442 | 274 | 3102 | 22 | 15 |
|      | Greg Cook, Cin, AFL | 197 | 106 | 1854 | 15 | 11 |
| 1970 | John Brodie, SF, NFC | 378 | 223 | 2941 | 24 | 10 |
|      | Daryle Lamonica, Oak, AFC | 356 | 179 | 2516 | 22 | 15 |
| 1971 | Roger Staubach, Dall, NFC | 211 | 126 | 1882 | 15 | 4 |
|      | Bob Griese, Mia, AFC | 263 | 145 | 2089 | 19 | 9 |

## Passing *(Cont.)*

| Year | Player, Team | Att. | Comp | Yards | TD | Int |
|------|--------------|------|------|-------|----|-----|
| 1972 | Norm Snead, NY, NFC | 325 | 196 | 2307 | 17 | 12 |
| | Earl Morrall, Mia, AFC | 150 | 83 | 1360 | 11 | 7 |
| 1973 | Roger Staubach, Dall, NFC | 286 | 179 | 2428 | 23 | 15 |
| | Ken Stabler, Oak, AFC | 260 | 163 | 1997 | 14 | 10 |
| 1974 | Ken Anderson, Cin, AFC | 328 | 213 | 2667 | 18 | 10 |
| | Sonny Jurgensen, Wash, NFC | 167 | 107 | 1185 | 11 | 5 |
| 1975 | Ken Anderson, Cin, AFC | 377 | 228 | 3169 | 21 | 11 |
| | Fran Tarkenton, Minn, NFC | 425 | 273 | 2994 | 25 | 13 |
| 1976 | Ken Stabler, Oak, AFC | 291 | 194 | 2737 | 27 | 17 |
| | James Harris, LA, NFC | 158 | 91 | 1460 | 8 | 6 |
| 1977 | Bob Griese, Mia, AFC | 307 | 180 | 2252 | 22 | 13 |
| | Roger Staubach, Dall, NFC | 361 | 210 | 2620 | 18 | 9 |
| 1978 | Roger Staubach, Dall, NFC | 413 | 231 | 3190 | 25 | 16 |
| | Terry Bradshaw, Pitt, AFC | 368 | 207 | 2915 | 28 | 20 |
| 1979 | Roger Staubach, Dall, NFC | 461 | 267 | 3586 | 27 | 11 |
| | Dan Fouts, SD, AFC | 530 | 332 | 4082 | 24 | 24 |
| 1980 | Brian Sipe, Clev, AFC | 554 | 337 | 4132 | 30 | 14 |
| | Ron Jaworski, Phi, NFC | 451 | 257 | 3529 | 27 | 12 |
| 1981 | Ken Anderson, Cin, AFC | 479 | 300 | 3754 | 29 | 10 |
| | Joe Montana, SF, NFC | 488 | 311 | 3565 | 19 | 12 |
| 1982 | Ken Anderson, Cin, AFC | 309 | 218 | 2495 | 12 | 9 |
| | Joe Theismann, Wash, NFC | 252 | 161 | 2033 | 13 | 9 |
| 1983 | Steve Bartkowski, Atl, NFC | 432 | 274 | 3167 | 22 | 5 |
| | Dan Marino, Mia, AFC | 296 | 173 | 2210 | 20 | 6 |
| 1984 | Dan Marino, Mia, AFC | 564 | 362 | 5084 | 48 | 17 |
| | Joe Montana, SF, NFC | 432 | 279 | 3630 | 28 | 10 |
| 1985 | Ken O'Brien, NY, AFC | 488 | 297 | 3888 | 25 | 8 |
| | Joe Montana, SF, NFC | 494 | 303 | 3653 | 27 | 13 |
| 1986 | Tommy Kramer, Minn, NFC | 372 | 208 | 3000 | 24 | 10 |
| | Dan Marino, Mia, AFC | 623 | 378 | 4746 | 44 | 23 |
| 1987 | Joe Montana, SF, NFC | 398 | 266 | 3054 | 31 | 13 |
| | Bernie Kosar, Clev, AFC | 389 | 241 | 3033 | 22 | 9 |
| 1988 | Boomer Esiason, Cin, AFC | 388 | 223 | 3572 | 28 | 14 |
| | Wade Wilson, Minn, NFC | 332 | 204 | 2746 | 15 | 9 |
| 1989 | Joe Montana, SF, NFC | 386 | 271 | 3521 | 26 | 8 |
| | Boomer Esiason, Cin, AFC | 455 | 258 | 3525 | 28 | 11 |
| 1990 | Jim Kelly, Buffalo, AFC | 346 | 219 | 2829 | 24 | 9 |
| | Phil Simms, NY, NFC | 311 | 184 | 2284 | 15 | 4 |
| 1991 | Steve Young, SF, NFC | 279 | 180 | 2517 | 17 | 8 |
| | Jim Kelly, Buff, AFC | 474 | 304 | 3844 | 33 | 17 |
| 1992 | Steve Young, SF, NFC | 402 | 268 | 3465 | 25 | 7 |
| | Warren Moon, Hou, AFC | 346 | 224 | 2521 | 18 | 12 |

## Pass Receiving

| Year | Player, Team | No. | Yds | Avg | TD |
|------|--------------|-----|-----|-----|----|
| 1932 | Ray Flaherty, NY | 21 | 350 | 16.7 | 3 |
| 1933 | John Kelly, Brooklyn | 22 | 246 | 11.2 | 3 |
| 1934 | Joe Carter, Phil | 16 | 238 | 14.9 | 4 |
| | Morris Badgro, NY | 16 | 206 | 12.9 | 1 |
| 1935 | Tod Goodwin, NY | 26 | 432 | 16.6 | 4 |
| 1936 | Don Hutson, GB | 34 | 536 | 15.8 | 8 |
| 1937 | Don Hutson, GB | 41 | 552 | 13.5 | 7 |
| 1938 | Gaynell Tinsley, Chi Cards | 41 | 516 | 12.6 | 1 |
| 1939 | Don Hutson, GB | 34 | 846 | 24.9 | 6 |
| 1940 | Don Looney, Phil | 58 | 707 | 12.2 | 4 |
| 1941 | Don Hutson, GB | 58 | 738 | 12.7 | 10 |
| 1942 | Don Hutson, GB | 74 | 1211 | 16.4 | 17 |
| 1943 | Don Hutson, GB | 47 | 776 | 16.5 | 11 |
| 1944 | Don Hutson, GB | 58 | 866 | 14.9 | 9 |
| 1945 | Don Hutson, GB | 47 | 834 | 17.7 | 9 |
| 1946 | Jim Benton, LA | 63 | 981 | 15.6 | 6 |
| 1947 | Jim Keane, Chi | 64 | 910 | 14.2 | 10 |
| 1948 | Tom Fears, LA | 51 | 698 | 13.7 | 4 |
| 1949 | Tom Fears, LA | 77 | 1013 | 13.2 | 9 |
| 1950 | Tom Fears, LA | 84 | 1116 | 13.3 | 7 |
| 1951 | Elroy Hirsch, LA | 66 | 1495 | 22.7 | 17 |
| 1952 | Mac Speedie, Clev | 62 | 911 | 14.7 | 5 |
| 1953 | Pete Pihos, Phil | 63 | 1049 | 16.7 | 10 |
| 1954 | Pete Pihos, Phil | 60 | 872 | 14.5 | 10 |
| | Billy Wilson, SF | 60 | 830 | 13.8 | 5 |
| 1955 | Pete Pihos, Phil | 62 | 864 | 13.9 | 7 |
| 1956 | Billy Wilson, SF | 60 | 889 | 14.8 | 5 |
| 1957 | Billy Wilson, SF | 52 | 757 | 14.6 | 6 |
| 1958 | Raymond Berry, Balt | 56 | 794 | 14.2 | 9 |
| | Pete Retzlaff, Phil | 56 | 766 | 13.7 | 2 |
| 1959 | Raymond Berry, Balt | 66 | 959 | 14.5 | 14 |
| 1960 | Lionel Taylor, Den, AFL | 92 | 1235 | 13.4 | 12 |
| | Raymond Berry, Baltimore, NFL | 74 | 1298 | 17.5 | 10 |
| 1961 | Lionel Taylor, Den, AFL | 100 | 1176 | 11.8 | 4 |
| | Jim Phillips, LA, NFL | 78 | 1092 | 14.0 | 5 |
| 1962 | Lionel Taylor, Den, AFL | 77 | 908 | 11.8 | 4 |
| | Bobby Mitchell, Wash, NFL | 72 | 1384 | 19.2 | 11 |
| 1963 | Lionel Taylor, Den, AFL | 78 | 1101 | 14.1 | 10 |
| | Bobby Joe Conrad, St. Louis, NFL | 73 | 967 | 13.2 | 10 |
| 1964 | Charley Hennigan, Houston, AFL | 101 | 1546 | 15.3 | 8 |
| | Johnny Morris, Chi, NFL | 93 | 1200 | 12.9 | 10 |
| 1965 | Lionel Taylor, Den, AFL | 85 | 1131 | 13.3 | 6 |
| | Dave Parks, SF, NFL | 80 | 1344 | 16.8 | 12 |
| 1966 | Lance Alworth, SD, AFL | 73 | 1383 | 18.9 | 13 |
| | Charley Taylor, Wash, NFL | 72 | 1119 | 15.5 | 12 |
| 1967 | George Sauer, NY, AFL | 75 | 1189 | 15.9 | 6 |
| | Charley Taylor, Wash, NFL | 70 | 990 | 14.1 | 9 |
| 1968 | Clifton McNeil, SF, NFL | 71 | 994 | 14.0 | 7* |
| | Lance Alworth, SD, AFL | 68 | 1312 | 19.3 | 10 |

## Pass Receiving *(Cont.)*

| Year | Player, Team | No. | Yds | Avg | TD |
|------|--------------|-----|-----|-----|----|
| 1969 | Dan Abramowicz, | | | | |
| | NO, NFL | 73 | 1015 | 13.9 | 7 |
| | Lance Alworth, SD, AFL | 64 | 1003 | 15.7 | 4 |
| 1970 | Dick Gordon, Chi, NFC | 71 | 1026 | 14.5 | 13 |
| | Marlin Briscoe, | | | | |
| | Buff, AFC | 57 | 1036 | 18.2 | 8 |
| 1971 | Fred Biletnikoff, | | | | |
| | Oak, AFC | 61 | 929 | 15.2 | 9 |
| | Bob Tucker, NY, NFC | 59 | 791 | 13.4 | 4 |
| 1972 | Harold Jackson, | | | | |
| | Phi, NFC | 62 | 1048 | 16.9 | 4 |
| | Fred Biletnikoff, | | | | |
| | Oak, AFC | 58 | 802 | 13.8 | 7 |
| 1973 | Harold Carmichael, | | | | |
| | Phi, NFC | 67 | 1116 | 16.7 | 9 |
| | Fred Willis, Hou, AFC | 57 | 371 | 6.5 | 1 |
| 1974 | Lydell Mitchell, | | | | |
| | Balt, AFC | 72 | 544 | 7.6 | 2 |
| | Charles Young, | | | | |
| | Phi, NFC | 63 | 696 | 11.0 | 3 |
| 1975 | Chuck Foreman, | | | | |
| | Minn, NFC | 73 | 691 | 9.5 | 9 |
| | Reggie Rucker, | | | | |
| | Clev, AFC | 60 | 770 | 12.8 | 3 |
| | Lydell Mitchell, Balt, AFC | 60 | 544 | 9.1 | 4 |
| 1976 | MacArthur Lane, KC, AFC | 66 | 686 | 10.4 | 1 |
| | Drew Pearson, Dall, NFC | 58 | 806 | 13.9 | 6 |
| 1977 | Lydell Mitchell, Balt, AFC | 71 | 620 | 8.7 | 4 |
| | Ahmad Rashad, | | | | |
| | Minn, NFC | 51 | 681 | 13.4 | 2 |
| 1978 | Rickey Young, Minn, NFC | 88 | 704 | 8.0 | 5 |
| | Steve Largent, Sea, AFC | 71 | 1168 | 16.5 | 8 |
| 1979 | Joe Washington, | | | | |
| | Balt, AFC | 82 | 750 | 9.1 | 3 |
| | Ahmad Rashad, | | | | |
| | Minn, NFC | 80 | 1156 | 14.5 | 9 |

| Year | Player, Team | No. | Yds | Avg | TD |
|------|--------------|-----|-----|-----|----|
| 1980 | Kellen Winslow, SD, AFC | 89 | 1290 | 14.5 | 9 |
| | Earl Cooper, SF, NFC | 83 | 567 | 6.8 | 4 |
| 1981 | Kellen Winslow, SD, AFC | 88 | 1075 | 12.2 | 10 |
| | Dwight Clark, SF, NFC | 85 | 1105 | 13.0 | 4 |
| 1982 | Dwight Clark, SF, NFC | 60 | 913 | 15.2 | 5 |
| | Kellen Winslow, SD, AFC | 54 | 721 | 13.4 | 6 |
| 1983 | Todd Christensen, | | | | |
| | Los Angeles, AFC | 92 | 1247 | 13.6 | 12 |
| | Roy Green, StL, NFC | 78 | 1227 | 15.7 | 14 |
| | Charlie Brown, | | | | |
| | Wash, NFC | 78 | 1225 | 15.7 | 8 |
| | Earnest Gray, NY, NFC | 78 | 1139 | 14.6 | 5 |
| 1984 | Art Monk, Wash, NFC | 106 | 1372 | 12.9 | 7 |
| | Ozzie Newsome, | | | | |
| | Clev, AFC | 89 | 1001 | 11.2 | 5 |
| 1985 | Roger Craig, SF, NFC | 92 | 1016 | 11.0 | 6 |
| | Lionel James, SD, AFC | 86 | 1027 | 11.9 | 6 |
| 1986 | Todd Christensen, | | | | |
| | Los Angeles, AFC | 95 | 1153 | 12.1 | 8 |
| | Jerry Rice, SF, NFC | 86 | 1570 | 18.3 | 15 |
| 1987 | J.T. Smith, StL, NFC | 91 | 1117 | 12.3 | 8 |
| | Al Toon, NY, AFC | 68 | 976 | 14.4 | 5 |
| 1988 | Al Toon, NY, AFC | 93 | 1067 | 11.5 | 5 |
| | Henry Ellard, LA Rams, NFC | 86 | 1414 | 16.4 | 10 |
| 1989 | Sterling Sharpe, GB, NFC | 90 | 1423 | 15.8 | 12 |
| | Andre Reed, Buff, AFC | 88 | 1312 | 14.9 | 9 |
| 1990 | Jerry Rice, SF, NFC | 100 | 1502 | 15.0 | 13 |
| | Haywood Jeffires, | | | | |
| | Houston, AFC | 74 | 1048 | 14.2 | 8 |
| | Drew Hill, Hou, AFC | 74 | 1019 | 13.8 | 5 |
| 1991 | Haywood Jeffires, Hou, AFC | 100 | 1181 | 11.8 | 7 |
| | Michael Irvin, Dall, NFC | 93 | 1523 | 16.4 | 8 |
| 1992 | Sterling Sharpe, GB | 108 | 1461 | 13.5 | 13 |
| | Haywood Jeffires, Hou | 90 | 913 | 10.1 | 9 |

## Scoring

| Year | Player, Team | TD | FG | PAT | TP |
|------|--------------|----|----|-----|----|
| 1932 | Earl Clark, Portsmouth | 6 | 3 | 10 | 55 |
| 1933 | Ken Strong, NY | 6 | 5 | 13 | 64 |
| | Glenn Presnell, Ports | 6 | 6 | 10 | 64 |
| 1934 | Jack Manders, Chi | 3 | 10 | 31 | 79 |
| 1935 | Earl Clark, Det | 6 | 1 | 16 | 55 |
| 1936 | Earl Clark, Det | 7 | 4 | 19 | 73 |
| 1937 | Jack Manders, Chi | 5 | 8 | 15 | 69 |
| 1938 | Clarke Hinkle, GB | 7 | 3 | 7 | 58 |
| 1939 | Andy Farkas, Wash | 11 | 0 | 2 | 68 |
| 1940 | Don Hutson, GB | 7 | 0 | 15 | 57 |
| 1941 | Don Hutson, GB | 12 | 1 | 20 | 95 |
| 1942 | Don Hutson, GB | 17 | 1 | 33 | 138 |
| 1943 | Don Hutson, GB | 12 | 3 | 36 | 117 |
| 1944 | Don Hutson, GB | 9 | 0 | 31 | 85 |
| 1945 | Steve Van Buren, Phil | 18 | 0 | 2 | 110 |
| 1946 | Ted Fritsch, GB | 10 | 9 | 13 | 100 |
| 1947 | Pat Harder, Chicago Cards | 7 | 7 | 39 | 102 |
| 1948 | Pat Harder, Chicago Cards | 6 | 7 | 53 | 110 |
| 1949 | Pat Harder, Chicago Cards | 8 | 3 | 45 | 102 |
| | Gene Roberts, NY | 17 | 0 | 0 | 102 |
| 1950 | Doak Walker, Det | 11 | 8 | 38 | 128 |
| 1951 | Elroy Hirsch, LA | 17 | 0 | 0 | 102 |
| 1952 | Gordy Soltau, SF | 7 | 6 | 34 | 94 |
| 1953 | Gordy Soltau, SF | 6 | 10 | 48 | 114 |
| 1954 | Bobby Walston, Phil | 11 | 4 | 36 | 114 |
| 1955 | Doak Walker, Det | 7 | 9 | 27 | 96 |
| 1956 | Bobby Layne, Det | 5 | 12 | 33 | 99 |

| Year | Player, Team | TD | FG | PAT | TP |
|------|--------------|----|----|-----|----|
| 1957 | Sam Baker, Wash | 1 | 14 | 29 | 77 |
| | Lou Groza, Clev | 0 | 15 | 32 | 77 |
| 1958 | Jim Brown, Clev | 18 | 0 | 0 | 108 |
| 1959 | Paul Hornung, GB | 7 | 7 | 31 | 94 |
| 1960 | Paul Hornung, GB, NFL | 15 | 15 | 41 | 176 |
| | Gene Mingo, Den, AFL | 6 | 18 | 33 | 123 |
| 1961 | Gino Cappelletti, Bos, AFL | 8 | 17 | 48 | 147 |
| | Paul Hornung, GB, NFL | 10 | 15 | 41 | 146 |
| 1962 | Gene Mingo, Den, AFL | 4 | 27 | 32 | 137 |
| | Jim Taylor, GB, NFL | 19 | 0 | 0 | 114 |
| 1963 | Gino Cappelletti, Bos, AFL | 2 | 22 | 35 | 113 |
| | Don Chandler, NY, NFL | 0 | 18 | 52 | 106 |
| 1964 | Gino Cappelletti, Bos, AFL | 7 | 25 | 36 | 155 |
| | Lenny Moore, Balt, NFL | 20 | 0 | 0 | 120 |
| 1965 | Gale Sayers, Chi, NFL | 22 | 0 | 0 | 132 |
| | Gino Cappelletti, Bos, AFL | 9 | 17 | 27 | 132 |
| 1966 | Gino Cappelletti, Bos, AFL | 6 | 16 | 35 | 119 |
| | Bruce Gossett, LA, NFL | 0 | 28 | 29 | 113 |
| 1967 | Jim Bakken, StL, NFL | 0 | 27 | 36 | 117 |
| | George Blanda, Oak, AFL | 0 | 20 | 56 | 116 |
| 1968 | Jim Turner, NY, AFL | 0 | 34 | 43 | 145 |
| | Leroy Kelly, Clev, NFL | 20 | 0 | 0 | 120 |
| 1969 | Jim Turner, NY, AFL | 0 | 32 | 33 | 129 |
| | Fred Cox, Minn, NFL | 0 | 26 | 43 | 121 |
| 1970 | Fred Cox, Minn, NFC | 0 | 30 | 35 | 125 |
| | Jan Stenerud, KC, AFC | 0 | 30 | 26 | 116 |

## Scoring *(Cont.)*

| Year | Player, Team | TD | FG | PAT | TP | Year | Player, Team | TD | FG | PAT | TP |
|---|---|---|---|---|---|---|---|---|---|---|---|
| 1971 | Garo Yepremian, Mia, AFC | 0 | 28 | 33 | 117 | 1982 | Marcus Allen, LA, AFC | 14 | 0 | 0 | 84 |
| | Curt Knight, Wash, NFC | 0 | 29 | 27 | 114 | | Wendell Tyler, LA, NFC | 13 | 0 | 0 | 78 |
| 1972 | Chester Marcol, GB, NFC | 0 | 33 | 29 | 128 | 1983 | Mark Moseley, Wash, NFC | 0 | 33 | 62 | 161 |
| | Bobby Howfield, NY AFC | 0 | 27 | 40 | 121 | | Gary Anderson, Pitt, AFC | 0 | 27 | 38 | 119 |
| 1973 | David Ray, LA, NFC | 0 | 30 | 40 | 130 | 1984 | Ray Wersching, SF, NFC | 0 | 25 | 56 | 131 |
| | Roy Gerela, Pitt, AFC | 0 | 29 | 36 | 123 | | Gary Anderson, Pitt, AFC | 0 | 24 | 45 | 117 |
| 1974 | Chester Marcol, GB, NFC | 0 | 25 | 19 | 94 | 1985 | Kevin Butler, Chi, NFC | 0 | 31 | 51 | 144 |
| | Roy Gerela, Pitt, AFC | 0 | 20 | 33 | 93 | | Gary Anderson, Pitt, AFC | 0 | 33 | 40 | 139 |
| 1975 | O.J. Simpson, Buff, AFC | 23 | 0 | 0 | 138 | 1986 | Tony Franklin, NE, AFC | 0 | 32 | 44 | 140 |
| | Chuck Foreman, Minn, NFC | 22 | 0 | 0 | 132 | | Kevin Butler, Chi, NFC | 0 | 28 | 36 | 120 |
| 1976 | Toni Linhart, Balt, AFC | 0 | 20 | 49 | 109 | 1987 | Jerry Rice, SF, NFC | 23 | 0 | 0 | 138 |
| | Mark Moseley, Wash, NFC | 0 | 22 | 31 | 97 | | Jim Breech, Cin, AFC | 0 | 24 | 25 | 97 |
| 1977 | Errol Mann, Oak, AFC | 0 | 20 | 39 | 99 | 1988 | Scott Norwood, Buff, AFC | 0 | 32 | 33 | 129 |
| | Walter Payton, Chi, NFC | 16 | 0 | 0 | 96 | | Mike Cofer, SF, NFC | 0 | 27 | 40 | 121 |
| 1978 | Frank Corral, LA, NFC | 0 | 29 | 31 | 118 | 1989 | Mike Cofer, SF, NFC | 0 | 29 | 49 | 136 |
| | Pat Leahy, NY, AFC | 0 | 22 | 41 | 107 | | David Treadwell, Den, AFC | 0 | 27 | 39 | 120 |
| 1979 | John Smith, NE, AFC | 0 | 23 | 46 | 115 | 1990 | Nick Lowery, KC, AFC | 0 | 34 | 37 | 139 |
| | Mark Moseley, Wash, NFC | 0 | 25 | 39 | 114 | | Chip Lohmiller, Wash, NFC | 0 | 30 | 41 | 131 |
| 1980 | John Smith, NE, AFC | 0 | 26 | 51 | 129 | 1991 | Chip Lohmiller, Wash, NFC | 0 | 31 | 56 | 149 |
| | Ed Murray, Det, NFC | 0 | 27 | 35 | 116 | | Pete Stoyanovich, Mia, AFC | 0 | 31 | 28 | 121 |
| 1981 | Ed Murray, Det, NFC | 0 | 25 | 46 | 121 | 1992 | Pete Stoyanovich, Mia, AFC | 0 | 30 | 34 | 124 |
| 1981 | Rafael Septien, Dall, NFC | 0 | 27 | 40 | 121 | | Morten Anderson, NO, NFC | 0 | 29 | 33 | 120 |
| | Jim Breech, Cin, AFC | 0 | 22 | 49 | 115 | | Chip Lohmiller, Wash, NFC | 0 | 30 | 30 | 120 |
| | Nick Lowery, KC, AFC | 0 | 26 | 37 | 115 | | | | | | |

## Interceptions

| Year | Player, Team | No. | Yds | TD | Year | Player, Team | No. | Yds | TD |
|---|---|---|---|---|---|---|---|---|---|
| 1940 | Clarence Parker, Brooklyn | 6 | 146 | 1 | 1964 | Dainard Paulson, NY, AFL | 12 | 157 | 1 |
| | Kent Ryan, Det | 6 | 65 | 0 | | Paul Krause, Wash, NFL | 12 | 140 | 1 |
| | Don Hutson, GB | 6 | 24 | 0 | 1965 | W.K. Hicks, Hous, AFL | 9 | 156 | 0 |
| 1941 | Marshall Goldberg, Chi Cards | 7 | 54 | 0 | | Bobby Boyd, Balt, NFL | 9 | 78 | 1 |
| | Art Jones, Pitt | 7 | 35 | 0 | 1966 | Larry Wilson, StL, NFL | 10 | 180 | 2 |
| 1942 | Clyde Turner, Chi | 8 | 96 | 1 | | Johnny Robinson, KC, AFL | 10 | 136 | 1 |
| 1943 | Sammy Baugh, Wash | 11 | 112 | 0 | | Bobby Hunt, KC, AFL | 10 | 113 | 0 |
| 1944 | Howard Livingston, NY | 9 | 172 | 0 | 1967 | Miller Farr, Hous, AFL | 10 | 264 | 3 |
| 1945 | Roy Zimmerman, Phil | 7 | 90 | 0 | | Lem Barney, Det, NFL | 10 | 232 | 3 |
| 1946 | Bill Dudley, Pitt | 10 | 242 | 1 | | Tom Janik, Buff, AFL | 10 | 222 | 2 |
| 1947 | Frank Reagan, NY | 10 | 100 | 0 | | Dave Whitsell, NO, NFL | 10 | 178 | 2 |
| | Frank Seno, Bos | 10 | 203 | 0 | | Dick Westmoreland, Miami, AFL | 10 | 127 | 1 |
| 1948 | Dan Sandifer, Wash | 13 | 258 | 2 | 1968 | Dave Grayson, Oak, AFL | 10 | 195 | 1 |
| 1949 | Bob Nussbaumer, Chi | 12 | 157 | 0 | | Willie Williams, NY, NFL | 10 | 103 | 0 |
| 1950 | Orban Sanders, NY Yanks | 13 | 199 | 0 | 1969 | Mel Renfro, Dall, NFL | 10 | 118 | 0 |
| 1951 | Otto Schnellbacher, NY | 11 | 194 | 2 | | Emmitt Thomas, KC, AFL | 9 | 146 | 1 |
| 1952 | Dick Lane, LA | 14 | 298 | 2 | 1970 | Johnny Robinson, KC, AFC | 10 | 155 | 0 |
| 1953 | Jack Christiansen, Det | 12 | 238 | 1 | | Dick LeBeau, Det, NFC | 9 | 96 | 0 |
| 1954 | Dick Lane, Chicago Cards | 10 | 181 | 0 | 1971 | Bill Bradley, Phil, NFC | 11 | 248 | 0 |
| 1955 | Will Sherman, LA | 11 | 101 | 0 | | Ken Houston, Hous, AFC | 9 | 220 | 4 |
| 1956 | Lindon Crow, Chicago Cards | 11 | 170 | 0 | 1972 | Bill Bradley, Phil, NFC | 9 | 73 | 0 |
| 1957 | Milt Davis, Balt | 10 | 219 | 2 | | Mike Sensibaugh, KC, AFC | 8 | 65 | 0 |
| | Jack Christiansen, Det | 10 | 137 | 1 | 1973 | Dick Anderson, Miami, AFC | 8 | 163 | 2 |
| | Jack Butler, Pitt | 10 | 85 | 0 | | Mike Wagner, Pitt, AFC | 8 | 134 | 0 |
| 1958 | Jim Patton, NY | 11 | 183 | 0 | | Bobby Bryant, Minn, NFC | 7 | 105 | 1 |
| 1959 | Dean Derby, Pitt | 7 | 127 | 0 | 1974 | Emmitt Thomas, KC, AFC | 12 | 214 | 2 |
| | Milt Davis, Balt | 7 | 119 | 1 | | Ray Brown, Atl, NFC | 8 | 164 | 1 |
| | Don Shinnick, Balt | 7 | 70 | 0 | 1975 | Mel Blount, Pitt, AFC | 11 | 121 | 0 |
| 1960 | Austin Gonsoulin, Den, AFL | 11 | 98 | 0 | | Paul Krause, Minn, NFC | 10 | 201 | 0 |
| | Dave Baker, SF, NFL | 10 | 96 | 0 | 1976 | Monte Jackson, LA, NFC | 10 | 173 | 3 |
| | Jerry Norton, StL, NFL | 10 | 96 | 0 | | Ken Riley, Cin, AFC | 9 | 141 | 1 |
| 1961 | Billy Atkins, Buff, AFL | 10 | 158 | 0 | 1977 | Lyle Blackwood, Balt, AFC | 10 | 163 | 0 |
| | Dick Lynch, NY, NFL | 9 | 60 | 0 | | Rolland Lawrence, Atl, NFC | 7 | 138 | 0 |
| 1962 | Lee Riley, NY, AFL | 11 | 122 | 0 | 1978 | Thom Darden, Clev, AFC | 10 | 200 | 0 |
| | Willie Wood, GB, NFL | 9 | 132 | 0 | | Ken Stone, StL, NFC | 9 | 139 | 0 |
| 1963 | Fred Glick, Hous, AFL | 12 | 180 | 1 | | Willie Buchanon, GB, NFC | 9 | 93 | 1 |
| | Dick Lynch, NY, NFL | 9 | 251 | 3 | 1979 | Mike Reinfeldt, Hous, AFC | 12 | 205 | 0 |
| | Roosevelt Taylor, Chi, NFL | 9 | 172 | 1 | | Lemar Parrish, Wash, NFC | 9 | 65 | 0 |

## Interceptions (Cont.)

| Year | Player, Team | No. | Yds | TD | Year | Player, Team | No. | Yds | TD |
|------|--------------|-----|-----|-----|------|--------------|-----|-----|-----|
| 1980 | Lester Hayes, Oak, AFC | 13 | 273 | 1 | 1986 | Ronnie Lott, SF, NFC | 10 | 134 | 1 |
| | Nolan Cromwell, LA, NFC | 8 | 140 | 1 | | Deron Cherry, KC, AFC | 9 | 150 | 0 |
| 1981 | Everson Walls, Dall, NFC | 11 | 133 | 0 | 1987 | Barry Wilburn, Wash, NFC | 9 | 135 | 1 |
| | John Harris, Sea, AFC | 10 | 155 | 2 | | Mike Prior, Ind, AFC | 6 | 57 | 0 |
| 1982 | Everson Walls, Dall, NFC | 7 | 61 | 0 | | Mark Kelso, Buff, AFC | 6 | 25 | 0 |
| | Ken Riley, Cin, AFC | 5 | 88 | 1 | | Keith Bostic, Hous, AFC | 6 | -14 | 0 |
| | Bobby Jackson, NY, AFC | 5 | 84 | 1 | 1988 | Scott Case, Atl, NFC | 10 | 47 | 0 |
| | Dwayne Woodruff, Pitt, AFC | 5 | 53 | 0 | | Erik McMillan, NY, AFC | 8 | 168 | 2 |
| | Donnie Shell, Pitt, AFC | 5 | 27 | 0 | 1989 | Felix Wright, Clev, AFC | 9 | 91 | 1 |
| 1983 | Mark Murphy, Wash, NFC | 9 | 127 | 0 | | Eric Allen, Phil, NFC | 8 | 38 | 0 |
| | Ken Riley, Cin, AFC | 8 | 89 | 2 | 1990 | Mark Carrier, Chi, NFC | 10 | 39 | 0 |
| | Vann McElroy, LA, AFC | 8 | 68 | 0 | | Richard Johnson, Hous, AFC | 8 | 100 | 1 |
| 1984 | Ken Easley, Sea, AFC | 10 | 126 | 2 | 1991 | Ronnie Lott, LA, AFC | 8 | 52 | 0 |
| | Tom Flynn, GB, NFC | 9 | 106 | 0 | | Four in NFC tied with 6 | | | |
| 1985 | Everson Walls, Dall, NFC | 9 | 31 | 0 | 1992 | Henry Jones, Buff, AFC | 8 | 263 | 2 |
| | Albert Lewis, KC, AFC | 8 | 59 | 0 | | Audray McMillian, Minn, NFC | 8 | 157 | 2 |
| | Eugene Daniel, Ind, AFC | 8 | 53 | 0 | | | | | |

## Sacks

| Year | Player, Team | No. | Year | Player, Team | No. |
|------|--------------|-----|------|--------------|-----|
| 1982 | Doug Martin, Minn, NFC | 11.5 | 1987 | Reggie White, Phil, NFC | 21.0 |
| | Jesse Baker, Hou, AFC | 7.5 | | Andre Tippett, NE, AFC | 12.5 |
| 1983 | Mark Gastineau, NY Jets, AFC | 19.0 | 1988 | Reggie White, Phil, NFC | 18.0 |
| | Fred Dean, SF, NFC | 17.5 | | Greg Townsend, LA, AFC | 11.5 |
| 1985 | Mark Gastineau, NY, AFC | 22.0 | 1989 | Chris Doleman, Minn, NFC | 21.0 |
| | Richard Dent, Chi, NFC | 17.5 | | Lee Williams, SD, AFC | 14.0 |
| 1985 | Richard Dent, Chi, NFC | 17.0 | 1990 | Derrick Thomas, KC, AFC | 20.0 |
| | Andre Tippett, NE, AFC | 16.5 | | Charles Haley, SF, NFC | 16.0 |
| 1986 | Lawrence Taylor, NY, NFC | 20.5 | 1991 | Pat Swilling, NO, NFC | 17.0 |
| | Sean Jones, LA, AFC | 15.5 | | William Fuller, Hou, AFC | 15.0 |
| | | | 1992 | Clyde Simmons, Phil, NFC | 19.0 |
| | | | | Leslie O'Neal, SD, AFC | 17.0 |

# Annual NFL Team Statistical Leaders

## Points Scored

| Year | Team | Points | Year | Team | Points |
|------|------|--------|------|------|--------|
| 1932 | Green Bay | 152 | 1958 | Baltimore | 381 |
| 1933 | NY Giants | 244 | 1959 | Baltimore | 374 |
| 1934 | Chicago Bears | 286 | 1960 | NY Titans, AFL | 382 |
| 1935 | Chicago Bears | 192 | | Cleveland, NFL | 362 |
| 1936 | Green Bay | 248 | 1961 | Houston, AFL | 513 |
| 1937 | Green Bay | 220 | | Green Bay, NFL | 391 |
| 1938 | Green Bay | 223 | 1962 | Green Bay, NFL | 415 |
| 1939 | Chicago Bears | 298 | | Dallas Texans, AFL | 389 |
| 1940 | Washington | 245 | 1963 | NY Giants, NFL | 448 |
| 1941 | Chicago Bears | 396 | | San Diego, AFL | 399 |
| 1942 | Chicago Bears | 376 | 1964 | Baltimore, NFL | 428 |
| 1943 | Chicago Bears | 303 | | Buffalo, AFL | 400 |
| 1944 | Philadelphia | 267 | 1965 | San Francisco, NFL | 421 |
| 1945 | Philadelphia | 272 | | San Diego, AFL | 340 |
| 1946 | Chicago Bears | 289 | 1966 | Kansas City, AFL | 448 |
| 1947 | Chicago Bears | 363 | | Dallas, NFL | 445 |
| 1948 | Chicago Cardinals | 395 | 1967 | Oakland, AFL | 468 |
| 1949 | Philadelphia | 364 | | Los Angeles, NFL | 398 |
| 1950 | Los Angeles | 466 | 1968 | Oakland, AFL | 453 |
| 1951 | Los Angeles | 392 | | Dallas, NFL | 431 |
| 1952 | Los Angeles | 349 | 1969 | Minnesota, NFL | 379 |
| 1953 | San Francisco | 372 | | Oakland, AFL | 377 |
| 1954 | Detroit | 337 | 1970 | San Francisco, NFC | 352 |
| 1955 | Cleveland | 349 | | Baltimore, AFC | 321 |
| 1956 | Chicago Bears | 363 | 1971 | Dallas, NFC | 406 |
| 1957 | Los Angeles | 307 | | Oakland, AFC | 344 |

## Points Scored *(Cont.)*

| Year | Team | Points | Year | Team | Points |
|------|------|--------|------|------|--------|
| 1972 | Miami, AFC | 385 | | Dallas, NFC | 226 |
| | San Francisco, NFC | 353 | 1983 | Washington, NFC | 541 |
| 1973 | Los Angeles, NFC | 388 | | LA Raiders, AFC | 442 |
| | Denver, AFC | 354 | 1984 | Miami, AFC | 513 |
| 1974 | Oakland, AFC | 355 | | San Francisco, NFC | 475 |
| | Washington, NFC | 320 | 1985 | San Diego, AFC | 467 |
| 1975 | Buffalo, AFC | 420 | | Chicago, NFC | 456 |
| | Minnesota, NFC | 377 | 1986 | Miami, AFC | 430 |
| 1976 | Baltimore, AFC | 417 | | Minnesota, NFC | 398 |
| | Los Angeles, NFC | 351 | 1987 | San Francisco, NFC | 459 |
| 1977 | Oakland, AFC | 351 | | Cleveland, AFC | 390 |
| | Dallas, NFC | 345 | 1988 | Cincinnati, AFC | 448 |
| 1978 | Dallas, NFC | 384 | | LA Rams, NFC | 407 |
| | Miami, AFC | 372 | 1989 | San Francisco, NFC | 442 |
| 1979 | Pittsburgh, AFC | 416 | | Buffalo, AFC | 409 |
| | Dallas, NFC | 371 | 1990 | Buffalo, AFC | 428 |
| 1980 | Dallas, NFC | 454 | | Philadelphia, NFC | 396 |
| | New England, AFC | 441 | 1991 | Washington, NFC | 485 |
| 1981 | San Diego, AFC | 478 | | Buffalo, AFC | 458 |
| | Atlanta, NFC | 426 | 1992 | San Francisco, NFC | 431 |
| 1982 | San Diego, AFC | 288 | | Buffalo, AFC | 381 |

## Total Yards Gained

| Year | Team | Yards | Year | Team | Yards |
|------|------|-------|------|------|-------|
| 1932 | Chicago Bears | 2,755 | 1966 | Dallas, NFL | 5,145 |
| 1933 | NY Giants | 2,973 | | Kansas City, AFL | 5,114 |
| 1934 | Chicago Bears | 3,900 | 1967 | NY Jets, AFL | 5,152 |
| 1935 | Chicago Bears | 3,454 | | Baltimore, NFL | 5,008 |
| 1936 | Detroit | 3,703 | 1968 | Oakland, AFL | 5,036 |
| 1937 | Green Bay | 3,201 | | Dallas, NFL | 5,117 |
| 1938 | Green Bay | 3,037 | 1969 | Dallas NFL | 5,122 |
| 1939 | Chicago Bears | 3,988 | | Oakland, AFL | 5,036 |
| 1940 | Green Bay | 3,400 | 1970 | Oakland, AFC | 4,829 |
| 1941 | Chicago Bears | 4,265 | | San Francisco, NFC | 4,503 |
| 1942 | Chicago Bears | 3,900 | 1971 | Dallas, NFC | 5,035 |
| 1943 | Chicago Bears | 4,045 | | San Diego, AFC | 4,738 |
| 1944 | Chicago Bears | 3,239 | 1972 | Miami, AFC | 5,036 |
| 1945 | Washington | 3,549 | | NY Giants, NFC | 4,483 |
| 1946 | Los Angeles | 3,793 | 1973 | Los Angeles, NFC | 4,906 |
| 1947 | Chicago Bears | 5,053 | | Oakland, AFC | 4,773 |
| 1948 | Chicago Cardinals | 4,705 | 1974 | Dallas, NFC | 4,983 |
| 1949 | Chicago Bears | 4,873 | | Oakland, AFC | 4,718 |
| 1950 | Los Angeles | 5,420 | 1975 | Buffalo, AFC | 5,467 |
| 1951 | Los Angeles | 5,506 | | Dallas, NFC | 5,025 |
| 1952 | Cleveland | 4,352 | 1976 | Baltimore, AFC | 5,236 |
| 1953 | Philadelphia | 4,811 | | St. Louis, NFC | 5,136 |
| 1954 | Los Angeles | 5,187 | 1977 | Dallas, NFC | 4,812 |
| 1955 | Chicago Bears | 4,316 | | Oakland, AFC | 4,736 |
| 1956 | Chicago Bears | 4,537 | 1978 | New England, AFC | 5,965 |
| 1957 | Los Angeles | 4,143 | | Dallas, NFC | 5,959 |
| 1958 | Baltimore | 4,539 | 1979 | Pittsburgh, AFC | 6,258 |
| 1959 | Baltimore | 4,458 | | Dallas, NFC | 5,968 |
| 1960 | Houston, AFL | 4,936 | 1980 | San Diego, AFC | 6,410 |
| | Baltimore, NFL | 4,245 | | Los Angeles, NFC | 6,006 |
| 1961 | Houston, AFL | 6,288 | 1981 | San Diego, AFC | 6,744 |
| | Philadelphia, NFL | 5,112 | | Detroit, NFC | 5,933 |
| 1962 | NY Giants, NFL | 5,005 | 1982 | San Diego, AFC | 4,048 |
| | Houston, AFL | 4,971 | | San Francisco, NFC | 3,242 |
| 1963 | San Diego, AFL | 5,153 | 1983 | San Diego, AFC | 6,197 |
| | NY Giants, NFL | 5,005 | | Green Bay, NFC | 6,172 |
| 1964 | Buffalo, AFL | 5,206 | 1984 | Miami, AFC | 6,936 |
| | Baltimore, NFL | 4,779 | | San Francisco, NFC | 6,366 |
| 1965 | San Francisco, NFL | 5,270 | 1985 | San Diego, AFC | 6,535 |
| | San Diego, AFL | 5,188 | | San Francisco, NFC | 5,920 |

## Total Yards Gained *(Cont.)*

| Year | Team | Yards | Year | Team | Yards |
|------|------|-------|------|------|-------|
| 1986 | Cincinnati, AFC | 6,490 | 1990 | Houston, AFC | 6,222 |
| | San Francisco, NFC | 6,082 | | San Francisco, NFC | 5,895 |
| 1987 | San Francisco, NFC | 5,987 | 1991 | Buffalo, AFC | 6,252 |
| | Denver, AFC | 5,624 | | San Francisco | 5,858 |
| 1988 | Cincinnati, AFC | 6,057 | 1992 | San Francisco, NFC | 6,195 |
| | San Francisco, NFC | 5,900 | | Buffalo, AFC | 5,893 |
| 1989 | San Francisco, NFC | 6,268 | | | |
| | Cincinnati, AFC | 6,101 | | | |

## Pro Bowl All-Time Results

| Date | Result | Date | Result | Date | Result |
|------|--------|------|--------|------|--------|
| 1-15-39 | NY Giants 13, Pro All-Stars 10 | 1-17-60 | West 38, East 21 | 1-23-72 | AFC 26, NFC 13 |
| 1-14-40 | Green Bay 16, NFL All-Stars 7 | 1-15-61 | West 35, East 31 | 1-21-73 | AFC 33, NFC 28 |
| 12-29-40 | Chi Bears 28, NFL All-Stars 14 | 1-7-62 | AFL West 47, East 27 | 1-20-74 | AFC 15, NFC 13 |
| | | 1-14-62 | NFL West 31, East 30 | 1-20-75 | NFC 17, AFC 10 |
| 1-4-42 | Chi Bears 35, NFL All-Stars 24 | 1-13-63 | AFL West 21, East 14 | 1-26-76 | NFC 23, AFC 20 |
| 12-27-42 | NFL All-Stars 17, Washington 14 | 1-13-63 | NFL East 30, West 20 | 1-17-77 | AFC 24, NFC 14 |
| 1-14-51 | American Conf 28, National Conf 27 | 1-12-64 | NFL West 31, East 17 | 1-23-78 | NFC 14, AFC 13 |
| | | 1-19-64 | AFL West 27, East 24 | 1-29-79 | NFC 13, AFC 7 |
| 1-12-52 | National Conf 30, American Conf 13 | 1-10-65 | NFL West 34, East 14 | 1-27-80 | NFC 37, AFC 27 |
| | | 1-16-65 | AFL West 38, East 14 | 2-1-81 | NFC 21, AFC 7 |
| 1-10-53 | National Conf 27, American Conf 7 | 1-15-66 | AFL All-Stars 30, Buffalo 19 | 1-31-82 | AFC 16, NFC 13 |
| | | | | 2-6-83 | NFC 20, AFC 19 |
| 1-17-54 | East 20, West 9 | 1-15-66 | NFL East 36, West 7 | 1-29-84 | NFC 45, AFC 3 |
| 1-16-55 | West 26, East 19 | 1-21-67 | AFL East 30, West 23 | 1-27-85 | AFC 22, NFC 14 |
| 1-15-56 | East 31, West 30 | 1-22-67 | NFL East 20, West 10 | 2-2-86 | NFC 28, AFC 24 |
| 1-13-57 | West 19, East 10 | 1-21-68 | AFL East 25, West 24 | 2-1-87 | AFC 10, NFC 6 |
| 1-12-58 | West 26, East 7 | 1-21-68 | NFL West 38, East 20 | 2-7-88 | AFC 15, NFC 6 |
| 1-11-59 | East 28, West 21 | 1-19-69 | AFL West 38, East 25 | 1-29-89 | NFC 34, AFC 3 |
| | | 1-19-69 | NFL West 10, East 7 | 2-4-90 | NFC 27, AFC 21 |
| | | 1-17-70 | AFL West 26, East 3 | 2-3-91 | AFC 23, NFC 21 |
| | | 1-18-70 | NFL West 16, East 13 | 2-2-92 | NFC 21, AFC 15 |
| | | 1-24-71 | NFC 27, AFC 6 | 2-7-93 | AFC 23, NFC 20 |

## All-Time Winningest NFL Coaches

### Most Career Wins

| Coach | Yrs | Teams | Regular Season | | | | Career | | | |
|-------|-----|-------|---|---|---|---|---|---|---|---|
| | | | W | L | T | Pct | W | L | T | Pct |
| George Halas | 40 | Bears | 319 | 148 | 31 | .672 | 325 | 151 | 31 | .672 |
| Don Shula | 30 | Colts, Dolphins | 300 | 136 | 6 | .685 | 318 | 151 | 6 | .676 |
| Tom Landry | 29 | Cowboys | 250 | 162 | 6 | .605 | 270 | 178 | 6 | .601 |
| Curly Lambeau | 33 | Packers, Cardinals, Redskins | 226 | 132 | 22 | .623 | 229 | 134 | 22 | .623 |
| Chuck Noll | 23 | Steelers | 193 | 148 | 1 | .566 | 209 | 156 | 1 | .572 |
| Chuck Knox | 20 | Rams, Bills, Seahawks | 177 | 124 | 1 | .588 | 184 | 135 | 1 | .577 |
| Paul Brown | 21 | Browns, Bengals | 166 | 100 | 6 | .621 | 170 | 108 | 6 | .609 |
| Bud Grant | 18 | Vikings | 158 | 96 | 5 | .620 | 168 | 108 | 5 | .607 |
| Steve Owen | 23 | Giants | 151 | 100 | 17 | .595 | 153 | 108 | 17 | .582 |
| Joe Gibbs | 12 | Redskins | 124 | 60 | 0 | .674 | 140 | 65 | 0 | .683 |
| Hank Stram | 17 | Chiefs, Saints | 131 | 97 | 10 | .571 | 136 | 100 | 10 | .573 |
| Weeb Ewbank | 20 | Colts, Jets | 130 | 129 | 7 | .502 | 134 | 130 | 7 | .507 |
| Sid Gillman | 18 | Rams, Chargers, Oilers | 122 | 99 | 7 | .550 | 123 | 104 | 7 | .541 |
| George Allen | 12 | Rams, Redskins | 116 | 47 | 5 | .705 | 118 | 54 | 5 | .681 |
| Dan Reeves | 12 | Broncos | 110 | 73 | 1 | .601 | 117 | 79 | 1 | .596 |
| Don Coryell | 14 | Cardinals, Chargers | 111 | 83 | 1 | .572 | 114 | 89 | 1 | .561 |
| John Madden | 10 | Raiders | 103 | 32 | 7 | .750 | 112 | 39 | 7 | .731 |
| Mike Ditka | 11 | Bears | 106 | 62 | 0 | .631 | 112 | 68 | 0 | .622 |
| Buddy Parker | 15 | Cardinals, Lions, Steelers | 104 | 75 | 9 | .577 | 107 | 76 | 9 | .581 |
| Marv Levy | 12 | Chiefs, Bills | 98 | 77 | 0 | .560 | 106 | 82 | 0 | .564 |

## All-Time Winningest NFL Coaches *(Cont.)*

### Top Winning Percentages

| | W | L | T | Pct | | W | L | T | Pct |
|---|---|---|---|---|---|---|---|---|---|
| Vince Lombardi | 105 | 35 | 6 | .740 | George Halas | 325 | 151 | 31 | .672 |
| John Madden | 112 | 39 | 7 | .731 | Curly Lambeau | 229 | 134 | 22 | .623 |
| Joe Gibbs | 140 | 65 | 0 | .683 | Mike Ditka | 112 | 68 | 0 | .622 |
| George Allen | 118 | 54 | 5 | .681 | Bill Walsh | 102 | 63 | 1 | .617 |
| Don Shula | 318 | 151 | 6 | .676 | Paul Brown | 170 | 108 | 6 | .609 |

## All-Time Number-One Draft Choices

| Year | Team | Selection | Position |
|---|---|---|---|
| 1936 | Philadelphia | Jay Berwanger, Chicago | HB |
| 1937 | Philadelphia | Sam Francis, Nebraska | FB |
| 1938 | Cleveland | Corbett Davis, Indiana | FB |
| 1939 | Chicago Cardinals | Ki Aldrich, Texas Christian | C |
| 1940 | Chicago Cardinals | George Cafego, Tennessee | HB |
| 1941 | Chicago Bears | Tom Harmon, Michigan | HB |
| 1942 | Pittsburgh | Bill Dudley, Virginia | HB |
| 1943 | Detroit | Frank Sinkwich, Georgia | HB |
| 1944 | Boston | Angelo Bertelli, Notre Dame | QB |
| 1945 | Chicago Cardinals | Charley Trippi, Georgia | HB |
| 1946 | Boston | Frank Dancewicz, Notre Dame | QB |
| 1947 | Chicago Bears | Bob Fenimore, Oklahoma A&M | HB |
| 1948 | Washington | Harry Gilmer, Alabama | QB |
| 1949 | Philadelphia | Chuck Bednarik, Pennsylvania | C |
| 1950 | Detroit | Leon Hart, Notre Dame | E |
| 1951 | New York Giants | Kyle Rote, Southern Methodist | HB |
| 1952 | Los Angeles | Bill Wade, Vanderbilt | QB |
| 1953 | San Francisco | Harry Babcock, Georgia | E |
| 1954 | Cleveland | Bobby Garrett, Stanford | QB |
| 1955 | Baltimore | George Shaw, Oregon | QB |
| 1956 | Pittsburgh | Gary Glick, Colorado A&M | DB |
| 1957 | Green Bay | Paul Hornung, Notre Dame | HB |
| 1958 | Chicago Cardinals | King Hill, Rice | QB |
| 1959 | Green Bay | Randy Duncan, Iowa | QB |
| 1960 | Los Angeles | Billy Cannon, Louisiana State | RB |
| 1961 | Minnesota | Tommy Mason, Tulane | RB |
| | Buffalo (AFL) | Ken Rice, Auburn | G |
| 1968 | Minnesota | Ron Yary, Southern California | T |
| 1969 | Buffalo (AFL) | O. J. Simpson, Southern California | RB |
| 1970 | Pittsburgh | Terry Bradshaw, Louisiana Tech | QB |
| 1971 | New England | Jim Plunkett, Stanford | QB |
| 1972 | Buffalo | Walt Patulski, Notre Dame | DE |
| 1973 | Houston | John Matuszak, Tampa | DE |
| 1974 | Dallas | Ed Jones, Tennessee State | DE |
| 1975 | Atlanta | Steve Bartkowski, California | QB |
| 1976 | Tampa Bay | Lee Roy Selmon, Oklahoma | DE |
| 1977 | Tampa Bay | Ricky Bell, Southern California | RB |
| 1978 | Houston | Earl Campbell, Texas | RB |
| 1979 | Buffalo | Tom Cousineau, Ohio State | LB |
| 1980 | Detroit | Billy Sims, Oklahoma | RB |
| 1981 | New Orleans | George Rogers, South Carolina | RB |
| 1982 | New England | Kenneth Sims, Texas | DT |
| 1983 | Baltimore | John Elway, Stanford | QB |
| 1984 | New England | Irving Fryar, Nebraska | WR |
| 1985 | Buffalo | Bruce Smith, Virginia Tech | DE |
| 1986 | Tampa Bay | Bo Jackson, Auburn | RB |
| 1987 | Tampa Bay | Vinny Testaverde, Miami | QB |
| 1988 | Atlanta | Aundray Bruce, Auburn | LB |
| 1989 | Dallas | Troy Aikman, UCLA | QB |
| 1990 | Indianapolis | Jeff George, Illinois | QB |
| 1991 | Dallas | Russell Maryland, Miami | DT |
| 1992 | Indianapolis | Steve Emtman, Washington | DT |
| 1993 | New England | Drew Bledsoe, Washington St | QB |

From 1947 through 1958, the first selection in the draft was a bonus pick, awarded to the winner of a random draw. That club, in turn, forfeited its last-round draft choice. The winner of the bonus choice was eliminated from future draws. The system was abolished after 1958, by which time all clubs had received a bonus choice.

# Annual NFL Standings

## 1991

### American Football Conference

#### EASTERN DIVISION

| | W | L | T | Pct. | Pts. | Op. |
|---|---|---|---|---|---|---|
| Buffalo | 13 | 3 | 0 | .813 | 458 | 318 |
| NY Jets | 8 | 8 | 0 | .500 | 314 | 293 |
| Miami | 8 | 8 | 0 | .500 | 343 | 349 |
| New England | 6 | 10 | 0 | .375 | 211 | 305 |
| Indianapolis | 1 | 15 | 0 | .063 | 143 | 381 |

#### CENTRAL DIVISION

| | W | L | T | Pct. | Pts. | Op. |
|---|---|---|---|---|---|---|
| Houston | 11 | 5 | 0 | .688 | 386 | 251 |
| Pittsburgh | 7 | 9 | 0 | .438 | 292 | 344 |
| Cleveland | 6 | 10 | 0 | .375 | 293 | 298 |
| Cincinnati | 3 | 13 | 0 | .188 | 263 | 435 |

#### WESTERN DIVISION

| | W | L | T | Pct. | Pts. | Op. |
|---|---|---|---|---|---|---|
| Denver | 12 | 4 | 0 | .750 | 304 | 235 |
| Kansas City | 10 | 6 | 0 | .625 | 322 | 252 |
| LA Raiders | 9 | 7 | 0 | .563 | 298 | 297 |
| Seattle | 7 | 9 | 0 | .438 | 276 | 261 |
| San Diego | 4 | 12 | 0 | .250 | 274 | 342 |

### National Football Conference

#### EASTERN DIVISION

| | W | L | T | Pct. | Pts. | Op. |
|---|---|---|---|---|---|---|
| Washington | 14 | 2 | 0 | .875 | 485 | 224 |
| Dallas | 11 | 5 | 0 | .688 | 342 | 310 |
| Philadelphia | 10 | 6 | 0 | .625 | 285 | 244 |
| NY Giants | 8 | 8 | 0 | .500 | 281 | 297 |
| Phoenix | 4 | 12 | 0 | .250 | 196 | 344 |

#### CENTRAL DIVISION

| | W | L | T | Pct. | Pts. | Op. |
|---|---|---|---|---|---|---|
| Detroit | 12 | 4 | 0 | .750 | 339 | 295 |
| Chicago | 11 | 5 | 0 | .688 | 299 | 269 |
| Minnesota | 8 | 8 | 0 | .500 | 301 | 306 |
| Green Bay | 4 | 12 | 0 | .250 | 273 | 313 |
| Tampa Bay | 3 | 13 | 0 | .188 | 199 | 365 |

#### WESTERN DIVISION

| | W | L | T | Pct. | Pts. | Op. |
|---|---|---|---|---|---|---|
| New Orleans | 11 | 5 | 0 | .688 | 341 | 211 |
| Atlanta | 10 | 6 | 0 | .625 | 361 | 338 |
| San Francisco | 10 | 6 | 0 | .625 | 393 | 239 |
| LA Rams | 3 | 13 | 0 | .188 | 234 | 390 |

## 1990

### American Football Conference

#### EASTERN DIVISION

| | W | L | T | Pct. | Pts. | Op. |
|---|---|---|---|---|---|---|
| Buffalo | 13 | 3 | 0 | .813 | 428 | 263 |
| Miami | 12 | 4 | 0 | .750 | 336 | 242 |
| Indianapolis | 7 | 9 | 0 | .438 | 281 | 353 |
| NY Jets | 6 | 10 | 0 | .375 | 295 | 345 |
| New England | 1 | 15 | 0 | .063 | 181 | 446 |

#### CENTRAL DIVISION

| | W | L | T | Pct. | Pts. | Op. |
|---|---|---|---|---|---|---|
| Cincinnati | 9 | 7 | 0 | .563 | 360 | 352 |
| Houston | 9 | 7 | 0 | .563 | 405 | 307 |
| Pittsburgh | 9 | 7 | 0 | .563 | 292 | 240 |
| Cleveland | 3 | 13 | 0 | .188 | 228 | 462 |

#### WESTERN DIVISION

| | W | L | T | Pct. | Pts. | Op. |
|---|---|---|---|---|---|---|
| LA Raiders | 12 | 4 | 0 | .750 | 337 | 268 |
| Kansas City | 11 | 5 | 0 | .688 | 369 | 257 |
| Seattle | 9 | 7 | 0 | .563 | 306 | 286 |
| San Diego | 6 | 10 | 0 | .375 | 315 | 281 |
| Denver | 5 | 11 | 0 | .313 | 331 | 374 |

### National Football Conference

#### EASTERN DIVISION

| | W | L | T | Pct. | Pts. | Op. |
|---|---|---|---|---|---|---|
| NY Giants | 13 | 3 | 0 | .813 | 335 | 211 |
| Philadelphia | 10 | 6 | 0 | .625 | 396 | 299 |
| Washington | 10 | 6 | 0 | .625 | 381 | 301 |
| Dallas | 7 | 9 | 0 | .438 | 244 | 308 |
| Phoenix | 5 | 11 | 0 | .313 | 268 | 396 |

#### CENTRAL DIVISION

| | W | L | T | Pct. | Pts. | Op. |
|---|---|---|---|---|---|---|
| Chicago | 11 | 5 | 0 | .688 | 348 | 280 |
| Tampa Bay | 6 | 10 | 0 | .375 | 264 | 367 |
| Detroit | 6 | 10 | 0 | .375 | 373 | 413 |
| Green Bay | 6 | 10 | 0 | .375 | 271 | 347 |
| Minnesota | 6 | 10 | 0 | .375 | 351 | 326 |

#### WESTERN DIVISION

| | W | L | T | Pct. | Pts. | Op. |
|---|---|---|---|---|---|---|
| San Francisco | 14 | 2 | 0 | .875 | 353 | 239 |
| New Orleans | 8 | 8 | 0 | .500 | 274 | 275 |
| LA Rams | 5 | 11 | 0 | .313 | 345 | 412 |
| Atlanta | 5 | 11 | 0 | .313 | 348 | 365 |

## 1989

### American Football Conference

#### EASTERN DIVISION

|            | W  | L  | T | Pct. | Pts. | Op. |
|------------|----|----|---|------|------|-----|
| Buffalo    | 9  | 7  | 0 | .563 | 409  | 317 |
| Indianapolis | 8 | 8  | 0 | .500 | 298  | 301 |
| Miami      | 8  | 8  | 0 | .500 | 331  | 379 |
| New England | 5 | 11 | 0 | .313 | 297  | 391 |
| N.Y. Jets  | 4  | 12 | 0 | .250 | 253  | 411 |

#### CENTRAL DIVISION

|            | W | L | T | Pct. | Pts. | Op. |
|------------|---|---|---|------|------|-----|
| Cleveland  | 9 | 6 | 1 | .594 | 334  | 254 |
| Houston    | 9 | 7 | 0 | .563 | 365  | 412 |
| Pittsburgh | 9 | 7 | 0 | .563 | 265  | 326 |
| Cincinnati | 8 | 8 | 0 | .500 | 404  | 285 |

#### WESTERN DIVISION

|             | W  | L  | T | Pct. | Pts. | Op. |
|-------------|----|----|---|------|------|-----|
| Denver      | 11 | 5  | 0 | .688 | 362  | 226 |
| Kansas City | 8  | 7  | 1 | .531 | 318  | 286 |
| L.A. Raiders | 8 | 8  | 0 | .500 | 315  | 297 |
| Seattle     | 7  | 9  | 0 | .438 | 241  | 327 |
| San Diego   | 6  | 10 | 0 | .375 | 266  | 290 |

### National Football Conference

#### EASTERN DIVISION

|              | W  | L  | T | Pct. | Pts. | Op. |
|--------------|----|----|---|------|------|-----|
| N.Y. Giants  | 12 | 4  | 0 | .750 | 348  | 252 |
| Philadelphia | 11 | 5  | 0 | .688 | 342  | 274 |
| Washington   | 10 | 6  | 0 | .625 | 386  | 308 |
| Phoenix      | 5  | 11 | 0 | .313 | 258  | 377 |
| Dallas       | 1  | 15 | 0 | .063 | 204  | 393 |

#### CENTRAL DIVISION

|            | W  | L  | T | Pct. | Pts. | Op. |
|------------|----|----|---|------|------|-----|
| Minnesota  | 10 | 6  | 0 | .625 | 351  | 275 |
| Green Bay  | 10 | 6  | 0 | .625 | 362  | 356 |
| Detroit    | 7  | 9  | 0 | .438 | 312  | 364 |
| Chicago    | 6  | 10 | 0 | .375 | 358  | 377 |
| Tampa Bay  | 5  | 11 | 0 | .313 | 320  | 419 |

#### WESTERN DIVISION

|               | W  | L  | T | Pct. | Pts. | Op. |
|---------------|----|----|---|------|------|-----|
| San Francisco | 14 | 2  | 0 | .875 | 442  | 253 |
| LA Rams       | 11 | 5  | 0 | .688 | 426  | 344 |
| New Orleans   | 9  | 7  | 0 | .563 | 386  | 301 |
| Atlanta       | 3  | 13 | 0 | .188 | 279  | 437 |

## 1988

### American Football Conference

#### EASTERN DIVISION

|             | W  | L  | T | Pct. | Pts. | Op. |
|-------------|----|----|---|------|------|-----|
| Buffalo     | 12 | 4  | 0 | .750 | 329  | 237 |
| Indianapolis | 9 | 7  | 0 | .563 | 354  | 315 |
| New England | 9  | 7  | 0 | .563 | 250  | 284 |
| NY Jets     | 8  | 7  | 1 | .531 | 372  | 354 |
| Miami       | 6  | 10 | 0 | .375 | 319  | 380 |

#### CENTRAL DIVISION

|            | W  | L  | T | Pct. | Pts. | Op. |
|------------|----|----|---|------|------|-----|
| Cincinnati | 12 | 4  | 0 | .750 | 448  | 329 |
| Cleveland  | 10 | 6  | 0 | .625 | 304  | 288 |
| Houston    | 10 | 6  | 0 | .625 | 424  | 365 |
| Pittsburgh | 5  | 11 | 0 | .313 | 336  | 421 |

#### WESTERN DIVISION

|             | W | L  | T | Pct. | Pts. | Op. |
|-------------|---|----|---|------|------|-----|
| Seattle     | 9 | 7  | 0 | .563 | 339  | 329 |
| Denver      | 8 | 8  | 0 | .500 | 327  | 352 |
| LA Raiders  | 7 | 9  | 0 | .438 | 325  | 369 |
| San Diego   | 6 | 10 | 0 | .375 | 231  | 332 |
| Kansas City | 4 | 11 | 1 | .281 | 254  | 320 |

### National Football Conference

#### EASTERN DIVISION

|              | W  | L  | T | Pct. | Pts. | Op. |
|--------------|----|----|---|------|------|-----|
| Philadelphia | 10 | 6  | 0 | .625 | 379  | 319 |
| NY Giants    | 10 | 6  | 0 | .625 | 359  | 304 |
| Washington   | 7  | 9  | 0 | .438 | 345  | 387 |
| Phoenix      | 7  | 9  | 0 | .438 | 344  | 398 |
| Dallas       | 3  | 13 | 0 | .188 | 265  | 381 |

#### CENTRAL DIVISION

|           | W  | L  | T | Pct. | Pts. | Op. |
|-----------|----|----|---|------|------|-----|
| Chicago   | 12 | 4  | 0 | .750 | 312  | 215 |
| Minnesota | 11 | 5  | 0 | .688 | 406  | 233 |
| Tampa Bay | 5  | 11 | 0 | .313 | 261  | 350 |
| Detroit   | 4  | 12 | 0 | .250 | 220  | 313 |
| Green Bay | 4  | 12 | 0 | .250 | 240  | 315 |

#### WESTERN DIVISION

|               | W  | L  | T | Pct. | Pts. | Op. |
|---------------|----|----|---|------|------|-----|
| San Francisco | 10 | 6  | 0 | .625 | 369  | 294 |
| LA Rams       | 10 | 6  | 0 | .625 | 407  | 293 |
| New Orleans   | 10 | 6  | 0 | .625 | 312  | 283 |
| Atlanta       | 5  | 11 | 0 | .313 | 244  | 315 |

## 1987

### American Football Conference

#### EASTERN DIVISION

|  | W | L | T | Pct. | Pts. | Op. |
|---|---|---|---|---|---|---|
| Indianapolis | 9 | 6 | 0 | .600 | 300 | 238 |
| New England | 8 | 7 | 0 | .533 | 320 | 293 |
| Miami | 8 | 7 | 0 | .533 | 362 | 335 |
| Buffalo | 7 | 8 | 0 | .467 | 270 | 305 |
| NY Jets | 6 | 9 | 0 | .400 | 334 | 360 |

#### CENTRAL DIVISION

|  | W | L | T | Pct. | Pts. | Op. |
|---|---|---|---|---|---|---|
| Cleveland | 10 | 5 | 0 | .667 | 390 | 239 |
| Houston | 9 | 6 | 0 | .600 | 345 | 349 |
| Pittsburgh | 8 | 7 | 0 | .533 | 285 | 299 |
| Cincinnati | 4 | 11 | 0 | .267 | 285 | 370 |

#### WESTERN DIVISION

|  | W | L | T | Pct. | Pts. | Op. |
|---|---|---|---|---|---|---|
| Denver | 10 | 4 | 1 | .700 | 379 | 288 |
| Seattle | 9 | 6 | 0 | .600 | 371 | 314 |
| San Diego | 8 | 7 | 0 | .533 | 253 | 317 |
| LA Raiders | 5 | 10 | 0 | .333 | 301 | 289 |
| Kansas City | 4 | 11 | 0 | .267 | 273 | 388 |

### National Football Conference

#### EASTERN DIVISION

|  | W | L | T | Pct. | Pts. | Op. |
|---|---|---|---|---|---|---|
| Washington | 11 | 4 | 0 | .733 | 379 | 285 |
| Dallas | 7 | 8 | 0 | .467 | 340 | 348 |
| St. Louis | 7 | 8 | 0 | .467 | 362 | 368 |
| Philadelphia | 7 | 8 | 0 | .467 | 337 | 380 |
| NY Giants | 6 | 9 | 0 | .400 | 280 | 312 |

#### CENTRAL DIVISION

|  | W | L | T | Pct. | Pts. | Op. |
|---|---|---|---|---|---|---|
| Chicago | 11 | 4 | 0 | .733 | 356 | 282 |
| Minnesota | 8 | 7 | 0 | .533 | 336 | 335 |
| Green Bay | 5 | 9 | 1 | .367 | 255 | 300 |
| Tampa Bay | 4 | 11 | 0 | .267 | 286 | 360 |
| Detroit | 4 | 11 | 0 | .267 | 269 | 384 |

#### WESTERN DIVISION

|  | W | L | T | Pct. | Pts. | Op. |
|---|---|---|---|---|---|---|
| San Francisco | 13 | 2 | 0 | .867 | 459 | 253 |
| New Orleans | 12 | 3 | 0 | .800 | 422 | 283 |
| LA Rams | 6 | 9 | 0 | .400 | 317 | 361 |
| Atlanta | 3 | 12 | 0 | .200 | 205 | 436 |

## 1986

### American Football Conference

#### EASTERN DIVISION

|  | W | L | T | Pct. | Pts. | Op. |
|---|---|---|---|---|---|---|
| New England | 11 | 5 | 0 | .688 | 412 | 307 |
| NY Jets | 10 | 6 | 0 | .625 | 364 | 386 |
| Miami | 8 | 8 | 0 | .500 | 430 | 405 |
| Buffalo | 4 | 12 | 0 | .250 | 287 | 348 |
| Indianapolis | 3 | 15 | 0 | .188 | 229 | 400 |

#### CENTRAL DIVISION

|  | W | L | T | Pct. | Pts. | Op. |
|---|---|---|---|---|---|---|
| Cleveland | 12 | 4 | 0 | .750 | 391 | 310 |
| Cincinnati | 10 | 6 | 0 | .625 | 409 | 394 |
| Pittsburgh | 6 | 10 | 0 | .375 | 307 | 336 |
| Houston | 5 | 11 | 0 | .313 | 274 | 329 |

#### WESTERN DIVISION

|  | W | L | T | Pct. | Pts. | Op. |
|---|---|---|---|---|---|---|
| Denver | 11 | 5 | 0 | .688 | 378 | 327 |
| Kansas City | 10 | 6 | 0 | .625 | 358 | 326 |
| Seattle | 10 | 7 | 0 | .625 | 366 | 293 |
| LA Raiders | 8 | 8 | 0 | .500 | 323 | 346 |
| San Diego | 4 | 12 | 0 | .250 | 335 | 396 |

### National Football Conference

#### EASTERN DIVISION

|  | W | L | T | Pct. | Pts. | Op. |
|---|---|---|---|---|---|---|
| NY Giants | 14 | 2 | 0 | .875 | 371 | 236 |
| Washington | 12 | 4 | 0 | .750 | 368 | 296 |
| Dallas | 7 | 9 | 0 | .438 | 346 | 337 |
| Philadelphia | 5 | 10 | 1 | .344 | 256 | 312 |
| St. Louis | 4 | 11 | 1 | .281 | 218 | 351 |

#### CENTRAL DIVISION

|  | W | L | T | Pct. | Pts. | Op. |
|---|---|---|---|---|---|---|
| Chicago | 14 | 2 | 0 | .875 | 352 | 187 |
| Minnesota | 9 | 7 | 0 | .563 | 398 | 273 |
| Detroit | 5 | 11 | 0 | .313 | 277 | 326 |
| Green Bay | 4 | 12 | 0 | .250 | 254 | 418 |
| Tampa Bay | 2 | 14 | 0 | .125 | 239 | 473 |

#### WESTERN DIVISION

|  | W | L | T | Pct. | Pts. | Op. |
|---|---|---|---|---|---|---|
| San Francisco | 10 | 5 | 1 | .656 | 374 | 247 |
| LA Rams | 10 | 6 | 0 | .625 | 309 | 267 |
| Atlanta | 7 | 8 | 1 | .469 | 280 | 280 |
| New Orleans | 7 | 9 | 0 | .438 | 288 | 287 |

## 1985

### American Football Conference

#### EASTERN DIVISION

|  | W | L | T | Pct. | Pts. | Op. |
|---|---|---|---|---|---|---|
| Miami | 12 | 4 | 0 | .750 | 428 | 320 |
| NY Jets | 11 | 5 | 0 | .688 | 393 | 264 |
| New England | 11 | 5 | 0 | .688 | 362 | 290 |
| Indianapolis | 5 | 11 | 0 | .313 | 320 | 386 |
| Buffalo | 2 | 14 | 0 | .125 | 200 | 381 |

#### CENTRAL DIVISION

|  | W | L | T | Pct. | Pts. | Op. |
|---|---|---|---|---|---|---|
| Cleveland | 8 | 8 | 0 | .500 | 287 | 294 |
| Cincinnati | 7 | 9 | 0 | .438 | 441 | 437 |
| Pittsburgh | 7 | 9 | 0 | .438 | 379 | 355 |
| Houston | 5 | 11 | 0 | .313 | 284 | 412 |

#### WESTERN DIVISION

|  | W | L | T | Pct. | Pts. | Op. |
|---|---|---|---|---|---|---|
| LA Raiders | 12 | 4 | 0 | .750 | 354 | 308 |
| Denver | 11 | 5 | 0 | .688 | 380 | 329 |
| Seattle | 8 | 8 | 0 | .500 | 349 | 303 |
| San Diego | 8 | 8 | 0 | .500 | 467 | 435 |
| Kansas City | 6 | 10 | 0 | .375 | 317 | 360 |

### National Football Conference

#### EASTERN DIVISION

|  | W | L | T | Pct. | Pts. | Op. |
|---|---|---|---|---|---|---|
| Dallas | 10 | 6 | 0 | .625 | 357 | 333 |
| NY Giants | 10 | 6 | 0 | .625 | 399 | 283 |
| Washington | 10 | 6 | 0 | .625 | 297 | 312 |
| Philadelphia | 7 | 9 | 0 | .438 | 286 | 310 |
| St. Louis | 5 | 11 | 0 | .313 | 278 | 414 |

#### CENTRAL DIVISION

|  | W | L | T | Pct. | Pts. | Op. |
|---|---|---|---|---|---|---|
| Chicago | 15 | 1 | 0 | .938 | 456 | 198 |
| Green Bay | 8 | 8 | 0 | .500 | 337 | 355 |
| Minnesota | 7 | 9 | 0 | .438 | 346 | 359 |
| Detroit | 7 | 9 | 0 | .438 | 307 | 366 |
| Tampa Bay | 2 | 14 | 0 | .125 | 294 | 448 |

#### WESTERN DIVISION

|  | W | L | T | Pct. | Pts. | Op. |
|---|---|---|---|---|---|---|
| LA Rams | 11 | 5 | 0 | .688 | 340 | 277 |
| San Francisco | 10 | 6 | 0 | .625 | 411 | 263 |
| New Orleans | 5 | 11 | 0 | .313 | 294 | 401 |
| Atlanta | 4 | 12 | 0 | .250 | 282 | 452 |

## 1984

### American Football Conference

#### EASTERN DIVISION

|  | W | L | T | Pct. | Pts. | Op. |
|---|---|---|---|---|---|---|
| Miami | 14 | 2 | 0 | .875 | 371 | 236 |
| New England | 9 | 7 | 0 | .563 | 362 | 352 |
| NY Jets | 7 | 9 | 0 | .438 | 332 | 364 |
| Indianapolis | 4 | 12 | 0 | .250 | 239 | 414 |
| Buffalo | 2 | 14 | 0 | .125 | 250 | 454 |

#### CENTRAL DIVISION

|  | W | L | T | Pct. | Pts. | Op. |
|---|---|---|---|---|---|---|
| Pittsburgh | 9 | 7 | 0 | .563 | 387 | 310 |
| Cincinnati | 8 | 8 | 0 | .500 | 339 | 339 |
| Cleveland | 5 | 11 | 0 | .313 | 250 | 297 |
| Houston | 3 | 13 | 0 | .188 | 240 | 437 |

#### WESTERN DIVISION

|  | W | L | T | Pct. | Pts. | Op. |
|---|---|---|---|---|---|---|
| Denver | 13 | 3 | 0 | .813 | 353 | 241 |
| Seattle | 12 | 4 | 0 | .750 | 418 | 282 |
| LA Raiders | 11 | 5 | 0 | .688 | 368 | 278 |
| Kansas City | 8 | 8 | 0 | .500 | 314 | 324 |
| San Diego | 7 | 9 | 0 | .438 | 394 | 413 |

### National Football Conference

#### EASTERN DIVISION

|  | W | L | T | Pct. | Pts. | Op. |
|---|---|---|---|---|---|---|
| Washington | 11 | 5 | 0 | .688 | 426 | 310 |
| NY Giants | 9 | 7 | 0 | .563 | 299 | 301 |
| St. Louis | 9 | 7 | 0 | .563 | 423 | 345 |
| Dallas | 9 | 7 | 0 | .563 | 308 | 308 |
| Philadelphia | 6 | 9 | 1 | .406 | 278 | 320 |

#### CENTRAL DIVISION

|  | W | L | T | Pct. | Pts. | Op. |
|---|---|---|---|---|---|---|
| Chicago | 10 | 6 | 0 | .625 | 325 | 248 |
| Green Bay | 8 | 8 | 0 | .500 | 390 | 309 |
| Tampa Bay | 6 | 10 | 0 | .375 | 335 | 380 |
| Detroit | 4 | 11 | 1 | .281 | 283 | 408 |
| Minnesota | 3 | 13 | 0 | .188 | 276 | 484 |

#### WESTERN DIVISION

|  | W | L | T | Pct. | Pts. | Op. |
|---|---|---|---|---|---|---|
| San Francisco | 15 | 1 | 0 | .938 | 475 | 227 |
| LA Rams | 10 | 6 | 0 | .625 | 346 | 316 |
| New Orleans | 7 | 9 | 0 | .438 | 298 | 361 |
| Atlanta | 4 | 12 | 0 | .250 | 281 | 382 |

## 1983

### American Football Conference

#### EASTERN DIVISION

|  | W | L | T | Pct. | Pts. | Op. |
|---|---|---|---|---|---|---|
| Miami | 12 | 4 | 0 | .750 | 389 | 250 |
| New England | 8 | 8 | 0 | .500 | 274 | 289 |
| Buffalo | 8 | 8 | 0 | .500 | 283 | 351 |
| Baltimore | 7 | 9 | 0 | .438 | 264 | 354 |
| NY Jets | 7 | 9 | 0 | .438 | 313 | 331 |

#### CENTRAL DIVISION

|  | W | L | T | Pct. | Pts. | Op. |
|---|---|---|---|---|---|---|
| Pittsburgh | 10 | 6 | 0 | .625 | 355 | 303 |
| Cleveland | 9 | 7 | 0 | .563 | 356 | 342 |
| Cincinnati | 7 | 9 | 0 | .438 | 346 | 302 |
| Houston | 2 | 14 | 0 | .125 | 288 | 460 |

#### WESTERN DIVISION

|  | W | L | T | Pct. | Pts. | Op. |
|---|---|---|---|---|---|---|
| LA Raiders | 12 | 4 | 0 | .750 | 442 | 338 |
| Seattle | 9 | 7 | 0 | .563 | 403 | 397 |
| Denver | 9 | 7 | 0 | .563 | 302 | 327 |
| San Diego | 6 | 10 | 0 | .375 | 358 | 462 |
| Kansas City | 6 | 10 | 0 | .375 | 386 | 367 |

### National Football Conference

#### EASTERN DIVISION

|  | W | L | T | Pct. | Pts. | Op. |
|---|---|---|---|---|---|---|
| Washington | 14 | 2 | 0 | .875 | 541 | 332 |
| Dallas | 12 | 4 | 0 | .750 | 479 | 360 |
| St. Louis | 8 | 7 | 1 | .531 | 374 | 428 |
| Philadelphia | 5 | 11 | 0 | .313 | 233 | 322 |
| NY Giants | 3 | 12 | 1 | .219 | 267 | 347 |

#### CENTRAL DIVISION

|  | W | L | T | Pct. | Pts. | Op. |
|---|---|---|---|---|---|---|
| Detroit | 9 | 7 | 0 | .563 | 347 | 286 |
| Green Bay | 8 | 8 | 0 | .500 | 429 | 439 |
| Chicago | 8 | 8 | 0 | .500 | 311 | 301 |
| Minnesota | 8 | 8 | 0 | .500 | 316 | 348 |
| Tampa Bay | 2 | 14 | 0 | .125 | 241 | 380 |

#### WESTERN DIVISION

|  | W | L | T | Pct. | Pts. | Op. |
|---|---|---|---|---|---|---|
| San Francisco | 10 | 6 | 0 | .625 | 432 | 293 |
| LA Rams | 9 | 7 | 0 | .563 | 361 | 344 |
| New Orleans | 8 | 8 | 0 | .500 | 319 | 337 |
| Atlanta | 7 | 9 | 0 | .438 | 370 | 389 |

## 1982

### American Football Conference

|  | W | L | T | Pct. | Pts. | Op. |
|---|---|---|---|---|---|---|
| LA Raiders | 8 | 1 | 0 | .889 | 260 | 200 |
| Miami | 7 | 2 | 0 | .778 | 198 | 131 |
| Cincinnati | 7 | 2 | 0 | .778 | 232 | 177 |
| Pittsburgh | 6 | 3 | 0 | .667 | 204 | 146 |
| San Diego | 6 | 3 | 0 | .667 | 288 | 221 |
| NY Jets | 6 | 3 | 0 | .667 | 245 | 166 |
| New England | 5 | 4 | 0 | .556 | 143 | 157 |
| Cleveland | 4 | 5 | 0 | .444 | 140 | 182 |
| Buffalo | 4 | 5 | 0 | .444 | 150 | 154 |
| Seattle | 4 | 5 | 0 | .444 | 127 | 147 |
| Kansas City | 3 | 6 | 0 | .333 | 176 | 184 |
| Denver | 2 | 7 | 0 | .222 | 148 | 226 |
| Houston | 1 | 8 | 0 | .111 | 136 | 245 |
| Baltimore | 0 | 8 | 1 | .056 | 113 | 236 |

### National Football Conference

|  | W | L | T | Pct. | Pts. | Op. |
|---|---|---|---|---|---|---|
| Washington | 8 | 1 | 0 | .889 | 190 | 128 |
| Dallas | 6 | 3 | 0 | .667 | 226 | 145 |
| Green Bay | 5 | 3 | 1 | .611 | 226 | 169 |
| Minnesota | 5 | 4 | 0 | .556 | 187 | 198 |
| Atlanta | 5 | 4 | 0 | .556 | 183 | 199 |
| St. Louis | 5 | 4 | 0 | .556 | 135 | 170 |
| Tampa Bay | 5 | 4 | 0 | .556 | 158 | 178 |
| Detroit | 4 | 5 | 0 | .444 | 181 | 176 |
| New Orleans | 4 | 5 | 0 | .444 | 129 | 160 |
| NY Giants | 4 | 5 | 0 | .444 | 164 | 160 |
| San Francisco | 3 | 6 | 0 | .333 | 209 | 206 |
| Chicago | 3 | 6 | 0 | .333 | 141 | 174 |
| Philadelphia | 3 | 6 | 0 | .333 | 191 | 195 |
| LA Rams | 2 | 7 | 0 | .222 | 200 | 250 |

### 1981

**American Football Conference**

#### EASTERN DIVISION

|  | W | L | T | Pct. | Pts. | Op. |
|---|---|---|---|---|---|---|
| Miami | 11 | 4 | 1 | .719 | 345 | 275 |
| NY Jets | 10 | 5 | 1 | .656 | 355 | 287 |
| Buffalo | 10 | 6 | 0 | .625 | 311 | 276 |
| Baltimore | 2 | 14 | 0 | .125 | 259 | 533 |
| New England | 2 | 14 | 0 | .125 | 322 | 370 |

#### CENTRAL DIVISION

|  | W | L | T | Pct. | Pts. | Op. |
|---|---|---|---|---|---|---|
| Cincinnati | 12 | 4 | 0 | .750 | 421 | 304 |
| Pittsburgh | 8 | 8 | 0 | .500 | 356 | 297 |
| Houston | 7 | 9 | 0 | .438 | 281 | 355 |
| Cleveland | 5 | 11 | 0 | .313 | 276 | 375 |

#### WESTERN DIVISION

|  | W | L | T | Pct. | Pts. | Op. |
|---|---|---|---|---|---|---|
| San Diego | 10 | 6 | 0 | .625 | 478 | 390 |
| Denver | 10 | 6 | 0 | .625 | 321 | 289 |
| Kansas City | 9 | 7 | 0 | .563 | 343 | 290 |
| Oakland | 7 | 9 | 0 | .438 | 273 | 343 |
| Seattle | 6 | 10 | 0 | .375 | 322 | 388 |

**National Football Conference**

#### EASTERN DIVISION

|  | W | L | T | Pct. | Pts. | Op. |
|---|---|---|---|---|---|---|
| Dallas | 12 | 4 | 0 | .750 | 367 | 277 |
| Philadelphia | 10 | 6 | 0 | .625 | 368 | 221 |
| NY Giants | 9 | 7 | 0 | .563 | 295 | 257 |
| Washington | 8 | 8 | 0 | .500 | 347 | 349 |
| St. Louis | 7 | 9 | 0 | .438 | 315 | 408 |

#### CENTRAL DIVISION

|  | W | L | T | Pct. | Pts. | Op. |
|---|---|---|---|---|---|---|
| Tampa Bay | 9 | 7 | 0 | .563 | 315 | 268 |
| Detroit | 8 | 8 | 0 | .500 | 397 | 322 |
| Green Bay | 8 | 8 | 0 | .500 | 324 | 361 |
| Minnesota | 7 | 9 | 0 | .438 | 325 | 369 |
| Chicago | 6 | 10 | 0 | .375 | 253 | 324 |

#### WESTERN DIVISION

|  | W | L | T | Pct. | Pts. | Op. |
|---|---|---|---|---|---|---|
| San Francisco | 13 | 3 | 0 | .813 | 357 | 250 |
| Atlanta | 7 | 9 | 0 | .438 | 426 | 355 |
| Los Angeles | 6 | 10 | 0 | .375 | 303 | 351 |
| New Orleans | 4 | 12 | 0 | .250 | 207 | 378 |

### 1980

**American Football Conference**

#### EASTERN DIVISION

|  | W | L | T | Pct. | Pts. | Op. |
|---|---|---|---|---|---|---|
| Buffalo | 11 | 5 | 0 | .688 | 320 | 260 |
| New England | 10 | 6 | 0 | .625 | 441 | 325 |
| Miami | 8 | 8 | 0 | .500 | 266 | 305 |
| Baltimore | 7 | 9 | 0 | .438 | 355 | 387 |
| NY Jets | 4 | 12 | 0 | .250 | 302 | 395 |

#### CENTRAL DIVISION

|  | W | L | T | Pct. | Pts. | Op. |
|---|---|---|---|---|---|---|
| Cleveland | 11 | 5 | 0 | .688 | 357 | 310 |
| Houston | 11 | 5 | 0 | .688 | 295 | 251 |
| Pittsburgh | 9 | 7 | 0 | .563 | 352 | 313 |
| Cincinnati | 6 | 10 | 0 | .375 | 244 | 312 |

#### WESTERN DIVISION

|  | W | L | T | Pct. | Pts. | Op. |
|---|---|---|---|---|---|---|
| San Diego | 11 | 5 | 0 | .688 | 418 | 327 |
| Oakland | 11 | 5 | 0 | .688 | 364 | 306 |
| Kansas City | 8 | 8 | 0 | .500 | 319 | 336 |
| Denver | 8 | 8 | 0 | .500 | 310 | 323 |
| Seattle | 4 | 12 | 0 | .250 | 291 | 408 |

**National Football Conference**

#### EASTERN DIVISION

|  | W | L | T | Pct. | Pts. | Op. |
|---|---|---|---|---|---|---|
| Philadelphia | 12 | 4 | 0 | .750 | 384 | 222 |
| Dallas | 12 | 4 | 0 | .750 | 454 | 311 |
| Washington | 6 | 10 | 0 | .375 | 261 | 293 |
| St. Louis | 5 | 11 | 0 | .313 | 299 | 350 |
| NY Giants | 4 | 12 | 0 | .250 | 249 | 425 |

#### CENTRAL DIVISION

|  | W | L | T | Pct. | Pts. | Op. |
|---|---|---|---|---|---|---|
| Minnesota | 9 | 7 | 0 | .563 | 317 | 308 |
| Detroit | 9 | 7 | 0 | .563 | 334 | 272 |
| Chicago | 7 | 9 | 0 | .438 | 304 | 264 |
| Tampa Bay | 5 | 10 | 1 | .344 | 271 | 341 |
| Green Bay | 5 | 10 | 1 | .344 | 231 | 371 |

#### WESTERN DIVISION

|  | W | L | T | Pct. | Pts. | Op. |
|---|---|---|---|---|---|---|
| Atlanta | 12 | 4 | 0 | .750 | 405 | 272 |
| Los Angeles | 11 | 5 | 0 | .688 | 424 | 289 |
| San Francisco | 6 | 10 | 0 | .375 | 320 | 415 |
| New Orleans | 1 | 15 | 0 | .063 | 291 | 487 |

## 1979

### American Football Conference

#### EASTERN DIVISION

| | W | L | T | Pct. | Pts. | Op. |
|---|---|---|---|---|---|---|
| Miami | 10 | 6 | 0 | .625 | 341 | 257 |
| New England | 9 | 7 | 0 | .563 | 411 | 326 |
| NY Jets | 8 | 8 | 0 | .500 | 337 | 383 |
| Buffalo | 7 | 9 | 0 | .438 | 268 | 279 |
| Baltimore | 5 | 11 | 0 | .313 | 271 | 351 |

#### CENTRAL DIVISION

| | W | L | T | Pct. | Pts. | Op. |
|---|---|---|---|---|---|---|
| Pittsburgh | 12 | 4 | 0 | .750 | 416 | 262 |
| Houston | 11 | 5 | 0 | .688 | 362 | 331 |
| Cleveland | 9 | 7 | 0 | .563 | 359 | 352 |
| Cincinnati | 4 | 12 | 0 | .250 | 337 | 421 |

#### WESTERN DIVISION

| | W | L | T | Pct. | Pts. | Op. |
|---|---|---|---|---|---|---|
| San Diego | 12 | 4 | 0 | .750 | 411 | 246 |
| Denver | 10 | 6 | 0 | .625 | 289 | 262 |
| Seattle | 9 | 7 | 0 | .563 | 378 | 372 |
| Oakland | 9 | 7 | 0 | .563 | 365 | 337 |
| Kansas City | 7 | 9 | 0 | .438 | 238 | 262 |

### National Football Conference

#### EASTERN DIVISION

| | W | L | T | Pct. | Pts. | Op. |
|---|---|---|---|---|---|---|
| Dallas | 11 | 5 | 0 | .688 | 371 | 313 |
| Philadelphia | 11 | 5 | 0 | .688 | 339 | 282 |
| Washington | 10 | 6 | 0 | .625 | 348 | 295 |
| NY Giants | 6 | 10 | 0 | .375 | 237 | 323 |
| St. Louis | 5 | 11 | 0 | .313 | 307 | 358 |

#### CENTRAL DIVISION

| | W | L | T | Pct. | Pts. | Op. |
|---|---|---|---|---|---|---|
| Tampa Bay | 10 | 6 | 0 | .625 | 273 | 237 |
| Chicago | 10 | 6 | 0 | .625 | 306 | 249 |
| Minnesota | 7 | 9 | 0 | .438 | 259 | 337 |
| Green Bay | 5 | 11 | 0 | .313 | 246 | 316 |
| Detroit | 2 | 14 | 0 | .125 | 219 | 365 |

#### WESTERN DIVISION

| | W | L | T | Pct. | Pts. | Op. |
|---|---|---|---|---|---|---|
| Los Angeles | 9 | 7 | 0 | .563 | 323 | 309 |
| New Orleans | 8 | 8 | 0 | .500 | 370 | 360 |
| Atlanta | 6 | 10 | 0 | .375 | 300 | 388 |
| San Francisco | 2 | 14 | 0 | .125 | 308 | 416 |

## 1978

### American Football Conference

#### EASTERN DIVISION

| | W | L | T | Pct. | Pts. | Op. |
|---|---|---|---|---|---|---|
| New England | 11 | 5 | 0 | .688 | 358 | 286 |
| Miami | 11 | 5 | 0 | .688 | 372 | 254 |
| NY Jets | 8 | 8 | 0 | .500 | 359 | 364 |
| Buffalo | 5 | 11 | 0 | .313 | 302 | 354 |
| Baltimore | 5 | 11 | 0 | .313 | 239 | 421 |

#### CENTRAL DIVISION

| | W | L | T | Pct. | Pts. | Op. |
|---|---|---|---|---|---|---|
| Pittsburgh | 14 | 2 | 0 | .875 | 356 | 195 |
| Houston | 10 | 6 | 0 | .625 | 283 | 298 |
| Cleveland | 8 | 8 | 0 | .500 | 334 | 356 |
| Cincinnati | 4 | 12 | 0 | .250 | 252 | 284 |

#### WESTERN DIVISION

| | W | L | T | Pct. | Pts. | Op. |
|---|---|---|---|---|---|---|
| Denver | 10 | 6 | 0 | .625 | 282 | 198 |
| Oakland | 9 | 7 | 0 | .563 | 311 | 283 |
| Seattle | 9 | 7 | 0 | .563 | 345 | 358 |
| San Diego | 9 | 7 | 0 | .563 | 355 | 309 |
| Kansas City | 4 | 12 | 0 | .250 | 243 | 327 |

### National Football Conference

#### EASTERN DIVISION

| | W | L | T | Pct. | Pts. | Op. |
|---|---|---|---|---|---|---|
| Dallas | 12 | 4 | 0 | .750 | 384 | 208 |
| Philadelphia | 9 | 7 | 0 | .563 | 270 | 250 |
| Washington | 8 | 8 | 0 | .500 | 273 | 283 |
| St. Louis | 6 | 10 | 0 | .375 | 248 | 296 |
| NY Giants | 6 | 10 | 0 | .375 | 264 | 298 |

#### CENTRAL DIVISION

| | W | L | T | Pct. | Pts. | Op. |
|---|---|---|---|---|---|---|
| Minnesota | 8 | 7 | 1 | .531 | 294 | 306 |
| Green Bay | 8 | 7 | 1 | .531 | 249 | 269 |
| Detroit | 7 | 9 | 0 | .438 | 290 | 300 |
| Chicago | 7 | 9 | 0 | .438 | 253 | 274 |
| Tampa Bay | 5 | 11 | 0 | .313 | 241 | 259 |

#### WESTERN DIVISION

| | W | L | T | Pct. | Pts. | Op. |
|---|---|---|---|---|---|---|
| Los Angeles | 12 | 4 | 0 | .750 | 316 | 245 |
| Atlanta | 9 | 7 | 0 | .563 | 240 | 290 |
| New Orleans | 7 | 9 | 0 | .438 | 281 | 298 |
| San Francisco | 2 | 14 | 0 | .125 | 219 | 350 |

## 1977

### American Football Conference

#### EASTERN DIVISION

|  | W | L | T | Pct. | Pts. | Op. |
|---|---|---|---|---|---|---|
| Baltimore | 10 | 4 | 0 | .714 | 295 | 221 |
| Miami | 10 | 4 | 0 | .714 | 313 | 197 |
| New England | 9 | 5 | 0 | .643 | 278 | 217 |
| NY Jets | 3 | 11 | 0 | .214 | 191 | 300 |
| Buffalo | 3 | 11 | 0 | .214 | 160 | 313 |

#### CENTRAL DIVISION

|  | W | L | T | Pct. | Pts. | Op. |
|---|---|---|---|---|---|---|
| Pittsburgh | 9 | 5 | 0 | .643 | 283 | 243 |
| Houston | 8 | 6 | 0 | .571 | 299 | 230 |
| Cincinnati | 8 | 6 | 0 | .571 | 238 | 235 |
| Cleveland | 6 | 8 | 0 | .429 | 269 | 267 |

#### WESTERN DIVISION

|  | W | L | T | Pct. | Pts. | Op. |
|---|---|---|---|---|---|---|
| Denver | 12 | 2 | 0 | .857 | 274 | 148 |
| Oakland | 11 | 3 | 0 | .786 | 351 | 230 |
| San Diego | 7 | 7 | 0 | .500 | 222 | 205 |
| Seattle | 5 | 9 | 0 | .357 | 282 | 373 |
| Kansas City | 2 | 12 | 0 | .143 | 225 | 349 |

### National Football Conference

#### EASTERN DIVISION

|  | W | L | T | Pct. | Pts. | Op. |
|---|---|---|---|---|---|---|
| Dallas | 12 | 2 | 0 | .857 | 345 | 212 |
| Washington | 9 | 5 | 0 | .643 | 196 | 189 |
| St. Louis | 7 | 7 | 0 | .500 | 272 | 287 |
| Philadelphia | 5 | 9 | 0 | .357 | 220 | 207 |
| NY Giants | 5 | 9 | 0 | .357 | 181 | 265 |

#### CENTRAL DIVISION

|  | W | L | T | Pct. | Pts. | Op. |
|---|---|---|---|---|---|---|
| Minnesota | 9 | 5 | 0 | .643 | 231 | 227 |
| Chicago | 9 | 5 | 0 | .643 | 255 | 253 |
| Detroit | 6 | 8 | 0 | .429 | 183 | 252 |
| Green Bay | 4 | 10 | 0 | .286 | 134 | 219 |
| Tampa Bay | 2 | 12 | 0 | .143 | 103 | 223 |

#### WESTERN DIVISION

|  | W | L | T | Pct. | Pts. | Op. |
|---|---|---|---|---|---|---|
| Los Angeles | 10 | 4 | 0 | .714 | 302 | 146 |
| Atlanta | 7 | 7 | 0 | .500 | 179 | 129 |
| San Francisco | 5 | 9 | 0 | .357 | 220 | 260 |
| New Orleans | 3 | 11 | 0 | .214 | 232 | 336 |

## 1976

### American Football Conference

#### EASTERN DIVISION

|  | W | L | T | Pct. | Pts. | Op. |
|---|---|---|---|---|---|---|
| Baltimore | 11 | 3 | 0 | .786 | 417 | 246 |
| New England | 11 | 3 | 0 | .786 | 376 | 236 |
| Miami | 6 | 8 | 0 | .429 | 263 | 264 |
| NY Jets | 3 | 11 | 0 | .214 | 169 | 383 |
| Buffalo | 2 | 12 | 0 | .143 | 245 | 363 |

#### CENTRAL DIVISION

|  | W | L | T | Pct. | Pts. | Op. |
|---|---|---|---|---|---|---|
| Pittsburgh | 10 | 4 | 0 | .714 | 342 | 138 |
| Cincinnati | 10 | 4 | 0 | .714 | 335 | 210 |
| Cleveland | 9 | 5 | 0 | .643 | 267 | 287 |
| Houston | 5 | 9 | 0 | .357 | 222 | 273 |

#### WESTERN DIVISION

|  | W | L | T | Pct. | Pts. | Op. |
|---|---|---|---|---|---|---|
| Oakland | 13 | 1 | 0 | .929 | 350 | 237 |
| Denver | 9 | 5 | 0 | .643 | 315 | 206 |
| San Diego | 6 | 8 | 0 | .429 | 248 | 285 |
| Kansas City | 5 | 9 | 0 | .357 | 290 | 376 |
| Tampa Bay | 0 | 14 | 0 | .000 | 125 | 412 |

### National Football Conference

#### EASTERN DIVISION

|  | W | L | T | Pct. | Pts. | Op. |
|---|---|---|---|---|---|---|
| Dallas | 11 | 3 | 0 | .786 | 296 | 194 |
| Washington | 10 | 4 | 0 | .714 | 291 | 217 |
| St. Louis | 10 | 4 | 0 | .714 | 309 | 267 |
| Philadelphia | 4 | 10 | 0 | .286 | 165 | 286 |
| NY Giants | 3 | 11 | 0 | .214 | 170 | 250 |

#### CENTRAL DIVISION

|  | W | L | T | Pct. | Pts. | Op. |
|---|---|---|---|---|---|---|
| Minnesota | 11 | 2 | 1 | .821 | 305 | 176 |
| Chicago | 7 | 7 | 0 | .500 | 253 | 216 |
| Detroit | 6 | 8 | 0 | .429 | 262 | 220 |
| Green Bay | 5 | 9 | 0 | .357 | 218 | 299 |

#### WESTERN DIVISION

|  | W | L | T | Pct. | Pts. | Op. |
|---|---|---|---|---|---|---|
| Los Angeles | 10 | 3 | 1 | .750 | 351 | 190 |
| San Francisco | 8 | 6 | 0 | .571 | 270 | 190 |
| Atlanta | 4 | 10 | 0 | .286 | 172 | 312 |
| New Orleans | 4 | 10 | 0 | .286 | 253 | 346 |
| Seattle | 2 | 12 | 0 | .143 | 229 | 429 |

## 1975

### American Football Conference

#### EASTERN DIVISION

|  | W | L | T | Pct. | Pts. | Op. |
|---|---|---|---|---|---|---|
| Baltimore | 10 | 4 | 0 | .714 | 395 | 269 |
| Miami | 10 | 4 | 0 | .714 | 357 | 222 |
| Buffalo | 8 | 6 | 0 | .571 | 420 | 355 |
| New England | 3 | 11 | 0 | .214 | 258 | 358 |
| NY Jets | 3 | 11 | 0 | .214 | 258 | 433 |

#### CENTRAL DIVISION

|  | W | L | T | Pct. | Pts. | Op. |
|---|---|---|---|---|---|---|
| Pittsburgh | 12 | 2 | 0 | .857 | 373 | 162 |
| Cincinnati | 11 | 3 | 0 | .786 | 340 | 246 |
| Houston | 10 | 4 | 0 | .714 | 293 | 226 |
| Cleveland | 3 | 11 | 0 | .214 | 218 | 372 |

#### WESTERN DIVISION

|  | W | L | T | Pct. | Pts. | Op. |
|---|---|---|---|---|---|---|
| Oakland | 11 | 3 | 0 | .786 | 375 | 255 |
| Denver | 6 | 8 | 0 | .429 | 254 | 307 |
| Kansas City | 5 | 9 | 0 | .357 | 282 | 341 |
| San Diego | 2 | 12 | 0 | .143 | 189 | 345 |

### National Football Conference

#### EASTERN DIVISION

|  | W | L | T | Pct. | Pts. | Op. |
|---|---|---|---|---|---|---|
| St. Louis | 11 | 3 | 0 | .786 | 356 | 276 |
| Dallas | 10 | 4 | 0 | .714 | 350 | 268 |
| Washington | 8 | 6 | 0 | .571 | 325 | 276 |
| NY Giants | 5 | 9 | 0 | .357 | 216 | 306 |
| Philadelphia | 4 | 10 | 0 | .286 | 225 | 302 |

#### CENTRAL DIVISION

|  | W | L | T | Pct. | Pts. | Op. |
|---|---|---|---|---|---|---|
| Minnesota | 12 | 2 | 0 | .857 | 377 | 180 |
| Detroit | 7 | 7 | 0 | .500 | 245 | 262 |
| Chicago | 4 | 10 | 0 | .286 | 191 | 379 |
| Green Bay | 4 | 10 | 0 | .286 | 226 | 285 |

#### WESTERN DIVISION

|  | W | L | T | Pct. | Pts. | Op. |
|---|---|---|---|---|---|---|
| Los Angeles | 12 | 2 | 0 | .857 | 312 | 135 |
| San Francisco | 5 | 9 | 0 | .357 | 255 | 286 |
| Atlanta | 4 | 10 | 0 | .286 | 240 | 289 |
| New Orleans | 2 | 12 | 0 | .143 | 165 | 360 |

## 1974

### American Football Conference

#### EASTERN DIVISION

|  | W | L | T | Pct. | Pts. | Op. |
|---|---|---|---|---|---|---|
| Miami | 11 | 3 | 0 | .786 | 327 | 216 |
| Buffalo | 9 | 5 | 0 | .643 | 264 | 244 |
| New England | 7 | 7 | 0 | .500 | 348 | 289 |
| NY Jets | 7 | 7 | 0 | .500 | 279 | 300 |
| Baltimore | 2 | 12 | 0 | .143 | 190 | 329 |

#### CENTRAL DIVISION

|  | W | L | T | Pct. | Pts. | Op. |
|---|---|---|---|---|---|---|
| Pittsburgh | 10 | 3 | 1 | .750 | 305 | 189 |
| Cincinnati | 7 | 7 | 0 | .500 | 283 | 259 |
| Houston | 7 | 7 | 0 | .500 | 236 | 282 |
| Cleveland | 4 | 10 | 0 | .286 | 251 | 344 |

#### WESTERN DIVISION

|  | W | L | T | Pct. | Pts. | Op. |
|---|---|---|---|---|---|---|
| Oakland | 12 | 2 | 0 | .857 | 355 | 228 |
| Denver | 7 | 6 | 1 | .536 | 302 | 294 |
| Kansas City | 5 | 9 | 0 | .357 | 233 | 293 |
| San Diego | 5 | 9 | 0 | .357 | 212 | 285 |

### National Football Conference

#### EASTERN DIVISION

|  | W | L | T | Pct. | Pts. | Op. |
|---|---|---|---|---|---|---|
| St. Louis | 10 | 4 | 0 | .714 | 285 | 218 |
| Washington | 10 | 4 | 0 | .714 | 320 | 196 |
| Dallas | 8 | 6 | 0 | .571 | 297 | 235 |
| Philadelphia | 7 | 7 | 0 | .500 | 242 | 217 |
| NY Giants | 2 | 12 | 0 | .143 | 195 | 299 |

#### CENTRAL DIVISION

|  | W | L | T | Pct. | Pts. | Op. |
|---|---|---|---|---|---|---|
| Minnesota | 10 | 4 | 0 | .714 | 310 | 195 |
| Detroit | 7 | 7 | 0 | .500 | 256 | 270 |
| Green Bay | 6 | 8 | 0 | .429 | 210 | 206 |
| Chicago | 4 | 10 | 0 | .286 | 152 | 279 |

#### WESTERN DIVISION

|  | W | L | T | Pct. | Pts. | Op. |
|---|---|---|---|---|---|---|
| Los Angeles | 10 | 4 | 0 | .714 | 263 | 181 |
| San Francisco | 6 | 8 | 0 | .429 | 226 | 236 |
| New Orleans | 5 | 9 | 0 | .357 | 166 | 263 |
| Atlanta | 3 | 11 | 0 | .214 | 111 | 271 |

## 1973

### American Football Conference

#### EASTERN DIVISION

| | W | L | T | Pct. | Pts. | Op. |
|---|---|---|---|---|---|---|
| Miami | 12 | 2 | 0 | .857 | 343 | 150 |
| Buffalo | 9 | 5 | 0 | .643 | 259 | 230 |
| New England | 5 | 9 | 0 | .357 | 258 | 300 |
| Baltimore | 4 | 10 | 0 | .286 | 226 | 341 |
| NY Jets | 4 | 10 | 0 | .286 | 240 | 306 |

#### CENTRAL DIVISION

| | W | L | T | Pct. | Pts. | Op. |
|---|---|---|---|---|---|---|
| Cincinnati | 10 | 4 | 0 | .714 | 286 | 231 |
| Pittsburgh | 10 | 4 | 0 | .714 | 347 | 210 |
| Cleveland | 7 | 5 | 2 | .571 | 234 | 255 |
| Houston | 1 | 13 | 0 | .071 | 199 | 447 |

#### WESTERN DIVISION

| | W | L | T | Pct. | Pts. | Op. |
|---|---|---|---|---|---|---|
| Oakland | 9 | 4 | 1 | .679 | 292 | 175 |
| Denver | 7 | 5 | 2 | .571 | 354 | 296 |
| Kansas City | 7 | 5 | 2 | .571 | 231 | 192 |
| San Diego | 2 | 11 | 1 | .179 | 188 | 386 |

### National Football Conference

#### EASTERN DIVISION

| | W | L | T | Pct. | Pts. | Op. |
|---|---|---|---|---|---|---|
| Dallas | 10 | 4 | 0 | .714 | 382 | 203 |
| Washington | 10 | 4 | 0 | .714 | 325 | 198 |
| Philadelphia | 5 | 8 | 1 | .393 | 310 | 393 |
| St. Louis | 4 | 9 | 1 | .321 | 286 | 365 |
| NY Giants | 2 | 11 | 1 | .179 | 226 | 362 |

#### CENTRAL DIVISION

| | W | L | T | Pct. | Pts. | Op. |
|---|---|---|---|---|---|---|
| Minnesota | 12 | 2 | 0 | .857 | 296 | 168 |
| Detroit | 6 | 7 | 1 | .464 | 271 | 247 |
| Green Bay | 5 | 7 | 2 | .429 | 202 | 259 |
| Chicago | 3 | 11 | 0 | .214 | 195 | 334 |

#### WESTERN DIVISION

| | W | L | T | Pct. | Pts. | Op. |
|---|---|---|---|---|---|---|
| Los Angeles | 12 | 2 | 0 | .857 | 388 | 178 |
| Atlanta | 9 | 5 | 0 | .643 | 318 | 224 |
| New Orleans | 5 | 9 | 0 | .357 | 163 | 312 |
| San Francisco | 5 | 9 | 0 | .357 | 262 | 319 |

## 1972

### American Football Conference

#### EASTERN DIVISION

| | W | L | T | Pct. | Pts. | Op. |
|---|---|---|---|---|---|---|
| Miami | 14 | 0 | 0 | 1.000 | 385 | 171 |
| NY Jets | 7 | 7 | 0 | .500 | 367 | 324 |
| Baltimore | 5 | 9 | 0 | .357 | 235 | 252 |
| Buffalo | 4 | 9 | 1 | .321 | 257 | 377 |
| New England | 3 | 11 | 0 | .214 | 192 | 446 |

#### CENTRAL DIVISION

| | W | L | T | Pct. | Pts. | Op. |
|---|---|---|---|---|---|---|
| Pittsburgh | 11 | 3 | 0 | .786 | 343 | 175 |
| Cleveland | 10 | 4 | 0 | .714 | 268 | 249 |
| Cincinnati | 8 | 6 | 0 | .571 | 299 | 229 |
| Houston | 1 | 13 | 0 | .071 | 164 | 380 |

#### WESTERN DIVISION

| | W | L | T | Pct. | Pts. | Op. |
|---|---|---|---|---|---|---|
| Oakland | 10 | 3 | 1 | .750 | 365 | 248 |
| Kansas City | 8 | 6 | 0 | .571 | 287 | 254 |
| Denver | 5 | 9 | 0 | .357 | 325 | 350 |
| San Diego | 4 | 9 | 1 | .321 | 264 | 344 |

### National Football Conference

#### EASTERN DIVISION

| | W | L | T | Pct. | Pts. | Op. |
|---|---|---|---|---|---|---|
| Washington | 11 | 3 | 0 | .786 | 336 | 218 |
| Dallas | 10 | 4 | 0 | .714 | 319 | 240 |
| NY Giants | 8 | 6 | 0 | .571 | 331 | 247 |
| St. Louis | 4 | 9 | 1 | .321 | 193 | 303 |
| Philadelphia | 2 | 11 | 1 | .179 | 145 | 352 |

#### CENTRAL DIVISION

| | W | L | T | Pct. | Pts. | Op. |
|---|---|---|---|---|---|---|
| Green Bay | 10 | 4 | 0 | .714 | 304 | 226 |
| Detroit | 8 | 5 | 1 | .607 | 339 | 290 |
| Minnesota | 7 | 7 | 0 | .500 | 301 | 252 |
| Chicago | 4 | 9 | 1 | .321 | 225 | 275 |

#### WESTERN DIVISION

| | W | L | T | Pct. | Pts. | Op. |
|---|---|---|---|---|---|---|
| San Francisco | 8 | 5 | 1 | .607 | 353 | 249 |
| Atlanta | 7 | 7 | 0 | .500 | 269 | 274 |
| Los Angeles | 6 | 7 | 1 | .464 | 291 | 286 |
| New Orleans | 2 | 11 | 1 | .179 | 215 | 361 |

## 1971

### American Football Conference

#### EASTERN DIVISION

|  | W | L | T | Pct. | Pts. | Op. |
|---|---|---|---|---|---|---|
| Miami | 10 | 3 | 1 | .769 | 315 | 174 |
| Baltimore | 10 | 4 | 0 | .714 | 313 | 140 |
| New England | 6 | 8 | 0 | .429 | 238 | 325 |
| NY Jets | 6 | 8 | 0 | .429 | 212 | 299 |
| Buffalo | 1 | 13 | 0 | .071 | 184 | 394 |

#### CENTRAL DIVISION

|  | W | L | T | Pct. | Pts. | Op. |
|---|---|---|---|---|---|---|
| Cleveland | 9 | 5 | 0 | .643 | 285 | 273 |
| Pittsburgh | 6 | 8 | 0 | .429 | 246 | 292 |
| Houston | 4 | 9 | 1 | .308 | 251 | 330 |
| Cincinnati | 4 | 10 | 0 | .286 | 284 | 265 |

#### WESTERN DIVISION

|  | W | L | T | Pct. | Pts. | Op. |
|---|---|---|---|---|---|---|
| Kansas City | 10 | 3 | 1 | .769 | 302 | 208 |
| Oakland | 8 | 4 | 2 | .667 | 344 | 278 |
| San Diego | 6 | 8 | 0 | .429 | 311 | 341 |
| Denver | 4 | 9 | 1 | .308 | 203 | 275 |

### National Football Conference

#### EASTERN DIVISION

|  | W | L | T | Pct. | Pts. | Op. |
|---|---|---|---|---|---|---|
| Dallas | 11 | 3 | 0 | .786 | 406 | 222 |
| Washington | 9 | 4 | 1 | .692 | 276 | 190 |
| Philadelphia | 6 | 7 | 1 | .462 | 221 | 302 |
| St. Louis | 4 | 9 | 1 | .308 | 231 | 279 |
| NY Giants | 4 | 10 | 0 | .286 | 228 | 362 |

#### CENTRAL DIVISION

|  | W | L | T | Pct. | Pts. | Op. |
|---|---|---|---|---|---|---|
| Minnesota | 11 | 3 | 0 | .786 | 245 | 139 |
| Detroit | 7 | 6 | 1 | .538 | 341 | 286 |
| Chicago | 6 | 8 | 0 | .429 | 185 | 276 |
| Green Bay | 4 | 8 | 2 | .333 | 274 | 298 |

#### WESTERN DIVISION

|  | W | L | T | Pct. | Pts. | Op. |
|---|---|---|---|---|---|---|
| San Francisco | 9 | 5 | 0 | .643 | 300 | 216 |
| Los Angeles | 8 | 5 | 1 | .615 | 313 | 260 |
| Atlanta | 7 | 6 | 1 | .538 | 274 | 277 |
| New Orleans | 4 | 8 | 2 | .333 | 266 | 347 |

## 1970

### American Football Conference

#### EASTERN DIVISION

|  | W | L | T | Pct. | Pts. | Op. |
|---|---|---|---|---|---|---|
| Baltimore | 11 | 2 | 1 | .846 | 321 | 234 |
| Miami | 10 | 4 | 0 | .714 | 297 | 228 |
| NY Jets | 4 | 10 | 0 | .286 | 255 | 286 |
| Buffalo | 3 | 10 | 1 | .231 | 204 | 337 |
| Boston Patriots | 2 | 12 | 0 | .143 | 149 | 361 |

#### CENTRAL DIVISION

|  | W | L | T | Pct. | Pts. | Op. |
|---|---|---|---|---|---|---|
| Cincinnati | 8 | 6 | 0 | .571 | 312 | 255 |
| Cleveland | 7 | 7 | 0 | .500 | 286 | 265 |
| Pittsburgh | 5 | 9 | 0 | .357 | 210 | 272 |
| Houston | 3 | 10 | 1 | .231 | 217 | 352 |

#### WESTERN DIVISION

|  | W | L | T | Pct. | Pts. | Op. |
|---|---|---|---|---|---|---|
| Oakland | 8 | 4 | 2 | .667 | 300 | 293 |
| Kansas City | 7 | 5 | 2 | .583 | 272 | 244 |
| San Diego | 5 | 6 | 3 | .455 | 282 | 278 |
| Denver | 5 | 8 | 1 | .385 | 253 | 264 |

### National Football Conference

#### EASTERN DIVISION

|  | W | L | T | Pct. | Pts. | Op. |
|---|---|---|---|---|---|---|
| Dallas | 10 | 4 | 0 | .714 | 299 | 221 |
| NY Giants | 9 | 5 | 0 | .643 | 301 | 270 |
| St. Louis | 8 | 5 | 1 | .615 | 325 | 228 |
| Washington | 6 | 8 | 0 | .429 | 297 | 314 |
| Philadelphia | 3 | 10 | 1 | .231 | 241 | 332 |

#### CENTRAL DIVISION

|  | W | L | T | Pct. | Pts. | Op. |
|---|---|---|---|---|---|---|
| Minnesota | 12 | 2 | 0 | .857 | 335 | 143 |
| Detroit | 10 | 4 | 0 | .714 | 347 | 202 |
| Chicago | 6 | 8 | 0 | .429 | 256 | 261 |
| Green Bay | 6 | 8 | 0 | .429 | 196 | 293 |

#### WESTERN DIVISION

|  | W | L | T | Pct. | Pts. | Op. |
|---|---|---|---|---|---|---|
| San Francisco | 10 | 3 | 1 | .769 | 352 | 267 |
| Los Angeles | 9 | 4 | 1 | .692 | 325 | 202 |
| Atlanta | 4 | 8 | 2 | .333 | 206 | 261 |
| New Orleans | 2 | 11 | 1 | .154 | 172 | 347 |

## 1969

## NATIONAL FOOTBALL LEAGUE

### Eastern Conference

#### CAPITOL DIVISION

|  | W | L | T | Pct. | Pts. | Op. |
|---|---|---|---|---|---|---|
| Dallas | 11 | 2 | 1 | .846 | 369 | 223 |
| Washington | 7 | 5 | 2 | .583 | 307 | 319 |
| New Orleans | 5 | 9 | 0 | .357 | 311 | 393 |
| Philadelphia | 4 | 9 | 1 | .308 | 279 | 377 |

#### CENTURY DIVISION

|  | W | L | T | Pct. | Pts. | Op. |
|---|---|---|---|---|---|---|
| Cleveland | 10 | 3 | 1 | .769 | 351 | 300 |
| NY Giants | 6 | 8 | 0 | .429 | 264 | 298 |
| St. Louis | 4 | 9 | 1 | .308 | 314 | 389 |
| Pittsburgh | 1 | 13 | 0 | .071 | 218 | 404 |

### Western Conference

#### COASTAL DIVISION

|  | W | L | T | Pct. | Pts. | Op. |
|---|---|---|---|---|---|---|
| Los Angeles | 11 | 3 | 0 | .786 | 320 | 243 |
| Baltimore | 8 | 5 | 1 | .615 | 279 | 268 |
| Atlanta | 6 | 8 | 0 | .429 | 276 | 268 |
| San Francisco | 4 | 8 | 2 | .333 | 277 | 319 |

#### CENTRAL DIVISION

|  | W | L | T | Pct. | Pts. | Op. |
|---|---|---|---|---|---|---|
| Minnesota | 12 | 2 | 0 | .857 | 379 | 133 |
| Detroit | 9 | 4 | 1 | .692 | 259 | 188 |
| Green Bay | 8 | 6 | 0 | .571 | 269 | 221 |
| Chicago | 1 | 13 | 0 | .071 | 210 | 339 |

## AMERICAN FOOTBALL LEAGUE

#### EASTERN DIVISION

|  | W | L | T | Pct. | Pts. | Op. |
|---|---|---|---|---|---|---|
| NY Jets | 10 | 4 | 0 | .714 | 353 | 269 |
| Houston | 6 | 6 | 2 | .500 | 278 | 279 |
| Boston Patriots | 4 | 10 | 0 | .286 | 266 | 316 |
| Buffalo | 4 | 10 | 0 | .286 | 230 | 359 |
| Miami | 3 | 10 | 1 | .231 | 233 | 332 |

#### WESTERN DIVISION

|  | W | L | T | Pct. | Pts. | Op. |
|---|---|---|---|---|---|---|
| Oakland | 12 | 1 | 1 | .923 | 377 | 242 |
| Kansas City | 11 | 3 | 0 | .786 | 359 | 177 |
| San Diego | 8 | 6 | 0 | .571 | 288 | 276 |
| Denver | 5 | 8 | 1 | .385 | 297 | 344 |
| Cincinnati | 4 | 9 | 1 | .308 | 280 | 367 |

## 1968

## NATIONAL FOOTBALL LEAGUE

### Eastern Conference

#### CAPITOL DIVISION

|  | W | L | T | Pct. | Pts. | Op. |
|---|---|---|---|---|---|---|
| Dallas | 12 | 2 | 0 | .857 | 431 | 186 |
| NY Giants | 7 | 7 | 0 | .500 | 294 | 325 |
| Washington | 5 | 9 | 0 | .357 | 249 | 358 |
| Philadelphia | 2 | 12 | 0 | .143 | 202 | 351 |

#### CENTURY DIVISION

|  | W | L | T | Pct. | Pts. | Op. |
|---|---|---|---|---|---|---|
| Cleveland | 10 | 4 | 0 | .714 | 394 | 273 |
| St. Louis | 9 | 4 | 1 | .692 | 325 | 289 |
| New Orleans | 4 | 9 | 1 | .308 | 246 | 327 |
| Pittsburgh | 2 | 11 | 1 | .154 | 244 | 397 |

### Western Conference

#### COASTAL DIVISION

|  | W | L | T | Pct. | Pts. | Op. |
|---|---|---|---|---|---|---|
| Baltimore | 13 | 1 | 0 | .929 | 402 | 144 |
| Los Angeles | 10 | 3 | 1 | .769 | 312 | 200 |
| San Francisco | 7 | 6 | 1 | .538 | 303 | 310 |
| Atlanta | 2 | 12 | 0 | .143 | 170 | 389 |

#### CENTRAL DIVISION

|  | W | L | T | Pct. | Pts. | Op. |
|---|---|---|---|---|---|---|
| Minnesota | 8 | 6 | 0 | .571 | 282 | 242 |
| Chicago | 7 | 7 | 0 | .500 | 250 | 333 |
| Green Bay | 6 | 7 | 1 | .462 | 281 | 227 |
| Detroit | 4 | 8 | 2 | .333 | 207 | 241 |

## AMERICAN FOOTBALL LEAGUE

#### EASTERN DIVISION

|  | W | L | T | Pct. | Pts. | Op. |
|---|---|---|---|---|---|---|
| NY Jets | 11 | 3 | 0 | .786 | 419 | 280 |
| Houston | 7 | 7 | 0 | .500 | 303 | 248 |
| Miami | 5 | 8 | 1 | .385 | 276 | 355 |
| Boston Patriots | 4 | 10 | 0 | .286 | 229 | 406 |
| Buffalo | 1 | 12 | 1 | .077 | 199 | 367 |

#### WESTERN DIVISION

|  | W | L | T | Pct. | Pts. | Op. |
|---|---|---|---|---|---|---|
| Oakland | 12 | 2 | 0 | .857 | 453 | 233 |
| Kansas City | 12 | 2 | 0 | .857 | 371 | 170 |
| San Diego | 9 | 5 | 0 | .643 | 382 | 310 |
| Denver | 5 | 9 | 0 | .357 | 255 | 404 |
| Cincinnati | 3 | 11 | 0 | .214 | 215 | 329 |

### 1967
## NATIONAL FOOTBALL LEAGUE

**Eastern Conference**                    **Western Conference**

#### CAPITOL DIVISION

| | W | L | T | Pct. | Pts. | Op. |
|---|---|---|---|---|---|---|
| Dallas | 9 | 5 | 0 | .643 | 342 | 268 |
| Philadelphia | 6 | 7 | 1 | .462 | 351 | 409 |
| Washington | 5 | 6 | 3 | .455 | 347 | 353 |
| New Orleans | 3 | 11 | 0 | .214 | 233 | 379 |

#### COASTAL DIVISION

| | W | L | T | Pct. | Pts. | Op. |
|---|---|---|---|---|---|---|
| Los Angeles | 11 | 1 | 2 | .917 | 398 | 196 |
| Baltimore | 11 | 1 | 2 | .917 | 394 | 198 |
| San Francisco | 7 | 7 | 0 | .500 | 273 | 337 |
| Atlanta | 1 | 12 | 1 | .077 | 175 | 422 |

#### CENTURY DIVISION

| | W | L | T | Pct. | Pts. | Op. |
|---|---|---|---|---|---|---|
| Cleveland | 9 | 5 | 0 | .643 | 334 | 297 |
| NY Giants | 7 | 7 | 0 | .500 | 369 | 379 |
| St. Louis | 6 | 7 | 1 | .462 | 333 | 356 |
| Pittsburgh | 4 | 9 | 1 | .308 | 281 | 320 |

#### CENTRAL DIVISION

| | W | L | T | Pct. | Pts. | Op. |
|---|---|---|---|---|---|---|
| Green Bay | 9 | 4 | 1 | .692 | 332 | 209 |
| Chicago | 7 | 6 | 1 | .538 | 239 | 218 |
| Detroit | 5 | 7 | 2 | .417 | 260 | 259 |
| Minnesota | 3 | 8 | 3 | .273 | 233 | 294 |

## AMERICAN FOOTBALL LEAGUE

#### EASTERN DIVISION

| | W | L | T | Pct. | Pts. | Op. |
|---|---|---|---|---|---|---|
| Houston | 9 | 4 | 1 | .692 | 258 | 199 |
| NY Jets | 8 | 5 | 1 | .615 | 371 | 329 |
| Buffalo | 4 | 10 | 0 | .286 | 237 | 285 |
| Miami | 4 | 10 | 0 | .286 | 219 | 407 |
| Boston Patriots | 3 | 10 | 1 | .231 | 280 | 389 |

#### WESTERN DIVISION

| | W | L | T | Pct. | Pts. | Op. |
|---|---|---|---|---|---|---|
| Oakland | 13 | 1 | 0 | .929 | 468 | 233 |
| Kansas City | 9 | 5 | 0 | .643 | 408 | 254 |
| San Diego | 8 | 5 | 1 | .615 | 360 | 352 |
| Denver | 3 | 11 | 0 | .214 | 256 | 409 |

### 1966
## NATIONAL FOOTBALL LEAGUE

#### EASTERN CONFERENCE

| | W | L | T | Pct. | Pts. | Op. |
|---|---|---|---|---|---|---|
| Dallas | 10 | 3 | 1 | .769 | 445 | 239 |
| Cleveland | 9 | 5 | 0 | .643 | 403 | 259 |
| Philadelphia | 9 | 5 | 0 | .643 | 326 | 340 |
| St. Louis | 8 | 5 | 1 | .615 | 264 | 265 |
| Washington | 7 | 7 | 0 | .500 | 351 | 355 |
| Pittsburgh | 5 | 8 | 1 | .385 | 316 | 347 |
| Atlanta | 3 | 11 | 0 | .214 | 204 | 437 |
| NY Giants | 1 | 12 | 1 | .077 | 263 | 501 |

#### WESTERN CONFERENCE

| | W | L | T | Pct. | Pts. | Op. |
|---|---|---|---|---|---|---|
| Green Bay | 12 | 2 | 0 | .857 | 335 | 163 |
| Baltimore | 9 | 5 | 0 | .643 | 314 | 226 |
| Los Angeles | 8 | 6 | 0 | .571 | 289 | 212 |
| San Francisco | 6 | 6 | 2 | .500 | 320 | 325 |
| Chicago | 5 | 7 | 2 | .417 | 234 | 272 |
| Detroit | 4 | 9 | 1 | .308 | 206 | 317 |
| Minnesota | 4 | 9 | 1 | .308 | 292 | 304 |

## AMERICAN FOOTBALL LEAGUE

#### EASTERN DIVISION

| | W | L | T | Pct. | Pts. | Op. |
|---|---|---|---|---|---|---|
| Buffalo | 9 | 4 | 1 | .692 | 358 | 255 |
| Boston Patriots | 8 | 4 | 2 | .677 | 315 | 283 |
| NY Jets | 6 | 6 | 2 | .500 | 322 | 312 |
| Houston | 3 | 11 | 0 | .214 | 335 | 396 |
| Miami | 3 | 11 | 0 | .214 | 213 | 362 |

#### WESTERN DIVISION

| | W | L | T | Pct. | Pts. | Op. |
|---|---|---|---|---|---|---|
| Kansas City | 11 | 2 | 1 | .846 | 448 | 276 |
| Oakland | 8 | 5 | 1 | .615 | 315 | 288 |
| San Diego | 7 | 6 | 1 | .538 | 335 | 284 |
| Denver | 4 | 10 | 0 | .286 | 196 | 381 |

## 1965
## NATIONAL FOOTBALL LEAGUE

### EASTERN CONFERENCE

| | W | L | T | Pct. | Pts. | Op. |
|---|---|---|---|---|---|---|
| Cleveland | 11 | 3 | 0 | .786 | 363 | 325 |
| Dallas | 7 | 7 | 0 | .500 | 325 | 280 |
| NY Giants | 7 | 7 | 0 | .500 | 270 | 338 |
| Washington | 6 | 8 | 0 | .429 | 257 | 301 |
| Philadelphia | 5 | 9 | 0 | .357 | 363 | 359 |
| St. Louis | 5 | 9 | 0 | .357 | 296 | 309 |
| Pittsburgh | 2 | 12 | 0 | .143 | 202 | 397 |

### WESTERN CONFERENCE

| | W | L | T | Pct. | Pts. | Op. |
|---|---|---|---|---|---|---|
| Green Bay | 10 | 3 | 1 | .769 | 316 | 224 |
| Baltimore | 10 | 3 | 1 | .769 | 389 | 284 |
| Chicago | 9 | 5 | 0 | .643 | 409 | 275 |
| San Francisco | 7 | 6 | 1 | .538 | 421 | 402 |
| Minnesota | 7 | 7 | 0 | .500 | 383 | 403 |
| Detroit | 6 | 7 | 1 | .462 | 257 | 295 |
| Los Angeles | 4 | 10 | 0 | .286 | 269 | 328 |

## AMERICAN FOOTBALL LEAGUE

### EASTERN DIVISION

| | W | L | T | Pct. | Pts. | Op. |
|---|---|---|---|---|---|---|
| Buffalo | 10 | 3 | 1 | .769 | 313 | 226 |
| NY Jets | 5 | 8 | 1 | .385 | 285 | 303 |
| Boston Patriots | 4 | 8 | 2 | .333 | 244 | 302 |
| Houston | 4 | 10 | 0 | .286 | 298 | 429 |

### WESTERN DIVISION

| | W | L | T | Pct. | Pts. | Op. |
|---|---|---|---|---|---|---|
| San Diego | 9 | 2 | 3 | .818 | 340 | 227 |
| Oakland | 8 | 5 | 1 | .615 | 298 | 239 |
| Kansas City | 7 | 5 | 2 | .583 | 322 | 285 |
| Denver | 4 | 10 | 0 | .286 | 303 | 392 |

## 1964
## NATIONAL FOOTBALL LEAGUE

### EASTERN CONFERENCE

| | W | L | T | Pct. | Pts. | Op. |
|---|---|---|---|---|---|---|
| Cleveland | 10 | 3 | 1 | .769 | 415 | 293 |
| St. Louis | 9 | 3 | 2 | .750 | 357 | 331 |
| Philadelphia | 6 | 8 | 0 | .429 | 312 | 313 |
| Washington | 6 | 8 | 0 | .429 | 307 | 305 |
| Dallas | 5 | 8 | 1 | .385 | 250 | 289 |
| Pittsburgh | 5 | 9 | 0 | .357 | 253 | 315 |
| NY Giants | 2 | 10 | 2 | .167 | 241 | 399 |

### WESTERN CONFERENCE

| | W | L | T | Pct. | Pts. | Op. |
|---|---|---|---|---|---|---|
| Baltimore | 12 | 2 | 0 | .857 | 428 | 225 |
| Green Bay | 8 | 5 | 1 | .615 | 342 | 245 |
| Minnesota | 8 | 5 | 1 | .615 | 355 | 296 |
| Detroit | 7 | 5 | 2 | .583 | 280 | 260 |
| Los Angeles | 5 | 7 | 2 | .417 | 283 | 339 |
| Chicago | 5 | 9 | 0 | .357 | 260 | 379 |
| San Francisco | 4 | 10 | 0 | .286 | 236 | 330 |

## AMERICAN FOOTBALL LEAGUE

### EASTERN DIVISION

| | W | L | T | Pct. | Pts. | Op. |
|---|---|---|---|---|---|---|
| Buffalo | 12 | 2 | 0 | .857 | 400 | 242 |
| Boston Patriots | 10 | 3 | 1 | .769 | 365 | 297 |
| NY Jets | 5 | 8 | 1 | .385 | 278 | 315 |
| Houston | 4 | 10 | 0 | .286 | 310 | 355 |

### WESTERN DIVISION

| | W | L | T | Pct. | Pts. | Op. |
|---|---|---|---|---|---|---|
| San Diego | 8 | 5 | 1 | .615 | 341 | 300 |
| Kansas City | 7 | 7 | 0 | .500 | 366 | 306 |
| Oakland | 5 | 7 | 2 | .417 | 303 | 350 |
| Denver | 2 | 11 | 1 | .154 | 240 | 438 |

## 1963
## NATIONAL FOOTBALL LEAGUE

### EASTERN CONFERENCE

| | W | L | T | Pct. | Pts. | Op. |
|---|---|---|---|---|---|---|
| NY Giants | 11 | 3 | 0 | .786 | 448 | 280 |
| Cleveland | 10 | 4 | 0 | .714 | 343 | 262 |
| St. Louis | 9 | 5 | 0 | .643 | 341 | 283 |
| Pittsburgh | 7 | 4 | 3 | .636 | 321 | 295 |
| Dallas | 4 | 10 | 0 | .286 | 305 | 378 |
| Washington | 3 | 11 | 0 | .214 | 279 | 398 |
| Philadelphia | 2 | 10 | 2 | .167 | 242 | 381 |

### WESTERN CONFERENCE

| | W | L | T | Pct. | Pts. | Op. |
|---|---|---|---|---|---|---|
| Chicago | 11 | 1 | 2 | .917 | 301 | 144 |
| Green Bay | 11 | 2 | 1 | .846 | 369 | 206 |
| Baltimore | 8 | 6 | 0 | .571 | 316 | 285 |
| Detroit | 5 | 8 | 1 | .385 | 326 | 265 |
| Minnesota | 5 | 8 | 1 | .385 | 309 | 390 |
| Los Angeles | 5 | 9 | 0 | .357 | 210 | 350 |
| San Francisco | 2 | 12 | 0 | .143 | 198 | 391 |

## 1963 *(Cont.)*
### AMERICAN FOOTBALL LEAGUE

| EASTERN DIVISION | W | L | T | Pct. | Pts. | Op. | WESTERN DIVISION | W | L | T | Pct. | Pts. | Op. |
|---|---|---|---|---|---|---|---|---|---|---|---|---|---|
| Boston Patriots ....7 | 6 | 1 | .538 | 327 | 257 | | San Diego .........11 | 3 | 0 | .786 | 399 | 256 |
| Buffalo .................7 | 6 | 1 | .538 | 304 | 291 | | Oakland ............10 | 4 | 0 | .714 | 363 | 288 |
| Houston ..............6 | 8 | 0 | .429 | 302 | 372 | | Kansas City .........5 | 7 | 2 | .417 | 347 | 263 |
| NY Jets .............5 | 8 | 1 | .385 | 249 | 399 | | Denver .................2 | 11 | 1 | .154 | 301 | 473 |

## 1962
### NATIONAL FOOTBALL LEAGUE

| EASTERN CONFERENCE | W | L | T | Pct. | Pts. | Op. | WESTERN CONFERENCE | W | L | T | Pct. | Pts. | Op. |
|---|---|---|---|---|---|---|---|---|---|---|---|---|---|
| NY Giants ..........12 | 2 | 0 | .857 | 398 | 283 | | Green Bay .........13 | 1 | 0 | .929 | 415 | 148 |
| Pittsburgh ...........9 | 5 | 0 | .643 | 312 | 363 | | Detroit ................11 | 3 | 0 | .786 | 315 | 177 |
| Cleveland ...........7 | 6 | 1 | .538 | 291 | 257 | | Chicago ..............9 | 5 | 0 | .643 | 321 | 287 |
| Washington.........5 | 7 | 2 | .417 | 305 | 376 | | Baltimore ............7 | 7 | 0 | .500 | 293 | 288 |
| Dallas Cowboys...5 | 8 | 1 | .385 | 398 | 402 | | San Francisco......6 | 8 | 0 | .429 | 282 | 331 |
| St. Louis..............4 | 9 | 1 | .308 | 287 | 361 | | Minnesota............2 | 11 | 1 | .154 | 254 | 410 |
| Philadelphia........3 | 10 | 1 | .231 | 282 | 356 | | Los Angeles.........1 | 12 | 1 | .077 | 220 | 334 |

### AMERICAN FOOTBALL LEAGUE

| EASTERN DIVISION | W | L | T | Pct. | Pts. | Op. | WESTERN DIVISION | W | L | T | Pct. | Pts. | Op. |
|---|---|---|---|---|---|---|---|---|---|---|---|---|---|
| Houston .............11 | 3 | 0 | .786 | 387 | 270 | | Dallas Texans ....11 | 3 | 0 | .786 | 389 | 233 |
| Boston Patriots ....9 | 4 | 1 | .692 | 346 | 295 | | Denver .................7 | 7 | 0 | .500 | 353 | 334 |
| Buffalo .................7 | 6 | 1 | .538 | 309 | 272 | | San Diego............4 | 10 | 0 | .286 | 314 | 392 |
| NY Titans .............5 | 9 | 0 | .357 | 278 | 423 | | Oakland ...............1 | 13 | 0 | .071 | 213 | 370 |

## 1961
### NATIONAL FOOTBALL LEAGUE

| EASTERN CONFERENCE | W | L | T | Pct. | Pts. | Op. | WESTERN CONFERENCE | W | L | T | Pct. | Pts. | Op. |
|---|---|---|---|---|---|---|---|---|---|---|---|---|---|
| NY Giants ..........10 | 3 | 1 | .769 | 368 | 220 | | Green Bay .........11 | 3 | 0 | .786 | 391 | 223 |
| Philadelphia.......10 | 4 | 0 | .714 | 361 | 297 | | Detroit .................8 | 5 | 1 | .615 | 270 | 258 |
| Cleveland ...........8 | 5 | 1 | .615 | 319 | 270 | | Baltimore ............8 | 6 | 0 | .571 | 302 | 307 |
| St. Louis..............7 | 7 | 0 | .500 | 279 | 267 | | Chicago ..............8 | 6 | 0 | .571 | 326 | 302 |
| Pittsburgh ...........6 | 8 | 0 | .429 | 295 | 287 | | San Francisco......7 | 6 | 1 | .538 | 346 | 272 |
| Dallas Cowboys...4 | 9 | 1 | .308 | 236 | 380 | | Los Angeles.........4 | 10 | 0 | .286 | 263 | 333 |
| Washington.........1 | 12 | 1 | .077 | 174 | 392 | | Minnesota............3 | 11 | 0 | .214 | 285 | 407 |

### AMERICAN FOOTBALL LEAGUE

| EASTERN DIVISION | W | L | T | Pct. | Pts. | Op. | WESTERN DIVISION | W | L | T | Pct. | Pts. | Op. |
|---|---|---|---|---|---|---|---|---|---|---|---|---|---|
| Houston .............10 | 3 | 1 | .769 | 513 | 242 | | San Diego..........12 | 2 | 0 | .857 | 396 | 219 |
| Boston Patriots ....9 | 4 | 1 | .692 | 413 | 313 | | Dallas Texans .....6 | 8 | 0 | .429 | 334 | 343 |
| NY Titans ............7 | 7 | 0 | .500 | 301 | 390 | | Denver .................3 | 11 | 0 | .214 | 251 | 432 |
| Buffalo .................6 | 8 | 0 | .429 | 294 | 342 | | Oakland ...............2 | 12 | 0 | .143 | 237 | 458 |

## 1960
## NATIONAL FOOTBALL LEAGUE

### EASTERN CONFERENCE

| | W | L | T | Pct. | Pts. | Op. |
|---|---|---|---|---|---|---|
| Philadelphia | 10 | 2 | 0 | .833 | 321 | 246 |
| Cleveland | 8 | 3 | 1 | .727 | 362 | 217 |
| NY Giants | 6 | 4 | 2 | .600 | 271 | 261 |
| St. Louis | 6 | 5 | 1 | .545 | 288 | 230 |
| Pittsburgh | 5 | 6 | 1 | .455 | 240 | 275 |
| Washington | 1 | 9 | 2 | .100 | 178 | 309 |

### WESTERN CONFERENCE

| | W | L | T | Pct. | Pts. | Op. |
|---|---|---|---|---|---|---|
| Green Bay | 8 | 4 | 0 | .667 | 332 | 209 |
| Detroit | 7 | 5 | 0 | .583 | 239 | 212 |
| San Francisco | 7 | 5 | 0 | .583 | 208 | 205 |
| Baltimore | 6 | 6 | 0 | .500 | 288 | 234 |
| Chicago | 5 | 6 | 1 | .455 | 194 | 299 |
| LA Rams | 4 | 7 | 1 | .364 | 265 | 297 |
| Dallas Cowboys | 0 | 11 | 1 | .000 | 177 | 369 |

## AMERICAN FOOTBALL LEAGUE

### EASTERN DIVISION

| | W | L | T | Pct. | Pts. | Op. |
|---|---|---|---|---|---|---|
| Houston | 10 | 4 | 0 | .714 | 379 | 285 |
| NY Titans | 7 | 7 | 0 | .500 | 382 | 399 |
| Buffalo | 5 | 8 | 1 | .385 | 296 | 303 |
| Boston | 5 | 9 | 1 | .357 | 286 | 349 |

### WESTERN DIVISION

| | W | L | T | Pct. | Pts. | Op. |
|---|---|---|---|---|---|---|
| LA Chargers | 10 | 4 | 0 | .714 | 373 | 336 |
| Dallas Texans | 8 | 6 | 0 | .571 | 362 | 253 |
| Oakland | 6 | 8 | 0 | .429 | 319 | 388 |
| Denver | 4 | 9 | 1 | .308 | 309 | 393 |

## 1959

### EASTERN CONFERENCE

| | W | L | T | Pct. | Pts. | Op. |
|---|---|---|---|---|---|---|
| NY Giants | 10 | 2 | 0 | .833 | 284 | 170 |
| Cleveland | 7 | 5 | 0 | .583 | 270 | 214 |
| Philadelphia | 7 | 5 | 0 | .583 | 268 | 278 |
| Pittsburgh | 6 | 5 | 1 | .545 | 257 | 216 |
| Washington | 3 | 9 | 0 | .250 | 185 | 350 |
| Chi Cardinals | 2 | 10 | 0 | .167 | 234 | 324 |

### WESTERN CONFERENCE

| | W | L | T | Pct. | Pts. | Op. |
|---|---|---|---|---|---|---|
| Baltimore | 9 | 3 | 0 | .750 | 374 | 251 |
| Chi Bears | 8 | 4 | 0 | .667 | 252 | 196 |
| Green Bay | 7 | 5 | 0 | .583 | 248 | 246 |
| San Francisco | 7 | 5 | 0 | .583 | 255 | 237 |
| Detroit | 3 | 8 | 1 | .273 | 203 | 275 |
| Los Angeles | 2 | 10 | 0 | .167 | 242 | 315 |

## 1958

### EASTERN CONFERENCE

| | W | L | T | Pct. | Pts. | Op. |
|---|---|---|---|---|---|---|
| NY Giants | 9 | 3 | 0 | .750 | 246 | 183 |
| Cleveland | 9 | 3 | 0 | .750 | 302 | 217 |
| Pittsburgh | 7 | 4 | 1 | .636 | 261 | 230 |
| Washington | 4 | 7 | 1 | .364 | 214 | 268 |
| Chi Cardinals | 2 | 9 | 1 | .182 | 261 | 356 |
| Philadelphia | 2 | 9 | 1 | .182 | 235 | 306 |

### WESTERN CONFERENCE

| | W | L | T | Pct. | Pts. | Op. |
|---|---|---|---|---|---|---|
| Baltimore | 9 | 3 | 0 | .750 | 381 | 203 |
| Chi Bears | 8 | 4 | 0 | .667 | 298 | 230 |
| Los Angeles | 8 | 4 | 0 | .667 | 344 | 278 |
| San Francisco | 6 | 6 | 0 | .500 | 257 | 324 |
| Detroit | 4 | 7 | 1 | .364 | 261 | 276 |
| Green Bay | 1 | 10 | 1 | .091 | 193 | 382 |

## 1957

### EASTERN CONFERENCE

| | W | L | T | Pct. | Pts. | Op. |
|---|---|---|---|---|---|---|
| Cleveland | 9 | 2 | 1 | .818 | 269 | 172 |
| NY Giants | 7 | 5 | 0 | .583 | 254 | 211 |
| Pittsburgh | 6 | 6 | 0 | .500 | 161 | 178 |
| Washington | 5 | 6 | 1 | .455 | 251 | 230 |
| Philadelphia | 4 | 8 | 0 | .333 | 173 | 230 |
| Chi Cardinals | 3 | 9 | 0 | .250 | 200 | 299 |

### WESTERN CONFERENCE

| | W | L | T | Pct. | Pts. | Op. |
|---|---|---|---|---|---|---|
| Detroit | 8 | 4 | 0 | .667 | 251 | 231 |
| San Francisco | 8 | 4 | 0 | .667 | 260 | 264 |
| Baltimore | 7 | 5 | 0 | .583 | 303 | 235 |
| Los Angeles | 6 | 6 | 0 | .500 | 307 | 278 |
| Chi Bears | 5 | 7 | 0 | .417 | 203 | 211 |
| Green Bay | 3 | 9 | 0 | .250 | 218 | 311 |

## 1956

### EASTERN CONFERENCE

| | W | L | T | Pct. | Pts. | Op. |
|---|---|---|---|---|---|---|
| NY Giants | 8 | 3 | 1 | .727 | 264 | 197 |
| Chi Cardinals | 7 | 5 | 0 | .583 | 240 | 182 |
| Washington | 6 | 6 | 0 | .500 | 183 | 225 |
| Cleveland | 5 | 7 | 0 | .417 | 167 | 177 |
| Pittsburgh | 5 | 7 | 0 | .417 | 217 | 250 |
| Philadelphia | 3 | 8 | 1 | .273 | 143 | 215 |

### WESTERN CONFERENCE

| | W | L | T | Pct. | Pts. | Op. |
|---|---|---|---|---|---|---|
| Chi Bears | 9 | 2 | 1 | .818 | 363 | 246 |
| Detroit | 9 | 3 | 0 | .750 | 300 | 188 |
| San Francisco | 5 | 6 | 1 | .455 | 233 | 284 |
| Baltimore | 5 | 7 | 0 | .417 | 270 | 322 |
| Green Bay | 4 | 8 | 0 | .333 | 264 | 342 |
| Los Angeles | 4 | 8 | 0 | .333 | 291 | 307 |

## 1955

### EASTERN CONFERENCE

| | W | L | T | Pct. | Pts. | Op. |
|---|---|---|---|---|---|---|
| Cleveland | 9 | 2 | 1 | .818 | 349 | 218 |
| Washington | 8 | 4 | 0 | .667 | 246 | 222 |
| NY Giants | 6 | 5 | 1 | .545 | 267 | 223 |
| Chi Cardinals | 4 | 7 | 1 | .364 | 224 | 252 |
| Philadelphia | 4 | 7 | 1 | .364 | 248 | 231 |
| Pittsburgh | 4 | 8 | 0 | .333 | 195 | 285 |

### WESTERN CONFERENCE

| | W | L | T | Pct. | Pts. | Op. |
|---|---|---|---|---|---|---|
| Los Angeles | 8 | 3 | 1 | .727 | 260 | 231 |
| Chi Bears | 8 | 4 | 0 | .667 | 294 | 251 |
| Green Bay | 6 | 6 | 0 | .500 | 258 | 276 |
| Baltimore | 5 | 6 | 1 | .455 | 214 | 239 |
| San Francisco | 4 | 8 | 0 | .333 | 216 | 298 |
| Detroit | 3 | 9 | 0 | .250 | 230 | 275 |

## 1954

### EASTERN CONFERENCE

| | W | L | T | Pct. | Pts. | Op. |
|---|---|---|---|---|---|---|
| Cleveland | 9 | 3 | 0 | .750 | 336 | 162 |
| Philadelphia | 7 | 4 | 1 | .636 | 284 | 230 |
| NY Giants | 7 | 5 | 0 | .583 | 293 | 184 |
| Pittsburgh | 5 | 7 | 0 | .417 | 219 | 263 |
| Washington | 3 | 9 | 0 | .250 | 207 | 432 |
| Chi Cardinals | 2 | 10 | 0 | .167 | 183 | 347 |

### WESTERN CONFERENCE

| | W | L | T | Pct. | Pts. | Op. |
|---|---|---|---|---|---|---|
| Detroit | 9 | 2 | 1 | .818 | 337 | 189 |
| Chi Bears | 8 | 4 | 0 | .667 | 301 | 279 |
| San Francisco | 7 | 4 | 1 | .636 | 313 | 251 |
| Los Angeles | 6 | 5 | 1 | .545 | 314 | 285 |
| Green Bay | 4 | 8 | 0 | .333 | 234 | 251 |
| Baltimore | 3 | 9 | 0 | .250 | 131 | 279 |

## 1953

### EASTERN CONFERENCE

| | W | L | T | Pct. | Pts. | Op. |
|---|---|---|---|---|---|---|
| Cleveland | 11 | 1 | 0 | .917 | 348 | 162 |
| Philadelphia | 7 | 4 | 1 | .636 | 352 | 215 |
| Washington | 6 | 5 | 1 | .545 | 208 | 215 |
| Pittsburgh | 6 | 6 | 0 | .500 | 211 | 263 |
| NY Giants | 3 | 9 | 0 | .250 | 179 | 277 |
| Chi Cardinals | 1 | 10 | 1 | .091 | 190 | 337 |

### WESTERN CONFERENCE

| | W | L | T | Pct. | Pts. | Op. |
|---|---|---|---|---|---|---|
| Detroit | 10 | 2 | 0 | .833 | 271 | 205 |
| San Francisco | 9 | 3 | 0 | .750 | 372 | 237 |
| Los Angeles | 8 | 3 | 1 | .727 | 366 | 236 |
| Chi Bears | 3 | 8 | 1 | .273 | 218 | 262 |
| Baltimore | 3 | 9 | 0 | .250 | 182 | 350 |
| Green Bay | 2 | 9 | 1 | .182 | 200 | 338 |

## 1952

### AMERICAN CONFERENCE

| | W | L | T | Pct. | Pts. | Op. |
|---|---|---|---|---|---|---|
| Cleveland | 8 | 4 | 0 | .667 | 310 | 213 |
| NY Giants | 7 | 5 | 0 | .583 | 234 | 231 |
| Philadelphia | 7 | 5 | 0 | .583 | 252 | 271 |
| Pittsburgh | 5 | 7 | 0 | .417 | 300 | 273 |
| Chi Cardinals | 4 | 8 | 0 | .333 | 172 | 221 |
| Washington | 4 | 8 | 0 | .333 | 240 | 287 |

### NATIONAL CONFERENCE

| | W | L | T | Pct. | Pts. | Op. |
|---|---|---|---|---|---|---|
| Detroit | 9 | 3 | 0 | .750 | 344 | 192 |
| Los Angeles | 9 | 3 | 0 | .750 | 349 | 234 |
| San Francisco | 7 | 5 | 0 | .583 | 285 | 221 |
| Green Bay | 6 | 6 | 0 | .500 | 295 | 312 |
| Chi Bears | 5 | 7 | 0 | .417 | 245 | 326 |
| Dallas Texans | 1 | 11 | 0 | .083 | 182 | 427 |

### 1951

| AMERICAN CONFERENCE | W | L | T | Pct. | Pts. | Op. |
|---|---|---|---|---|---|---|
| Cleveland | 11 | 1 | 0 | .917 | 331 | 152 |
| NY Giants | 9 | 2 | 1 | .818 | 254 | 161 |
| Washington | 5 | 7 | 0 | .417 | 183 | 296 |
| Pittsburgh | 4 | 7 | 1 | .364 | 183 | 235 |
| Philadelphia | 4 | 8 | 0 | .333 | 234 | 264 |
| Chi Cardinals | 3 | 9 | 0 | .250 | 210 | 287 |

| NATIONAL CONFERENCE | W | L | T | Pct. | Pts. | Op. |
|---|---|---|---|---|---|---|
| Los Angeles | 8 | 4 | 0 | .667 | 392 | 261 |
| Detroit | 7 | 4 | 1 | .636 | 336 | 259 |
| San Francisco | 7 | 4 | 1 | .636 | 255 | 205 |
| Chi Bears | 7 | 5 | 0 | .583 | 286 | 282 |
| Green Bay | 3 | 9 | 0 | .250 | 254 | 375 |
| NY Yanks | 1 | 9 | 2 | .100 | 241 | 382 |

### 1950

| AMERICAN CONFERENCE | W | L | T | Pct. | Pts. | Op. |
|---|---|---|---|---|---|---|
| Cleveland | 10 | 2 | 0 | .833 | 310 | 144 |
| NY Giants | 10 | 2 | 0 | .833 | 268 | 150 |
| Philadelphia | 6 | 6 | 0 | .500 | 254 | 141 |
| Pittsburgh | 6 | 6 | 0 | .500 | 180 | 195 |
| Chi Cardinals | 5 | 7 | 0 | .417 | 233 | 287 |
| Washington | 3 | 9 | 0 | .250 | 232 | 326 |

| NATIONAL CONFERENCE | W | L | T | Pct. | Pts. | Op. |
|---|---|---|---|---|---|---|
| Los Angeles | 9 | 3 | 0 | .750 | 466 | 309 |
| Chi. Bears | 9 | 3 | 0 | .750 | 279 | 207 |
| NY Yanks | 7 | 5 | 0 | .583 | 366 | 367 |
| Detroit | 6 | 6 | 0 | .500 | 321 | 285 |
| Green Bay | 3 | 9 | 0 | .250 | 244 | 406 |
| San Francisco | 3 | 9 | 0 | .250 | 213 | 300 |
| Baltimore | 1 | 11 | 0 | .083 | 213 | 462 |

### 1949

| EASTERN DIVISION | W | L | T | Pct. | Pts. | Op. |
|---|---|---|---|---|---|---|
| Philadelphia | 11 | 1 | 0 | .917 | 364 | 134 |
| Pittsburgh | 6 | 5 | 1 | .545 | 224 | 214 |
| NY Giants | 6 | 6 | 0 | .500 | 287 | 298 |
| Washington | 4 | 7 | 1 | .364 | 268 | 339 |
| NY Bulldogs | 1 | 10 | 1 | .091 | 153 | 365 |

| WESTERN DIVISION | W | L | T | Pct. | Pts. | Op. |
|---|---|---|---|---|---|---|
| Los Angeles | 8 | 2 | 2 | .800 | 360 | 239 |
| Chi Bears | 9 | 3 | 0 | .750 | 332 | 218 |
| Chi Cardinals | 6 | 5 | 1 | .545 | 360 | 301 |
| Detroit | 4 | 8 | 0 | .333 | 237 | 259 |
| Green Bay | 2 | 10 | 0 | .167 | 114 | 329 |

### 1948

| EASTERN DIVISION | W | L | T | Pct. | Pts. | Op. |
|---|---|---|---|---|---|---|
| Philadelphia | 9 | 2 | 1 | .818 | 376 | 156 |
| Washington | 7 | 5 | 0 | .583 | 291 | 287 |
| NY Giants | 4 | 8 | 0 | .333 | 297 | 388 |
| Pittsburgh | 4 | 8 | 0 | .333 | 200 | 243 |
| Boston | 3 | 9 | 0 | .250 | 174 | 372 |

| WESTERN DIVISION | W | L | T | Pct. | Pts. | Op. |
|---|---|---|---|---|---|---|
| Chi Cardinals | 11 | 1 | 0 | .917 | 395 | 226 |
| Chi Bears | 10 | 2 | 0 | .833 | 375 | 151 |
| Los Angeles | 6 | 5 | 1 | .545 | 327 | 269 |
| Green Bay | 3 | 9 | 0 | .250 | 154 | 290 |
| Detroit | 2 | 10 | 0 | .167 | 200 | 407 |

### 1947

| EASTERN DIVISION | W | L | T | Pct. | Pts. | Op. |
|---|---|---|---|---|---|---|
| Philadelphia | 8 | 4 | 0 | .667 | 308 | 242 |
| Pittsburgh | 8 | 4 | 0 | .667 | 240 | 259 |
| Boston | 4 | 7 | 1 | .364 | 168 | 256 |
| Washington | 4 | 8 | 0 | .333 | 295 | 367 |
| NY Giants | 2 | 8 | 2 | .200 | 190 | 309 |

| WESTERN DIVISION | W | L | T | Pct. | Pts. | Op. |
|---|---|---|---|---|---|---|
| Chi Cardinals | 9 | 3 | 0 | .750 | 306 | 231 |
| Chi Bears | 8 | 4 | 0 | .667 | 363 | 241 |
| Green Bay | 6 | 5 | 1 | .545 | 274 | 210 |
| Los Angeles | 6 | 6 | 0 | .500 | 259 | 214 |
| Detroit | 3 | 9 | 0 | .250 | 231 | 305 |

## 1946

| EASTERN DIVISION | W | L | T | Pct. | Pts. | Op. |
|---|---|---|---|---|---|---|
| NY Giants | 7 | 3 | 1 | .700 | 236 | 162 |
| Philadelphia | 6 | 5 | 0 | .545 | 231 | 220 |
| Washington | 5 | 5 | 1 | .500 | 171 | 191 |
| Pittsburgh | 5 | 5 | 1 | .500 | 136 | 117 |
| Boston | 2 | 8 | 1 | .200 | 189 | 273 |

| WESTERN DIVISION | W | L | T | Pct. | Pts. | Op. |
|---|---|---|---|---|---|---|
| Chi Bears | 8 | 2 | 1 | .800 | 289 | 193 |
| Los Angeles | 6 | 4 | 1 | .600 | 277 | 257 |
| Green Bay | 6 | 5 | 0 | .545 | 148 | 158 |
| Chi Cardinals | 6 | 5 | 0 | .545 | 260 | 198 |
| Detroit | 1 | 10 | 0 | .091 | 142 | 310 |

## 1945

| EASTERN DIVISION | W | L | T | Pct. | Pts. | Op. |
|---|---|---|---|---|---|---|
| Washington | 8 | 2 | 0 | .800 | 209 | 121 |
| Philadelphia | 7 | 3 | 0 | .700 | 272 | 133 |
| NY Giants | 3 | 6 | 1 | .333 | 179 | 198 |
| Boston | 3 | 6 | 1 | .333 | 123 | 211 |
| Pittsburgh | 2 | 8 | 0 | .200 | 79 | 220 |

| WESTERN DIVISION | W | L | T | Pct. | Pts. | Op. |
|---|---|---|---|---|---|---|
| Cleveland | 9 | 1 | 0 | .900 | 244 | 136 |
| Detroit | 7 | 3 | 0 | .700 | 195 | 194 |
| Green Bay | 6 | 4 | 0 | .600 | 258 | 173 |
| Chi Bears | 3 | 7 | 0 | .300 | 192 | 235 |
| Chi Cardinals | 1 | 9 | 0 | .100 | 98 | 228 |

## 1944

| EASTERN DIVISION | W | L | T | Pct. | Pts. | Op. |
|---|---|---|---|---|---|---|
| NY Giants | 8 | 1 | 1 | .889 | 206 | 75 |
| Philadelphia | 7 | 1 | 2 | .875 | 267 | 131 |
| Washington | 6 | 3 | 1 | .667 | 169 | 180 |
| Boston | 2 | 8 | 0 | .200 | 82 | 233 |
| Brooklyn | 0 | 10 | 0 | .000 | 69 | 166 |

| WESTERN DIVISION | W | L | T | Pct. | Pts. | Op. |
|---|---|---|---|---|---|---|
| Green Bay | 8 | 2 | 0 | .800 | 238 | 141 |
| Chi Bears | 6 | 3 | 1 | .667 | 258 | 172 |
| Detroit | 6 | 3 | 1 | .667 | 216 | 151 |
| Cleveland | 4 | 6 | 0 | .400 | 188 | 224 |
| Card-Pitt | 0 | 10 | 0 | .000 | 108 | 328 |

## 1943

| EASTERN DIVISION | W | L | T | Pct. | Pts. | Op. |
|---|---|---|---|---|---|---|
| Washington | 6 | 3 | 1 | .667 | 229 | 137 |
| NY Giants | 6 | 3 | 1 | .667 | 197 | 170 |
| Phil-Pitt. | 5 | 4 | 1 | .556 | 225 | 230 |
| Brooklyn | 2 | 8 | 0 | .200 | 65 | 234 |

| WESTERN DIVISION | W | L | T | Pct. | Pts. | Op. |
|---|---|---|---|---|---|---|
| Chi Bears | 8 | 1 | 1 | .889 | 303 | 157 |
| Green Bay | 7 | 2 | 1 | .778 | 264 | 172 |
| Detroit | 3 | 6 | 1 | .333 | 178 | 218 |
| Chi Cardinals | 0 | 10 | 0 | .000 | 95 | 238 |

## 1942

| EASTERN DIVISION | W | L | T | Pct. | Pts. | Op. |
|---|---|---|---|---|---|---|
| Washington | 10 | 1 | 0 | .909 | 227 | 102 |
| Pittsburgh | 7 | 4 | 0 | .636 | 167 | 119 |
| NY Giants | 5 | 5 | 1 | .500 | 155 | 139 |
| Brooklyn | 3 | 8 | 0 | .273 | 100 | 168 |
| Philadelphia | 2 | 9 | 0 | .182 | 134 | 239 |

| WESTERN DIVISION | W | L | T | Pct. | Pts. | Op. |
|---|---|---|---|---|---|---|
| Chi Bears | 11 | 0 | 0 | 1.000 | 376 | 84 |
| Green Bay | 8 | 2 | 1 | .800 | 300 | 215 |
| Cleveland | 5 | 6 | 0 | .455 | 150 | 207 |
| Chi Cardinals | 3 | 8 | 0 | .273 | 98 | 209 |
| Detroit | 0 | 11 | 0 | .000 | 38 | 263 |

## 1941

### EASTERN DIVISION

| | W | L | T | Pct. | Pts. | Op. |
|---|---|---|---|---|---|---|
| NY Giants | 8 | 3 | 0 | .727 | 238 | 114 |
| Brooklyn | 7 | 4 | 0 | .636 | 158 | 127 |
| Washington | 6 | 5 | 0 | .545 | 176 | 174 |
| Philadelphia | 2 | 8 | 1 | .200 | 119 | 218 |
| Pittsburgh | 1 | 9 | 1 | .100 | 103 | 276 |

### WESTERN DIVISION

| | W | L | T | Pct. | Pts. | Op. |
|---|---|---|---|---|---|---|
| Chi Bears | 10 | 1 | 0 | .909 | 396 | 147 |
| Green Bay | 10 | 1 | 0 | .909 | 258 | 120 |
| Detroit | 4 | 6 | 1 | .400 | 121 | 195 |
| Chi Cardinals | 3 | 7 | 1 | .300 | 127 | 197 |
| Cleveland | 2 | 9 | 0 | .182 | 116 | 244 |

## 1940

### EASTERN DIVISION

| | W | L | T | Pct. | Pts. | Op. |
|---|---|---|---|---|---|---|
| Washington | 9 | 2 | 0 | .818 | 245 | 142 |
| Brooklyn | 8 | 3 | 0 | .727 | 186 | 120 |
| NY Giants | 6 | 4 | 1 | .600 | 131 | 133 |
| Pittsburgh | 2 | 7 | 2 | .222 | 60 | 178 |
| Philadelphia | 1 | 10 | 0 | .091 | 111 | 211 |

### WESTERN DIVISION

| | W | L | T | Pct. | Pts. | Op. |
|---|---|---|---|---|---|---|
| Chi Bears | 8 | 3 | 0 | .727 | 238 | 152 |
| Green Bay | 6 | 4 | 1 | .600 | 238 | 155 |
| Detroit | 5 | 5 | 1 | .500 | 138 | 153 |
| Cleveland | 4 | 6 | 1 | .400 | 171 | 191 |
| Chi Cardinals | 2 | 7 | 2 | .222 | 139 | 222 |

## 1939

### EASTERN DIVISION

| | W | L | T | Pct. | Pts. | Op. |
|---|---|---|---|---|---|---|
| NY Giants | 9 | 1 | 1 | .900 | 168 | 85 |
| Washington | 8 | 2 | 1 | .800 | 242 | 94 |
| Brooklyn | 4 | 6 | 1 | .400 | 108 | 219 |
| Philadelphia | 1 | 9 | 1 | .100 | 105 | 200 |
| Pittsburgh | 1 | 9 | 1 | .100 | 114 | 216 |

### WESTERN DIVISION

| | W | L | T | Pct. | Pts. | Op. |
|---|---|---|---|---|---|---|
| Green Bay | 9 | 2 | 0 | .818 | 233 | 153 |
| Chi Bears | 8 | 3 | 0 | .727 | 298 | 157 |
| Detroit | 6 | 5 | 0 | .545 | 145 | 150 |
| Cleveland | 5 | 5 | 1 | .500 | 195 | 164 |
| Chi Cardinals | 1 | 10 | 0 | .091 | 84 | 254 |

## 1938

### EASTERN DIVISION

| | W | L | T | Pct. | Pts. | Op. |
|---|---|---|---|---|---|---|
| NY Giants | 8 | 2 | 1 | .800 | 194 | 79 |
| Washington | 6 | 3 | 2 | .667 | 148 | 154 |
| Brooklyn | 4 | 4 | 3 | .500 | 131 | 161 |
| Philadelphia | 5 | 6 | 0 | .455 | 154 | 164 |
| Pittsburgh | 2 | 9 | 0 | .182 | 79 | 169 |

### WESTERN DIVISION

| | W | L | T | Pct. | Pts. | Op. |
|---|---|---|---|---|---|---|
| Green Bay | 8 | 3 | 0 | .727 | 223 | 118 |
| Detroit | 7 | 4 | 0 | .636 | 119 | 108 |
| Chi Bears | 6 | 5 | 0 | .545 | 194 | 148 |
| Cleveland | 4 | 7 | 0 | .364 | 131 | 215 |
| Chi Cardinals | 2 | 9 | 0 | .182 | 111 | 168 |

## 1937

### EASTERN DIVISION

| | W | L | T | Pct. | Pts. | Op. |
|---|---|---|---|---|---|---|
| Washington | 8 | 3 | 0 | .727 | 195 | 120 |
| NY Giants | 6 | 3 | 2 | .667 | 128 | 109 |
| Pittsburgh | 4 | 7 | 0 | .364 | 122 | 145 |
| Brooklyn | 3 | 7 | 1 | .300 | 82 | 174 |
| Philadelphia | 2 | 8 | 1 | .200 | 86 | 177 |

### WESTERN DIVISION

| | W | L | T | Pct. | Pts. | Op. |
|---|---|---|---|---|---|---|
| Chi Bears | 9 | 1 | 1 | .900 | 201 | 100 |
| Green Bay | 7 | 4 | 0 | .636 | 220 | 122 |
| Detroit | 7 | 4 | 0 | .636 | 180 | 105 |
| Chi Cardinals | 5 | 5 | 1 | .500 | 135 | 165 |
| Cleveland | 1 | 10 | 0 | .091 | 75 | 207 |

## 1936

### EASTERN DIVISION

| | W | L | T | Pct. | Pts. | Op. |
|---|---|---|---|---|---|---|
| Boston | 7 | 5 | 0 | .583 | 149 | 110 |
| Pittsburgh | 6 | 6 | 0 | .500 | 98 | 187 |
| NY Giants | 5 | 6 | 1 | .455 | 115 | 163 |
| Brooklyn | 3 | 8 | 1 | .273 | 92 | 161 |
| Philadelphia | 1 | 11 | 0 | .083 | 51 | 206 |

### WESTERN DIVISION

| | W | L | T | Pct. | Pts. | Op. |
|---|---|---|---|---|---|---|
| Green Bay | 10 | 1 | 1 | .909 | 248 | 118 |
| Chi Bears | 9 | 3 | 0 | .750 | 222 | 94 |
| Detroit | 8 | 4 | 0 | .667 | 235 | 102 |
| Chi Cardinals | 3 | 8 | 1 | .273 | 74 | 143 |

## 1935

### EASTERN DIVISION

| | W | L | T | Pct. | Pts. | Op. |
|---|---|---|---|---|---|---|
| NY Giants | 9 | 3 | 0 | .750 | 180 | 96 |
| Brooklyn | 5 | 6 | 1 | .455 | 90 | 141 |
| Pittsburgh | 4 | 8 | 0 | .333 | 100 | 209 |
| Boston | 2 | 8 | 1 | .200 | 65 | 123 |
| Philadelphia | 2 | 9 | 0 | .182 | 60 | 179 |

### WESTERN DIVISION

| | W | L | T | Pct. | Pts. | Op. |
|---|---|---|---|---|---|---|
| Detroit | 7 | 3 | 2 | .700 | 191 | 111 |
| Green Bay | 8 | 4 | 0 | .667 | 181 | 96 |
| Chi Bears | 6 | 4 | 2 | .600 | 192 | 106 |
| Chi Cardinals | 6 | 4 | 2 | .600 | 99 | 97 |

## 1934

### EASTERN DIVISION

| | W | L | T | Pct. | Pts. | Op. |
|---|---|---|---|---|---|---|
| NY Giants | 8 | 5 | 0 | .615 | 147 | 107 |
| Boston | 6 | 6 | 0 | .500 | 107 | 94 |
| Brooklyn | 4 | 7 | 0 | .364 | 61 | 153 |
| Philadelphia | 4 | 7 | 0 | .364 | 127 | 85 |
| Pittsburgh | 2 | 10 | 0 | .167 | 51 | 206 |

### WESTERN DIVISION

| | W | L | T | Pct. | Pts. | Op. |
|---|---|---|---|---|---|---|
| Chi Bears | 13 | 0 | 0 | 1.000 | 286 | 86 |
| Detroit | 10 | 3 | 0 | .769 | 238 | 59 |
| Green Bay | 7 | 6 | 0 | .538 | 156 | 112 |
| Chi Cardinals | 5 | 6 | 0 | .455 | 80 | 84 |
| St. Louis | 1 | 2 | 0 | .333 | 27 | 61 |
| Cincinnati | 0 | 8 | 0 | .000 | 10 | 243 |

## 1933

### EASTERN DIVISION

| | W | L | T | Pct. | Pts. | Op. |
|---|---|---|---|---|---|---|
| NY Giants | 11 | 3 | 0 | .786 | 244 | 101 |
| Brooklyn | 5 | 4 | 1 | .556 | 93 | 54 |
| Boston | 5 | 5 | 2 | .500 | 103 | 97 |
| Philadelphia | 3 | 5 | 1 | .375 | 77 | 158 |
| Pittsburgh | 3 | 6 | 2 | .333 | 67 | 208 |

### WESTERN DIVISION

| | W | L | T | Pct. | Pts. | Op. |
|---|---|---|---|---|---|---|
| Chi Bears | 10 | 2 | 1 | .833 | 133 | 82 |
| Portsmouth | 6 | 5 | 0 | .545 | 128 | 87 |
| Green Bay | 5 | 7 | 1 | .417 | 170 | 107 |
| Cincinnati | 3 | 6 | 1 | .333 | 38 | 110 |
| Chi Cardinals | 1 | 9 | 1 | .100 | 52 | 101 |

## 1932

| | W | L | T | Pct. |
|---|---|---|---|---|
| Chicago Bears | 7 | 1 | 6 | .875 |
| Green Bay Packers | 10 | 3 | 1 | .769 |
| Portsmouth Spartans | 6 | 2 | 4 | .750 |
| Boston Braves | 4 | 4 | 2 | .500 |
| New York Giants | 4 | 6 | 2 | .400 |
| Brooklyn Dodgers | 3 | 9 | 0 | .250 |
| Chicago Cardinals | 2 | 6 | 2 | .250 |
| Staten Island Stapletons | 2 | 7 | 3 | .222 |

## 1931

| | W | L | T | Pct. |
|---|---|---|---|---|
| Green Bay Packers | 12 | 2 | 0 | .857 |
| Portsmouth Spartans | 11 | 3 | 0 | .786 |
| Chicago Bears | 8 | 5 | 0 | .615 |
| Chicago Cardinals | 5 | 4 | 0 | .556 |
| New York Giants | 7 | 6 | 1 | .538 |
| Providence Steam Roller | 4 | 4 | 3 | .500 |
| Staten Island Stapletons | 4 | 6 | 1 | .400 |
| Cleveland Indians | 2 | 8 | 0 | .200 |
| Brooklyn Dodgers | 2 | 12 | 0 | .143 |
| Frankford Yellow Jackets | 1 | 6 | 1 | .143 |

## 1930

| | W | L | T | Pct. |
|---|---|---|---|---|
| Green Bay Packers | 10 | 3 | 1 | .769 |
| New York Giants | 13 | 4 | 0 | .765 |
| Chicago Bears | 9 | 4 | 1 | .692 |
| Brooklyn Dodgers | 7 | 4 | 1 | .636 |
| Providence Steam Roller | 6 | 4 | 1 | .600 |
| Staten Island Stapletons | 5 | 5 | 2 | .500 |
| Chicago Cardinals | 5 | 6 | 2 | .455 |
| Portsmouth Spartans | 5 | 6 | 3 | .455 |
| Frankford Yellow Jackets | 4 | 13 | 1 | .222 |
| Minneapolis Red Jackets | 1 | 7 | 1 | .125 |
| Newark Tornadoes | 1 | 10 | 1 | .091 |

## 1929

| | W | L | T | Pct. |
|---|---|---|---|---|
| Green Bay Packers | 12 | 0 | 1 | 1.000 |
| New York Giants | 13 | 1 | 1 | .929 |
| Frankford Yellow Jackets | 9 | 4 | 5 | .692 |
| Chicago Cardinals | 6 | 6 | 1 | .500 |
| Boston Bulldogs | 4 | 4 | 0 | .500 |
| Orange Tornadoes | 3 | 4 | 4 | .429 |
| Staten Island Stapletons | 3 | 4 | 3 | .429 |
| Providence Steam Roller | 4 | 6 | 2 | .400 |
| Chicago Bears | 4 | 9 | 2 | .308 |
| Buffalo Bisons | 1 | 7 | 1 | .125 |
| Minneapolis Red Jackets | 1 | 9 | 0 | .100 |
| Dayton Triangles | 0 | 6 | 0 | .000 |

## 1928

| | W | L | T | Pct. |
|---|---|---|---|---|
| Providence Steam Roller | 8 | 1 | 2 | .889 |
| Frankford Yellow Jackets | 11 | 3 | 2 | .786 |
| Detroit Wolverines | 7 | 2 | 1 | .778 |
| Green Bay Packers | 6 | 4 | 3 | .600 |
| Chicago Bears | 7 | 5 | 1 | .583 |
| New York Giants | 4 | 7 | 2 | .364 |
| New York Yankees | 4 | 8 | 1 | .333 |
| Pottsville Maroons | 2 | 8 | 0 | .200 |
| Chicago Cardinals | 1 | 5 | 0 | .167 |
| Dayton Triangles | 0 | 7 | 0 | .000 |

## 1927

| | W | L | T | Pct. |
|---|---|---|---|---|
| New York Giants | 11 | 1 | 1 | .917 |
| Green Bay Packers | 7 | 2 | 1 | .778 |
| Chicago Bears | 9 | 3 | 2 | .750 |
| Cleveland Bulldogs | 8 | 4 | 1 | .667 |
| Providence Steam Roller | 8 | 5 | 1 | .615 |
| New York Yankees | 7 | 8 | 1 | .467 |
| Frankford Yellow Jackets | 6 | 9 | 3 | .400 |
| Pottsville Maroons | 5 | 8 | 0 | .385 |
| Chicago Cardinals | 3 | 7 | 1 | .300 |
| Dayton Triangles | 1 | 6 | 1 | .143 |
| Duluth Eskimos | 1 | 8 | 0 | .111 |
| Buffalo Bisons | 0 | 5 | 0 | .000 |

## 1926

| | W | L | T | Pct. |
|---|---|---|---|---|
| Frankford Yellow Jackets | 14 | 1 | 1 | .933 |
| Chicago Bears | 12 | 1 | 3 | .923 |
| Pottsville Maroons | 10 | 2 | 1 | .833 |
| Kansas City Cowboys | 8 | 3 | 0 | .727 |
| Green Bay Packers | 7 | 3 | 3 | .700 |
| Los Angeles Buccaneers | 6 | 3 | 1 | .667 |
| New York Giants | 8 | 4 | 1 | .667 |
| Duluth Eskimos | 6 | 5 | 3 | .545 |
| Buffalo Rangers | 4 | 4 | 2 | .500 |
| Chicago Cardinals | 5 | 6 | 1 | .455 |
| Providence Steam Roller | 5 | 7 | 1 | .417 |
| Detroit Panthers | 4 | 6 | 2 | .400 |
| Hartford Blues | 3 | 7 | 0 | .300 |
| Brooklyn Lions | 3 | 8 | 0 | .273 |
| Milwaukee Badgers | 2 | 7 | 0 | .222 |
| Akron Pros | 1 | 4 | 3 | .200 |
| Dayton Triangles | 1 | 4 | 1 | .200 |
| Racine Tornadoes | 1 | 4 | 0 | .200 |
| Columbus Tigers | 1 | 6 | 0 | .143 |
| Canton Bulldogs | 1 | 9 | 3 | .100 |
| Hammond Pros | 0 | 4 | 0 | .000 |
| Louisville Colonels | 0 | 4 | 0 | .000 |

## 1925

| | W | L | T | Pct. |
|---|---|---|---|---|
| Chicago Cardinals | 11 | 2 | 1 | .846 |
| Pottsville Maroons | 10 | 2 | 0 | .833 |
| Detroit Panthers | 8 | 2 | 2 | .800 |
| New York Giants | 8 | 4 | 0 | .667 |
| Akron Indians | 4 | 2 | 2 | .667 |
| Frankford Yellow Jackets | 13 | 7 | 0 | .650 |
| Chicago Bears | 9 | 5 | 3 | .643 |
| Rock Island Independents | 5 | 3 | 3 | .625 |
| Green Bay Packers | 8 | 5 | 0 | .615 |
| Providence Steam Roller | 6 | 5 | 1 | .545 |
| Canton Bulldogs | 4 | 4 | 0 | .500 |
| Cleveland Bulldogs | 5 | 8 | 1 | .385 |
| Kansas City Cowboys | 2 | 5 | 1 | .286 |
| Hammond Pros | 1 | 4 | 0 | .250 |
| Buffalo Bisons | 1 | 6 | 2 | .143 |
| Duluth Kelleys | 0 | 3 | 0 | .000 |
| Rochester Jeffersons | 0 | 6 | 1 | .000 |
| Milwaukee Badgers | 0 | 6 | 0 | .000 |
| Dayton Triangles | 0 | 7 | 1 | .000 |
| Columbus Tigers | 0 | 9 | 0 | .000 |

### 1924

| | W | L | T | Pct. |
|---|---|---|---|---|
| Cleveland Bulldogs | 7 | 1 | 1 | .875 |
| Chicago Bears | 6 | 1 | 4 | .857 |
| Frankford Yellow Jackets | 11 | 2 | 1 | .846 |
| Duluth Kelleys | 5 | 1 | 0 | .833 |
| Rock Island Independents | 6 | 2 | 2 | .750 |
| Green Bay Packers | 7 | 4 | 0 | .636 |
| Racine Legion | 4 | 3 | 3 | .571 |
| Chicago Cardinals | 5 | 4 | 1 | .556 |
| Buffalo Bisons | 6 | 5 | 0 | .545 |
| Columbus Tigers | 4 | 4 | 0 | .500 |
| Hammond Pros | 2 | 2 | 1 | .500 |
| Milwaukee Badgers | 5 | 8 | 0 | .385 |
| Akron Indians | 2 | 6 | 0 | .333 |
| Dayton Triangles | 2 | 6 | 0 | .333 |
| Kansas City Blues | 2 | 7 | 0 | .222 |
| Kenosha Maroons | 0 | 5 | 1 | .000 |
| Minneapolis Marines | 0 | 6 | 0 | .000 |
| Rochester Jeffersons | 0 | 7 | 0 | .000 |

### 1922

| | W | L | T | Pct. |
|---|---|---|---|---|
| Canton Bulldogs | 10 | 0 | 2 | 1.000 |
| Chicago Bears | 9 | 3 | 0 | .750 |
| Chicago Cardinals | 8 | 3 | 0 | .727 |
| Toledo Maroons | 5 | 2 | 2 | .714 |
| Rock Island Independents | 4 | 2 | 1 | .667 |
| Racine Legion | 6 | 4 | 1 | .600 |
| Dayton Triangles | 4 | 3 | 1 | .571 |
| Green Bay Packers | 4 | 3 | 3 | .571 |
| Buffalo All-Americans | 5 | 4 | 1 | .556 |
| Akron Pros | 3 | 5 | 2 | .375 |
| Milwaukee Badgers | 2 | 4 | 3 | .333 |
| Oorang Indians | 2 | 6 | 0 | .250 |
| Minneapolis Marines | 1 | 3 | 0 | .250 |
| Louisville Brecks | 1 | 3 | 0 | .250 |
| Evansville Crimson Giants | 0 | 3 | 0 | .000 |
| Rochester Jeffersons | 0 | 4 | 1 | .000 |
| Hammond Pros | 0 | 5 | 1 | .000 |
| Columbus Panhandles | 0 | 7 | 0 | .000 |

### 1923

| | W | L | T | Pct. |
|---|---|---|---|---|
| Canton Bulldogs | 11 | 0 | 1 | 1.000 |
| Chicago Bears | 9 | 2 | 1 | .818 |
| Green Bay Packers | 7 | 2 | 1 | .778 |
| Milwaukee Badgers | 7 | 2 | 3 | .778 |
| Cleveland Indians | 3 | 1 | 3 | .750 |
| Chicago Cardinals | 8 | 4 | 0 | .667 |
| Duluth Kelleys | 4 | 3 | 0 | .571 |
| Columbus Tigers | 5 | 4 | 1 | .556 |
| Buffalo All-Americans | 4 | 4 | 3 | .500 |
| Racine Legion | 4 | 4 | 2 | .500 |
| Toledo Maroons | 2 | 3 | 2 | .400 |
| Rock Island Independents | 2 | 3 | 3 | .400 |
| Minneapolis Marines | 2 | 5 | 2 | .286 |
| St. Louis All-Stars | 1 | 4 | 2 | .200 |
| Hammond Pros | 1 | 5 | 1 | .167 |
| Dayton Triangles | 1 | 6 | 1 | .143 |
| Akron Indians | 1 | 6 | 0 | .143 |
| Oorang Indians | 1 | 10 | 0 | .091 |
| Rochester Jeffersons | 0 | 2 | 0 | .000 |
| Louisville Brecks | 0 | 3 | 0 | .000 |

### 1921

| | W | L | T | Pct. |
|---|---|---|---|---|
| Chicago Staleys | 9 | 1 | 1 | .900 |
| Buffalo All-Americans | 9 | 1 | 2 | .900 |
| Akron Pros | 8 | 3 | 1 | .727 |
| Canton Bulldogs | 5 | 2 | 3 | .714 |
| Rock Island Independents | 4 | 2 | 1 | .667 |
| Evansville Crimson Giants | 3 | 2 | 0 | .600 |
| Green Bay Packers | 3 | 2 | 1 | .600 |
| Dayton Triangles | 4 | 4 | 1 | .500 |
| Chicago Cardinals | 3 | 3 | 2 | .500 |
| Rochester Jeffersons | 2 | 3 | 0 | .400 |
| Cleveland Indians | 3 | 5 | 0 | .375 |
| Washington Senators | 1 | 2 | 0 | .333 |
| Cincinnati Celts | 1 | 3 | 0 | .250 |
| Hammond Pros | 1 | 3 | 1 | .250 |
| Minneapolis Marines | 1 | 3 | 0 | .250 |
| Detroit Heralds | 1 | 5 | 1 | .167 |
| Columbus Panhandles | 1 | 8 | 0 | .111 |
| Tonawanda Kardex | 0 | 1 | 0 | .000 |
| Muncie Flyers | 0 | 2 | 0 | .000 |
| Louisville Brecks | 0 | 2 | 0 | .000 |
| New York Giants | 0 | 2 | 0 | .000 |

### 1920

| | W | L | T | Pct. |
|---|---|---|---|---|
| Akron Pros | 8 | 0 | 3 | 1.000 |
| Decatur Staleys | 10 | 1 | 2 | .909 |
| Buffalo All-Americans | 9 | 1 | 1 | .900 |
| Chicago Cardinals | 6 | 2 | 2 | .750 |
| Rock Island Independents | 6 | 2 | 2 | .750 |
| Dayton Triangles | 5 | 2 | 2 | .714 |
| Rochester Jeffersons | 6 | 3 | 2 | .667 |
| Canton Bulldogs | 7 | 4 | 2 | .636 |
| Detroit Heralds | 2 | 3 | 3 | .400 |
| Cleveland Tigers | 2 | 4 | 2 | .333 |
| Chicago Tigers | 2 | 5 | 1 | .286 |
| Hammond Pros | 2 | 5 | 0 | .286 |
| Columbus Panhandles | 2 | 6 | 2 | .250 |
| Muncie Flyers | 0 | 1 | 0 | .000 |

### Canadian Football League Grey Cup

| Year | Results | Site | Attendance |
|---|---|---|---|
| 1909 | U of Toronto 26, Parkdale 6 | Toronto | 3,807 |
| 1910 | U of Toronto 16, Hamilton Tigers 7 | Hamilton | 12,000 |
| 1911 | U of Toronto 14, Toronto 7 | Toronto | 13,687 |
| 1912 | Hamilton Alerts 11, Toronto 4 | Hamilton | 5,337 |
| 1913 | Hamilton Tigers 44, Parkdale 2 | Hamilton | 2,100 |
| 1914 | Toronto 14, U of Toronto 2 | Toronto | 10,500 |
| 1915 | Hamilton Tigers 13, Toronto RAA 7 | Toronto | 2,808 |
| 1916-19 | No game | | |
| 1920 | U of Toronto 16, Toronto 3 | Toronto | 10,088 |
| 1921 | Toronto 23, Edmonton 0 | Toronto | 9,558 |
| 1922 | Queen's U 13, Edmonton 1 | Kingston | 4,700 |
| 1923 | Queen's U 54, Regina 0 | Toronto | 8,629 |
| 1924 | Queen's U 11, Balmy Beach 3 | Toronto | 5,978 |
| 1925 | Ottawa Senators 24, Winnipeg 1 | Ottawa | 6,900 |
| 1926 | Ottawa Senators 10, Toronto U 7 | Toronto | 8,276 |
| 1927 | Balmy Beach 9, Hamilton Tigers 6 | Toronto | 13,676 |
| 1928 | Hamilton Tigers 30, Regina 0 | Hamilton | 4,767 |
| 1929 | Hamilton Tigers 14, Regina 3 | Hamilton | 1,906 |
| 1930 | Balmy Beach 11, Regina 6 | Toronto | 3,914 |
| 1931 | Montreal AAA 22, Regina 0 | Montreal | 5,112 |
| 1932 | Hamilton Tigers 25, Regina 6 | Hamilton | 4,806 |
| 1933 | Toronto 4, Sarnia 3 | Sarnia | 2,751 |
| 1934 | Sarnia 20, Regina 12 | Toronto | 8,900 |
| 1935 | Winnipeg 18, Hamilton Tigers 12 | Hamilton | 6,405 |
| 1936 | Sarnia 26, Ottawa RR 20 | Toronto | 5,883 |
| 1937 | Toronto 4, Winnipeg 3 | Toronto | 11,522 |
| 1938 | Toronto 30, Winnipeg 7 | Toronto | 18,778 |
| 1939 | Winnipeg 8, Ottawa 7 | Ottawa | 11,738 |
| 1940 | Ottawa 12, Balmy Beach 5 | Ottawa | 1,700 |
| 1940 | Ottawa 8, Balmy Beach 2 | Toronto | 4,998 |
| 1941 | Winnipeg 18, Ottawa 16 | Toronto | 19,065 |
| 1942 | Toronto RCAF 8, Winnipeg RCAF 5 | Toronto | 12,455 |
| 1943 | Hamilton F Wild 23, Winnipeg RCAF 14 | Toronto | 16,423 |
| 1944 | Montreal St H-D Navy 7, Hamilton F Wild 6 | Hamilton | 3,871 |
| 1945 | Toronto 35, Winnipeg 0 | Toronto | 18,660 |
| 1946 | Toronto 28, Winnipeg 6 | Toronto | 18,960 |
| 1947 | Toronto 10, Winnipeg 9 | Toronto | 18,885 |
| 1948 | Calgary 12, Ottawa 7 | Toronto | 20,013 |
| 1949 | Montreal Als 28, Calgary 15 | Toronto | 20,087 |
| 1950 | Toronto 13, Winnipeg 0 | Toronto | 27,101 |
| 1951 | Ottawa 21, Saskatchewan 14 | Toronto | 27,341 |
| 1952 | Toronto 21, Edmonton 11 | Toronto | 27,391 |
| 1953 | Hamilton Ticats 12, Winnipeg 6 | Toronto | 27,313 |
| 1954 | Edmonton 26, Montreal 25 | Toronto | 27,321 |
| 1955 | Edmonton 34, Montreal 19 | Vancouver | 39,417 |
| 1956 | Edmonton 50, Montreal 27 | Toronto | 27,425 |
| 1957 | Hamilton 32, Winnipeg 7 | Toronto | 27,051 |
| 1958 | Winnipeg 35, Hamilton 28 | Vancouver | 36,567 |
| 1959 | Winnipeg 21, Hamilton 7 | Toronto | 33,133 |
| 1960 | Ottawa 16, Edmonton 6 | Vancouver | 38,102 |
| 1961 | Winnipeg 21, Hamilton 14 | Toronto | 32,651 |
| 1962 | Winnipeg 28, Hamilton 27 | Toronto | 32,655 |
| 1963 | Hamilton 21, British Columbia 10 | Vancouver | 36,545 |
| 1964 | British Columbia 34, Hamilton 24 | Toronto | 32,655 |
| 1965 | Hamilton 22, Winnipeg 16 | Toronto | 32,655 |
| 1966 | Saskatchewan 29, Ottawa 14 | Vancouver | 36,553 |
| 1967 | Hamilton 24, Saskatchewan 1 | Ottawa | 31,358 |
| 1968 | Ottawa 24, Calgary 21 | Toronto | 32,655 |
| 1969 | Ottawa 29, Saskatchewan 11 | Montreal | 33,172 |
| 1970 | Montreal 23, Calgary 10 | Toronto | 32,669 |
| 1971 | Calgary 14, Toronto 11 | Vancouver | 34,484 |
| 1972 | Hamilton 13, Saskatchewan 10 | Hamilton | 33,993 |
| 1973 | Ottawa 22, Edmonton 18 | Toronto | 36,653 |
| 1974 | Montreal 20, Edmonton 7 | Vancouver | 34,450 |
| 1975 | Edmonton 9, Montreal 8 | Calgary | 32,454 |

## Canadian Football League Grey Cup (Cont.)

| Year | Results | Site | Attendance |
|---|---|---|---|
| 1976 | Ottawa 23, Saskatchewan 20 | Toronto | 53,467 |
| 1977 | Montreal 41, Edmonton 6 | Montreal | 68,318 |
| 1978 | Edmonton 20, Montreal 13 | Toronto | 54,695 |
| 1979 | Edmonton 17, Montreal 9 | Montreal | 65,113 |
| 1980 | Edmonton 48, Hamilton 10 | Toronto | 54,661 |
| 1981 | Edmonton 26, Ottawa 23 | Montreal | 52,478 |
| 1982 | Edmonton 32, Toronto 16 | Toronto | 54,741 |
| 1983 | Toronto 18, British Columbia 17 | Vancouver | 59,345 |
| 1984 | Winnipeg 47, Hamilton 17 | Edmonton | 60,081 |
| 1985 | British Columbia 37, Hamilton 24 | Montreal | 56,723 |
| 1986 | Hamilton 39, Edmonton 15 | Vancouver | 59,621 |
| 1987 | Edmonton 38, Toronto 36 | Vancouver | 59,478 |
| 1988 | Winnipeg 22, British Columbia 21 | Ottawa | 50,604 |
| 1989 | Saskatchewan 43, Hamilton 40 | Toronto | 54,088 |
| 1990 | Winnipeg 50, Edmonton 11 | Vancouver | 46,968 |
| 1991 | Toronto 36, Calgary 21 | Winnipeg | 51,985 |
| 1992 | Calgary 24, Winnepeg 10 | Toronto | 45,863 |

In 1909, Earl Grey, the Governor-General of Canada, donated a trophy for the Rugby Football Championship of Canada. The trophy, whic h subsequently became known as the Grey Cup, was originally open only to teams registered with the Canada Rugby Union. Since 1954, i t has been awarded to the winner of the Canadian Football League's championship game.

### AMERICAN FOOTBALL LEAGUE I

| Year | Champion | Record |
|---|---|---|
| 1926 | Philadelphia Quakers | 7-2 |

### AMERICAN FOOTBALL LEAGUE II

| Year | Champion | Record |
|---|---|---|
| 1936 | Boston Shamrocks | 8-3 |
| 1937 | LA Bulldogs | 8-0 |

### AMERICAN FOOTBALL LEAGUE III

| Year | Champion | Record |
|---|---|---|
| 1940 | Columbus Bullies | 8-1-1 |
| 1941 | Columbus Bullies | 5-1-2 |

### ALL-AMERICAN FOOTBALL CONFERENCE

| Year | Championship Game |
|---|---|
| 1946 | Cleveland 14, NY Yankees 9 |
| 1947 | Cleveland 14, NY Yankees 3 |
| 1948 | Cleveland 49, Buffalo 7 |
| 1949 | Cleveland 21, San Francisco 7 |

### WORLD FOOTBALL LEAGUE

| Year | World Bowl Championship |
|---|---|
| 1974 | Birmingham 22, Florida 21 |
| 1975 | Disbanded midseason |

### UNITED STATES FOOTBALL LEAGUE

| Year | Championship Game |
|---|---|
| 1983 | Michigan 24, Philadelphia 22, at Denver |
| 1984 | Philadelphia 23, Arizona 3, at Tampa |
| 1985 | Baltimore 28, Oakland 24, at East Rutherford |

## To Market We Go

Reduced to its essentials, the NFL labor settlement announced last January gives the players increased free agency in exchange for a salary cap for the owners. To be sure, the cap won't kick in until next year at the earliest, and free agency will be available only to veterans—at the outset those with five years' service, later those with four—and, for the most part, only during late winter and spring. In addition, each team can deny free agency to one so-called franchise player it designates and can asset the right of first refusal for two players in 1993 and one in '94. Also, the four conference finalists from last season can't sign any free agents in 1993 until they lose one or more of their own players to free agency.

Even with these restrictions, the seven-year deal is a triumph for the players. The agreement will result in higher player salaries, and its complexities will test the mettle of front offices, which will have to beef up their scouting of other teams; one team that's particularly deficient in this area is the Cincinnati Bengals.

Teams will also have to make hard decisions about their own personnel. Who, if anybody, should be designated a franchise player? Should they try to sign one player or another to a long-term contract? Who should be their right-of-first-refusal guys?

This much is clear: The NFL can now pursue plans, shelved because of the labor rancor that has dogged the league, to expand to two new cities, probably by the 1995 season. The most immediate beneficiaries, though, were a handful of players—most notably Pro Bowl defensive end Reggie White, who left Philadelphia for Green Bay—who had an antitrust suit pending against the NFL and were able to sell themselves to the highest bidder. On Feb. 1, 298 players became free agents too. One of them, Steeler linebacker Hardy Nickersen, exulted after the labor truce: "I couldn't ask for anything more basic than my basic freedom. In baseball, basketball and society in general, you can at some point of your life shop yourself around. Now I have that right, too."

**Herb Adderley, CB (b. 6-8-39)**
**SERVICE:** Green Bay Packers 1961-69, Dallas
Cowboys 1970-72.
**CAREER STATS:** 48 int.; 1,046 ret. yds.; 7 TDs.
Originally a running back in college at Michigan
State, Adderley was switched to defense late in his
rookie season by Packers coach Vince Lombardi.
Adderley went on to play in five Pro Bowls and four
Super Bowls. In the second Super Bowl against the
Oakland Raiders, Adderley intercepted a pass and
returned it 60 yards for a touchdown.

**Lance Alworth, WR (b. 8-3-40)**
**SERVICE:** San Diego Chargers 1962-70, Dallas
Cowboys 1971-72.
**CAREER STATS:** 542 rec.; 10,266 yds.; 85 TDs.
Nicknamed Bambi for his speed and grace, Alworth
was the premier receiver in the first decade of the
American Football League. He caught at least one
pass in every one of the 96 AFL games in which he
played and is one of only eight players to gain over
10,000 receiving yards in his career.

**Doug Atkins, DE (b. 5-8-30)**
**SERVICE:** Cleveland Browns 1953-54, Chicago
Bears 1955-66, New Orleans Saints 1967-69.
At 6'8" and 275 pounds, Atkins was known primarily
as a fearsome pass rusher during his 17-year career.
His height and mobility made him a model for future
tall, pass-batting defensive linemen. He was a No. 1
pick of the Browns out of the University of Tennessee
in 1953 and went on to make the Pro Bowl eight times.

**Morris (Red) Badgro, E (b. 12-1-02)**
**SERVICE:** New York Yankees 1927, New York Giants
1930-35, Brooklyn Dodgers 1936.
One of the stars in the early days of the league, Badgro
was named to the all-NFL team in 1931, '33 and '34. He
tied for the league lead in receptions in 1934 with 16. A
two-way player, he also proved himself an able tackler
on defense. During the first NFL championship game in
1933, he scored the first touchdown with a 26-yard
reception in the Giants' 23-21 loss to the Chicago Bears.

**Lem Barney, DB, (b. 9-8-45)**
**SERVICE:** Detroit Lions 1967-77.
**CAREER STATS:** 56 int., 7 TDs.
In his 11-year career with the Lions, Barney was a
masterful thief. His 56 interceptions ranks tenth
alltime. He was also a dangerous runner, totaling
seven touchdowns on interception returns, second to
Ken Houston's alltime mark of nine.

**Cliff Battles, HB (b. 5-1-10, d. 4-28-81)**
**SERVICE:** Boston Braves 1932, Boston Redskins
1933-36, Washington Redskins 1937.
**CAREER STATS:** 873 att.; 3,622 yds.; 23 TDs.
Battles was a star from the moment he stepped on
the field, winning the rushing title in his rookie
season. The next year he became the first player
ever to gain more than 200 yards in a game. In his
final season, he won the rushing title with 874 yards
and led the Redskins to their first NFL championship.

**Sammy Baugh, QB-P (b. 3-17-14)**
**SERVICE:** Washington Redskins 1937-52.
**CAREER STATS:** 1,693 comp.; 21,886 yds.; 186 TDs.
With his whiplike arm, "Slingin' Sammy" was largely

responsible for bringing the forward pass into prominence in the NFL. He led the league in passing in his
rookie year, capping the season with a three TD performance against the Bears as the Redskins won the
NFL title. During his 16-year career, he led the league
in passing five more times and still holds the record
for the highest punting average at 45.1 yards.

**Chuck Bednarik, C-LB (b. 5-1-25)**
**SERVICE:** Philadelphia Eagles 1949-62.
**CAREER STATS:** 20 int.
Bednarik was the prototypical linebacker, combining
agility with jarring power. His most famous tackle was
a hit on the New York Giants' Frank Gifford that put
the Giants' star out of action for a year. In the 1960
championship game against Green Bay, he stopped
the Packers' Jimmy Taylor short of the goal line to
insure a title for the Eagles. He played on both
offense and defense even after platooning had
become accepted practice, and he was an all-NFL
selection for seven straight years.

**Bert Bell, Owner-Commissioner (b. 2-25-
1895, d. 10-11-1959)**
**SERVICE:** Philadelphia Eagles 1933-40; Pittsburgh
Steelers 1941-46; NFL Commissioner 1946-59.
During his first few years as the league's second
commissioner, Bell guided the National Football
League through a battle with the All-America Football
Conference, which ultimately resulted in the absorp-
tion of three AAFC teams into the NFL. He later instituted the television blackout policy which prevented
the networks from televising a game in the home
team's city, thus preserving strong attendance.

**Bobby Bell, LB-DE (b. 6-17-40)**
**SERVICE:** Kansas City Chiefs 1963-74.
**CAREER STATS:** 26 int.; 6 TDs.
Moved from defensive end after his first three seasons, Bell became one of the league's greatest outside linebackers. He was selected as either all-AFL
or all-AFC nine times. Though he was 6'4" and
weighed 225 pounds, he had the mobility to track
down backs coming out of the backfield as well as
the speed to cover receivers out on a pattern.

**Raymond Berry, E (b. 2-27-33)**
**SERVICE:** Baltimore Colts 1955-67.
**CAREER STATS:** 631 rec.; 9,275 yds.; 68 TDs.
Though not gifted with great speed, Berry made himself into a great receiver by running pass patterns of
mathematical precision. He led the NFL in receiving
for three consecutive years from 1958 to 1960 and
caught 12 passes for 178 yards and one touchdown
in the Colts' dramatic overtime win in the 1958 NFL
Championship Game.

**Charles W. Bidwill, Sr., Owner (b. 9-16-1895,
d. 4-19-1947)**
**SERVICE:** Chicago Cardinals 1933-47.
Bidwill bought the Chicago Cardinals in 1933 and ran
the team until his death in 1947. In 1946, he signed
Georgia's Charley Trippi to a $100,000 contract, then
the richest ever. His team won the NFL title in 1947
behind the Dream Backfield of Paul Christman, Pat
Harder, Marshall Goldberg and Trippi. Along with the
Bears, the Cardinals, now based in Phoenix, are one
of only two charter NFL franchises still in existence.

## Fred Biletnikoff, WR (b. 2-23-43)
**SERVICE:** Oakland Raiders 1965-78
**CAREER STATS:** 589 rec.; 8,974 yds.; 76 TDs.
Biletnikoff, his blond hair flying out from under his helmet and his hands covered with grip-enhancing goo, led the league in catches only once, but his sure-handedness and consistency made him the Raiders' clutch receiver during their glory years. His greatest game came in one of the biggest, Super Bowl XI, where he caught four passes for 79 yards and was named the game's Most Valuable player.

## George Blanda, QB-K (b. 9-17-27)
**SERVICE:** Chicago Bears 1949-58; Baltimore Colts 1951 (one game); Houston Oilers 1960-66; Oakland Raiders 1967-75.
**CAREER STATS:** 4,007 att.; 1,911 comp.; 26,920 yds.; 236 TDs; 335 FGs; 2,002 pts.
Blanda's playing career spanned four decades and 26 years. He began as a backup with the Chicago Bears. In his fifth season he became a starter and led the league in attempts and completions. After suffering an injury the following season, he was again relegated to the bench for four years until retiring in 1959. The formation of the AFL brought him out of retirement, and he quarterbacked the Houston Oilers for seven seasons, leading the league in touchdown passes in 1961 with 36. Even with 20 years of professional football behind him, Blanda would likely have been a forgotten man were it not for a remarkable string of games in 1970. Picked up by the Oakland Raiders at age 43 as a backup, Blanda stepped in to lead the team to four wins and one tie on last second touchdown passes and field goals. For his efforts, he was named the AFC's Player of the Year. He played for five more seasons, remaining productive to the end when, at the age of 48, he kicked 44 extra points and 13 field goals for a total of 83 points.

## Mel Blount, CB (b. 4-10-48)
**SERVICE:** Pittsburgh Steelers 1970-83.
**CAREER STATS:** 57 int.; 2 TDs.
With the speed of a sprinter and the aggressiveness of a linebacker, Blount was an intimidating player on the Steelers' Super Bowl teams. He arrived in the same year as Terry Bradshaw and was as much a force on defense as Bradshaw was on offense. He led the league in interceptions in 1975 with 11, and his total of 57 career pickoffs was more than any Steeler who preceded him.

## Terry Bradshaw, QB (b. 9-2-48)
**SERVICE:** Pittsburgh Steelers 1970-83.
**CAREER STATS:** 2,105 comp.; 27,989 yds.; 212 TDs.
Great expectations were heaped upon Bradshaw when he was chosen first in the collegiate draft in 1970. Though he suffered through criticism that he was "dumb" during his first few seasons, he led the Steelers to four Super Bowl wins, something no other quarterback can boast. His career passing statistics don't match those of other Hall of Famers, but in the playoffs he was peerless. He was the Most Valuable Player in Super Bowls XIII and XIV.

## Jim Brown, FB (b. 2-17-36)
**SERVICE:** Cleveland Browns 1957-65.
**CAREER STATS:** 2,359 att.; 12,312 yds.; 106 TDs.
Thought by many to be the greatest running back in pro football history, Brown dominated the game during his nine-year career. After winning All-America honors in football and lacrosse at Syracuse University, Brown entered the NFL in 1957 and led the league with 942 yards rushing on the way to being named Rookie of the Year. He led the league in rushing seven more times, and his career average of 5.2 yards per carry is the best ever. His 126 touchdowns is still a record. He was named Player of the Year four times (1957, '58, '63, '65). Despite the pounding he took, he never missed a game and retired at the peak of his career in 1966.

## Paul Brown, Coach (b. 9-7-08, d. 8-5-91)
**SERVICE:** Cleveland Browns 1946-62, Cincinnati Bengals 1968-75
**CAREER RECORD:** 222 wins, 113 losses, 9 ties.
Heralded as one of the game's great pioneers, Brown's innovations included the playbook, the signaling of plays from the sidelines, college scouting, training camps and the use of a full-time coaching staff. After coaching in high school in his native Ohio and at Ohio State, he joined the Cleveland Browns of the newly formed All-America Football Conference in 1946. The Browns won four straight league titles, then three more titles after the team joined the NFL in 1950 (1950, 1954-55). He later formed the Cincinnati Bengals and was their first coach.

## Roosevelt Brown, OT (b. 10-20-32)
**SERVICE:** New York Giants 1953-65.
During his 13-year career, Brown was a mainstay of the Giants offensive line, earning ten trips to the Pro Bowl. Coming from predominantly black Morgan State College, Brown was an all-America but an untested player when he reported to Giants training camp in 1953. He quickly gained a starting spot and became the premier tackle in the league.

## Willie Brown, CB (b. 12-2-40)
**SERVICE:** Denver Broncos 1963-66; Oakland Raiders 1967-78
**CAREER STATS:** 54 int.; 2 TDs.
Brown was the most respected of the Oakland Raiders cover men during his nine-year tenure with the club, a period that saw the Raiders play in nine AFL/AFC Championship Games and two Super Bowls. His most memorable pickoff was a 75-yard interception return for a touchdown against Minnesota in Super Bowl XI.

## Buck Buchanan, DT (b. 9-10-40, d. 7-16-92)
**SERVICE:** Kansas City Chiefs 1963-75
Buchanan was a massive pillar (6'7", 274 pounds) in the Kansas City defensive line that helped the team win three division titles, two AFL championships and one Super Bowl. He missed only one game in his 13-year career, and he earned trips to eight pro football All-Star Games.

## Dick Butkus, MLB (b. 12-9-42)
**SERVICE:** Chicago Bears 1965-73.
**CAREER STATS:** 22 int.; 25 fumb. recoveries.
Few players have shown the intensity and aggressiveness of Butkus, the middle linebacker against whom all others will forever be measured. He had the agility to range from sideline to sideline to make tackles on running backs and receivers, and no player met a running back in the hole with more ferocity. A first-round draft choice from the University

of Illinois in 1965, Butkus immediately stepped into the starting lineup and remained there until a knee injury forced him to retire. He was selected to the Pro Bowl in eight of his nine seasons.

### Earl Campbell, RB (b. 3-29-55)
SERVICE: Houston Oilers 1978-84; New Orleans Saints 1984-85.
CAREER STATS: 2,187 rush. att.; 9,407 yds.; 81 TDs.
The No. 1 collegiate draft pick after winning the Heisman Trophy, Campbell burst into the NFL, winning both the Rookie and Player of the Year awards in 1978. A punishing back who was almost impossible to bring down with one defender, Campbell had the third-best rushing season of all time in 1980 when he ran for 1,934 yards. He led the league in rushing three straight seasons and is ninth in career rushing yards.

### Tony Canadeo, HB (b. 5-5-19)
SERVICE: Green Bay Packers 1941-44, 1946-52.
CAREER STATS: 1,025 rush. att.; 4,197 yds.; 26 TDs.
In 1949, Canadeo became only the third player in NFL history to rush for over 1,000 yards. More impressive was his 5.1 yards per carry that year. He began his career as a quarterback, but during his 11-year tenure with the Packers, he played offense and defense as well as returning kickoffs and punts.

### Joe Carr, League Administrator (b. 10-22-1880, d. 5-20-1939)
SERVICE: American Professional Football Association 1921; National Football League 1922-39.
A former Columbus, Ohio, newspaperman, Carr was one of the first administrators to bring to professional football a more rigorous organization. He established a standard player contract and pushed the league to expand to big cities. He was instrumental in bringing the New York Giants into the league in 1925.

### Guy Chamberlin, Coach-End (b. 1-16-1894, d. 4-4-1967)
SERVICE: Canton Bulldogs 1919; Decatur Staleys 1920; Chicago Staleys 1921; Canton Bulldogs 1922-23; Cleveland Bulldogs 1924; Frankford Yellowjackets 1925-26; Chicago Cardinals 1927-28.
CAREER RECORD: 56 wins; 14 losses; 5 ties.
Chamberlin was an outstanding receiver as well as a successful coach. In 1922 and '23, he led the Canton Bulldogs to undefeated seasons and consecutive NFL titles. The next season he won another NFL title as coach after the team had moved to Cleveland.

### Jack Christiansen, DB (b. 12-20-28, d. 6-29-86)
SERVICE: Detroit Lions 1951-58.
CAREER STATS: 46 int.; 85 punt ret.; 1,084 yds.
As a rookie in 1951, Christiansen, an unheralded sixth-round draft pick out of Colorado State, returned four punts for touchdowns. The next season he led the league with an average of 21.5 per return. He was also an outstanding defensive back, leading the NFL twice in interceptions, with 12 in 1953 and 10 in 1957. He was selected to the all-NFL team for six consecutive years.

### Earl (Dutch) Clark, QB (b. 10-11-06, d. 8-5-78)
SERVICE: Portsmouth Spartans 1931-32; Detroit Lions 1934-38.
CAREER STATS: 580 rush. att.; 2,757 yds.; 23 TDs.
Clark was an outstanding all-around player during the early years of the league. He was an all-NFL quarterback six times, and though he was known primarily as a runner, he once completed 53.5% of his passes at a time when the league average was much lower. He was the league's leading scorer three times.

### George Connor, T-LB (b. 1-21-25)
SERVICE: Chicago Bears 1948-55.
A versatile performer, Connor was named all-NFL at three different positions: offensive tackle, defensive tackle and linebacker. A native of Chicago, Connor was 6'3" and 240 pounds and earned All-America honors at both Holy Cross and Notre Dame. He became a linebacker in 1949 when the Bears shifted him to a more upright position on defense to stop the end sweep of the Philadelphia Eagles and their star halfback Steve Van Buren. Connor snuffed the Eagles attack and helped the Bears to a 38–21 win.

### Jimmy Conzelman, QB-Coach-Owner (b. 3-6-1898, d. 7-31-1970)
SERVICE: Decatur Staleys 1920; Rock Island Independents 1921-22; Milwaukee Badgers 1923-24; Detroit Panthers 1925-26; Providence Steam Roller 1927-30; Chicago Cardinals 1940-42, 1946-48.
CAREER RECORD: 89 wins; 68 losses; 17 ties.
Conzelman wore many hats during his NFL career, which included a two-year stint with the Detroit Panthers as their player, coach and owner. He won his first NFL title as a player-coach in 1928 with Providence. He left football to pursue other interests but was brought back into the league in 1940 as coach of the Chicago Cardinals, whom he coached to consecutive NFL titles in 1947 and '48.

### Larry Csonka, FB (b. 12-25-46)
SERVICE: Miami Dolphins 1968-74, 1979; New York Giants, 1976-79.
CAREER STATS: 1,891 att.; 8,081 yds.; 64 TDs.
A bruising fullback with a straight-ahead style, Csonka was the workhorse for the Dolphins in the early 1970s when they won three AFC titles and two Super Bowls. He totaled 112 yards rushing in Super Bowl VII and gained 145 yards in Super Bowl VIII, for which he was named the Most Valuable Player. His rushed for over 1,000 yards for three consecutive years, and his 5.4 yards per carry in 1971 led the league.

### Al Davis, Owner (b. 7-4-29)
SERVICE: Oakland Raiders 1963-81; Los Angeles Raiders 1982-present.
A maverick among NFL owners, Davis built the Raiders into one of the most successful sports franchises in history. His teams have won three Super Bowls (1976, '80 and '83). He was commissioner of the AFL in 1966 and was a prominent player in the merger negotiations with the NFL. He incurred the ire of the other owners when he invoked antitrust laws to move his franchise to Los Angeles over their objections.

### Len Dawson, QB (b. 6-20-35)
SERVICE: Pittsburgh Steelers 1957-59; Cleveland Browns 1960-61; Dallas Texans 1962; Kansas City Chiefs 1963-75.
CAREER STATS: 2,136 comp.; 28,711 yds.; 252 TDs.
After being a No. 1 draft pick for the Pittsburgh Steelers in 1957, Dawson suffered for five years as a backup before he found new life in the AFL. He started

for 14 seasons for the Dallas Texans and Kansas City Chiefs, winning four AFL passing titles and leading the Chiefs to two Super Bowls. In Super Bowl IV, the last between the AFL and NFL, Dawson won the MVP Award, completing 12 of 17 passes for 142 yards in a 23-7 upset of the Minnesota Vikings.

### Mike Ditka, TE-Coach (b. 10-18-39)
**SERVICE:** Chicago Bears 1961-66; Philadelphia 1967-68; Dallas Cowboys 1969-72.
**CAREER STATS:** 427 rec.; 5,812 yds.; 43 TDs.
Ditka broke into the NFL with a sensational year, making 56 catches for 1,076 yards and 12 touchdowns, a performance that gained him Rookie of the Year honors and established new standards for tight ends. A powerful blocker, Ditka helped the Bears win the NFL title in 1963 and was named to the Pro Bowl five times. He finished his career with the Dallas Cowboys, scoring the team's clinching touchdown in Super Bowl VI. He remained a winner as a coach, leading the Bears to a Super Bowl victory in 1986.

### Art Donovan, DT (b. 6-5-25)
**SERVICE:** Baltimore Colts 1950; New York Yanks 1951; Dallas Texans 1952; Baltimore Colts 1953-61.
At 6'3" and 265 pounds, Donovan was a heavy force on the defensive line and a light-hearted joker in the locker room. His sense of humor helped him endure a miserable three-year record of 3-31-2 early in his career. As the Colts improved, however, so did Donovan's stock. He was named all-NFL for four straight years from 1954 to '57.

### John (Paddy) Driscoll, QB (b. 1-11-1896, d. 6-29-1968)
**SERVICE:** Hammond Pros 1919; Decatur Staleys 1920; Chicago Cardinals 1920-25; Chicago Bears 1926-29.
Driscoll was one of the first stars of the league. He was adept in every aspect of the game but made his mark with his kicking. In 1925, he drop-kicked four field goals, one of them a 50-yarder.

### Bill Dudley, HB (b. 12-24-21)
**SERVICE:** Pittsburgh Steelers 1942, 1945-46; Detroit Lions 1947-49; Washington Redskins 1950-51, 1953.
**CAREER STATS:** 765 rush. att.; 3,57 yds.; 20 TDs.
Dudley was a versatile performer who had a knack for the big play. In 1946, he won the league's MVP award and led the NFL in rushing, punt returns and interceptions. In 1947, he scored 13 touchdowns, one on a punt return, one on a kickoff return, seven on receptions and four on the ground. He was also an able kicker, making 121 extra points and 33 field goals.

### Albert Glen (Turk) Edwards, T (b. 9-28-07, d. 1-12-73)
**SERVICE:** Boston Braves 1932; Boston Redskins 1933-36; Washington Redskins 1937-40.
Even in an era of two-way players, Edwards showed remarkable stamina. During one 15-game season in Boston, he missed only 10 minutes of action. At 6'2", 260 pounds, he was one of the largest players in his era and won all-NFL honors four times.

### Weeb Ewbank, Coach (b. 5-6-07)
**SERVICE:** Baltimore Colts 1954-62; NY Jets 1963-73.
**CAREER RECORD:** 134 wins, 130 losses, 7 ties.
In his stints in Baltimore and New York, Ewbank took young, losing teams and built them into champions. He holds the distinction of being the only coach to win titles in both the NFL and AFL. His championships came in two significant games: the Colts' 1958 overtime win over the New York Giants and the Jets stunning defeat of the Colts in Super Bowl III.

### Tom Fears, E (b. 12-3-23)
**SERVICE:** Los Angeles Rams 1948-56.
**CAREER STATS:** 400 rec.; 5,397 yds.; 38 TDs.
As part of an innovative three-receiver Rams passing attack, Fears became one of the most prolific pass catchers of his day. He led the league in receiving in each of his first three years, hauling in 84 passes in 1950. During a 51-14 win over Green Bay that season, he caught 18 passes, still a single-game record. Originally a defensive back, he was switched to offense after his first game, when he intercepted two passes and ran one back for a touchdown.

### Ray Flaherty, Coach (b. 9-1-04)
**SERVICE:** Boston Redskins 1936; Washington Redskins 1937-42; New York Yankees (AAFC) 1946-48; Chicago Hornets (AAFC) 1949.
**CAREER RECORD:** 82 wins, 41 losses, 5 ties.
Though he was on the losing end of Washington's 73-0 loss to Chicago in the 1940 NFL title game, Flaherty had a successful tenure as the Redskins coach. In two other title games—against the Bears in 1937 and 1942—Flaherty and the Redskins were the winners. He is credited with developing the screen pass, as a way to take the pressure off rookie quarterback Sammy Baugh in 1937.

### Len Ford, DE (b. 2-18-26, d. 3-14-72)
**SERVICE:** Los Angeles Dons (AAFC) 1948-49; Cleveland Browns 1950-57; Green Bay Packers 1958.
**CAREER STATS:** 20 fumble recoveries; 3 int.
Ford was the anchor of a Cleveland defensive unit that allowed the fewest points in the league for six seasons. He was a superior pass rusher, whose talents led to the development of the first defensive alignment where the ends take a three-point stance closer to the ball. In the 1954 championship game against Detroit, he intercepted two passes in a 56-10 Browns victory.

### Dan Fortmann, G (b. 4-11-16)
**SERVICE:** Chicago Bears 1936-43.
A Phi Beta Kappa student from Colgate, Fortmann was small (6', 210 lbs.) for a lineman, but he was one of the bedrock players for the Bears. During his eight-year career, the Bears won five division titles.

### Dan Fouts, QB (b. 6-10-51)
**SERVICE:** San Diego Chargers 1973-87.
**CAREER STATS:** 3,297 comp; 43,040 yds; 254 TDs.
The bionic arm of the pass-happy Charger offense of the late 70's and early 80's, Fouts set numerous NFL passing marks during his 15-year career. Among them were records—all since broken—for passing attempts in a season (609 in 1981); 300-yard games in a career (48); and 400-yard games in a career (six). From 1979 through '82, Fouts led the NFL in passing yardage. Against Miami on January 2, 1982, he completed 33 of 53 pass attempts for 433 yards, all of which were NFL postseason marks. When Fouts retired in 1987, only Fran Tarkenton had completed more passes for more yards than Fouts.

### Frank Gatski, C (b. 3-13-22)

**SERVICE:** Cleveland Browns 1946-56; Detroit Lions 1957.

Raised in the coal mining region of West Virginia, Gatski played for Marshall College in West Virginia and then Auburn University before moving on to the Cleveland Browns in the All-America Football Conference. As the tough center for the Browns and, in his last year, the Lions, he helped his teams win eight championships, four each in the AAFC and the NFL.

### Bill George, MLB (b. 10-27-30, d. 9-30-82)

**SERVICE:** Chicago Bears 1952-65; LA Rams 1966.
**CAREER STATS:** 18 int.

George was one of the first middle guards in the league to move to what we now know as middle linebacker, a role he helped define. He was named all-NFL twice as a middle guard and six times as a linebacker. In the Bears scheme, he also called the defensive signals and was a fierce blitzer.

### Frank Gifford, HB-FL (b. 8-16-30)

**SERVICE:** New York Giants 1952-60, 1962-64.
**CAREER STATS:** 840 att.; 3,609 yards; 34 rush. TDs; 367 rec.; 5,434 yds.; 43 rec. TDs.

Gifford was a gifted athlete who first made his mark as a running back, then later in his career as a flanker. He was the NFL player of the Year in 1956 when he rushed for 819 yards and caught 51 passes. He played in seven Pro Bowls. After a hit from Philadelphia linebacker Chuck Bednarik ended his season in 1960, he decided to retire and sat out all of the '61 season. He returned to the field in '62 as a flanker and caught 110 passes in three seasons before retiring for the final time. He also threw 14 touchdown passes in his career

### Sid Gillman, Coach (b. 10-26-11)

**SERVICE:** Los Angeles Rams 1955-59; Los Angeles Chargers 1960; San Diego Chargers 1961-69, 1971; Houston Oilers 1973-74.
**CAREER RECORD:** 123 wins, 104 losses, 7 ties.

Gillman was one of the first coaches to tap the full potential of the forward pass. His Chargers teams won their division in five of the AFL's first six years, primarily because of his exciting, high-powered offense. He moved to the Houston Oilers in 1973 and was named the AFC Coach of the Year in '74.

### Otto Graham, QB (b. 12-6-21)

**SERVICE:** Cleveland Browns 1946-55
**CAREER STATS:** 1,464 comp.; 23,584 yds.; 174 TDs.

A music major and basketball player at Northwestern University, Graham became one of the winningest quarterbacks in pro football history. Graham executed the T-formation to perfection in leading the Browns to four titles in the All-America Football Conference and three in the NFL. He was twice the NFL's passing leader, but his best performances came in big games. He threw four TD passes in the 1950 championship game win over the Rams, scored three TDs and threw for three more in the 1954 title game victory over Detroit, and scored two TDs and passed for two more the next year in a win over the Rams.

### Harold (Red) Grange, HB
### (b. 6-13-03, d. 1-28-91)

**SERVICE:** Chicago Bears 1925; New York Yankees (AFL) 1926; New York Yankees (NFL) 1927; Chicago Bears 1929-34.

More than any other player, Grange is responsible for the widespread success and popularity of professional football. A major star at the University of Illinois, Grange joined the Bears just 10 days after his last college game and drew a crowd of 36,000 for his debut against the Chicago Cardinals. He then embarked on a barnstorming tour with the Bears, drawing crowds of over 70,000 in both New York's Polo Grounds and the Los Angeles Coliseum.

### Joe Greene, DT (b. 9-24-46)

**SERVICE:** Pittsburgh Steelers 1969-81.

Drafted No. 1 by the Steelers out of North Texas State University in 1969, Mean Joe Greene made an immediate impact on his new team. He was named Defensive Rookie of the Year and became the pivotal player on the great Steeler defenses of the 1970s that helped produce four Super Bowl victories. He was chosen for the Pro Bowl 10 times and was named the league's Most Valuable Defensive Player twice. His great strength allowed him to dominate a game from his position as few had before him.

### Forrest Gregg, OT-G (b. 10-18-33)

**SERVICE:** Green Bay Packers 1956, 1958-70; Dallas Cowboys 1971.

Gregg's consistent play was one of the factors that made Green Bay into a champion in the 1960s. He didn't miss a game from 1956 to 1971, a then-record total of 188 straight. He lacked overpowering strength so he studied his rivals and controlled them by finesse. He won all-NFL honors for eight straight years beginning in 1960.

### Bob Griese, QB (b. 2-3-45)

**SERVICE:** Miami Dolphins 1967-80.
**CAREER STATS:** 1,926 comp.; 25,092 yds.; 192 TDs.

Griese was never the most talented athlete on the field, but he was always one of the smartest. He guided the Dolphins to 10 winning seasons in his last 11 with the team, including a 17–0 record in 1972. Under his leadership the Dolphins won consecutive Super Bowls after the 1972 and '73 seasons. He was selected to play in six Pro Bowls.

### Lou Groza, OT-K (b. 1-25-24)

**SERVICE:** Cleveland Browns 1946-59, 1961-67.
**CAREER STATS:** 810 XPs, 264 FGs, 1,608 points.

Nicknamed The Toe, Groza was a six-time starting tackle in the Pro Bowl as well as an accurate and prolific kicker. He led the league in number of field goals five times. His most crucial kick came in the 1950 championship game when he hit a 16-yarder in the final seconds to give the Browns their first NFL title by a score of 30–28 over the Rams. He was one of the original Browns in 1946 and remained with the team until 1967, then the longest career in league history.

### Joe Guyon, HB
### (b. 11-26-1892, d. 11-27-1971)

**SERVICE:** Canton Bulldogs 1919-20; Cleveland Indians 1921; Oorang Indians 1922-23; Rock Island Independents 1924; Kansas City Cowboys 1924-25; New York Giants 1927.

A native American who was born on a reservation in Minnesota, Guyon was an all-around player who starred during the NFL's first decade. He teamed with Jim Thorpe on the Oorang Indians teams of the early '20s and helped lead the 1927 New York Giants to the league championship.

### George Halas, Founder-Owner-Coach (b. 2-2-1895, d. 10-31-1983)
**SERVICE:** Decatur Staleys 1920; Chicago Bears 1922-83.
**CAREER RECORD:** 325 wins, 151 losses, 31 ties.
Along with Paul Brown, Halas was one of the founding fathers of football. He was an innovator who was the first to hold daily practices, the first to study game films of opponents, and the first to have games broadcast to the public via radio. His coaching career spanned five decades and included six NFL titles. Only six of his teams in 40 years finished below .500.

### Jack Ham, LB (b. 12-23-48)
**SERVICE:** Pittsburgh Steelers 1971-82.
**CAREER STATS:** 32 int.; 1 TD.; 19 fumb. recoveries.
Playing behind the Steel Curtain defensive line of the Pittsburgh teams of the 1970s, Ham was required to run with receivers and track down backs coming out of the backfield. Though smaller than most linebackers, he was perfect for that role. His nose for the ball enabled him to make big plays, including two interceptions in the 1974 AFC title game against Oakland that sent the Steelers to their first Super Bowl. He was named the NFL Defensive Player of the Year in 1975 and made the Pro Bowl eight times.

### John Hannah, G (b. 4-4-51)
**SERVICE:** New England Patriots 1973-85.
Touted as the best offensive lineman of all time, Hannah was a brutally effective blocker and one of the strongest players in the league. He played for teams that were mostly mediocre, but still earned Pro Bowl honors in eight seasons.

### Franco Harris, HB (b. 3-7-50)
**SERVICE:** Pittsburgh Steelers 1972-83; Seattle Seahawks 1984.
**CAREER STATS:** 2,949 rush. att.; 12,120 yds.; 91 TDs.
The fifth alltime leading rusher in NFL history, Harris is perhaps best known as the recipient of the "Immaculate Reception," an improbable last-second touchdown catch which allowed Pittsburgh to beat Oakland in a 1972 playoff game. He rushed for over 1,000 yards in eight seasons and was selected for the Pro Bowl nine times. He was the Most Valuable Player in Super Bowl IX when he rushed for 158 yards in Pittsburgh's 16–6 defeat of Minnesota. He is also the alltime Super Bowl rushing leader.

### Ed Healey, T (b. 12-28-1894, d. 12-9-1978)
**SERVICE:** Rock Island Independents 1920-22; Chicago Bears 1922-27.
A graduate of Dartmouth who was only a mediocre end on the football team there, Healey joined the Rock Island Independents after quitting his job loading meat onto railroad cars. Because of his size and his love of contact, he was switched to tackle where he blossomed, becoming a five time all-league pick.

### Mel Hein, C (b. 8-22-09, d. 1-31-92)
**SERVICE:** New York Giants 1931-45.
The captain of the New York Giants for 10 years, Hein was a consistent and sturdy player. He was named all-league at the center position for eight straight years, and in 1938, he was the league's Most Valuable Player. He was an accurate snapper in the single wing formation, and on defense from his linebacker's position he was adept at containing receivers by "jamming" them before they could get into their patterns.

### Ted Hendricks, LB (b. 11-1-47)
**SERVICE:** Baltimore Colts 1969-73; Green Bay Packers 1974; Oakland Raiders 1975-81; Los Angeles Raiders 1982-83
**CAREER STATS:** 26 int.
Nicknamed The Mad Stork because of his size and build (6'7", 225 pounds), Hendricks was a free spirit off the field and a terror for opponents on it. His best tactic of intimidation was the blitz, and if he didn't get a sack, he was big enough to bat down the pass or at least make the quarterback adjust his throw. He was also one of the great kick blockers in pro football history, batting away 25 field goal attempts or PATs.

### Wilbur (Pete) Henry, T (b. 10-31-1897, d. 2-7-1952)
**SERVICE:** Canton Bulldogs 1920-23, 1925-26; New York Giants 1927: Pottsville Maroons 1927-28.
At 6' and 250 pounds, Henry was a massive force on both the offensive and defensive lines in the early days of the league. Despite his appearance, which earned him the nickname Fats, Henry was agile and strong, as proved by his extraordinary kicking ability. He recorded a 50-yard dropkicked field goal in 1922 and a 94-yard punt in 1923.

### Arnie Herber, QB (b. 4-2-10, d. 10-14-69)
**SERVICE:** Green Bay Packers 1930-40; New York Giants 1944-45.
**CAREER STATS:** 487 comp.; 8,033 yds.; 79 TDs.
A Green Bay native, Herber first saw the Packers play while selling programs at the stadium as a teenager. Later he teamed with Don Hutson to form the league's first great passing combination. Herber led the league in passing three times and guided the Packers to league titles in 1930, '31, '36 and '39.

### Bill Hewitt, E (b. 10-8-09, d. 1-14-47)
**SERVICE:** Chicago Bears 1932-36; Philadelphia Eagles 1937-39; Phil-Pitt 1943.
**CAREER STATS:** 101 rec.; 1,606 yds.; 24 TDs.
One of the best of the two-way ends, Hewitt was named to the all-league team four times. Stocky and solidly built, he had such a fast start off the line of scrimmage that he was nicknamed The Offside Kid. He enjoyed his best season in 1936 when he caught 15 passes for an average of 23.9 yards per catch and scored six touchdowns.

### Clarke Hinkle, FB (b. 4-10-10)
**SERVICE:** Green Bay Packers 1932-41.
**CAREER STATS:** 1,171 rush. att.; 3,860 yds.; 33 TDs.
Hinkle was a stocky fullback for the Packers, whose matchups of the '30s with the Chicago Bears pitted him against another two-way power player, Bronko Nagurski. Even in those days when Nagurski was the preeminent fullback, Hinkle made all-NFL four times. His best season came in 1937 when he gained 552 yards and scored five touchdowns.

## Elroy (Crazylegs) Hirsch, HB-E (b. 6-17-23)

**SERVICE:** Chicago Rockets (AAFC) 1946-48; Los Angeles Rams 1949-57.

**CAREER STATS:** 387 rec.; 7,029 yds.; 60 TDs.

After a fractured skull nearly ended his career in 1948, Hirsch moved from halfback to end where he blossomed into a star. In 1951, as the Rams marched to the NFL title, he enjoyed one of the best seasons in league history. With Bob Waterfield and Norm Van Brocklin throwing, Hirsch caught 66 passes for 1,495 yards, a 22.7 average and 17 touchdowns, all of which led the league. His touchdown catches included one 91-yarder and five of more than 70 yards.

## Paul Hornung, HB-K (b. 12-23-35)

**SERVICE:** Green Bay Packers 1957-62, 1964-66.

**CAREER STATS:** 893 att.; 3,711 yds.; 50 TDs; 760 pts.

A Heisman Trophy winner from Notre Dame, Hornung, nicknamed The Golden Boy, was a multi-talented player who spent the first two years of his career moving between quarterback and halfback. When Vince Lombardi finally installed him as the left halfback he became a major star, leading the league in scoring three straight years from 1959 to '61, and in two of those seasons (1960 and '61) being named the league's MVP. His 176 points in a season still stands as a record. Commissioner Pete Rozelle suspended him from the league in 1963 for gambling.

## Ken Houston, S (b. 11-12-44)

**SERVICE:** Houston Oilers 1967-72; Washington Redskins 1973-80.

**CAREER STATS:** 49 int.; 9 TDs.

From little Prairie View A&M, Houston become one of the best safeties of all time. In his first five seasons with the Oilers, Houston set a career record for interceptions returned for touchdowns with nine. In 1971, he intercepted nine passes and returned four of them for touchdowns. He was selected to the Pro Bowl 12 times, but remained largely unknown until he showcased his talents before a Monday Night Football audience in 1973. With the Redskins leading the Cowboys 14-7 with only seconds remaining, Houston met fullback Walt Garrison and stopped him cold, inches short of the goal line, to preserve the victory.

## Robert (Cal) Hubbard, T (b. 10-31-00, d. 10-17-77)

**SERVICE:** New York Giants 1927-28, 1936; Green Bay Packers 1929-33, 1935; Pittsburgh Pirates 1936.

Hubbard was one of the first lineman to combine great size (6'5", 250 lbs.) and quickness. On defense, he was able to bat down passes and fill holes other linemen could not reach. He was an all-league tackle for five years and was part of the 1927 New York defense which allowed just 20 points in 13 games. After his football career, he took up baseball umpiring and is the only person elected to the halls of fame in both pro football and baseball.

## Sam Huff, MLB (b. 10-4-34)

**SERVICE:** New York Giants 1956-63; Washington Redskins 1964-67, 1969.

**CAREER STATS:** 30 int.

Huff was among the first middle linebackers—a fairly new position when he started his career—to become a star. He appeared on the cover of *Time* magazine and was the subject of a television special. He battled

great running backs of his day like Jim Taylor and Jim Brown and was named to the all-NFL team four times.

## Lamar Hunt, League Founder and Owner (b. 8-2-32)

**SERVICE:** Dallas Texans 1960-2; Kansas City Chiefs 1963-present.

Frustrated in his attempts to purchase an NFL team, Hunt, a young Texas oil man, joined with other investors to start the rival AFL in 1959. Though few gave the league a chance, the AFL used television and huge player contracts to compete with the established league and eventually to force a merger. In 10 years in the AFL, Hunt's Dallas/Kansas City team won three titles and played in the first Super Bowl. Hunt is also credited with giving the Super Bowl its name.

## Don Hutson, E (b. 1-31-13)

**SERVICE:** Green Bay Packers 1935-45.

**CAREER STATS:** 488 rec.; 7,991 yds.; 99 TDs.

Hutson was far and away the best receiver of his day. He was faster than almost any other player, and defenses were forced to double-team him. When he retired after the 1945 season, he had totaled 99 touchdown catches, a record that stood for 45 years until Steve Largent broke it in 1990. He led the league in receptions eight times and in TD catches nine times. He was also a defensive back who intercepted 24 passes and a kicker who scored 193 points. His best season came in 1942 when he caught 74 passes for 1,211 yards and 17 touchdowns.

## John Henry Johnson, FB (b. 11-24-29)

**SERVICE:** San Francisco 49ers 1954-56; Detroit Lions 1957-59; Pittsburgh Steelers 1960-65; Houston Oilers 1966.

**CAREER STATS:** 1,571 rush. att.; 6,803 yds.; 48 TDs.

Johnson opted for the Canadian Football League when he was drafted by the woeful Steelers in 1953, and in his single season there he was named MVP. The 49ers acquired him for the next season, and he became part of San Francisco's Million Dollar Backfield, which included future Hall of Famers Y.A. Tittle, Joe Perry and Hugh McElhenny. During his rookie year with the 49ers, Johnson rushed for 681 yards and nine touchdowns. Twice he rushed for over 1,000 yards with the Steelers, employing a slashing, slightly crouched running style. He was also known as an oustanding blocking back.

## David (Deacon) Jones, DE (b. 12-9-38)

**SERVICE:** Los Angeles Rams 1961-71; San Diego Chargers 1972-73; Washington Redskins 1974.

As part of the Rams' Fearsome Foursome defensive line, Jones brought notoriety to a formerly obscure position. He coined the term "sack" and though the league did not start keeping official statistics for the sack until after his career was over, his 26 sacks in 1967 would be a league record. He teamed with Merlin Olsen to develop stunts in order to foil blocking schemes, a tactic now universally used. He was twice named the NFL Defensive Player of the Year.

## Stan Jones, G-DT (b. 11-24-31)

**SERVICE:** Chicago Bears 1954-65; Washington Redskins 1966.

At 6'1" and 250 pounds, Jones was not a big lineman,

but during his career he succeeded as a versatile player on both offense and defense. Early in his career, he opened holes for Willie Gallimore and a potent Bears offense, but in 1963 he switched to defensive tackle and helped the Bears to their first championship in 17 years as part of a unit that allowed only 10 points per game.

### Sonny Jurgensen, QB (b. 8-23-34)
**SERVICE:** Philadelphia Eagles 1957-63; Washington Redskins 1964-74.
**CAREER STATS:** 2,433 comp.; 32,224 yds.; 255 TDs.
After four seasons as a backup to the Eagles' Norm Van Brocklin, Jurgensen, a classic dropback passer, came into his own in the 1961 season when he led the league in completions, yards and touchdowns. His most productive years, however, came after he was traded to the Redskins. Twice he was the individual league passing champion, and he ranks seventh on the alltime passing list.

### Walt Kiesling, Coach-G (b. 5-27-03, d. 3-2-62)
**SERVICE:** Duluth Eskimos 1926-27; Pottsville Maroons 1928; Chicago Cardinals 1929-33; Chicago Bears 1934; Green Bay Packers 1935-36; Pittsburgh Pirates 1937-39; Pittsburgh Steelers 1940-42, 1954-56 (coach).
**CAREER RECORD:** 25 wins, 39 losses, 4 ties.
Kiesling's devoted 34-year service to the game extended from his early days in the 1920s as a player to the late 1950s as a coach. He held three separate head coaching jobs, but most of his tenure in the league was as an assistant coach.

### Frank (Bruiser) Kinard, T (b. 10-23-14, d. 9-7-85)
**SERVICE:** Brooklyn Dodgers 1938-44; New York Yankees 1946-47.
As a tackle with the Brooklyn Dodgers, Kinard was an all-league selection in five of his seven seasons. As his nicknamed implies, he was a tough blocker and defender, even though he was relatively small at 6'1" and 218 pounds. He moved over to the AAFC for his final two seasons of football and earned all-league honors there in 1946.

### Earl (Curly) Lambeau, Founder-Coach (b. 4-9-1898, d. 6-1-1965)
**SERVICE:** Green Bay Packers 1919-49; Chicago Cardinals 1950-51; Washington Redskins 1952-53.
**CAREER RECORD:** 229 wins, 134 losses, 22 ties.
As the founder of the Green Bay Packers and the chief architect of their early success, Lambeau assured that the small-town franchise was able to compete with the larger city outfits. He employed the forward pass as no one had before, recruiting such prolific quarterbacks and receivers as Arnie Herber, Cecil Isbell and Don Hutson. With Lambeau as coach, the Packers won six NFL titles. His 229 victories ranks fourth alltime.

### Jack Lambert (b. 7-8-52)
**SERVICE:** Pittsburgh Steelers 1974-84.
**CAREER STATS:** 28 int.
As part of the Steelers' Iron Curtain defense, Lambert earned four Super Bowl rings and made nine straight Pro Bowl appearances. At a lean 6'4" and 220 pounds, he was agile enough to drop back into pass coverage or to track down a runner. He led his team in tackles for 10 straight seasons.

### Tom Landry (b. 9-11-24)
**SERVICE:** Dallas Cowboys 1960-88.
**CAREER RECORD:** 270 wins, 178 losses, 6 ties.
For his placid demeanor and his sterling record, Landry is one of the most respected coaches of all time. He ranks third on the alltime list of winning coaches, and he posted a string of 20 consecutive winning seasons. Under his direction the Cowboys appeared in five Super Bowls, winning two.

### Dick (Night Train) Lane, CB (b. 4-16-28)
**SERVICE:** Los Angeles Rams 1952-53; Chicago Cardinals 1954-59; Detroit Lions 1960-65.
**CAREER STATS:** 68 int.; 5 TDs.
With little experience in football outside high school, junior college and the Army, Lane was a long shot prospect when he tried out for the Los Angeles Rams in 1952. He was originally seen as a receiver but was shut out because of Rams stars Tom Fears and Crazylegs Hirsch. When he was moved to defense, he quickly came into his own, intercepting 14 passes in 12 games and scoring two touchdowns on interception returns in his rookie season. A fierce tackler, Lane was named to the all-league team once during his five-year stint with the Chicago Cardinals and four times during his tenure with the Lions.

### Jim Langer, C (b. 5-16-48)
**SERVICE:** Miami Dolphins 1970-79; Minnesota Vikings 1980-81.
Signed as a free agent with the Dolphins after he was cut by the Browns, Langer developed into one of the finest centers in the league. He didn't become a starter until 1972, but from '73 to '78, he was selected for the Pro Bowl every year. His consistency helped Miami achieve its perfect season in 1972, when he played on every offensive down.

### Willie Lanier, MLB (8-21-45)
**SERVICE:** Kansas City Chiefs 1967-77.
**CAREER STATS:** 27 int.; 2 TDs.
Lanier was one of the first black players to star at the middle linebacker position. His play was marked by the ferocity of his tackles, and he was at the center of the Kansas City defense that carried the team to a Super Bowl championship in 1970. He recovered 15 fumbles during his career and was named to the all-AFL/AFC team seven times.

### Yale Lary, S-P (b. 11-24-30)
**SERVICE:** Detroit Lions 1952-53, 1956-64.
**CAREER STATS:** 50 int.; 2 TDs; 503 punts; 44.3 avg.
Lary's versatility was a key to the Lions' winning teams of the 1950s. During his 11-year tenure, the Lions won three NFL titles and Lary played safety, punted and returned punts. He won three league punting titles, and his career average of 44.3 is the third best of all time. As a defensive back, he played in nine Pro Bowls and was elected to the all-NFL team three times.

### Dante Lavelli, E (b. 2-23-23)
**SERVICE:** Cleveland Browns 1946-56
**CAREER STATS:** 386 rec.; 6,488 yds.; 62 TDs.
Even as a rookie with the Browns, Lavelli was a star, catching 40 passes for 843 yards, both of which totals led the AAFC. His greatest game came in the 1950 NFL Championship against the Rams where he

caught 11 passes and scored two touchdowns to help the Browns to a 30–28 win. He was named to the all-AAFC team twice and earned all-league honors twice after the Browns joined the NFL.

### Bobby Layne, QB (b. 12-19-26, d. 12-1-86)
**SERVICE:** Chicago Bears 1948; New York Bulldogs 1949; Detroit Lions 1950-58; Pittsburgh Steelers 1958-62.
**CAREER STATS:** 1,814 comp.; 26,768 yds.; 196 TDs.
A fun-loving Texan with a heavy drawl, Layne's off-the-field activities got him as much publicity as his on-the-field performance. Nevertheless, he was a leader who guided the Lions to league championships in 1952 and '53. His leadership was most apparent in the 1953 title game against the Browns. With a minute remaining and the Lions trailing 16–10 at their own 20, Layne completed five of seven passes, including a 33-yarder for the touchdown that won the game. His greatest statistical season came in 1952 when he led the league in attempts, completions, yards and touchdowns.

### Alphonse (Tuffy) Leemans, HB-FB (b. 11-12-12, d. 1-19-79)
**SERVICE:** New York Giants 1936-43.
**CAREER STATS:** 919 rush. att.; 3,142 yds.; 17 TDs.
Leemans was an all-around offensive player who contributed to three divisional championships and one NFL title during his eight-year career. After a standout career at George Washington University, Leemans entered the league in 1936 and led the NFL in both attempts and yards rushing. In addition to his rushing exploits, Leemans threw 25 touchdown passes.

### Bob Lilly, DT (b. 7-26-39)
**SERVICE:** Dallas Cowboys 1961-74.
Lilly, the quintessential Texan, was born in Olney, Texas, attended Texas Christian University, and was the Cowboys first draft pick ever, first Pro Bowl player and first all-NFL choice. As part of Dallas's Doomsday Defense, Lilly was a devastating force in stopping opposing rushers. He made the all-NFL team eight times and played in five NFL/NFC Championship Games and two Super Bowls. He was one of the few defensive linemen whom opposing teams chose to run at directly so that he wouldn't beat them with his quick pursuit.

### Larry Little, G (b. 11-2-45)
**SERVICE:** San Diego Chargers 1967-68, Miami Dolphins 1969-80.
Only the third guard to be inducted into the Hall of Fame (after John Hannah and Gene Upshaw), Little was the Miami captain and the anchor of Miami's offensive line throughout the Dolphins' dynasty years of the early 1970's. At 6'1", 265-pounds, the Bethune-Cookman graduate set crushing blocks for backs Mercury Morris, Larry Csonka and Jim Kiick. Little played in three straight Super Bowls from 1971 through '73 and was named to the Pro Bowl team six times.

### Vince Lombardi, Coach (b. 6-11-13, d. 10-3-70)
**SERVICE:** Green Bay Packers 1959-67; Washington Redskins 1969.
**CAREER RECORD:** 105 wins, 35 losses, 6 ties.
Regarded as among the greatest coaches ever,

Lombardi was a tough disciplinarian who turned a failing Green Bay franchise into a dynasty. When he took over the team in 1959 after five years as an assistant coach with the New York Giants, the Packers had just finished a 1–10–1 season. The next year, they produced a winning record of 7–5–0 and went on in the next eight years to win five NFL championships and the first two Super Bowls. His .736 winning percentage is the highest ever. The Super Bowl trophy is named for him.

### Sid Luckman, QB (b. 11-21-1916)
**SERVICE:** Chicago Bears 1939-50.
**CAREER STATS:** 904 comp.; 14,683 yds.; 137 TDs.
Luckman was the first quarterback to master the T formation, and he was rewarded with four NFL championships and five all-league selections. He was the NFL Player of the Year in 1943, when he led the league in passing yardage (2,194) and touchdown passes (28). That year, in a game against the Giants, he threw for a record seven touchdowns, and in the title game against the Redskins, he threw for 276 yards and five touchdowns.

### William Roy "Link" Lyman, T (b. 11-30-1898, d. 12-16-1972)
**SERVICE:** Canton Bulldogs 1922-23, 1925; Cleveland Bulldogs 1924; Frankford Yellowjackets 1925; Chicago Bears 1926-28, 1930-31, 1933-34.
Lyman is credited with being the first player to employ the tactic of shifting defensive position in order to frustrate offensive attempts at blocking. He played on championship teams in Canton in 1922 and '23 and in Cleveland in '24. He was a part of one more title team with the Bears in 1933.

### John Mackey, TE (b. 9-09-41)
**SERVICE:** Baltimore Colts 1963-71; San Diego Chargers 1972.
**CAREER STATS:** 331 rec.; 5,236 yds.; 38 TDs.
Considered by many to be the prototypical tight end, Mackey was a fierce blocker on running plays and a fleet receiver who could outrun defensive backs. He enjoyed his best season in 1966 when he caught 50 passes for 829 yards and nine touchdowns.

### Tim Mara, Founder-Administrator (b. 7-29-1887, d. 2-17-1959)
**SERVICE:** New York Giants 1925-59.
When the NFL needed to start a franchise in New York City in 1925, bookmaker Mara put up the $500 and started the Giants. Mara quickly got the Giants on a winning track and in 1927, the team finished 11–1–1 and won their first NFL title. The Giants franchise remains in the Mara family today.

### Gino Marchetti, DE (b. 1-2-27)
**SERVICE:** Dallas Texans 1952; Baltimore Colts 1953-64, 1966.
Primarily known as a fierce pass rusher, Marchetti was named to the all-NFL team seven times. Raised in California of Italian immigrant parents, Marchetti was drafted by the New York Yanks, who became the Dallas Texans before folding after one season. Marchetti was assigned to the new Baltimore franchise, where he helped the Colts to two NFL titles.

## George Preston Marshall, Founder-Administrator (b. 10-13-1897, d. 8-9-1969)
**SERVICE:** Boston Braves 1932; Boston Redskins 1933-36; Washington Redskins 1937-69.
Marshall was the first owner to realize the value of promoting his team and of entertaining the fans. After losing money in Boston, he move the franchise to Washington, D.C., where it flourished. He introduced the idea of a halftime show and also used public relations methods to create media interest in his team.

## Ollie Matson, HB (b. 5-1-30)
**SERVICE:** Chicago Cardinals 1952, 1954-58; Los Angeles Rams 1959-62; Detroit Lions 1963; Philadelphia Eagles 1964-66.
**CAREER STATS:** 1,170 rush. att.; 5,173 yds.; 40 TDs
Matson was a versatile player who had the misfortune never to play for a championship team. He was a world class sprinter who won a bronze and a gold medal at the 1952 Olympics. He was a powerful rusher, a steady receiver out of the backfield and a speedy return man. His career total of nine touchdowns on kickoff and punt returns is an NFL record. In 1955 he led the league with an average of 18.8 per punt return.

## Don Maynard, WR (b. 1-25-37)
**SERVICE:** New York Giants 1958; New York Titans 1960-62; New York Jets 1963-72; St. Louis Cardinals 1973.
**CAREER STATS:** 633 rec.; 11,834 yds.; 88 TDs.
By the time of his retirement in 1973, Maynard, a speedy Texan, had totaled more yards than any other receiver in history. He was already a productive receiver when Joe Namath joined the Jets in 1965, but the two of them quickly set new standards for passing duos. In 1967 and '68, Maynard led the AFL in average yards per catch with 20.2 and 22.8, respectively. He now ranks seventh among alltime receivers.

## George McAfee, HB (b. 3-13-18)
**SERVICE:** Chicago Bears 1940-41, 1945-50.
**CAREER STATS:** 341 rush. att.; 1,685 yds.; 22 TDs.
At a slender 6', 177 pounds, McAfee was an unlikely looking pro football halfback. Fleet-footed with a variety of moves, he was a shifty runner, who also caught passes, returned punts and kickoffs and played defensive back. His career punt return average of 12.8 is still the best ever. He also intercepted 21 passes during his career.

## Mike McCormack, T (b. 6-21-30)
**SERVICE:** New York Yanks 1951; Cleveland Browns 1954-62.
McCormack was a mainstay of the Browns' offensive line for nine years, protecting quarterback Otto Graham and opening holes for Jim Brown. He was named to the Pro Bowl six times and was the team captain from 1956 until the end of the career.

## Hugh McElhenny, HB (b. 12-31-28)
**SERVICE:** San Francisco 49ers 1952-60; Minnesota Vikings 1961-62; New York Giants 1963; Detroit Lions 1964.
**CAREER STATS:** 1,124 rush. att.; 5,281 yds.; 38 TDs.
When McElhenny joined the San Francisco 49ers in 1952, the franchise was struggling, but after his rookie year, the team could boast a star. He was named Rookie of the Year for his all-around excellence,

which included a league-leading 7.0 yards per carry and a punt return average of 14.2. He also had the year's longest punt return and run from scrimmage, 94 and 89 yards respectively. A durable and versatile player, McElhenny was a six-time Pro Bowl selection.

## Johnny (Blood) McNally, HB (b. 11-27-03, d. 11-28-85)
**SERVICE:** Milwaukee Badgers 1925-26; Duluth Eskimos 1926-27; Pottsville Maroons 1928; Green Bay Packers 1935-36; Pittsburgh Pirates 1934, 1937-39.
McNally adopted the name Johnny Blood in order to disguise his identity so he could play both professional and college football. During 15 seasons in the league, he showed himself to be a versatile player, but his forte was receiving.

## Mike Michalske, G (b. 4-24-03, d. 10-26-83)
**SERVICE:** New York Yankees 1926 (AFL); New York Yankees (NFL) 1927-28; Green Bay Packers 1929-35, 1937.
Michalske was the premier lineman for the Packers during his career, when the team won three titles. He was equally adept at pulling on sweeps and blocking straight ahead. He was named all-NFL four times.

## Wayne Millner, E (b. 1-31-13, d. 11-19-76)
**SERVICE:** Boston Redskins 1936; Washington Redskins 1937-41, 1945.
**CAREER STATS:** 124 rec.; 1,578 yds.; 12 TDs.
Millner was the favorite target of Sammy Baugh, and the duo helped the team win an NFL championship in 1937. In that year's title game against the Bears, Baugh and Millner connected on eight passes for 181 yards and two TDs.

## Bobby Mitchell, WR-HB (b. 6-6-35)
**SERVICE:** Cleveland Browns 1958-61; Washington Redskins 1962-68.
**CAREER STATS:** 521 rec.; 7,954 yds.; 65 TDs.
Mitchell began his career as a running back, but after he was traded to the Washington Redskins in 1962, he was moved to wide receiver, where he flourished at the receiving end of passes from Sonny Jurgensen. As a running back with the Browns, he teamed with Jim Brown and in one game gained 232 yards. At Washington, he was always a threat to go long, and in his first year as a Redskin, he caught 72 passes for 1,384 yards, both league-leading numbers. His career total of 14,708 yards ranks eighth alltime.

## Ron Mix, T (b. 3-10-38)
**SERVICE:** Los Angeles Chargers 1960; San Diego Chargers 1961-69; Oakland Raiders 1971.
Mix was the top lineman in the AFL during his 10-year career with the Chargers. Even though San Diego employed a passing offense under coach Sid Gillman, Mix was called for only two holding penalties in 10 seasons. His superior balance allowed him to stay with blocks longer than other linemen, and he could often be seen downfield, helping to spring runners for longer gains. He made the all-AFL team nine times.

## Lenny Moore, FL-RB (b. 11-25-33)
**SERVICE:** Baltimore Colts 1956-67.
**CAREER STATS:** 1,069 rush. att.; 5,174 yds.; 63 TDs; 363 rec.; 42 TDs.
Excelling both as a runner and as a receiver, Moore

gained 12,449 combined net yards and scored 113 touchdowns, fourth on the alltime TD list. He led the league in average gain per carry four times, his top number being 7.5 in his rookie season. In 1964 he scored a touchdown in 11 straight games. Five times he was an all-NFL selection.

### Marion Motley, FB (b. 6-5-20)
**SERVICE:** Cleveland Browns 1946-53; Pittsburgh Steelers 1955.
**CAREER STATS:** 828 rush. att.; 4,720 yds.; 31 TDs.
One of the first of the big bruising fullbacks, Motley kept Browns' opponents from concentrating entirely on Cleveland's strong passing game. In 1948, he led the AAFC in rushing, and when the Browns joined the NFL in 1950, he led the league in rushing with 810 yards. Over his career he averaged 5.7 yards per carry.

### George Musso, T-G (b. 4-8-10)
**SERVICE:** Chicago Bears 1933-44.
At 6'2" and 270 pounds, Musso was the largest of the Monsters of the Midway. A durable two-way player, Musso was hard to get around on defense and a fearsome blocker for Bear runners like Bronko Nagurski on offense. He won all-NFL honors twice.

### Bronko Nagurski, FB (b. 11-3-08, d. 1-07-90)
**SERVICE:** Chicago Bears 1930-37, 1943.
**CAREER STATS:** 610 rush. att.; 2,708 yds.; 18 TDs.
After becoming an all-America at both fullback and tackle, Nagurski plowed through the NFL, helping the Bears win three championships in 1932, '33 and '43. He never averaged less than 4.2 yards per carry in any one season. He was also a passer, throwing two touchdown passes in the 1933 championship game. After the 1937 season, he left for a career in professional wrestling, but in 1943 returned to football and scored a touchdown in the NFL title game.

### Joe Namath, QB (b. 5-31-43)
**SERVICE:** New York Jets 1965-76; Los Angeles Rams 1977.
**CAREER STATS:** 1,886 comp.; 27,663 yds.; 173 TDs.
Namath is almost as famous for his off-the-field exploits as his performance on it, but by all measures he had a lasting effect on the sport. In 1965 he became the AFL's prime catch in the bidding war with the NFL by signing a contract for the then astounding figure of $400,000. Dubbed Broadway Joe for his after-hours activities, Namath brought glamor and viability to his upstart league. When the Jets earned a place in Super Bowl III, he guaranteed victory and made good on that promise by leading the Jets to a 16-7 upset victory over the Colts. Widely acknowledged as having the quickest release in history, Namath led the league in passing yards three times and was named Player of the Year in 1968.

### Earle (Greasy) Neale, Coach (b. 11-5-1891, d. 11-2-1973)
**SERVICE:** Philadelphia Eagles 1941-50.
**CAREER RECORD:** 66 wins, 44 losses, 5 ties.
A college star at West Virginia Wesleyan and a Cincinnati Reds outfielder, Neale became coach of the Philadelphia Eagles in 1941. He installed a T formation offense and the Eagles went on to become one of the powers in the league throughout the decade of the 1940s, winning three division titles and two NFL championships.

### Ernie Nevers, FB (b. 6-11-03, d. 5-3-76)
**SERVICE:** Duluth Eskimos 1926-27; Chicago Cardinals 1929-31.
After starring in baseball, basketball and football at Stanford, Nevers joined the Duluth Eskimos in 1926, and in those barnstorming days, played 29 games that season. Nevers did everything for the team, playing offense and defense, punting, placekicking and returning kicks. In 1929, with the Chicago Cardinals, he erupted for 40 points in a win over the Bears, a record that still stands.

### Ray Nitschke, MLB (b. 12-29-36)
**SERVICE:** Green Bay Packers 1958-72
**CAREER STATS:** 25 int.; 2 TDs.
The famed number 66, Nitschke was at the heart of the defense during the Packers' glory years. Lining up opposite Nitschke's fearsome visage intimidated opponents, who knew that Nitschke would tear through them to get to the ball. During his 15-year career, the Packers won five NFL championships.

### Chuck Noll, Coach (b. 1-5-32)
**SERVICE:** Pittsburgh Steelers 1969-91
**CAREER RECORD:** 209–156–1; four Super Bowl wins.
Noll is the only coach to win four Super Bowls, leading Pittsburgh to victory in 1975, '76, '79, and '80. In 23 years as the Steelers' head coach, Noll won 11 division titles and compiled a record of 209–156–1, including a 16–8 mark in postseason competition. Noll, who played seven seasons (1953–60) at guard for the Cleveland Browns, spent nine seasons as an NFL assistant coach before becoming Pittsburgh's head coach in 1969.

### Leo Nomellini, T (b. 6-19-24)
**SERVICE:** San Francisco 49ers 1950-63
Nomellini was the 49ers first ever draft choice, and he played in every game for them for 14 years. At 6'3", 284 pounds, he was a huge force on both offense and defense, becoming one of the few players to earn all-NFL status on both units. He played in 10 Pro Bowls.

### Merlin Olsen, DT (b. 9-15-40)
**SERVICE:** Los Angeles Rams 1962-76.
Olsen, a Phi Beta Kappa student at Utah State, was part of The Fearsome Foursome of the Rams that dominated the league in the 1960s and '70s. With Deacon Jones, he developed stunts and moves that brought new finesse to defensive line play. He was named to the Pro Bowl for 14 straight years.

### Jim Otto, C (b. 1-5-38)
**SERVICE:** Oakland Raiders 1960-74.
With a unique number (00) and a palindromic surname, Otto gained a measure of fame unusual for a center. But his consistency on the field helped him achieve the respect of his peers. In his 15-year career, he started every game the Raiders played, a total of 308. The strength of the offensive line during his tenure helped the Raiders to win seven divisional titles and one AFL championship.

# Members of the Pro Football Hall of Fame *(Cont.)*

### Steve Owen, T-Coach
### (b. 4-21-1898, d. 5-17-1964)
**SERVICE:** Kansas City Cowboys 1924-25; New York
Giants 1926-53.
**CAREER RECORD:** 153 wins, 108 losses, 17 ties.
As a tackle with the Giants for nine seasons, Owen led
a defense that gave up points sparingly. He went on
to serve the Giants as a coach for 23 seasons, winning two NFL championships and eight division titles.
He was also an innovator, developing a defense in
which the ends drop back into pass coverage, an
alignment which later became the standard 4-3-3. He
also used a two-platoon substitution plan, in which
two different units played both offense and defense.

### Alan Page, DT (b. 8-7-45)
**SERVICE:** Minnesota Vikings 1967-78; Chicago
Bears 1978-81.
**CAREER STATS:** 224 fumb. recoveries; 28 blocked kicks;
164 sacks.
Page was the dominant player in Minnesota's Purple
People Eaters front four of the 1970s. During his
career, the Vikings made four trips to the Super Bowl
and won nine NFC Central titles. He was the first
defensive player ever to be named the Player of the
Year, an honor he earned in 1972. Possessing
superior mobility and quickness, Page was a
relentless pursuer of the ballcarrier, and teams found
it wisest to run right at him to neutralize his speed.

### Clarence (Ace) Parker, QB (b. 5-17-12)
**SERVICE:** Brooklyn Dodgers 1937-41; Boston Yanks
1945; New York Yankees (AAFC) 1946.
**CAREER STATS:** 335 comp.; 4,701 yds.; 30 TDs.
Though small in stature at 5'11" and 168 pounds,
Parker was a two-way powerhouse for the Brooklyn
Dodgers of the 1940s. In 1940 he won the league's
Most Valuable Player award, throwing for 10 touch-
downs and scoring three more on runs.

### Jim Parker, T-G (b. 4-3-34)
**SERVICE:** Baltimore Colts 1957-67.
At a massive 6'3" and 273 pounds, Parker was the
primary force that separated Johnny Unitas from an
oncoming pass rush. He was an all-league selection
as a tackle four times and four times as a guard. He
was a two-way lineman at Ohio State and an Outland
Trophy winner.

### Walter Payton, RB (b. 7-25-54)
**SERVICE:** Chicago Bears 1975–87.
**CAREER STATS:** 16,726 yds.; 110 TDs.
The NFL's all-time leading rusher, Payton ran for
16,726 yards and 110 touchdowns in his 13 years
with the Bears. Nicknamed "Sweetness" for his
running style, Payton broke Jim Brown's career
rushing mark in 1984 and just kept going. In 10 of his
13 seasons, Payton topped 1,000 yards; in 77 games
he rushed for more than 100 yards. Against Minnesota
in 1977, Payton carried 40 times for an NFL-record
275 yards. Also a fine receiver, Payton caught 492
passes for 4,538 yards and 15 TDs in his career.

### Joe Perry, FB (b. 1-27-27)
**SERVICE:** San Francisco 49ers 1948-60, 1963;
Baltimore Colts 1961-62.
**CAREER STATS:** 1,929 rush. att.; 9,723 yds.; 71 TDs.
When he retired in 1963, Perry's 9,723 yard rushing

in the AAFC and NFL ranked second behind Jim
Brown. Of the top 20 NFL yardage gainers of all time,
Perry's 4.8 yards per carry ranks second again only
to Jim Brown's 5.2. He twice rushed for over 1,000
yards (1953 and '54), leading the NFL in both
seasons.

### Pete Pihos, E (b. 10-22-23)
**SERVICE:** Philadelphia Eagles 1947-55.
**CAREER STATS:** 373 rec.; 5,619 yds.; 61 TDs.
With his career covering the era when football moved
from two-way players to a two-platoon system, Pihos
proved himself both an all-around star and a superior
specialist. After a college career as an all-America fullback and end at the University of Indiana, Pihos joined
the Eagles in 1947 and was part of the Eagles teams
that won two straight NFL championships in 1948 and
'49. He played defensive end full-time in 1952 and was
named all-league. In 1953, he switched to offensive
end and won three straight NFL pass catching crowns,
hauling in over 60 passes each season.

### Hugh (Shorty) Ray, Supervisor of Officials
### (b. 9-21-1884, d. 9-16-1956)
**SERVICE:** National Football League 1938-52.
Ray was one of the first people to codify the rules of
football, which he did in the 1920s in a book for the
National Federation of State High School Athletic
Associations. When he joined the NFL, he made sure
that officials mastered the rules so as to minimize on-
field disputes.

### Dan Reeves, Owner-Administrator
### (b. 6-30-12, d. 4-15-71)
**SERVICE:** Cleveland Rams 1941-45; Los Angeles
Rams 1946-71.
In 1946, a year after the Cleveland Rams won the
NFL Championship, Reeves moved the team to Los
Angeles. He was the first owner in the new league to
relocate on the West Coast and after some tough
financial years the risk paid off as the Rams often
drew crowds of over 80,000 fans. Reeves was also
the first owner to employ a full-time scouting staff. In
1946, he signed UCLA star Kenny Washington to a
contract, making him the first black player to enter
the league since 1933.

### John Riggins, RB (b. 8-4-49)
**SERVICE:** New York Jets 1971-75; Washington
Redskins 1976-85.
**CAREER STATS:** 2,916 att.; 11,352 yds.; 104 TDs.
A big back blessed with sprinter's speed, Riggins ran
through the NFL for the sixth leading rushing total of all
time. He is also the third leading touchdown scorer of
all time. He set two Super Bowl records in 1983 when
he rushed 38 times for 166 yds. A free spirit off the
field, Riggins once showed up at the Jets' training
camp with a Mohawk haircut.

### Jim Ringo, C (b. 11-21-31)
**SERVICE:** Green Bay Packers 1953-63; Philadelphia
Eagles 1964-67.
As the Packers' starting center for 10 years, Ringo
made the all-NFL team six times. Altogether he
started in 182 consecutive games. At 235 pounds, he
wasn't large but his quickness and reliability made
him a stalwart on the Packers line.

PRO FOOTBALL    **141**

**Andy Robustelli, DE (b. 12-6-25)**
SERVICE: Los Angeles Rams 1951-55; New York Giants 1956-64.
Robustelli was a standout offensive player at little Arnold College, but when the Rams installed him at defensive end during his rookie season, he became a standout pass rusher. During his 14-year career in the NFL, he made the all-league team seven times.

**Art Rooney, Founder-Administrator (b. 1-27-01, d. 8-25-88)**
SERVICE: Pittsburgh Steelers 1933-88.
For years the Steelers were one of the worst teams in the league, but Rooney, the patriarch of the franchise, continued to love the game and his players. He bought the franchise in 1933 and ran it until his death in '88. After 42 years in the league, the Steelers gave Rooney his first championship, in 1975, and they went on to win three more in that decade.

**Pete Rozelle, Commissioner (b. 3-1-26)**
SERVICE: National Football League 1960-89.
Rozelle was the 33-year-old general manager of the Los Angeles Rams when he was named commissioner in 1960. He shepherded the NFL through its most volatile and popular period, overseeing television contracts, strikes, the merger with the AFL, and drug and gambling scandals. He saw the league through massive expansion, as the size of the NFL has more than doubled.

**Bob St. Clair, T (b. 2-18-31)**
SERVICE: San Francisco 49ers 1953-63.
At 6'9" and 265 pounds St. Clair was a tower on the offensive line, but he was perhaps most effective as a special teams player. In 1956 he blocked 10 field goals and extra point attempts.

**Gayle Sayers, HB (b. 5-30-43)**
SERVICE: Chicago Bears 1965-71.
CAREER STATS: 991 rush. att.; 4,956 yds.; 39 TDs.
One of the most exciting players in NFL history, Sayers, in his brief career, displayed moves that had never been seen before on a football field. In his rookie year, he scored 22 touchdowns—14 on runs, six on pass receptions and two on returns. In one game against San Francisco he scored six touchdowns. He rushed for over 1,000 yards twice, in 1966 and 1969, leading the league both times. Knee injuries in 1968 and '70 ended his career.

**Joe Schmidt, MLB (b. 1-18-32)**
SERVICE: Detroit Lions 1953-65.
CAREER STATS: 24 int.; 2 TDs.
For nine of his 13 seasons, Schmidt was the captain of a Lions' defense known for its gambling, blitzing style. He was named all-NFL eight times.

**Tex Schramm, Administrator (b. 6-20-20)**
SERVICE: Dallas Cowboys 1960-88.
Along with coach Tom Landry and superscout Gil Brandt, president and general manager Schramm helped build the Dallas Cowboys into a dynasty. Schramm headed up a peerless scouting system and put together teams that won five Super Bowls and posted 20 consecutive winning seasons.

**Art Shell, T (b. 11-25-46)**
SERVICE: Oakland Raiders 1968-81; Los Angeles Raiders 1982.
Teaming with guard Gene Upshaw on the left side of the offensive line for 14 years, Shell helped create a formidable wall between the defense and the quarterback. He played in eight Pro Bowls and is now the coach of the Raiders.

**O.J. Simpson, RB (b. 7-9-47)**
SERVICE: Buffalo Bills 1969-77; San Francisco 49ers 1978-79.
CAREER STATS: 2,404 att.; 11,236 yds.; 61 TDs.
Simpson was expected to be the savior of the woeful Bills when he entered the league in 1969. Out of place in his first three seasons, he was used only sparingly as a rusher. When Lou Saban took over as coach, he began to give the ball to Simpson 30 and 40 times a game, with immediate results. Simpson rushed for over 1,000 yards in each of the next five seasons, leading the league in four of them and rushing for a then-record 2,003 yards in 1973. He won the Player of the Year Award in 1972, '73 and '75 and is seventh on the alltime career rushing list.

**Bart Starr, QB (b. 1-9-34)**
SERVICE: Green Bay Packers 1956-71.
CAREER STATS: 3,149 pass. att.; 1,808 comp.; 24,718 yds.; 152 TDs.
Though he didn't play much early in his career, Starr, under the tutelage of Vince Lombardi, became one of the best ever. He perfectly fit the Packers ball-control offense and proved adept at changing plays at the line of scrimmage. He led the league in passing three times and was always at or near the top of the league in completion percentage. He was the Player of the Year in 1966 and the MVP in Super Bowls I and II.

**Roger Staubach, QB (b. 2-3-42)**
SERVICE: Dallas Cowboys 1969-79.
CAREER STATS: 2,958 pass. att.; 1,685 comp.; 22,700 yds.; 153 TDs.
Feared as much for his running ability as for his passing arm, Staubach was a master at getting his team out of seemingly hopeless situations. He was known for leading the Cowboys to come-from-behind wins, as in a 1972 playoff game against the 49ers when he threw two TDs in the last 1:10 to produce a 30-28 victory. He won the NFL passing title four times and led Dallas to six divisional titles and two Super Bowl victories. He was named Player of the Year in 1971.

**Ernie Stautner, DT (b. 4-20-25)**
SERVICE: Pittsburgh Steelers 1950-63.
At 6'2" and 235 pounds, Stautner seemed too small to be a defensive lineman. But he became a regular for the Steelers at defensive tackle, missing only six games in 14 years. During that time of hardship for Pittsburgh, Stautner was often the only bright spot, playing in nine Pro Bowls.

**Jan Stenerud, K (b. 11-26-42)**
SERVICE: Kansas City Chiefs 1967-79; Green Bay Packers 1980-83; Minnesota Vikings 1984-85.
CAREER STATS: 580 XPs.; 373 FGs.; 1,699 pts.
Stenerud was the first pure kicker elected to the Hall of Fame. He holds the record for most career field goals and is second to George Blanda in total points.

# Members of the Pro Football Hall of Fame *(Cont.)*

**Ken Strong, HB (b. 8-6-06, d. 10-5-79)**
**SERVICE:** Staten Island Stapletons 1929-32;
New York Giants 1933-35, 1939, 1944-47;
New York Yanks (AFL) 1936-37.
**CAREER STATS:** 35 TDs; 169 XPs.; 39 FGs; 496 pts.
After a career as an all-America at New York
University, Strong embarked on a 14-year career with
three teams and two leagues. A great all-around ath-
lete, he displayed all his skills in the 1934 NFL
Championship game, scoring two touchdowns and
kicking four extra points and a field goal in the
Giants' 30-13 win over the Bears.

**Joe Stydahar, T (b. 3-17-12, d. 3-23-77)**
**SERVICE:** Chicago Bears 1936-42, 1945-46.
A little-known tackle out of West Virginia, Stydahar
became the rock of a lineman on which George
Halas built his championship teams of the 1940s. A
60-minute player who was fast for his size, Stydahar
helped the Bears win three NFL titles.

**Fran Tarkenton, QB (b. 2-3-40)**
**SERVICE:** Minnesota Vikings 1961-66, 1972-78;
New York Giants 1967-71.
**CAREER STATS:** 6,467 pass. att.; 3,686 comp.;
47,003 yds.; 342 TDs.
In 18 seasons with the Vikings and Giants, Tarkenton
became the alltime leader in attempts, completions,
yards passing and touchdowns. He took Minnesota
to the Super Bowl three times and was the Player of
the Year in 1975. He was always a threat to run as his
scrambling style frustrated attempts to defense him.

**Charley Taylor, WR-HB (b. 9-28-41)**
**SERVICE:** Washington Redskins 1964-75, 1977.
**CAREER STATS:** 649 rec.; 9,140 yds.; 79 TDs.
Taylor was the NFL's rookie of the year as a running
back in 1964, but in his third year, the Redskins shifted him to wide receiver. In his first full season at that
position, he led the league with 72 catches. He led
the league again the next year with 70 catches, and
when he retired in 1977, he was the alltime leader
with 649 catches. He now ranks fifth on the career list.

**Jim Taylor, FB (b. 9-20-35)**
**SERVICE:** Green Bay Packers 1958-66;
New Orleans Saints 1967.
**CAREER STATS:** 1,941 att.; 8,597 yds.; 83 TDs.
As the hard-nose fullback in Vince Lombardi's
scheme, Taylor was often called upon to pick up the
two or three yards the Packers needed for a first
down. In each of the five seasons from 1960 to '64,
he gained over 1,000 yards. In the 1962 title game,
he gained 85 yards on 31 carries in the Packers' 16-7
win over the Giants.

**Jim Thorpe, HB (b. 5-28-1888, d. 3-28-1953)**
**SERVICE:** Canton Bulldogs 1915-17, 1919-20;
Cleveland Indians 1921; Oorang Indians 1922-23;
Rock Island Independents 1924; New York Giants 1925;
Canton Bulldogs 1926; Chicago Cardinals 1928.
Though Thorpe was past his prime when he began
playing professional football, he still played for 12
years and led the Canton Bulldogs to championships
in 1916, '17 and '19. The most telling statistical measure of his ability in football comes from his days at
the Carlisle Indian School, when he scored 25 touchdowns in leading Carlisle to the national collegiate

championship. He was a runner of stunning speed
and an exceptional kicker, and he brought popularity
to the game when its survival was in question.

**Y.A. Tittle, QB (b. 10-24-26)**
**SERVICE:** Baltimore Colts 1948-50; San Francisco
49ers 1951-60; New York Giants 1961-64.
**CAREER STATS:** 2,427 comp.; 33,070 yds.; 242 TDs.
Tittle had an illustrious 13-year career behind him
when he joined the Giants in 1961. After unseating
the popular Charley Conerly for the starting job, Tittle
led the Giants to the division title and earned Most
Valuable Player honors. The next season he threw 33
touchdown passes, 13 more than he had ever thrown,
and in 1963, at age 37, he threw 36 TD passes and
was the league's overall passing champion.

**George Trafton, C
(b. 12-6-1896, d. 9-5-1971)**
**SERVICE:** Decatur Staleys 1920; Chicago Staleys 1921;
Chicago Bears 1922-32.
By all accounts, Trafton's rough style of play made
opponents angry, but he was also an innovative player who was the first center to use a one-hand snap.
During his 13-year career, he played for only one
team—the Staleys later became the Bears—a rare
occurrence in the early days of pro football.

**Charley Trippi, HB-QB (b. 12-14-22)**
**SERVICE:** Chicago Cardinals 1947-55.
**CAREER STATS:** 687 att.; 3,506 yds.; 23 TDs.
Trippi, an all-America from the University of Georgia,
was a major figure in the war between the AAFC and
the NFL and his signing by the Cardinals was a big
blow to the AAFC. He was a versatile performer,
leading the Cardinals to the championship in his
rookie year, rushing for 206 yards and two TDs in the
title game. Later in his career he played quarterback,
and during his last two years, defensive back.

**Emlen Tunnell, DB (b. 3-29-25, d. 7-22-75)**
**SERVICE:** New York Giants 1948-58; Green Bay
Packers 1959-61.
**CAREER STATS:** 79 int.; 4 TDs.
The first black player on the Giants, Tunnell was an
elusive runner after interceptions and on punt and
kickoff returns. He never led the league in pickoffs,
but his 79 career interceptions ranks second alltime.
He did lead the league in punt return yardage for
three straight years in the early 1950s.

**Clyde (Bulldog) Turner, C-LB (b. 11-10-19)**
**SERVICE:** Chicago Bears 1940-52.
**CAREER STATS:** 16 int.; 2 TDs.
Turner was an all-NFL selection six times during the
1940s, when the Bears won four championships. As
a linebacker, he had his finest season in 1942 when
he intercepted a league-leading eight passes.
Blessed with exceptional speed, Turner also saw
action at running back and once returned an interceptions 96 yards for a touchdown.

**Johnny Unitas, QB (b. 5-7-33)**
**SERVICE:** Baltimore Colts 1956-72; San Diego
Chargers 1973.
**CAREER STATS:** 2,830 comp.; 40,239 yds.; 290 TDs.
Cut by the Pittsburgh Steelers, Unitas played semi-
pro football for a year before joining the Colts as a

backup. When the starter was hurt, Unitas got his chance and eventually became one of the greatest quarterbacks in history. He was at his best in the 1958 championship game, when he directed an 84-yard drive for a tying field goal and then an 80-yard drive in overtime to win the game. He threw touchdown passes in a record 47 consecutive games from 1956 to '60. For four seasons from 1957 through '60, he led the league in touchdown passes. He was Player of the Year three times, in 1959, '64 and '67.

## Gene Upshaw, G (b. 8-15-45)
**SERVICE:** Oakland Raiders 1967-81.
As a 6'5", 255-pound pulling guard on the Raiders' powerful sweeps, Upshaw was a fearsome sight. He started all but one game in his 15 seasons with the Raiders and played in six Pro Bowls.

## Norm Van Brocklin, QB (b. 3-15-26, d. 5-2-83)
**SERVICE:** Los Angeles Rams 1949-57; Philadelphia Eagles 1958-60.
**CAREER STATS:** 1,553 comp.; 23,611 yds.; 173 TDs.
Van Brocklin alternated with Bob Waterfield and other quarterbacks through much of his career with the Rams, but in spite of that, he won the individual passing crown three times. In 1951 he passed for 554 yards in a game against the New York Yanks, a record that still stands. After being traded to the Eagles in 1960, he led the team to the NFL title.

## Steve Van Buren, HB (b. 12-28-20)
**SERVICE:** Philadelphia Eagles 1944-51.
**CAREER STATS:** 1,320 att.; 5,860 yds.; 69 TDs.
A powerful, punishing runner, Van Buren was the key to the Eagles' 1948 and 1949 NFL championship teams. He led the league in rushing both years—as well as in two other seasons—and in the title games he rushed for 198 and 196 yards respectively. He also led the league in rushing touchdowns four times.

## Doak Walker, HB (b. 1-1-27)
**SERVICE:** Detroit Lions 1950-55.
**CAREER STATS:** 309 rush. att.; 1,520 yds.; 152 rec.; 2,539 yds; 34 total TDs; 534 pts.
Though he played for only five seasons, Walker finished his career as the third leading scorer of all time. His versatility was legendary. In addition to rushing and receiving, he returned punts and kick-offs, passed occasionally, punted and even played defense, nabbing two interceptions in his career. He twice led the league in scoring.

## Bill Walsh, Coach (b. 11-30-31)
**SERVICE:** San Francisco 49ers 1979-88.
**CAREER RECORD:** 102–63–1; three Super Bowl wins.
Taking over a San Francisco team that went 2–14 in 1978, Walsh led the 49ers to their first Super Bowl title in 1981. They also won the Super Bowl in both 1985 and '89. Walsh then retired from NFL coaching. In 1992, after spending three years as an analyst for NBC-TV, Walsh returned to Stanford, where he had begun his coaching career, and led the Cardinal to a 10–3 record and a win over Penn State in the Blockbuster Bowl.

## Paul Warfield, WR (b. 11-28-42)
**SERVICE:** Cleveland 1964-69, 1976-77; Miami Dolphins 1970-74.
**CAREER STATS:** 427 rec.; 8,565 yds.; 85 TDs.
Warfield was a graceful, speedy receiver, who often exhibited his best moves after he caught the football. It was not unusual to see Warfield turn an opponent completely around with an effective fake. He twice led the league in touchdown catches.

## Bob Waterfield, QB (b. 7-26-20, d. 3-25-83)
**SERVICE:** Cleveland Rams 1945; Los Angeles Rams 1946-52.
**CAREER STATS:** 814 comp.; 11,849 yds.; 98 TDs.
In his rookie season, Waterfield was named the league's Most Valuable Player as he led the league in touchdown passes and quarterbacked the Rams to a 15–14 victory over the Redskins in the NFL Championship Game. The next year he improved to 18 touchdown passes, again leading the league. He was also a superior punter with a 42.4 career average.

## Arnie Weinmeister, DT (b. 3-23-23)
**SERVICE:** New York Yankees (AAFC) 1948-49; New York Giants 1950-53.
Though a sizable 6'4" and 235 pounds, Weinmeister had oustanding speed, regularly roaming all over the field, forcing quarterbacks to hurry their passes and pulling down runners from behind. He left American pro football after only six season to return to his native Canada and play in the CFL.

## Bill Willis, MG (b. 10-5-21)
**SERVICE:** Cleveland Browns 1946-53.
As one of the first blacks to play pro football since the early 1930s, Willis attracted a lot of attention. He quickly gained acclaim for his abilities as well. He was lightning-quick off the defensive line and superb at tracking down running backs on sweeps.

## Larry Wilson, S (b. 3-24-38)
**SERVICE:** St. Louis Cardinals 1960-72.
**CAREER STATS:** 52 int.; 5 TDs.
Quarterbacks in the 1960s got accustomed to seeing Wilson's craggy face staring right at them as he prepared for one of his patented safety blitzes. He played in eight Pro Bowl games and led the league in interceptions in 1966 with 10.

## Alex Wojciechowicz, C-LB (b. 8-12-15, d. 7-13-92)
**SERVICE:** Detroit Lions 1938-46; Philadelphia Eagles 1946-50.
**CAREER STATS:** 16 int.
First gaining fame as one of Fordham's Seven Blocks of Granite, Wojciechowicz was an anchor at center and linebacker for the Lions and, later, for the Eagles. He had sure hands on pass coverage, intercepting seven passes in 1944.

## Willie Wood, S (b. 12-23-36)
**SERVICE:** Green Bay 1960-71.
**CAREER STATS:** 48 int.
Only 5'10" and 190 pounds, Wood was known nevertheless for his willingness to take on anybody on the field and for his great leaping ability. A ferocious hitter, he particularly like to tangle with opposing tight ends. He led the league in interceptions in 1962 with nine.

# College Football

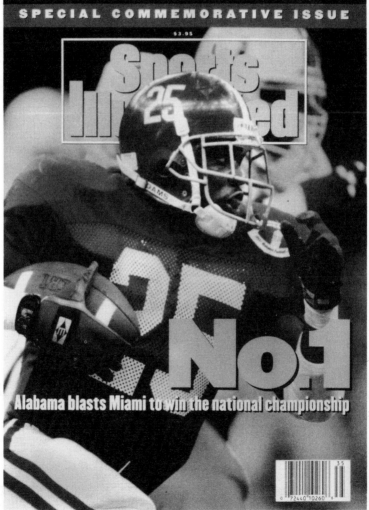

SPECIAL COMMEMORATIVE ISSUE

$3.95

*Sports Illustrated*

No1

Alabama blasts Miami to win the national championship

AL TIELEMANS

# The Tide Rolled In

*Alabama defeated Miami to become the national champion in a
season of surprises in college football* | by AUSTIN MURPHY

**W**IRE TO WIRE, IT WAS A
season of surprises. Ask
Jack Crowe, the former
Arkansas coach who got
the ax after a single game,
a humiliating 10–3 loss to
The Citadel. Ask former
Washington quarterback Billy Joe Hobert,
who discovered that yes, there *was* a prob-
lem with accepting no-interest, five-figure
loans from a pal's relatives. Ask Lamar
Thomas, the talented, loquacious Miami
wide receiver who on New Year's night in
the Louisiana Superdome thought he was
home free.

Thomas became a symbol of his team's
stunning downfall. After hauling in a pass
from Gino Torretta in the Sugar Bowl, the
lanky wideout had clear sailing to the end
zone until—what's this?—he was run down
and stripped of the ball by Alabama cornerback George Teague. Teague's larceny was
college football's play of the season. It
broke Miami's spirit and provided the

Crimson Tide with an instant slogan for its
34–13 win over the defending national
champion Hurricanes: We'll take that!

It took the Crimson Tide an even 100
years to win this, its 12th national football
championship. Miami had won four from
1983 through '91 alone. The Hurricanes
had also been stunned by Penn State in the
'87 Fiesta Bowl with a title on the line. Thus
did Alabama serve the ever braggadocious
Hurricanes with their second cosmic come-
uppance in six years.

Getting the nation's top two teams into a
title game was an upset in itself. Before the
newfangled, untested Bowl Coalition—
designed to produce a No. 1 versus No. 2
matchup—could work, traditionally back-
stabbing bowl representatives would be
forced to cooperate for the common good.
Remarkably, they did ... for the most part.

While the bowl system, which had been
threatened with extinction by a playoff
system, was strengthened, several head
coaches lost influence. Joining Crowe in the

**When Teague stripped Thomas of the ball and a sure six points, he broke Miami's spirit.**

unemployment line was 16-year Tennessee coach Johnny Majors, a former All-America halfback at Tennessee. Majors was dumped despite an 8–3 regular-season record in a rebuilding year in which he had missed the first three games while recuperating from heart surgery. Critics heaped scorn on Volunteer athletic director Doug Dickey, for such a heartless move and on Majors' replacement, assistant head coach Phil Fulmer, whom they accused—but never proved guilty—of unseemly maneuvering for the job. After Southern Cal's stunning 24–7 loss to Fresno State in the Freedom Bowl (USC's seniors had been so insulted by the prospect of having to play the lowly Bulldogs that they had to be talked out of boycotting the bowl), Trojan coach Larry Smith was sacrificed to quell alumni outrage.

Coaches were getting heat from both sides: their bosses and their underlings. Players in at least four programs fomented rebellions. After losing their first three games the Tigers of Memphis State boycotted practice one day, demanding the firing of authoritarian head coach Chuck Stobart. Stobart stayed. The Tigers won four straight. After an 0–5 start, South Carolina players called for the firing of head coach Sparky Woods. But Woods' job was saved by an earringed, longhaired true freshman quarterback named Steve Taneyhill, who guaranteed reporters that the Gamecocks would not lose another game. He was wrong—they went 5–1 the rest of the way, falling to Florida 14–9. Taneyhill has since promised that his team will go 11–0 in '93.

The off-season event with potentially the most resounding impact occurred in early February, with the stroke of an 18-year-old's pen. Scott Bentley signed a letter of intent to attend Florida State. The Seminoles finally had themselves a kicker.

Many college football followers felt that the Seminoles concluded the 1992 season playing the best football in the country. But for the second year running, Florida State had dropped a game to Miami by missing a makable last-second field goal. Which is why Florida State fans were so cheered by the news that Bentley, the top schoolboy kicker in the country, from Aurora, Colo., had snubbed Notre Dame and signed with the Seminoles. Bentley booted seven field goals of at least 50 yards in high school; 34

**Dan Mowrey's Miami miss: a disaster Seminole fans hope Bentley will render obsolete.**

of his kickoffs sailed through the uprights. His task will be made even easier next season by a rule change moving the hashmarks 20 yards closer to the middle of the field.

Perhaps, this Oct. 6 in Tallahassee, if the Seminoles find themselves within field goal range in a close game, Bentley will help Florida State do what it has not been able to do since 1989—beat Miami—and give Bobby Bowden the only significant achievement that has eluded him in 27 years of college coaching, a national title.

The anemia of Miami's offense in the Sugar Bowl had been prefigured by its performance over a three-game stretch earlier in the season. Against Arizona, the Hurricanes were held to two rushing yards, but eked out an 8–7 victory, thanks to a last-second Wildcat field goal attempt that missed by two feet. After squeaking past Florida State the next week, the Hurricanes flew north, to State College, Pa., where for the third straight Saturday they owed victory to an ornery defense and the vagaries of the human instep. Penn State kicker Craig Fayak had his first field goal attempt

blocked, and pulled his second, a 20-yard chip shot, wide left. Miami won 17–14.

In that three-game gantlet Torretta completed 57 of 125 passes, and the Hurricane offense scored just four touchdowns. Miami coach Dennis Erickson said he "could care less." Since the beginning of the previous season, Erickson pointed out, "Gino is 17–0." And for the second straight season the Hurricanes looked to be the best team in the country.

Only Washington could dispute that. The Huskies, with whom Miami had shared the '91 national championship, were also undefeated. It had been apparent from the beginning of the season, however, that this was an inferior edition—particularly on defense. For their '91 success Washington owed a large debt to Steve Emtman, the junior defensive tackle who left college after the season and was the first pick in that spring's NFL draft.

But it was another large debt that began the unraveling of the '92 Huskies. Two days before Washington's Nov. 7 game at Arizona, part-time starting quarterback Hobert was suspended from the team for having accepted three loans, totaling $50,000, from the father-in-law of a friend. Hobert blew the dough on guns, good times and a new Camaro, which he equipped with a $4,000 sound system. Borrowing the money "wasn't the smartest thing I've ever done, because I ended up blowing it," said Hobert. It also got him thrown off the team. Hobert's folly was thrown into even sharper relief when it was learned that his benefactor was … a rocket scientist.

With Hobert *finito* as a Husky, part-time starter Mark Brunell had the starting job all to himself against Arizona. A swarming Wildcat defense anchored by nosetackle Rob Waldrop forced four Washington turnovers, limited the Huskies to a field goal and spoiled their hopes of repeating as national champions in a 16–3 upset. Embattled and distracted by the Hobert scandal—in addition to several other embarassments to the program—the Huskies would go on to drop two more games.

PETER READ MILLER

**Hobert learned a hard lesson: Don't take no-interest loans from the family of a friend.**

During 'Bama's game against Louisiana State, news of Washington's loss reached the Alabama players. The Tide poured it on, taming the Tigers 31–11, improving their record to 8–0 and leapfrogging from No. 6 in the AP poll to No. 2. By Thanksgiving two obstacles stood between the Tide and a No. 1 versus No. 2 Sugar Bowl showdown with Miami. The first was its annual Turkey Day jihad against Auburn. The Tigers gained added incentive when, on the eve of the game, 12-year head coach Pat Dye resigned, citing poor health and a pending NCAA investigation. Inspired, Auburn held Alabama to a scoreless tie at halftime. But on the first series of the second half, 'Bama cornerback Antonio Langham went 61 yards with an interception for the winning touchdown.

Langham reprised his heroics nine days later. His fourth-quarter interception return

RICHARD MACKSON

against Florida won for Alabama the inaugural Southeastern Conference Championship Game and thus a Sugar Bowl berth. Having expanded to 12 members in 1990, the SEC split into eastern and western divisions and scheduled, beginning with the '92 season, a title game between the division champs. It was a great deal for the SEC, which reaped $6 million selling the TV rights to the game. Not all the players and coaches could muster as much enthusiasm. "We've won 11 games," said 'Bama coach Gene Stallings before beating Florida, "and we still haven't won anything."

The Hurricanes were coming off a thrashing of San Diego State, a game which had been hyped as the Heisman Bowl—featuring leading Heisman candidates Torretta (25–1 as a starter; over 7,000 career passing yards) and sophomore tailback Marshall Faulk (15 touchdowns, nation-leading 163 rushing yards per game). The game, alas, came to be known as Dud Bowl I as the Aztecs lost 63–17, with Torretta throwing for 310 yards. Faulk, nursing a sprained right knee, did not play, virtually handing the 58th Heisman to Torretta, who won it

**Faulk had another fine season but finished behind Torretta in the Heisman balloting.**

with 1,400 points to Faulk's 1,080. Finishing third, with 982 points, was Georgia tailback Garrison Hearst, who finished the season with an average of 6.8 yards per carry.

To the delight of the engineers of the Bowl Coalition, a No. 1 versus No. 2 matchup fell neatly into place. Once Miami and Alabama were locked into the Sugar Bowl, however, the spirit of cooperation among the fraternity of tasteless-blazer-clad Bowl reps began to fray. As Southwestern Conference champs, the 12–0, fourth-ranked Aggies of Texas A&M received an automatic invitation to the Cotton Bowl. As a member of the coalition, the raison d'être of which was to ensure better bowl matchups than in past seasons, the Cotton Bowl was obligated to invite the best team available: Florida State. After the Miami loss, the Seminoles had switched to a no-back, shotgun attack that better enabled quarterback Charlie Ward—starting point guard on the Seminole hoops team—to exploit his multiple talents. The

Seminoles started to flat out annihilate defenses.

But Cotton Bowl chairman Jim (Hoss) Brock could not resist the better television ratings his bowl would reap with an invitation to No. 5 Notre Dame. The ensuing howls of outrage from the Aggies, who saw their slim national championship hopes evanesce, gave way to whimpers of embarrassment when, a week before the game, A&M head coach R.C. Slocum was forced to suspend four players, including starting tailback Greg Hill, pending an investigation into irregularities with their school-arranged summer jobs. All the A&M national title talk rang hollow after Notre Dame's resounding 28–3 victory.

The SWC sent a meager two teams to bowl games, one less than the Big Eight and the Big Ten, which critics referred to as "Michigan and the Nine Dwarves." Among the best-represented conferences in the postseason was, surprisingly, the WAC. Five Western Athletic Conference teams went bowling. (The Pac-10 and the SEC sent six teams apiece to bowls.) The Wolverines, who won the Big Ten despite three ties, salvaged a modicum of respect for their once mighty conference by beating Washington in the Rose Bowl 38–31. Elsewhere the Big Ten took gas as usual, with Illinois losing to Hawaii in the Holiday Bowl; Ohio State lost the Citrus to Georgia 21–14, then lost junior running back Robert Smith, who announced that he would make himself available in the NFL draft. This news would not have been extraordinary—in all, 46 underclassmen made themselves eligible— had Smith not *sat out* his sophomore season after accusing coaches of encouraging him to skip classes to attend practice. Now Smith, who was taken in the first round by the Minnesota Vikings, had decided that school could wait, after all.

And in what was billed as the "Battle of the Geniuses," Joe Paterno's Nittany Lions, who commence playing a Big Ten football schedule in '93, were humbled by Bill Walsh–led Stanford, 24–3 in the Blockbuster Bowl. All-everything wideout O.J. McDuffie

was shut down by the Cardinal's cornerback Darrien Gordon, who said after the game that as McDuffie's frustration mounted, the receiver took to shouting at Gordon, "Hey man, I'm an All-American!" It was Penn State's fourth defeat in their last seven bowl appearances: The Nittany Lions should feel right at home in the Big Ten.

The Sugar Bowl would be Torretta's best chance to vindicate his Heisman electors and make believers of the large body of players, coaches and members of the media who felt that the fifth-year senior was not even the best player on his own team. The supreme overconfidence with which the Hurricanes came into the game was personified by Thomas, the mouthy receiver, who questioned the manliness of Alabama's defensive backs, who had played lots of

**Reggie Brooks rambled for 115 yards in Notre Dame's 28–3 thumping of the Aggies.**

DAMIAN STROHMEYER

PETER READ MILLER

Bowl. He threw three interceptions, each of which led to an Alabama touchdown. "In the second quarter he looked over at me and froze for a second," recalled Tide defensive end John Copeland. "I saw fear."

Pick No. 3 was a 31-yard interception return for a touchdown by Teague that made the score 27–6. The play was a highlight film effort, to be sure, but bloodless and uninspired next to the heroics Teague was about to perform. With less than 10 minutes left in the third quarter, Thomas, who had already lost one fumble, gathered in a pass from Torretta at the Miami 36-yard line and had clear sailing to the goal line. Teague overtook him at the Alabama 15. Not content to make the tackle, he reached over Thomas's right shoulder and stole the ball, effecting a remarkable, full-gallop fumble recovery. "Probably the worst moment I've ever had playing football," said Thomas.

Thus did Teague break the Hurricanes' spirit, just as Alabama broke the back of the nascent Hurricane dynasty. As far as cultivating a dynasty of its own, Alabama has an uphill fight. Just after 'Bama's triumph, new Auburn coach Terry Bowden announced his intention of sweet-talking the state's best recruits while the Crimson Tide celebrated. Sure enough, come signing day, two of the nation's top prospects, jumbo offensive tackle Willie Anderson of Whistler and tight end Jesse McCovery from St. Elmo, signed with Auburn.

But the best recruiting was done not by Terry Bowden, but by his old man, down in Tallahassee. A consensus of experts agreed that Bowden had reeled in the best class in the nation, including five of the top 10 players in talent-rich Florida. And one from Aurora, Colo. Beware Florida State in '93. The Seminoles finally have a kicker.

zone defense that season. "Real men play man," said Thomas. Not that he questioned the widsom of staying in safe zones against Miami's receivers, whom Thomas had dubbed the Ruthless Posse and whom he had anointed "probably the best receiving corps ever assembled."

The best receiving corps ever assembled got itself taken apart in the Superdome. When Miami had the ball the Crimson Tide put five, six, sometimes even seven defensive backs on the field. Occasionally the Tide brought all 11 men up to the line of scrimmage—a naked challenge to the Ruthless Posse: beat us deep if you can. "Sometimes we'd play man, sometimes we'd show man and drop into zone," said cornerback Tommy Johnson. "Torretta didn't know *what* was going on."

Torretta had gone 26–1 as a starter by deciphering coverages and keeping his cool. Both talents deserted him in the Sugar

## Final Polls

### Associated Press

| | Record | Pts | Head Coach | SI Preseason Top 20 |
|---|---|---|---|---|
| 1............................Alabama (62) | 13-0-0 | 1550 | Gene Stallings | 7 |
| 2............................Florida State | 11-1-0 | 1470 | Bobby Bowden | 4 |
| 3............................Miami | 11-1-0 | 1410 | Dennis Erickson | 1 |
| 4............................Notre Dame | 10-1-1 | 1375 | Lou Holtz | 6 |
| 5............................Michigan | 9-0-3 | 1266 | Gary Moeller | 8 |
| 6............................Syracuse | 10-2-0 | 1209 | Paul Pasqualoni | 11 |
| 7............................Texas A&M | 12-1-0 | 1167 | R.C. Slocum | 14 |
| 8............................Georgia | 10-2-0 | 1159 | Ray Goff | 10 |
| 9............................Stanford | 10-3-0 | 1058 | Bill Walsh | |
| 10..........................Florida | 9-4-0 | 931 | Steve Spurrier | 3 |
| 11..........................Washington | 9-3-0 | 892 | Don James | 5 |
| 12..........................Tennessee | 9-3-0 | 819 | Johnny Majors | |
| 13..........................Colorado | 9-2-1 | 818 | Bill McCartney | 12 |
| 14..........................Nebraska | 9-3-0 | 771 | Tom Osborne | 17 |
| 15..........................Washington State | 9-3-0 | 618 | Mike Price | |
| 16..........................Mississippi | 9-3-0 | 580 | Billy Brewer | |
| 17..........................North Carolina State | 9-3-1 | 582 | Dick Sheridan | |
| 18..........................Ohio State | 8-3-1 | 493 | John Cooper | 13 |
| 19..........................North Carolina | 9-3-0 | 491 | Mack Brown | |
| 20..........................Hawaii | 11-2-0 | 354 | Bob Wagner | |
| 21..........................Boston College | 8-3-1 | 314 | Tom Coughlin | |
| 22..........................Kansas | 8-4-0 | 183 | Glenn Mason | |
| 23..........................Mississippi State | 7-5-0 | 167 | Jackie Sherrill | 18 |
| 24..........................Fresno State | 9-4-0 | 124 | Jim Sweeney | |
| 25..........................Wake Forest | 8-4-0 | 107 | Bill Dooley | |

Note: As voted by panel of 60 sportswriters and broadcasters following bowl games (1st-place votes in parentheses).

### USA Today/CNN

| | Pts | Prev Rank | | Pts | Prev Rank |
|---|---|---|---|---|---|
| 1..............Alabama | 1500 | 2 | 14.............Nebraska | 749 | 10 |
| 2..............Florida State | 1422 | 4 | 15.............North Carolina State | 572 | 12 |
| 3..............Miami | 1356 | 1 | 16.............Mississippi | 538 | 19 |
| 4..............Notre Dame | 1327 | 5 | 17.............Washington State | 495 | 18 |
| 5..............Michigan | 1231 | 7 | 18.............North Carolina | 450 | 20 |
| 6..............Texas A&M | 1149 | 3 | 19.............Ohio State | 426 | 14 |
| 7..............Syracuse | 1135 | 9 | 20.............Hawaii | 424 | 24 |
| 8..............Georgia | 1134 | 8 | 21.............Boston College | 303 | 16 |
| 9..............Stanford | 982 | 13 | 22.............Fresno State | 243 | — |
| 10............Washington | 846 | 11 | 23.............Kansas | 201 | — |
| 11............Florida | 845 | 15 | 24.............Penn State | 138 | 21 |
| 12............Tennessee | 818 | 17 | 25.............Wake Forest | 128 | — |
| 13............Colorado | 806 | 6 | | | |

Note: As voted by panel of 60 Division I-A head coaches; 25 points for 1st, 24 for 2nd, etc. (1st-place votes in parentheses).

## Bowls and Playoffs

### NCAA Division I-A Bowl Results

| Date | Bowl | Result | Payout/Team ($) | Attendance |
|---|---|---|---|---|
| 12-18-92..............Las Vegas | | Bowling Green 35, Nevada 34 | 150,000 | 15,476 |
| 12-25-92..............Aloha | | Kansas 23, Brigham Young 20 | 750,000 | 42,933 |
| 12-29-92..............Copper | | Washington State 31, Utah 28 | 650,000 | 40,876 |
| 12-29-92..............Freedom | | Fresno State 24, Southern California 7 | 650,000 | 50,745 |
| 12-30-92..............Holiday | | Hawaii 27, Illinois 17 | 1.5 million | 44,457 |
| 12-31-92..............Independence | | Wake Forest 39, Oregon 35 | 650,000 | 31,337 |
| 12-31-92..............Hancock | | Baylor 20, Arizona 15 | 1.1 million | 41,622 |

## NCAA Division I-A Bowl Results

| Date | Bowl | Result | Payout/Team ($) | Attendance |
|---|---|---|---|---|
| 12-31-92 | Gator | Florida 27, N Carolina St 10 | 1.6 million | 71,233 |
| 12-31-92 | Liberty | Mississippi 13, Air Force 0 | 900,000 | 32,107 |
| 1-1-93 | Hall of Fame | Tennessee 38, Boston College 23 | 1 million | 52,056 |
| 1-1-93 | Citrus | Georgia 21, Ohio St 14 | 2 million | 65,861 |
| 1-1-93 | Cotton | Notre Dame 28, Texas A&M 3 | 3 million | 71,615 |
| 1-1-92 | Blockbuster | Stanford 24, Penn St 3 | 1.525 million | 45,554 |
| 1-1-93 | Fiesta | Syracuse 26, Colorado 22 | 3 million | 70,224 |
| 1-1-93 | Rose | Michigan 38, Washington 31 | 6.5 million | 94,236 |
| 1-1-93 | Orange | Florida St 27, Nebraska 14 | 4.2 million | 57,324 |
| 1-1-93 | Sugar | Alabama 38, Miami 13 | 3.8 million | 76,789 |
| 1-2-93 | Peach | N Carolina 21, Mississippi St 17 | 1 million | 69,125 |

## NCAA Division I-AA Championship Boxscore

| | | | | |
|---|---|---|---|---|
| Youngstown St | 0 | 0 | 14 | 14—28 |
| Marshall | 0 | 14 | 14 | 3—31 |

### SECOND QUARTER

MU: Mark Bartrum 6 pass from Michael Payton (Willy Merrick kick), 4:27.
MU: Orlando Hatchett 5 run (Merrick kick), 11:30.

### THIRD QUARTER

MU: Glenn Pedro 1 run (Merrick kick), 4:47.
MU: Hatchett 22 pass from Payton (Merrick kick), 9:14.
YSU: Herb Williams 30 pass from Nick Cothran (Jeff Wilkins kick), 11:19.
YSU: Tamron Smith 4 run (Wilkins kick), 14:44.

### FOURTH QUARTER

YSU: Smith 1 run (Wilkins kick), 2:56.
YSU: Smith 10 run (Wilkins kick), 12:32.
MU: FG Merrick 22 FG, 14:50.

| | YSU | MU |
|---|---|---|
| First downs | 17 | 26 |
| Rushing yardage | 166 | 185 |
| Passing yardage | 256 | 270 |
| Return yardage | 35 | 70 |
| Passes (comp-att-int) | 25-40-1 | 18-31-2 |
| Punts (no.-avg) | 6-41.6 | 5-39.8 |
| Fumbles (no.-lost) | 0-0 | 1-1 |
| Penalties (no.-yards) | 3-20 | 7-40 |

## Small College Championship Summaries

### NCAA DIVISION II

**First round:** Ferris St 19, Edinboro 15; New Haven 38, West Chester 26; Jacksonville St 41, Savannah St 16; North Alabama 33, Hampton 21; Texas A&I 22, Western St 13; Portland St 42, UC Davis 28; Pittsburg St 26, North Dakota 21; North Dakota St 42, Northeast Missouri St 7.
**Quarterfinals:** New Haven 35, Ferris 13; Jacksonville St 14, North Alabama 12; Portland St 35, Texas A&I 30; Pittsburg 38, North Dakota St 37 (OT).
**Semifinals:** Jacksonville St 46, New Haven 35; Pittsburg St 41, Portland St 38.
**Championship:** 12-12-92 Florence, AL

| | | | | |
|---|---|---|---|---|
| Pittsburg St | 6 | 7 | 0 | 0—13 |
| Jacksonville St | 0 | 10 | 7 | 0—17 |

### NCAA DIVISION III

**First round:** Mount Union 27, Dayton 10; Illinois Wesleyan 21, Aurora 12; Central Iowa 20, Carleton 8; Wisconsin-La Crosse 47, Redlands 26; Emory & Henry 17, Thomas More 0; Washington & Jefferson 33, Lycoming 0; Rowan 41, Worcester Tech 14; Buffalo St 28, Ithaca 26.
**Quarterfinals:** Mount Union 49, Illinois Wesleyan 27; Wisconsin-La Crosse 34, Central Iowa 9; Washington & Jefferson 51, Emory & Henry 15; Rowan 28, Buffalo St 19.
**Semifinals:** Wisconsin-La Crosse 29, Mount Union 24; Washington & Jefferson 18, Rowan 13.
**Championship:** 12-12-92 Bradenton, FL

| | | | | |
|---|---|---|---|---|
| Wisconsin-La Crosse | 0 | 14 | 2 | 0—16 |
| Washington & Jeff | 0 | 0 | 12 | 0—12 |

### NAIA DIVISION I PLAYOFFS

**First Round:** Central St (OH) 34, Harding (AR) 0; Central Arkansas 14, Soutwestern Oklahoma 2; Gardner-Webb (NC) 28, Concord (WV) 21; Shepherd (WV) 6, Carson-Newman (TN) 3.
**Semifinals:** Central St (OH) 30, Central Arkansas 23; Gardner-Webb (NC) 22, Shepherd (WV) 7.

**Championship:** 12-12-92 Boiling Springs, NC

| | | | | |
|---|---|---|---|---|
| Central St (OH) | 6 | 0 | 0 | 13—19 |
| Gardner-Webb (NC) | 2 | 14 | 0 | 0—16 |

### NAIA DIVISION II PLAYOFFS

**First round:** Baker (KS) 21, Northwestern (IA) 20; Benedictine (KS) 17, Hastings (NE) 15; Findlay (OH) 32, Georgetown (KY) 14; Hardin-Simmons (TX) 42, Howard Payne (TX) 28; Linfield (OR) 26, Western Washington 0; Minot St (ND) 31, Dakota Wesleyan (SD) 21; Pacific Lutheran (WA) 37, Montan Tech 0; Westminster (PA) 28, Friends (KS) 0.
**Quarterfinals:** Benedictine (KS) 21, Baker (KS) 14; Findlay (OH) 13, Westminster (PA) 7; Linfield (OR) 44, Pacific Lutheran (WA) 30; Minot St (ND) 21, Hardin-Simmons (TX) 14.
**Semifinals:** Findlay (OH) 27, Benedictine (KS) 24; Linfield (OR) 47, Minot St (ND) 12.

**Championship:** 12-19-92 Portland, OR

| | | | | |
|---|---|---|---|---|
| Findlay (OH) | 0 | 14 | 12 | 0—26 |
| Linfield (OR) | 7 | 0 | 0 | 6—13 |

## Heisman Memorial Trophy

| Player/School | Class | Pos | 1st | 2nd | 3rd | Total |
|---|---|---|---|---|---|---|
| Gino Torretta, Miami | Sr | QB | 310 | 179 | 112 | 1,400 |
| Marshall Faulk, San Diego St. | So | RB | 164 | 207 | 174 | 1,080 |
| Garrison Hearst, Georgia | Jr | RB | 140 | 196 | 170 | 982 |
| Marvin Jones, Florida St. | Jr | LB | 81 | 51 | 47 | 392 |
| Reggie Brooks, Notre Dame | Sr | RB | 42 | 53 | 62 | 294 |
| Charlie Ward, Florida St. | Jr | QB | 18 | 18 | 36 | 126 |
| Micheal Barrow, Miami | Sr | LB | 10 | 10 | 14 | 64 |
| Drew Bledsoe, Washington St. | Jr | QB | 6 | 8 | 14 | 48 |
| Glyn Milburn, Stanford | Sr | RB/KR | 5 | 11 | 10 | 47 |
| Eric Curry, Alabama | Sr | DE | 3 | 13 | 12 | 47 |

Note: Former Heisman winners and the media vote, with ballots allowing for 3 names (3 points for 1st, 2 for 2nd, 1 for 3rd).

## Offensive Players of the Year

Maxwell Award (Player)..............................Gino Torretta, Miami, QB
Walter Camp Player of the Year (Back).....Gino Torretta, Miami, QB
Davey O'Brien Award (QB)........................Gino Torretta, Miami, QB
Doak Walker Award (RB)..........................Garrison Hearst, Georgia, RB

## Other Awards

Vince Lombardi/Rotary Award (Lineman)..Marvin Jones, Florida St., LB
Outland Trophy (Interior lineman)..............Will Shields, Nebraska, OG
Butkus Award (Linebacker).......................Marvin Jones, Florida St, LB
Jim Thorpe Award (Defensive back)..........Deon Figures, Colorado, CB
Sporting News Player of the Year.............Marvin Jones, Miami, LB
Walter Payton Award (Div I-AA Player)......Michael Payton, Marshall, QB
Harlon Hill Trophy (Div II Player)...............Ronald Moore, Pittsburg St, RB

## Coaches' Awards

Walter Camp Award...................................Gene Stallings, Alabama
Eddie Robinson Award (Div I-AA).............Charlie Taaffe, Citadel
Bobby Dodd Award..................................Eddie Robinson, Grambling
Bear Bryant Award...................................Gene Stallings, Alabama

### AFCA COACHES OF THE YEAR

Division I-A.................................................Gene Stallings, Alabama
Division I-AA..............................................Charlie Taaffe, Citadel
Division II and NAIA Division I....................Bill Burgess, Jacksonville St
Division III and NAIA Division II..................John Luckhardt, Washington & Jefferson

## Football Writers Association of America All-America Team

### OFFENSE

Sean Dawkins, California, Jr...............Wide receiver
Ryan Yarborough, Wyoming, Jr.........Wide receiver
Chris Gedney, Syracuse, Sr...............Tight end
Lincoln Kennedy, Washington, Sr.......OL
Will Shields, Nebraska, Sr..................OL
Everett Lindsay, Mississippi, Sr..........OL
Willie Roaf, Louisiana Tech, Sr...........OL
Gino Torretta, Miami, Sr.....................Quarterback
Marshall Faulk, San Diego St, Soph....Running back
Garrison Hearst, Georgia, Jr..............Running back
Joe Allison, Memphis St, Jr................PK
Curtis Conway, Southern Cal, Jr.........Kick returner

### DEFENSE

Chris Hutchinson, Michigan, Sr..........DL
Rob Waldrop, Arizona, Jr...................DL
John Copeland, Alabama, Sr..............DL
Chris Slade, Virginia, Sr.....................DL
Marvin Jones, Florida St, Jr................Linebacker
Micheal Barrow, Miami, Sr.................Linebacker
Marcus Buckley, Texas A & M, Sr.......Linebacker
Carlton McDonald, Air Force, Sr.........Defensive back
Patrick Bates, Texas A & M, Jr...........Defensive back
Deon Figures. Colorado, Sr................Defensive back
Lance Gunn, Texas, Sr.......................Defensive back
Josh Miller, Arizona, Sr......................Punter

## Division I-A

### ATLANTIC COAST CONFERENCE

| | Conference | | | Full Season | | | |
|---|---|---|---|---|---|---|---|
| | W | L | T | W | L | T | Pct |
| Florida St | 8 | 0 | 0 | 10 | 1 | 0 | .909 |
| N Carolina St | 6 | 2 | 0 | 9 | 2 | 1 | .792 |
| N Carolina | 5 | 3 | 0 | 8 | 3 | 0 | .727 |
| Virginia | 4 | 4 | 0 | 7 | 4 | 0 | .636 |
| Wake Forest | 4 | 4 | 0 | 7 | 4 | 0 | .636 |
| Georgia Tech | 4 | 4 | 0 | 5 | 6 | 0 | .454 |
| Clemson | 3 | 5 | 0 | 5 | 6 | 0 | .454 |
| Maryland | 2 | 6 | 0 | 3 | 8 | 0 | .273 |
| Duke | 0 | 8 | 0 | 2 | 9 | 0 | .182 |

### BIG EAST CONFERENCE

| | Conference | | | Full Season | | | |
|---|---|---|---|---|---|---|---|
| | W | L | T | W | L | T | Pct |
| Miami | 4 | 0 | 0 | 11 | 0 | 0 | 1.000 |
| Syracuse | 6 | 1 | 0 | 9 | 2 | 0 | .818 |
| Rutgers | 4 | 2 | 0 | 7 | 4 | 0 | .636 |
| Boston College | 2 | 1 | 1 | 8 | 2 | 1 | .773 |
| W Virginia | 2 | 3 | 1 | 5 | 4 | 2 | .545 |
| Pittsburgh | 1 | 3 | 0 | 3 | 9 | 0 | .250 |
| Virginia Tech | 1 | 4 | 0 | 2 | 8 | 0 | .227 |
| Temple | 0 | 6 | 0 | 1 | 10 | 0 | .091 |

Note: As it was in 1991, the Big East champion is determined by the CNN/USA Today coaches' poll. Miami was ranked the highest and thereby recognized as conference champion. Beginning in 1993, the Big East will have a full round-robin schedule to determine its champion.

### BIG EIGHT CONFERENCE

| | Conference | | | Full Season | | | |
|---|---|---|---|---|---|---|---|
| | W | L | T | W | L | T | Pct |
| Nebraska | 6 | 1 | 0 | 9 | 2 | 0 | .818 |
| Colorado | 5 | 1 | 1 | 9 | 1 | 1 | .864 |
| Kansas | 4 | 3 | 0 | 7 | 4 | 0 | .636 |
| Oklahoma | 3 | 2 | 2 | 5 | 4 | 2 | .545 |
| Oklahoma St | 2 | 4 | 1 | 4 | 6 | 1 | .409 |
| Kansas St | 2 | 5 | 0 | 5 | 6 | 0 | .455 |
| Iowa St | 2 | 5 | 0 | 4 | 7 | 0 | .364 |
| Missouri | 2 | 5 | 0 | 3 | 8 | 0 | .273 |

### BIG TEN CONFERENCE

| | Conference | | | Full Season | | | |
|---|---|---|---|---|---|---|---|
| | W | L | T | W | L | T | Pct |
| Michigan | 6 | 0 | 2 | 8 | 0 | 3 | .864 |
| Ohio St | 5 | 2 | 1 | 8 | 2 | 1 | .773 |
| Michigan St | 5 | 3 | 0 | 5 | 6 | 0 | .455 |
| Illinois | 4 | 3 | 1 | 6 | 4 | 1 | .591 |
| Iowa | 4 | 4 | 0 | 5 | 7 | 0 | .417 |
| Indiana | 3 | 5 | 0 | 5 | 6 | 0 | .455 |
| Wisconsin | 3 | 5 | 0 | 5 | 6 | 0 | .455 |
| Purdue | 3 | 5 | 0 | 4 | 7 | 0 | .364 |
| Northwestern | 3 | 5 | 0 | 3 | 8 | 0 | .273 |
| Minnesota | 2 | 6 | 0 | 2 | 9 | 0 | .182 |

### BIG WEST CONFERENCE

| | Conference | | | Full Season | | | |
|---|---|---|---|---|---|---|---|
| | W | L | T | W | L | T | Pct |
| Nevada | 5 | 1 | 0 | 7 | 4 | 0 | .636 |
| San Jose St | 4 | 2 | 0 | 7 | 4 | 0 | .636 |
| Utah St | 4 | 2 | 0 | 5 | 6 | 0 | .455 |
| New Mexico St | 3 | 3 | 0 | 6 | 5 | 0 | .545 |
| NV-Las Vegas | 3 | 3 | 0 | 6 | 5 | 0 | .545 |
| Pacific | 2 | 4 | 0 | 3 | 8 | 0 | .273 |
| Cal St-Fullerton | 0 | 6 | 0 | 2 | 9 | 0 | .182 |

## Division I-A (Cont.)

### MID-AMERICAN CONFERENCE

| | Conference | | | Full Season | | | |
|---|---|---|---|---|---|---|---|
| | W | L | T | W | L | T | Pct |
| Bowling Green | 8 | 0 | 0 | 9 | 2 | 0 | .818 |
| Western Michigan | 6 | 3 | 0 | 7 | 3 | 1 | .682 |
| Toledo | 5 | 3 | 0 | 8 | 3 | 0 | .727 |
| Akron | 5 | 3 | 0 | 7 | 3 | 1 | .682 |
| Miami (Ohio) | 5 | 3 | 0 | 6 | 4 | 1 | .591 |
| Ball St | 5 | 4 | 0 | 5 | 6 | 0 | .455 |
| Central Michigan | 4 | 5 | 0 | 5 | 6 | 0 | .455 |
| Kent State | 2 | 7 | 0 | 2 | 9 | 0 | .182 |
| Eastern Michigan | 1 | 7 | 0 | 1 | 10 | 0 | .091 |
| Ohio | 1 | 7 | 0 | 1 | 10 | 0 | .091 |

### PACIFIC-10 CONFERENCE

| | Conference | | | Full Season | | | |
|---|---|---|---|---|---|---|---|
| | W | L | T | W | L | T | Pct |
| Washington | 6 | 2 | 0 | 9 | 2 | 0 | .818 |
| Stanford | 6 | 2 | 0 | 9 | 3 | 0 | .750 |
| Washington St | 5 | 3 | 0 | 8 | 3 | 0 | .727 |
| Southern Cal | 5 | 3 | 0 | 6 | 4 | 1 | .591 |
| Arizona | 4 | 3 | 1 | 6 | 4 | 1 | .591 |
| Oregon | 4 | 4 | 0 | 6 | 5 | 0 | .545 |
| Arizona St | 4 | 4 | 0 | 6 | 5 | 0 | .545 |
| UCLA | 3 | 5 | 0 | 6 | 5 | 0 | .545 |
| California | 2 | 6 | 0 | 4 | 7 | 0 | .364 |
| Oregon St | 0 | 7 | 1 | 1 | 9 | 1 | .136 |

### SOUTHEASTERN CONFERENCE

| | Conference | | | Full Season | | | |
|---|---|---|---|---|---|---|---|
| **East** | W | L | T | W | L | T | Pct |
| Florida* | 6 | 2 | 0 | 8 | 4 | 0 | .667 |
| Georgia | 6 | 2 | 0 | 9 | 2 | 0 | .818 |
| Tennessee | 5 | 3 | 0 | 8 | 3 | 0 | .727 |
| South Carolina | 3 | 5 | 0 | 5 | 6 | 0 | .455 |
| Vanderbilt | 2 | 6 | 0 | 4 | 7 | 0 | .364 |
| Kentucky | 2 | 6 | 0 | 4 | 7 | 0 | .364 |
| **West** | | | | | | | |
| Alabama* | 8 | 0 | 0 | 12 | 0 | 0 | 1.000 |
| Mississippi | 5 | 3 | 0 | 8 | 3 | 0 | .727 |
| Mississippi St | 4 | 4 | 0 | 7 | 4 | 0 | .636 |
| Arkansas | 3 | 4 | 1 | 3 | 7 | 1 | .318 |
| Auburn | 2 | 5 | 1 | 5 | 5 | 1 | .500 |
| Louisiana St | 1 | 7 | 0 | 2 | 9 | 0 | .182 |

*Overall record includes first SEC Championship Game in which Alabama defeated Florida, 28-21, on Dec 5.

### SOUTHWEST ATHLETIC CONFERENCE

| | Conference | | | Full Season | | | |
|---|---|---|---|---|---|---|---|
| | W | L | T | W | L | T | Pct |
| Texas A&M | 7 | 0 | 0 | 12 | 0 | 0 | 1.000 |
| Baylor | 4 | 3 | 0 | 6 | 5 | 0 | .545 |
| Rice | 4 | 3 | 0 | 6 | 5 | 0 | .545 |
| Texas | 4 | 3 | 0 | 6 | 5 | 0 | .545 |
| Texas Tech | 4 | 3 | 0 | 5 | 6 | 0 | .455 |
| Southern Meth | 2 | 5 | 0 | 5 | 6 | 0 | .455 |
| Houston | 2 | 5 | 0 | 4 | 7 | 0 | .364 |
| Texas Christian | 1 | 6 | 0 | 2 | 8 | 1 | .227 |

## Division I-A (Cont.)

### WESTERN ATHLETIC CONFERENCE

| | Conference | | | Full Season | | | |
|---|---|---|---|---|---|---|---|
| | W | L | T | W | L | T | Pct |
| Hawaii | 6 | 2 | 0 | 10 | 2 | 0 | .833 |
| Brigham Young | 6 | 2 | 0 | 8 | 4 | 0 | .667 |
| Fresno St | 6 | 2 | 0 | 8 | 4 | 0 | .667 |
| San Diego St | 5 | 3 | 0 | 5 | 5 | 1 | .500 |
| Air Force | 4 | 4 | 0 | 7 | 4 | 0 | .636 |
| Utah | 4 | 4 | 0 | 6 | 5 | 0 | .545 |
| Wyoming | 3 | 5 | 0 | 5 | 7 | 0 | .417 |
| Colorado St | 3 | 5 | 0 | 5 | 7 | 0 | .417 |
| New Mexico | 2 | 6 | 0 | 3 | 8 | 0 | .273 |
| UTEP | 1 | 7 | 0 | 1 | 10 | 0 | .091 |

### INDEPENDENTS

| | Full Season | | | |
|---|---|---|---|---|
| | W | L | T | Pct |
| Notre Dame | 9 | 1 | 1 | .864 |
| Penn St | 7 | 4 | 0 | .636 |
| Southern Miss | 7 | 4 | 0 | .636 |
| Memphis St | 6 | 5 | 0 | .545 |
| Army | 5 | 6 | 0 | .455 |
| E Carolina | 5 | 6 | 0 | .455 |
| Louisiana Tech | 5 | 6 | 0 | .455 |
| Louisville | 5 | 6 | 0 | .455 |
| Northern Illinois | 5 | 6 | 0 | .455 |
| Tulsa | 4 | 7 | 0 | .364 |
| Cincinnati | 3 | 8 | 0 | .273 |
| Arkansas St | 2 | 9 | 0 | .182 |
| Southwestern Louisiana | 2 | 9 | 0 | .182 |
| Tulane | 2 | 9 | 0 | .182 |
| Navy | 1 | 10 | 0 | .091 |

## Division I-AA

### BIG SKY CONFERENCE

| | Conference | | | Full Season | | | |
|---|---|---|---|---|---|---|---|
| | W | L | T | W | L | T | Pct |
| Idaho | 6 | 1 | 0 | 9 | 2 | 0 | .818 |
| Eastern Washington | 6 | 1 | 0 | 7 | 3 | 0 | .700 |
| Weber St | 4 | 3 | 0 | 6 | 5 | 0 | .545 |
| Montana | 4 | 3 | 0 | 6 | 5 | 0 | .545 |
| Boise St | 3 | 4 | 0 | 5 | 6 | 0 | .455 |
| Northern Arizona | 2 | 5 | 0 | 4 | 7 | 0 | .364 |
| Montana St | 2 | 5 | 0 | 4 | 7 | 0 | .364 |
| Idaho St | 1 | 6 | 0 | 3 | 8 | 0 | .273 |

### GATEWAY COLLEGIATE ATHLETIC CONFERENCE

| | Conference | | | Full Season | | | |
|---|---|---|---|---|---|---|---|
| | W | L | T | W | L | T | Pct |
| Northern Iowa | 5 | 1 | 0 | 10 | 1 | 0 | .909 |
| Western Illinois | 4 | 2 | 0 | 7 | 4 | 0 | .636 |
| SW Missouri St | 4 | 2 | 0 | 6 | 5 | 0 | .545 |
| Illinois St | 2 | 4 | 0 | 5 | 6 | 0 | .455 |
| Eastern Illinois | 2 | 4 | 0 | 5 | 6 | 0 | .455 |
| Southern Illinois | 2 | 4 | 0 | 4 | 7 | 0 | .364 |
| Indiana St | 2 | 4 | 0 | 4 | 7 | 0 | .364 |

## Division I-AA (Cont.)

### IVY GROUP

| | Conference | | | Full Season | | | |
|---|---|---|---|---|---|---|---|
| | W | L | T | W | L | T | Pct |
| Dartmouth | 6 | 1 | 0 | 8 | 2 | 0 | .800 |
| Princeton | 6 | 1 | 0 | 8 | 2 | 0 | .800 |
| Pennsylvania | 5 | 2 | 0 | 7 | 3 | 0 | .700 |
| Cornell | 4 | 3 | 0 | 7 | 3 | 0 | .700 |
| Harvard | 3 | 4 | 0 | 3 | 7 | 0 | .300 |
| Yale | 2 | 5 | 0 | 4 | 6 | 0 | .400 |
| Columbia | 2 | 5 | 0 | 3 | 7 | 0 | .300 |
| Brown | 0 | 7 | 0 | 0 | 10 | 0 | .000 |

### MID-EASTERN ATHLETIC CONFERENCE

| | Conference | | | Full Season | | | |
|---|---|---|---|---|---|---|---|
| | W | L | T | W | L | T | Pct |
| N Carolina A&T | 5 | 1 | 0 | 9 | 2 | 0 | .818 |
| Florida A&M | 4 | 2 | 0 | 7 | 4 | 0 | .636 |
| S Carolina St | 4 | 2 | 0 | 7 | 4 | 0 | .636 |
| Howard | 3 | 3 | 0 | 7 | 4 | 0 | .636 |
| Delaware St | 3 | 3 | 0 | 6 | 5 | 0 | .545 |
| Bethune-Cookman | 2 | 4 | 0 | 3 | 7 | 0 | .300 |
| Morgan St | 0 | 6 | 0 | 2 | 8 | 0 | .200 |

### OHIO VALLEY CONFERENCE

| | Conference | | | Full Season | | | |
|---|---|---|---|---|---|---|---|
| | W | L | T | W | L | T | Pct |
| Middle Tennessee St | 8 | 0 | 0 | 9 | 2 | 0 | .818 |
| Eastern Kentucky | 7 | 1 | 0 | 9 | 2 | 0 | .818 |
| Tennessee Tech | 6 | 2 | 0 | 7 | 4 | 0 | .636 |
| Tennessee St | 5 | 3 | 0 | 5 | 6 | 0 | .455 |
| Morehead St | 3 | 5 | 0 | 3 | 8 | 0 | .273 |
| Austin Peay | 2 | 6 | 0 | 3 | 8 | 0 | .273 |
| Tenn-Martin | 2 | 6 | 0 | 3 | 8 | 0 | .273 |
| Southeast Mo St | 2 | 6 | 0 | 2 | 9 | 0 | .182 |
| Murray St | 1 | 7 | 0 | 2 | 9 | 0 | .182 |

### PATRIOT LEAGUE

| | Conference | | | Full Season | | | |
|---|---|---|---|---|---|---|---|
| | W | L | T | W | L | T | Pct |
| Lafayette | 5 | 0 | 0 | 8 | 3 | 0 | .727 |
| Holy Cross | 4 | 1 | 0 | 6 | 5 | 0 | .545 |
| Colgate | 2 | 3 | 0 | 4 | 7 | 0 | .364 |
| Lehigh | 2 | 3 | 0 | 3 | 8 | 0 | .273 |
| Bucknell | 1 | 4 | 0 | 4 | 7 | 0 | .364 |
| Fordham | 1 | 4 | 0 | 1 | 9 | 0 | .100 |

### SOUTHERN CONFERENCE

| | Conference | | | Full Season | | | |
|---|---|---|---|---|---|---|---|
| | W | L | T | W | L | T | Pct |
| Citadel | 6 | 1 | 0 | 10 | 1 | 0 | .909 |
| Marshall | 5 | 2 | 0 | 8 | 3 | 0 | .727 |
| Appalachian St | 5 | 2 | 0 | 7 | 4 | 0 | .636 |
| Western Carolina | 5 | 2 | 0 | 7 | 4 | 0 | .636 |
| Furman | 4 | 3 | 0 | 6 | 5 | 0 | .545 |
| E Tennessee St | 2 | 5 | 0 | 5 | 6 | 0 | .455 |
| Virginia Military | 1 | 6 | 0 | 3 | 8 | 0 | .273 |
| TN-Chattanooga | 0 | 7 | 0 | 2 | 9 | 0 | .182 |
| Georgia Southern* | - | - | - | 7 | 4 | 0 | .636 |

*Georgia Southern did not compete for title in 1992.

## Division I-AA (Cont.)

### SOUTHLAND CONFERENCE

| | Conference | | | Full Season | | | |
|---|---|---|---|---|---|---|---|
| | W | L | T | W | L | T | Pct |
| NE Louisiana | 7 | 0 | 0 | 9 | 2 | 0 | .818 |
| McNeese St | 6 | 1 | 0 | 8 | 3 | 0 | .727 |
| Sam Houston St | 3 | 2 | 2 | 6 | 3 | 2 | .636 |
| Northwestern (La) | 4 | 3 | 0 | 7 | 4 | 0 | .636 |
| N Texas | 3 | 4 | 0 | 4 | 7 | 0 | .364 |
| SW Texas St | 2 | 4 | 1 | 5 | 5 | 1 | .500 |
| SF Austin St | 1 | 6 | 0 | 3 | 8 | 0 | .273 |
| Nicholls St | 0 | 6 | 1 | 1 | 9 | 1 | .136 |

### SOUTHWESTERN ATHLETIC CONFERENCE

| | Conference | | | Full Season | | | |
|---|---|---|---|---|---|---|---|
| | W | L | T | W | L | T | Pct |
| Alcorn St | 7 | 0 | 0 | 7 | 3 | 0 | .700 |
| Grambling | 6 | 1 | 0 | 9 | 2 | 0 | .818 |
| Jackson St | 4 | 3 | 0 | 7 | 4 | 0 | .636 |
| Alabama St | 3 | 4 | 0 | 5 | 6 | 0 | .455 |
| Southern-B.R. | 3 | 4 | 0 | 5 | 6 | 0 | .455 |
| Texas Southern | 3 | 4 | 0 | 5 | 6 | 0 | .455 |
| Mississippi Valley | 2 | 5 | 0 | 4 | 5 | 0 | .444 |
| Prairie View A&M | 0 | 7 | 0 | 0 | 11 | 0 | .000 |

### YANKEE CONFERENCE

| | Conference | | | Full Season | | | |
|---|---|---|---|---|---|---|---|
| | W | L | T | W | L | T | Pct |
| Delaware | 7 | 1 | 0 | 9 | 2 | 0 | .818 |
| Villanova | 6 | 2 | 0 | 9 | 2 | 0 | .818 |
| Massachusetts | 5 | 3 | 0 | 7 | 3 | 0 | .700 |
| Richmond | 5 | 3 | 0 | 7 | 4 | 0 | .636 |
| Maine | 4 | 4 | 0 | 6 | 5 | 0 | .545 |
| Connecticut | 4 | 4 | 0 | 5 | 6 | 0 | .455 |
| New Hampshire | 3 | 5 | 0 | 5 | 5 | 1 | .500 |
| Boston U | 2 | 6 | 0 | 3 | 8 | 0 | .273 |
| Rhode Island | 0 | 8 | 0 | 1 | 10 | 0 | .091 |

### INDEPENDENTS

| | Full Season | | | |
|---|---|---|---|---|
| | W | L | T | Pct |
| Samford | 9 | 2 | 0 | .818 |
| William & Mary | 9 | 2 | 0 | .818 |
| Youngstown St | 8 | 2 | 1 | .773 |
| Liberty | 7 | 4 | 0 | .636 |
| Central Florida | 6 | 4 | 0 | .600 |
| Towson St | 5 | 5 | 0 | .500 |
| Northeastern | 5 | 5 | 1 | .500 |
| Western Kentucky | 4 | 6 | 0 | .400 |
| James Madison | 4 | 7 | 0 | .364 |

## THEY SAID IT

*Jim Muldoon, Pac-10 p.r. man, denigrating the record of conference champion Washington's Rose Bowl opponent, Michigan: "Eight-oh-three isn't a record. It's an area code."*

## Division I-A

### SCORING

| | Class | GP | TD | XP | FG | Pts | Pts/Game |
|---|---|---|---|---|---|---|---|
| Garrison Hearst, Georgia | Jr | 11 | 21 | 0 | 0 | 126 | 11.45 |
| Richie Anderson, Penn St | Sr | 11 | 19 | 2 | 0 | 116 | 10.55 |
| Marshall Faulk, San Diego St | So | 10 | 15 | 2 | 0 | 92 | 9.20 |
| Joe Allison, Memphis St | Jr | 11 | 0 | 32 | 23 | 101 | 9.18 |
| Greg Hill, Texas A&M | So | 12 | 17 | 0 | 0 | 102 | 8.50 |
| Tyrone Wheatley, Michigan | So | 10 | 14 | 0 | 0 | 84 | 8.40 |
| Trevor Cobb, Rice | Sr | 11 | 15 | 2 | 0 | 92 | 8.36 |
| Calvin Jones, Nebraska | So | 11 | 15 | 0 | 0 | 90 | 8.18 |
| Craig Thomas, Michigan St | Jr | 11 | 15 | 0 | 0 | 90 | 8.18 |
| Rusty Hanna, Toledo | Sr | 11 | 0 | 26 | 21 | 89 | 8.09 |
| Nelson Welch, Clemson | So | 11 | 0 | 23 | 22 | 89 | 8.09 |

### FIELD GOALS

| | Class | GP | FGA | FG | Pct | FG/Game |
|---|---|---|---|---|---|---|
| Joe Allison, Memphis St | Jr | 11 | 25 | 23 | 92.0 | 2.09 |
| Scott Ethridge, Auburn | So | 11 | 28 | 22 | 78.6 | 2.00 |
| Nelson Welch, Clemson | So | 11 | 28 | 22 | 78.6 | 2.00 |
| Rick Thompson, Wisconsin | Sr | 11 | 32 | 22 | 68.8 | 2.00 |
| Rusty Hanna, Toledo | Sr | 11 | 29 | 21 | 72.4 | 1.91 |
| Tommy Thompson, Oregon | Jr | 11 | 31 | 20 | 64.5 | 1.82 |
| Eric Lange, Tulsa | Sr | 11 | 23 | 19 | 82.6 | 1.73 |
| Scott Sisson, Georgia Tech | Sr | 11 | 24 | 19 | 79.2 | 1.73 |
| Sean Jones, Utah St | Sr | 11 | 24 | 18 | 75.0 | 1.64 |
| Daron Alcorn, Akron | Sr | 11 | 26 | 18 | 69.2 | 1.64 |

### TOTAL OFFENSE

| | | | Rushing | | Passing | | Total Offense | | | |
|---|---|---|---|---|---|---|---|---|---|---|
| | Class | GP | Car | Net | Att | Yds | Yds | Yds/Play | TDR* | Yds/Game |
| Jimmy Klingler, Houston | So | 11 | 40 | -50 | 504 | 3818 | 3768 | 6.93 | 32 | 342.55 |
| John Kaleo, Maryland | Sr | 11 | 106 | 80 | 482 | 3392 | 3472 | 5.90 | 22 | 315.64 |
| Ryan Hancock, BYU | So | 9 | 33 | -49 | 288 | 2635 | 2586 | 8.06 | 17 | 287.33 |
| Charlie Ward, Florida St | Jr | 11 | 100 | 504 | 365 | 2647 | 3151 | 6.78 | 28 | 286.45 |
| Gino Torretta, Miami (FL) | Sr | 11 | 34 | -24 | 402 | 3060 | 3036 | 6.96 | 19 | 276.00 |
| Shane Matthews, Florida | Sr | 12 | 73 | -29 | 463 | 3205 | 3176 | 5.93 | 25 | 264.67 |
| Frank Dolce, Utah | Sr | 9 | 60 | 5 | 322 | 2369 | 2374 | 6.21 | 22 | 263.78 |
| Alex Van Pelt, Pittsburgh | Sr | 12 | 27 | 0 | 407 | 3163 | 3163 | 7.29 | 20 | 263.58 |
| Drew Bledsoe, Washington St | Jr | 11 | 78 | -53 | 386 | 2770 | 2717 | 5.86 | 22 | 247.00 |
| Trent Dilfer, Fresno St | So | 12 | 73 | 82 | 331 | 2828 | 2910 | 7.20 | 22 | 242.50 |

*Touchdowns responsible for.

### RUSHING

| | Class | GP | Car | Yds | Avg | TD | Yds/Game |
|---|---|---|---|---|---|---|---|
| Marshall Faulk, San Diego St | So | 10 | 265 | 1630 | 6.2 | 15 | 163.00 |
| Garrison Hearst, Georgia | Jr | 11 | 228 | 1547 | 6.8 | 19 | 140.64 |
| Ryan Benjamin, Pacific | Sr | 11 | 231 | 1441 | 6.2 | 13 | 131.00 |
| Chuckie Dukes, Boston College | Sr | 11 | 238 | 1387 | 5.8 | 10 | 126.09 |
| Trevor Cobb, Rice | Sr | 11 | 279 | 1386 | 5.0 | 11 | 126.00 |
| Travis Sims, Hawaii | Sr | 12 | 220 | 1498 | 6.8 | 9 | 124.83 |
| Reggie Brooks, Notre Dame | Sr | 11 | 167 | 1343 | 8.0 | 13 | 122.09 |
| LeShon Johnson, N Illinois | Jr | 11 | 265 | 1338 | 5.0 | 6 | 121.64 |
| Byron Morris, Texas Tech | So | 11 | 242 | 1279 | 5.3 | 10 | 116.27 |
| Deland McCullough, Miami (Ohio) | Fr | 9 | 227 | 1026 | 4.5 | 6 | 114.00 |

**Whole Lot of W's**

At the start of the 1992 season there were two Division III football teams with 500 or more wins—Wittenberg and Widener. Now there are three more. Washington and Jefferson is one of them, having joined the elite by beating Widener. Williams is another, thanks to a win over Wesleyan. The third is Franklin and Marshall, which doesn't belong in this item except that its milestone W occured at home on Williamson Field against Western Maryland.

## Division I-A (Cont.)

### PASSING EFFICIENCY

| | Class | GP | Att | Comp | Pct Comp | Yds | Yds/Att | TD | Int | Rating Pts |
|---|---|---|---|---|---|---|---|---|---|---|
| Elvis Grbac, Michigan | Sr | 9 | 169 | 112 | 66.27 | 1465 | 8.67 | 15 | 12 | 154.2 |
| Marvin Graves, Syracuse | Jr | 11 | 242 | 146 | 60.33 | 2296 | 9.49 | 14 | 12 | 149.2 |
| Ryan Hancock, Brigham Young | So | 9 | 288 | 165 | 57.29 | 2635 | 9.15 | 17 | 13 | 144.6 |
| Bert Emmanuel, Rice | Jr | 11 | 179 | 94 | 52.51 | 1558 | 8.70 | 11 | 6 | 139.2 |
| Kordell Stewart, Colorado | So | 9 | 252 | 151 | 59.92 | 2109 | 8.37 | 12 | 9 | 138.8 |
| Eric Zeier, Georgia | So | 11 | 258 | 151 | 58.53 | 2248 | 8.71 | 12 | 12 | 137.8 |
| Jimmy Klingler, Houston | So | 11 | 504 | 303 | 60.12 | 3818 | 7.58 | 32 | 18 | 137.6 |
| Bobby Goodman, Virginia | Sr | 11 | 232 | 130 | 56.03 | 1707 | 7.36 | 21 | 12 | 137.4 |
| Joe Youngblood, Cent Michigan | Jr | 11 | 278 | 161 | 57.91 | 2209 | 7.95 | 18 | 13 | 136.7 |
| Trent Dilfer, Fresno St | So | 12 | 331 | 174 | 52.57 | 2828 | 8.54 | 20 | 14 | 135.8 |

Note: Minimum 15 attempts per game.

### RECEPTIONS PER GAME

| | Class | GP | No. | Yds | TD | R/Game |
|---|---|---|---|---|---|---|
| Sherman Smith, Houston | Jr | 11 | 103 | 923 | 6 | 9.36 |
| Bryan Reeves, Nevada | Jr | 11 | 81 | 1114 | 10 | 7.36 |
| Aaron Turner, Pacific | Sr | 11 | 79 | 1171 | 11 | 7.18 |
| Ryan Yarborough, Wyoming | Jr | 12 | 86 | 1351 | 12 | 7.17 |
| Lloyd Hill, Texas Tech | Jr | 11 | 76 | 1261 | 12 | 6.91 |
| Michael Westbrook, Colorado | So | 11 | 76 | 1060 | 8 | 6.91 |

### RECEIVING YARDS PER GAME

| | Class | GP | No. | Yds | TD | Yds/Game |
|---|---|---|---|---|---|---|
| Lloyd Hill, Texas Tech | Jr | 11 | 76 | 1261 | 12 | 114.64 |
| Marcus Badgett, Maryland | Sr | 11 | 75 | 1240 | 9 | 112.73 |
| Ryan Yarborough, Wyoming | Jr | 12 | 86 | 1351 | 12 | 112.58 |
| Victor Bailey, Missouri | Sr | 11 | 75 | 1210 | 6 | 110.00 |
| Aaron Turner, Pacific | Sr | 11 | 79 | 1171 | 11 | 106.45 |

### ALL-PURPOSE RUNNERS

| | Class | GP | Rush | Rec | PR | KOR | Yds* | Yds/Game |
|---|---|---|---|---|---|---|---|---|
| Ryan Benjamin, Pacific | Sr | 11 | 1441 | 434 | 96 | 626 | 2597 | 236.09 |
| Glyn Milburn, Stanford | Sr | 12 | 851 | 405 | 573 | 292 | 2121 | 176.75 |
| Marshall Faulk, San Diego St | So | 10 | 1630 | 128 | 0 | 0 | 1758 | 175.80 |
| Garrison Hearst, Georgia | Jr | 11 | 1547 | 324 | 0 | 39 | 1910 | 173.64 |
| Henry Bailey, Nevada-Las Vegas | So | 11 | 15 | 832 | 219 | 817 | 1883 | 171.18 |

*Includes interceptions return yards

### INTERCEPTIONS

| | Class | GP | No. | Yds | TD | Int/Game |
|---|---|---|---|---|---|---|
| Carlton McDonald, Air Force | Sr | 11 | 8 | 109 | 1 | .73 |
| C.J. Masters, Kansas St | Sr | 11 | 7 | 152 | 2 | .64 |
| Greg Evans, Texas Christian | Jr | 11 | 7 | 121 | 0 | .64 |
| T. Drakeford, Virginia Tech | Jr | 11 | 7 | 121 | 1 | .64 |
| Joe Bair, Bowling Green | Jr | 11 | 7 | 51 | 0 | .64 |
| Chris Owens, Akron | Sr | 11 | 7 | 49 | 0 | .64 |
| Corey Sawyer, Florida St | So | 11 | 7 | 0 | 0 | .64 |

### PUNTING

| | Class | No. | Avg |
|---|---|---|---|
| Ed Bunn, UTEP | Sr | 41 | 47.68 |
| Mitch Berger, Colorado | Jr | 53 | 47.04 |
| Brian Parvin, Nevada-Las Vegas | Sr | 57 | 46.26 |
| Sean Snyder, Kansas St | Sr | 80 | 44.65 |
| Jeff Buffaloe, Memphs St | Sr | 52 | 44.56 |

Note: Minimum of 3.6 per game.

### PUNT RETURNS

| | Class | No. | Yds | TD | Avg |
|---|---|---|---|---|---|
| Lee Gissender, Northwestern | Jr | 15 | 327 | 1 | 21.80 |
| James McMillion, Iowa St | Jr | 23 | 435 | 3 | 18.91 |
| Glyn Milburn, Stanford | Sr | 31 | 573 | 3 | 18.48 |
| Jamie Mouton, Houston | Sr | 18 | 278 | 1 | 15.44 |
| Corey Sawyer, Florida St | So | 33 | 488 | 1 | 14.79 |

Note: Minimum 1.2 per game.

## Division I-A (Cont.)

### KICKOFF RETURNS

| | Class | No. | Yds | TD | Avg |
|---|---|---|---|---|---|
| Fred Montgomery, New Mexico St | Sr | 14 | 457 | 0 | 32.64 |
| Leroy Gallman, Duke | Sr | 14 | 433 | 0 | 30.93 |
| Lew Lawhorn, Temple | So | 20 | 600 | 2 | 30.00 |
| Chris Singleton, Nevada | Jr | 17 | 497 | 0 | 29.24 |
| Brad Breedlove, Duke | Sr | 15 | 438 | 0 | 29.20 |

Note: Minimum of 1.2 per game.

## Division I-A Single-Game Highs

### RUSHING AND PASSING

Rushing and passing plays: 77—Jeff Handy, Missouri, Oct 17 (vs Oklahoma St).

Rushing and passing yards: 612—Jimmy Klingler, Houston, Nov 28 (vs Rice).

Rushing plays: 44—Kevin Galbreath, Arizona St, Oct 24 (vs UCLA).

Net rushing yards: 300—Marshall Faulk, San Diego St, Nov 14 (vs Hawaii).

Passes attempted: 75—Chris Vargas, Nevada, Sep 19 (vs McNeese St).

Passes completed: 46—Jimmy Klingler, Houston, Nov 28 (vs Rice).

Passing yards: 613—Jimmy Klingler, Houston, Nov 28 (vs Rice).

### RECEIVING AND RETURNS

Passes caught: 16—Bryan Reeves, Nevada, Oct 3 (vs Cal St Fullerton).

Receiving yards: 274—Darnay Scott, San Diego St, Oct 17 (vs UTEP).

Punt return yards: 164—Deon Figures, Colorado, Oct 24 (vs Kansas St).

Kickoff return yards: 231—Leroy Gallman, Duke, Nov 14 (vs North Carolina St).

## Division I-AA

### SCORING

| | Class | GP | TD | XP | FG | Pts | Pts/Game |
|---|---|---|---|---|---|---|---|
| Sherriden May, Idaho | So | 11 | 25 | 0 | 0 | 150 | 13.64 |
| Keith Elias, Princeton | Jr | 10 | 18 | 2 | 0 | 110 | 11.00 |
| Toby Davis, Illinois St | Sr | 11 | 20 | 0 | 0 | 120 | 10.91 |
| Markus Thomas, Eastern Kentucky | Sr | 11 | 18 | 0 | 0 | 108 | 9.82 |
| Harry Brown, Alcorn St | Jr | 9 | 14 | 0 | 0 | 84 | 9.33 |
| Kenny Sims, James Madison | Sr | 9 | 14 | 0 | 0 | 84 | 9.33 |

### FIELD GOALS

| | Class | GP | FGA | FG | Pct | FG/Game |
|---|---|---|---|---|---|---|
| Mike Dodd, Boise St | Sr | 11 | 31 | 22 | .710 | 2.00 |
| Scott Obermeier, Northern Iowa | Fr | 11 | 19 | 17 | .895 | 1.55 |
| Terry Belden, Northern Arizona | Jr | 11 | 24 | 15 | .625 | 1.36 |
| Dennis Durkin, Dartmouth | Sr | 10 | 13 | 13 | 1.000 | 1.30 |
| Mike Cochrane, Cornell | Sr | 10 | 22 | 13 | .591 | 1.30 |

## Division I-AA (Cont.)

### TOTAL OFFENSE

| | Class | GP | Rushing | | | | Passing | | Total Offense | | | |
|---|---|---|---|---|---|---|---|---|---|---|---|---|
| | | | Car | Gain | Loss | Net | Att | Yds | Yds | Yds/Play | TDR* | Yds/Game |
| Steve McNair, Alcorn St | So | 10 | 92 | 633 | 117 | 516 | 427 | 3541 | 4057 | 7.82 | 39 | 405.70 |
| Doug Nussmeier, Idaho | Jr | 11 | 97 | 620 | 211 | 409 | 333 | 3028 | 3437 | 7.99 | 28 | 312.45 |
| Jay Fiedler, Dartmouth | Jr | 10 | 80 | 326 | 140 | 186 | 273 | 2748 | 2934 | 8.31 | 31 | 293.40 |
| S. Semptimphelter, Lehigh | Jr | 11 | 107 | 272 | 288 | -16 | 405 | 3190 | 3174 | 6.20 | 20 | 288.55 |
| Jamie Martin, Weber St | Sr | 11 | 86 | 200 | 278 | -78 | 463 | 3207 | 3129 | 5.70 | 22 | 284.45 |

*Touchdowns responsible for.

### RUSHING

| | Class | GP | Car | Yds | Avg | TD | Yds/Game |
|---|---|---|---|---|---|---|---|
| Keith Elias, Princeton | Jr | 10 | 245 | 1575 | 6.4 | 18 | 157.50 |
| Toby Davis, Illinois State | Sr | 11 | 341 | 1561 | 4.6 | 20 | 141.91 |
| Carl Tremble, Furman | Sr | 11 | 228 | 1555 | 6.8 | 13 | 141.36 |
| Kelvin Anderson, Southeast Missouri | So | 10 | 205 | 1371 | 6.7 | 13 | 137.10 |
| Erik Marsh, Lafayette | So | 10 | 284 | 1365 | 4.8 | 10 | 136.50 |

### PASSING EFFICIENCY

| | Class | GP | Att | Comp | Pct Comp | Yds | Yds/Att | TD | Int | Rating Pts |
|---|---|---|---|---|---|---|---|---|---|---|
| Jay Fiedler, Dartmouth | Jr | 10 | 273 | 175 | 64.10 | 2748 | 10.07 | 25 | 13 | 169.4 |
| Lonnie Galloway, W Carolina | Jr | 11 | 211 | 128 | 60.66 | 2181 | 10.34 | 20 | 12 | 167.4 |
| Wendal Lowrey, NE Louisiana | Sr | 11 | 227 | 147 | 64.76 | 2190 | 9.65 | 16 | 9 | 161.1 |
| Donny Simmons, W Illinois | Sr | 11 | 281 | 182 | 64.77 | 2496 | 8.88 | 25 | 11 | 160.9 |
| Michael Payton, Marshall | Sr | 11 | 313 | 200 | 63.90 | 2788 | 8.91 | 26 | 11 | 159.1 |

Note: Minimum 15 attempts per game.

### RECEPTIONS PER GAME

| | Class | GP | No. | Yds | TD | R/Game |
|---|---|---|---|---|---|---|
| Glenn Krupa, Southeast Missouri | Sr | 11 | 77 | 773 | 4 | 7.00 |
| Mike Wilson, Boise St | Jr | 11 | 76 | 913 | 2 | 6.91 |
| Darren Rizzi, Rhode Island | Sr | 11 | 74 | 1102 | 6 | 6.73 |
| Yo Murphy, Idaho | Sr | 11 | 68 | 1156 | 9 | 6.18 |
| Troy Brown, Marshall | Sr | 11 | 67 | 1109 | 11 | 6.09 |

### RECEIVING YARDS PER GAME

| | Class | GP | No. | Yds | TD | Yds/Game |
|---|---|---|---|---|---|---|
| Jason Cristino, Lehigh | Sr | 11 | 65 | 1282 | 9 | 116.55 |
| Yo Murphy, Idaho | Sr | 11 | 68 | 1156 | 9 | 105.09 |
| Vincent Brisby, NE Louisiana | Sr | 10 | 56 | 1050 | 9 | 105.00 |
| Rod Boothes, Richmond | Jr | 11 | 47 | 1115 | 10 | 101.36 |
| Troy Brown, Marshall | Sr | 11 | 67 | 1109 | 11 | 100.82 |

### ALL-PURPOSE RUNNERS

| | Class | GP | Rush | Rec | PR | KOR | Yds* | Yds/Game |
|---|---|---|---|---|---|---|---|---|
| David Wright, Indiana State | Fr | 11 | 1313 | 108 | 0 | 593 | 2014 | 183.09 |
| Kelvin Anderson, SE Missouri | So | 10 | 1371 | 171 | 0 | 253 | 1795 | 179.50 |
| Troy Brown, Marshall | Sr | 11 | 152 | 1109 | 101 | 482 | 1844 | 167.64 |
| Keith Elias, Princeton | Jr | 10 | 1575 | 98 | 0 | 0 | 1673 | 167.30 |
| Patrick Robinson, Tennessee St | Sr | 10 | 0 | 803 | 150 | 665 | 1618 | 161.80 |

*Includes interceptions return yards

### INTERCEPTIONS

| | Class | GP | No. | Yds | TD | Int/Game |
|---|---|---|---|---|---|---|
| Dave Roberts, Youngstown St | Sr | 11 | 9 | 39 | 0 | .82 |
| Mark Chapman, Connecticut | Sr | 11 | 8 | 67 | 0 | .73 |
| Don Caparotti, Massachusetts | Sr | 10 | 7 | 15 | 0 | .70 |
| Torrence Forney, Citadel | Sr | 11 | 7 | 71 | 1 | .64 |
| Bob Jordan, New Hampshire | Jr | 11 | 7 | 35 | 0 | .64 |

## Division I-AA (Cont.)

### PUNTING

| | Class | No. | Avg |
|---|---|---|---|
| Harold Alexander, Appalachian St | Sr | 55 | 44.45 |
| Terry Belden, Northern Arizona | Jr | 59 | 44.31 |
| Rob Sims, Pennsylvania | Sr | 67 | 43.43 |
| Colin Godfrey, Tennessee St | Sr | 54 | 42.20 |
| Tim Mosley, Northern Iowa | Jr | 50 | 42.04 |
| Leo Araguz, Stephen F. Austin | Sr | 54 | 42.04 |

Note: Minimum 3.6 per game.

## Division II

### SCORING

| | Class | GP | TD | XP | FG | Pts | Pts/Game |
|---|---|---|---|---|---|---|---|
| David McCartney, Chadron St | Jr | 10 | 25 | 4 | 0 | 154 | 15.4 |
| Ronald Moore, Pittsburg St | Sr | 11 | 27 | 4 | 0 | 166 | 15.1 |
| Roger Graham, New Haven | So | 10 | 22 | 0 | 0 | 132 | 13.2 |
| Chad Guthrie, NE Missouri St | Sr | 11 | 22 | 2 | 0 | 134 | 12.2 |
| Larry Jackson, Edinboro | So | 10 | 19 | 0 | 0 | 114 | 11.4 |
| Greg Marshall, Colorado Mines | Sr | 10 | 18 | 6 | 0 | 114 | 11.4 |
| A.J. Livingston, New Haven | Jr | 10 | 19 | 0 | 0 | 114 | 11.4 |

### FIELD GOALS

| | Class | GP | FGA | FG | Pct | FG/Game |
|---|---|---|---|---|---|---|
| Mike Estrella, St Mary's (Calif) | Jr | 9 | 27 | 15 | 55.6 | 1.67 |
| Billy Watkins, E Texas St | Jr | 11 | 26 | 15 | 57.7 | 1.36 |
| Roy Miller, Fort Hays St | Sr | 11 | 21 | 15 | 71.4 | 1.36 |
| Ed Detwiler, East Stroudsburg | Sr | 10 | 25 | 13 | 52.0 | 1.30 |
| Jason Monday, Lenoir-Rhyne | Sr | 10 | 15 | 13 | 86.7 | 1.30 |

### TOTAL OFFENSE

| | Class | GP | Yds | Yds/Game |
|---|---|---|---|---|
| John Charles, Portland St | Sr | 8 | 2708 | 338.5 |
| Thad Trujillo, Fort Lewis | So | 10 | 3047 | 304.7 |
| John Craven, Gardner-Webb | So | 11 | 3216 | 292.4 |
| Vernon Buck, Wingate | So | 10 | 2838 | 283.8 |
| Dave McDonald, West Chester | So | 10 | 2771 | 277.1 |
| Steve Smith, Western St | Sr | 10 | 2771 | 277.1 |

### RUSHING

| | Class | GP | Car | Yds | TD | Yds/Game |
|---|---|---|---|---|---|---|
| Roger Graham, New Haven | So | 10 | 200 | 1717 | 22 | 171.7 |
| Ronald Moore, Pittsburg St | Sr | 11 | 239 | 1864 | 26 | 169.5 |
| Karl Evans, Missouri Southern St | Sr | 10 | 327 | 1586 | 14 | 158.6 |
| Thelbert Withers, N. Mexico Highlands | Jr | 11 | 240 | 1621 | 15 | 147.4 |
| Scott Schulte, Hillsdale | Jr | 11 | 271 | 1582 | 16 | 143.8 |

### PASSING EFFICIENCY

| | Class | GP | Att | Comp | Yds | Pct Comp | TD | Int | Rating Pts |
|---|---|---|---|---|---|---|---|---|---|
| Steve Smith, Western St | Sr | 10 | 271 | 180 | 2719 | 66.4 | 30 | 5 | 183.5 |
| John Charles, Portland St | Sr | 8 | 263 | 179 | 2770 | 68.0 | 24 | 7 | 181.3 |
| Ken Suhl, New Haven | Sr | 10 | 239 | 148 | 2336 | 61.9 | 26 | 5 | 175.7 |
| Kurt Coduti, Michigan Tech | Sr | 9 | 155 | 92 | 1518 | 59.3 | 15 | 3 | 169.7 |
| Rovell McMillien, Winston-Salem | Jr | 11 | 165 | 83 | 1532 | 50.3 | 14 | 5 | 150.2 |

### RECEPTIONS PER GAME

| | Class | GP | No. | Yds | TD | C/Game |
|---|---|---|---|---|---|---|
| Randy Bartosh, Southwest Baptist | Sr | 8 | 65 | 860 | 2 | 8.1 |
| Rodney Robinson, Gardner-Webb | Sr | 11 | 89 | 1496 | 16 | 8.1 |
| Troy Walker, California State Chico | Jr | 10 | 79 | 874 | 5 | 7.9 |
| Matt Carman, Livingston | Jr | 9 | 66 | 759 | 3 | 7.3 |
| Damon Thomas, Wayne St (Neb) | Jr | 10 | 71 | 821 | 3 | 7.1 |
| Calvin Walker, Valdosta St | Jr | 10 | 71 | 867 | 8 | 7.1 |

## Division II (Cont.)

### RECEIVING YARDS PER GAME

| | Class | GP | No. | Yds | TD | Yds/Game |
|---|---|---|---|---|---|---|
| Rodney Robinson, Gardner-Webb | Sr | 11 | 89 | 1496 | 16 | 136.0 |
| Johnny Cox, Fort Lewis | Jr | 10 | 65 | 1331 | 12 | 133.1 |
| Charles Guy, Sonoma St | Sr | 10 | 64 | 1260 | 12 | 126.0 |
| Randy Bartosh, Southwest Baptist | Sr | 8 | 65 | 860 | 2 | 107.5 |
| Steve Weaver, West Chester | Sr | 10 | 53 | 1037 | 11 | 103.7 |

### INTERCEPTIONS

| | Class | GP | No. | Yds | Int/Game |
|---|---|---|---|---|---|
| Pat Williams, East Texas St | Jr | 11 | 13 | 145 | 1.2 |
| Joseph Best, Fort Valley St | Jr | 11 | 12 | 129 | 1.1 |
| Tom McKenney, West Liberty St | So | 10 | 10 | 59 | 1.0 |
| Jason Johnson, Shepherd | So | 10 | 9 | 66 | .9 |
| Seven tied with .8 int/game | | | | | |

### PUNTING

| | Class | No. | Avg |
|---|---|---|---|
| Jimmy Morris, Angelo St | So | 45 | 44.5 |
| Eric Fadness, Fort Lewis | Sr | 43 | 43.9 |
| Chris Carter, Henderson St | Jr | 57 | 43.6 |
| Alex Campbell, Morris Brown | Fr | 54 | 42.6 |
| Jon Waugh, Sonoma St | Jr | 46 | 42.5 |

Note: Minimum 3.6 per game.

## Division III

### SCORING

| | Class | GP | TD | XP | FG | Pts | Pts/Game |
|---|---|---|---|---|---|---|---|
| Chris Babirad, Wash. & Jeff. | Sr | 9 | 24 | 0 | 0 | 144 | 16.0 |
| Trent Nauholz, Simpson | Jr | 8 | 21 | 2 | 0 | 128 | 16.0 |
| Greg Novarro, Bentley | Sr | 10 | 25 | 0 | 0 | 150 | 15.0 |
| Carey Bender, Coe | Jr | 9 | 21 | 4 | 0 | 130 | 14.4 |
| Stanley Drayton, Allegheny | Sr | 9 | 20 | 0 | 0 | 120 | 13.3 |

### FIELD GOALS

| | Class | GP | FGA | FG | Pct | FG/Game |
|---|---|---|---|---|---|---|
| Todd Holthaus, Rose-Hulman | Jr | 10 | 19 | 13 | 68.4 | 1.30 |
| T.J. Robles, Catholic | So | 10 | 26 | 12 | 46.2 | 1.20 |
| Scott Rubinetti, Montclair St | Fr | 9 | 14 | 10 | 71.4 | 1.11 |
| Tim Dreslinski, Mount Union | So | 10 | 17 | 11 | 64.7 | 1.10 |
| Garret Skipper, Redlands | So | 9 | 14 | 9 | 64.3 | 1.00 |
| Joop De Groot, Blackburn | Sr | 9 | 12 | 9 | 75.0 | 1.00 |
| Chris DiMaggio, Alfred | Sr | 10 | 15 | 10 | 66.7 | 1.00 |

### TOTAL OFFENSE

| | Class | GP | Yds | Yds/Game |
|---|---|---|---|---|
| Jordan Poznick, Principia | Jr | 8 | 2747 | 343.4 |
| Steve Austin, Mass-Boston | Sr | 9 | 3003 | 333.7 |
| Scott Isphording, Hanover | Jr | 10 | 3150 | 315.0 |
| Chip Chevalier, Swarthmore | Sr | 9 | 2564 | 284.9 |
| Leroy Williams, Upsala | So | 10 | 2822 | 282.2 |

## Division III *(Cont.)*

### RUSHING

| | Class | GP | Car | Yds | TD | Yds/Game |
|---|---|---|---|---|---|---|
| Kirk Matthieu, Maine Maritime | Jr | 9 | 327 | 1733 | 16 | 192.6 |
| Chris Babirad, Wash. & Jeff. | Sr | 9 | 243 | 1589 | 22 | 176.6 |
| Wes Stearns, Merchant Marine | Sr | 9 | 247 | 1477 | 12 | 164.1 |
| Trent Nauholz, Simpson | Jr | 8 | 254 | 1302 | 21 | 162.8 |
| Rob Johnson, W Maryland | Jr | 10 | 330 | 1560 | 18 | 156.0 |

### PASSING EFFICIENCY

| | Class | GP | Att | Comp | Yds | Pct Comp | TD | Int | Rating Pts |
|---|---|---|---|---|---|---|---|---|---|
| Steve Keller, Dayton | Sr | 10 | 153 | 99 | 1350 | 64.7 | 17 | 5 | 168.9 |
| Jim Ballard, Mount Union | Jr | 10 | 292 | 186 | 2656 | 63.7 | 29 | 8 | 167.4 |
| Tom Miles, Grove City | Jr | 9 | 192 | 113 | 1767 | 58.8 | 15 | 9 | 152.5 |
| Jason Gonnion, Wisconsin-La Crosse | Jr | 9 | 219 | 127 | 1904 | 57.9 | 17 | 5 | 152.0 |
| John Koz, Baldwin-Wallace | Jr | 10 | 293 | 182 | 2382 | 62.1 | 22 | 6 | 151.1 |

Note: Minimum 15 attempts per game

### RECEPTIONS PER GAME

| | Class | GP | No. | Yds | TD | C/Game |
|---|---|---|---|---|---|---|
| Matt Newton, Principia | Jr | 8 | 98 | 1487 | 14 | 12.3 |
| Sean Monroe, Mass-Boston | Sr | 9 | 95 | 1693 | 17 | 10.6 |
| Matt Hess, Ripon | Jr | 9 | 71 | 1208 | 16 | 7.9 |
| Brian Vendergrift, Rhodes | Jr | 10 | 78 | 881 | 4 | 7.8 |
| Rod Tranum, MIT | Sr | 8 | 61 | 745 | 5 | 7.6 |

### RECEIVING YARDS PER GAME

| | Class | GP | No. | Yds | TD | Yds/Game |
|---|---|---|---|---|---|---|
| Sean Monroe, Mass-Boston | Sr | 9 | 95 | 1693 | 17 | 188.1 |
| Matt Newton, Principia | Jr | 8 | 98 | 1487 | 14 | 185.9 |
| Matt Hess, Ripon | Jr | 9 | 71 | 1208 | 16 | 134.2 |
| Eric Green, Illinois Benedictine | Sr | 10 | 74 | 1189 | 12 | 118.9 |
| Josh Drake, Swarthmore | Jr | 9 | 67 | 1042 | 9 | 115.8 |

### INTERCEPTIONS

| | Class | GP | No. | Yds | Int/Game |
|---|---|---|---|---|---|
| Chris Butts, Worcester St | Jr | 9 | 12 | 109 | 1.3 |
| Randy Simpson, Wis-Stevens Pt | So | 8 | 8 | 127 | 1.0 |
| Andrew Ostrand, Carroll (Wis) | Sr | 9 | 9 | 91 | 1.0 |
| Curtis Turner, Hampden-Sydney | So | 10 | 9 | 109 | .9 |
| Brent Sands, Cornell College | Sr | 10 | 9 | 163 | .9 |
| Greg Thoma, St John's (Minn) | Jr | 10 | 9 | 149 | .9 |

### PUNTING

| | Class | No. | Avg |
|---|---|---|---|
| Robert Ray, San Diego | So | 44 | 42.3 |
| Joel Blackerby, Ferrum | Sr | 45 | 41.0 |
| Bob Ehret, Washington & Lee | Sr | 54 | 40.7 |
| Andy Mahle, Otterbein | So | 59 | 40.1 |
| Ryan Haley, John Carroll | Jr | 51 | 40.1 |

Note: Minimum 3.6 per game

## Offense

### SCORING

| | GP | Pts | Avg |
|---|---|---|---|
| Fresno St | 12 | 486 | 40.5 |
| Nebraska | 11 | 427 | 38.8 |
| Florida St | 11 | 419 | 38.1 |
| Notre Dame | 11 | 409 | 37.2 |
| Michigan | 11 | 393 | 35.7 |
| Penn State | 11 | 388 | 35.3 |
| Houston | 11 | 378 | 34.4 |
| Hawaii | 12 | 394 | 32.8 |
| Miami (Fla) | 11 | 356 | 32.4 |
| Georgia | 11 | 352 | 32.0 |

### RUSHING

| | GP | Car | Yds | Avg | TD | Yds/Game |
|---|---|---|---|---|---|---|
| Nebraska | 11 | 618 | 3610 | 5.8 | 40 | 328.2 |
| Hawaii | 12 | 630 | 3519 | 5.6 | 32 | 293.3 |
| Notre Dame | 11 | 555 | 3090 | 5.6 | 34 | 280.9 |
| Army | 11 | 667 | 2934 | 4.4 | 23 | 266.7 |
| Michigan | 11 | 531 | 2909 | 5.5 | 28 | 264.5 |
| Clemson | 11 | 580 | 2828 | 4.9 | 21 | 257.1 |
| Air Force | 11 | 610 | 2665 | 4.4 | 26 | 242.3 |
| Baylor | 11 | 570 | 2641 | 4.6 | 24 | 240.1 |
| Colorado State | 12 | 571 | 2881 | 5.0 | 25 | 240.1 |
| Virginia | 11 | 513 | 2589 | 5.0 | 19 | 235.4 |

### TOTAL OFFENSE

| | GP | Plays | Yds | Avg | TD* | Yds/Game |
|---|---|---|---|---|---|---|
| Houston | 11 | 842 | 5714 | 6.8 | 48 | 519.45 |
| Fresno St | 12 | 881 | 5791 | 6.6 | 61 | 482.58 |
| Notre Dame | 11 | 808 | 5174 | 6.4 | 52 | 470.36 |
| Maryland | 11 | 945 | 5131 | 5.4 | 37 | 466.45 |
| Michigan | 11 | 806 | 5120 | 6.4 | 51 | 465.45 |
| Florida State | 11 | 851 | 5080 | 6.0 | 41 | 461.82 |
| Brigham Young | 12 | 879 | 5517 | 6.3 | 44 | 459.75 |
| Pittsburgh | 12 | 919 | 5429 | 5.9 | 35 | 452.42 |
| Georgia | 11 | 732 | 4954 | 6.8 | 40 | 450.36 |
| Boston College | 11 | 817 | 4822 | 5.9 | 41 | 438.36 |

*Defensive and special teams TDs not included.

### PASSING

| | P | Att | Comp | Yds | Pct Comp | Yds/Att | TD | Int | Yds/Game |
|---|---|---|---|---|---|---|---|---|---|
| Houston | 11 | 619 | 368 | 4478 | 59.5 | 7.2 | 36 | 24 | 407.1 |
| Maryland | 11 | 514 | 304 | 3628 | 59.1 | 7.1 | 18 | 23 | 329.8 |
| Miami (Fla) | 11 | 457 | 259 | 3476 | 56.7 | 7.6 | 23 | 7 | 316.0 |
| Nevada | 11 | 497 | 268 | 3328 | 53.9 | 6.7 | 23 | 27 | 302.5 |
| Brigham Young | 12 | 405 | 222 | 3575 | 54.8 | 8.8 | 27 | 19 | 297.9 |
| Colorado | 11 | 398 | 232 | 3271 | 58.3 | 8.2 | 22 | 20 | 297.4 |
| Missouri | 11 | 442 | 258 | 3223 | 58.4 | 7.3 | 13 | 12 | 293.0 |
| Pittsburgh | 12 | 455 | 266 | 3483 | 58.5 | 7.7 | 23 | 20 | 290.3 |
| Florida | 12 | 503 | 290 | 3440 | 57.7 | 6.8 | 25 | 18 | 286.7 |
| East Carolina | 11 | 497 | 272 | 3085 | 54.7 | 6.2 | 27 | 27 | 280.5 |

### Single-Game Highs

Points scored: 70—Florida St, Nov 14 (vs Tulane).
Net rushing yards: 490—Nebraska, Sep 12 (vs Middle Tenn St).
Passing yards: 654—Houston, Nov 28 (vs Rice).
Total yards: 787—Nebraska, Sep 7 (vs Utah St).
Fewest total yards allowed: 13—Arizona St, Sep 19 (vs Louisville).
Passes attempted: 77—East Carolina, Sep 5 (vs Syracuse).
Passes completed: 49—Houston, Nov 28 (vs Rice).

## Defense

### SCORING

| | GP | Pts | Avg |
|---|---|---|---|
| Arizona | 11 | 98 | 8.9 |
| Alabama | 12 | 109 | 9.1 |
| Miami (Fla) | 11 | 127 | 11.5 |
| Ohio State | 11 | 137 | 12.5 |
| Michigan | 11 | 140 | 12.7 |
| Georgia | 11 | 141 | 12.8 |
| Washington | 11 | 148 | 13.5 |
| Toledo | 11 | 153 | 13.9 |
| Texas A&M | 12 | 168 | 14.0 |
| Louisiana Tech | 11 | 167 | 15.2 |

### TOTAL DEFENSE

| | GP | Plays | Yds | Avg | Yds/Game |
|---|---|---|---|---|---|
| Alabama | 12 | 725 | 2330 | 3.2 | 194.2 |
| Arizona | 11 | 747 | 2783 | 3.7 | 253.0 |
| Memphis State | 11 | 766 | 2788 | 3.6 | 253.5 |
| Louisiana Tech | 11 | 698 | 2822 | 4.0 | 256.5 |
| Auburn | 11 | 699 | 2837 | 4.1 | 257.9 |
| Mississippi | 11 | 775 | 2909 | 3.8 | 264.5 |
| Arizona State | 11 | 734 | 2957 | 4.0 | 268.8 |
| Miami (Fla) | 11 | 764 | 2979 | 3.9 | 270.8 |
| Colorado | 11 | 731 | 3058 | 4.2 | 278.0 |
| Stanford | 12 | 821 | 3369 | 4.1 | 280.8 |

## Defense (Cont.)

### RUSHING

| | GP | Car | Yds | Avg | TD | Yds/Game |
|---|---|---|---|---|---|---|
| Alabama | 12 | 395 | 660 | 1.7 | 5 | 55.0 |
| Arizona | 11 | 384 | 716 | 1.9 | 4 | 65.1 |
| Mississippi | 11 | 413 | 895 | 2.2 | 10 | 81.4 |
| Michigan | 11 | 369 | 985 | 2.7 | 6 | 89.5 |
| Syracuse | 11 | 339 | 1007 | 3.0 | 10 | 91.5 |
| Florida State | 11 | 400 | 1103 | 2.8 | 3 | 100.3 |
| Memphis State | 11 | 447 | 1107 | 2.5 | 9 | 100.6 |
| Miami (Fla) | 11 | 406 | 1118 | 2.8 | 4 | 101.6 |
| Notre Dame | 11 | 399 | 1222 | 3.1 | 9 | 111.1 |
| Toledo | 11 | 466 | 1248 | 2.7 | 8 | 113.5 |

### TURNOVER MARGIN

| | | Turnovers Gained | | | Turnovers Lost | | | Margin/ |
|---|---|---|---|---|---|---|---|---|
| | GP | Fum | Int | Total | Fum | Int | Total | Game |
| Nebraska | 11 | 14 | 16 | 30 | 5 | 7 | 12 | 1.64 |
| Akron | 11 | 10 | 24 | 34 | 7 | 11 | 18 | 1.45 |
| Miami (Fla) | 11 | 11 | 18 | 29 | 6 | 7 | 13 | 1.45 |
| Alabama | 12 | 15 | 22 | 37 | 10 | 10 | 20 | 1.42 |
| Tennessee | 11 | 14 | 11 | 25 | 7 | 4 | 11 | 1.27 |
| S Mississippi | 11 | 11 | 19 | 30 | 6 | 10 | 16 | 1.27 |
| Rice | 11 | 12 | 18 | 30 | 8 | 8 | 16 | 1.27 |
| Wake Forest | 11 | 15 | 13 | 28 | 7 | 9 | 16 | 1.09 |
| Stanford | 12 | 16 | 18 | 34 | 12 | 9 | 21 | 1.08 |
| Arizona | 11 | 10 | 16 | 26 | 8 | 7 | 15 | 1.00 |

### PASSING EFFICIENCY

| | GP | Att | Comp | Yds | Pct Comp | Yds/Att | TD | Pct TD | Int | Pct Int | Rating Pts |
|---|---|---|---|---|---|---|---|---|---|---|---|
| Western Michigan | 11 | 283 | 121 | 1522 | 42.76 | 5.38 | 5 | 1.77 | 15 | 5.30 | 83.16 |
| Alabama | 12 | 330 | 164 | 1670 | 49.70 | 5.06 | 6 | 1.82 | 22 | 6.67 | 84.87 |
| Colorado | 11 | 257 | 105 | 1461 | 40.86 | 5.68 | 8 | 3.11 | 18 | 7.00 | 84.87 |
| Stanford | 12 | 354 | 161 | 1869 | 45.48 | 5.28 | 10 | 2.82 | 18 | 5.08 | 88.98 |
| Miami (Fla) | 11 | 358 | 173 | 1861 | 48.32 | 5.20 | 10 | 2.79 | 16 | 5.93 | 91.15 |
| Auburn | 11 | 270 | 117 | 1565 | 43.33 | 5.80 | 10 | 3.70 | 17 | 4.70 | 92.39 |
| Mississippi | 11 | 362 | 169 | 2014 | 46.69 | 5.56 | 10 | 2.76 | 19 | 6.40 | 93.14 |
| Southern Mississippi | 11 | 297 | 143 | 1692 | 48.15 | 5.70 | 9 | 3.03 | 13 | 4.00 | 93.21 |
| Toledo | 11 | 325 | 148 | 1880 | 45.54 | 5.78 | 7 | 2.15 | 12 | 3.97 | 93.24 |
| Georgia | 11 | 302 | 151 | 1699 | 50.00 | 5.63 | 5 | 1.66 | 13 | 4.08 | 94.77 |

# 1992 NCAA Division I-AA Team Leaders

## Offense

### SCORING

| | GP | Pts | Avg |
|---|---|---|---|
| Marshall | 11 | 466 | 42.4 |
| Idaho | 11 | 446 | 40.5 |
| Grambling | 11 | 438 | 39.8 |
| Alcorn State | 10 | 398 | 39.8 |
| Central Florida | 10 | 373 | 37.3 |

### RUSHING

| | GP | Car | Yds | Avg | TD | Yds/Game |
|---|---|---|---|---|---|---|
| Citadel | 11 | 672 | 3800 | 5.7 | 33 | 345.5 |
| Western Kentucky | 10 | 592 | 2871 | 4.8 | 26 | 287.1 |
| Delaware State | 11 | 618 | 3099 | 5.0 | 31 | 281.7 |
| SW Missouri St | 11 | 646 | 3037 | 4.7 | 30 | 276.1 |
| Indiana State | 11 | 578 | 3029 | 5.2 | 33 | 275.4 |

### TOTAL OFFENSE

| | GP | Plays | Yds | Avg | TD* | Yds/Game |
|---|---|---|---|---|---|---|
| Alcorn State | 10 | 728 | 5029 | 6.9 | 57 | 502.90 |
| Marshall | 11 | 796 | 5397 | 6.8 | 62 | 490.64 |
| Idaho | 11 | 856 | 5390 | 6.3 | 56 | 490.00 |
| Central Florida | 10 | 708 | 4768 | 6.7 | 49 | 476.80 |
| Dartmouth | 10 | 751 | 4740 | 6.3 | 45 | 474.00 |

*Defensive and special teams TDs not included.

### PASSING

| | GP | Att | Comp | Yds | Pct Comp | Yds/Att | TD | Int | Yds/Game |
|---|---|---|---|---|---|---|---|---|---|
| Alcorn State | 10 | 436 | 236 | 3605 | 54.1 | 8.3 | 30 | 13 | 360.5 |
| Montana | 11 | 503 | 283 | 3582 | 56.3 | 7.1 | 22 | 20 | 325.6 |
| Morgan State | 10 | 394 | 207 | 2985 | 52.5 | 7.6 | 19 | 25 | 298.5 |
| Weber State | 11 | 476 | 286 | 3271 | 60.1 | 6.9 | 21 | 16 | 297.4 |
| Central Florida | 10 | 359 | 190 | 2973 | 52.9 | 8.3 | 29 | 19 | 297.3 |

## Defense

### SCORING

| | GP | Pts | Avg |
|---|---|---|---|
| Citadel | 11 | 143 | 13.0 |
| Middle Tennessee St | 11 | 144 | 13.1 |
| Georgia Southern | 11 | 151 | 13.7 |
| Villanova | 11 | 153 | 13.9 |
| Pennsylvania | 10 | 144 | 14.4 |

### TOTAL DEFENSE

| | GP | Plays | Yds | Avg | Yds/Game |
|---|---|---|---|---|---|
| South Carolina St | 11 | 691 | 2760 | 4.0 | 250.9 |
| Massachusetts | 10 | 699 | 2705 | 3.9 | 270.5 |
| Holy Cross | 11 | 798 | 3026 | 3.8 | 275.1 |
| Villanova | 11 | 750 | 3055 | 4.1 | 277.7 |
| North Carolina A&T | 11 | 713 | 3085 | 4.3 | 280.5 |

### RUSHING

| | GP | Car | Yds | Avg | TD | Yds/Game |
|---|---|---|---|---|---|---|
| Villanova | 11 | 401 | 856 | 2.1 | 8 | 77.8 |
| E Washington | 10 | 340 | 830 | 2.4 | 11 | 83.0 |
| Montana | 11 | 417 | 1086 | 2.6 | 11 | 98.7 |
| Princeton | 10 | 398 | 1011 | 2.5 | 10 | 101.1 |
| Fordham | 10 | 415 | 1067 | 2.6 | 16 | 106.7 |

### TURNOVER MARGIN

| | Turnovers Gained | | | Turnovers Lost | | | |
|---|---|---|---|---|---|---|---|
| | Fum | Int | Total | Fum | Int | Total | Marg/Gm |
| Youngstown St | 9 | 21 | 30 | 6 | 6 | 12 | 1.64 |
| Howard | 20 | 23 | 43 | 13 | 12 | 25 | 1.64 |
| Grambling | 18 | 23 | 41 | 14 | 10 | 24 | 1.55 |
| Montana St | 11 | 20 | 31 | 5 | 10 | 15 | 1.45 |
| Cornell | 13 | 13 | 26 | 8 | 4 | 12 | 1.40 |

### PASSING EFFICIENCY

| | GP | Att | Comp | Yds | Pct Comp | Yds/Att | TD | Pct TD | Int | Pct Int | Rating Pts |
|---|---|---|---|---|---|---|---|---|---|---|---|
| Middle Tennessee St | 11 | 254 | 107 | 1300 | 42.13 | 5.12 | 4 | 1.57 | 17 | 6.69 | 76.93 |
| South Carolina St | 11 | 259 | 106 | 1423 | 40.93 | 5.49 | 10 | 3.86 | 19 | 7.34 | 85.15 |
| Pennsylvania | 10 | 269 | 126 | 1453 | 46.84 | 5.40 | 7 | 2.60 | 14 | 5.20 | 90.39 |
| Sam Houston St | 11 | 306 | 140 | 1840 | 45.75 | 6.01 | 6 | 1.96 | 17 | 5.56 | 91.62 |
| Howard | 11 | 264 | 117 | 1660 | 44.32 | 6.29 | 10 | 3.79 | 23 | 8.71 | 92.21 |

# 1992 NCAA Division II Team Leaders

## Offense

### SCORING

| | GP | Pts | Avg |
|---|---|---|---|
| New Haven | 10 | 505 | 50.5 |
| Western State | 10 | 471 | 47.1 |
| Gardner-Webb | 11 | 498 | 45.3 |
| Hampton | 11 | 475 | 43.2 |
| Michigan Tech | 9 | 353 | 39.2 |

### TOTAL OFFENSE

| | GP | Plays | Yds | Avg | Yds/Game |
|---|---|---|---|---|---|
| New Haven | 10 | 741 | 5877 | 7.9 | 587.7 |
| Western St | 10 | 770 | 5644 | 7.3 | 564.4 |
| NM Highlands | 11 | 818 | 5394 | 6.6 | 490.4 |
| Portland St | 9 | 562 | 4403 | 7.8 | 489.2 |
| Gardner-Webb | 11 | 854 | 5311 | 6.2 | 482.8 |

### RUSHING

| | GP | Car | Yds | Avg | Yds/Game |
|---|---|---|---|---|---|
| Pittsburg St | 11 | 651 | 3892 | 6.0 | 353.8 |
| NW Missouri St | 11 | 653 | 3775 | 5.8 | 343.2 |
| New Haven | 10 | 487 | 3397 | 7.0 | 339.7 |
| Wofford | 11 | 616 | 3606 | 5.9 | 327.8 |
| Elon | 10 | 568 | 2889 | 5.1 | 288.9 |

### PASSING

| | GP | Att | Comp | Yds | Pct Comp | Yds/Att | Int | Yds/Game |
|---|---|---|---|---|---|---|---|---|
| Gardner-Webb | 11 | 501 | 282 | 4046 | 56.3 | 8.1 | 19 | 367.8 |
| Portland St | 9 | 318 | 216 | 3250 | 67.9 | 10.2 | 7 | 361.1 |
| Western State | 10 | 348 | 223 | 3460 | 64.1 | 9.9 | 7 | 346.0 |
| Fort Lewis | 10 | 433 | 227 | 3200 | 52.4 | 7.4 | 14 | 320.0 |
| Livingston | 9 | 443 | 237 | 2824 | 53.5 | 6.4 | 16 | 313.8 |

## Defense

### SCORING

| | GP | Pts | Avg |
|---|---|---|---|
| Ferris State | 11 | 115 | 10.5 |
| Troy State | 11 | 118 | 10.7 |
| Central Missouri St | 10 | 108 | 10.8 |
| Edinboro | 10 | 112 | 11.2 |
| North Alabama | 11 | 128 | 11.6 |

### RUSHING

| | GP | Car | Yds | Avg | Yds/Game |
|---|---|---|---|---|---|
| Ashland | 11 | 407 | 708 | 1.7 | 64.4 |
| Humboldt St | 11 | 369 | 772 | 2.1 | 70.2 |
| Wayne St (Neb) | 10 | 380 | 704 | 1.9 | 70.4 |
| Slippery Rock | 11 | 323 | 804 | 2.5 | 73.1 |
| Carson-Newman | 10 | 333 | 782 | 2.3 | 78.2 |

## Defense (Cont.)

### TOTAL DEFENSE

|  | GP | Plays | Yds | Avg | Yds/Game |
|---|---|---|---|---|---|
| Ashland | 11 | 705 | 2326 | 3.3 | 211.5 |
| Eastern New Mexico | 10 | 663 | 2227 | 3.4 | 222.7 |
| East Texas St. | 11 | 718 | 2450 | 3.4 | 222.7 |
| Central Arkansas | 10 | 634 | 2293 | 3.6 | 229.3 |
| Augustana (SD) | 11 | 743 | 2539 | 3.4 | 230.8 |

### PASS EFFICIENCY

|  | GP | Att | Comp | Yds | Pct Comp | Yds/Att | TD | Int | Ratings Pts |
|---|---|---|---|---|---|---|---|---|---|
| East Texas State | 11 | 260 | 89 | 1276 | 34.2 | 4.9 | 5 | 26 | 61.8 |
| Fort Valley State | 11 | 266 | 96 | 1267 | 36.0 | 4.8 | 13 | 28 | 71.2 |
| Central Missouri State | 10 | 181 | 72 | 789 | 39.7 | 4.4 | 6 | 12 | 74.1 |
| Gardner-Webb | 11 | 335 | 140 | 1848 | 41.7 | 5.5 | 11 | 35 | 78.1 |
| Central Arkansas | 10 | 256 | 109 | 1197 | 42.5 | 4.7 | 8 | 17 | 78.9 |

# 1992 NCAA Division III Team Leaders

## Offense

### SCORING

|  | GP | Pts | Avg |
|---|---|---|---|
| Coe | 9 | 418 | 46.4 |
| Central Iowa | 9 | 378 | 42.0 |
| Washington & Jefferson | 9 | 373 | 41.4 |
| Dayton | 10 | 408 | 40.8 |
| Ithaca | 10 | 399 | 39.9 |

### RUSHING

|  | GP | Car | Yds | Avg | Yds/Game |
|---|---|---|---|---|---|
| Wisc-River Falls | 9 | 516 | 2840 | 5.5 | 315.6 |
| Chicago | 10 | 560 | 3083 | 5.5 | 308.3 |
| Ithaca | 10 | 561 | 3065 | 5.5 | 306.5 |
| Simpson | 9 | 558 | 2622 | 4.7 | 291.3 |
| Occidental | 9 | 485 | 2619 | 5.4 | 291.0 |

### TOTAL OFFENSE

|  | GP | Plays | Yds | Avg | Yds/Game |
|---|---|---|---|---|---|
| Mount Union | 10 | 752 | 4637 | 6.2 | 463.7 |
| Upper Iowa | 10 | 763 | 4568 | 6.0 | 456.8 |
| Hanover | 10 | 731 | 4492 | 6.1 | 449.2 |
| Wash & Jeff | 9 | 660 | 4004 | 6.1 | 444.9 |
| Illinois Wesleyan | 9 | 682 | 3997 | 5.9 | 444.1 |

### PASSING

|  | GP | Att | Comp | Yds | Pct | Yds/Game |
|---|---|---|---|---|---|---|
| Mass-Boston | 9 | 402 | 184 | 3033 | 45.8 | 337.0 |
| Principia | 8 | 454 | 242 | 2633 | 53.3 | 329.1 |
| Hanover | 10 | 375 | 212 | 3181 | 56.5 | 318.1 |
| Upper Iowa | 10 | 399 | 243 | 2879 | 60.9 | 287.9 |
| Mount Union | 10 | 323 | 205 | 2875 | 63.5 | 287.5 |

## Defense

### SCORING

|  | GP | Pts | Avg |
|---|---|---|---|
| Dayton | 10 | 67 | 6.7 |
| Dickinson | 10 | 76 | 7.6 |
| Emory & Henry | 10 | 76 | 7.6 |
| St John's (Minn) | 10 | 81 | 8.1 |
| Aurora | 9 | 76 | 8.4 |

### RUSHING

|  | GP | Car | Yds | Yds/Game |
|---|---|---|---|---|
| Bridgewater (Mass) | 10 | 343 | 432 | 43.2 |
| Defiance | 10 | 373 | 594 | 59.4 |
| Merchant Marine | 9 | 260 | 582 | 64.7 |
| Wisconsin-River Falls | 9 | 300 | 587 | 65.2 |
| Bentley | 10 | 350 | 669 | 66.9 |

### PASSING EFFICIENCY

|  | GP | Att | Comp | Yds | Pct Comp | Yds/Att | TD | Int | Rating Pts |
|---|---|---|---|---|---|---|---|---|---|
| St Peter's | 9 | 223 | 83 | 766 | 37.2 | 3.4 | 3 | 21 | 51.7 |
| Mass-Boston | 9 | 194 | 74 | 899 | 38.1 | 4.6 | 4 | 20 | 63.2 |
| Emory & Henry | 10 | 254 | 96 | 1076 | 37.8 | 4.2 | 5 | 20 | 64.2 |
| Rochester | 9 | 230 | 82 | 944 | 35.6 | 4.1 | 5 | 15 | 64.2 |
| Cornell College | 10 | 235 | 94 | 929 | 40.0 | 4.0 | 8 | 21 | 66.5 |

# FOR THE RECORD · Year to Year

## National Champions

| Year | Champion | Record | Bowl Game | Head Coach |
|------|----------|--------|-----------|------------|
| 1883 | Yale | 8-0-0 | No bowl | Ray Tompkins (Captain) |
| 1884 | Yale | 9-0-0 | No bowl | Eugene L. Richards (Captain) |
| 1885 | Princeton | 9-0-0 | No bowl | Charles DeCamp (Captain) |
| 1886 | Yale | 9-0-1 | No bowl | Robert N. Corwin (Captain) |
| 1887 | Yale | 9-0-0 | No bowl | Harry W. Beecher (Captain) |
| 1888 | Yale | 13-0-0 | No bowl | Walter Camp |
| 1889 | Princeton | 10-0-0 | No bowl | Edgar Poe (Captain) |
| 1890 | Harvard | 11-0-0 | No bowl | George A. Stewart |
|  |  |  |  | George C. Adams |
| 1891 | Yale | 13-0-0 | No bowl | Walter Camp |
| 1892 | Yale | 13-0-0 | No bowl | Walter Camp |
| 1893 | Princeton | 11-0-0 | No bowl | Tom Trenchard (Captain) |
| 1894 | Yale | 16-0-0 | No bowl | William C. Rhodes |
| 1895 | Pennsylvania | 14-0-0 | No bowl | George Woodruff |
| 1896 | Princeton | 10-0-1 | No bowl | Garrett Cochran |
| 1897 | Pennsylvania | 15-0-0 | No bowl | George Woodruff |
| 1898 | Harvard | 11-0-0 | No bowl | W. Cameron Forbes |
| 1899 | Harvard | 10-0-1 | No bowl | Benjamin H. Dibblee |
| 1900 | Yale | 12-0-0 | No bowl | Malcolm McBride |
| 1901 | Michigan | 11-0-0 | Won Rose | Fielding Yost |
| 1902 | Michigan | 11-0-0 | No bowl | Fielding Yost |
| 1903 | Princeton | 11-0-0 | No bowl | Art Hillebrand |
| 1904 | Pennsylvania | 12-0-0 | No bowl | Carl Williams |
| 1905 | Chicago | 11-0-0 | No bowl | Amos Alonzo Stagg |
| 1906 | Princeton | 9-0-1 | No bowl | Bill Roper |
| 1907 | Yale | 9-0-1 | No bowl | Bill Knox |
| 1908 | Pennsylvania | 11-0-1 | No bowl | Sol Metzger |
| 1909 | Yale | 10-0-0 | No bowl | Howard Jones |
| 1910 | Harvard | 8-0-1 | No bowl | Percy Houghton |
| 1911 | Princeton | 8-0-2 | No bowl | Bill Roper |
| 1912 | Harvard | 9-0-0 | No bowl | Percy Houghton |
| 1913 | Harvard | 9-0-0 | No bowl | Percy Houghton |
| 1914 | Army | 9-0-0 | No bowl | Charley Daly |
| 1915 | Cornell | 9-0-0 | No bowl | Al Sharpe |
| 1916 | Pittsburgh | 8-0-0 | No bowl | Pop Warner |
| 1917 | Georgia Tech | 9-0-0 | No bowl | John Heisman |
| 1918 | Pittsburgh | 4-1-0 | No bowl | Pop Warner |
| 1919 | Harvard | 9-0-1 | Won Rose | Bob Fisher |
| 1920 | California | 9-0-0 | Won Rose | Andy Smith |
| 1921 | Cornell | 8-0-0 | No bowl | Gil Dobie |
| 1922 | Cornell | 8-0-0 | No bowl | Gil Dobie |
| 1923 | Illinois | 8-0-0 | No bowl | Bob Zuppke |
| 1924 | Notre Dame | 10-0-0 | Won Rose | Knute Rockne |
| 1925 | Alabama (H) | 10-0-0 | Won Rose | Wallace Wade |
|  | Dartmouth (D) | 8-0-0 | No bowl | Jesse Hawley |
| 1926 | Alabama (H) | 9-0-1 | Tied Rose | Wallace Wade |
|  | Stanford (D)(H) | 10-0-1 | Tied Rose | Pop Warner |
| 1927 | Illinois | 7-0-1 | No bowl | Bob Zuppke |
| 1928 | Georgia Tech (H) | 10-0-0 | Won Rose | Bill Alexander |
|  | Southern Cal (D) | 9-0-1 | No bowl | Howard Jones |
| 1929 | Notre Dame | 9-0-0 | No bowl | Knute Rockne |
| 1930 | Notre Dame | 10-0-0 | No bowl | Knute Rockne |
| 1931 | Southern Cal | 10-1-0 | Won Rose | Howard Jones |
| 1932 | Southern Cal (H) | 10-0-0 | Won Rose | Howard Jones |
|  | Michigan (D) | 8-0-0 | No bowl | Harry Kipke |
| 1933 | Michigan | 7-0-1 | No bowl | Harry Kipke |
| 1934 | Minnesota | 8-0-0 | No bowl | Bernie Bierman |
| 1935 | Minnesota (H) | 8-0-0 | No bowl | Bernie Bierman |
|  | Southern Meth (D) | 12-1-0 | Lost Rose | Matty Bell |
| 1936 | Minnesota | 7-1-0 | No bowl | Bernie Bierman |
| 1937 | Pittsburgh | 9-0-1 | No bowl | Jock Sutherland |
| 1938 | Texas Christian (AP) | 11-0-0 | Won Sugar | Dutch Meyer |
|  | Notre Dame (D) | 8-1-0 | No bowl | Elmer Layden |

| Year | Champion | Record | Bowl Game | Head Coach |
|------|----------|--------|-----------|------------|
| 1939 | Southern Cal (D) | 8-0-2 | Won Rose | Howard Jones |
| | Texas A&M (AP) | 11-0-0 | Won Sugar | Homer Norton |
| 1940 | Minnesota | 8-0-0 | No bowl | Bernie Bierman |
| 1941 | Minnesota | 8-0-0 | No bowl | Bernie Bierman |
| 1942 | Ohio St | 9-1-0 | No bowl | Paul Brown |
| 1943 | Notre Dame | 9-1-0 | No bowl | Frank Leahy |
| 1944 | Army | 9-0-0 | No bowl | Red Blaik |
| 1945 | Army | 9-0-0 | No bowl | Red Blaik |
| 1946 | Notre Dame | 8-0-1 | No bowl | Frank Leahy |
| 1947 | Notre Dame | 9-0-0 | No bowl | Frank Leahy |
| | Michigan* | 10-0-0 | Won Rose | Fritz Crisler |
| 1948 | Michigan | 9-0-0 | No bowl | Bennie Oosterbaan |
| 1949 | Notre Dame | 10-0-0 | No bowl | Frank Leahy |
| 1950 | Oklahoma | 10-1-0 | Lost Sugar | Bud Wilkinson |
| 1951 | Tennessee | 10-1-0 | Lost Sugar | Bob Neyland |
| 1952 | Michigan St | 9-0-0 | No bowl | Biggie Munn |
| 1953 | Maryland | 10-1-0 | Lost Orange | Jim Tatum |
| 1954 | Ohio St | 10-0-0 | Won Rose | Woody Hayes |
| | UCLA (UP) | 9-0-0 | No bowl | Red Sanders |
| 1955 | Oklahoma | 11-0-0 | Won Orange | Bud Wilkinson |
| 1956 | Oklahoma | 10-0-0 | No bowl | Bud Wilkinson |
| 1957 | Auburn | 10-0-0 | No bowl | Shug Jordan |
| | Ohio St (UP) | 9-1-0 | Won Rose | Woody Hayes |
| 1958 | Louisiana St | 11-0-0 | Won Sugar | Paul Dietzel |
| 1959 | Syracuse | 11-0-0 | Won Cotton | Ben Schwartzwalder |
| 1960 | Minnesota | 8-2-0 | Lost Rose | Murray Warmath |
| 1961 | Alabama | 11-0-0 | Won Sugar | Bear Bryant |
| 1962 | Southern Cal | 11-0-0 | Won Rose | John McKay |
| 1963 | Texas | 11-0-0 | Won Cotton | Darrell Royal |
| 1964 | Alabama | 10-1-0 | Lost Orange | Bear Bryant |
| 1965 | Alabama | 9-1-1 | Won Orange | Bear Bryant |
| | Michigan St (UPI) | 10-1-0 | Lost Rose | Duffy Daugherty |
| 1966 | Notre Dame | 9-0-1 | No bowl | Ara Parseghian |
| 1967 | Southern Cal | 10-1-0 | Won Rose | John McKay |
| 1968 | Ohio St | 10-0-0 | Won Rose | Woody Hayes |
| 1969 | Texas | 11-0-0 | Won Cotton | Darrell Royal |
| 1970 | Nebraska | 11-0-1 | Won Orange | Bob Devaney |
| | Texas (UPI) | 10-1-0 | Lost Cotton | Darrell Royal |
| 1971 | Nebraska | 13-0-0 | Won Orange | Bob Devaney |
| 1972 | Southern Cal | 12-0-0 | Won Rose | John McKay |
| 1973 | Notre Dame | 11-0-0 | Won Sugar | Ara Parseghian |
| | Alabama (UPI) | 11-1-0 | Lost Sugar | Bear Bryant |
| 1974 | Oklahoma | 11-0-0 | No bowl | Barry Switzer |
| | Southern Cal (UPI) | 10-1-1 | Won Rose | John McKay |
| 1975 | Oklahoma | 11-1-0 | Won Orange | Barry Switzer |
| 1976 | Pittsburgh | 12-0-0 | Won Sugar | Johnny Majors |
| 1977 | Notre Dame | 11-1-0 | Won Cotton | Dan Devine |
| 1978 | Alabama | 11-1-0 | Won Sugar | Bear Bryant |
| | Southern Cal (UPI) | 12-1-0 | Won Rose | John Robinson |
| 1979 | Alabama | 12-0-0 | Won Sugar | Bear Bryant |
| 1980 | Georgia | 12-0-0 | Won Sugar | Vince Dooley |
| 1981 | Clemson | 12-0-0 | Won Orange | Danny Ford |
| 1982 | Penn St | 11-1-0 | Won Sugar | Joe Paterno |
| 1983 | Miami (FL) | 11-1-0 | Won Orange | Howard Schnellenberger |
| 1984 | Brigham Young | 13-0-0 | Won Holiday | LaVell Edwards |
| 1985 | Oklahoma | 11-1-0 | Won Orange | Barry Switzer |
| 1986 | Penn St | 12-0-0 | Won Fiesta | Joe Paterno |
| 1987 | Miami (FL) | 12-0-0 | Won Orange | Jimmy Johnson |
| 1988 | Notre Dame | 12-0-0 | Won Fiesta | Lou Holtz |
| 1989 | Miami (FL) | 11-1-0 | Won Sugar | Dennis Erickson |
| 1990 | Colorado | 11-1-1 | Won Orange | Bill McCartney |
| | Georgia Tech (UPI) | 11-0-1 | Won Citrus | Bobby Ross |
| 1991 | Miami (FL) | 12-0-0 | Won Orange | Dennis Erickson |
| | Washington (CNN) | 12-0-0 | Won Rose | Don James |
| 1992 | Alabama | 13-0-0 | Won Sugar | Gene Stallings |

*The AP, which had voted Notre Dame No. 1, took a second vote, giving the national title to Michigan after its 49-0 win over Southern Cal in the Rose Bowl.

Note: Selectors: Helms Athletic Foundation (H) 1883-1935, The Dickinson System (D) 1924-40, The Associated Press (AP) 1936-90, United Press International (UPI) 1958-90, and USA Today/CNN(CNN) 1991.

# Results of Major Bowl Games

## Rose Bowl

1-1-2 ............Michigan 49, Stanford 0
1-1-16 ..........Washington St 14, Brown 0
1-1-17 ..........Oregon 14, Pennsylvania 0
1-1-18 ..........Mare Island 19, Camp Lewis 7
1-1-19 ..........Great Lakes 17, Mare Island 0
1-1-20 ..........Harvard 7, Oregon 6
1-1-21 ..........California 28, Ohio St 0
1-2-22 ..........Washington & Jefferson 0, California 0
1-1-23 ..........Southern Cal 14, Penn St 3
1-1-24 ..........Navy 14, Washington 14
1-1-25 ..........Notre Dame 27, Stanford 10
1-1-26 ..........Alabama 20, Washington 19
1-1-27 ..........Alabama 7, Stanford 7
1-2-28 ..........Stanford 7, Pittsburgh 6
1-1-29 ..........Georgia Tech 8, California 7
1-1-30 ..........Southern Cal 47, Pittsburgh 14
1-1-31 ..........Alabama 24, Washington St 0
1-1-32 ..........Southern Cal 21, Tulane 12
1-2-33 ..........Southern Cal 35, Pittsburgh 0
1-1-34 ..........Columbia 7, Stanford 0
1-1-35 ..........Alabama 29, Stanford 13
1-1-36 ..........Stanford 7, Southern Meth 0
1-1-37 ..........Pittsburgh 21, Washington 0
1-1-38 ..........California 13, Alabama 0
1-2-39 ..........Southern Cal 7, Duke 3
1-1-40 ..........Southern Cal 14, Tennessee 0
1-1-41 ..........Stanford 21, Nebraska 13
1-1-42 ..........Oregon St 20, Duke 16
1-1-43 ..........Georgia 9, UCLA 0
1-1-44 ..........Southern Cal 29, Washington 0
1-1-45 ..........Southern Cal 25, Tennessee 0
1-1-46 ..........Alabama 34, Southern Cal 14
1-1-47 ..........Illinois 45, UCLA 14
1-1-48 ..........Michigan 49, Southern Cal 0
1-1-49 ..........Northwestern 20, California 14
1-2-50 ..........Ohio St 17, California 14
1-1-51 ..........Michigan 14, California 6
1-1-52 ..........Illinois 40, Stanford 7
1-1-53 ..........Southern Cal 7, Wisconsin 0
1-1-54 ..........Michigan St 28, UCLA 20
1-1-55 ..........Ohio St 20, Southern Cal 7
1-2-56 ..........Michigan St 17, UCLA 14
1-1-57 ..........Iowa 35, Oregon St 19
1-1-58 ..........Ohio St 10, Oregon 7
1-1-59 ..........Iowa 38, California 12
1-1-60 ..........Washington 44, Wisconsin 8
1-2-61 ..........Washington 17, Minnesota 7
1-1-62 ..........Minnesota 21, UCLA 3
1-1-63 ..........Southern Cal 42, Wisconsin 37
1-1-64 ..........Illinois 17, Washington 7
1-1-65 ..........Michigan 34, Oregon St 7
1-1-66 ..........UCLA 14, Michigan St 12
1-2-67 ..........Purdue 14, Southern Cal 13
1-1-68 ..........Southern Cal 14, Indiana 3
1-1-69 ..........Ohio St 27, Southern Cal 16
1-1-70 ..........Southern Cal 10, Michigan 3
1-1-71 ..........Stanford 27, Ohio St 17
1-1-72 ..........Stanford 13, Michigan 12
1-1-73 ..........Southern Cal 42, Ohio St 17
1-1-74 ..........Ohio St 42, Southern Cal 21
1-1-75 ..........Southern Cal 18, Ohio St 17
1-1-76 ..........UCLA 23, Ohio St 10
1-1-77 ..........Southern Cal 14, Michigan 6
1-2-78 ..........Washington 27, Michigan 20
1-1-79 ..........Southern Cal 17, Michigan 10
1-1-80 ..........Southern Cal 17, Ohio St 16
1-1-81 ..........Michigan 23, Washington 6

1-1-82 ..........Washington 28, Iowa 0
1-1-83 ..........UCLA 24, Michigan 14
1-2-84 ..........UCLA 45, Illinois 9
1-1-85 ..........Southern Cal 20, Ohio St 17
1-1-86 ..........UCLA 45, Iowa 28
1-1-87 ..........Arizona St 22, Michigan 15
1-1-88 ..........Michigan St 20, Southern Cal 17
1-2-89 ..........Michigan 22, Southern Cal 14
1-1-90 ..........Southern Cal 17, Michigan 10
1-1-91 ..........Washington 46, Iowa 34
1-1-92 ..........Washington 34, Michigan 14
1-1-93 ..........Michigan 38, Washington 31

City: Pasadena.

Stadium: Rose Bowl.

Capacity: 104,091.

Automatic Berths: Pacific-10 champ vs Big 10 champ (since 1947).

Playing Sites: Tournament Park (1902, 1916-22), Rose Bowl (1923-41, since 1943), Duke Stadium, Durham, NC (1942).

## Orange Bowl

1-1-35 ..........Bucknell 26, Miami (FL) 0
1-1-36 ..........Catholic 20, Mississippi 19
1-1-37 ..........Duquesne 13, Mississippi St 12
1-1-38 ..........Auburn 6, Michigan St 0
1-2-39 ..........Tennessee 17, Oklahoma 0
1-1-40 ..........Georgia Tech 21, Missouri 7
1-1-41 ..........Mississippi St 14, Georgetown 7
1-1-42 ..........Georgia 40, Texas Christian 26
1-1-43 ..........Alabama 37, Boston College 21
1-1-44 ..........Louisiana St 19, Texas A&M 14
1-1-45 ..........Tulsa 26, Georgia Tech 12
1-1-46 ..........Miami (FL) 13, Holy Cross 6
1-1-47 ..........Rice 8, Tennessee 0
1-1-48 ..........Georgia Tech 20, Kansas 14
1-1-49 ..........Texas 41, Georgia 28
1-2-50 ..........Santa Clara 21, Kentucky 13
1-1-51 ..........Clemson 15, Miami (FL) 14
1-1-52 ..........Georgia Tech 17, Baylor 14
1-1-53 ..........Alabama 61, Syracuse 6
1-1-54 ..........Oklahoma 7, Maryland 0
1-1-55 ..........Duke 34, Nebraska 7
1-2-56 ..........Oklahoma 20, Maryland 6
1-1-57 ..........Colorado 27, Clemson 21
1-1-58 ..........Oklahoma 48, Duke 21
1-1-59 ..........Oklahoma 21, Syracuse 6
1-1-60 ..........Georgia 14, Missouri 0
1-2-61 ..........Missouri 21, Navy 14
1-1-62 ..........Louisiana St 25, Colorado 7
1-1-63 ..........Alabama 17, Oklahoma 0
1-1-64 ..........Nebraska 13, Auburn 7
1-1-65 ..........Texas 21, Alabama 17
1-1-66 ..........Alabama 39, Nebraska 28
1-2-67 ..........Florida 27, Georgia Tech 12
1-1-68 ..........Oklahoma 26, Tennessee 24
1-1-69 ..........Penn St 15, Kansas 14
1-1-70 ..........Penn St 10, Missouri 3
1-1-71 ..........Nebraska 17, Louisiana St 12
1-1-72 ..........Nebraska 38, Alabama 6
1-1-73 ..........Nebraska 40, Notre Dame 6
1-1-74 ..........Penn St 16, Louisiana St 9
1-1-75 ..........Notre Dame 13, Alabama 11
1-1-76 ..........Oklahoma 14, Michigan 6
1-1-77 ..........Ohio St 27, Colorado 10
1-2-78 ..........Arkansas 31, Oklahoma 6

### Orange Bowl *(Cont.)*

1-1-79..............Oklahoma 31, Nebraska 24
1-1-80..............Oklahoma 24, Florida St 7
1-1-81..............Oklahoma 18, Florida St 17
1-1-82..............Clemson 22, Nebraska 15
1-1-83..............Nebraska 21, Louisiana St 20
1-2-84..............Miami (FL) 31, Nebraska 30
1-1-85..............Washington 28, Oklahoma 17
1-1-86..............Oklahoma 25, Penn St 10
1-1-87..............Oklahoma 42, Arkansas 8
1-1-88..............Miami (FL) 20, Oklahoma 14
1-2-89..............Miami (FL) 23, Nebraska 3
1-1-90..............Notre Dame 21, Colorado 6
1-1-91..............Colorado 10, Notre Dame 9
1-1-92..............Miami 22, Nebraska 0
1-1-93..............Florida State 27, Nebraska 14

City: Miami.
Stadium: Orange Bowl.
Capacity: 75,500.
Automatic Berths: Big 8 champ (1954-64, since 1976).

### Sugar Bowl

1-1-35..............Tulane 20, Temple 14
1-1-36..............Texas Christian 3, Louisiana St 2
1-1-37..............Santa Clara 21, Louisiana St 14
1-1-38..............Santa Clara 6, Louisiana St 0
1-2-39..............Texas Christian 15, Carnegie Tech 7
1-1-40..............Texas A&M 14, Tulane 13
1-1-41..............Boston Col 19, Tennessee 13
1-1-42..............Fordham 2, Missouri 0
1-1-43..............Tennessee 14, Tulsa 7
1-1-44..............Georgia Tech 20, Tulsa 18
1-1-45..............Duke 29, Alabama 26
1-1-46..............Oklahoma St 33, St Mary's (CA) 13
1-1-47..............Georgia 20, N Carolina 10
1-1-48..............Texas 27, Alabama 7
1-1-49..............Oklahoma 14, N Carolina 6
1-2-50..............Oklahoma 35, Louisiana St 0
1-1-51..............Kentucky 13, Oklahoma 7
1-1-52..............Maryland 28, Tennessee 13
1-1-53..............Georgia Tech 24, Mississippi 7
1-1-54..............Georgia Tech 42, W Virginia 19
1-1-55..............Navy 21, Mississippi 0
1-2-56..............Georgia Tech 7, Pittsburgh 0
1-1-57..............Baylor 13, Tennessee 7
1-1-58..............Mississippi 39, Texas 7
1-1-59..............Louisiana St 7, Clemson 0
1-1-60..............Mississippi 21, Louisiana St 0
1-2-61..............Mississippi 14, Rice 6
1-1-62..............Alabama 10, Arkansas 3
1-1-63..............Mississippi 17, Arkansas 13
1-1-64..............Alabama 12, Mississippi 7
1-1-65..............Louisiana St 13, Syracuse 10
1-1-66..............Missouri 20, Florida 18
1-2-67..............Alabama 34, Nebraska 7
1-1-68..............Louisiana St 20, Wyoming 13
1-1-69..............Arkansas 16, Georgia 2
1-1-70..............Mississippi 27, Arkansas 22
1-1-71..............Tennessee 34, Air Force 13
1-1-72..............Oklahoma 40, Auburn 22
12-31-72..........Oklahoma 14, Penn St 0
12-31-73..........Notre Dame 24, Alabama 23
12-31-74..........Nebraska 13, Florida 10
12-31-75..........Alabama 13, Penn St 6
1-1-77..............Pittsburgh 27, Georgia 3
1-2-78..............Alabama 35, Ohio St 6

### Sugar Bowl *(Cont.)*

1-1-79..............Alabama 14, Penn St 7
1-1-80..............Alabama 24, Arkansas 9
1-1-81..............Georgia 17, Notre Dame 10
1-1-82..............Pittsburgh 24, Georgia 20
1-1-83..............Penn St 27, Georgia 23
1-2-84..............Auburn 9, Michigan 7
1-1-85..............Nebraska 28, Louisiana St 10
1-1-86..............Tennessee 35, Miami (FL) 7
1-1-87..............Nebraska 30, Louisiana St 15
1-1-88..............Syracuse 16, Aurburn 16
1-2-89..............Florida St 13, Auburn 7
1-1-90..............Miami (FL) 33, Alabama 25
1-1-91..............Tennessee 23, Virginia 22
1-1-92..............Notre Dame 39, Florida 28
1-1-93..............Alabama 34, Miami 13

City: New Orleans.
Stadium: Louisiana Superdome.
Capacity: 69,548.
Automatic Berths: Southeastern champ (since 1977).
Playing Sites: Tulane Stadium (1935-74), Superdome (since 1974).

### Cotton Bowl

1-1-37..............Texas Christian 16, Marquette 6
1-1-38..............Rice 28, Colorado 14
1-2-39..............St. Mary's (CA) 20, Texas Tech 13
1-1-40..............Clemson 6, Boston Col 3
1-1-41..............Texas A&M 13, Fordham 12
1-1-42..............Alabama 29, Texas A&M 21
1-1-43..............Texas 14, Georgia Tech 7
1-1-44..............Texas 7, Randolph Field 7
1-1-45..............Oklahoma St 34, Texas Christian 0
1-1-46..............Texas 40, Missouri 27
1-1-47..............Arkansas 0, Louisiana St 0
1-1-48..............Southern Meth 13, Penn St 13
1-1-49..............Southern Meth 21, Oregon 13
1-2-50..............Rice 27, N Carolina 13
1-1-51..............Tennessee 20, Texas 14
1-1-52..............Kentucky 20, Texas Christian 7
1-1-53..............Texas 16, Tennessee 0
1-1-54..............Rice 28, Alabama 6
1-1-55..............Georgia Tech 14, Arkansas 6
1-2-56..............Mississippi 14, Texas Christian 13
1-1-57..............Texas Christian 28, Syracuse 27
1-1-58..............Navy 20, Rice 7
1-1-59..............Texas Christian 0, Air Force 0
1-1-60..............Syracuse 23, Texas 14
1-2-61..............Duke 7, Arkansas 6
1-1-62..............Texas 12, Mississippi 7
1-1-63..............Louisiana St 13, Texas 0
1-1-64..............Texas 28, Navy 6
1-1-65..............Arkansas 10, Nebraska 7
1-1-66..............Louisiana St 14, Arkansas 7
12-31-66..........Georgia 24, Southern Meth 9
1-1-68..............Texas A&M 20, Alabama 16
1-1-69..............Texas 36, Tennessee 13
1-1-70..............Texas 21, Notre Dame 17
1-1-71..............Notre Dame 24, Texas 11
1-1-72..............Penn St 30, Texas 6
1-1-73..............Texas 17, Alabama 13
1-1-74..............Nebraska 19, Texas 3
1-1-75..............Penn St 41, Baylor 20
1-1-76..............Arkansas 31, Georgia 10
1-1-77..............Houston 30, Maryland 21
1-2-78..............Notre Dame 38, Texas 10

## Results of Major Bowl Games *(Cont.)*

### Cotton Bowl *(Cont.)*

1-1-79 .............Notre Dame 35, Houston 34
1-1-80 .............Houston 17, Nebraska 14
1-1-81 .............Alabama 30, Baylor 2
1-1-82 .............Texas 14, Alabama 12
1-1-83 .............Southern Meth 7, Pittsburgh 3
1-2-84 .............Georgia 10, Texas 9
1-1-85 .............Boston Col 45, Houston 28
1-1-86 .............Texas A&M 36, Auburn 16
1-1-87 .............Ohio St 28, Texas A&M 12
1-1-88 .............Texas A&M 35, Notre Dame 10
1-2-89 .............UCLA 17, Arkansas 3
1-1-90 .............Tennessee 31, Arkansas 27
1-1-91 .............Miami (FL) 46, Texas 3
1-1-92 .............Florida St 10, Texas A&M 2
1-1-93 .............Notre Dame 28, Texas A&M 3

City: Dallas.
Stadium: Cotton Bowl.
Capacity: 72,032.
Automatic Berths: Southwest champ (since 1942).
Playing Sites: Fair Park Stadium (1937), Cotton Bowl (since 1938).

### John Hancock Bowl

1-1-36 .............Hardin-Simmons 14, New Mexico St 14
1-1-37 .............Hardin-Simmons 34, UTEP 6
1-1-38 .............W Virginia 7, Texas Tech 6
1-2-39 .............Utah 26, New Mexico 0
1-1-40 .............Catholic 0, Arizona St 0
1-1-41 .............Case Reserve 26, Arizona St 13
1-1-42 .............Tulsa 6, Texas Tech 0
1-1-43 .............2nd Air Force 13, Hardin-Simmons 7
1-1-44 .............Southwestern (TX) 7, New Mexico 0
1-1-45 .............Southwestern (TX) 35, New Mexico 0
1-1-46 .............New Mexico 34, Denver 24
1-1-47 .............Cincinnati 18, Virginia Tech 6
1-1-48 .............Miami (OH) 13, Texas Tech 12
1-1-49 .............W Virginia 21, UTEP 12
1-2-50 .............UTEP 33, Georgetown 20
1-1-51 .............West Texas St 14, Cincinnati 13
1-1-52 .............Texas Tech 25, Pacific 14
1-1-53 .............Pacific 26, Southern Miss 7
1-1-54 .............UTEP 37, Southern Miss 14
1-1-55 .............UTEP 47, Florida St 20
1-2-56 .............Wyoming 21, Texas Tech 14
1-1-57 .............George Washington 13, UTEP 0
1-1-58 .............Louisville 34, Drake 20
12-31-58 .............Wyoming 14, Hardin-Simmons 6
12-31-59 .............New Mexico St 28, N Texas 8
12-31-60 .............New Mexico St 20, Utah St 13
12-30-61 .............Villanova 17, Wichita St 9
12-31-62 .............W Texas St 15, Ohio 14
12-31-63 .............Oregon 21, Southern Meth 14
12-26-64 .............Georgia 7, Texas Tech 0
12-31-65 .............UTEP 13, Texas Christian 12
12-24-66 .............Wyoming 28, Florida St 20
12-30-67 .............UTEP 14, Mississippi 7
12-28-68 .............Auburn 34, Arizona 10
12-20-69 .............Nebraska 45, Georgia 6
12-19-70 .............Georgia Tech 17, Texas Tech 9
12-18-71 .............Louisiana St 33, Iowa St 15
12-30-72 .............N Carolina 32, Texas Tech 28
12-29-73 .............Missouri 34, Auburn 17
12-28-74 .............Mississippi St 26, N Carolina 24
12-26-75 .............Pittsburgh 33, Kansas 19
1-2-77 .............Texas A&M 37, Florida 14

### John Hancock Bowl *(Cont.)*

12-31-77 .........Stanford 24, Louisiana St 14
12-23-78 .........Texas 42, Maryland 0
12-22-79 .........Washington 14, Texas 7
12-27-80 .........Nebraska 31, Mississippi St 17
12-26-81 .........Oklahoma 40, Houston 14
12-25-82 .........N Carolina 26, Texas 10
12-24-83 .........Alabama 28, Southern Meth 7
12-22-84 .........Maryland 28, Tennessee 27
12-28-85 .........Georgia 13, Arizona 13
12-25-86 .........Alabama 28, Washington 6
12-25-87 .........Oklahoma St 35, W Virginia 33
12-24-88 .........Alabama 29, Army 28
12-30-89 .........Pittsburgh 31, Texas A&M 28
12-31-90 .........Michigan St 17, Southern Cal 16
12-31-91 .........UCLA 6, Illinois 3
12-31-92 .........Baylor 20, Arizona 15

City: El Paso.
Stadium: Sun Bowl.
Capacity: 52,000.
Automatic Berths: None.
Name Changes: Sun Bowl (1936-86), John Hancock Sun Bowl (1987-88), John Hancock Bowl (since 1989).
Playing Sites: Kidd Field (1936-62), Sun Bowl (since 1963).

### Gator Bowl

1-1-46 .............Wake Forest 26, S Carolina 14
1-1-47 .............Oklahoma 34, N Carolina St 13
1-1-48 .............Maryland 20, Georgia 20
1-1-49 .............Clemson 24, Missouri 23
1-2-50 .............Maryland 20, Missouri 7
1-1-51 .............Wyoming 20, Washington & Lee 7
1-1-52 .............Miami (FL) 14, Clemson 0
1-1-53 .............Florida 14, Tulsa 13
1-1-54 .............Texas Tech 35, Auburn 13
12-31-54 .........Auburn 33, Baylor 13
12-31-55 .........Vanderbilt 25, Auburn 13
12-29-56 .........Georgia Tech 21, Pittsburgh 14
12-28-57 .........Tennessee 3, Texas A&M 0
12-27-58 .........Mississippi 7, Florida 3
1-2-60 .............Arkansas 14, Georgia Tech 7
12-31-60 .........Florida 13, Baylor 12
12-30-61 .........Penn St 30, Georgia Tech 15
12-29-62 .........Florida 17, Penn St 7
12-28-63 .........N Carolina 35, Air Force 0
1-2-65 .............Florida St 36, Oklahoma 19
12-31-65 .........Georgia Tech 31, Texas Tech 21
12-31-66 .........Tennessee 18, Syracuse 12
12-30-67 .........Penn St 17, Florida St 17
12-28-68 .........Missouri 35, Alabama 10
12-27-69 .........Florida 14, Tennessee 13
1-2-71 .............Auburn 35, Mississippi 28
12-31-71 .........Georgia 7, N Carolina 3
12-30-72 .........Auburn 24, Colorado 3
12-29-73 .........Texas Tech 28, Tennessee 19
12-30-74 .........Auburn 27, Texas 3
12-29-75 .........Maryland 13, Florida 0
12-27-76 .........Notre Dame 20, Penn St 9
12-30-77 .........Pittsburgh 34, Clemson 3
12-29-78 .........Clemson 17, Ohio St 15
12-28-79 .........N Carolina 17, Michigan 15
12-29-80 .........Pittsburgh 37, S Carolina 9
12-28-81 .........N Carolina 31, Arkansas 27
12-30-82 .........Florida St 31, W Virginia 12
12-30-83 .........Florida 14, Iowa 6
12-28-84 .........Oklahoma St 21, S Carolina 14
12-30-85 .........Florida St 34, Oklahoma St 23

## Gator Bowl *(Cont.)*

12-27-86 .........Clemson 27, Stanford 21
12-31-87 .........Louisiana St 30, S Carolina 13
1-1-89 .............Georgia 34, Michigan St 27
12-30-89 .........Clemson 27, W Virginia 7
1-1-91 .............Michigan 35, Mississippi 3
12-29-91 .........Oklahoma 48, Virginia 14
12-31-92 .........Florida 27, NC State 10

City: Jacksonville, FL.
Stadium: Gator Bowl.
Capacity: 82,000. Automatic Berths: None.

## Florida Citrus Bowl

1-1-47 .............Catawba 31, Maryville (TN) 6
1-1-48 .............Catawba 7, Marshall 0
1-1-49 .............Murray St 21, Sul Ross St 21
1-2-50 .............St Vincent 7, Emory & Henry 6
1-1-51 .............Morris Harvey 35, Emory & Henry 14
1-1-52 .............Stetson 35, Arkansas St 20
1-1-53 .............E Texas St 33, Tennessee Tech 0
1-1-54 .............E Texas St 7, Arkansas St 7
1-1-55 .............NE-Omaha 7, Eastern Kentucky 6
1-2-56 .............Juniata 6, Missouri Valley 6
1-1-57 .............W Texas St 20, Southern Miss 13
1-1-58 .............E Texas St 10, Southern Miss 9
12-27-58 .........E Texas St 26, Missouri Valley 7
1-1-60 .............Middle Tennessee St 21, Presbyterian 12
12-30-60 .........Citadel 27, Tennessee Tech 0
12-29-61 .........Lamar 21, Middle Tennessee St 14
12-22-62 .........Houston 49, Miami (OH) 21
12-28-63 .........Western Kentucky 27, Coast Guard 0
12-12-64 .........E Carolina 14, Massachusetts 13
12-11-65 .........E Carolina 31, Maine 0
12-10-66 .........Morgan St 14, West Chester 6
12-16-67 .........TN-Martin 25, West Chester 8
12-27-68 .........Richmond 49, Ohio 42
12-26-69 .........Toledo 56, Davidson 33
12-28-70 .........Toledo 40, William & Mary 12
12-28-71 .........Toledo 28, Richmond 3
12-29-72 .........Tampa 21, Kent St 18
12-22-73 .........Miami (OH) 16, Florida 7
12-21-74 .........Miami (OH) 21, Georgia 10
12-20-75 .........Miami (OH) 20, S Carolina 7
12-18-76 .........Oklahoma St 49, Brigham Young 21
12-23-77 .........Florida St 40, Texas Tech 17
12-23-78 .........N Carolina St 30, Pittsburgh 17
12-22-79 .........Louisiana St 34, Wake Forest 10
12-20-80 .........Florida 35, Maryland 20
12-19-81 .........Missouri 19, Southern Miss 17
12-18-82 .........Auburn 33, Boston Col 26
12-17-83 .........Tennessee 30, Maryland 23
12-22-84 .........Georgia 17, Florida St 17

## Florida Citrus Bowl *(Cont.)*

12-28-85 .........Ohio St 10, Brigham Young 7
1-1-87 .............Auburn 16, Southern Cal 7
1-1-88 .............Clemson 35, Penn St 10
1-2-89 .............Clemson 13, Oklahoma 6
1-1-90 .............Illinois 31, Virginia 21
1-1-91 .............Georgia Tech 45, Nebraska 21
1-1-92 .............California 37, Clemson 13
1-1-93 .............Georgia 21, Ohio State 14

City: Orlando, FL.
Stadium: Florida Citrus Bowl-Orlando.
Capacity: 52,300. Automatic Berths: None.
Name Change: Tangerine Bowl (1947-82), Florida Citrus Bowl (since 1983).
Playing Sites: Tangerine Bowl (1947-72, 1974-82); Florida Field, Gainesville (1973); Orlando Stadium (1983-85); Florida Citrus Bowl- Orlando (since 1986). Tangerine Bowl, Orlando Stadium and Florida Citrus Bowl-Orlando are identical site.

## Liberty Bowl

12-19-59 .........Penn St 7, Alabama 0
12-17-60 .........Penn St 41, Oregon 12
12-16-61 .........Syracuse 15, Miami (FL) 14
12-15-62 .........Oregon St 6, Villanova 0
12-21-63 .........Mississippi St 16, N Carolina St
12-19-64 .........Utah 32, W Virginia 6
12-18-65 .........Mississippi 13, Auburn 7
12-10-66 .........Miami (FL) 14, Virginia Tech 7
12-16-67 .........N Carolina St 14, Georgia 7
12-14-68 .........Mississippi 34, Virginia Tech 17
12-13-69 .........Colorado 47, Alabama 33
12-12-70 .........Tulane 17, Colorado 3
12-20-71 .........Tennessee 14, Arkansas 13
12-18-72 .........Georgia Tech 31, Iowa St 30
12-17-73 .........N Carolina St 31, Kansas 18
12-16-74 .........Tennessee 7, Maryland 3
12-22-75 .........Southern Cal 20, Texas A&M 0
12-20-76 .........Alabama 36, UCLA 6
12-19-77 .........Nebraska 21, N Carolina 17
12-23-78 .........Missouri 20, Louisiana St 15
12-22-79 .........Penn St 9, Tulane 6
12-27-80 .........Purdue 28, Missouri 25
12-30-81 .........Ohio St 31, Navy 28
12-29-82 .........Alabama 21, Illinois 15
12-29-83 .........Notre Dame 19, Boston Col 18
12-27-84 .........Auburn 21, Arkansas 15
12-27-85 .........Baylor 21, Louisiana St 7
12-29-86 .........Tennessee 21, Minnesota 14
12-29-87 .........Georgia 20, Arkansas 17
12-28-88 .........Indiana 34, S Carolina 10
12-28-89 .........Mississippi 42, Air Force 29
12-27-90 .........Air Force 23, Ohio St 11
12-29-91 .........Air Force 38, Mississippi St 15
12-31-92 .........Mississippi 13, Air Force 0

City: Memphis.
Stadium: Liberty Bowl Memorial Stadium.
Capacity: 63,000.
Automatic Berths: Since 1989, winner of Commander-in-Chief's Trophy (Air Force, Army, Navy).
Playing Sites: Philadelphia (Municipal Stadium, 1959-63), Atlantic City (Convention Center, 1964); Memphis (since 1965).

### Peach Bowl

12-30-68..........Louisiana St 31, Florida St 27
12-30-69..........W Virginia 14, S Carolina 3
12-30-70..........Arizona St 48, N Carolina 26
12-30-71..........Mississippi 41, Georgia Tech 18
12-29-72..........N Carolina St 49, W Virginia 13
12-28-73..........Georgia 17, Maryland 16
12-28-74..........Vanderbilt 6, Texas Tech 6
12-31-75..........W Virginia 13, N Carolina St 10
12-31-76..........Kentucky 21, N Carolina 0
12-31-77..........N Carolina St 24, Iowa St 14
12-25-78..........Purdue 41, Georgia Tech 21
12-31-79..........Baylor 24, Clemson 18
1-2-81..............Miami (FL) 20, Virginia Tech 10
12-31-81..........W Virginia 26, Florida 6
12-31-82..........Iowa 28, Tennessee 22
12-30-83..........Florida St 28, N Carolina 3
12-31-84..........Virginia 27, Purdue 24
12-31-85..........Army 31, Illinois 29
12-31-86..........Virginia Tech 25, N Carolina St 24
1-2-88..............Tennessee 27, Indiana 22
12-31-88..........N Carolina St 28, Iowa 23
12-30-89..........Syracuse 19, Georgia 18
12-29-90..........Auburn 27, Indiana 23
1-1-92..............E Carolina 37, N Carolina St 34
1-2-93..............North Carolina 21, Miss. St 17

City: Atlanta.
Stadium: Atlanta Fulton County Stadium.
Capacity: 59,800.
Automatic Berths: None.
Playing Sites: Grant Field (1968-70), Atlanta Stadium (since 1971).

### Fiesta Bowl

12-27-71..........Arizona St 45, Florida St 38
12-23-72..........Arizona St 49, Missouri 35
12-21-73..........Arizona St 28, Pittsburgh 7
12-28-74..........Oklahoma St 16, Brigham Young 6
12-26-75..........Arizona St 17, Nebraska 14
12-25-76..........Oklahoma 41, Wyoming 7
12-25-77..........Penn St 42, Arizona St 30
12-25-78..........Arkansas 10, UCLA 10
12-25-79..........Pittsburgh 16, Arizona 10
12-26-80..........Penn St 31, Ohio St 19
1-1-82..............Penn St 26, Southern Cal 10
1-1-83..............Arizona St 32, Oklahoma 21
1-2-84..............Ohio St 28, Pittsburgh 23
1-1-85..............UCLA 39, Miami (FL) 37
1-1-86..............Michigan 27, Nebraska 23
1-2-87..............Penn St 14, Miami (FL) 10
1-1-88..............Florida St 31, Nebraska 28
1-2-89..............Notre Dame 34, W Virginia 21
1-1-90..............Florida St 41, Nebraska 17
1-1-91..............Louisville 34, Alabama 7
1-1-92..............Penn St 42, Tennessee 17
1-1-93..............Syracuse 26, Colorado 22

City: Tempe, AZ.
Stadium: Sun Devil Stadium.
Capacity: 74,000.
Automatic Berths: None.

### Independence Bowl

12-13-76..........McNeese St 20, Tulsa 16
12-17-77..........Louisiana Tech 24, Louisville 14

### Independence Bowl *(Cont.)*

12-16-78..........E Carolina 35, Louisiana Tech 13
12-15-79..........Syracuse 31, McNeese St 7
12-13-80..........Southern Miss 16, McNeese St 14
12-12-81..........Texas A&M 33, Oklahoma St 16
12-11-82..........Wisconsin 14, Kansas St 3
12-10-83..........Air Force 9, Mississippi 3
12-15-84..........Air Force 23, Virginia Tech 7
12-21-85..........Minnesota 20, Clemson 13
12-20-86..........Mississippi 20, Texas Tech 17
12-19-87..........Washington 24, Tulane 12
12-23-88..........Southern Miss 38, UTEP 18
12-16-89..........Oregon 27, Tulsa 24
12-15-90..........Louisiana Tech 34, Maryland 34
12-29-91..........Georgia 24, Arkansas 15
12-31-92..........Wake Forest 39, Oregon 35

City: Shreveport, LA.
Stadium: Independence Stadium.
Capacity: 50,560.
Automatic Berths: None.

### All-American Bowl (Discontinued)

12-22-77..........Maryland 17, Minnesota 7
12-20-78..........Texas A&M 28, Iowa St 12
12-29-79..........Missouri 24, S Carolina 14
12-27-80..........Arkansas 34, Tulane 15
12-31-81..........Mississippi St 10, Kansas 0
12-31-82..........Air Force 36, Vanderbilt 28
12-22-83..........W Virginia 20, Kentucky 16
12-29-84..........Kentucky 20, Wisconsin 19
12-31-85..........Georgia Tech 17, Michigan St 14
12-31-86..........Florida St 27, Indiana 13
12-22-87..........Virginia 22, Brigham Young 16
12-29-88..........Florida 14, Illinois 10
12-28-89..........Texas Tech 49, Duke 21
12-28-90..........N Carolina St 31, Southern Mississippi 27

City: Birmingham, AL.
Stadium: Legion Field.
Capacity: 75,808.
Automatic Berths: None.
Name Change: Hall of Fame Classic (1977-84), All-American Bowl (1985–90).

### Holiday Bowl

12-22-78..........Navy 23, Brigham Young 16
12-21-79..........Indiana 38, Brigham Young 37
12-19-80..........Brigham Young 46, Southern Meth 45
12-18-81..........Brigham Young 38, Washington St 36
12-17-82..........Ohio St 47, Brigham Young 17
12-23-83..........Brigham Young 21, Missouri 17
12-21-84..........Brigham Young 24, Michigan 17
12-22-85..........Arkansas 18, Arizona St 17
12-30-86..........Iowa 39, San Diego St 38
12-30-87..........Iowa 20, Wyoming 19
12-30-88..........Oklahoma St 62, Wyoming 14
12-29-89..........Penn St 50, Brigham Young 39
12-29-90..........Texas A&M 65, Brigham Young 14
12-30-91..........Iowa 13, Brigham Young 13
12-30-92..........Hawaii 27, Illinois 17

City: San Diego.
Stadium: Jack Murphy Stadium.
Capacity: 60,750.
Automatic Berths: Western Athletic champ (except 1985).

### Las Vegas Bowl

12-19-81 ..........Toledo 27, San Jose St 25
12-18-82 ..........Fresno St 29, Bowling Green 28
12-17-83 ..........Northern Illinois 20, Cal St-Fullerton 13
12-15-84 ..........NV-Las Vegas 30, Toledo 13*
12-14-85 ..........Fresno St 51, Bowling Green 7
12-13-86 ..........San Jose St 37, Miami (OH) 7
12-12-87 ..........Eastern Michigan 30, San Jose St 27
12-10-88 ..........Fresno St 35, Western Michigan 30
12-9-89 ...........Fresno St 27, Ball St 6
12-8-90 ...........San Jose St 48, Central Michigan 24
12-14-91 ..........Bowling Green 28, Fresno St 21
12-18-92 ..........Bowling Green 35, Nevada 34

* Toledo won later by forfeit.
City: Fresno, CA.
Stadium: Bulldog Stadium.
Capacity: 30,000.
Automatic Berths: Mid-American and Big West champs.
Name change: California Bowl (1981-91)

### Aloha Bowl

12-25-82 ..........Washington 21, Maryland 20
12-26-83 ..........Penn St 13, Washington 10
12-29-84 ..........Southern Meth 27, Notre Dame 20
12-28-85 ..........Alabama 24, Southern Cal 3
12-27-86 ..........Arizona 30, N Carolina 21
12-25-87 ..........UCLA 20, Florida 16
12-25-88 ..........Washington St 24, Houston 22
12-25-89 ..........Michigan St 33, Hawaii 13
12-25-90 ..........Syracuse 28, Arizona 0
12-25-91 ..........Georgia Tech 18, Stanford 17
12-25-92 ..........Kansas 23, BYU 20

City: Honolulu.
Stadium: Aloha Stadium.
Capacity: 50,000.
Automatic Berths: None.

### Freedom Bowl

12-16-84 ..........Iowa 55, Texas 17
12-30-85 ..........Washington 20, Colorado 17
12-30-86 ..........UCLA 31, Brigham Young 10
12-30-87 ..........Arizona St 33, Air Force 28
12-29-88 ..........Brigham Young 20, Colorado 17
12-30-89 ..........Washington 34, Florida 7
12-29-90 ..........Colorado St 32, Oregon 31
12-30-91 ..........Tulsa 28, San Diego St 17
12-29-92 ..........Fresno St 24, Southern Cal 7

City: Anaheim.
Stadium: Anaheim Stadium.
Capacity: 70,500.
Automatic Berths: None.

### Hall of Fame Bowl

12-23-86 ..........Boston Col 27, Georgia 24
1-2-88 .............Michigan 28, Alabama 24
1-2-89 .............Syracuse 23, Louisiana St 10
1-1-90 .............Auburn 31, Ohio St 14
1-1-91 .............Clemson 30, Illinois 0
1-1-92 .............Syracuse 24, Ohio St 17
1-1-93 .............Tennessee 38, Boston College 23

City: Tampa.
Stadium: Tampa Stadium.
Capacity: 74,315.
Automatic Berths: None.

### Copper Bowl

12-31-89 ..........Arizona 17, N Carolina St 10
12-31-90 ..........California 17, Wyoming 15
12-31-91 ..........Indiana 24, Baylor 0
12-29-92 ..........Washington St 31, Utah 28

City: Tucson.
Stadium: Arizona Stadium.
Capacity: 57,000.
Automatic Berths: None.

### Blockbuster Bowl

12-28-90 ..........Florida St 24, Penn St 17
12-28-91 ..........Alabama 30, Colorado 25
1-1-93 .............Stanford 24, Penn St 3

City: Miami.
Stadium: Joe Robbie.
Capacity: 75,000.
Automatic Berths: None.

### Bluebonnet Bowl (Discontinued)

12-19-59 ..........Clemson 23, Texas Christian 7
12-17-60 ..........Texas 3, Alabama 3
12-16-61 ..........Kansas 33, Rice 7
12-22-62 ..........Missouri 14, Georgia Tech 10
12-21-63 ..........Baylor 14, LSU 7
12-19-64 ..........Tulsa 14, Mississippi 7
12-18-65 ..........Tennessee 27, Tulsa 6
12-17-66 ..........Texas 19, Mississippi 0
12-23-67 ..........Colorado 31, Miami (FL) 21
12-31-68 ..........Southern Meth 28, Oklahoma 27
12-31-69 ..........Houston 36, Auburn 7
12-31-70 ..........Alabama 24, Oklahoma 24
12-31-71 ..........Colorado 29, Houston 17
12-30-72 ..........Tennessee 24, LSU 17
12-29-73 ..........Houston 47, Tulane 7
12-23-74 ..........N Carolina St 31, Houston 31
12-27-75 ..........Texas 38, Colorado 21
12-31-76 ..........Nebraska 27, Texas Tech 24
12-31-77 ..........Southern Cal 47, Texas A&M 28
12-31-78 ..........Stanford 25, Georgia 22
12-31-79 ..........Purdue 27, Tennessee 22
12-31-80 ..........N Carolina 16, Texas 7
12-31-81 ..........Michigan 33, UCLA 14
12-31-82 ..........Arkansas 28, Florida 24
12-31-83 ..........Oklahoma St 24, Baylor 14
12-31-84 ..........W Virginia 31, Texas Christian 14
12-31-85 ..........Air Force 24, Texas 16
12-31-86 ..........Baylor 21, Colorado 9
12-31-87 ..........Texas 32, Pittsburgh 27

City: Houston.
Name change: Astro-Bluebonnet Bowl (1968-76).
Playing sites: Rice Stadium (1959-67, 1985-86),
Astrodome (1968-84, 1987).

## Division I-AA

| Year | Winner | Runner-Up | Score |
|---|---|---|---|
| 1978 | Florida A&M | Massachusetts | 35-28 |
| 1979 | Eastern Kentucky | Lehigh | 30-7 |
| 1980 | Boise St | Eastern Kentucky | 3l-29 |
| 1981 | Idaho St | Eastern Kentucky | 34-23 |
| 1982 | Eastern Kentucky | Delaware | 17-14 |
| 1983 | Southern Illinois | Western Carolina | 43-7 |
| 1984 | Montana St | Louisiana Tech | 19-6 |
| 1985 | Georgia Southern | Furman | 44-42 |
| 1986 | Georgia Southern | Arkansas St | 48-21 |
| 1987 | NE Louisiana | Marshall | 43-42 |
| 1988 | Furman | Georgia Southern | 17-12 |
| 1989 | Georgia Southern | SF Austin St | 37-34 |
| 1990 | Georgia Southern | NV-Reno | 36-13 |
| 1991 | Youngstown St | Marshall | 25-17 |
| 1992 | Marshall | Youngstown St | 31-28 |

## Division II

| Year | Winner | Runner-Up | Score |
|---|---|---|---|
| 1973 | Louisiana Tech | Western Kentucky | 34-0 |
| 1974 | Central Michigan | Delaware | 54-14 |
| 1975 | Northern Michigan | Western Kentucky | 16-14 |
| 1976 | Montana St | Akron | 24-13 |
| 1977 | Lehigh | Jacksonville St | 33-0 |
| 1978 | Eastern Illinois | Delaware | 10-9 |
| 1979 | Delaware | Youngstown St | 38-21 |
| 1980 | Cal Poly SLO | Eastern Illinois | 21-13 |
| 1981 | SW Texas St | N Dakota St | 42-13 |
| 1982 | SW Texas St | UC-Davis | 34-9 |
| 1983 | N Dakota St | Central St (OH) | 41-21 |
| 1984 | Troy St | N Dakota St | 18-17 |
| 1985 | N Dakota St | N Alabama | 35-7 |
| 1986 | N Dakota St | S Dakota | 27-7 |
| 1987 | Troy St | Portland St | 31-17 |
| 1988 | N Dakota St | Portland St | 35-21 |
| 1989 | Mississippi Col | Jacksonville St | 3-0 |
| 1990 | N Dakota St | Indiana (PA) | 51-11 |
| 1991 | Pittsburg St | Jacksonville St | 23-6 |
| 1992 | Jacksonville St | Pittsburg St | 17-13 |

## Division III

| Year | Winner | Runner-Up | Score |
|---|---|---|---|
| 1973 | Wittenberg | Juniata | 41-0 |
| 1974 | Central (IA) | Ithaca | 10-8 |
| 1975 | Wittenberg | Ithaca | 28-0 |
| 1976 | St John's (MN) | Towson St | 31-28 |
| 1977 | Widener | Wabash | 39-36 |
| 1978 | Baldwin-Wallace | Wittenberg | 24-10 |
| 1979 | Ithaca | Wittenberg | 14-10 |
| 1980 | Dayton | Ithaca | 63-0 |
| 1981 | Widener | Dayton | 17-10 |
| 1982 | W Georgia | Augustana (IL) | 14-0 |
| 1983 | Augustana (IL) | Union (NY) | 21-17 |
| 1984 | Augustana (IL) | Central (IA) | 21-12 |
| 1985 | Augustana (IL) | Ithaca | 20-7 |
| 1986 | Augustana (IL) | Salisbury St | 31-3 |
| 1987 | Wagner | Dayton | 19-3 |
| 1988 | Ithaca | Central (IA) | 39-24 |
| 1989 | Dayton | Union (NY) | 17-7 |
| 1990 | Allegheny | Lycoming | 21-14 (OT) |
| 1991 | Ithaca | Dayton | 34-20 |
| 1992 | Wisconsin-LaCrosse | Washington and Jefferson | 16-12 |

## Division I

| Year | Winner | Runner-Up | Score |
|------|--------|-----------|-------|
| 1956 | St Joseph's (IN) Montana State | | 0-0 |
| 1957 | Kansas St-Pittsburg | Hillsdale (MI) | 27-26 |
| 1958 | Northeastern Oklahoma | Northern Arizona | 19-13 |
| 1959 | Texas A&I | Lenoir-Rhyne (NC) | 20-7 |
| 1960 | Lenoir-Rhyne | Humboldt St (CA) | 15-14 |
| 1961 | Kansas St-Pittsburg | Linfield (OR) | 12-7 |
| 1962 | Central St (OK) | Lenoir-Rhyne (NC) | 28-13 |
| 1963 | St John's (MN) | Prairie View (TX) | 33-27 |
| 1964 | Concordia-Moorhead Sam Houston | | 7-7 |
| 1965 | St John's (MN) | Linfield (OR) | 33-0 |
| 1966 | Waynesburg (PA) | WI-Whitewater | 42-21 |
| 1967 | Fairmont St (WV) | Eastern Washington | 28-21 |
| 1968 | Troy St (MI) | Texas A&I | 43-35 |
| 1969 | Texas A&I | Concordia-Moorhead | 32-7 |
| 1970 | Texas A&I | Wofford (SC) | 48-7 |
| 1971 | Livingston (AL) | Arkansas Tech | 14-12 |
| 1972 | E Texas St | Carson-Newman | 21-18 |
| 1973 | Abilene Christian | Elon (NC) | 42-14 |
| 1974 | Texas A&I | Henderson St (AR) | 34-23 |
| 1975 | Texas A&I | Salem (WV) | 37-0 |
| 1976 | Texas A&I | Central Arkansas | 26-0 |
| 1977 | Abilene Christian | Southwestern Oklahoma | 24-7 |
| 1978 | Angelo St | Elon (NC) | 34-14 |
| 1979 | Texas A&I | Central St (OK) | 20-14 |
| 1980 | Elon (NC) | Northeastern Oklahoma | 17-10 |
| 1981 | Elon (NC) | Pittsburg St | 3-0 |
| 1982 | Central St (OK) | Mesa (CO) | 14-11 |
| 1983 | Carson-Newman (TN) | Mesa (CO) | 36-28 |
| 1984 | Carson-Newman (TN) Central Arkansas | | 19-19 |
| 1985 | Central Arkansas Hillsdale (MI) | | 10-10 |
| 1986 | Carson-Newman (TN) | Cameron (OK) | 17-0 |
| 1987 | Cameron (OK) | Carson-Newman (TN) | 30-2 |
| 1988 | Carson-Newman (TN) | Adams St (CO) | 56-21 |
| 1989 | Carson-Newman (TN) | Emporia St (KS) | 34-20 |
| 1990 | Central St (OH) | Mesa St (CO) | 38-16 |
| 1991 | Central Arkansas | Central St (OH) | 19-16 |
| 1992 | Central St (OH) | Gardner-Webb (NC) | 19-16 |

## Division II

| Year | Winner | Runner-Up | Score |
|------|--------|-----------|-------|
| 1970 | Westminster (PA) | Anderson (IN) | 21-16 |
| 1971 | California Lutheran | Westminster (PA) | 30-14 |
| 1972 | Missouri Southern | Northwestern (IA) | 21-14 |
| 1973 | Northwestern (IA) | Glenville St (WV) | 10-3 |
| 1974 | Texas Lutheran | Missouri Valley | 42-0 |
| 1975 | Texas Lutheran | California Lutheran | 34-8 |
| 1976 | Westminster (PA) | Redlands (CA) | 20-13 |
| 1977 | Westminster (PA) | California Lutheran | 17-9 |
| 1978 | Concordia-Moorhead | Findlay (OH) | 7-0 |
| 1979 | Findlay (OH) | Northwestern (IA) | 51-6 |
| 1980 | Pacific Lutheran | Wilmington | 38-10 |
| 1981 | Austin Col Concordia-Moorhead | | 24-24 |
| 1982 | Linfield (OR) | William Jewell (MO) | 33-15 |
| 1983 | Northwestern (IA) | Pacific Lutheran | 25-21 |
| 1984 | Linfield (OR) | Northwestern (IA) | 33-22 |
| 1985 | WI-La Crosse | Pacific Lutheran | 24-7 |
| 1986 | Linfield (OR) | Baker (KS) | 17-0 |
| 1987 | Pacific Lutheran | WI-Stevens Point* | 16-16 |
| 1988 | Westminster (PA) | WI-La Crosse | 21-14 |
| 1989 | Westminster (PA) | WI-La Crosse | 51-30 |
| 1990 | Peru St (NEB) | Westminster (PA) | 17-7 |
| 1991 | Georgetown (KY) | Pacific Lutheran | 28-20 |
| 1992 | Findlay (OH) | Linfield (OR) | 26-13 |

*Forfeited 1987 season due to use of an ineligible player.

## Heisman Memorial Trophy

Awarded to the best college player by the Downtown Athletic Club of New York City. The trophy is named after John W. Heisman, who coached Georgia Tech to the national championship in 1917 and later served as DAC athletic director.

| Year | Winner, College, Position<br>Winner's Season Statistics | Runner-up, College |
|---|---|---|
| 1935 | **Jay Berwanger, Chicago, HB**<br>Rush: 119 Yds: 577 TD: 6 | Monk Meyer, Army |
| 1936 | **Larry Kelley, Yale, E**<br>Rec: 17 Yds: 372 TD: 6 | Sam Francis, Nebraska |
| 1937 | **Clint Frank, Yale, HB**<br>Rush: 157 Yds: 667 TD: 11 | Byron White, Colorado |
| 1938 | **†Davey O'Brien, Texas Christian, QB**<br>Att/Comp: 194/110 Yds: 1733 TD: 19 | Marshall Goldberg, Pittsburgh |
| 1939 | **Nile Kinnick, Iowa, HB**<br>Rush: 106 Yds: 374 TD: 5 | Tom Harmon, Michigan |
| 1940 | **Tom Harmon, Michigan, HB**<br>Rush: 191 Yds: 852 TD: 16 | John Kimbrough, Texas A&M |
| 1941 | **†Bruce Smith, Minnesota, HB**<br>Rush: 98 Yds: 480 TD: 6 | Angelo Bertelli, Notre Dame |
| 1942 | **Frank Sinkwich, Georgia, HB**<br>Att/Comp: 166/84 Yds: 1392 TD: 10 | Paul Governali, Columbia |
| 1943 | **Angelo Bertelli, Notre Dame, QB**<br>Att/Comp: 36/25 Yds: 511 TD: 10 | Bob Odell, Pennsylvania |
| 1944 | **Les Horvath, Ohio State, QB**<br>Rush: 163 Yds: 924 TD: 12 | Glenn Davis, Army |
| 1945 | *****†Doc Blanchard, Army, FB**<br>Rush: 101 Yds: 718 TD: 13 | Glenn Davis, Army |
| 1946 | **Glenn Davis, Army, HB**<br>Rush: 123 Yds: 712 TD: 7 | Charley Trippi, Georgia |
| 1947 | **†John Lujack, Notre Dame, QB**<br>Att/Comp: 109/61 Yds: 777 TD: 9 | Bob Chappius, Michigan |
| 1948 | ***Doak Walker, Southern Methodist, HB**<br>Rush: 108 Yds: 532 TD: 8 | Charlie Justice, N Carolina |
| 1949 | **†Leon Hart, Notre Dame, E**<br>Rec: 19 Yds: 257 TD: 5 | Charlie Justice, N Carolina |
| 1950 | ***Vic Janowicz, Ohio St, HB**<br>Att/Comp: 77/32 Yds: 561 TD: 12 | Hank Lauricella, Tennessee |
| 1951 | **Dick Kazmaier, Princeton, HB**<br>Rush: 149 Yds: 861 TD: 9 | Hank Lauricella, Tennessee |
| 1952 | **Billy Vessels, Oklahoma, HB**<br>Rush: 167 Yds: 1072 TD: 17 | Jack Scarbath, Maryland |
| 1953 | **John Lattner, Notre Dame, HB**<br>Rush: 134 Yds: 651 TD: 6 | Paul Geil, Minnesota |
| 1954 | **Alan Ameche, Wisconsin, FB**<br>Rush: 146 Yds: 641 TD: 9 | Kurt Burris, Oklahoma |
| 1955 | **Howard Cassady, Ohio St, HB**<br>Rush: 161 Yds: 958 TD: 15 | Jim Swink, Texas Christian |
| 1956 | **Paul Hornung, Notre Dame, QB**<br>Att/Comp: 111/59 Yds: 917 TD: 3 | Johnny Majors, Tennessee |
| 1957 | **John David Crow, Texas A&M, HB**<br>Rush: 129 Yds: 562 TD: 10 | Alex Karras, Iowa |
| 1958 | **Pete Dawkins, Army, HB**<br>Rush: 78 Yds: 428 TD: 6 | Randy Duncan, Iowa |
| 1959 | **Billy Cannon, Louisiana St, HB**<br>Rush: 139 Yds: 598 TD: 6 | Rich Lucas, Penn St |
| 1960 | **Joe Bellino, Navy, HB**<br>Rush: 168 Yds: 834 TD: 18 | Tom Brown, Minnesota |
| 1961 | **Ernie Davis, Syracuse, HB**<br>Rush: 150 Yds: 823 TD: 15 | Bob Ferguson, Ohio St |
| 1962 | **Terry Baker, Oregon St, QB**<br>Att/Comp: 203/112 Yds: 1738 TD: 15 | Jerry Stovall, Louisiana St |
| 1963 | ***Roger Staubach, Navy, QB**<br>Att/Comp: 161/107 Yds: 1474 TD: 7 | Billy Lothridge, Georgia Tech |
| 1964 | **John Huarte, Notre Dame, QB**<br>Att/Comp: 205/114 Yds: 2062 TD: 16 | Jerry Rhome, Tulsa |

## Heisman Memorial Trophy (Cont.)

| Year | Winner, College, Position<br>Winner's Season Statistics | Runner-up, College |
|------|------|------|
| 1965 | **Mike Garrett, Southern Cal, HB**<br>Rush: 267 TD: 1440 TD: 16 | Howard Twilley, Tulsa |
| 1966 | **Steve Spurrier, Florida, QB**<br>Att/Comp: 291/179 Yds: 2012 TD: 16 | Bob Griese, Purdue |
| 1967 | **Gary Beban, UCLA, QB**<br>Att/Comp: 156/87 Yds: 1359 TD: 8 | O.J. Simpson, Southern Cal |
| 1968 | **O.J. Simpson, Southern Cal, HB**<br>Rush: 383 Yds: 1880 TD: 23 | Leroy Keyes, Purdue |
| 1969 | **Steve Owens, Oklahoma, FB**<br>Rush: 358 Yds: 1523 TD: 23 | Mike Phipps, Purdue |
| 1970 | **Jim Plunkett, Stanford, QB**<br>Att/Comp: 358/191 Yds: 2715 TD: 18 | Joe Theismann, Notre Dame |
| 1971 | **Pat Sullivan, Auburn, QB**<br>Att/Comp: 281/162 Yds: 2012 TD: 20 | Ed Marinaro, Cornell |
| 1972 | **Johnny Rodgers, Nebraska, FL**<br>Rec: 55 Yds: 942 TD: 17 | Greg Pruitt, Oklahoma |
| 1973 | **John Cappelletti, Penn St, HB**<br>Rush: 286 Yds: 1522 TD: 17 | John Hicks, Ohio St |
| 1974 | **\*Archie Griffin, Ohio St, HB**<br>Rush: 256 Yds: 1695 TD: 12 | Anthony Davis, Southern Cal |
| 1975 | **Archie Griffin, Ohio St, HB**<br>Rush: 262 Yds: 1450 TD: 4 | Chuck Muncie, California |
| 1976 | **†Tony Dorsett, Pittsburgh, HB**<br>Rush: 370 Yds: 2150 TD: 23 | Ricky Bell, Southern Cal |
| 1977 | **Earl Campbell, Texas, FB**<br>Rush: 267 Yds: 1744 TD: 19 | Terry Miller, Oklahoma St |
| 1978 | **\*Billy Sims, Oklahoma, HB**<br>Rush: 231 Yds: 1762 TD: 20 | Chuck Fusina, Penn St |
| 1979 | **Charles White, Southern Cal, HB**<br>Rush: 332 Yds: 1803 TD: 19 | Billy Sims, Oklahoma |
| 1980 | **George Rogers, S Carolina, HB**<br>Rush: 324 Yds: 1894 TD: 14 | Hugh Green, Pittsburgh |
| 1981 | **Marcus Allen, Southern Cal, HB**<br>Rush: 433 Yds: 2427 TD: 23 | Herschel Walker, Georgia |
| 1982 | **\*Herschel Walker, Georgia, HB**<br>Rush: 335 Yds: 1752 TD: 17 | John Elway, Stanford |
| 1983 | **Mike Rozier, Nebraska, HB**<br>Rush: 275 Yds: 2148 TD: 29 | Steve Young, Brigham Young |
| 1984 | **Doug Flutie, Boston College, QB**<br>Att/Comp: 396/233 Yds: 3454 TD: 27 | Keith Byars, Ohio St |
| 1985 | **Bo Jackson, Auburn, HB**<br>Rush: 278 Yds: 1786 TD: 17 | Chuck Long, Iowa |
| 1986 | **Vinny Testaverde, Miami, QB**<br>Att/Comp: 276/175 Yds: 2557 TD: 26 | Paul Palmer, Temple |
| 1987 | **Tim Brown, Notre Dame, WR**<br>Rec: 39 Yds: 846 TD: 7 | Don McPherson, Syracuse |
| 1988 | **\*Barry Sanders, Oklahoma St, RB**<br>Rush: 344 Yds: 2628 TD: 39 | Rodney Peete, Southern Cal |
| 1989 | **\*Andre Ware, Houston, QB**<br>Att/Comp: 578/365 Yds: 4699 TD: 46 | Anthony Thompson, Indiana |
| 1990 | **\*Ty Detmer, Brigham Young, QB**<br>Att/Comp: 562/361 Yds: 5188 TD: 41 | Raghib Ismail, Notre Dame |
| 1991 | **\*Desmond Howard, Michigan, WR**<br>Rec: 61 Yds: 950 TD: 23 | Casey Weldon, Florida St |
| 1992 | **Gino Torretta, Miami, QB**<br>Att/Comp: 402/228 Yds: 3060 TD: 19 | Marshall Faulk, San Diego St |

*Juniors (all others seniors). †Winners who played for national championship teams the same year.

Note: Former Heisman winners and national media cast votes, with ballots allowing for three names (3 points for first, 2 for second and 1 for third).

# Awards

## Jim Thorpe Award

Given to the best defensive back of the year, the award is presented by the Jim Thorpe Athletic Club of Oklahoma City.

| Year | Player, College | Year | Player, College |
|------|-----------------|------|-----------------|
| 1986 | Thomas Everett, Baylor | 1989 | Mark Carrier, Southern Cal |
| 1987 | Bennie Blades, Miami (FL) | 1990 | Darryl Lewis, Arizona |
| | Rickey Dixon, Oklahoma | 1991 | Terrell Buckley, Florida St |
| 1988 | Deion Sanders, Florida St | 1992 | Deon Figures, Colorado |

## Outland Trophy

Given to the outstanding interior lineman, selected by the Football Writers Association of America.

| Year | Player, College, Position | Year | Player, College, Position |
|------|---------------------------|------|---------------------------|
| 1946 | George Connor, Notre Dame, T | 1969 | Mike Reid, Penn St, DT |
| 1947 | Joe Steffy, Army, G | 1970 | Jim Stillwagon, Ohio St, MG |
| 1948 | Bill Fischer, Notre Dame, G | 1971 | Larry Jacobson, Nebraska, DT |
| 1949 | Ed Bagdon, Michigan St, G | 1972 | Rich Glover, Nebraska, MG |
| 1950 | Bob Gain, Kentucky, T | 1973 | John Hicks, Ohio St, OT |
| 1951 | Jim Weatherall, Oklahoma, T | 1974 | Randy White, Maryland, DE |
| 1952 | Dick Modzelewski, Maryland, T | 1975 | Lee Roy Selmon, Oklahoma, DT |
| 1953 | J. D. Roberts, Oklahoma, G | 1976 | *Ross Browner, Notre Dame, DE |
| 1954 | Bill Brooks, Arkansas, G | 1977 | Brad Shearer, Texas, DT |
| 1955 | Calvin Jones, Iowa, G | 1978 | Greg Roberts, Oklahoma, G |
| 1956 | Jim Parker, Ohio St, G | 1979 | Jim Ritcher, N Carolina St, C |
| 1957 | Alex Karras, Iowa, T | 1980 | Mark May, Pittsburgh, OT |
| 1958 | Zeke Smith, Auburn, G | 1981 | *Dave Rimington, Nebraska, C |
| 1959 | Mike McGee, Duke, T | 1982 | Dave Rimington, Nebraska, C |
| 1960 | Tom Brown, Minnesota, G | 1983 | Dean Steinkuhler, Nebraska, G |
| 1961 | Merlin Olsen, Utah St, T | 1984 | Bruce Smith, Virginia Tech, DT |
| 1962 | Bobby Bell, Minnesota, T | 1985 | Mike Ruth, Boston Col, NG |
| 1963 | Scott Appleton, Texas, T | 1986 | Jason Buck, Brigham Young, DT |
| 1964 | Steve DeLong, Tennessee, T | 1987 | Chad Hennings, Air Force, DT |
| 1965 | Tommy Nobis, Texas, G | 1988 | Tracy Rocker, Auburn, DT |
| 1966 | Loyd Phillips, Arkansas, T | 1989 | Mohammed Elewonibi, Brigham Young, G |
| 1967 | Ron Yary, Southern Cal, T | 1990 | Russell Maryland, Miami (FL), DT |
| 1968 | Bill Stanfill, Georgia, T | 1991 | *Steve Emtman, Washington, DT |
| 1968 | Bill Stanfill, Georgia, T | 1992 | Will Shields, Nebraska, G |

*Juniors (all others seniors).

## Vince Lombardi/Rotary Award

Given to the outstanding college lineman of the year, the award is sponsored by the Rotary Club of Houston.

| Year | Player, College, Position | Year | Player, College, Position |
|------|---------------------------|------|---------------------------|
| 1970 | Jim Stillwagon, Ohio St, MG | 1982 | Dave Rimington, Nebraska, C |
| 1971 | Walt Patulski, Notre Dame, DE | 1983 | Dean Steinkuhler, Nebraska, G |
| 1972 | Rich Glover, Nebraska, MG | 1984 | Tony Degrate, Texas, DT |
| 1973 | John Hicks, Ohio St, OT | 1985 | Tony Casillas, Oklahoma, NG |
| 1974 | Randy White, Maryland, DT | 1986 | Cornelius Bennett, Alabama, LB |
| 1975 | Lee Roy Selmon, Oklahoma, DT | 1987 | Chris Spielman, Ohio St, LB |
| 1976 | Wilson Whitley, Houston, DT | 1988 | Tracy Rocker, Auburn, DT |
| 1977 | Ross Browner, Notre Dame, DE | 1989 | Percy Snow, Michigan St, LB |
| 1978 | Bruce Clark, Penn St, DT | 1990 | Chris Zorich, Notre Dame, NG |
| 1979 | Brad Budde, Southern Cal, G | 1991 | Steve Emtman, Washington, DT |
| 1980 | Hugh Green, Pittsburgh, DE | 1992 | Marvin Jones, Florida St, LB |
| 1981 | Kenneth Sims, Texas, DT | | |

## Butkus Award

Given to the top collegiate linebacker, the award was established by the Downtown Athletic Club of Orlando and named for college hall of famer Dick Butkus of Illinois.

| Year | Player, College | Year | Player, College |
|------|-----------------|------|-----------------|
| 1985 | Brian Bosworth, Oklahoma | 1989 | Percy Snow, Michigan St |
| 1986 | Brian Bosworth, Oklahoma | 1990 | Alfred Williams, Colorado |
| 1987 | Paul McGowan, Florida St | 1991 | Erick Anderson, Michigan |
| 1988 | Derrick Thomas, Alabama | 1992 | Marvin Jones, Florida St |

## Davey O'Brien National Quarterback Award

Given to the No. 1 quarterback in the nation by the Davey O'Brien Educational and Charitable Trust of Fort Worth. Named for Texas Christian hall of fame quarterback Davey O'Brien (1936-38).

| Year | Player, College | Year | Player, College |
|------|-----------------|------|-----------------|
| 1981 | Jim McMahon, Brigham Young | 1987 | Don McPherson, Syracuse |
| 1982 | Todd Blackledge, Penn St | 1988 | Troy Aikman, UCLA |
| 1983 | Steve Young, Brigham Young | 1989 | Andre Ware, Houston |
| 1984 | Doug Flutie, Boston Col | 1990 | Ty Detmer, Brigham Young |
| 1985 | Chuck Long, Iowa | 1991 | Ty Detmer, Brigham Young |
| 1986 | Vinny Testaverde, Miami (FL) | 1992 | Gino Torretta, Miami |

Note: Originally known as the Davey O'Brien Memorial Trophy, honoring the outstanding football player in the Southwest as follows: 1977—Earl Campbell, Texas, RB; 1978—Billy Sims, Oklahoma, RB; 1979—Mike Singletary, Baylor, LB; 1980—Mike Singletary, Baylor, LB.

## Maxwell Award

Given to the nation's outstanding college football player by the Maxwell Football Club of Philadelphia.

| Year | Player, College, Position | Year | Player, College, Position |
|------|---------------------------|------|---------------------------|
| 1937 | Clint Frank, Yale, HB | 1965 | Tommy Nobis, Texas, LB |
| 1938 | Davey O'Brien, Texas Christian, QB | 1966 | Jim Lynch, Notre Dame, LB |
| 1939 | Nile Kinnick, Iowa, HB | 1967 | Gary Beban, UCLA, QB |
| 1940 | Tom Harmon, Michigan, HB | 1968 | O. J. Simpson, Southern Cal, RB |
| 1941 | Bill Dudley, Virginia, HB | 1969 | Mike Reid, Penn St, DT |
| 1942 | Paul Governali, Columbia, QB | 1970 | Jim Plunkett, Stanford, QB |
| 1943 | Bob Odell, Pennsylvania, HB | 1971 | Ed Marinaro, Cornell, RB |
| 1944 | Glenn Davis, Army, HB | 1972 | Brad Van Pelt, Michigan St, DB |
| 1945 | Doc Blanchard, Army, FB | 1973 | John Cappelletti, Penn St, RB |
| 1946 | Charley Trippi, Georgia, HB | 1974 | Steve Joachim, Temple, QB |
| 1947 | Doak Walker, Southern Meth, HB | 1975 | Archie Griffin, Ohio St, RB |
| 1948 | Chuck Bednarik, Pennsylvania, C | 1976 | Tony Dorsett, Pittsburgh, RB |
| 1949 | Leon Hart, Notre Dame, E | 1977 | Ross Browner, Notre Dame, DE |
| 1950 | Reds Bagnell, Pennsylvania, HB | 1978 | Chuck Fusina, Penn St, QB |
| 1951 | Dick Kazmaier, Princeton, HB | 1979 | Charles White, Southern Cal, RB |
| 1952 | John Lattner, Notre Dame, HB | 1980 | Hugh Green, Pittsburgh, DE |
| 1953 | John Lattner, Notre Dame, HB | 1981 | Marcus Allen, Southern Cal, RB |
| 1954 | Ron Beagle, Navy, E | 1982 | Herschel Walker, Georgia, RB |
| 1955 | Howard Cassady, Ohio St, HB | 1983 | Mike Rozier, Nebraska, RB |
| 1956 | Tommy McDonald, Oklahoma, HB | 1984 | Doug Flutie, Boston Col, QB |
| 1957 | Bob Reifsnyder, Navy, T | 1985 | Chuck Long, Iowa, QB |
| 1958 | Pete Dawkins, Army, HB | 1986 | Vinny Testaverde, Miami (FL), QB |
| 1959 | Rich Lucas, Penn St, QB | 1987 | Don McPherson, Syracuse, QB |
| 1960 | Joe Bellino, Navy, HB | 1988 | Barry Sanders, Oklahoma St, RB |
| 1961 | Bob Ferguson, Ohio St, FB | 1989 | Anthony Thompson, Indiana, RB |
| 1962 | Terry Baker, Oregon St, QB | 1990 | Ty Detmer, Brigham Young, QB |
| 1963 | Roger Staubach, Navy, QB | 1991 | Desmond Howard, Michigan, WR |
| 1964 | Glenn Ressler, Penn St, C | 1992 | Gino Torretta, Miami (FL), QB |

## Walter Payton Player of the Year Award

Given to the top Division I-AA football player, the award is sponsored by Sports Network and voted on by Division I-AA sports information directors.

| Year | Player, College, Position |
|------|---------------------------|
| 1987 | Kenny Gamble, Colgate, RB |
| 1988 | Dave Meggett, Towson St, RB |
| 1989 | John Friesz, Idaho, QB |
| 1990 | Walter Dean, Grambling, RB |
| 1991 | Jamie Martin, Weber St, QB |
| 1992 | Michael Payton, Marshall, QB |

## The Harlon Hill Trophy

Given to the outstanding NCAA Division II college football player, the award is sponsored by the National Harlon Hill Awards Committee, Florence, AL.

| Year | Player, College, Position |
|------|---------------------------|
| 1986 | Jeff Bentrim, N Dakota St, QB |
| 1987 | Johnny Bailey, Texas A&I, RB |
| 1988 | Johnny Bailey, Texas A&I, RB |
| 1989 | Johnny Bailey, Texas A&I, RB |
| 1990 | Chris Simdorn, N Dakota St, QB |
| 1991 | Ronnie West, Pittsburg St, WR |
| 1992 | Ronald Moore, Pittsburg St, RB |

## Career

### SCORING

**Most Points Scored:** 423 — Roman Anderson, Houston, 1988-91
**Most Points Scored per Game:** 11.9 — Bob Gaiters, New Mexico St, 1959-60
**Most Touchdowns Scored:** 65 — Anthony Thompson, Indiana, 1986-89
**Most Touchdowns Scored per Game:** 1.93 — Ed Marinaro, Cornell, 1969-71
**Most Touchdowns Scored, Rushing:** 64 — Anthony Thompson, Indiana, 1986-89
**Most Touchdowns Scored, Passing:** 121 — Ty Detmer, Brigham Young, 1988-91
**Most Touchdowns Scored, Receiving:** 43 — Aaron Turner, Pacific, 1989-92
**Most Touchdowns Scored, Interception Returns:** 5 — Ken Thomas, San Jose St, 1979-82; Jackie Walker, Tennessee, 1969-71
**Most Touchdowns Scored, Punt Returns:** 7 — Johnny Rodgers, Nebraska, 1970-72; Jack Mitchell, Oklahoma, 1946-48
**Most Touchdowns Scored, Kickoff Returns:** 6 — Anthony Davis, Southern Cal, 1972-74

### TOTAL OFFENSE

**Most Plays:** 1722 — Todd Santos, San Diego St, 1984-87
**Most Plays per Game:** 48.5 — Doug Gaynor, Long Beach St, 1984-85
**Most Yards Gained:** 14,665 — Ty Detmer, Brigham Young, 1988-91 (15,031 passing, -366 rushing)
**Most Yards Gained per Game:** 318.8 — Ty Detmer, Brigham Young, 1988-91
**Most 300+ Yard Games:** 18 — Steve Young, Brigham Young, 1981-83

### RUSHING

**Most Rushes:** 1215 — Steve Bartalo, Colorado St, 1983-86 (4813 yds)
**Most Rushes per Game:** 34.0 — Ed Marinaro, Cornell, 1969-71
**Most Yards Gained:** 6082 — Tony Dorsett, Pittsburgh, 1973-76
**Most Yards Gained per Game:** 174.6 — Ed Marinaro, Cornell, 1969-71
**Most 100+ Yard Games:** 33 — Tony Dorsett, Pittsburgh, 1973-76; Archie Griffin, Ohio St, 1972-75
**Most 200+ Yard Games:** 11 — Marcus Allen, Southern Cal, 1978-81

### SPECIAL TEAMS

**Highest Punt Return Average:** 23.6 — Jack Mitchell, Oklahoma, 1946-48
**Highest Kickoff Return Average:** 36.2 — Forrest Hall, San Francisco, 1946-47
**Highest Average Yards per Punt:** 45.6 — Reggie Roby, Iowa, 1979-82

### PASSING

**Highest Passing Efficiency Rating:** 162.7 — Ty Detmer, Brigham Young, 1988-91 (1530 attempts, 958 completions, 65 interceptions, 15,031 yards, 121 TD passes)
**Most Passes Attempted:** 1,530 — Ty Detmer, Brigham Young, 1988-91
**Most Passes Attempted per Game:** 39.6 — Mike Perez, San Jose St, 1986-87
**Most Passes Completed:** 958 — Ty Detmer, Brigham Young, 1988-91
**Most Passes Completed per Game:** 25.9 — Doug Gaynor, Long Beach St, 1984-85
**Highest Completion Percentage:** 65.2 — Steve Young, Brigham Young, 1981-83
**Most Yards Gained:** 15,031 — Ty Detmer, Brigham Young, 1988-91
**Most Yards Gained per Game:** 326.7 — Ty Detmer, Brigham Young, 1988-91

### RECEIVING

**Most Passes Caught:** 266 — Aaron Turner, Pacific, 1989-92
**Most Passes Caught per Game:** 10.5 — Emmanuel Hazard, Houston, 1989-90
**Most Yards Gained:** 4345 — Aaron Turner, Pacific, 1989-92
**Most Yards Gained per Game:** 128.6 — Howard Twilley, Tulsa, 1963-65
**Highest Average Gain per Reception:** 25.7 — Wesley Walker, California, 1973-75

### ALL-PURPOSE RUNNING

**Most Plays:** 1347 — Steve Bartalo, Colorado St, 1983-86 (1215 rushes, 132 receptions)
**Most Yards Gained:** 7172 — Napoleon McCallum, Navy, 1981-85 (4179 rushing, 796 receiving, 858 punt returns, 1339 kickoff returns)
**Most Yards Gained per Game:** 237.8 — Ryan Benjamin, Pacific, 1990-92
**Highest Average Gain per Play:** 17.4 — Anthony Carter, Michigan, 1979-82.

### INTERCEPTIONS

**Most Passes Intercepted:** 29 — Al Brosky, Illinois, 1950-52
**Most Passes Intercepted per Game:** 1.07 — Al Brosky, Illinois, 1950-52
**Most Yards on Interception Returns:** 470 — John Provost, Holy Cross, 1972-74
**Highest Average Gain per Interception:** 26.5 — Tom Pridemore, W Virginia, 1975-77

## Single Season

### SCORING

**Most Points Scored:** 234 — Barry Sanders, Oklahoma St, 1988
**Most Points Scored per Game:** 21.27 — Barry Sanders, Oklahoma St, 1988
**Most Touchdowns Scored:** 39 — Barry Sanders, Oklahoma St, 1988
**Most Touchdowns Scored, Rushing:** 37 — Barry Sanders, Oklahoma St, 1988
**Most Touchdowns Scored, Passing:** 54 — David Klingler, Houston, 1990
**Most Touchdowns Scored, Receiving:** 22 — Emmanuel Hazard, Houston, 1989
**Most Touchdowns Scored, Interception Returns:** 3 — by many players
**Most Touchdowns Scored, Punt Returns:** 4 — James Henry, Southern Miss, 1987; Golden Richards, Brigham Young, 1971; Cliff Branch , Colorado1971
**Most Touchdowns Scored, Kickoff Returns:** 3 — Terance Mathis, New Mexico, 1989; Willie Gault, Tennessee, 1980; Anthony Davis, Southern Cal, 1974; Stan Brown, Purdue, 1970; Forrest Hall, San Francisco, 1946

### TOTAL OFFENSE

**Most Plays:** 704 — David Klingler, Houston, 1990
Most Yards Gained: 5221 — David Klingler, Houston, 1990
**Most Yards Gained per Game:** 474.6 — David Klingler, Houston, 1990
**Most 300+ Yard Games:** 11 — Jim McMahon, Brigham Young, 1980

### RUSHING

**Most Rushes:** 403 — Marcus Allen, Southern Cal, 1981
**Most Rushes per Game:** 39.6 — Ed Marinaro, Cornell, 1971
**Most Yards Gained:** 2628 — Barry Sanders, Oklahoma St, 1988
**Most Yards Gained per Game:** 238.9 — Barry Sanders, Oklahoma St, 1988
**Most 100+ Yard Games:** 11 — By nine players, most recently Barry Sanders, Oklahoma St, 1988

### PASSING

**Highest Passing Efficiency Rating:** 176.9 — Jim McMahon, Brigham Young, 1980 (445 attempts, 284 completions, 18 interceptions, 4571 yards, 47 TD passes)
**Most Passes Attempted:** 643 — David Klingler, Houston, 1990
**Most Passes Attempted per Game:** 58.4 — David Klingler, Houston, 1990
**Most Passes Completed:** 374 — David Klingler, Houston, 1990
**Most Passes Completed per Game:** 34.0 — David Klingler, Houston, 1990
**Highest Completion Percentage:** 71.3 — Steve Young, Brigham Young, 1983
**Most Yards Gained:** 5188 — Ty Detmer, Brigham Young, 1990
**Most Yards Gained per Game:** 471.6 — Ty Detmer, Brigham Young, 1990

### RECEIVING

**Most Passes Caught:** 142 — Emmanuel Hazard, Houston, 1989
**Most Passes Caught per Game:** 13.4 — Howard Twilley, Tulsa, 1965
**Most Yards Gained:** 1779 — Howard Twilley, Tulsa, 1965
**Most Yards Gained per Game:** 177.9 — Howard Twilley, Tulsa, 1965
**Highest Average Gain per Reception:** 27.9 — Elmo Wright, Houston, 1968

### ALL-PURPOSE RUNNING

**Most Plays:** 432 — Marcus Allen, Southern Cal, 1981
**Most Yards Gained:** 3250 — Barry Sanders, Oklahoma St, 1988
**Most Yards Gained per Game:** 295.5 — Barry Sanders, Oklahoma St, 1988
**Highest Average Gain per Play:** 18.6 — Craig Thompson, Eastern Michigan, 1992

### INTERCEPTIONS

**Most Passes Intercepted:** 14 — Al Worley, Washington, 1968
**Most Yards on Interception Returns:** 302 — Charles Phillips, Southern Cal, 1974
**Highest Average Gain per Interception:** 50.6 — Norm Thompson, Utah, 1969

### SPECIAL TEAMS

**Highest Punt Return Average:** 25.9 — Bill Blackstock, Tennessee, 1951
**Highest Kickoff Return Average:** 38.2 — Forrest Hall, San Francisco, 1946
**Highest Average Yards per Punt:** 49.8 — Reggie Roby, Iowa, 1981

### THEY SAID IT

*Drew Bledsoe, former Washington State quarterback, after the New England Patriots made him the top choice in the NFL draft, recalling that he once thought the No. 1 pick was someone special: "But now that it's me, it loses some of its mystique."*

# Division I-A Individual Records (Cont.)

## Single Game

### SCORING

**Most Points Scored:** 48 — Howard Griffith, Illinois, 1990 (vs Southern Illinois)
**Most Field Goals:** 7 — Dale Klein, Nebraska, 1985 (vs Missouri); Mike Prindle, Western Michigan, 1984 (vs Marshall)
**Most Extra Points (Kick):** 13 — Terry Leiweke, Houston, 1968 (vs Tulsa)
**Most Extra Points (2-Pts):** 6 — Jim Pilot, New Mexico St, 1961 (vs Hardin-Simmons)

### TOTAL OFFENSE

**Most Yards Gained:** 732 — David Klingler, Houston, 1990 (vs Arizona St)

### RUSHING

**Most Yards Gained:** 396 — Tony Sands, Kansas, 1991 (vs Missouri)
**Most Touchdowns Rushed:** 8 — Howard Griffith, Illinois, 1990 (vs Southern Illinois)

### PASSING

**Most Passes Completed:** 48 — David Klingler, Houston, 1990 (vs Southern Methodist)
**Most Yards Gained:** 716 — David Klingler, Houston, 1990 (vs Arizona St)
**Most Touchdowns Passed:** 11 — David Klingler, Houston, 1990 [vs Eastern Washington (I-AA)]

### RECEIVING

**Most Passes Caught:** 22 — Jay Miller, Brigham Young, 1973 (vs New Mexico)
**Most Yards Gained:** 349 — Chuck Hughes, UTEP, 1965 (vs N Texas St)
**Most Touchdown Catches:** 6 — Tim Delaney, San Diego St, 1969 (vs New Mexico St)

# NCAA Division I-AA Individual Records

## Career

### SCORING

**Most Points Scored:** 385 — Marty Zendejas, NV-Reno, 1984-87
**Most Touchdowns Scored:** 60 — Charvez Foger, NV-Reno, 1985-88
**Most Touchdowns Scored, Rushing:** 55 — Kenny Gamble, Colgate, 1984-87
**Most Touchdowns Scored, Passing:** 139 — Willie Totten, Mississippi Valley, 1982-85
**Most Touchdowns Scored, Receiving:** 50 — Jerry Rice, Mississippi Valley, 1981-84

### PASSING

**Highest Passing Efficiency Rating:** 148.9 — Jay Johnson, Northern Iowa, 1989-92
**Most Passes Attempted:** 1,606 — Neil Lomax, Portland St, 1977-80
**Most Passes Completed:** 938 — Neil Lomax, Portland St, 1977-80
**Most Passes Completed per Game:** 23.8 — Stan Greene, Boston U, 1989-90
**Highest Completion Percentage:** 66.9 — Jason Garrett, Princeton, 1987-88

**Most Yards Gained:** 13,220 — Neil Lomax, Portland St, 1977-80
**Most Yards Gained per Game:** 317.8 — Willie Totten, Mississippi Valley, 1982-85

### RUSHING

**Most Rushes:** 963 — Kenny Gamble, Colgate, 1984-87
**Most Rushes per Game:** 23.7 — Paul Lewis, Boston U, 1981-84
**Most Yards Gained:** 5,333 — Frank Hawkins, NV-Reno, 1977-80
**Most Yards Gained per Game:** 133.0 — Mike Clark, Akron, 1984-86

### RECEIVING

**Most Passes Caught:** 301 — Jerry Rice, Mississippi Valley, 1981-84
**Most Yards Gained:** 4,693 — Jerry Rice, Mississippi Valley, 1981-84
**Most Yards Gained per Game:** 114.5 — Jerry Rice, Mississippi Valley, 1981-84
**Highest Average Gain per Reception:** 24.3 — John Taylor, Delaware St, 1982-85

## Single Season

### SCORING

**Most Points Scored:** 170 — Geoff Mitchell, Weber St, 1991
**Most Touchdowns Scored:** 28 — Geoff Mitchell, Weber St, 1991
**Most Touchdowns Scored, Rushing:** 24 — Geoff Mitchell, Weber St, 1991
**Most Touchdowns Scored, Passing:** 56 — Willie Totten, Mississippi Valley, 1984
**Most Touchdowns Scored, Receiving:** 27 — Jerry Rice, Mississippi Valley, 1984

### PASSING

**Highest Passing Efficiency Rating:** 181.3 — Michael Payton, Marshall, 1991
**Most Passes Attempted:** 518 — Willie Totten, Mississippi Valley, 1984
**Most Passes Completed:** 324 — Willie Totten, Mississippi Valley, 1984
**Most Passes Completed per Game:** 32.4 — Willie Totten, Mississippi Valley, 1984
**Highest Completion Percentage:** 68.2 — Jason Garrett, Princeton, 1984
**Most Yards Gained:** 4,557 — Willie Totten, Mississippi Valley, 1984
**Most Yards Gained per Game:** 455.7 — Willie Totten, Mississippi Valley, 1984

## Single Season (Cont.)

### RUSHING

**Most Rushes:** 351 — James Black, Akron, 1983
**Most Rushes per Game:** 34.0 — James Black, Akron, 1983
**Most Yards Gained:** 1,883 — Rich Erenberg, Colgate, 1983
**Most Yards Gained per Game:** 172.2 — Gene Lake, Deleware St, 1984

### RECEIVING

**Most Passes Caught:** 115 — Brian Forster, Rhode Island, 1985
**Most Yards Gained:** 1,682 — Jerry Rice, Mississippi Valley, 1984
**Most Yards Gained per Game:** 168.2 — Jerry Rice, Mississippi Valley, 1984
**Highest Average Gain per Reception:** 37.0 — Kenny Shedd, Northern Iowa, 1992

## Single Game

### SCORING

**Most Points Scored:** 36 — By five players. Most recently Erwin Matthews, Richmond, 1987 (vs Massachusetts)
**Most Field Goals:** 8 — Goran Lingmerth, Northern Arizona, 1986 (vs Idaho)

### PASSING

**Most Passes Completed:** 47 — Jamie Martin, Weber St, 1991 (vs Idaho St)
**Most Yards Gained:** 624 — Jamie Martin, Weber St, 1991 (vs Idaho St)
**Most Touchdowns Passed:** 9 — Willie Totten, Mississippi Valley, 1984 (vs Kentucky St)

### RUSHING

**Most Yards Gained:** 345 — Russell Davis, Idaho, 1981 (vs Portland St)
**Most Touchdowns Rushed:** 6 — Gene Lake, Delaware St, 1984 (vs. Howard); Gill Fenerty, Holy Cross, 1983 (vs Columbia); Henry Odom, S Carolina St, 1980 (vs Morgan St)

### RECEIVING

**Most Passes Caught:** 24 — Jerry Rice, Mississippi Valley 1983 (vs Southern-Baton Rouge)
**Most Yards Gained:** 370— Michael Lerch, Princeton, 1991 (vs Brown)
**Most Touchdown Catches:** 5 — Rennie Benn, Lehigh, 1985 [vs Indiana (PA)]; Jerry Rice, Mississippi Valley, 1984 (vs Prairie View and vs Kentucky St)

# NCAA Division II Individual Records

## Career

### SCORING

**Most Points Scored:** 464 — Walter Payton, Jackson St, 1971-74
**Most Touchdowns Scored:** 72 — Shawn Graves, Wofford, 1989-92
**Most Touchdowns Scored, Rushing:** 66 — Johnny Bailey, Texas A&I, 1986-89
**Most Touchdowns Scored, Passing:** 93 — Doug Williams, Grambling, 1974-77
**Most Touchdowns Scored, Receiving:** 49 — Bruce Cerone, Yankton/Emporia St, 1966-69

### PASSING

**Highest Passing Efficiency Rating:** 164.4 — Tony Aliucci, Indiana (PA)
**Most Passes Attempted:** 1,442 — Earl Harvey, N Carolina Central, 1985-88
**Most Passes Completed:** 690 — Earl Harvey, N Carolina Central, 1985-88
**Most Passes Completed per Game:** 25.0 — Tim Von Dulm, Portland St, 1969-70
**Highest Completion Percentage:** 69.6 — Chris Peterson, UC-Davis, 1985-86
**Most Yards Gained:** 10,621 — Earl Harvey, N Carolina Central, 1985-88
**Most Yards Gained per Game:** 320.1 — Tom Ehrhardt, Rhode Island, 1984-85

### RUSHING

**Most Rushes:** 1,072 — Bernie Peeters, Luther, 1968-71
**Most Rushes per Game:** 29.8 — Bernie Peeters, Luther, 1968-71
**Most Yards Gained:** 6,320 — Johnny Bailey, Texas A&I, 1986-89
**Most Yards Gained per Game:** 162.1 — Johnny Bailey, Texas A&I, 1986-89

### RECEIVING

**Most Passes Caught:** 253 — Chris Myers, Kenyon, 1967-70
**Most Yards Gained:** 4,354 — Bruce Cerone, Yankton/Emporia St, 1966-69
**Most Yards Gained per Game:** 137.3 — Ed Bell, Idaho St, 1968-69
**Highest Average Gain per Reception:** 21.8 — Willie Richardson, Jackson St, 1959-62

## Single Season

### SCORING

**Most Points Scored:** 178 — Terry Metcalf, Long Beach St, 1971
**Most Touchdowns Scored:** 29 — Terry Metcalf, Long Beach St, 1971
**Most Touchdowns Scored, Rushing:** 28 — Terry Metcalf, Long Beach St, 1971
**Most Touchdowns Scored, Passing:** 45 — Bob Toledo, San Francisco St, 1967
**Most Touchdowns Scored, Receiving:** 20 — Ed Bell, Idaho St, 1969

### PASSING

**Highest Passing Efficiency Rating:** 210.1 — Boyd Crawford, College of Idaho, 1953
**Most Passes Attempted:** 515 — Todd Mayfield, W Texas St, 1986
**Most Passes Completed:** 317 — Todd Mayfield, W Texas St, 1986
**Most Passes Completed per Game:** 28.8 — Todd Mayfield, W Texas St, 1986
**Highest Completion Percentage:** 70.1 — Chris Peterson, UC-Davis, 1986
**Most Yards Gained:** 3,741 — Chris Hegg, NE Missouri St, 1985
**Most Yards Gained per Game:** 351.3 — Bob Toledo, San Francisco St, 1967

### RUSHING

**Most Rushes:** 350 — Leon Burns, Long Beach St, 1969
**Most Rushes per Game:** 38.6 — Mark Perkins, Hobart, 1968
**Most Yards Gained:** 2,011 — Johnny Bailey, Texas A&I, 1986
**Most Yards Gained per Game:** 182.8 — Johnny Bailey, Texas A&I, 1986

### RECEIVING

**Most Passes Caught:** 106 — Barry Wagner, Alabama A&M, 1989
**Most Yards Gained:** 1,812 — Barry Wagner, Alabama A&M, 1989
**Most Yards Gained per Game:** 164.7 — Barry Wagner, Alabama A&M, 1989
**Highest Average Gain per Reception:** 28.7 — Kevin Collins, Santa Clara, 1983

## Single Game

### SCORING

**Most Points Scored:** 48 — Paul Zaeske, N Park, 1968 (vs N Central); Junior Wolf, Panhandle St, 1958 [vs St Mary (KS)]
**Most Field Goals:** 6 — Steve Huff, Central Missouri St, 1985 (vs SE Missouri St)

### PASSING

**Most Passes Completed:** 44 — Tom Bonds, Cal Lutheran, 1986 [vs St Mary's (CA)]
**Most Yards Gained:** 592 — John Charles, Portland State, 1991 (vs Cal-Poly San Luis Obispo)
**Most Touchdowns Passed:** 10 — Bruce Swanson, N Park, 1968 (vs N Central)

### RUSHING

**Most Yards Gained:** 382 — Kelly Ellis, Northern Iowa, 1979 (vs Western Illinois)
**Most Touchdowns Rushed:** 8 — Junior Wolf, Panhandle St, 1958 [vs St Mary (KS)]

### RECEIVING

**Most Passes Caught:** 23 — Barry Wagner, Alabama A&M, 1989 (vs Clark Atlanta)
**Most Yards Gained:** 370 — Barry Wagner, Alabama A&M, 1989 (vs Clark Atlanta)
**Most Touchdown Catches:** 8 — Paul Zaeske, N Park, 1968 (vs N Central)

# Division III Individual Records

## Career

### SCORING

**Most Points Scored:** 474 — Joe Dudek, Plymouth St, 1982-85
**Most Touchdowns Scored:** 79 — Joe Dudek, Plymouth St, 1982-85
**Most Touchdowns Scored, Rushing:** 76 — Joe Dudek, Plymouth St, 1982-85
**Most Touchdowns Scored, Passing:** 110 — Kirk Baumgartner, WI-Stevens Point, 1986-89
**Most Touchdowns Scored, Receiving:** 55 — Chris Bisaillon, Illinois Wesleyan, 1989-92

### RUSHING

**Most Rushes:** 1,112 — Mike Birosak, Dickinson, 1986-89
**Most Rushes per Game:** 32.7 — Chris Sizemore, Bridgewater (VA), 1972-74
**Most Yards Gained:** 5,570 — Joe Dudek, Plymouth St, 1982-85
**Most Yards Gained per Game:** 151.8 — Terry Underwood, Wagner, 1985-88

## Career *(Cont.)*

### PASSING

**Highest Passing Efficiency Rating:** 153.3 — Joe Blake, Simpson, 1987-90
**Most Passes Attempted:** 1,696 — Kirk Baumgartner, WI-Stevens Point, 1986-89
**Most Passes Completed:** 883 — Kirk Baumgartner, WI-Stevens Point, 1986-89
**Most Passes Completed per Game:** 24.9 — Keith Bishop, Illinois Wesleyan, 1981; Wheaton (IL), 1983-85
**Highest Completion Percentage:** 62.2 — Brian Moore, Baldwin-Wallace, 1981-84
**Most Yards Gained:** 13,028 — Kirk Baumgartner, WI-Stevens Point, 1986-89
**Most Yards Gained per Game:** 317.8 — Kirk Baumgartner, WI-Stevens Point, 1986-89

### RECEIVING

**Most Passes Caught:** 258 — Bill Stromberg, Johns Hopkins, 1978-81
**Most Yards Gained:** 3,846 — Dale Amos, Franklin & Marshall, 1986-89
**Most Yards Gained per Game:** 110.1 — Tim McNamara, Trinity (CT), 1981-84
**Highest Average Gain per Reception:** 20.0 — Marty Redlawsk, Concordia (IL), 1984-87

## Single Season

### SCORING

**Most Points Scored:** 168 — Stanley Drayton, Allegheny, 1991
**Most Points Scored per Game:** 16.8 — Stanley Drayton, Allegheny, 1991
**Most Touchdowns Scored:** 28 — Stanley Drayton, Allegheny, 1991
**Most Touchdowns Scored, Rushing:** 26 — Ricky Gales, Simpson, 1989
**Most Touchdowns Scored, Passing:** 39 — Kirk Baumgartner, WI-Stevens Point, 1989
**Most Touchdowns Scored, Receiving:** 20 — John Aromando, Trenton St, 1983

### RUSHING

**Most Rushes:** 380 — Mike Birosak, Dickinson, 1989
**Most Rushes per Game:** 38.0 — Mike Birosak, Dickinson, 1989
**Most Yards Gained:** 2,035 — Ricky Gales, Simpson, 1989
**Most Yards Gained per Game:** 203.5 — Ricky Gales, Simpson, 1989

### PASSING

**Highest Passing Efficiency Rating:** 203.3 — Joe Blake, Simpson, 1989
**Most Passes Attempted:** 527 — Kirk Baumgartner, WI-Stevens Point, 1988
**Most Passes Completed:** 276 — Kirk Baumgartner, WI-Stevens Point, 1988
**Most Passes Completed per Game:** 29.1 — Keith Bishop, Illinois Wesleyan, 1985
**Highest Completion Percentage:** 64.0 — Willie Reyna, La Verne, 1992
**Most Yards Gained:** 3,828 — Kirk Baumgartner, WI-Stevens Point, 1988
**Most Yards Gained per Game:** 369.2 — Kirk Baumgartner, WI-Stevens Point, 1989

### RECEIVING

**Most Passes Caught:** 106 — Theo Blanco, WI-Stevens Point, 1987
**Most Yards Gained:** 1,693 — Sean Munroe, Mass-Boston, 1992
**Most Yards Gained per Game:** 188.1 — Sean Munroe, Mass-Boston 1992
**Highest Average Gain per Reception:** 26-9 — Marty Redlawsk, Concordia (IL), 1985

## Single Game

### SCORING

**Most Field Goals:** 6 — Jim Hever, Rhodes, 1984 (vs Millsaps)

### PASSING

**Most Passes Completed:** 50 — Tim Lynch, Hofstra, 1991 (vs Fordham)
**Most Yards Gained:** 585 — Tim Lynch, Hofstra, 1991 (vs Fordham)
**Most Touchdowns Passed:** 8 — Kirk Baumgartner, WI-Stevens Point, 1989 (vs WI-Superior); Steve Austin, Mass-Boston, 1992 (vs Framingham St)

### RUSHING

**Most Yards Gained:** 382 — Pete Baranek, Carthage, 1985 (vs N Central)
**Most Touchdowns Rushed:** 6 — Rob Sinclair, Simpson, 1990 (vs Upper Iowa); Eric Leiser, Eureka, 1991, (vs Concordia)

### RECEIVING

**Most Passes Caught:** 23 — Sean Munroe, Mass-Boston, 1992 (vs Mass-Maritime)
**Most Yards Gained:** 332 — Sean Munroe, Mass-Boston, 1992 (vs Mass-Maritime)
**Most Touchdown Catches:** 5 — By 10 players. Most Recent: Sean Munroe, Mass-Boston, 1992 (vs Mass-Maritime)

# Career

## Scoring

### POINTS (KICKERS)

| | Years | Pts |
|---|---|---|
| Roman Anderson, Houston | 1988-91 | 423 |
| Carlos Huerta, Miami (FL) | 1988-91 | 397 |
| Jason Elam, Hawaii | 1988-92 | 395 |
| Derek Schmidt, Florida St | 1984-87 | 393 |
| Luis Zendejas, Arizona St | 1981-84 | 368 |
| Jeff Jaeger, Washington | 1983-86 | 358 |
| John Lee, UCLA | 1982-85 | 353 |
| Max Zendejas, Arizona | 1982-85 | 353 |

### POINTS (NON-KICKERS)

| | Years | Pts |
|---|---|---|
| Anthony Thompson, Indiana | 1986-89 | 394 |
| Tony Dorsett, Pittsburgh | 1973-76 | 356 |
| Glenn Davis, Army | 1943-46 | 354 |
| Art Luppino, Arizona | 1953-56 | 337 |
| Steve Owens, Oklahoma | 1967-69 | 336 |

### POINTS PER GAME (NON-KICKERS)

| | Years | Pts/Game |
|---|---|---|
| Bob Gaiters, New Mexico St | 1959-60 | 11.9 |
| Ed Marinaro, Cornell | 1969-71 | 11.8 |
| Bill Burnett, Arkansas | 1968-70 | 11.3 |
| Steve Owens, Oklahoma | 1967-69 | 11.2 |
| Eddie Talboom, Wyoming | 1948-50 | 10.8 |

## Total Offense

### YARDS GAINED

| | Years | Yds |
|---|---|---|
| Ty Detmer, Brigham Young | 1988-91 | 14,665 |
| Doug Flutie, Boston Col | 1981-84 | 11,317 |
| Alex Van Pelt, Pittsburgh | 1989-92 | 10,814 |
| Todd Santos, San Diego St | 1984-87 | 10,513 |
| Kevin Sweeney, Fresno St | 1982-86 | 10,252 |

### YARDS PER GAME

| | Years | Yds/Game |
|---|---|---|
| Ty Detmer, Brigham Young | 1988-91 | 318.8 |
| Mike Perez, San Jose St | 1986-87 | 309.1 |
| Doug Gaynor, Long Beach St | 1984-85 | 305.0 |
| Tony Eason, Illinois | 1981-82 | 299.5 |
| Steve Young, Brigham Young | 1981-83 | 284.4 |
| Doug Flutie, Boston Col | 1981-84 | 269.5 |

## Rushing

### YARDS GAINED

| | Years | Yds |
|---|---|---|
| Tony Dorsett, Pittsburgh | 1973-76 | 6082 |
| Charles White, Southern Cal | 1976-79 | 5598 |
| Herschel Walker, Georgia | 1980-82 | 5259 |
| Archie Griffin, Ohio St | 1972-75 | 5177 |
| Anthony Thompson, Indiana | 1986-89 | 4965 |

### YARDS PER GAME

| | Years | Yds/Game |
|---|---|---|
| Ed Marinaro, Cornell | 1969-71 | 174.6 |
| O. J. Simpson, Southern Cal | 1967-68 | 164.4 |
| Herschel Walker, Georgia | 1980-82 | 159.4 |
| Tony Dorsett, Pittsburgh | 1973-76 | 141.4 |
| Mike Rozier, Nebraska | 1981-83 | 136.6 |

### TOUCHDOWNS RUSHING

| | Years | TD |
|---|---|---|
| Anthony Thompson, Indiana | 1986-89 | 64 |
| Steve Owens, Oklahoma | 1967-69 | 56 |
| Tony Dorsett, Pittsburgh | 1973-76 | 55 |
| Ed Marinaro, Cornell | 1969-71 | 50 |
| Mike Rozier, Nebraska | 1981-83 | 49 |

## Passing

### PASSING EFFICIENCY

| | Years | Rating |
|---|---|---|
| Ty Detmer, Brigham Young | 1988-91 | 162.7 |
| Jim McMahon, Brigham Young | 1977-78, 80-81 | 156.9 |
| Steve Young, Brigham Young | 1982, 84-86 | 149.8 |
| Robbie Bosco, Brigham Young | 1981-83 | 149.4 |
| Chuck Long, Iowa | 1981-85 | 148.9 |

Note: Minimum 500 completions.

### YARDS GAINED

| | Years | Yds |
|---|---|---|
| Ty Detmer, Brigham Young | 1988-91 | 15,031 |
| Todd Santos, San Diego St | 1984-87 | 11,425 |
| Alex Van Pelt, Pittsburgh | 1989-92 | 10,913 |
| Kevin Sweeney, Fresno St | 1982-86 | 10,623 |
| Doug Flutie, Boston Col | 1981-84 | 10,579 |
| Brian McClure, Bowling Green | 1982-85 | 10,280 |

Note: Minimum 500 completions.

### COMPLETIONS

| | Years | Comp |
|---|---|---|
| Ty Detmer, Brigham Young | 1988-91 | 958 |
| Todd Santos, San Diego St | 1984-87 | 910 |
| Brian McClure, Bowling Green | 1982-85 | 900 |
| Eric Wilhelm, Oregon St | 1989-92 | 870 |
| Alex Van Pelt, Pittsburgh | 1989-92 | 845 |

Note: Minimum 500 completions.

### TOUCHDOWNS PASSING

| | Years | TD |
|---|---|---|
| Ty Detmer, Brigham Young | 1988-91 | 121 |
| David Klingler, Houston | 1988-91 | 92 |
| Troy Kopp, Pacific | 1989-92 | 87 |
| Jim McMahon, Brigham Young | 1977-78,80-81 | 84 |
| Joe Adams, Tennessee St | 1977-80 | 81 |

## Receiving

### CATCHES

| | Years | No. |
|---|---|---|
| Aaron Turner, Pacific | 1989-92 | 266 |
| Terance Mathis, New Mexico | 1985-87, 89 | 263 |
| Mark Templeton, Long Beach St | 1983-86 | 262 |
| Howard Twilley, Tulsa | 1963-65 | 261 |
| David Williams, Illinois | 1983-85 | 245 |

### CATCHES PER GAME

| | Years | No./Game |
|---|---|---|
| Emmanuel Hazard, Houston | 1989-90 | 10.5 |
| Howard Twilley, Tulsa | 1963-65 | 10.0 |
| Jason Phillips, Houston | 1987-88 | 9.4 |
| Neal Sweeney, Tulsa | 1965-66 | 7.4 |
| David Williams, Illinois | 1983-85 | 7.4 |

### YARDS GAINED

| | Years | Yds |
|---|---|---|
| Aaron Turner, Pacific | 1989-92 | 4345 |
| Terance Mathis, New Mexico | 1985-87,89 | 4254 |
| Marc Zeno, Tulane | 1984-87 | 3725 |
| Ron Sellers, Florida St | 1966-68 | 3598 |
| Elmo Wright, Houston | 1968-70 | 3347 |

### TOUCHDOWN CATCHES

| | Years | TD |
|---|---|---|
| Aaron Turner, Pacific | 1989-92 | 43 |
| Clarkston Hines, Duke | 1986-89 | 38 |
| Terance Mathis, New Mexico | 1985-87,89 | 36 |
| Elmo Wright, Houston | 1968-70 | 34 |
| Howard Twilley, Tulsa | 1963-65 | 32 |

## Career (Cont.)

### All-Purpose Running

#### YARDS GAINED

| | Years | Yds |
|---|---|---|
| Napoleon McCallum, Navy | 1981-85 | 7172 |
| Darrin Nelson, Stanford | 1977-78,80-81 | 6885 |
| Terance Mathis, New Mexico | 1985-87,89 | 6691 |
| Tony Dorsett, Pittsburgh | 1973-76 | 6615 |
| Paul Palmer, Temple | 1983-86 | 6609 |

#### YARDS PER GAME

| | Years | Yds/Game |
|---|---|---|
| Ryan Benjamin, Pacific, | 1990-92 | 237.8 |
| Sheldon Canley, San Jose St | 1988-90 | 205.8 |
| Howard Stevens, Louisville | 1971-72 | 193.7 |
| O. J. Simpson, Southern Cal | 1967-68 | 192.9 |
| Ed Marinaro, Cornell | 1969-71 | 183.0 |

### Interceptions

| PLAYER/SCHOOL | Years | Int |
|---|---|---|
| Al Brosky, Illinois | 1950-52 | 29 |
| John Provost, Holy Cross | 1972-74 | 27 |
| Martin Bayless, Bowling Green | 1980-83 | 27 |
| Tom Curtis, Michigan | 1967-69 | 25 |
| Tony Thurman, Boston Col | 1981-84 | 25 |
| Tracy Saul, Texas Tech | 1989-92 | 25 |

### Punting Average

| PLAYER/SCHOOL | Years | Avg |
|---|---|---|
| Reggie Roby, Iowa | 1979-82 | 45.6 |
| Greg Montgomery, Michigan St | 1985-87 | 45.4 |
| Tom Tupa, Ohio St | 1984-87 | 45.2 |
| Barry Helton, Colorado | 1984-87 | 44.9 |
| Ray Guy, Southern Miss | 1970-72 | 44.7 |

Note: At least 150 punts kicked.

### Punt Return Average

| PLAYER/SCHOOL | Years | Avg |
|---|---|---|
| Jack Mitchell, Oklahoma | 1946-48 | 23.6 |
| Gene Gibson, Cincinnati | 1949-50 | 20.5 |
| Eddie Macon, Pacific | 1949-51 | 18.9 |
| Jackie Robinson, UCLA | 1939-40 | 18.8 |
| Mike Fuller, Auburn | 1972-74 | 17.7 |
| Bobby Dillon, Texas | 1949-51 | 17.7 |

Note: At least 1.2 punt returns per game.

### Kickoff Return Average

| PLAYER/SCHOOL | Years | Avg |
|---|---|---|
| Forrest Hall, San Francisco | 1946-47 | 36.2 |
| Anthony Davis, Southern Cal | 1972-74 | 35.1 |
| Overton Curtis, Utah St | 1957-58 | 31.0 |
| Fred Montgomery, New Mexico St | 1991-92 | 30.5 |
| Altie Taylor, Utah St | 1966-68 | 29.3 |
| Stan Brown, Purdue | 1968-70 | 28.8 |

Note: At least 1.2 kickoff returns per game.

---

### Safety Patrol

All of Charleston, S.C., is hailing the heroism of Daniel Johnson, a strong safety on The Citadel football team, who in one 48-hour span in February:

• saved the life of a Citadel teammate whose throat was slashed with a broken bottle when two strangers attacked them in the street. The friend's carotid artery was cut, and as the attackers fled, Johnson stuck his fingers into the wound to stanch the bleeding;

• ran down a purse snatcher, turned the suspect over to the police and comforted the victim. Johnson even gave fair warning to the hapless thief, calling out during the chase, "I'm all-conference in track. I'm going to catch you."

---

## Single Season

### Scoring

#### POINTS

| | Year | Pts |
|---|---|---|
| Barry Sanders, Oklahoma St | 1988 | 234 |
| Mike Rozier, Nebraska | 1983 | 174 |
| Lydell Mitchell, Penn St | 1971 | 174 |
| Art Luppino, Arizona | 1954 | 166 |
| Bobby Reynolds, Nebraska | 1950 | 157 |

#### FIELD GOALS

| | Year | FG |
|---|---|---|
| John Lee, UCLA | 1984 | 29 |
| Paul Woodside, W Virginia | 1982 | 28 |
| Luis Zendejas, Arizona St | 1983 | 28 |
| Fuad Reveiz, Tennessee | 1982 | 27 |

Note: Three tied with 25 each.

### All-Purpose Running

#### YARDS GAINED

| | Year | Yds |
|---|---|---|
| Barry Sanders, Oklahoma St | 1988 | 3250 |
| Ryan Benjamin, Pacific | 1991 | 2995 |
| Mike Pringle, Fullerton St | 1989 | 2690 |
| Paul Palmer, Temple | 1986 | 2633 |
| Ryan Benjamin, Pacific | 1992 | 2597 |
| Marcus Allen, Southern Cal | 1981 | 2559 |

#### YARDS PER GAME

| | Years | Yds/Game |
|---|---|---|
| Barry Sanders, Oklahoma St | 1988 | 295.5 |
| Ryan Benjamin, Pacific | 1991 | 249.6 |
| Byron (Whizzer) White, Colorado | 1937 | 246.3 |
| Mike Pringle, Fullerton St | 1989 | 244.6 |
| Paul Palmer, Temple | 1986 | 239.4 |
| Ryan Benjamin, Pacific | 1992 | 236.1 |

## Total Offense

### YARDS GAINED

| | Year | Yds |
|---|---|---|
| David Klingler, Houston | 1990 | 5221 |
| Ty Detmer, Brigham Young | 1990 | 5022 |
| Andre Ware, Houston | 1989 | 4661 |
| Jim McMahon, Brigham Young | 1980 | 4627 |
| Ty Detmer, Brigham Young | 1989 | 4433 |

### YARDS PER GAME

| | Year | Yds/Game |
|---|---|---|
| David Klingler, Houston | 1990 | 474.6 |
| Andre Ware, Houston | 1989 | 423.7 |
| Ty Detmer, Brigham Young | 1990 | 418.5 |
| Steve Young, Brigham Young | 1983 | 395.1 |
| Scott Mitchell, Utah | 1988 | 390.8 |

## Rushing

### YARDS GAINED

| | Year | Yds |
|---|---|---|
| Barry Sanders, Oklahoma St | 1988 | 2628 |
| Marcus Allen, Southern Cal | 1981 | 2342 |
| Mike Rozier, Nebraska | 1983 | 2148 |
| Tony Dorsett, Pittsburgh | 1976 | 1948 |
| Lorenzo White, Michigan St | 1985 | 1908 |

### YARDS PER GAME

| | Year | Yds/Game |
|---|---|---|
| Barry Sanders, Oklahoma St | 1988 | 238.9 |
| Marcus Allen, Southern Cal | 1981 | 212.9 |
| Ed Marinaro, Cornell | 1971 | 209.0 |
| Charles White, Southern Cal | 1979 | 180.3 |
| Mike Rozier, Nebraska | 1983 | 179.0 |

### TOUCHDOWNS RUSHING

| | Year | TD |
|---|---|---|
| Barry Sanders, Oklahoma St | 1988 | 37 |
| Mike Rozier, Nebraska | 1983 | 29 |
| Ed Marinaro, Cornell | 1971 | 24 |
| Anthony Thompson, Indiana | 1988 | 24 |
| Anthony Thompson, Indiana | 1989 | 24 |

## Receiving

### CATCHES

| | Year | GP | No. |
|---|---|---|---|
| Emmanuel Hazard, Houston | 1989 | 11 | 142 |
| Howard Twilley, Tulsa | 1965 | 10 | 134 |
| Jason Phillips, Houston | 1988 | 11 | 108 |
| Fred Gilbert, Houston | 1991 | 11 | 106 |
| Sherman Smith, Houston | 1992 | 11 | 103 |

### CATCHES PER GAME

| | Year | No. | No./Game |
|---|---|---|---|
| Howard Twilley, Tulsa | 1965 | 134 | 13.4 |
| Emmanuel Hazard, Houston | 1989 | 142 | 12.9 |
| Jason Phillips, Houston | 1988 | 108 | 9.8 |
| Fred Gilbert, Houston | 1991 | 106 | 9.6 |
| Jerry Hendren, Idaho | 1969 | 95 | 9.5 |
| Howard Twilley, Tulsa | 1964 | 95 | 9.5 |

## Passing

### PASSING EFFICIENCY

| | Year | Rating |
|---|---|---|
| Jim McMahon, Brigham Young | 1980 | 176.9 |
| Ty Detmer, Brigham Young | 1989 | 175.6 |
| Jerry Rhome, Tulsa | 1964 | 172.6 |
| Steve Young, Brigham Young | 1983 | 168.5 |
| Vinny Testaverde, Miami (FL) | 1986 | 165.8 |
| Brian Dowling, Yale | 1968 | 165.8 |

### YARDS GAINED

| | Year | Yds |
|---|---|---|
| Ty Detmer, Brigham Young | 1990 | 5188 |
| David Klingler, Houston | 1990 | 5140 |
| Andre Ware, Houston | 1989 | 4699 |
| Jim McMahon, Brigham Young | 1980 | 4571 |
| Ty Detmer, Brigham Young | 1989 | 4560 |

### COMPLETIONS

| | Year | Att | Comp |
|---|---|---|---|
| David Klingler, Houston | 1990 | 643 | 374 |
| Andre Ware, Houston | 1989 | 578 | 365 |
| Ty Detmer, Brigham Young | 1990 | 562 | 361 |
| Robbie Bosco, Brigham Young | 1985 | 511 | 338 |
| Scott Mitchell, Utah | 1988 | 533 | 323 |

Note: Minimum 15 attempts per game.

### TOUCHDOWNS PASSING

| | Year | TD |
|---|---|---|
| David Klingler, Houston | 1990 | 54 |
| Jim McMahon, Brigham Young | 1980 | 47 |
| Andre Ware, Houston | 1989 | 46 |
| Ty Detmer, Brigham Young | 1990 | 41 |
| Dennis Shaw, San Diego St | 1969 | 39 |

### YARDS GAINED

| | Year | Yds |
|---|---|---|
| Howard Twilley, Tulsa | 1965 | 1779 |
| Emmanuel Hazard, Houston | 1989 | 1689 |
| Chuck Hughes, UTEP* | 1965 | 1519 |
| Henry Ellard, Fresno St | 1982 | 1510 |

*UTEP was Texas Western in 1965.

### TOUCHDOWN CATCHES

| | Year | TD |
|---|---|---|
| Emmanuel Hazard, Houston | 1989 | 22 |
| Desmond Howard, Michigan | 1991 | 19 |
| Tom Reynolds, San Diego St | 1969 | 18 |
| Dennis Smith, Utah | 1989 | 18 |
| Aaron Turner, Pacific | 1991 | 18 |

## Single Game
### Scoring

### POINTS

| | Opponent | Year | Pts |
|---|---|---|---|
| Howard Griffith, Illinois | Southern Illinois | 1990 | 48 |
| Jim Brown, Syracuse | Colgate | 1956 | 43 |
| Showboat Boykin, Mississippi | Mississippi St | 1951 | 42 |
| Fred Wendt, UTEP* | New Mexico St | 1948 | 42 |
| Marshall Faulk, San Diego St | Pacific | 1991 | 42 |
| Dick Bass, Pacific | San Diego St | 1958 | 38 |

*UTEP was Texas Mines in 1948.

### FIELD GOALS

| | Opponent | Year | FG |
|---|---|---|---|
| Dale Klein, Nebraska | Missouri | 1985 | 7 |
| Mike Prindle, Western Michigan | Marshall | 1984 | 7 |

Note: Klein's distances were 32-22-43-44-29-43-43.
Prindle's distances were 32-44-42-23-48-41-27.

## Single Game (Cont.)

### Total Offense

| YARDS GAINED | Opponent | Year | Yds |
|---|---|---|---|
| David Klingler, Houston | Arizona St | 1990 | 732 |
| Matt Vogler, Texas Christian | Houston | 1990 | 696 |
| David Klingler, Houston | Texas Christian | 1990 | 625 |
| Scott Mitchell, Utah | Air Force | 1988 | 625 |
| Jimmy Klingler, Houston | Rice | 1992 | 612 |

### Passing

| YARDS GAINED | Opponent | Year | Yds |
|---|---|---|---|
| David Klingler, Houston | Arizona St | 1990 | 716 |
| Matt Vogler, Texas Christian | Houston | 1990 | 690 |
| Scott Mitchell, Utah | Air Force | 1988 | 631 |
| Jeremy Leach, New Mexico | Utah | 1989 | 622 |
| Dave Wilson, Illinois | Ohio St | 1980 | 621 |

| COMPLETIONS | Opponent | Year | Comp |
|---|---|---|---|
| David Klingler, Houston | Southern Methodist | 1990 | 48 |
| Jimmy Klingler, Houston | Rice | 1992 | 46 |
| Sandy Schwab, Northwestern | Michigan | 1982 | 45 |
| Chuck Hartlieb, Iowa | Indiana | 1988 | 44 |
| Jim McMahon, Brigham Young | Colorado St | 1981 | 44 |

| TOUCHDOWNS PASSING | Opponent | Year | TD |
|---|---|---|---|
| David Klingler, Houston | E. Wash | 1990 | 11 |

Note: Klingler's TD passes were 5-48-29-7-3-7-40-10-7-8-51.

### Rushing

| YARDS GAINED | Opponent | Year | Yds |
|---|---|---|---|
| Tony Sands, Kansas | Missouri | 1991 | 396 |
| Marshall Faulk, San Diego St | Pacific | 1991 | 386 |
| Anthony Thompson, Indiana | Wisconsin | 1989 | 377 |
| Rueben Mayes, Washington St | Oregon | 1984 | 357 |
| Mike Pringle, California St-Fullerton | New Mexico St | 1989 | 357 |

| TOUCHDOWNS RUSHING | Opponent | Year | TD |
|---|---|---|---|
| Howard Griffith, Illinois | Southern Illinois | 1990 | 8 |

Note: Griffith's TD runs were 5-51-7-41-5-18-5-3.

### Receiving

| CATCHES | Opponent | Year | No. |
|---|---|---|---|
| Jay Miller, Brigham Young | New Mexico | 1973 | 22 |
| Rick Eber, Tulsa | Idaho St | 1967 | 20 |
| Howard Twilley, Tulsa | Colorado St | 1965 | 19 |
| Ron Fair, Arizona St | Washington St | 1989 | 19 |
| Emmanuel Hazard, Houston | Texas Christian | 1989 | 19 |
| Emmanuel Hazard, Houston | Texas | 1989 | 19 |

| YARDS GAINED | Opponent | Year | Yds |
|---|---|---|---|
| Chuck Hughes, UTEP* | N Texas St | 1965 | 349 |
| Rick Eber, Tulsa | Idaho St | 1967 | 322 |
| Harry Wood, Tulsa | Idaho St | 1967 | 318 |
| Jeff Evans, New Mexico St | Southern Illinois | 1978 | 316 |
| Tom Reynolds, San Diego St | Utah St | 1971 | 290 |

*UTEP was Texas Western in 1965.

| TOUCHDOWN CATCHES | Opponent | Year | TD |
|---|---|---|---|
| Tim Delaney, San Diego St | New Mexico St | 1969 | 6 |

Note: Delaney's TD catches were 2-22-34-31-30-9.

## Longest Plays (since 1941)

| RUSHING | Opponent | Year | Yds |
|---|---|---|---|
| Gale Sayers, Kansas | Nebraska | 1963 | 99 |
| Max Anderson, Arizona St | Wyoming | 1967 | 99 |
| Ralph Thompson, W Texas St | Wichita St | 1970 | 99 |
| Kelsey Finch, Tennessee | Florida | 1977 | 99 |

| PASSING | Opponent | Year | Yds |
|---|---|---|---|
| Fred Owens to Jack Ford, Portland | St Mary's (CA) | 1947 | 99 |
| Bo Burris to Warren McVea, Houston | Washington St | 1966 | 99 |
| Colin Clapton to Eddie Jenkins, Holy Cross | Boston U | 1970 | 99 |
| Terry Peel to Robert Ford, Houston | Syracuse | 1970 | 99 |
| Terry Peel to Robert Ford, Houston | San Diego St | 1972 | 99 |
| Cris Collinsworth to Derrick Gaffney, Florida | Rice | 1977 | 99 |
| Scott Ankrom to James Maness, Texas Christian | Rice | 1984 | 99 |

| FIELD GOALS | Opponent | Year | Yds |
|---|---|---|---|
| Steve Little, Arkansas | Texas | 1977 | 67 |
| Russell Erxleben, Texas | Rice | 1977 | 67 |
| Joe Williams, Wichita St | Southern Illinois | 1978 | 67 |
| Tony Franklin, Texas A&M | Baylor | 1976 | 65 |
| Russell Erxleben, Texas | Oklahoma | 1977 | 64 |
| Tony Franklin, Texas A&M | Baylor | 1976 | 64 |

| PUNTS | Opponent | Year | Yds |
|---|---|---|---|
| Pat Brady, Nevada* | Loyola (CA) | 1950 | 99 |
| George O'Brien, Wisconsin | Iowa | 1952 | 96 |

*Note: Nevada was Nevada-Reno in 1950.

## Rushing

| Year | Player, Team | Att. | Yards | Avg. |
|---|---|---|---|---|
| 1937 | Byron White, Colorado | 181 | 1121 | 6.2 |
| 1938 | Len Eshmont, Fordham | 132 | 831 | 6.3 |
| 1939 | John Polanski, Wake Forest | 137 | 882 | 6.4 |
| 1940 | Al Ghesquiere, Detroit Mercy | 146 | 957 | 6.6 |
| 1941 | Frank Sinkwich, Georgia | 209 | 1103 | 5.3 |
| 1942 | Rudy Mobley, Hardin-Simmons | 187 | 1281 | 6.9 |
| 1943 | Creighton Miller, Notre Dame | 151 | 911 | 6.0 |
| 1944 | Wayne Williams, Minnesota | 136 | 911 | 6.7 |
| 1945 | Bob Fenimore, Oklahoma State | 142 | 1048 | 7.4 |
| 1946 | Rudy Mobley, Hardin-Simmons | 227 | 1262 | 5.6 |
| 1947 | Wilton Davis, Hardin-Simmons | 193 | 1173 | 6.1 |
| 1948 | Fred Wendt, UTEP | 184 | 1570 | 8.5 |
| 1949 | John Dottley, Mississippi | 208 | 1312 | 6.3 |
| 1950 | Wilford White, Arizona St | 199 | 1502 | 7.5 |
| 1951 | Ollie Matson, San Francisco | 245 | 1566 | 6.4 |
| 1952 | Howie Waugh, Tulsa | 164 | 1372 | 8.4 |
| 1953 | J. C. Caroline, Illinois | 194 | 1256 | 6.5 |
| 1954 | Art Luppino, Arizona | 179 | 1359 | 7.6 |
| 1955 | Art Luppino, Arizona | 209 | 1313 | 6.3 |
| 1956 | Jim Crawford, Wyoming | 200 | 1104 | 5.5 |
| 1957 | Leon Burton, Arizona St | 117 | 1126 | 9.6 |
| 1958 | Dick Bass, Pacific (Cal) | 205 | 1361 | 6.6 |
| 1959 | Pervis Atkins, New Mexico State | 130 | 971 | 7.5 |
| 1960 | Bob Gaiters, New Mexico State | 197 | 1338 | 6.8 |
| 1961 | Jim Pilot, New Mexico St | 191 | 1278 | 6.7 |
| 1962 | Jim Pilot, New Mexico St | 208 | 1247 | 6.0 |
| 1963 | Dave Casinelli, Memphis St | 219 | 1016 | 4.6 |
| 1964 | Brian Piccolo, Wake Forest | 252 | 1044 | 4.1 |
| 1965 | Mike Garrett, Southern Cal | 267 | 1440 | 5.4 |

| Year | Player, Team | Att. | Yards | Avg. |
|---|---|---|---|---|
| 1966 | Ray McDonald, Idaho | 259 | 1329 | 5.1 |
| 1967 | O.J. Simpson, Southern Cal | 266 | 1415 | 5.3 |
| 1968 | O. J. Simpson, Southern Cal | 355 | 1709 | 4.8 |
| 1969 | Steve Owens, Oklahoma | 358 | 1523 | 4.3 |

| Year | Player, Team | G | Att. | Yards | Avg./g. |
|---|---|---|---|---|---|
| 1970 | Ed Marinaro, Cornell | 9 | 285 | 1425 | 158.3 |
| 1971 | Ed Marinaro, Cornell | 9 | 356 | 1881 | 209.0 |
| 1972 | Pete VanValkenburg, Brigham Young | 10 | 232 | 1386 | 138.6 |
| 1973 | Mark Kellar, N Illinois | 11 | 291 | 1719 | 156.3 |
| 1974 | Louie Giammona, Utah State | 10 | 329 | 1534 | 153.4 |
| 1975 | Ricky Bell, Southern Cal | 11 | 357 | 1875 | 170.5 |
| 1976 | Tony Dorsett, Pittsburgh | 11 | 338 | 1948 | 177.1 |
| 1977 | Earl Campbell, Texas | 11 | 267 | 1744 | 158.5 |
| 1978 | Billy Sims, Oklahoma | 11 | 231 | 1762 | 160.2 |
| 1979 | Charles White, Southern Cal | 10 | 293 | 1803 | 180.3 |
| 1980 | George Rogers, South Carolina | 11 | 297 | 1781 | 161.9 |
| 1981 | Marcus Allen, Southern Cal | 11 | 403 | 2342 | 212.9 |
| 1982 | Ernest Anderson, Oklahoma State | 11 | 353 | 1877 | 170.6 |
| 1983 | Mike Rozier, Nebraska | 12 | 275 | 2148 | 179.0 |
| 1984 | Keith Byars, Ohio State | 11 | 313 | 1655 | 150.5 |
| 1985 | Lorenzo White, Michigan State | 11 | 386 | 1908 | 173.5 |
| 1986 | Paul Palmer, Temple | 11 | 386 | 1908 | 173.5 |
| 1987 | Ickey Woods, UNLV | 11 | 259 | 1658 | 150.7 |
| 1988 | Barry Sanders, Oklahoma State | 11 | 344 | 2628 | 232.1 |
| 1989 | Anthony Thompson | 11 | 358 | 1793 | 163.0 |
| 1990 | Gerald Hudson, Oklahoma State | 11 | 279 | 1642 | 149.3 |
| 1991 | Marshall Faulk, San Diego State | 9 | 201 | 1429 | 158.8 |
| 1992 | Marshall Faulk, San Diego State | 10 | 265 | 1630 | 163.0 |

Note: Annual rushing champion was based on total yards from 1937–69 and on yards per game from 1970 to the present.

## Passing

| Year | Player, Team | Att. | Comp | Int. | Pct. | Yards | TD |
|---|---|---|---|---|---|---|---|
| 1937 | Davey O'Brien, Texas Christian | 234 | 94 | 18 | .402 | 969 | — |
| 1938 | Davey O'Brien, Texas Christian | 167 | 93 | 4 | .557 | 1457 | — |
| 1939 | Kay Eakin, Arkansas | 193 | 78 | 18 | .404 | 962 | — |
| 1940 | Billy Sewell, Washington St | 174 | 86 | 17 | .494 | 1023 | — |
| 1941 | Bud Schwenk, Washington (Mo) | 234 | 114 | 19 | .487 | 1457 | — |
| 1942 | Ray Evans, Kansas | 200 | 101 | 9 | .505 | 1117 | — |
| 1943 | Johnny Cook, Georgia | 157 | 73 | 20 | .465 | 1007 | — |
| 1944 | Paul Rickards, Pittsburgh | 178 | 84 | 20 | .472 | 997 | — |
| 1945 | Al Dekdebrun, Cornell | 194 | 90 | 15 | .464 | 1227 | — |
| 1946 | Travis Tidwell, Auburn | 158 | 79 | 10 | .500 | 943 | 5 |
| 1947 | Charlie Conerly, Mississippi | 233 | 133 | 7 | .571 | 1367 | 18 |
| 1948 | Stan Heath, Nevada | 222 | 126 | 9 | .568 | 2005 | 22 |
| 1949 | Adrian Burk, Baylor | 191 | 110 | 6 | .576 | 1428 | 14 |
| 1950 | Don Heinrich, Washington | 221 | 134 | 9 | .606 | 1846 | 14 |
| 1951 | Don Klosterman, Loyola (Cal) | 315 | 159 | 21 | .505 | 1843 | 9 |
| 1952 | Don Heinrich, Washington | 270 | 137 | 17 | .507 | 1647 | 13 |
| 1953 | Bob Garrett, Stanford | 205 | 118 | 10 | .576 | 1637 | 17 |

## Passing (Cont.)

| Year | Player, Team | Att. | Comp | Int | Pct | Yards | TD |
|------|--------------|------|------|-----|-----|-------|-----|
| 1954 | Paul Larson, California | 195 | 125 | 8 | .641 | 1537 | 10 |
| 1955 | George Welsh, Navy | 150 | 94 | 6 | .627 | 1319 | 8 |
| 1956 | John Brodie, Stanford | 240 | 139 | 14 | .579 | 1633 | 12 |
| 1957 | Ken Ford, Hardin-Simmons | 205 | 115 | 11 | .561 | 1254 | 14 |
| 1958 | Buddy Humphrey, Baylor | 195 | 112 | 8 | .574 | 1316 | 7 |
| 1959 | Dick Norman, Stanford | 263 | 152 | 12 | .578 | 1963 | 11 |
| 1960 | Harold Stephens, Hardin-Simmons | 256 | 145 | 14 | .566 | 1254 | 3 |
| 1961 | Chon Gallegos, San Jose St | 197 | 117 | 13 | .594 | 1480 | 14 |
| 1962 | Don Trull, Baylor | 229 | 125 | 12 | .546 | 1627 | 11 |
| 1963 | Don Trull, Baylor | 308 | 174 | 12 | .565 | 2157 | 12 |
| 1964 | Jorry Rhome, Tulsa | 326 | 224 | 4 | .687 | 2870 | 32 |
| 1965 | Bill Anderson, Tulsa | 509 | 296 | 14 | .582 | 3464 | 30 |
| 1966 | John Eckman, Wichita State | 458 | 195 | 34 | .426 | 2339 | 7 |
| 1967 | Terry Stone, New Mexico | 336 | 160 | 19 | .476 | 1946 | 9 |
| 1968 | Chuck Hixson, Southern Methodist | 468 | 265 | 23 | .566 | 3103 | 21 |
| 1969 | John Reaves, Florida | 396 | 222 | 19 | .561 | 2896 | 24 |

| Year | Player, Team | G | Att | Comp | Avg | Int | Pct | Yards | TD |
|------|--------------|---|-----|------|-----|-----|-----|-------|-----|
| 1970 | Sonny Sixkiller, Washington | 10 | 362 | 186 | 18.6 | 22 | .514 | 2303 | 15 |
| 1971 | Brian Sipe, San Diego State | 11 | 369 | 196 | 17.8 | 21 | .531 | 2532 | 17 |
| 1972 | Don Strock, Virginia Tech | 11 | 427 | 228 | 20.7 | 27 | .534 | 3243 | 16 |
| 1973 | Jesse Freitas, San Diego State | 11 | 347 | 227 | 20.6 | 17 | .654 | 2993 | 21 |
| 1974 | Steve Bartkowski, California | 11 | 325 | 182 | 16.5 | 7 | .560 | 2580 | 12 |
| 1975 | Craig Penrose, San Diego State | 11 | 349 | 198 | 18.0 | 24 | .567 | 2660 | 15 |
| 1976 | Tommy Kramer, Rice | 11 | 501 | 269 | 24.5 | 19 | .537 | 3317 | 21 |
| 1977 | Guy Benjamin, Stanford | 10 | 330 | 208 | 20.8 | 15 | .630 | 2521 | 19 |
| 1978 | Steve Dils, Stanford | 11 | 391 | 247 | 22.5 | 15 | .632 | 2943 | 22 |

| Year | Player, Team | G | Att | Comp | Int | Pct | Yards | TD | Pts |
|------|--------------|---|-----|------|-----|-----|-------|-----|-----|
| 1979 | Turk Schonert, Stanford | 11 | 221 | 148 | 6 | .670 | 1922 | 19 | 163.0 |
| 1980 | Jim McMahon, Brigham Young | 12 | 445 | 284 | 18 | .638 | 4571 | 47 | 176.9 |
| 1981 | Jim McMahon, Brigham Young | 10 | 423 | 272 | 7 | .643 | 3555 | 30 | 155.0 |
| 1982 | Tom Ramsey, UCLA | 11 | 311 | 191 | 10 | .614 | 2824 | 21 | 153.5 |
| 1983 | Steve Young, Brigham Young | 11 | 429 | 306 | 10 | .713 | 3902 | 33 | 168.5 |
| 1984 | Doug Flutie, Boston College | 11 | 386 | 233 | 11 | .604 | 3454 | 27 | 152.9 |
| 1985 | Jim Harbaugh, Michigan | 11 | 212 | 139 | 6 | .656 | 1913 | 18 | 163.7 |
| 1986 | Vinny Testaverde, Miami | 10 | 276 | 175 | 9 | .634 | 2557 | 26 | 165.8 |
| 1987 | Don McPherson, Syracuse | 11 | 229 | 129 | 11 | .563 | 2341 | 22 | 164.3 |
| 1988 | Timm Rosenbach, Washington St | 11 | 302 | 199 | 10 | .659 | 2791 | 23 | 162.0 |
| 1989 | Ty Detmer, Brigham Young | 12 | 412 | 265 | 15 | .643 | 4560 | 32 | 175.6 |
| 1990 | Shawn Moore, Virginia | 10 | 241 | 144 | 8 | .598 | 2262 | 21 | 160.7 |
| 1991 | Elvis Grbac, Michigan | 11 | 228 | 152 | 5 | .667 | 1955 | 24 | 169.0 |
| 1992 | Elvis Grbac, Michigan | 9 | 169 | 112 | 12 | .663 | 1465 | 15 | 154.2 |

Note: Annual passing champion was based on total completions from 1937–69, on completions per game from 1970–78 and on passing efficiency points from 1979 to the present.

## Receiving

| Year | Player, Team | No. | Yds | Avg | TD |
|------|--------------|-----|-----|-----|-----|
| 1937 | Jim Benton, Arkansas | 47 | 754 | 16.0 | — |
| 1938 | Sam Boyd, Baylor | 32 | 537 | 16.8 | — |
| 1939 | Ken Kavanaugh, LSU | 30 | 467 | 15.6 | — |
| 1940 | Eddie Bryant, Virginia | 30 | 222 | 7.4 | 2 |
| 1941 | Hank Stanton | 50 | 820 | 16.4 | — |
| 1942 | Bill Rogers, Texas A&M | 39 | 432 | 11.1 | — |
| 1943 | Neil Armstrong, Okla St. | 39 | 317 | 8.1 | — |
| 1944 | Reid Moseley, Georgia | 32 | 506 | 15.8 | — |
| 1945 | Reid Moseley, Georgia | 31 | 662 | 21.4 | — |
| 1946 | Neil Armstrong, Okla St. | 32 | 479 | 15.0 | 1 |
| 1947 | Barney Poole, Mississippi | 52 | 513 | 9.9 | 8 |
| 1948 | Johnny O'Quinn, Wake Forest | 39 | 605 | 15.5 | 7 |
| 1949 | Art Weiner, North Carolina | 52 | 762 | 14.7 | 7 |
| 1950 | Gordon Cooper, Denver | 46 | 569 | 12.4 | 8 |

| Year | Player, Team | No. | Yds | Avg | TD |
|------|--------------|-----|-----|-----|-----|
| 1951 | Dewey McConnell, Wyoming | 47 | 725 | 15.4 | 9 |
| 1952 | Ed Brown, Fordham | 57 | 774 | 13.6 | 6 |
| 1953 | John Carson, Georgia | 45 | 663 | 14.7 | 4 |
| 1954 | Jim Hanifan, California | 44 | 569 | 12.9 | 7 |
| 1955 | Hank Burnine, Missouri | 44 | 594 | 13.5 | 2 |
| 1956 | Art Powell, San Jose St | 40 | 583 | 14.6 | 5 |
| 1957 | Stuart Vaughan, Utah | 53 | 756 | 14.3 | 5 |
| 1958 | Dave Hibbert, Arizona | 61 | 606 | 9.9 | 4 |
| 1959 | Chris Burford, Stanford | 61 | 756 | 12.4 | 6 |
| 1960 | Hugh Campbell, Washington State | 66 | 881 | 13.3 | 10 |
| 1961 | Hugh Campbell, Washington State | 53 | 723 | 13.6 | 5 |
| 1962 | Vern Burke, Oregon St | 69 | 1007 | 14.6 | 10 |
| 1963 | Lawrence Elkins, Baylor | 70 | 873 | 12.5 | 8 |
| 1964 | Howard Twilley, Tulsa | 95 | 1178 | 12.4 | 13 |

## Receiving (Cont.)

| Year | Player, Team | No. | Yds | Avg | TD |
|------|--------------|-----|-----|-----|-----|
| 1965 | Howard Twilley, Tulsa | 134 | 1779 | 13.3 | 16 |
| 1966 | Glenn Meltzer, Wichita St | 91 | 1115 | 12.3 | 4 |
| 1967 | Bob Goodridge, Vanderbilt | 79 | 1114 | 14.1 | 6 |
| 1968 | Ron Sellars, Florida St | 86 | 1496 | 13.4 | 12 |
| 1969 | Jerry Hendren, Idaho | 95 | 1452 | 15.3 | 12 |

| Year | Player, Team | G | No. | Avg | Yds | TD |
|------|--------------|---|-----|-----|-----|-----|
| 1970 | Mike Mikolayunas, Davidson | 10 | 87 | 8.7 | 1128 | 8 |
| 1971 | Tom Reynolds, San Diego State | 10 | 67 | 6.7 | 1070 | 7 |
| 1972 | Tom Forzani, Utah St | 11 | 85 | 7.7 | 1169 | 8 |
| 1973 | Jay Miller, Brigham Young | 11 | 100 | 9.1 | 1181 | 8 |
| 1974 | Dwight McDonald, San Diego State | 11 | 88 | 7.8 | 1157 | 7 |
| 1975 | Bob Farnham, Brown | 9 | 56 | 6.2 | 701 | 2 |
| 1976 | Billy Ryckman, Lousiana Tech | 11 | 77 | 7.0 | 1382 | 10 |
| 1977 | Wayne Tolleson, Western Carolina | 11 | 73 | 6.6 | 1101 | 7 |
| 1978 | Dave Petzke, Northern Illinois | 11 | 91 | 8.3 | 1217 | 11 |
| 1979 | Rick Beasley, Appalachian St | 11 | 74 | 6.7 | 1205 | 12 |
| 1980 | Dave Young, Purdue | 11 | 67 | 6.1 | 917 | 8 |

| Year | Player, Team | G | No. | Avg | Yds | TD |
|------|--------------|---|-----|-----|-----|-----|
| 1981 | Pete Harvey, North Texas | 9 | 57 | 6.3 | 743 | 3 |
| 1982 | Vincent White, Stanford | 10 | 68 | 6.8 | 677 | 8 |
| 1983 | Keith Edwards, Vanderbilt | 11 | 97 | 8.8 | 909 | 8 |
| 1984 | David Williams, Illinois | 11 | 101 | 9.2 | 1278 | 8 |
| 1985 | Rodney Carter, Purdue | 11 | 98 | 8.9 | 1099 | 4 |
| 1986 | Mark Templeton, Long Beach St | 11 | 99 | 9.0 | 875 | 3 |
| 1987 | Jason Phillips, Houston | 11 | 99 | 9.0 | 875 | 3 |
| 1988 | Jason Phillips, Houston | 11 | 108 | 9.8 | 1444 | 15 |
| 1989 | Manny Hazard, Houston | 11 | 142 | 12.9 | 1689 | 22 |

| Year | Player, Team | G | No. | Avg | Yds | TD |
|------|--------------|---|-----|-----|-----|-----|
| 1990 | Manny Hazard, Houston | 10 | 78 | 7.8 | 946 | 9 |
| 1991 | Fred Gilbert, Houston | 11 | 108 | 9.6 | 957 | 7 |
| 1992 | Sherman Smith, Houston | 11 | 103 | 9.4 | 923 | 6 |

| Year | Player, Team | G | No. | Yds | Avg | TD |
|------|--------------|---|-----|-----|-----|-----|
| 1990 | Patrick Rowe, San Diego State | 11 | 71 | 1392 | 126.6 | 8 |
| 1991 | Aaron Turner, Pacific (Cal) | 11 | 92 | 1604 | 145.8 | 8 |
| 1992 | Lloyd Hill, Texas Tech | 11 | 76 | 1261 | 114.6 | 12 |

Note: Annual receiving champion was based on total catches from 1937–1969, on catches per game from 1970–89 and on catches per game and yards per game from 1990 to the present.

## Scoring

| Year | Player, Team | TD | FG | PAT | TP |
|------|--------------|-----|-----|-----|-----|
| 1937 | Byron White, Colorado | 16 | 1 | 23 | 122 |
| 1938 | Parker Hall, Mississippi | 11 | 0 | 7 | 73 |
| 1939 | Tom Harmon, Michigan | 14 | 1 | 15 | 102 |
| 1940 | Tom Harmon, Michigan | 16 | 1 | 18 | 117 |
| 1941 | Bill Dudley, Virginia | 18 | 1 | 23 | 134 |
| 1942 | Bob Steuber, Missouri | 18 | 0 | 13 | 121 |
| 1943 | Steve Van Buren, LSU | 14 | 0 | 14 | 98 |
| 1944 | Glenn Davis, Army | 20 | 0 | 0 | 120 |
| 1945 | Doc Blanchard, Army | 19 | 0 | 1 | 115 |
| 1946 | Gene Roberts, Tenn-Chatt | 18 | 0 | 9 | 117 |
| 1947 | Lou Gambino, Maryland | 16 | 0 | 0 | 96 |
| 1948 | Fred Wendt, UTEP | 20 | 0 | 32 | 152 |
| 1949 | George Thomas, Oklahoma | 19 | 0 | 3 | 117 |
| 1950 | Bobby Reynolds, Nebraska | 22 | 0 | 25 | 157 |
| 1951 | Ollie Matson, San Francisco | 21 | 0 | 0 | 126 |
| 1952 | Jackie Parker, Mississippi St | 16 | 0 | 24 | 120 |
| 1953 | Earl Lindley, Utah St | 13 | 0 | 3 | 81 |

| Year | Player, Team | TD | FG | PAT | TP |
|------|--------------|-----|-----|-----|-----|
| 1954 | Art Luppino, Arizona | 24 | 0 | 22 | 166 |
| 1955 | Jim Swink, Texas Christian | 20 | 0 | 5 | 125 |
| 1956 | Clendon Thomas, Oklahoma | 18 | 0 | 0 | 108 |
| 1957 | Leon Burton, Arizona St | 16 | 0 | 0 | 96 |
| 1958 | Dick Bass, Pacific | 18 | 0 | 8 | 116 |
| 1959 | Pervis Atkins, New Mexico St | 17 | 0 | 5 | 107 |
| 1960 | Bob Gaiters, New Mexico St | 23 | 0 | 7 | 145 |
| 1961 | Jim Pilot, New Mexico St | 21 | 0 | 12 | 138 |
| 1962 | Jerry Logan, West Texas St | 13 | 0 | 32 | 110 |
| 1963 | Cosmo Iacavazzi, Princeton | 14 | 0 | 0 | 84 |
| 1963 | Dave Casinelli, Memphis St | 14 | 0 | 0 | 84 |
| 1964 | Brian Piccolo, Wake Forest | 17 | 0 | 9 | 111 |
| 1965 | Howard Twilley, Tulsa | 16 | 0 | 31 | 127 |
| 1966 | Ken Hebert, Houston | 11 | 2 | 41 | 113 |
| 1967 | Leroy Keyes, Purdue | 19 | 0 | 0 | 114 |
| 1968 | Jim O'Brien, Cincinnati | 12 | 13 | 31 | 142 |
| 1969 | Steve Owens, Oklahoma | 23 | 0 | 0 | 138 |

### Thanks for the Memorooskis

In January the NCAA football rules committee whistled dead the guard-around play, a.k.a. the fumblerooski, after concluding that the play was so difficult to officiate that it was often run illegally. For the record, the last successful execution of the now extinct ploy—in which the center, instead of snapping the ball to the quarterback, sets it on the ground for a guard to pick up—occurred at the Blue-Gray Game on Dec. 25, producing the spectacle of a 290-pounder from Houston, Jason Youngblood, lumbering 18 yards for a TD. As witnesses to Youngblood's earth-rattling romp can attest, eliminating the fumblerooski takes some fun out of the game.

## Scoring (Cont.)

| Year | Player, Team | TD | FG | PAT | TP | Avg |
|------|--------------|-----|-----|-----|-----|-----|
| 1970 | Brian Bream, Air Force | 20 | 0 | 0 | 120 | 12.0 |
| | Gary Kosins, Dayton | 18 | 0 | 0 | 108 | 12.0 |
| 1971 | Ed Marinaro, Cornell | 24 | 0 | 4 | 148 | 16.4 |
| 1972 | Harold Henson, Ohio St | 20 | 0 | 0 | 120 | 12.0 |
| 1973 | Jim Jennings, Rutgers | 21 | 0 | 2 | 128 | 11.6 |
| 1974 | Bill Marek, Wisconsin | 19 | 0 | 0 | 114 | 12.7 |
| 1975 | Pete Johnson, Ohio St | 25 | 0 | 0 | 150 | 13.6 |
| 1976 | Tony Dorsett, Pittsburgh | 22 | 0 | 2 | 134 | 12.2 |
| 1977 | Earl Campbell, Texas | 19 | 0 | 0 | 114 | 10.4 |
| 1978 | Billy Sims, Oklahoma | 20 | 0 | 0 | 120 | 10.9 |
| 1979 | Billy Sims, Oklahoma | 22 | 0 | 0 | 132 | 12.0 |
| 1980 | Sammy Winder, S Mississippi | 20 | 0 | 0 | 120 | 10.9 |
| 1981 | Marcus Allen, USC | 23 | 0 | 0 | 138 | 12.5 |
| 1982 | Greg Allen, Florida St | 21 | 0 | 0 | 126 | 11.5 |

| Year | Player, Team | TD | FG | PAT | TP | Avg |
|------|--------------|-----|-----|-----|-----|-----|
| 1983 | Mike Rozier, Nebraska | 29 | 0 | 0 | 174 | 14.5 |
| 1984 | Keith Byars, Ohio St | 24 | 0 | 0 | 144 | 13.1 |
| 1985 | Bernard White, Bowling Green | 19 | 0 | 0 | 114 | 10.4 |
| 1986 | Steve Bartalo, Colorado St | 19 | 0 | 0 | 114 | 10.4 |
| 1987 | Paul Hewitt, San Diego St | 24 | 0 | 0 | 144 | 12.0 |
| 1988 | Barry Sanders, Oklahoma St | 39 | 0 | 0 | 234 | 21.3 |
| 1989 | Anthony Thompson, Indiana | 25 | 0 | 4 | 154 | 14.0 |
| 1990 | Stacey Robinson, N Illinois | 19 | 0 | 6 | 120 | 10.9 |
| 1991 | Marshall Faulk, San Diego St | 23 | 0 | 2 | 140 | 15.6 |
| 1992 | Garrison Hearst, Georgia | 21 | 0 | 0 | 126 | 11.5 |

Note: Annual scoring champion based on total points from 1937–69 and on points per game from 1970 to the present.

## Interceptions

| Year | Player, Team | No. | Yards |
|------|--------------|-----|-------|
| 1938 | Elmer Tarbox, Texas Tech | 11 | 89 |
| 1939 | Harold Van Every, Minnesota | 8 | 59 |
| 1940 | Dick Morgan, Tulsa | 7 | 210 |
| 1941 | Bobby Robertson, USC | 9 | 126 |
| 1942 | Ray Evans, Kansas | 10 | 76 |
| 1943 | Jay Stoves, Washington | 7 | 139 |
| 1944 | Joe Stuart, California | 7 | 76 |
| 1945 | Jake Leicht, Oregon | 9 | 195 |
| 1946 | Larry Hatch, Washington | 8 | 114 |
| 1947 | John Bruce, William & Mary | 9 | 78 |
| 1948 | Jay Van Noy, Utah St | 8 | 228 |
| 1949 | Bobby Wilson, Mississippi | 10 | 70 |
| 1950 | Hank Rich, Arizona St | 12 | 135 |
| 1951 | George Shaw, Oregon | 13 | 136 |
| 1952 | Cecil Ingram, Alabama | 10 | 163 |
| 1953 | Bob Garrett, Stanford | 9 | 80 |
| 1954 | Gary Glick, Colorado St | 8 | 168 |
| 1955 | Sam Wesley, Oregon St | 7 | 61 |
| 1956 | Jack Hill, Utah St | 7 | 132 |
| 1957 | Ray Toole, North Texas | 7 | 133 |
| 1958 | Jim Norton, Idaho | 9 | 222 |
| 1959 | Bud Whitehead, Florida St | 6 | 111 |
| 1960 | Bob O'Billovich, Montana | 7 | 71 |
| 1961 | Joe Zuger, Arizona St | 10 | 121 |
| 1962 | Byron Beaver, Houston | 10 | 56 |
| 1963 | Dick Kern, William & Mary | 8 | 116 |
| 1964 | Tony Carey, Notre Dame | 8 | 121 |
| 1965 | Bob Sullivan, Maryland | 10 | 61 |
| 1966 | Henry King, Utah St | 11 | 180 |
| 1967 | Steve Haterius, West Texas St | 11 | 90 |
| 1968 | Al Worley, Washington | 14 | 130 |
| 1969 | Seth Miller, Arizona St | 11 | 63 |

| Year | Player, Team | G | No. | Avg | Yards |
|------|--------------|-----|-----|-----|-------|
| 1970 | Mike Sensibaugh, Ohio St | 8 | 8 | 1.0 | 40 |
| 1971 | Frank Polito, Villanova | 10 | 12 | 1.2 | 261 |
| 1972 | Mike Townsend, Notre Dame | 10 | 10 | 1.0 | 39 |
| 1973 | Mike Gow, Illinois | 11 | 10 | .91 | 142 |
| 1974 | Mike Haynes, Arizona St | 11 | 10 | .91 | 115 |
| 1975 | Jim Bolding, E Carolina | 10 | 10 | 1.0 | 51 |
| 1976 | Anthony Francis, Houston | 11 | 10 | .91 | 118 |
| 1977 | Paul Lawler, Colgate | 9 | 7 | .78 | 53 |
| 1978 | Pete Harris, Penn St | 11 | 10 | .91 | 155 |
| 1979 | Joe Callan, Ohio | 9 | 9 | 1.0 | 110 |
| 1980 | Ronnie Lott, USC | 11 | 8 | .73 | 166 |
| | Steve McNamee, William & Mary | 11 | 8 | .73 | 125 |
| | Greg Benton, Drake | 11 | 8 | .73 | 119 |
| | Jeff Hip, Georgia | 11 | 8 | .73 | 104 |
| | Mike Richardson, Arizona St | 11 | 8 | .73 | 89 |
| | Vann McElroy, Baylor | 11 | 8 | .73 | 73 |
| 1981 | Sam Shaffer, Temple | 10 | 9 | .90 | 76 |
| 1982 | Terry Hoage, Georgia | 10 | 12 | 1.20 | 51 |
| 1983 | Martin Bayless, Bowling Green | 11 | 10 | .91 | 64 |
| 1984 | Tony Thurman, Boston College | 11 | 12 | 1.09 | 99 |
| 1985 | Chris White, Tennessee | 11 | 9 | .82 | 168 |
| 1986 | Bennie Blades, Miami (Fla) | 11 | 10 | .91 | 128 |
| 1987 | Keith McMeans, Virginia | 10 | 9 | .90 | 35 |
| 1988 | Kurt Larson, Michigan St | 11 | 8 | .73 | 78 |
| | Andy Logan, Kent | 11 | 8 | .73 | 54 |
| 1989 | Cornelius Price, Houston | 11 | 12 | 1.09 | 187 |
| | Bob Navarro, E Michigan | 11 | 12 | 1.09 | 73 |
| 1990 | Jerry Parks, Houston | 11 | 8 | .73 | 124 |
| 1991 | Terrell Buckley, Florida St | 12 | 12 | 1.0 | 238 |
| 1992 | Carlton McDonald, USAF | 11 | 8 | .73 | 109 |

Note: Annual interceptions champion was based on total interceptions from 1938–1969 and on interceptions per game from 1970 to the present.

## 1991

| | | Record | Coach |
|---|---|---|---|
| 1. | Miami (FL) | 12-0-0 | Dennis Erickson |
| 2. | #Washington | 12-0-0 | Don James |
| 3. | Penn St. | 11-2-0 | Joe Paterno |
| 4. | Florida St. | 11-2-0 | Bobby Bowden |
| 5. | Alabama | 11-1-0 | Gene Stallings |
| 6. | Michigan | 10-2-0 | Gary Moeller |
| 7. | Florida | 10-2-0 | Steve Spurrier |
| 8. | California | 10-2-0 | Bruce Snyder |
| 9. | E Carolina | 11-1-0 | Bill Lewis |
| 10. | Iowa | 10-1-1 | Hayden Fry |
| 11. | Syracuse | 10-2-0 | Paul Pasqualoni |
| 12. | Texas A&M | 10-2-0 | R.C. Slocum |
| 13. | Notre Dame | 10-3-0 | Lou Holtz |
| 14. | Tennessee | 9-3-0 | Johnny Majors |
| 15. | Nebraska | 9-2-1 | Tom Osborne |
| 16. | Oklahoma | 9-3-0 | Gary Gibbs |
| 17. | Georgia | 9-3-0 | Ray Goff |
| 18. | Clemson | 9-2-1 | Ken Hatfield |
| 19. | UCLA | 9-3-0 | Terry Donahue |
| 20. | Colorado | 8-3-1 | Bill McCartney |

#Selected No. 1 by CNN

## 1989

| | | Record | Coach |
|---|---|---|---|
| 1. | Miami (FL) | 11-1-0 | Dennis Erickson |
| 2. | Notre Dame | 12-1-0 | Lou Holtz |
| 3. | Florida St. | 10-2-0 | Bobby Bowden |
| 4. | Colorado | 11-1-0 | Bill McCartney |
| 5. | Tennessee | 11-1-0 | Johnny Majors |
| 6. | Auburn | 10-2-0 | Pat Dye |
| 7. | Michigan | 10-2-0 | Bo Schembechler |
| 8. | Southern Cal | 9-2-1 | Larry Smith |
| 9. | Alabama | 10-2-0 | Bill Curry |
| 10. | Illinois | 10-2-0 | John Mackovic |
| 11. | Nebraska | 10-2-0 | Tom Osborne |
| 12. | Clemson | 10-2-0 | Danny Ford |
| 13. | Arkansas | 10-2-0 | Ken Hatfield |
| 14. | Houston | 9-2-0 | Jack Pardee |
| 15. | Penn St. | 8-3-1 | Joe Paterno |
| 16. | Michigan St | 8-4-0 | George Perles |
| 17. | Pittsburgh | 8-3-1 | Mike Gottfried |
| 18. | Virginia | 10-3-0 | George Welsh |
| 19. | Texas Tech | 9-3-0 | Spike Dykes |
| 20. | Texas A&M | 8-4-0 | R.C. Slocum |

## 1990

| | | Record | Coach |
|---|---|---|---|
| 1. | Colorado | 11-1-1 | Bill McCartney |
| 2. | #Georgia Tech | 11-0-1 | Bobby Ross |
| 3. | Miami (FL) | 10-2-0 | Dennis Erickson |
| 4. | Florida St. | 10-2-0 | Bobby Bowden |
| 5. | Washington | 10-2-0 | Don James |
| 6. | Notre Dame | 9-3-0 | Lou Holtz |
| 7. | Michigan | 9-3-0 | Gary Moeller |
| 8. | Tennessee | 9-2-2 | Johnny Majors |
| 9. | Clemson | 10-2-0 | Ken Hatfield |
| 10. | Houston | 10-1-0 | John Jenkins |
| 11. | Penn St. | 9-3-0 | Joe Paterno |
| 12. | Texas | 10-2-0 | David McWilliams |
| 13. | Florida | 9-2-0 | Steve Spurrier |
| 14. | Louisville | 10-1-1 | H. Schnellenberger |
| 15. | Texas A&M | 9-3-1 | R.C. Slocum |
| 16. | Michigan St | 8-3-1 | George Perles |
| 17. | Oklahoma | 8-3-0 | Gary Gibbs |
| 18. | Iowa | 8-4-0 | Hayden Fry |
| 19. | Auburn | 8-3-1 | Pat Dye |
| 20. | Southern Cal | 8-4-1 | Larry Smith |

#Selected No. 1 by UPI

## 1988

| | | Record | Coach |
|---|---|---|---|
| 1. | Notre Dame | 12-0-0 | Lou Holtz |
| 2. | Miami (FL) | 11-1-0 | Jimmy Johnson |
| 3. | Florida State | 11-1-0 | Bobby Bowden |
| 4. | Michigan | 9-2-1 | Bo Schembechler |
| 5. | W. Virginia | 11-1-0 | Don Nehlen |
| 6. | UCLA | 10-2-0 | Terry Donahue |
| 7. | Southern Cal | 10-2-0 | Larry Smith |
| 8. | Auburn | 10-2-0 | Pat Dye |
| 9. | Clemson | 10-2-0 | Danny Ford |
| 10. | Nebraska | 11-2-0 | Tom Osborne |
| 11. | Oklahoma State | 10-2-0 | Pat Jones |
| 12. | Arkansas | 10-2-0 | Ken Hatfield |
| 13. | Syracuse | 10-2-0 | Dick MacPherson |
| 14. | Oklahoma | 9-3-0 | Barry Switzer |
| 15. | Georgia | 9-3-0 | Vince Dooley |
| 16. | Washington State | 9-3-0 | Dennis Erickson |
| 17. | Alabama | 9-3-0 | Bill Curry |
| 18. | Houston | 9-3-0 | Jack Pardee |
| 19. | LSU | 8-4-0 | Mike Archer |
| 20. | Indiana | 8-3-1 | Bill Mallory |

Note: Except where indicated with an asterisk, the polls from 1936 through 1964 were taken before the bowl games and those from 1965 through 1991 were taken after the bowl games.

## 1987

| | | Record | Coach |
|---|---|---|---|
| 1. | Miami (FL) | 12–0–0 | Jimmy Johnson |
| 2. | Florida State | 11–1–0 | Bobby Bowden |
| 3. | Oklahoma | 11–1–0 | Barry Switzer |
| 4. | Syracuse | 11–0–1 | Dick MacPherson |
| 5. | LSU | 10–1–1 | Mike Archer |
| 6. | Nebraska | 10–2–0 | Tom Osborne |
| 7. | Auburn | 9–1–2 | Pat Dye |
| 8. | Michigan State | 9–2–1 | George Perles |
| 9. | UCLA | 10–2–0 | Terry Donahue |
| 10. | Texas A&M | 10–2–0 | Jackie Sherrill |
| 11. | Oklahoma State | 10–2–0 | Pat Jones |
| 12. | Clemson | 10–2–0 | Danny Ford |
| 13. | Georgia | 9–3–0 | Vince Dooley |
| 14. | Tennessee | 10–2–1 | Johnny Majors |
| 15. | S. Carolina | 8–4–0 | Joe Morrison |
| 16. | Iowa | 10–3–0 | Hayden Fry |
| 17. | Notre Dame | 8–4–0 | Lou Holtz |
| 18. | Southern Cal | 8–4–0 | Larry Smith |
| 19. | Michigan | 8–4–0 | Bo Schembechler |
| 20. | Arizona State | 7–4–1 | John Cooper |

## 1985

| | | Record | Coach |
|---|---|---|---|
| 1. | Oklahoma | 11–1–0 | Barry Switzer |
| 2. | Michigan | 10–1–1 | Bo Schembechler |
| 3. | Penn St | 11–1–0 | Joe Paterno |
| 4. | Tennessee | 9–1–2 | Johnny Majors |
| 5. | Florida | 9–1–1 | Galen Hall |
| 6. | Texas A&M | 10–2–0 | Jackie Sherrill |
| 7. | UCLA | 9–2–1 | Terry Donahue |
| 8. | Air Force | 12–1–0 | Fisher De Berry |
| 9. | Miami (FL) | 10–2–0 | Jimmy Johnson |
| 10. | Iowa | 10–2–0 | Hayden Fry |
| 11. | Nebraska | 9–3–0 | Tom Osborne |
| 12. | Arkansas | 10–2–0 | Ken Hatfield |
| 13. | Alabama | 9–2–1 | Ray Perkins |
| 14. | Ohio State | 9–3–0 | Earle Bruce |
| 15. | Florida State | 9–3–0 | Bobby Bowden |
| 16. | BYU | 11–3–0 | LaVell Edwards |
| 17. | Baylor | 9–3–0 | Grant Teaff |
| 18. | Maryland | 9–3–0 | Bobby Ross |
| 19. | Georgia Tech | 9–2–1 | Bill Curry |
| 20. | LSU | 9–2–1 | Bill Arnsparger |

## 1986

| | | Record | Coach |
|---|---|---|---|
| 1. | Penn. St | 12–0–0 | Joe Paterno |
| 2. | Miami (FL) | 11–1–0 | Jimmy Johnson |
| 3. | Oklahoma | 11–1–0 | Barry Switzer |
| 4. | Arizona State | 10–1–1 | John Cooper |
| 5. | Nebraska | 10–2–0 | Tom Osborne |
| 6. | Auburn | 10–2–0 | Pat Dye |
| 7. | Ohio State | 10–3–0 | Earle Bruce |
| 8. | Michigan | 11–2–0 | Bo Schembechler |
| 9. | Alabama | 10–3–0 | Ray Perkins |
| 10. | LSU | 9–3–0 | Bill Arnsparger |
| 11. | Arizona | 9–3–0 | Larry Smith |
| 12. | Baylor | 9–3–0 | Grant Teaff |
| 13. | Texas A&M | 9–3–0 | Jackie Sherrill |
| 14. | UCLA | 8–3–1 | Terry Donahue |
| 15. | Arkansas | 9–3–0 | Ken Hatfield |
| 16. | Iowa | 9–3–0 | Hayden Fry |
| 17. | Clemson | 8–2–2 | Danny Ford |
| 18. | Washington | 8–3–1 | Don James |
| 19. | Boston College | 9–3–0 | Jack Bicknell |
| 20. | Virginia Tech | 9–2–1 | Bill Dooley |

## 1984

| | | Record | Coach |
|---|---|---|---|
| 1. | BYU | 13–0–0 | LaVell Edwards |
| 2. | Washington | 11–1–0 | Don James |
| 3. | Florida | 9–1–1 | Chas Pell (0–1–1) |
| | | | Galen Hall (9–0) |
| 4. | Nebraska | 10–2–0 | Tom Osborne |
| 5. | Boston College | 10–2–0 | Jack Bicknell |
| 6. | Oklahoma | 9–2–1 | Barry Switzer |
| 7. | Oklahoma State | 10–2–0 | Pat Jones |
| 8. | SMU | 10–2–0 | Bobby Collins |
| 9. | UCLA | 9–3–0 | Terry Donahue |
| 10. | Southern Cal | 10–3–0 | Ted Tollner |
| 11. | S. Carolina | 10–2–0 | Joe Morrison |
| 12. | Maryland | 9–3–0 | Bobby Ross |
| 13. | Ohio State | 9–3–0 | Earle Bruce |
| 14. | Auburn | 9–4–0 | Pat Dye |
| 15. | LSU | 8–3–1 | Bill Arnsparger |
| 16. | Iowa | 8–4–1 | Hayden Fry |
| 17. | Florida State | 7–3–2 | Bobby Bowden |
| 18. | Miami (FL) | 8–5–0 | Jimmy Johnson |
| 19. | Kentucky | 9–3–0 | Jerry Claiborne |
| 20. | Virginia | 8–2–2 | George Welsh |

## 1983

| | | Record | Coach |
|---|---|---|---|
| 1. | Miami (FL) | 11–1–0 | Howard Schnellenberger |
| 2. | Nebraska | 12–1–0 | Tom Osborne |
| 3. | Auburn | 11–1–0 | Pat Dye |
| 4. | Georgia | 10–1–1 | Vince Dooley |
| 5. | Texas | 11–1–0 | Fred Akers |
| 6. | Florida | 9–2–1 | Charlie Pell |
| 7. | BYU | 11–1–0 | LaVell Edwards |
| 8. | Michigan | 9–3–0 | Bo Schembechler |
| 9. | Ohio State | 9–3–0 | Earle Bruce |
| 10. | Illinois | 10–2–0 | Mike White |
| 11. | Clemson | 9–1–1 | Danny Ford |
| 12. | SMU | 10–2–0 | Bobby Collins |
| 13. | Air Force | 10–2–0 | Ken Hatfield |
| 14. | Iowa | 9–3–0 | Hayden Fry |
| 15. | Alabama | 8–4–0 | Ray Perkins |
| 16. | W. Virginia | 9–3–0 | Don Nehlen |
| 17. | UCLA | 7–4–1 | Terry Donahue |
| 18. | Pittsburgh | 8–3–1 | Foge Fazio |
| 19. | Boston College | 9–3–0 | Jack Bicknell |
| 20. | E. Carolina | 8–3–0 | Ed Emory |

## 1981

| | | Record | Coach |
|---|---|---|---|
| 1. | Clemson | 12–0–0 | Danny Ford |
| 2. | Texas | 10–1–1 | Fred Akers |
| 3. | Penn St | 10–2–0 | Joe Paterno |
| 4. | Pittsburgh | 11–1–0 | Jackie Sherrill |
| 5. | SMU | 10–1–0 | Ron Meyer |
| 6. | Georgia | 10–2–0 | Vince Dooley |
| 7. | Alabama | 9–2–1 | Bear Bryant |
| 8. | Miami (FL) | 9–2–0 | H.Schnellenberger |
| 9. | N. Carolina | 10–2–0 | Dick Crum |
| 10. | Washington | 10–2–0 | Don James |
| 11. | Nebraska | 9–3–0 | Tom Osborne |
| 12. | Michigan | 9–3–0 | Bo Schembechler |
| 13. | BYU | 11–2–0 | LaVell Edwards |
| 14. | Southern Cal | 9–3–0 | John Robinson |
| 15. | Ohio State | 9–3–0 | Earle Bruce |
| 16. | Arizona State | 9–2–0 | Darryl Rogers |
| 17. | W. Virginia | 9–3–0 | Don Nehlen |
| 18. | Iowa | 8–4–0 | Hayden Fry |
| 19. | Missouri | 8–4–0 | Warren Powers |
| 20. | Oklahoma | 7–4–1 | Barry Switzer |

## 1982

| | | Record | Coach |
|---|---|---|---|
| 1. | Penn St | 11–1–0 | Joe Paterno |
| 2. | SMU | 11–0–1 | Bobby Collins |
| 3. | Nebraska | 12–1–0 | Tom Osborne |
| 4. | Georgia | 11–1–0 | Vince Dooley |
| 5. | UCLA | 10–1–1 | Terry Donahue |
| 6. | Arizona State | 10–2–0 | Darryl Rogers |
| 7. | Washington | 10–2–0 | Don James |
| 8. | Clemson | 9–1–1 | Danny Ford |
| 9. | Arkansas | 9–2–1 | Lou Holtz |
| 10. | Pittsburgh | 9–3–0 | Foge Fazio |
| 11. | LSU | 8–3–1 | Jerry Stovall |
| 12. | Ohio State | 9–3–0 | Earle Bruce |
| 13. | Florida State | 9–3–0 | Bobby Bowden |
| 14. | Auburn | 9–3–0 | Pat Dye |
| 15. | Southern Cal | 8–3–0 | John Robinson |
| 16. | Oklahoma | 8–4–0 | Barry Switzer |
| 17. | Texas | 9–3–0 | Fred Akers |
| 18. | N. Carolina | 8–4–0 | Dick Crum |
| 19. | W. Virginia | 9–3–0 | Don Nehlen |
| 20. | Maryland | 8–4–0 | Bobby Ross |

## 1980

| | | Record | Coach |
|---|---|---|---|
| 1. | Georgia | 12–0–0 | Vince Dooley |
| 2. | Pittsburgh | 11–1–0 | Jackie Sherrill |
| 3. | Oklahoma | 10–2–0 | Barry Switzer |
| 4. | Michigan | 10–2–0 | Bo Schembechler |
| 5. | Florida State | 10–2–0 | Bobby Bowden |
| 6. | Alabama | 10–2–0 | Bear Bryant |
| 7. | Nebraska | 10–2–0 | Tom Osborne |
| 8. | Penn St | 10–2–0 | Joe Paterno |
| 9. | Notre Dame | 9–2–1 | Dan Devine |
| 10. | N. Carolina | 11–1–0 | Dick Crum |
| 11. | Southern Cal | 8–2–1 | John Robinson |
| 12. | BYU | 12–1–0 | LaVell Edwards |
| 13. | UCLA | 9–2–0 | Terry Donahue |
| 14. | Baylor | 10–2–0 | Grant Teaff |
| 15. | Ohio State | 9–3–0 | Earle Bruce |
| 16. | Washington | 9–3–0 | Don James |
| 17. | Purdue | 9–3–0 | Jim Young |
| 18. | Miami (FL) | 9–3–0 | H. Schnellenberger |
| 19. | Miss. State | 9–3–0 | Emory Bellard |
| 20. | SMU | 8–4–0 | Ron Meyer |

## 1979

| | | Record | Coach |
|---|---|---|---|
| 1. | Alabama | 12–0–0 | Bear Bryant |
| 2. | Southern Cal | 11–0–1 | John Robinson |
| 3. | Oklahoma | 11–1–0 | Barry Switzer |
| 4. | Ohio State | 11–1–0 | Earle Bruce |
| 5. | Houston | 11–1–0 | Bill Yeoman |
| 6. | Florida State | 11–1–0 | Bobby Bowden |
| 7. | Pittsburgh | 11–1–0 | Jackie Sherrill |
| 8. | Arkansas | 10–2–0 | Lou Holtz |
| 9. | Nebraska | 10–2–0 | Tom Osborne |
| 10. | Purdue | 10–2–0 | Jim Young |
| 11. | Washington | 10–1–0 | Don James |
| 12. | Texas | 9–3–0 | Fred Akers |
| 13. | BYU | 11–1–0 | LaVell Edwards |
| 14. | Baylor | 8–4–0 | Grant Teaff |
| 15. | N. Carolina | 8–3–1 | Dick Crum |
| 16. | Auburn | 8–3–0 | Doug Barfield |
| 17. | Temple | 10–2–0 | Wayne Hardin |
| 18. | Michigan | 8–4–0 | Bo Schembechler |
| 19. | Indiana | 8–4–0 | Lee Corso |
| 20. | Penn St | 8–4–0 | Joe Paterno |

## 1977

| | | Record | Coach |
|---|---|---|---|
| 1. | Notre Dame | 11–1–0 | Dan Devine |
| 2. | Alabama | 11–1–0 | Bear Bryant |
| 3. | Arkansas | 11–1–0 | Lou Holtz |
| 4. | Texas | 11–1–0 | Fred Akers |
| 5. | Penn St | 11–1–0 | Joe Paterno |
| 6. | Kentucky | 10–1–0 | Fran Curci |
| 7. | Oklahoma | 10–2–0 | Barry Switzer |
| 8. | Pittsburgh | 9–2–1 | Jackie Sherrill |
| 9. | Michigan | 10–2–0 | Bo Schembechler |
| 10. | Washington | 10–2–0 | Don James |
| 11. | Ohio State | 9–3–0 | Woody Hayes |
| 12. | Nebraska | 9–3–0 | Tom Osborne |
| 13. | Southern Cal | 8–4–0 | John Robinson |
| 14. | Florida State | 10–2–0 | Bobby Bowden |
| 15. | Stanford | 9–3–0 | Bill Walsh |
| 16. | San Diego State | 10–1–0 | Claude Gilbert |
| 17. | N Carolina | 8–3–1 | Bill Dooley |
| 18. | Arizona State | 9–3–0 | Frank Kush |
| 19. | Clemson | 8–3–1 | Charley Pell |
| 20. | BYU | 9–2–0 | LaVell Edwards |

## 1978

| | | Record | Coach |
|---|---|---|---|
| 1. | Alabama | 11–1–0 | Bear Bryant |
| 2. | #Southern Cal | 12–1–0 | John Robinson |
| 3. | Oklahoma | 11–1–0 | Barry Switzer |
| 4. | Penn St | 11–1–0 | Joe Paterno |
| 5. | Michigan | 10–2–0 | Bo Schembechler |
| 6. | Clemson | 11–1–0 | Charley Pell |
| 7. | Notre Dame | 9–3–0 | Dan Devine |
| 8. | Nebraska | 9–3–0 | Tom Osborne |
| 9. | Texas | 9–3–0 | Fred Akers |
| 10. | Houston | 9–3–0 | Bill Yeoman |
| 11. | Arkansas | 9–2–1 | Lou Holtz |
| 12. | Michigan State | 8–3–0 | Darryl Rogers |
| 13. | Purdue | 9–2–1 | Jim Young |
| 14. | UCLA | 8–3–1 | Terry Donahue |
| 15. | Missouri | 8–4–0 | Warren Powers |
| 16. | Georgia | 9–2–1 | Vince Dooley |
| 17. | Stanford | 8–4–0 | Bill Walsh |
| 18. | N.C. State | 9–3–0 | Bo Rein |
| 19. | Texas A&M | 8–4–0 | Emory Bellard (4–2) Tom Wilson (4–2) |
| 20. | Maryland | 9–3–0 | Jerry Claiborne |

#Selected No. 1 by UPI

## 1976

| | | Record | Coach |
|---|---|---|---|
| 1. | Pittsburgh | 12–0–0 | Johnny Majors |
| 2. | Southern Cal | 11–1–0 | John Robinson |
| 3. | Michigan | 10–2–0 | Bo Schembeclhler |
| 4. | Houston | 10–2–0 | Bill Yeoman |
| 5. | Oklahoma | 9–2–1 | Barry Switzer |
| 6. | Ohio State | 9–2–1 | Woody Hayes |
| 7. | Texas A&M | 10–2–0 | Emory Bellard |
| 8. | Maryland | 11–1–0 | Jerry Claiborne |
| 9. | Nebraska | 9–3–1 | Tom Osborne |
| 10. | Georgia | 10–2–0 | Vince Dooley |
| 11. | Alabama | 9–3–0 | Bear Bryant |
| 12. | Notre Dame | 9–3–0 | Dan Devine |
| 13. | Texas Tech | 10–2–0 | Steve Sloan |
| 14. | Oklahoma State | 9–3–0 | Jim Stanley |
| 15. | UCLA | 9–2–1 | Terry Donahue |
| 16. | Colorado | 8–4–0 | Bill Mallory |
| 17. | Rutgers | 11–0–0 | Frank Burns |
| 18. | Kentucky | 9–3–0 | Fran Curci |
| 19. | Iowa State | 8–3–0 | Earle Bruce |
| 20. | Miss. State | 9–2–0 | Bob Tyler |

## 1975

| | | Record | Coach |
|---|---|---|---|
| 1. | Oklahoma | 11–1–0 | Barry Switzer |
| 2. | Arizona State | 12–0–0 | Frank Kush |
| 3. | Alabama | 11–1–0 | Bear Bryant |
| 4. | Ohio State | 11–1–0 | Woody Hayes |
| 5. | UCLA | 9–2–1 | Dick Vermeil |
| 6. | Texas | 10–2–0 | Darrell Royal |
| 7. | Arkansas | 10–2–0 | Frank Broyles |
| 8. | Michigan | 8–2–2 | Bo Schembechler |
| 9. | Nebraska | 10–2–0 | Tom Osborne |
| 10. | Penn St | 9–3–0 | Joe Paterno |
| 11. | Texas A&M | 10–2–0 | Emory Bellard |
| 12. | Miami (OH) | 11–1–0 | Dick Crum |
| 13. | Maryland | 9–2–1 | Jerry Claiborne |
| 14. | California | 8–3–0 | Mike White |
| 15. | Pittsburgh | 8–4–0 | Johnny Majors |
| 16. | Colorado | 9–3–0 | Bill Mallory |
| 17. | Southern Cal | 8–4–0 | John McKay |
| 18. | Arizona | 9–2–0 | Jim Young |
| 19. | Georgia | 9–3–0 | Vince Dooley |
| 20. | West Virginia | 9–3–0 | Bobby Bowden |

## 1973

| | | Record | Coach |
|---|---|---|---|
| 1. | Notre Dame | 11–0–0 | Ara Parseghian |
| 2. | Ohio State | 10–0–1 | Woody Hayes |
| 3. | Oklahoma | 10–0–1 | Barry Switzer |
| 4. | #Alabama | 11–1–0 | Bear Bryant |
| 5. | Penn St | 12–0–0 | Joe Paterno |
| 6. | Michigan | 10–0–1 | Bo Schembechler |
| 7. | Nebraska | 9–2–1 | Tom Osborne |
| 8. | Southern Cal | 9–2–1 | John McKay |
| 9. | Arizona State | 11–1–0 | Frank Kush |
| | Houston | 11–1–0 | Bill Yeoman |
| 11. | Texas Tech | 11–1–0 | Jim Carlen |
| 12. | UCLA | 9–2–0 | Pepper Rodgers |
| 13. | LSU | 9–3–0 | Charlie McClendon |
| 14. | Texas | 8–3–0 | Darrell Royal |
| 15. | Miami (OH) | 11–0–0 | Bill Mallory |
| 16. | N.C. State | 9–3–0 | Lou Holtz |
| 17. | Missouri | 8–4–0 | Al Onofrio |
| 18. | Kansas | 7–4–1 | Don Fambrough |
| 19. | Tennessee | 8–4–0 | Bill Battle |
| 20. | Maryland | 8–4–0 | Jerry Claiborne |
| | Tulane | 9–3–0 | Bennie Ellender |

#Selected No. 1 by UPI

## 1974

| | | Record | Coach |
|---|---|---|---|
| 1. | Oklahoma | 11–0–0 | Barry Switzer |
| 2. | #Southern Cal | 10–1–1 | John McKay |
| 3. | Michigan | 10–1–0 | Bo Schembechler |
| 4. | Ohio State | 10–2–0 | Woody Hayes |
| 5. | Alabama | 11–1–0 | Bear Bryant |
| 6. | Notre Dame | 10–2–0 | Ara Parseghian |
| 7. | Penn St | 10–2–0 | Joe Paterno |
| 8. | Auburn | 10–2–0 | Shug Jordan |
| 9. | Nebraska | 9–3–0 | Tom Osborne |
| 10. | Miami (OH) | 10–0–1 | Dick Crum |
| 11. | N.C. State | 9–2–1 | Lou Holtz |
| 12. | Michigan State | 7–3–1 | Denny Stolz |
| 13. | Maryland | 8–4–0 | Jerry Claiborne |
| 14. | Baylor | 8–4–0 | Grant Teaff |
| 15. | Florida | 8–4–0 | Doug Dickey |
| 16. | Texas A&M | 8–3–0 | Emory Ballard |
| 17. | Miss. State | 9–3–0 | Bob Tyler |
| | Texas | 8–4–0 | Darrell Royal |
| 19. | Houston | 8–3–1 | Bill Yeoman |
| 20. | Tennessee | 7–3–2 | Bill Battle |

#Selected No. 1 by UPI

## 1972

| | | Record | Coach |
|---|---|---|---|
| 1. | Southern Cal | 12–0–0 | John McKay |
| 2. | Oklahoma | 11–1–0 | Chuck Fairbanks |
| 3. | Texas | 10–1–0 | Darrell Royal |
| 4. | Nebraska | 9–2–1 | Bob Devaney |
| 5. | Auburn | 10–1–0 | Shug Jordan |
| 6. | Michigan | 10–1–0 | Bo Schembechler |
| 7. | Alabama | 10–2–0 | Bear Bryant |
| 8. | Tennessee | 10–2–0 | Bill Battle |
| 9. | Ohio State | 9–2–0 | Woody Hayes |
| 10. | Penn St | 10–2–0 | Joe Paterno |
| 11. | LSU | 9–2–1 | Charlie McClendon |
| 12. | N. Carolina | 11–1–0 | Bill Dooley |
| 13. | Arizona State | 10–2–0 | Frank Kush |
| 14. | Notre Dame | 8–3–0 | Ara Parseghian |
| 15. | UCLA | 8–3–0 | Pepper Rodgers |
| 16. | Colorado | 8–4–0 | Eddie Crowder |
| 17. | N.C. State | 8–3–1 | Lou Holtz |
| 18. | Louisville | 9–1–0 | Lee Corso |
| 19. | Washington State | 7–4–0 | Jim Sweeney |
| 20. | Georgia Tech | 7–4–1 | Bill Fulcher |

## 1971

| | | Record | Coach |
|---|---|---|---|
| 1. | Nebraska | 13–0–0 | Bob Devaney |
| 2. | Oklahoma | 11–1–0 | Chuck Fairbanks |
| 3. | Colorado | 10–2–0 | Eddie Crowder |
| 4. | Alabama | 11–1–0 | Bear Bryant |
| 5. | Penn St | 11–1–0 | Joe Paterno |
| 6. | Michigan | 11–1–0 | Bo Schembechler |
| 7. | Georgia | 11–1–0 | Vince Dooley |
| 8. | Arizona State | 11–1–0 | Frank Kush |
| 9. | Tennessee | 10–2–0 | Bill Battle |
| 10. | Stanford | 9–3–0 | John Ralston |
| 11. | LSU | 9–3–0 | Charlie McClendon |
| 12. | Auburn | 9–2–0 | Shug Jordan |
| 13. | Notre Dame | 8–2–0 | Ara Parseghian |
| 14. | Toledo | 12–0–0 | John Murphy |
| 15. | Mississippi | 10–2–0 | Billy Kinard |
| 16. | Arkansas | 8–3–1 | Frank Broyles |
| 17. | Houston | 9–3–0 | Bill Yeoman |
| 18. | Texas | 8–3–0 | Darrell Royal |
| 19. | Washington | 8–3–0 | Jim Owens |
| 20. | Southern Cal | 6–4–1 | John McKay |

## 1969

| | | Record | Coach |
|---|---|---|---|
| 1. | Texas | 11–0–0 | Darrell Royal |
| 2. | Penn St | 11–0–0 | Joe Paterno |
| 3. | Southern Cal | 10–0–1 | John McKay |
| 4. | Ohio State | 8–1–0 | Woody Hayes |
| 5. | Notre Dame | 8–2–1 | Ara Parseghian |
| 6. | Missouri | 9–2–0 | Dan Devine |
| 7. | Arkansas | 9–2–0 | Frank Broyles |
| 8. | Mississippi | 8–3–0 | Johnny Vaught |
| 9. | Michigan | 8–3–0 | Bo Schembechler |
| 10. | LSU | 9–1–0 | Charlie McClendon |
| 11. | Nebraska | 9–2–0 | Bob Devaney |
| 12. | Houston | 9–2–0 | Bill Yeoman |
| 13. | UCLA | 8–1–1 | Tommy Prothro |
| 14. | Florida | 9–1–1 | Ray Graves |
| 15. | Tennessee | 9–2–0 | Doug Dickey |
| 16. | Colorado | 8–3–0 | Eddie Crowder |
| 17. | W. Virginia | 10–0–1 | Jim Carlen |
| 18. | Purdue | 8–2–0 | Jack Mollenkopf |
| 19. | Stanford | 7–2–1 | John Ralston |
| 20. | Auburn | 8–3–0 | Shug Jordan |

## 1970

| | | Record | Coach |
|---|---|---|---|
| 1. | Nebraska | 11–0–1 | Bob Devaney |
| 2. | Notre Dame | 10–1–0 | Ara Parseghian |
| 3. | #Texas | 10–1–0 | Darrell Royal |
| 4. | Tennessee | 11–0–0 | Bill Battle |
| 5. | Ohio State | 9–1–0 | Woody Hayes |
| 6. | Arizona State | 11–0–0 | Frank Kush |
| 7. | LSU | 9–3–0 | Charlie McClendon |
| 8. | Stanford | 9–3–0 | John Ralston |
| 9. | Michigan | 9–1–0 | Bo Schembechler |
| 10. | Auburn | 9–2–0 | Shug Jordan |
| 11. | Arkansas | 9–2–0 | Frank Broyles |
| 12. | Toledo | 12–0–0 | Frank Lauterbur |
| 13. | Georgia Tech | 9–3–0 | Bud Carson |
| 14. | Dartmouth | 9–0–0 | Bob Blackman |
| 15. | Southern Cal | 6–4–1 | John McKay |
| 16. | Air Force | 9–3–0 | Ben Martin |
| 17. | Tulane | 8–4–0 | Jim Pittman |
| 18. | Penn St | 7–3–0 | Joe Paterno |
| 19. | Houston | 8–3–0 | Bill Yeoman |
| 20. | Oklahoma | 7–4–1 | Chuck Fairbanks |
| | Mississippi | 7–4–0 | Johnny Vaught |

#Selected No. 1 by UPI

## 1968

| | | Record | Coach |
|---|---|---|---|
| 1. | Ohio State | 10–0–0 | Woody Hayes |
| 2. | Penn St | 11–0–0 | Joe Paterno |
| 3. | Texas | 9–1–1 | Darrell Royal |
| 4. | Southern Cal | 9–1–1 | John McKay |
| 5. | Notre Dame | 7–2–1 | Ara Parseghian |
| 6. | Arkansas | 10–1–0 | Frank Broyles |
| 7. | Kansas | 9–2–0 | Pepper Rodgers |
| 8. | Georgia | 8–1–2 | Vince Dooley |
| 9. | Missouri | 8–3–0 | Dan Devine |
| 10. | Purdue | 8–2–0 | Jack Mollenkopf |
| 11. | Oklahoma | 7–4–0 | Chuck Fairbanks |
| 12. | Michigan | 8–2–0 | Bump Elliott |
| 13. | Tennessee | 8–2–1 | Doug Dickey |
| 14. | SMU | 8–3–0 | Hayden Fry |
| 15. | Oregon State | 7–3–0 | Dee Andros |
| 16. | Auburn | 7–4–0 | Shug Jordan |
| 17. | Alabama | 8–3–0 | Bear Bryant |
| 18. | Houston | 6–2–2 | Bill Yeoman |
| 19. | LSU | 8–3–0 | Charlie McClendon |
| 20. | Ohio University | 10–1–0 | Bill Hess |

## 1967*

| | | Record | Coach |
|---|---|---|---|
| 1. | Southern Cal | 9-1-0 | John McKay |
| 2. | Tennessee | 9-1-0 | Doug Dickey |
| 3. | Oklahoma | 9-1-0 | Chuck Fairbanks |
| 4. | Indiana | 9-1-0 | John Pont |
| 5. | Notre Dame | 8-2-0 | Ara Parseghian |
| 6. | Wyoming | 10-0-0 | Lloyd Eaton |
| 7. | Oregon State | 7-2-1 | Dee Andros |
| 8. | Alabama | 8-1-1 | Bear Bryant |
| 9. | Purdue | 8-2-0 | Jack Mollenkopf |
| 10. | Penn St | 8-2-0 | Joe Paterno |
| 11–20: UPI† | | | |
| 11. | UCLA | 7-2-1 | Tommy Prothro |
| 12. | Syracuse | 8-2-0 | Ben Schwartzwalder |
| 13. | Colorado | 8-2-0 | Eddie Crowder |
| 14. | Minnesota | 8-2-0 | Murray Warmath |
| 15. | Florida State | 7-2-1 | Bill Peterson |
| 16. | Miami (FL) | 7-3-0 | Charlie Tate |
| 17. | N.C. State | 8-2-0 | Earle Edwards |
| 18. | Georgia | 7-3-0 | Vince Dooley |
| 19. | Houston | 9-2-0 | Bill Yeoman |
| 20. | Arizona State | 8-2-0 | Frank Kush |

†UPI ranked Penn St 11th and did not rank Alabama, which was on probation

## 1966

| | | Record | Coach |
|---|---|---|---|
| 1. | Notre Dame | 9-0-1 | Ara Parseghian |
| 2. | Michigan State | 9-0-1 | Duffy Daugherty |
| 3. | Alabama | 10-0-0 | Bear Bryant |
| 4. | Georgia | 9-1-0 | Vince Dooley |
| 5. | UCLA | 9-1-0 | Tommy Prothro |
| 6. | Nebraska | 9-1-0 | Bob Devaney |
| 7. | Purdue | 8-2-0 | Jack Mollenkopf |
| 8. | Georgia Tech | 9-1-0 | Bobby Dodd |
| 9. | Miami (FL) | 7-2-1 | Charlie Tate |
| 10. | SMU | 8-2-0 | Hayden Fry |
| 11–20: UPI | | | |
| 11. | Florida | 8-2-0 | Ray Graves |
| 12. | Mississippi | 8-2-0 | Johnny Vaught |
| 13. | Arkansas | 8-2-0 | Frank Broyles |
| 14. | Tennessee | 7-3-0 | Doug Dickey |
| 15. | Wyoming | 9-1-0 | Lloyd Eaton |
| 16. | Syracuse | 8-2-0 | Ben Schwartzwalder |
| 17. | Houston | 8-2-0 | Bill Yeoman |
| 18. | Southern Cal | 7-3-0 | John McKay |
| 19. | Oregon State | 7-3-0 | Dee Andros |
| 20. | Virginia Tech | 8-1-1 | Jerry Claiborne |

## 1965

| | | Record | Coach |
|---|---|---|---|
| 1. | Alabama | 9-1-1 | Bear Bryant |
| 2. | #Michigan State | 10-1-0 | Duffy Daugherty |
| 3. | Arkansas | 10-1-0 | Frank Broyles |
| 4. | UCLA | 8-2-1 | Tommy Prothro |
| 5. | Nebraska | 10-1-0 | Bob Devaney |
| 6. | Missouri | 8-2-1 | Dan Devine |
| 7. | Tennessee | 8-1-2 | Doug Dickey |
| 8. | LSU | 8-3-0 | Charlie McClendon |
| 9. | Notre Dame | 7-2-1 | Ara Parseghian |
| 10. | Southern Cal | 7-2-1 | John McKay |
| 11–20: UPI† | | | |
| 11. | Texas Tech | 8-2-0 | JT King |
| 12. | Ohio State | 7-2-0 | Woody Hayes |
| 13. | Florida | 7-3-0 | Ray Graves |
| 14. | Purdue | 7-2-1 | Jack Mollenkopf |
| 15. | Georgia | 6-4-0 | Vince Dooley |
| 16. | Tulsa | 8-2-0 | Glenn Dobbs |
| 17. | Mississippi | 6-4-0 | Johnny Vaught |
| 18. | Kentucky | 6-4-0 | Charlie Bradshaw |
| 19 | Syracuse | 7-3-0 | Ben Schwartzwalder |
| 20. | Colorado | 6-2-2 | Eddie Crowder |

#Selected No. 1 by UPI

†UPI ranked Louisiana St 14th

## 1964

| | | Record | Coach |
|---|---|---|---|
| 1. | Alabama | 10-0-0 | Bear Bryant |
| 2. | Arkansas | 10-0-0 | Frank Broyles |
| 3. | Notre Dame | 9-1-0 | Ara Parseghian |
| 4. | Michigan | 8-1-0 | Bump Elliott |
| 5. | Texas | 9-1-0 | Darrell Royal |
| 6. | Nebraska | 9-1-0 | Bob Devaney |
| 7. | LSU | 7-2-1 | Charlie McClendon |
| 8. | Oregon State | 8-2-0 | Tommy Prothro |
| 9. | Ohio State | 7-2-0 | Woody Hayes |
| 10. | Southern Cal | 7-3-0 | John McKay |
| 11–20: UPI | | | |
| 11. | Florida State | 8-1-1 | Bill Peterson |
| 12. | Syracuse | 7-3-0 | Ben Schwartzwalder |
| 13. | Princeton | 9-0-0 | Dick Colman |
| 14. | Penn St | 6-4-0 | Rip Engle |
| | Utah | 8-2-0 | Ray Nagel |
| 16. | Illinois | 6-3-0 | Pete Elliott |
| | New Mexico | 9-2-0 | Bill Weeks |
| 18. | Tulsa | 8-2-0 | Glenn Dobbs |
| 19. | Missouri | 6-3-1 | Dan Devine |
| 20. | Mississippi | 5-4-1 | Johnny Vaught |
| | Michigan State | 4-5-1 | Duffy Daugherty |

## 1963

| | | Record | Coach |
|---|---|---|---|
| 1. | Texas | 10–0–0 | Darrell Royal |
| 2. | Navy | 9–1–0 | Wayne Hardin |
| 3. | Illinois | 7–1–1 | Pete Elliott |
| 4. | Pittsburgh | 9–1–0 | John Michelosen |
| 5. | Auburn | 9–1–0 | Shug Jordan |
| 6. | Nebraska | 9–1–0 | Bob Devaney |
| 7. | Mississippi | 7–0–2 | Johnny Vaught |
| 8. | Alabama | 8–2–0 | Bear Bryant |
| 9. | Oklahoma | 8–2–0 | Bud Wilkinson |
| 10. | Michigan State | 6–2–1 | Duffy Daugherty |
| 11–20: UPI | | | |
| 11. | Miss. State | 6–2–2 | Paul Davis |
| 12. | Syracuse | 8–2–0 | Ben Schwartzwalder |
| 13. | Arizona State | 8–1–0 | Frank Kush |
| 14. | Memphis State | 9–0–1 | Billy J. Murphy |
| 15. | Washington | 6–4–0 | Jim Owens |
| 16. | Penn St | 7–3–0 | Rip Engle |
| | Southern Cal | 7–3–0 | John McKay |
| | Missouri | 7–3–0 | Dan Devine |
| 19. | N. Carolina | 8–2–0 | Jim Hickey |
| 20. | Baylor | 7–3–0 | John Bridgers |

## 1961

| | | Record | Coach |
|---|---|---|---|
| 1. | Alabama | 10–0–0 | Bear Bryant |
| 2. | Ohio State | 8–0–1 | Woody Hayes |
| 3. | Texas | 9–1–0 | Darrell Royal |
| 4. | LSU | 9–1–0 | Paul Dietzel |
| 5. | Mississippi | 9–1–0 | Johnny Vaught |
| 6. | Minnesota | 7–2–0 | Murray Warmath |
| 7. | Colorado | 9–1–0 | Sonny Grandelius |
| 8. | Michigan State | 7–2–0 | Duffy Daugherty |
| 9. | Arkansas | 8–2–0 | Frank Broyles |
| 10. | Utah State | 9–0–1 | John Ralston |
| 11. | Missouri | 7–2–1 | Dan Devine |
| 12. | Purdue | 6–3–0 | Jack Mollenkopf |
| 13. | Georgia Tech | 7–3–0 | Bobby Dodd |
| 14. | Syracuse | 7–3–0 | Ben Schwartzwalder |
| 15. | Rutgers | 9–0–0 | John Bateman |
| 16. | UCLA | 7–3–0 | Bill Barnes |
| 17. | Rice | 7–3–0 | Jess Neely |
| | Penn St | 7–3–0 | Rip Engle |
| | Arizona | 8–1–1 | Jim LaRue |
| 20. | Duke | 7–3–0 | Bill Murray |

## 1962

| | | Record | Coach |
|---|---|---|---|
| 1. | Southern Cal | 10–0–0 | John McKay |
| 2. | Wisconsin | 8–1–0 | Milt Bruhn |
| 3. | Mississippi | 9–0–0 | Johnny Vaught |
| 4. | Texas | 9–0–1 | Darrell Royal |
| 5. | Alabama | 9–1–0 | Bear Bryant |
| 6. | Arkansas | 9–1–0 | Frank Broyles |
| 7. | LSU | 8–1–1 | Charlie McClendon |
| 8. | Oklahoma | 8–2–0 | Bud Wilkinson |
| 9. | Penn St | 9–1–0 | Rip Engle |
| 10. | Minnesota | 6–2–1 | Murray Warmath |
| 11–20: UPI | | | |
| 11. | Georgia Tech | 7–2–1 | Bobby Dodd |
| 12. | Missouri | 7–1–2 | Dan Devine |
| 13. | Ohio State | 6–3–0 | Woody Hayes |
| 14. | Duke | 8–2–0 | Bill Murray |
| | Washington | 7–1–2 | Jim Owens |
| 16. | Northwestern | 7–2–0 | Ara Parseghian |
| | Oregon State | 8–2–0 | Tommy Prothro |
| 18. | Arizona State | 7–2–1 | Frank Kush |
| | Miami (FL) | 7–3–0 | Andy Gustafson |
| | Illinois | 2–7–0 | Pete Elliott |

## 1960

| | | Record | Coach |
|---|---|---|---|
| 1. | Minnesota | 8–1–0 | Murray Warmath |
| 2. | Mississippi | 9–0–1 | Johnny Vaught |
| 3. | Iowa | 8–1–0 | Forest Evashevski |
| 4. | Navy | 9–1–0 | Wayne Hardin |
| 5. | Missouri | 9–1–0 | Dan Devine |
| 6. | Washington | 9–1–0 | Jim Owens |
| 7. | Arkansas | 8–2–0 | Frank Broyles |
| 8. | Ohio State | 7–2–0 | Woody Hayes |
| 9. | Alabama | 8–1–1 | Bear Bryant |
| 10. | Duke | 7–3–0 | Bill Murray |
| 11. | Kansas | 7–2–1 | Jack Mitchell |
| 12. | Baylor | 8–2–0 | John Bridgers |
| 13. | Auburn | 8–2–0 | Shug Jordan |
| 14. | Yale | 9–0–0 | Jordan Oliver |
| 15. | Michigan State | 6–2–1 | Duffy Daugherty |
| 16. | Penn St | 6–3–0 | Rip Engle |
| 17. | New Mexico St. | 10–0–0 | Warren Woodson |
| 18. | Florida | 8–2–0 | Ray Graves |
| 19. | Syracuse | 7–2–0 | Ben Schwartzwalder |
| | Purdue | 4–4–1 | Jack Mollenkopf |

# Annual Associated Press Top 20 *(Cont.)*

## 1959

| | | Record | Coach |
|---|---|---|---|
| 1. | Syracuse | 10–0–0 | Ben Schwartzwalder |
| 2. | Mississippi | 9–1–0 | Johnny Vaught |
| 3. | LSU | 9–1–0 | Paul Dietzel |
| 4. | Texas | 9–1–0 | Darrell Royal |
| 5. | Georgia | 9–1–0 | Wally Butts |
| 6. | Wisconsin | 7–2–0 | Milt Bruhn |
| 7. | TCU | 8–2–0 | Abe Martin |
| 8. | Washington | 9–1–0 | Jim Owens |
| 9. | Arkansas | 8–2–0 | Frank Broyles |
| 10. | Alabama | 7–1–2 | Bear Bryant |
| 11. | Clemson | 8–2–0 | Frank Howard |
| 12. | Penn St | 8–2–0 | Rip Engle |
| 13. | Illinois | 5–3–1 | Ray Eliot |
| 14. | Southern Cal | 8–2–0 | Don Clark |
| 15. | Oklahoma | 7–3–0 | Bud Wilkinson |
| 16. | Wyoming | 9–1–0 | Bob Devaney |
| 17. | Notre Dame | 5–5–0 | Joe Kuharich |
| 18. | Missouri | 6–4–0 | Dan Devine |
| 19. | Florida | 5–4–1 | Bob Woodruff |
| 20. | Pittsburgh | 6–4–0 | John Michelosen |

## 1957

| | | Record | Coach |
|---|---|---|---|
| 1. | Auburn | 10–0–0 | Shug Jordan |
| 2. | #Ohio State | 8–1–0 | Woody Hayes |
| 3. | Michigan State | 8–1–0 | Duffy Daugherty |
| 4. | Oklahoma | 9–1–0 | Bud Wilkinson |
| 5. | Navy | 8–1–1 | Eddie Erdelatz |
| 6. | Iowa | 7–1–1 | Forest Evashevski |
| 7. | Mississippi | 8–1–1 | Johnny Vaught |
| 8. | Rice | 7–3–0 | Jess Neely |
| 9. | Texas A&M | 8–2–0 | Bear Bryant |
| 10. | Notre Dame | 7–3–0 | Terry Brennan |
| 11. | Texas | 6–3–1 | Darrell Royal |
| 12. | Arizona State | 10–0–0 | Dan Devine |
| 13. | Tennessee | 7–3–0 | Bowden Wyatt |
| 14. | Mississippi State | 6–2–1 | Wade Walker |
| 15. | N.C. State | 7–1–2 | Earle Edwards |
| 16. | Duke | 6–2–2 | Bill Murray |
| 17. | Florida | 6–2–1 | Bob Woodruff |
| 18. | Army | 7–2–0 | Red Blaik |
| 19. | Wisconsin | 6–3–0 | Milt Brunt |
| 20. | VMI | 9–0–1 | John McKenna |

#Selected No. 1 by UP

## 1958

| | | Record | Coach |
|---|---|---|---|
| 1. | LSU | 10–0–0 | Paul Dietzel |
| 2. | Iowa | 7–1–1 | Forest Evashevski |
| 3. | Army | 8–0–1 | Red Blaik |
| 4. | Auburn | 9–0–1 | Shug Jordan |
| 5. | Oklahoma | 9–1–0 | Bud Wilkinson |
| 6. | Air Force | 9–0–1 | Ben Martin |
| 7. | Wisconsin | 7–1–1 | Milt Bruhn |
| 8. | Ohio State | 6–1–2 | Woody Hayes |
| 9. | Syracuse | 8–1–0 | Ben Schwartzwalder |
| 10. | TCU | 8–2–0 | Abe Martin |
| 11. | Mississippi | 8–2–0 | Johnny Vaught |
| 12. | Clemson | 8–2–0 | Frank Howard |
| 13. | Purdue | 6–1–2 | Jack Mollenkopf |
| 14. | Florida | 6–3–1 | Bob Woodruff |
| 15. | South Carolina | 7–3–0 | Warren Giese |
| 16. | California | 7–3–0 | Pete Elliott |
| 17. | Notre Dame | 6–4–0 | Terry Brennan |
| 18. | SMU | 6–4–0 | Bill Meek |
| 19. | Oklahoma State | 7–3–0 | Cliff Speegle |
| 20. | Rutgers | 8–1–0 | John Stiegman |

## 1956

| | | Record | Coach |
|---|---|---|---|
| 1. | Oklahoma | 10–0–0 | Bud Wilkinson |
| 2. | Tennessee | 10–0–0 | Bowden Wyatt |
| 3. | Iowa | 8–1–0 | Forest Evashevski |
| 4. | Georgia Tech | 9–1–0 | Bobby Dodd |
| 5. | Texas A&M | 9–0–1 | Bear Bryant |
| 6. | Miami (FL) | 8–1–1 | Andy Gustafson |
| 7. | Michigan | 7–2–0 | Bennie Oosterbaan |
| 8. | Syracuse | 7–1–0 | Ben Schwartzwalder |
| 9. | Michigan State | 7–2–0 | Duffy Daugherty |
| 10. | Oregon State | 7–2–1 | Tommy Prothro |
| 11. | Baylor | 8–2–0 | Sam Boyd |
| 12. | Minnesota | 6–1–2 | Murray Warmath |
| 13. | Pittsburgh | 7–2–1 | John Michelosen |
| 14. | TCU | 7–3–0 | Abe Martin |
| 15. | Ohio State | 6–3–0 | Woody Hayes |
| 16. | Navy | 6–1–2 | Eddie Erdelatz |
| 17. | G. Washington | 7–1–1 | Gene Sherman |
| 18. | Southern Cal. | 8–2–0 | Jess Hill |
| 19. | Clemson | 7–1–2 | Frank Howard |
| 20. | Colorado | 7–2–1 | Dallas Ward |
| | Penn St | 6–2–1 | Rip Engle |

## 1955

| | | Record | Coach |
|---|---|---|---|
| 1. | Oklahoma | 10–0–0 | Bud Wilkinson |
| 2. | Michigan State | 8–1–0 | Duffy Daugherty |
| 3. | Maryland | 10–0–0 | Jim Tatum |
| 4. | UCLA | 9–1–0 | Red Sanders |
| 5. | Ohio State | 7–2–0 | Woody Hayes |
| 6. | TCU | 9–1–0 | Abe Martin |
| 7. | Georgia Tech | 8–1–1 | Bobby Dodd |
| 8. | Auburn | 8–1–1 | Shug Jordan |
| 9. | Notre Dame | 8–2–0 | Terry Brennan |
| 10. | Mississippi | 9–1–0 | Johnny Vaught |
| 11. | Pittsburgh | 7–3–0 | John Michelosen |
| 12. | Michigan | 7–2–0 | Bennie Oosterbaan |
| 13. | Southern Cal | 6–4–0 | Jess Hill |
| 14. | Miami (FL) | 6–3–0 | Andy Gustafson |
| 15. | Miami (OH) | 9–0–0 | Ara Parseghian |
| 16. | Stanford | 6–3–1 | Chuck Taylor |
| 17. | Texas A&M | 7–2–1 | Bear Bryant |
| 18. | Navy | 6–2–1 | Eddie Erdelatz |
| 19. | West Virginia | 8–2–0 | Art Lewis |
| 20. | Army | 6–3–0 | Red Blaik |

## 1953

| | | Record | Coach |
|---|---|---|---|
| 1. | Maryland | 10–0–0 | Jim Tatum |
| 2. | Notre Dame | 9–0–1 | Frank Leahy |
| 3. | Michigan State | 8–1–0 | Biggie Munn |
| 4. | Oklahoma | 8–1–1 | Bud Wilkinson |
| 5. | UCLA | 8–1–0 | Red Sanders |
| 6. | Rice | 8–2–0 | Jess Neely |
| 7. | Illinois | 7–1–1 | Ray Eliot |
| 8. | Georgia Tech | 8–2–1 | Bobby Dodd |
| 9. | Iowa | 5–3–1 | Forest Evashevski |
| 10. | West Virginia | 8–1–0 | Art Lewis |
| 11. | Texas | 7–3–0 | Ed Price |
| 12. | Texas Tech | 10–1–0 | DeWitt Weaver |
| 13. | Alabama | 6–2–3 | Red Drew |
| 14. | Army | 7–1–1 | Red Blaik |
| 15. | Wisconsin | 6–2–1 | Ivy Williamson |
| 16. | Kentucky | 7–2–1 | Bear Bryant |
| 17. | Auburn | 7–2–1 | Shug Jordan |
| 18. | Duke | 7–2–1 | Bill Murray |
| 19. | Stanford | 6–3–1 | Chuck Taylor |
| 20. | Michigan | 6–3–0 | Bennie Oosterbaan |

## 1954

| | | Record | Coach |
|---|---|---|---|
| 1. | Ohio State | 9–0–0 | Woody Hayes |
| 2. | #UCLA | 9–0–0 | Red Sanders |
| 3. | Oklahoma | 10–0–0 | Bud Wilkinson |
| 4. | Notre Dame | 9–1–0 | Terry Brennan |
| 5. | Navy | 7–2–0 | Eddie Erdelatz |
| 6. | Mississippi | 9–1–0 | Johnny Vaught |
| 7. | Army | 7–2–0 | Red Blaik |
| 8. | Maryland | 7–2–1 | Jim Tatum |
| 9. | Wisconsin | 7–2–0 | Ivy Williamson |
| 10. | Arkansas | 8–2–0 | Bowden Wyatt |
| 11. | Miami (FL) | 8–1–0 | Andy Gustafson |
| 12. | West Virginia | 8–1–0 | Art Lewis |
| 13. | Auburn | 7–3–0 | Shug Jordan |
| 14. | Duke | 7–2–1 | Bill Murray |
| 15. | Michigan | 6–3–0 | Bennie Oosterbaan |
| 16. | Virginia Tech | 8–0–1 | Frank Moseley |
| 17. | Southern Cal | 8–3–0 | Jess Hill |
| 18. | Baylor | 7–3–0 | George Sauer |
| 19. | Rice | 7–3–0 | Jess Neely |
| 20. | Penn St | 7–2–0 | Rip Engle |

#Selected No. 1 by UP

## 1952

| | | Record | Coach |
|---|---|---|---|
| 1. | Michigan State | 9–0–0 | Biggie Munn |
| 2. | Georgia Tech | 11–0–0 | Bobby Dodd |
| 3. | Notre Dame | 7–2–1 | Frank Leahy |
| 4. | Oklahoma | 8–1–1 | Bud Wilkinson |
| 5. | Southern Cal | 9–1–0 | Jess Hill |
| 6. | UCLA | 8–1–0 | Red Sanders |
| 7. | Mississippi | 8–0–2 | Johnny Vaught |
| 8. | Tennessee | 8–1–1 | Bob Neyland |
| 9. | Alabama | 9–2–0 | Red Drew |
| 10. | Texas | 8–2–0 | Ed Price |
| 11. | Wisconsin | 6–2–1 | Ivy Williamson |
| 12. | Tulsa | 8–1–1 | J.O. Brothers |
| 13. | Maryland | 7–2–0 | Jim Tatum |
| 14. | Syracuse | 7–2–0 | Ben Schwartzwalder |
| 15. | Florida | 7–3–0 | Bob Woodruff |
| 16. | Duke | 8–2–0 | Bill Murray |
| 17. | Ohio State | 6–3–0 | Woody Hayes |
| 18. | Purdue | 4–3–2 | Stu Holcomb |
| 19. | Princeton | 8–1–0 | Charlie Caldwell |
| 20. | Kentucky | 5–4–2 | Bear Bryant |

## 1951

| | | Record | Coach |
|---|---|---|---|
| 1. | Tennessee | 10–0–0 | Bob Neyland |
| 2. | Michigan State | 9–0–0 | Biggie Munn |
| 3. | Maryland | 9–0–0 | Jim Tatum |
| 4. | Illinois | 8–0–1 | Ray Eliot |
| 5. | Georgia Tech | 10–0–1 | Bobby Dodd |
| 6. | Princeton | 9–0–0 | Charlie Caldwell |
| 7. | Stanford | 9–1–0 | Chuck Taylor |
| 8. | Wisconsin | 7–1–1 | Ivy Williamson |
| 9. | Baylor | 8–1–1 | George Sauer |
| 10. | Oklahoma | 8–2–0 | Bud Wilkinson |
| 11. | TCU | 6–4–0 | Dutch Meyer |
| 12. | California | 8–2–0 | Pappy Waldorf |
| 13. | Virginia | 8–1–0 | Art Guepe |
| 14. | San Francisco | 9–0–0 | Joe Kuharich |
| 15. | Kentucky | 7–4–0 | Bear Bryant |
| 16. | Boston Univ. | 6–4–0 | Buff Donelli |
| 17. | UCLA | 5–3–1 | Red Sanders |
| 18. | Washington State | 7–3–0 | Forest Evashevski |
| 19. | Holy Cross | 8–2–0 | Eddie Anderson |
| 20. | Clemson | 7–2–0 | Frank Howard |

## 1949

| | | Record | Coach |
|---|---|---|---|
| 1. | Notre Dame | 10–0–0 | Frank Leahy |
| 2. | Oklahoma | 10–0–0 | Bud Wilkinson |
| 3. | California | 10–0–0 | Pappy Waldorf |
| 4. | Army | 9–0–0 | Red Blaik |
| 5. | Rice | 9–1–0 | Jess Neely |
| 6. | Ohio State | 6–1–2 | Wes Fesler |
| 7. | Michigan | 6–2–1 | Bennie Oosterbaan |
| 8. | Minnesota | 7–2–0 | Bernie Bierman |
| 9. | LSU | 8–2–0 | Gaynell Tinsley |
| 10. | Pacific | 11–0–0 | Larry Siemering |
| 11. | Kentucky | 9–2–0 | Bear Bryant |
| 12. | Cornell | 8–1–0 | Lefty James |
| 13. | Villanova | 8–1–0 | Jim Leonard |
| 14. | Maryland | 8–1–0 | Jim Tatum |
| 15. | Santa Clara | 7–2–1 | Len Casanova |
| 16. | North Carolina | 7–3–0 | Carl Snavely |
| 17. | Tennessee | 7–2–1 | Bob Neyland |
| 18. | Princeton | 6–3–0 | Charlie Caldwell |
| 19. | Michigan State | 6–3–0 | Biggie Munn |
| 20. | Missouri | 7–3–0 | Don Faurot |
| | Baylor | 8–2–0 | Bob Woodruff |

## 1950

| | | Record | Coach |
|---|---|---|---|
| 1. | Oklahoma | 10–0–0 | Bud Wilkinson |
| 2. | Army | 8–1–0 | Red Blaik |
| 3. | Texas | 9–1–0 | Blair Cherry |
| 4. | Tennessee | 10–1–0 | Bob Neyland |
| 5. | California | 9–0–1 | Pappy Waldorf |
| 6. | Princeton | 9–0–0 | Charlie Caldwell |
| 7. | Kentucky | 10–1–0 | Bear Bryant |
| 8. | Michigan State | 8–1–0 | Biggie Munn |
| 9. | Michigan | 5–3–1 | Bennie Oosterhaan |
| 10. | Clemson | 8–0–1 | Frank Howard |
| 11. | Washington | 8–2–0 | Howard Odell |
| 12. | Wyoming | 9–0–0 | Bowden Wyatt |
| 13. | Illinois | 7–2–0 | Ray Eliot |
| 14. | Ohio State | 6–3–0 | Wes Fesler |
| 15. | Miami (FL) | 9–0–1 | Andy Gustafson |
| 16. | Alabama | 9–2–0 | Red Drew |
| 17. | Nebraska | 6–2–1 | Bill Glassford |
| 18. | Wash. & Lee | 8–2–0 | George Barclay |
| 19. | Tulsa | 9–1–1 | J.O. Brothers |
| 20. | Tulane | 6–2–1 | Henry Frnka |

## 1948

| | | Record | Coach |
|---|---|---|---|
| 1. | Michigan | 9–0–0 | Bennie Oosterbaan |
| 2. | Notre Dame | 9–0–1 | Frank Leahy |
| 3. | North Carolina | 9–0–1 | Carl Snavely |
| 4. | California | 10–0–0 | Pappy Waldorf |
| 5. | Oklahoma | 9–1–0 | Bud Wilkinson |
| 6. | Army | 8–0–1 | Red Blaik |
| 7. | Northwestern | 7–2–0 | Bob Voigts |
| 8. | Georgia | 9–1–0 | Wally Butts |
| 9. | Oregon | 9–1–0 | Jim Aiken |
| 10. | SMU | 8–1–1 | Matty Bell |
| 11. | Clemson | 10–0–0 | Frank Howard |
| 12. | Vanderbilt | 8–2–1 | Red Sanders |
| 13. | Tulane | 9–1–0 | Henry Frnka |
| 14. | Michigan State | 6–2–2 | Biggie Munn |
| 15. | Mississippi | 8–1–0 | Johnny Vaught |
| 16. | Minnesota | 7–2–0 | Bernie Bierman |
| 17. | William & Mary | 6–2–2 | Rube McCray |
| 18. | Penn St | 7–1–1 | Bob Higgins |
| 19. | Cornell | 8–1–0 | Lefty James |
| 20. | Wake Forest | 6–3–0 | Peahead Walker |

## 1947

| | | Record | Coach |
|---|---|---|---|
| 1. | Notre Dame | 9–0–0 | Frank Leahy |
| 2. | #Michigan | 9–0–0 | Fritz Crisler |
| 3. | SMU | 9–0–1 | Matty Bell |
| 4. | Penn St | 9–0–0 | Bob Higgins |
| 5. | Texas | 9–1–0 | Blair Cherry |
| 6. | Alabama | 8–2–0 | Red Drew |
| 7. | Pennsylvania | 7–0–1 | George Munger |
| 8. | Southern Cal | 7–1–1 | Jeff Cravath |
| 9. | North Carolina | 8–2–0 | Carl Snavely |
| 10. | Georgia Tech | 9–1–0 | Bobby Dodd |
| 11. | Army | 5–2–2 | Red Blaik |
| 12. | Kansas | 8–0–2 | George Sauer |
| 13. | Mississippi | 8–2–0 | Johnny Vaught |
| 14. | William & Mary | 9–1–0 | Rube McCray |
| 15. | California | 9–1–0 | Pappy Waldorf |
| 16. | Oklahoma | 7–2–1 | Bud Wilkinson |
| 17. | N.C. State | 5–3–1 | Beattie Feathers |
| 18. | Rice | 6–3–1 | Jess Neely |
| 19. | Duke | 4–3–2 | Wallace Wade |
| 20. | Columbia | 7–2–0 | Lou Little |

The AP, which had voted Notre Dame No. 1 before the bowl games, took a second vote, giving the title to Michigan after its 49-0 win over Southern Cal in the Rose Bowl.

## 1945

| | | Record | Coach |
|---|---|---|---|
| 1. | Army | 9–0–0 | Red Blaik |
| 2. | Alabama | 9–0–0 | Frank Thomas |
| 3. | Navy | 7–1–1 | Oscar Hagberg |
| 4. | Indiana | 9–0–1 | Bo McMillan |
| 5. | Oklahoma A&M | 8–0–0 | Jim Lookabaugh |
| 6. | Michigan | 7–3–0 | Fritz Crisler |
| 7. | St. Mary's | 7–1–0 | Jimmy Phelan |
| 8. | Pennsylvania | 6–2–0 | George Munger |
| 9. | Notre Dame | 7–2–1 | Hugh Devore |
| 10. | Texas | 9–1–0 | Dana X. Bible |
| 11. | Southern Cal | 7–3–0 | Jeff Cravath |
| 12. | Ohio State | 7–2–0 | Carroll Widdoes |
| 13. | Duke | 6–2–0 | Eddie Cameron |
| 14. | Tennessee | 8–1–0 | John Barnhill |
| 15. | LSU | 7–2–0 | Bernie Moore |
| 16. | Holy Cross | 8–1–0 | John DeGrosa |
| 17. | Tulsa | 8–2–0 | Henry Frnka |
| 18. | Georgia | 8–2–0 | Wally Butts |
| 19. | Wake Forest | 4–3–1 | Peahead Walker |
| 20. | Columbia | 8–1–0 | Lou Little |

## 1946

| | | Record | Coach |
|---|---|---|---|
| 1. | Notre Dame | 8–0–1 | Frank Leahy |
| 2. | Army | 9–0–1 | Red Blaik |
| 3. | Georgia | 10–0–0 | Wally Butts |
| 4. | UCLA | 10–0–0 | B. LaBrucherie |
| 5. | Illinois | 7–2–0 | Ray Eliot |
| 6. | Michigan | 6–2–1 | Fritz Crisler |
| 7. | Tennessee | 9–1–0 | Bob Neyland |
| 8. | LSU | 9–1–0 | Bernie Moore |
| 9. | North Carolina | 8–1–1 | Carl Snavely |
| 10. | Rice | 8–2–0 | Jess Neely |
| 11. | Georgia Tech | 8–2–0 | Bobby Dodd |
| 12. | Yale | 7–1–1 | Howard Odell |
| 13. | Pennsylvania | 6–2–0 | George Munger |
| 14. | Oklahoma | 7–3–0 | Jim Tatum |
| 15. | Texas | 8–2–0 | Dana X. Bible |
| 16. | Arkansas | 6–3–1 | John Barnhill |
| 17. | Tulsa | 9–1–0 | J.O. Brothers |
| 18. | N.C. State | 8–2–0 | Beattie Feathers |
| 19. | Delaware | 9–0–0 | Bill Murray |
| 20. | Indiana | 6–3–0 | Bo McMillan |

## 1944

| | | Record | Coach |
|---|---|---|---|
| 1. | Army | 9–0–0 | Red Blaik |
| 2. | Ohio State | 9–0–0 | Carroll Widdoes |
| 3. | Randolph Field | 11–0–0 | Frank Tritico |
| 4. | Navy | 6–3–0 | Oscar Hagberg |
| 5. | Bainbridge NTS | 9–0–0 | Joe Maniaci |
| 6. | Iowa Pre-Flight | 10–1–0 | Jack Meagher |
| 7. | Southern Cal | 7–0–2 | Jeff Cravath |
| 8. | Michigan | 8–2–0 | Fritz Crisler |
| 9. | Notre Dame | 8–2–0 | Ed McKeever |
| 10. | March Field | 7–1–2 | Paul Schissler |
| 11. | Duke | 5–4–0 | Eddie Cameron |
| 12. | Tennessee | 8–0–1 | John Barnhill |
| 13. | Georgia Tech | 8–2–0 | Bill Alexander |
| | Norman P-F | 6–0–0 | John Gregg |
| 15. | Illinois | 5–4–1 | Ray Eliot |
| 16. | El Toro Marines | 8–1–0 | Dick Hanley |
| 17. | Great Lakes | 9–2–1 | Paul Brown |
| 18. | Fort Pierce | 9–0–0 | Hamp Pool |
| 19. | St. Mary's P-F | 4–4–0 | Jules Sikes |
| 20. | 2nd Air Force | 7–2–1 | Bill Reese |

## 1943

| | | Record | Coach |
|---|---|---|---|
| 1. | Notre Dame | 9–1–0 | Frank Leahy |
| 2. | Iowa Pre-Flight | 9–1–0 | Don Faurot |
| 3. | Michigan | 8–1–0 | Fritz Crisler |
| 4. | Navy | 8–1–0 | Billick Whelchel |
| 5. | Purdue | 9–0–0 | Elmer Burnham |
| 6. | Great Lakes | 10–2–0 | Tony Hinkle |
| 7. | Duke | 8–1–0 | Eddie Cameron |
| 8. | Del Monte P-F | 7–1–0 | Bill Kern |
| 9. | Northwestern | 6–2–0 | Pappy Waldorf |
| 10. | March Field | 9–1–0 | Paul Schissler |
| 11. | Army | 7–2–1 | Red Balik |
| 12. | Washington | 4–0–0 | Ralph Welch |
| 13. | Georgia Tech | 7–3–0 | Bill Alexander |
| 14. | Texas | 7–1–0 | Dana X. Bible |
| 15. | Tulsa | 6–0–1 | Henry Frnka |
| 16. | Dartmouth | 6–1–0 | Earl Brown |
| 17. | Bainbridge NTS | 7–1–0 | Joe Maniaci |
| 18. | Colorado Col. | 7–0–0 | Hal White |
| 19. | Pacific | 7–2–0 | Amos A. Stagg |
| 20. | Pennsylvania | 6–2–1 | George Munger |

## 1941

| | | Record | Coach |
|---|---|---|---|
| 1. | Minnesota | 8–0–0 | Bernie Bierman |
| 2. | Duke | 9–0–0 | Wallace Wade |
| 3. | Notre Dame | 8–0–1 | Frank Leahy |
| 4. | Texas | 8–1–1 | Dana X. Bible |
| 5. | Michigan | 6–1–1 | Fritz Crisler |
| 6. | Fordham | 7–1–0 | Jim Crowley |
| 7. | Missouri | 8–1–0 | Don Faurot |
| 8. | Duquesne | 8–0–0 | Buff Donelli |
| 9. | Texas A&M | 9–1–0 | Homer Norton |
| 10. | Navy | 7–1–1 | Swede Larson |
| 11. | Northwestern | 5–3–0 | Pappy Waldorf |
| 12. | Oregon State | 7–2–0 | Lon Stiner |
| 13. | Ohio State | 6–1–1 | Paul Brown |
| 14. | Georgia | 8–1–1 | Wally Butts |
| 15. | Pennsylvania | 7–1–1 | George Munger |
| 16. | Mississipi State | 8–1–1 | Allyn McKeen |
| 17. | Mississippi | 6–2–1 | Harry Mehre |
| 18. | Tennessee | 8–2–0 | John Barnhill |
| 19. | Washington State | 6–4–0 | Babe Hollingbery |
| 20. | Alabama | 8–2–0 | Frank Thomas |

## 1942

| | | Record | Coach |
|---|---|---|---|
| 1. | Ohio State | 9–1–0 | Paul Brown |
| 2. | Georgia | 10–1–0 | Wally Butts |
| 3. | Wisconsin | 8–1–1 | H. Stuhldreher |
| 4. | Tulsa | 10–0–0 | Henry Frnka |
| 5. | Georgia Tech | 9–1–0 | Bill Alexander |
| 6. | Notre Dame | 7–2–2 | Frank Leahy |
| 7. | Tennessee | 8–1–1 | John Barnhill |
| 8. | Boston College | 8–1–0 | Denny Myers |
| 9. | Michigan | 7–3–0 | Fritz Crisler |
| 10. | Alabama | 7–3–0 | Frank Thomas |
| 11. | Texas | 8–2–0 | Dana X. Bible |
| 12. | Stanford | 6–4–0 | Marchie Schwartz |
| 13. | UCLA | 7–3–0 | Babe Horrell |
| 14. | William & Mary | 9–1–1 | Carl Voyles |
| 15. | Santa Clara | 7–2–0 | Buck Shaw |
| 16. | Auburn | 6–4–1 | Jack Meagher |
| 17. | Washington State | 6–2–2 | Babe Hollingbery |
| 18. | Mississippi State | 8–2–0 | Allyn McKeen |
| 19. | Minnesota | 5–4–0 | George Hauser |
| | Holy Cross | 5–4–1 | Ank Scanlon |
| | Penn St | 6–1–1 | Bob Higgins |

## 1940

| | | Record | Coach |
|---|---|---|---|
| 1. | Minnesota | 8–0–0 | Bernie Bierman |
| 2. | Stanford | 9–0–0 | C. Shaughnessy |
| 3. | Michigan | 7–1–0 | Fritz Crisler |
| 4. | Tennessee | 10–0–0 | Bob Neyland |
| 5. | Boston College | 10–0–0 | Frank Leahy |
| 6. | Texas A&M | 8–1–0 | Homer Norton |
| 7. | Nebraska | 8–1–0 | Biff Jones |
| 8. | Northwestern | 6–2–0 | Pappy Waldorf |
| 9. | Mississippi State | 9–0–1 | Allyn McKeen |
| 10. | Washington | 7–2–0 | Jimmy Phelan |
| 11. | Santa Clara | 6–1–1 | Buck Shaw |
| 12. | Fordham | 7–1–0 | Jim Crowley |
| 13. | Georgetown | 8–1–0 | Jack Hagerty |
| 14. | Pennsylvania | 6–1–1 | George Munger |
| 15. | Cornell | 6–2–0 | Carl Snavely |
| 16. | SMU | 8–1–1 | Matty Bell |
| 17. | Hard.-Simmons | 9–0–0 | Abe Woodson |
| 18. | Duke | 7–2–0 | Wallace Wade |
| 19. | Lafayette | 9–0–0 | Hooks Mylin |
| 20. | — | | |

## 1939

| | | Record | Coach |
|---|---|---|---|
| 1. | Texas A&M | 10–0–0 | Homer Norton |
| 2. | Tennessee | 10–0–0 | Bob Neyland |
| 3. | #Southern Cal | 7–0–2 | Howard Jones |
| 4. | Cornell | 8–0–0 | Carl Snavely |
| 5. | Tulane | 8–0–1 | Red Dawson |
| 6. | Missouri | 8–1–0 | Don Faurot |
| 7. | UCLA | 6–0–4 | Babe Horrell |
| 8. | Duke | 8–1–0 | Wallace Wade |
| 9. | Iowa | 6–1–1 | Eddie Anderson |
| 10. | Duquesne | 8–0–1 | Buff Donelli |
| 11. | Boston College | 9–1–0 | Frank Leahy |
| 12. | Clemson | 8–1–0 | Jess Neely |
| 13. | Notre Dame | 7–2–0 | Elmer Layden |
| 14. | Santa Clara | 5–1–3 | Buck Shaw |
| 15. | Ohio State | 6–2–0 | Francis Schmidt |
| 16. | Georgia Tech | 7–2–0 | Bill Alexander |
| 17. | Fordham | 6–2–0 | Jim Crowley |
| 18. | Nebraska | 7–1–1 | Biff Jones |
| 19. | Oklahoma | 6–2–1 | Tom Stidham |
| 20. | Michigan | 6–2–0 | Fritz Crisler |

#Selected No. 1 by the Dickinson System.

## 1937

| | | Record | Coach |
|---|---|---|---|
| 1. | Pittsburgh | 9–0–1 | Jack Sutherland |
| 2. | California | 9–0–1 | Stub Allison |
| 3. | Fordham | 7–0–1 | Jim Crowley |
| 4. | Alabama | 9–0–0 | Frank Thomas |
| 5. | Minnesota | 6–2–0 | Bernie Bierman |
| 6. | Villanova | 8–0–1 | Clipper Smith |
| 7. | Dartmouth | 7–0–2 | Red Blaik |
| 8. | LSU | 9–1–0 | Bernie Moore |
| 9. | Notre Dame | 6–2–1 | Elmer Layden |
| | Santa Clara | 8–0–0 | Buck Shaw |
| 11. | Nebraska | 6–1–2 | Biff Jones |
| 12. | Yale | 6–1–1 | Ducky Pond |
| 13. | Ohio State | 6–2–0 | Francis Schmidt |
| 14. | Holy Cross | 8–0–2 | Eddie Anderson |
| | Arkansas | 6–2–2 | Fred Thomsen |
| 16. | TCU | 4–2–2 | Dutch Meyer |
| 17. | Colorado | 8–0–0 | Bunnie Oakes |
| 18. | Rice | 5–3–2 | Jimmy Kitts |
| 19. | North Carolina | 7–1–1 | Ray Wolf |
| 20. | Duke | 7–2–1 | Wallace Wade |

## 1938

| | | Record | Coach |
|---|---|---|---|
| 1. | TCU | 10–0–0 | Dutch Meyer |
| 2. | Tennessee | 10–0–0 | Bob Neyland |
| 3. | Duke | 9–0–0 | Wallace Wade |
| 4. | Oklahoma | 10–0–0 | Tom Stidham |
| 5. | Notre Dame | 8–1–0 | Elmer Layden |
| 6. | Carnegie Tech | 7–1–0 | Bill Kern |
| 7. | Southern Cal | 8–2–0 | Howard Jones |
| 8. | Pittsburgh | 8–2–0 | Jack Sutherland |
| 9. | Holy Cross | 8–1–0 | Eddie Anderson |
| 10. | Minnesota | 6–2–0 | Bernie Bierman |
| 11. | Texas Tech | 10–0–0 | Pete Cawthon |
| 12. | Cornell | 5–1–1 | Carl Snavely |
| 13. | Alabama | 7–1–1 | Frank Thomas |
| 14. | California | 10–1–0 | Stub Allison |
| 15. | Fordham | 6–1–2 | Jim Crowley |
| 16. | Michigan | 6–1–1 | Fritz Crisler |
| 17. | Northwestern | 4–2–2 | Pappy Waldorf |
| 18. | Villanova | 8–0–1 | Clipper Smith |
| 19. | Tulane | 7–2–1 | Red Dawson |
| 20. | Dartmouth | 7–2–0 | Red Blaik |

#Selected No. 1 by the Dickinson System.

## 1936

| | | Record | Coach |
|---|---|---|---|
| 1. | Minnesota | 7–1–0 | Bernie Bierman |
| 2. | LSU | 9–0–1 | Bernie Moore |
| 3. | Pittsburgh | 7–1–1 | Jack Sutherland |
| 4. | Alabama | 8–0–1 | Frank Thomas |
| 5. | Washington | 7–1–0 | Jimmy Phelan |
| 6. | Santa Clara | 7–1–0 | Buck Shaw |
| 7. | Northwestern | 7–1–0 | Pappy Waldorf |
| 8. | Notre Dame | 6–2–1 | Elmer Layden |
| 9. | Nebraska | 7–2–0 | Dana X. Bible |
| 10. | Pennsylvania | 7–1–0 | Harvey Harman |
| 11. | Duke | 9–1–0 | Wallace Wade |
| 12. | Yale | 7–1–0 | Ducky Pond |
| 13. | Dartmouth | 7–1–1 | Red Blaik |
| 14. | Duquesne | 7–2–0 | John Smith |
| 15. | Fordham | 5–1–2 | Jim Crowley |
| 16. | TCU | 8–2–2 | Dutch Meyer |
| 17. | Tennessee | 6–2–2 | Bob Neyland |
| 18. | Arkansas | 7–3–0 | Fred Thomsen |
| 19. | Navy | 6–3–0 | Tom Hamilton |
| 20. | Marquette | 7–1–0 | Frank Murray |

## DIVISION I-A WINNINGEST TEAMS

### All-Time Winning Percentage

|  | Yrs | W | L | T | Pct | GP | Bowl Record |
|---|---|---|---|---|---|---|---|
| Notre Dame | 104 | 712 | 210 | 41 | .761 | 963 | 12-6-0 |
| Michigan | 113 | 731 | 238 | 36 | .743 | 1006 | 11-13-0 |
| Alabama | 97 | 682 | 236 | 43 | .734 | 959 | 25-17-3 |
| Oklahoma | 98 | 650 | 237 | 52 | .719 | 939 | 19-10-1 |
| Texas | 100 | 682 | 268 | 31 | .711 | 981 | 16-16-2 |
| Southern Cal | 100 | 622 | 249 | 52 | .702 | 923 | 22-13-0 |
| Ohio St | 103 | 649 | 264 | 52 | .699 | 965 | 11-14-0 |
| Penn St | 106 | 664 | 289 | 41 | .689 | 994 | 17-10-2 |
| Nebraska | 103 | 662 | 285 | 40 | .687 | 991 | 14-17-0 |
| Tennessee | 96 | 627 | 274 | 52 | .684 | 953 | 18-15-0 |
| Central Michigan | 92 | 475 | 249 | 36 | .649 | 760 | 3-1-0 |
| Washington | 103 | 555 | 306 | 49 | .637 | 910 | 12-8-1 |
| Miami (OH) | 104 | 542 | 301 | 42 | .636 | 885 | 5-2-0 |
| Army | 103 | 581 | 323 | 50 | .635 | 954 | 2-1-0 |
| Georgia | 99 | 584 | 327 | 53 | .633 | 964 | 15-13-3 |
| Louisiana St | 99 | 568 | 319 | 46 | .633 | 933 | 11-16-1 |
| Florida St | 46 | 304 | 175 | 16 | .632 | 494 | 13-7-2 |
| Arizona St | 80 | 436 | 252 | 24 | .629 | 712 | 9-5-1 |
| Auburn | 100 | 547 | 335 | 46 | .614 | 928 | 12-9-2 |
| Michigan St | 96 | 515 | 322 | 43 | .610 | 880 | 5-5-0 |
| Minnesota | 109 | 551 | 352 | 43 | .605 | 946 | 2-3-0 |
| Arkansas | 99 | 545 | 356 | 39 | .601 | 940 | 9-15-3 |
| UCLA | 74 | 429 | 276 | 37 | .603 | 742 | 10-7-1 |
| Pittsburgh | 103 | 563 | 375 | 42 | .596 | 980 | 8-10-0 |

Note: Includes bowl games.

### All-Time Victories

| | | |
|---|---|---|
| Michigan ......731 | Georgia ......584 | Auburn ......547 |
| Notre Dame ......712 | Army ......581 | Arkansas ......545 |
| Texas ......682 | Syracuse ......576 | W Virginia ......546 |
| Alabama ......682 | Louisiana St ......568 | Miami (OH) ......542 |
| Penn State ......664 | Pittsburgh ......563 | N Carolina St ......540 |
| Nebraska ......662 | Washington ......555 | Texas A&M ......538 |
| Oklahoma ......650 | Minnesota ......551 | Rutgers ......526 |
| Ohio St ......649 | Colorado ......549 | California ......520 |
| Tennessee ......627 | Georgia Tech ......549 | Clemson ......517 |
| Southern Cal ......622 | Navy ......543 | Michigan St ......515 |

## NUMBER ONE VS NUMBER TWO

The number 1 and number 2 teams, according to the Associated Press Poll, have met 27 times, including 9 bowl games, since the poll's inception in 1936. The number 1 teams have a 16-9-2 record in these matchups. Notre Dame (3-3-2) has played in 8 of the games.

| Date | Results | Stadium |
|---|---|---|
| 10-9-43 | No. 1 Notre Dame 35, No. 2 Michigan 12 | Michigan (Ann Arbor) |
| 11-20-43 | No. 1 Notre Dame 14, No. 2 Iowa Pre-Flight 13 | Notre Dame (South Bend) |
| 12-2-44 | No. 1 Army 23, No. 2 Navy 7 | Municipal (Baltimore) |
| 11-10-45 | No. 1 Army 48, No. 2 Notre Dame 0 | Yankee (New York) |
| 12-1-45 | No. 1 Army 32, No. 2 Navy 13 | Municipal (Philadelphia) |
| 11-9-46 | No. 1 Army 0, No. 2 Notre Dame 0 | Yankee (New York) |
| 1-1-63 | No. 1 Southern Cal 42, No. 2 Wisconsin 37 (Rose Bowl) | Rose Bowl (Pasadena) |
| 10-12-63 | No. 2 Texas 28, No. 1 Oklahoma 7 | Cotton Bowl (Dallas) |
| 1-1-64 | No. 1 Texas 28, No. 2 Navy 6 (Cotton Bowl) | Cotton Bowl (Dallas) |
| 11-19-66 | No. 1 Notre Dame 10, No. 2 Michigan St 10 | Spartan (East Lansing) |
| 9-28-68 | No. 1 Purdue 37, No. 2 Notre Dame 22 | Notre Dame (South Bend) |
| 1-1-69 | No. 1 Ohio St 27, No. 2 Southern Cal 16 (Rose Bowl) | Rose Bowl (Pasadena) |
| 12-6-69 | No. 1 Texas 15, No. 2 Arkansas 14 | Razorback (Fayetteville) |
| 11-25-71 | No. 1 Nebraska 35, No. 2 Oklahoma 31 | Owen Field (Norman) |
| 1-1-72 | No. 1 Nebraska 38, No. 2 Alabama 6 (Orange Bowl) | Orange Bowl (Miami) |

## NUMBER ONE VS NUMBER TWO *(Cont.)*

| Date | Results | Stadium |
|---|---|---|
| 1-1-79 | No. 2 Alabama 14, No. 1 Penn St 7 (Sugar Bowl) | Sugar Bowl (New Orleans) |
| 9-26-81 | No. 1 Southern Cal 28, No. 2 Oklahoma 24 | Coliseum (Los Angeles) |
| 1-1-83 | No. 2 Penn St 27, No. 1 Georgia 23 (Sugar Bowl) | Sugar Bowl (New Orleans) |
| 10-19-85 | No. 1 Iowa 12, No. 2 Michigan 10 | Kinnick (Iowa City) |
| 9-27-86 | No. 2 Miami (FL) 28, No. 1 Oklahoma 16 | Orange Bowl (Miami) |
| 1-2-87 | No. 2 Penn St 14, No. 1 Miami (FL) 10 (Fiesta Bowl) | Fiesta Bowl (Tempe) |
| 11-21-87 | No. 2 Oklahoma 17, No. 1 Nebraska 7 | Memorial (Lincoln) |
| 1-1-88 | No. 2 Miami (FL) 20, No. 1 Oklahoma 14 (Orange Bowl) | Orange Bowl (Miami) |
| 11-26-88 | No. 1 Notre Dame 27, No. 2 Southern Cal 10 | Coliseum (Los Angeles) |
| 9-16-89 | No. 1 Notre Dame 24, No. 2 Michigan 19 | Michigan (Ann Arbor) |
| 11-16-91 | No. 2 Miami 17, No. 1 Florida St 16 | Campbell (Tallahassee) |
| 1-1-93 | No. 2 Alabama 34, No. 1 Miami 13 | Superdome (New Orleans) |

## Longest Winning Streaks

| Wins | Team | Yrs | Ended by | Score |
|---|---|---|---|---|
| 47 | Oklahoma | 1953-57 | Notre Dame | 7-0 |
| 39 | Washington | 1908-14 | Oregon St | 0-0 |
| 37 | Yale | 1890-93 | Princeton | 6-0 |
| 37 | Yale | 1887-89 | Princeton | 10-0 |
| 35 | Toledo | 1969-71 | Tampa | 21-0 |
| 34 | Pennsylvania | 1894-96 | Lafayette | 6-4 |
| 31 | Oklahoma | 1948-50 | Kentucky | 13-7 |
| 31 | Pittsburgh | 1914-18 | Cleveland Naval Reserve | 10-9 |
| 31 | Pennsylvania | 1896-98 | Harvard | 10-0 |
| 30 | Texas | 1968-70 | Notre Dame | 24-11 |
| 29 | Michigan | 1901-03 | Minnesota | 6-6 |
| 29 | Miami (FL) | 1990-92 | Alabama | 34-13 |
| 28 | Alabama | 1978-80 | Mississippi St | 6-3 |
| 28 | Oklahoma | 1973-75 | Kansas | 23-3 |
| 28 | Michigan St | 1950-53 | Purdue | 6-0 |

## Longest Unbeaten Streaks

| No. | W | T | Team | Yrs | Ended by | Score |
|---|---|---|---|---|---|---|
| 63 | 59 | 4 | Washington | 1907-17 | California | 27-0 |
| 56 | 55 | 1 | Michigan | 1901-05 | Chicago | 2-0 |
| 50 | 46 | 4 | California | 1920-25 | Olympic Club | 15-0 |
| 48 | 47 | 1 | Oklahoma | 1953-57 | Notre Dame | 7-0 |
| 48 | 47 | 1 | Yale | 1885-89 | Princeton | 10-0 |
| 47 | 42 | 5 | Yale | 1879-85 | Princeton | 6-5 |
| 44 | 42 | 2 | Yale | 1894-96 | Princeton | 24-6 |
| 42 | 39 | 3 | Yale | 1904-08 | Harvard | 4-0 |
| 39 | 37 | 2 | Notre Dame | 1946-50 | Purdue | 28-14 |
| 37 | 36 | 1 | Oklahoma | 1972-75 | Kansas | 23-3 |
| 35 | 34 | 1 | Minnesota | 1903-05 | Wisconsin | 16-12 |
| 34 | 33 | 1 | Nebraska | 1912-16 | Kansas | 7-3 |
| 34 | 32 | 2 | Princeton | 1884-87 | Harvard | 12-0 |
| 34 | 29 | 5 | Princeton | 1877-82 | Harvard | 1-0 |
| 33 | 30 | 3 | Tennessee | 1926-30 | Alabama | 18-6 |
| 33 | 31 | 2 | Georgia Tech | 1914-18 | Pittsburgh | 32-0 |
| 33 | 30 | 3 | Harvard | 1911-15 | Cornell | 10-0 |
| 32 | 31 | 1 | Nebraska | 1969-71 | UCLA | 20-17 |
| 32 | 30 | 2 | Army | 1944-47 | Columbia | 21-20 |
| 32 | 31 | 1 | Harvard | 1898-1900 | Yale | 28-0 |
| 31 | 30 | 1 | Penn St | 1967-70 | Colorado | 41-13 |
| 31 | 30 | 1 | San Diego St | 1967-70 | Long Beach St | 27-11 |
| 31 | 29 | 2 | Georgia Tech | 1950-53 | Notre Dame | 27-14 |
| 30 | 25 | 5 | Penn St | 1919-22 | Navy | 14-0 |
| 30 | 28 | 2 | Pennsylvania | 1903-06 | Swarthmore | 4-0 |
| 28 | 26 | 2 | Southern Cal | 1978-80 | Washington | 20-10 |
| 28 | 26 | 2 | Army | 1947-50 | Navy | 14-2 |
| 28 | 24 | 4 | Minnesota | 1933-36 | Northwestern | 6-0 |
| 28 | 26 | 2 | Tennessee | 1930-33 | Duke | 10-2 |
| 27 | 26 | 1 | Southern Cal | 1931-33 | Stanford | 13-7 |
| 27 | 24 | 3 | Notre Dame | 1910-14 | Yale | 28-0 |

Note: Includes bowl games.

# Notable Achievements (Cont.)

## Longest Losing Streaks

| L | | Seasons | Ended Against | Score |
|---|---|---|---|---|
| 44 | Columbia | 1983-88 | Princeton | 16-14 |
| 34 | Northwestern | 1979-82 | Northern Illinois | 31-6 |
| 28 | Virginia | 1958-61 | William & Mary | 21-6 |
| 28 | Kansas St | 1945-48 | Arkansas St | 37-6 |
| 27 | Eastern Michigan | 1980-82 | Kent St | 9-7 |

## Longest Series

| GP | Opponents (Series Leader Listed First) | Record | First Game | GP | Opponents (Series Leader Listed First) | Record | First Game |
|---|---|---|---|---|---|---|---|
| 102 | Minnesota-Wisconsin | 55-39-8 | 1890 | 95 | Stanford-California | 47-37-11 | 1892 |
| 101 | Missouri-Kansas | 48-44-9 | 1891 | 93 | Navy-Army | 44-42-7 | 1890 |
| 99 | Nebraska-Kansas | 75-21-3 | 1892 | 91 | Auburn-Georgia Tech | 47-39-4 | 1892 |
| 99 | Texas Christian-Baylor | 46-46-7 | 1899 | 92 | Penn St-Pittsburgh | 47-41-4 | 1893 |
| 99 | Texas-Texas A&M | 64-30-5 | 1894 | 90 | Louisiana St-Tulane* | 61-22-7 | 1893 |
| 97 | N Carolina-Virginia | 54-39-4 | 1892 | 90 | Clemson-S Carolina | 53-33-4 | 1896 |
| 97 | Miami (OH)-Cincinnati | 53-38-6 | 1888 | 90 | Kansas-Kansas St | 61-24-5 | 1902 |
| 96 | Auburn-Georgia | 45-44-7 | 1892 | 90 | Oklahoma-Kansas | 60-24-6 | 1903 |
| 96 | Oregon-Oregon St | 47-39-10 | 1894 | 90 | Utah-Utah St | 59-27-4 | 1892 |
| 95 | Purdue-Indiana | 58-31-6 | 1891 | | | | |

*Disputed series record. Tulane claims 23-59-7 record.

# NCAA Coaches' Records

## ALL-TIME WINNINGEST DIVISION I-A COACHES

### By Percentage

| Coach (Alma mater) | Colleges Coached | Yrs | W | L | T | Pct |
|---|---|---|---|---|---|---|
| Knute Rockne (Notre Dame '14)† | Notre Dame 1918-30 | 13 | 105 | 12 | 5 | .881 |
| Frank W. Leahy (Notre Dame '31)† | Boston Col 1939-40; Notre Dame 1941-43, 1946-53 | 13 | 107 | 13 | 9 | .864 |
| George W. Woodruff (Yale '89)† | Pennsylvania 1892-01; Illinois 1903; Carlisle 1905 | 12 | 142 | 25 | 2 | .846 |
| Barry Switzer (Arkansas '60) | Oklahoma 1973-88 | 16 | 157 | 29 | 4 | .837 |
| Percy D. Haughton (Harvard '99)† | Cornell 1899-1900; Harvard 1908-16; Columbia 1923-24 | 13 | 96 | 17 | 6 | .832 |
| Bob Neyland (Army '16)† | Tennessee 1926-34, 1936-40, 1946-52 | 21 | 173 | 31 | 12 | .829 |
| Fielding "Hurry Up" Yost (Lafayette '97)† | Ohio Wesleyan 1897; Nebraska 1898; Kansas 1899; Stanford 1900; Michigan 1901-23, 1925-26 | 29 | 196 | 36 | 12 | .828 |
| Bud Wilkinson (Minnesota '37)† | Oklahoma 1947-63 | 17 | 145 | 29 | 4 | .826 |
| Jock Sutherland (Pittsburgh '18)† | Lafayette 1919-23; Pittsburgh 1924-38 | 20 | 144 | 28 | 14 | .812 |
| Bob Devaney (Alma, MI '39)† | Wyoming 1957-61; Nebraska 1962-72 | 16 | 136 | 30 | 7 | .806 |
| Tom Osborne (Hastings '59)* | Nebraska 1973-present | 20 | 195 | 46 | 3 | .805 |
| Frank W. Thomas (Notre Dame '23)† | Chattanooga 1925-28; Alabama 1931-42, 1944-46 | 19 | 141 | 33 | 9 | .795 |
| Henry L. Williams (Yale '91)† | Army 1891; Minnesota 1900-21 | 23 | 141 | 34 | 12 | .786 |
| Joe Paterno (Brown '50)* | Penn St 1966-present | 27 | 247 | 67 | 3 | .784 |
| Gil Dobie (Minnesota '02)† | N Dakota St 1906-07; Washington 1908-16; Navy 1917-19; Cornell 1920-35; Boston Col 1936-38 | 33 | 180 | 45 | 15 | .781 |
| Paul W. "Bear" Bryant (Alabama '36)† | Maryland 1945; Kentucky 1946-53; Texas A&M 1954-57; Alabama 1958-82 | 38 | 323 | 85 | 17 | .780 |

*Active coach. †Hall of Fame member.

Note: Minimum 10 years as head coach at Division I institutions; record at 4-year colleges only; bowl games included; ties computed as half won, half lost.

## Top Winners by Victories

| | Yrs | W | L | T | Pct | | Yrs | W | L | T | Pct |
|---|---|---|---|---|---|---|---|---|---|---|---|
| Paul "Bear" Bryant | 38 | 323 | 85 | 17 | .780 | Warren Woodson | 31 | 203 | 95 | 14 | .673 |
| Amos Alonzo Stagg | 57 | 314 | 199 | 35 | .605 | Vince Dooley | 25 | 201 | 77 | 10 | .715 |
| Glenn "Pop" Warner | 44 | 313 | 106 | 32 | .729 | Eddie Anderson | 39 | 201 | 128 | 15 | .606 |
| Joe Paterno | 27 | 247 | 67 | 3 | .784 | Dana Bible | 33 | 198 | 72 | 23 | .715 |
| Woody Hayes | 33 | 238 | 72 | 10 | .759 | Dan McGugin | 30 | 197 | 55 | 19 | .762 |
| Bo Schembechler | 27 | 234 | 65 | 8 | .775 | Fielding Yost | 29 | 196 | 36 | 12 | .828 |
| Bobby Bowden | 27 | 227 | 77 | 3 | .744 | Howard Jones | 29 | 194 | 64 | 21 | .733 |
| Jess Neely | 40 | 207 | 176 | 19 | .539 | John Vaught | 25 | 190 | 61 | 12 | .745 |

## Most Bowl Victories

| | W | L | T | | W | L | T |
|---|---|---|---|---|---|---|---|
| Paul "Bear" Bryant | 15 | 12 | 2 | Darrell Royal | 8 | 7 | 1 |
| *Joe Paterno | 14 | 8 | 1 | *Tom Osborne | 8 | 12 | 0 |
| *Bobby Bowden | 12 | 3 | 1 | Vince Dooley | 8 | 10 | 2 |
| John Vaught | 10 | 8 | 0 | *Terry Donahue | 8 | 2 | 1 |
| *Don James | 10 | 5 | 0 | Bob Devaney | 7 | 3 | 0 |
| *Johnny Majors | 9 | 7 | 0 | Dan Devine | 7 | 3 | 0 |
| Bobby Dodd | 9 | 4 | 0 | *Lou Holtz | 9 | 6 | 2 |
| Barry Switzer | 8 | 5 | 0 | Charlie McClendon | 7 | 6 | 0 |

*Active coach.

## WINNINGEST ACTIVE COACHES
### By Percentage

| Coach | College Years | W | L | T | Pct* | Bowls W | L | T |
|---|---|---|---|---|---|---|---|---|
| John Robinson, Southern Cal | 7 | 67 | 14 | 2 | .819 | 4 | 1 | 0 |
| Tom Osborne, Nebraska | 20 | 195 | 46 | 3 | .805 | 8 | 12 | 0 |
| Joe Paterno, Penn St | 26 | 247 | 67 | 3 | .784 | 14 | 8 | 1 |
| Danny Ford, Arkansas | 12 | 96 | 29 | 4 | .760 | 6 | 2 | 0 |
| Bobby Bowden, Florida St | 27 | 227 | 77 | 3 | .744 | 12 | 3 | 1 |
| LaVell Edwards, Brigham Young | 21 | 191 | 67 | 3 | .738 | 5 | 11 | 1 |
| Dennis Erickson, Miami (FL) | 11 | 94 | 35 | 1 | .727 | 4 | 1 | 0 |
| Dick Sheridan, North Carolina State | 15 | 121 | 52 | 5 | .694 | 5 | 7 | 0 |
| Steve Spurrier, Florida | 6 | 48 | 21 | 1 | .693 | 1 | 2 | 0 |
| Don James, Washington | 22 | 176 | 78 | 3 | .691 | 10 | 5 | 0 |

*Ties computed as half win, half loss. Bowl games included.

Note: Minimum 5 years as Division I-A head coach; record at 4-year colleges only.

## Relatively Speaking

Every football season, colleges send us hundreds of slick publicity packets touting players. This year, however, two homemade packets caught our eye. One was from the mother of Penn's aptly named running back, Sundiata Rush. The other was from an aunt of Louisiana Tech offensive lineman Willy Roaf. Could this be a trend? We'll see next season.

In the meantime: "Sundi's strength is his perseverence," writes his mom, Brenda Brooks. "He is a good motivator, has good work habits, a clean character and is well liked by his teammates."

The Roaf recommendation, as penned by his aunt Mary Layton, leans heavily on his career in Pee-Wee football and on the fact that he was a choirboy at Grace Episcopal Church in Pine Bluff, Arkansas: "Willy is a big good-natured guy with the proverbial heart of gold who has never met a person he didn't like." Roaf, who is indeed big—6'5'' and 295 pounds—will likely be a first-round pick in next year's NFL draft. When he was 13, he served as a page in the Arkansas legislature and met one person he particularly liked, the state's kid governor, another comer, named Bill Clinton.

## By Victories

| Coach | Won | Coach | Won |
|-------|-----|-------|-----|
| Joe Paterno, Penn St | 247 | Don James, Washington | 176 |
| Bobby Bowden, Florida St | 227 | Grant Teaff, Baylor | 170 |
| Hayden Fry, Iowa | 194 | Bill Dooley, Wake Forest | 161 |
| Tom Osborne, Nebraska | 195 | Earle Bruce, Colorado St | 154 |
| LaVell Edwards, Brigham Young | 191 | Pat Dye, Auburn | 153 |
| Lou Holtz, Notre Dame | 182 | Jim Wacker, Minnesota | 146 |
| Jim Sweeney, Fresno St | 178 | Bill Mallory, Indiana | 147 |
| Johnny Majors, Tennessee | 176 | | |

## WINNINGEST ACTIVE DIVISION I-AA COACHES
### By Percentage

| Coach, College | Yrs | W | L | T | Pct* |
|----------------|-----|---|---|---|------|
| Roy Kidd, Eastern Kentucky | 29 | 239 | 84 | 8 | .734 |
| Eddie Robinson, Grambling | 50 | 381 | 136 | 15 | .730 |
| Tubby Raymond, Delaware | 27 | 223 | 88 | 2 | .716 |
| Jimmy Satterfield, Furman | 7 | 61 | 24 | 2 | .713 |
| Houston Markham, Alabama St | 6 | 44 | 19 | 3 | .674 |
| Andy Talley, Villanova | 13 | 84 | 42 | 2 | .675 |
| Bill Davis, Tennessee St | 14 | 100 | 51 | 1 | .662 |
| Bill Hayes, N Carolina A&T | 17 | 123 | 63 | 2 | .660 |
| William Collick, Delaware St | 8 | 56 | 29 | 0 | .659 |
| James Donnelly, Middle Tennessee St | 16 | 119 | 64 | 1 | .649 |

*Ties computed as half win, half loss. Playoff games included.
Note: Minimum 5 years as a Division I-A and/or Division I-AA head coach; record at 4-year colleges only.

### By Victories

| | | | |
|---|---|---|---|
| Eddie Robinson, Grambling | 381 | Bill Bowes, New Hampshire | 136 |
| Roy Kidd, Eastern Kentucky | 239 | Willie Jeffries, S Carolina St | 124 |
| Tubby Raymond, Delaware | 223 | Bill Hayes, N Carolina A&T | 123 |
| Carmen Cozza, Yale | 166 | Don Read, Montana | 120 |
| Marino Casem, Southern-B.R. | 159 | James Donnelly, Middle Tennessee St | 119 |
| Ron Randleman, Sam Houston St | 151 | Joe Restic, Harvard | 114 |

## WINNINGEST ACTIVE DIVISION II COACHES
### By Percentage

| Coach, College | Yrs | W | L | T | Pct* |
|----------------|-----|---|---|---|------|
| Rocky Hager, N Dakota St | 6 | 59 | 12 | 1 | .826 |
| Ken Sparks, Carson-Newman | 13 | 119 | 37 | 1 | .761 |
| Danny Hale, Bloomsburg | 5 | 40 | 13 | 0 | .755 |
| Bob Cortese, Fort Hays St | 13 | 106 | 34 | 3 | .752 |
| Bill Burgess, Jacksonville St | 8 | 69 | 22 | 4 | .747 |
| Dick Lowry, Hillsdale | 19 | 145 | 59 | 2 | .709 |
| Mark Whipple, New Haven | 5 | 37 | 16 | 0 | .698 |
| Gene Carpenter, Millersville | 24 | 159 | 69 | 5 | .693 |
| Tom Hollman, Edinboro | 9 | 61 | 27 | 3 | .687 |
| Joe Taylor, Hampton | 10 | 70 | 31 | 4 | .686 |

*Ties computed as half win, half loss. Playoff games included.
Note: Minimum 5 years as a college head coach; record at 4-year colleges only.

### By Victories

| | | | |
|---|---|---|---|
| Jim Malosky, MN-Duluth | 223 | Dick Lowry, Hillsdale | 145 |
| Fred Martinelli, Ashland | 208 | Douglas Porter, Fort Valley St | 135 |
| Gene Carpenter, Millersville | 159 | Bud Elliott, NW Missouri St | 134 |
| Ron Harms, Texas A&I | 156 | Claire Boroff, Kearney St | 129 |
| Ross Fortier, Moorhead St | 152 | Ken Sparks, Carson-Newman | 119 |

## WINNINGEST ACTIVE DIVISION III COACHES
### By Percentage

| Coach, College | Yrs | W | L | T | Pct* |
|---|---|---|---|---|---|
| Bob Reade, Augustana (IL) | 14 | 131 | 19 | 1 | .871 |
| Dick Farley, Williams | 6 | 38 | 8 | 2 | .813 |
| Larry Kehres, Mount Union | 7 | 60 | 13 | 3 | .809 |
| Ron Schipper, Central (IA) | 32 | 252 | 61 | 3 | .802 |
| Lou Desloges, Plymouth St | 7 | 55 | 14 | 3 | .785 |
| John Luckhardt, Washington & Jefferson | 11 | 86 | 24 | 2 | .777 |
| Jack Siedlecki, Amherst | 5 | 36 | 10 | 1 | .777 |
| Bob Packard, Baldwin-Wallace | 12 | 93 | 27 | 2 | .770 |
| Roger Harring, WI-La Crosse | 24 | 199 | 59 | 7 | .764 |
| Bill Manlove, Delaware Valley | 24 | 185 | 60 | 1 | .754 |

*Ties computed as half win, half loss. Playoff games included.

Note: Minimum 5 years as a college head coach; record at 4-year colleges only.

### By Victories (Minimum of 100)

| | |
|---|---|
| John Gagliardi, St John's (MN) ...............294 | Jim Christopherson, Concordia-Moorhead...........169 |
| Ron Schipper, Central (IA) ......................252 | Frank Girardi, Lycoming..........................................150 |
| Jim Butterfield, Ithaca ............................200 | Don Miller, Trinity (Conn)......................................140 |
| Roger Harring, WI-LaCrosse....................199 | Joe McDaniel, Centre.............................................138 |
| Bill Manlove, Delaware Valley .................185 | Ray Smith, Hope .....................................................138 |

## NAIA Coaches' Records

## WINNINGEST ACTIVE NAIA COACHES
### By Percentage

| Coach, College | Yrs | W | L | T | Pct* |
|---|---|---|---|---|---|
| Charlie Richard, Baker (KS) | 12 | 107 | 22 | 1 | .827 |
| Ted Kessinger, Bethany | 17 | 138 | 31 | 1 | .815 |
| †Billy Joe, Central St (OH) | 19 | 161 | 51 | 3 | .759 |
| Frosty Westering, Pacific Lutheran | 26 | 213 | 71 | 5 | .746 |
| Hank Biesiot, Dickinson St (ND) | 17 | 103 | 37 | 1 | .734 |
| Larry Korver, Northwestern (IA) | 26 | 197 | 70 | 6 | .733 |
| Max Bowman, Greenville (IL) | 6 | 36 | 13 | 1 | .730 |
| Jim Svoboda, Nebraska Wesleyan | 6 | 44 | 17 | 0 | .721 |
| Dick Strahm, Findlay (OH) | 18 | 127 | 50 | 3 | .714 |
| †Jim Malosky, Minnesota-Duluth | 35 | 216 | 113 | 10 | .667 |

*Ties computed as half win, half loss. Playoff games included.

†Denotes Division I coach.

Note: Minimum five years as a collegiate head coach and includes record against four-year institutions only.

### Victories

| | |
|---|---|
| †Jim Malosky, MN-Duluth .......................216 | Ted Kessinger, Bethany (KS)................................138 |
| Frosty Westering, Pacific Lutheran (WA) ...............213 | Dick Strahm, Findlay (OH) ....................................127 |
| Larry Korver, Northwestern (IA) ............197 | Rollie Greeno, Jamestown (ND)...........................125 |
| †Billy Joe, Central St (OH) .....................161 | Bob Petrino, Carroll (MT)......................................124 |
| Buddy Benson, Ouachita Baptist (AR)..................152 | Bill Ramseyer, Clinch Valley (VA)........................119 |

†Denotes Division I coach.

**Marcus Allen, HB (b. 3-26-60)**
**COLLEGE:** USC **YEAR:** 1981
**HEISMAN STATS:** 403 att.; 2,342 yds.; 212.9 per game. 2,550 all-purpose yds.; 22 rushing TDs.
Allen rushed for 649 yards and eight TDs as a sophomore, but his primary role that season was to block for Heisman Trophy–winning teammate Charles White. With White's graduation, Allen took over the top spot in the Trojan backfield as a junior, scoring 14 TDs and rushing for 1,563 yards to rank second among the nation's rushers, behind Georgia's Herschel Walker. Allen's senior season was the finest he—or any other college rusher—had ever had. He became the first NCAA player to rush for more than 2,000 yards in a season (2,342) and set 14 other NCAA records. Allen went on to a superb career with the L.A. Raiders, being named NFL Rookie of the Year in 1982 and Player of the Year in '85.

**Alan Ameche, FB (b. 6-1-33; d. 8-8-88)**
**COLLEGE:** Wisconsin **YEAR:** 1954
**HEISMAN STATS:** 146 att.; 641 yds.; 9 TDs.
The son of Italian immigrants, Ameche grew up in Kenosha, Wis., and excelled at both football and track and field. He rushed for 946 yards as a sophomore and gained a further 133 in the Badgers' 7–0 loss to USC. Nicknamed the Horse for his speed and size (6' 1", 217), Ameche played both linebacker and fullback his junior and senior years, averaging 55 minutes a game. He rushed for 802 yards as a junior and 641 as a senior, winning the Heisman in the latter season. Ameche went on to play six seasons with the Baltimore Colts, from 1955 to '60. In 1955 he led NFL rushers with 961 yards, earning All-Pro and Rookie of the Year honors. In the 1958 NFL Championship Game between the Colts and the Giants, considered by many to be the greatest game ever played, Ameche scored two TDs, including the winner in pro football's first sudden-death overtime.

**Terry Baker, QB (b. 5-5-41)**
**COLLEGE:** Oregon St **YEAR:** 1962
**HEISMAN STATS:** 112 comp.; 203 att.; 1,738 yds.; 15 TDs.
Baker was the first player from a school west of the Rockies to win the Heisman. A true scholar-athlete, he was also honored in 1962 as *Sports Illustrated's* Sportsman of the Year. Recruited by Oregon State as a basketball player, Baker made the football team as a walk-on and was the Beavers' second-string tailback in his sophomore season when the starting quarterback was injured. Baker stepped in and went on to compile 1,473 yards rushing and passing to rank sixth nationally. As a senior Baker led Oregon State to a 9–2 record and scored the only touchdown in the Beavers' 6–0 win over Villanova in the Liberty Bowl. He also led the nation in total offense (2,276 yards).

**Gary Beban, QB (b. 8-5-46)**
**COLLEGE:** UCLA **YEAR:** 1967
**HEISMAN STATS:** 87 comp.; 156 att.; 1,359 yards; 8 TDs.
Even though his senior year may have been the least productive of his three at UCLA, Beban edged crosstown-rival O.J. Simpson for the 1967 Heisman. Beban took over as Bruin quarterback in 1965, leading them to a 9–1 season capped by a stirring 14–12 win over previously undefeated Michigan State in the Rose Bowl. In three seasons under Beban, UCLA was 25–4–1.

**Joe Bellino, HB (b. 3-13-38)**
**COLLEGE:** Navy **YEAR:** 1960
**HEISMAN STATS:** 168 att.; 834 yds.; 18 TDs.
Built like a spark plug (5'8", 185), Bellino played three seasons for the Naval Academy, the finest of them being his last. In leading Navy to an 8–1 record, Bellino did everything: He rushed for 834 yards; caught 17 passes for 280 yards and three TDs; threw two TD passes; returned punts and kickoffs; and even punted. In a brief pro career Bellino played for the New England Patriots from 1965 through '67, primarily returning kickoffs and punts and scoring just one TD.

**Angelo Bertelli, QB (b. 6-18-21)**
**COLLEGE:** Notre Dame **YEAR:** 1943
**HEISMAN STATS:** 25 comp.; 36 att.; 511 yds.; 10 TDs.
Bertelli was Heisman runner-up as a sophomore, when he led the Irish to an 8-0-1 record. If his stats for 1943 look thin, it's because he played just six games before entering the Marine Corps in November. The Fighting Irish were a perfect 6–0 before Bertelli's departure, and under his replacement, future Heisman winner Johnny Lujack, they won the national championship with a 9–1 record. Bertelli served in the Pacific and then returned to Notre Dame to complete his education. He played one season with the L.A. Dons and two with the Chicago Rockets before retiring with knee injuries.

**Jay Berwanger, HB (b. 3-19-14)**
**COLLEGE:** University of Chicago **YEAR:** 1935
**HEISMAN STATS:** 119 att.; 577 yds.; 6 TDs.
The first Heisman Trophy winner, Berwanger starred for three seasons at the University of Chicago. Nicknamed the Man in the Iron Mask for the face protector he wore after breaking his nose as a freshman, Berwanger played both ways, but won renown as a runner. Against Ohio State his senior year, he ran 85 yards for a touchdown. Berwanger scored another historic first when he was the first player selected (by Philadelphia) in the first pro draft. Berwanger, however, did not sign, choosing instead to pursue more lucrative opportunities in business.

**Doc Blanchard, FB, (12-11-24)**
**COLLEGE:** Army **YEAR:** 1945
**HEISMAN STATS:** 101 att.; 718 yds.; 19 TDs.
Blanchard, "Mr. Inside" to backfield mate Glenn Davis's "Mr Outside," was the foundation of Army's football dynasty in the mid-40's, when the cadets went undefeated three straight seasons (1944 through '46). Compared to other backs of his era, Blanchard was unusually big (6', 205), strong (he won the 1945 IC4A shot put) and fast (10.0 100 yds). In his Heisman-winning junior season, Blanchard scored 19 TDs and rushed for 718 yards, an average of 7.1 yards per carry. In the 25 games he played for Army, Blanchard gained 1,666 yards rushing (5.9 yards per carry) and scored 39 TDs. In 1945 he became the first football player to win the Sullivan Award as the nation's top amateur athlete. He never played pro football, choosing instead a career as a jet fighter pilot.

**Tim Brown, HB-QB (b. 6-22-66)**
**COLLEGE:** Notre Dame **YEAR:** 1987
**HEISMAN STATS:** 39 rec.; 846 yds.; 7 TDs.
The seventh player from Notre Dame to win the Heisman, Brown attended Woodrow Wilson High in Dallas, the alma mater of 1938 Heisman winner Davey

O'Brien. Brown, a flashy six-foot, 195-pound flanker and kick return specialist, looked like a lock for the Heisman until he suffered a painful separation of his right shoulder midway through the season. Despite subpar performances against Penn State and Miami that seemed to allow Syracuse quarterback Don McPherson back into the race, Brown was a surprisingly easy winner. For the season he accumulated 1,847 all-purpose yards on 130 plays, an average of 14.2 yards every time he got the ball. Taken in the first round of the 1988 draft by the L.A. Raiders, Brown is now a wide receiver for the Raiders.

### Earl Campbell, TB (b. 3-29-55)
**COLLEGE:** Texas **YEAR:** 1977
**HEISMAN STATS:** 335 att.; 1,744 yds.; 19 TDs.
Campbell overcame an impoverished childhood in Tyler, Texas, to become one of the greatest—and probably the most punishing—back in college football history. The first player to be named All-SWC for four straight years, Campbell flourished in his senior season. Possessed of massive thighs, he led the nation in both rushing (1,744 yards) and scoring (114 points on 19 TDs). His finest game may have come against Texas A&M, when he ran for 222 yards and four TDs. The first player chosen in the NFL draft, by Houston, Campbell led the league in rushing and was named league MVP in each of his first three pro seasons.

### Billy Cannon, HB (b. 2-8-37)
**COLLEGE:** LSU **YEAR:** 1959
**HEISMAN STATS:** 139 att.; 598 yds.; 6 TDs.
The law has figured twice in Billy Cannon's life, fortuitously in one case, sadly in the other. Legend has it that Cannon, after a minor scrape with the law as a teen, was lucky enough to appear before a judge who was a rabid LSU football fan. In exchange for a suspended sentence, the judge ordered Cannon to matriculate at LSU, an arrangement that brought glory to both school and athlete. Cannon's finest season in Baton Rouge probably came his junior year, when he led the Tigers to a 7–0 win over Clemson in the Sugar Bowl, an 11–0 record and the national title. Cannon's senior year was memorable for a single flash of brilliance. The top-ranked Tigers were trailing No. 3-ranked Mississippi 3–0 late in a rainy game when Cannon took a punt on his own 11-yard line and raced 89 yards for the winning touchdown. Cannon played 11 pro seasons, the finest of which came in 1961, when he led Houston to the AFL title by rushing for a league-leading total of 948 yards. Cannon retired after the 1970 season and set up an orthodontics practice in Baton Rouge. In 1983 he pleaded guilty to participating in a counterfeiting scheme and was sentenced to five years in prison.

### John Cappelletti, HB (b. 8-9-52)
**COLLEGE:** Penn State **YEAR:** 1973
**HEISMAN STATS:** 286 att.; 1,522 yds.; 17 TDs.
Cappelletti spent his first two seasons at Penn State as a defensive back. Switched to offense in his junior year, Cappelletti rushed 233 times for 1,117 yards and scored 13 TDs. Dedicating his senior year to his younger brother, Joey, who had leukemia, Cappelletti led the Nittany Lions to a 12–0 record, rushing for 1,522 yards to rank fifth nationally. Cappelletti played seven seasons in the NFL, with the Rams and the Chargers, retiring in 1982.

### Howard Cassady, HB (b. 3-2-34)
**COLLEGE:** Ohio State **YEAR:** 1955
**HEISMAN STATS:** 161 att.; 958 yds.;15 TDs.
Plucked from the playing fields of Columbus, Ohio's Central High by eagle-eyed Woody Hayes, Cassady was an instant success at Ohio State, scoring three TDs in his first game as a freshman, against Indiana. Nicknamed Hopalong for the popular movie and TV character, Cassady was an explosive runner who also played defensive back, twice leading the team in interceptions. Cassady was a unanimous All-America selection in both 1954 and '55. In 1954 he led the Buckeyes to a 10–0 season, a 20–7 win over USC at the Rose Bowl and the national title. In 1955 he rushed for 958 yards and scored 15 TDs, as the Buckeyes went 7–2. Cassady played eight seasons in the NFL, but because of his size (5'10", 172) he was used primarily as a defensive back and kick returner. He retired in 1963.

### John David Crow, HB (b. 7-8-35)
**COLLEGE:** Texas A&M **YEAR:** 1957
**HEISMAN STATS:** 129 att.; 562 yds.; 6 touchdowns.
Crow, a Louisiana native, played three seasons at Texas A&M under Bear Bryant, starring on both offense and defense. At 6'2", 220-pounds, Crow was big for a running back. "Watching him play was like watching a grown man play with boys," Bryant said. Crow's Heisman stats might have been even more impressive had he not suffered a rash of early season injuries. In his three-year collegiate career, he rushed 296 times for 1,455 yards; caught 13 passes for 280 yards; intercepted eight passes for 45 yards; and scored 115 points on 19 TDs and one PAT. An outstanding pro for 11 seasons, with the Cardinals and the 49ers, Crow was named to four All-Pro teams. From 1975 to '80 he was head coach at Northeast Louisiana University (20-34-1).

### Ernie Davis, HB (b. 12-14-39; d. 5-18-63)
**COLLEGE:** Syracuse **YEAR:** 1961
**HEISMAN STATS:** 150 att.; 823 yds.; 15 TDs.
The first black player to win the Heisman, Davis also won the closest vote in history, edging Bob Ferguson of Ohio State by 53 points. At Syracuse, Davis broke numerous school records that had been held by the great Jim Brown, including total yards (3,303), TDs (35) and points (220). He broke open the 1960 Cotton Bowl with a TD reception of 87 yards, a major bowl record, as Syracuse beat Texas 23–14. He also played basketball at Syracuse and was chosen senior marshal at his graduation. The first player taken in the 1962 pro football draft (by the Redskins, who traded him to the Browns, where he would have played next to Jim Brown), Davis became ill with leukemia while preparing for the 1962 College All-Star game and died without having played a single professional down.

### Glenn Davis, HB (b. 12-26-24)
**COLLEGE:** Army **YEAR:** 1946
**HEISMAN STATS:** 123 att.; 712 yds.; 7 TDs.
Twice the Heisman runner-up before winning it in 1946, Davis was "Mr. Outside" to backfield mate Doc Blanchard's "Mr. Inside." A four-year starter on the Army football juggernaut of the mid '40s, Davis also played baseball and basketball at West Point and ran on the track team. As a sophomore he averaged a

collegiate-record 11.5 yards per carry, then broke it the following year, when he averaged 11.51 yards per carry. Indeed, over his four-year career Davis rushed for 6,464 yards on 637 attempts (10.1 per carry), passed for 12 TDs and scored another 59. In undermanned Army's 20–13 defeat of powerful Michigan, Davis ran for 105 yards, completed all seven of his pass attempts, for 159 yards, made two interceptions and a game-saving defensive play at the finish. Davis played two seasons with the L.A. Rams before aggravating an old knee injury and retiring in 1951.

### Pete Dawkins, HB (b. 3-8-38)
**COLLEGE:** Army **YEAR:** 1958
**HEISMAN STATS:** 78 att.; 428 yds.; 6 TDs.
Dawkins, a versatile performer for West Point in his junior season, rushed for 665 yards (5.4 yards per carry) and eight TDs, and caught 11 passes for 225 yards and three TDs. As a senior he rushed for 428 yards (5.5 average per carry). Dawkins also played three seasons as a defenseman for the Cadet hockey team, and as a senior achieved an unprecedented sweep of West Point honors—as "first captain" of Cadets, class president, one of his class's "star men" (top 5% of class) and football captain. Dawkins won a Rhodes scholarship and studied at Oxford, where he earned a "blue" in rugby. Despite becoming at 45 the Army's youngest general, Dawkins left the service to go into banking. In 1988 he was beaten by Bill Bradley in his bid to become a U.S. senator from New Jersey.

### Ty Detmer, QB (b. 10-30-67)
**COLLEGE:** Brigham Young **YEAR:** 1990
**HEISMAN STATS:** 361 comp.; 562 att.; 5,188 yds.; 41 TDs.
One in a long line of Cougar quarterbacks with seemingly bionic arms, Detmer set a total of 29 NCAA records in 1990, including passing yards in a season (5,188). Still, as a Heisman candidate, the six-foot, 175-pound junior had his detractors. Some argued that he played in a relatively weak conference, the Western Athletic Conference; some that his gaudy numbers were the product of the pass-oriented BYU offense. On the plus side was Detmer's performance against top-ranked Miami: He completed 38 of 54 passes for 406 yards and three TDs. As a senior, when he finished third in Heisman voting, Detmer increased his record-passing yardage total to 15,031 and retired as the highest-rated college quarterback ever (162.7). Picked in the ninth round of the NFL draft by Green Bay, he saw no playing time as a rookie.

### Tony Dorsett, HB (b. 4-7-54)
**COLLEGE:** Pittsburgh **YEAR:** 1976
**HEISMAN STATS:** 356 att.; 2,150 yds.; 23 TDs.
Dorsett, a 5'11", 160-pounder from Hopewell Township, Pa., was a superb running back long before he won the Heisman. In just his third game as a freshman, Dorsett rushed for 265 yards against Northwestern, a record for college freshmen. That year he became the first legitimate freshman All-America since 1944. Dorsett rushed for over 1,000 yards in each of his four years at Pitt, winding up with an NCAA career-record 6,082 yards (141.1 yards per game) and 58 TDs. In the 1977 Sugar Bowl he rushed for 202 yards and one TD, helping Pitt beat Georgia 27–3 to clinch the national championship with a 12–0 record. Drafted in the first round by the Dallas Cowboys, Dorsett played almost his entire 12-year

career with them. When Dorsett retired at the end of the 1988 season, he was second only to Walter Payton among NFL career rushers, with 12,739 yards.

### Doug Flutie, QB, (b. 10-23-62)
**COLLEGE:** Boston College. **YEAR:** 1984.
**HEISMAN STATS:** 233 comp.; 386 att.; 3,454 yards; 27 TDs.
That no quarterback had won the Heisman in 13 years cannot have concerned Doug Flutie. He was used to beating the odds. Deemed too small at 5'10", 173 pounds to be a Division I quarterback, Flutie was all set to attend the University of New Hampshire when Boston College offered him its final football scholarship. He began his freshman year as the Eagles' fifth quarterback but was starting by midseason. As a sophomore Flutie threw for 520 yards against Penn State and led BC to an 8-2-1 record. Hampered early in his career by a tendency to throw more interceptions than TDs, Flutie threw for 27 TDs and just 11 interceptions in his Heisman-winning season. His most memorable pass came on Nov. 23, 1984, when his 48-yard Hail Mary to Gerard Phelan beat defending national champion Miami 47–45. His 10,579 career passing yards set an NCAA record. Flutie played briefly in the NFL, for the Bears and the Patriots, but has had his greatest success as a pro in the CFL, leading the Calgary Stampeders to the 1992 Grey Cup title.

### Clint Frank, TB (b. 9-13-15, d. 7-7-92)
**COLLEGE:** Yale **YEAR:** 1937
**HEISMAN STATS:** 157 att.; 667 yds.; 11 TDs.
Frank succeeded Yale teammate Larry Kelley as Heisman winner. A 5'10", 175-pound tailback, Frank ran, in the words of one admirer, "with the speed and power of a wild buffalo in mad flight." Although he had great games against virtually every Ivy League opponent—as a junior he beat Dartmouth with a 35-yard TD pass with three seconds on the clock and as a senior he scored all three Yale TDs against Brown—Frank always saved his best for Princeton. Against the heavily favored Tigers his junior year, he marched the Eli 81 yards down the field, throwing a 50-yard pass and then running the final 13 yards for the winning TD. Against Princeton the following year he scored four TDs on runs of 79, 51, five and four yards and totaled 191 yards for the day on 19 carries.

### Mike Garrett, HB (b. 4-12-44)
**COLLEGE:** USC **YEAR:** 1965
**HEISMAN STATS:** 267 att.; 1,440 yds.; 16 TDs.
The second player from a school in the far West and the second black player to win the Heisman, Garrett led the nation in rushing his senior year, gaining 144 yards per game. In his career Garrett gained 3,221 yards, then an NCAA career record, and averaged 5.3 yards per carry. Also a fine baseball player at USC, Garrett toyed briefly with the idea of playing major league baseball. Garrett played eight NFL seasons, for the K.C. Chiefs and the S.D. Chargers, retiring after the 1973 season.

### Archie Griffin, HB (b. 8-21-54)
**COLLEGE:** Ohio State **YEAR:** 1974–75
**1974 HEISMAN STATS:** 256 att.; 1,695 yds.; 12 TDs.
**1975 HEISMAN STATS:** 262 att.; 1,450 yds.; 4 TDs.
Of the 57 men who have won the Heisman, Griffin is the only one to have won it twice. An overweight child,

Griffin was known as Butterball to his family. He grew to 5'8", 182 pounds and was persuaded by Woody Hayes to come to Ohio State. In the second game of his freshman year, against North Carolina, he came off the bench to rush for a Buckeye record 239 yards. The following year, in Ohio State's opener, he began an incredible streak of 31 straight games with over 100 yards rushing, gaining 129 against Minnesota. In the second of his four Rose Bowl appearances, Griffin ran for 149 yards on 22 carries as Ohio State beat USC 42–21. In his two Heisman-winning seasons, Griffin rushed for 1,620 and 1,357 yards, and in the latter led the Buckeyes to an 11–0 record and the national title. Michigan, however, did stop Griffin's streak, holding him to just 46 yards on 19 carries. In his four-year career Griffin rushed for 5,177 yards—the first college player to top 5,000—on 845 carries, an average of 6.1 yards per carry. The second player taken in the 1976 NFL draft, Griffin played eight seasons with the Cincinnati Bengals, retiring in 1983.

## Tom Harmon, HB (b. 9-28-19; d. 3-17-90)
**COLLEGE:** Michigan **YEAR:** 1940
**CAREER STATS:** 191 att.; 852 yds.; 16 TDs.
As a 60-minute player, Harmon was capable of dominating a game on both offense and defense. Against Iowa in 1939, he scored all 27 points for the Wolverines, six of them coming on a 95-yard pass interception. Dubbed the Gary Ghost for his hometown in Indiana, Harmon led the nation in scoring in both 1939 (102 points) and '40 (117) and broke many of Red Grange's Big Ten records. For his career Harmon rushed 398 times for 2,134 yards and completed 101 of 233 passes for 1,396 yards. Harmon served in the Air Force in World War II. Twice forced to bail out over enemy territory, Harmon was awarded both the Silver Star and the Purple Heart. He played two seasons (1946 and '47) for the L.A. Rams, and though his legs had been badly burned in the war, he averaged 5.1 yards per rush and 19.2 per reception.

## Leon Hart, End (b. 11-2-28)
**COLLEGE:** Notre Dame **YEAR:** 1949
**HEISMAN STATS:** 19 rec.; 257 yds.; 5 TDs.
Notre Dame did not lose a game during Hart's four years on the varsity, compiling a record of 36-0-2 and winning three straight national championships from 1947 to '49. One of only two ends to win the Heisman (Larry Kelley was the other), Hart stood 6'4" and weighed 245 pounds and was exceedingly hard to bring down. During his four-year career at Notre Dame, Hart caught 49 passes for 742 yards and 13 TDs. He played end for the Detroit Lions from 1950 to '58, earning All-Pro honors in '51 and '52 and playing on three NFL championship teams ('52, '53, '57). Hart was a founder of the NFL Players Association.

## Paul Hornung, QB (b. 12-23-35)
**COLLEGE:** Notre Dame **YEAR:** 1956
**HEISMAN STATS:** 59 comp.; 111 att.; 917 yards; 3 TDs.
In retrospect two things seem odd about the 1956 Heisman race. First, Jim Brown, arguably the greatest running back of all-time, finished fifth in the voting. And second, the award went to a player whose team won just two games. Not that you could blame Hornung. At Notre Dame the two-time All America completed 105 of 214 passes for 1,660 yards and 12

TDs. Chosen by the Green Bay Packers in the first round of the 1957 NFL draft, Hornung was ineffective at quarterback for two seasons, then coach Vince Lombardi shifted him to halfback. He was named league MVP in both '60 and '61. Hornung led the league in scoring three straight years (1959–61), and his total of 176 points in '60 still stands as the NFL record.

## Les Horvath, HB-QB (b. 9-12-21)
**COLLEGE:** Ohio State **YEAR:** 1944
**CAREER STATS:** 163 att.; 924 yds.; 12 TDs.
After leading Ohio State to a 9–1 record and the national championship in 1942, his senior year, Horvath spent the following year in a special Army dentistry program. Granted an extra year of eligibility, he returned to the gridiron in 1944 and led Ohio State to its first perfect season since 1920. He scored two TDs in the Buckeyes' 18–14 come-from-behind win over Michigan, and for the season ranked second nationally in rushing, third in total offense. Horvath spent three relatively undistinguished seasons with the L.A. Rams and the Cleveland Browns and upon retiring set up a dental practice in Glendale, Calif.

## Desmond Howard, WR (b. 1-13-72)
**SERVICE:** Michigan. **YEAR:** 1991
**HEISMAN STATS:** 61 rec.; 950 yds.; 23 TDs.
Howard got the highest percentage of first-place votes (85%) in Heisman history. Teamed at Michigan with his former high school quarterback, Elvis Grabac, the 5'9", 174-pound junior earned the Heisman with routinely spectacular catches, many of them clutched in his fingertips while diving or leaping acrobatically. Probably the most important catch Howard made all year was a 25-yarder on fourth down in the fourth quarter against Notre Dame that preserved a narrow Wolverine win. Against Ohio State Howard returned a punt 93 yards for a TD. The fourth player taken in the 1992 NFL draft, by Washington, Howard spent his rookie season mostly returning kickoffs and punts.

## John Huarte, QB (b. 5-20-43)
**SERVICE:** Notre Dame **YEAR:** 1964
**HEISMAN STATS:** 114 comp.; 205 att.; 2,062 yds.; 6 TDs.
It would be hard to imagine a Heisman winner ever again coming from the same obscurity that Huarte did in winning the 1964 trophy. Not only had he never won a varsity letter, he had played a grand total of 50 varsity minutes. But Huarte impressed coach Ara Parseghian during spring practice and got the starter's job his senior year. He took the Irish from 2–7 in 1963 to 9–2 in '64, completing 55.6% of his passes for 2,080 yards, 16 TDs and an average gain of 18.1 yards per completion.

## Bo Jackson, HB (b. 11-30-62)
**COLLEGE:** Auburn **YEAR:** 1985
**HEISMAN STATS:** 278 att.; 1,786 yds.; 17 TDs.
The only person ever to play in both the All-Star Game and the Pro Bowl, Jackson first showed his prodigious talents at McAdory High School in McCalla, Ala., where he was two-time state champ in the decathlon, hit a national high school record 20 home runs in one season and gained 1,173 yards on 108 carries and scored 17 TDs in his senior year. Auburn's first three-sport letterman in 30 years, the 6'1", 220-pound Jackson ran 100 meters in 10.39 and, as the Tigers'

centerfielder in 1985, batted .401 with 17 homers and 43 RBIs. On the gridiron Jackson retired as Auburn's alltime leading rusher, with 4,303 yards, an average of 6.6 per carry, and scored 43 TDs. He led Auburn in the Tangerine, Sugar, Liberty and Cotton Bowls, earning MVP honors in the last three. The first player taken in the 1986 NFL draft, by Tampa Bay, Jackson signed instead with baseball's Kansas City Royals. Renowned for his tape-measure blasts, Jackson's homer off Rick Reuschel to lead off the 1989 All Star Game helped earn him MVP honors for the game. Signed by the LA Raiders in 1987, Jackson played four seasons with them before an injury to his left hip, suffered on Jan. 13, 1991 in a game with the Cincinnati Bengals, forced him out of football. In his four pro seasons Jackson carried 515 times for 2,782 yards (5.4 yards per carry) and 16 TDs and also had two receiving TDs. Signed as a free agent by the Chicago White Sox on April 3, 1991, he had his left hip replaced in April 5, 1992. At the start of the 1993 season he had played five seasons for Kansas City and one for Chicago and had a career batting average of .249, with 112 homers and 327 RBIs. In his first at bat of the 1993 season Jackson homered.

## Vic Janowicz, HB (b. 2-26-30)
**COLLEGE:** Ohio State **YEAR:** 1950
**HEISMAN STATS:** 32 comp.; 77 att.; 561 yds.; 12 TDs.
Janowicz won the Heisman as a junior, when Ohio State coach Wes Fesler made him the centerpiece of the Buckeyes' single wing offense. In it, Janowicz ran, passed, called offensive signals, punted and kicked extra points and field goals; on defense, he played safety. His best game probably came against Iowa, when he ran for two TDs, passed for four more; kicked 10 extra points; and recovered two fumbles. The following year the Buckeyes had trouble adjusting to new coach Woody Hayes's split T offense, and neither Janowicz nor his team had a great year. Upon graduating, Janowicz returned to his first love—baseball—playing two seasons for the Pittsburgh Pirates and batting .214.

## Dick Kazmaier, HB (b. 11-23-30)
**COLLEGE:** Princeton **YEAR:** 1951
**HEISMAN STATS:** 149 att.; 861 yds.; 9 TDs.
The last Ivy League player to win the Heisman, Kazmaier was a tailback in Princeton's single wing offense. In the 27 games he played for the Tigers, Kazmaier ran for 20 TDs and threw for another 35. A two-time All-America, he rushed 368 times for 1,964 yards and completed 179 of 289 pass attempts for 2,393 yards. During the Kazmaier era, Princeton won 22 straight games. Kazmaier is one of the few Heisman winners never to play pro football. After graduating cum laude, he earned an MBA at Harvard and went into business.

## Larry Kelley, End (b. 5-30-15)
**COLLEGE:** Yale **YEAR:** 1936
**HEISMAN STATS:** 17 rec.; 372 yds.; 6 TDs.
One of only two ends to win the Heisman (Leon Hart was the other), Kelley played two seasons at Yale with Clint Frank, the 1937 Heisman winner. Kelley scored at least one TD against Harvard and Princeton in each of his three seasons. Kelley also played basketball at Yale and captained the Eli baseball team.

## Nile Kinnick, QB-HB (b. 7-9-18; d. 6-2-43)
**COLLEGE:** Iowa **YEAR:** 1939
**HEISMAN STATS:** 106 att.; 374 yds.; 5 TDs.
The grandson of an Iowa governor, Kinnick was a superb athlete and student, a young man whom many expected to have a glowing future in public office. In 1939 the 5'10", 175-pound Kinnick led the NCAA in kickoff return yardage, with 377 yards on 15 returns. In his three-year collegiate career Kinnick rushed for 724 yards on 254 carries, completed 88 of 229 passes for 1,445 yards and intercepted 18 passes. After graduating Phi Beta Kappa in 1940, he went to Iowa Law School. A member of the Naval Reserve, Kinnick entered active duty soon after the attack on Pearl Harbor. He was killed when his Navy fighter plane crashed into the Gulf of Paria, Venezuela.

## John Lattner, HB (b. 10-24-32)
**COLLEGE:** Notre Dame **YEAR:** 1953
**HEISMAN STATS:** 134 att.; 651 yds.; 6 TDs.
Lattner may have been the most self-deprecating of all the Heisman winners. As a self-imposed penalty for fumbling five times against Michigan State in 1952, he carried a football around the Notre Dame campus for a week. Though not overwhelmingly fast or a great passer, Lattner always found ways to beat opponents. Against Oklahoma in his senior year he cut through three blockers in the open field to make the "defensive play of the season"; later in the game he intercepted a pass to preserve the Irish's 28–21 win. He returned kickoffs for TDs 86 yards against Purdue and 92 yards against Pennsylvania and scored four TDs in Notre Dame's 48–14 defeat of USC at the Los Angeles Coliseum. In his three years at Notre Dame, the 6'2", 195-pound Lattner scored 20 TDs, rushed for 1,724 yards on 350 carries (a 4.9 yard average) and gained 3,116 all-purpose yards, as the Fighting Irish compiled a cumulative 23-4-2 record. Lattner played one season for the Pittsburgh Steelers, making the Pro Bowl, then served two years in the Air Force. He tried to return to the Steelers, but a knee injury sustained in the service ended his hopes of playing again. When Lattner's Heisman Trophy melted during a fire, he asked for and was given a new one.

## John Lujack, QB (b. 1-4-25)
**COLLEGE:** Notre Dame **YEAR:** 1947
**HEISMAN STATS:** 61 comp.; 109 att.; 777 yds.; 9 TDs.
Though he was one of the finest T-formation quarterbacks in the history of college football, Lujack first got the attention of Notre Dame coaches with his fierce tackling. Indeed, in his junior year he made one of the most famous tackles ever, nailing Army's Doc Blanchard single-handedly in the open field to save a TD. Lujack's first start at quarterback came in 1943 when eventual Heisman-winner Angelo Bertelli went into the service. In his first start, against Army, Lujack threw two TD passes, ran for another and intercepted a pass. After two years in the Navy he returned to play two more seasons in South Bend. Lujack spent four years with the Chicago Bears. In his rookie season he tied a club record with eight interceptions. The following year he threw for six TDs and a league-record 468 yards against the Chicago Cardinals. Despite being named All-Pro in 1950 and '51, Lujack retired to become the Notre Dame backfield coach.

## Davey O'Brien, QB (b. 6-22-17; d. 11-18-77)
**COLLEGE:** Texas Christian **YEAR:** 1938
**HEISMAN STATS:** 110 comp.; 194 att.; 1,733 yds.; 19 TDs.

The tiniest of Heisman winners at 5'7'', 150-pounds, O'Brien began his TCU career as backup to Sammy Baugh before taking over as the starting quarterback in 1937. The next year he led TCU to an 11–0 record and the national title, throwing for 19 TDs and only four interceptions and rushing 466 yards on 127 carries. O'Brien played two seasons with the Philadelphia Eagles and was named quarterback on the coaches' All-Star team as a rookie. Though he set long-standing NFL records with 33 completions of 60 attempts in his final game with the Eagles, O'Brien retired after the 1940 season to join the FBI. He died of cancer in 1977.

## Steve Owens, FB (b. 12-9-47)
**COLLEGE:** Oklahoma **YEAR:** 1969
**HEISMAN STATS:** 358 att.; 1,523 yds.; 23 TDs.

By his own account, the 6'2'', 215-pound Owens was neither especially fast or shifty. He was, however, a workhorse, averaging over 35 carries a game in his last two years with the Sooners. In his senior year he set an NCAA record with 55 rushing attempts against Oklahoma State. Owens led the nation in attempts in both his junior and senior seasons and in rushing yards (1,523) and TDs (23) in the latter. Owens rushed for 100 yards in 17 straight games, and he finished his three-year Sooner career as the NCAA's all-time leader in both rushing yards (3,867) and scoring (336 points). Owens played seven seasons with the Detroit Lions, becoming, in 1971, the first Lion to top the 1,000-yard mark, with 1,035. Hampered by injuries throughout his pro career, he retired in 1977.

## Jim Plunkett, QB (b. 12-5-47)
**COLLEGE:** Stanford **YEAR:** 1970
**HEISMAN STATS:** 191 comp.; 358 att.; 2,715 yds.; 18 TDs.

No Heisman winner has had more potential obstacles to overcome than Plunkett, who was born to blind parents and raised in poverty. A month before he was to enroll at Stanford, a tumor developed in Plunkett's neck. Fearing the worst, Plunkett had it removed. It turned out to be benign. The Stanford coaching staff wanted Plunkett to move to defensive end, but he refused and in his sophomore year became the Cardinal's starting quarterback. As a senior he became the first Division I player to surpass 7,000 total yards in a career, with 7,887. Plunkett completed 530 of 962 passing attempts for 7,544 yards and 52 TDs. He led Stanford to a 27–17 win over Ohio State in the Rose Bowl and was named Player of the Game. The first player taken by the New England Patriots in the 1971 draft, Plunkett justified their faith by passing for 2,158 yards and 19 TDs and earning Rookie of the Year honors. After four injury-troubled years with the Pats and two mediocre seasons with the 49ers, Plunkett was signed by the Oakland Raiders. Midway through the 1980 season he replaced injured Dan Pastorini and led the Raiders to the Super Bowl, where they beat the Eagles 27–10. Plunkett came off the bench again in 1983 to lead Oakland into the Super Bowl, where the Raiders beat the Redskins 38–10 and Plunkett earned MVP honors. After sitting out the 1987 season with injuries, he retired.

## Johnny Rodgers, FL (b. 7-5-51)
**COLLEGE:** Nebraska **YEAR:** 1972
**HEISMAN STATS:** 55 rec.; 942 yds.; 17 TDs.

It surprised a lot of people when Rodgers won the 1972 Heisman Trophy by a landslide, not because he lacked credentials on the field, but because he had taken part in a gas station robbery as a freshman. Nebraska coaches Bob Devaney and Tom Osborne acted as Rodgers's guardians during his two-year probation. During his three-year career Rodgers amassed 5,691 all-purpose yards, an NCAA record, and the Cornhuskers won 31 straight games, claiming national titles in 1970 and '71. He led Nebraska to three straight Orange Bowl victories: a 17–12 win over LSU; a 38–6 trouncing of Alabama; and a 40–7 defeat of Notre Dame. In that game Rodgers scored four TDs himself and threw for a fifth. Deeming the 5'9'', 165-pound Rodgers too small for the NFL, the San Diego Chargers allowed the Montreal Alouettes to outbid them for his services. Rodgers earned CFL Rookie of the Year honors in 1973 and starred for the Alouettes through the 1976 season, after which he played two years for the Chargers before retiring.

## George Rogers, HB (b. 12-8-58)
**COLLEGE:** South Carolina **YEAR:** 1980
**HEISMAN STATS:** 324 att.; 1,894 yds.; 14 TDs.

The odds were heavily stacked against Rogers's winning the Heisman: The son of a convicted murderer, he was the first black from a southern school to win the Heisman, and he did so at a school that had virtually no national TV coverage. In his last two seasons the 6'2'', 224-pound tailback gained over 100 yards in 22 games and wound up his career with 5,204 yards. Rogers was selected in the first round of the 1981 draft by the New Orleans Saints. As a rookie he led the NFL in rushing, with 1,674 yards on 378 carries, earning Pro Bowl and Rookie of the Year honors. Traded to Washington before the 1985 season, Rogers retired in 1988.

## Mike Rozier, HB (b. 3-1-61)
**COLLEGE:** Nebraska **YEAR:** 1983
**HEISMAN STATS:** 275 att.; 2,148 yds.; 29 TDs.

Rozier spent a year at Coffeyville (KS) Community College before transferring to Nebraska, which went 33–5 in his three seasons. The 5'11'', 210-pound Rozier became only the second collegiate back, after Marcus Allen, to top the 2,000-yard mark in a season. In his three seasons at Nebraska, Rozier rushed for 4,780 yards, scored 50 TDs and averaged 136.6 yards per game and 7.17 per carry. The first player chosen in the 1984 USFL draft, Rozier played two seasons in that league before signing with the Houston Oilers.

## Barry Sanders, RB (b. 7-16-68)
**COLLEGE:** Oklahoma State **YEAR:** 1988
**HEISMAN STATS:** 344 att.; 2,628 yds.; 39 TDs.

Barely recruited out of high school in Wichita because of his size (5'8'', 180 pounds), Sanders went on to have the greatest season of any running back in NCAA history. Among the many records he set during his Heisman-winning junior year were season marks for TDs (39), yards gained rushing (2,628 for an average of 238.9 per game) and all-purpose running yards (3,250). Sanders topped 300 yards in a game four times that season, something no one had done more than once in an entire career. His best game was his last, against Texas Tech in Tokyo, when he ran for 332 yards and four TDs. Sanders passed up his final year of eligibility and was drafted by the Detroit Lions with the third pick of the 1989 draft. As a rookie he led the NFC in rushing, with 1,470 yards, and the next year gained 1,304 to lead the NFL.

### O.J. Simpson, HB (b. 7-9-47)
**COLLEGE:** Southern Cal **YEAR:** 1968
**HEISMAN STATS:** 383 att.; 1,880 yds.; 23 TDs.
Considered by some to be the greatest running back ever, Orenthal James Simpson possessed all the tools. He was strong and agile and ran 100 yards in 9.3—fast enough to run a leg on USC's world-record setting 440-yard relay team. Simpson's grades, however, were not good enough to get him into USC, his first choice. So he went to San Francisco City College—the first Heisman winner to have started his career at a junior college—and set J.C. records for both season TDs (54) and single-game yardage (310). Transferring to USC in 1967, he led the nation in rushing, with 1,415 yards, an NCAA record. Simpson broke that mark the following year, with 1,709. In his two years at USC, Simpson rushed for 3,295 yards on 649 carries (5.1 yards per carry) and scored 34 touchdowns in 22 games as the Trojans went 19-2-1. Selected in the first round of the 1969 NFL draft by the Buffalo Bills, Simpson was used sparingly for three seasons before hitting his stride in 1972. The next year Simpson broke Jim Brown's season rushing record, becoming the first player to top 2,000 yards, with 2,003. Easily the most ubiquitous of Heisman winners, Simpson has done TV commentary and starred in Hertz commercials and films such as *The Towering Inferno* and *Naked Gun*.

### Billy Sims, HB (b. 9-18-55)
**COLLEGE:** Oklahoma **YEAR:** 1978
**HEISMAN STATS:** 231 att.; 1,762 yds.; 20 TDs.
Sims was a superstar at Hooks High in Texas, rushing for 7,738 yards in his career and gaining at least 123 in every game he played. Injured his first two seasons at Oklahoma, Sims came alive as a junior. Running behind the blocking of his roommate, eventual Outland Trophy winner Greg Roberts, Sims led the nation with 1,762 yards and 20 TDs. He topped 200 yards in three straight games and was named offensive MVP in the 1979 Orange Bowl, helping the Sooners to a 31–24 win over Nebraska. Sims had another great year in 1979, rushing for 1,506 yards and scoring 22 TDs, yet lost in the Heisman balloting to Charles White of USC.

### Frank Sinkwich, HB (b. 10-10-20; d. 10-22-90)
**COLLEGE:** Georgia **YEAR:** 1942
**HEISMAN STATS:** 84 comp.; 166 att.; 1,392 yds.; 10 TDs.
Sinkwich was truly a double-threat player, rushing for 30 TDs in his career and passing for another 30. Renowned for his willingness to play in spite of injury, he broke his jaw as a junior and played with an aluminum face mask. In leading the Bulldogs to a 40–26 win over Texas Christian in the 1942 Orange Bowl, Sinkwich set a bowl game record with 382 yards of total offense, throwing three TD passes and running 43 yards for a fourth TD. Despite playing most of his senior year with two sprained ankles, Sinkwich led the nation in total offense, with 2,187 yards, passing for

1,392 and rushing for 795. Sinkwich played five seasons of pro football, his best season coming in 1944 when he led the NFL in punting and was named league MVP.

### Bruce Smith, HB (b. 2-8-20; d. 8-28-67)
**COLLEGE:** Minnesota **YEAR:** 1941
**HEISMAN STATS:** 98 att.; 480 yds.; 6 TDs.
Smith was the star halfback of a Golden Gopher backfield that included three All-Americas—Smith, George Franck and Bill Daley. Minnesota won 17 straight games and won national titles in 1940 and '41. Against undefeated Michigan in 1940, Smith ran 80 yards for the game-winning touchdown in Minnesota's 7–6 victory. Smith played his senior year with a bad knee. After Iowa held the Golden Gophers to negative yardage in the first quarter, Smith limped into the game and turned it into a 34–14 win for Minnesota. In his three-year career at Minnesota, Smith rushed for 1,214 yards (4.9 per carry), passed for 496 and had a 39.6-yard average as a punter. After serving in the Navy during World War II, Smith played five pro seasons with the Green Bay Packers and the L.A. Rams, most of it on defense. Smith died of cancer in 1967.

### Steve Spurrier, QB (b. 4-20-45)
**COLLEGE:** Florida **YEAR:** 1966
**HEISMAN STATS:** 179 comp.; 291 att.; 2,012 yds.; 16 TDs.
Spurrier had a knack for the dramatic. Eight times in his three-year career at Florida, he brought the Gators from behind to win in the fourth quarter. The most impressive of those comebacks may have been one that fell short. Trailing Missouri 20–0 in the fourth quarter of the 1966 Sugar Bowl, Spurrier scored one TD and passed for two more. The Gators, however, missed three tries at two-point conversions. Spurrier, with 27 completions and 352 passing yards, was named the game's MVP. The next year he kicked a 40-yard field goal with 2:12 left to beat Auburn 30–27. Overall he completed 392 of 692 pass attempts for 4,848 yards and 36 TDs. A first-round draft pick of the San Francisco 49ers, Spurrier spent nine seasons with the Niners, mainly as a backup to John Brodie. Currently he is the head coach at his alma mater.

### Roger Staubach, QB (b. 2-5-42)
**COLLEGE:** Navy **YEAR:** 1963
**HEISMAN STATS:** 107 comp.; 161 att.; 1,474 yds.; 7 TDs.
After failing the Naval Academy entrance exam, Staubach spent a year at the New Mexico Military Institute. In his three years at Navy, Staubach completed 292 of 463 passes (63%) for 3,571 yards. Staubach also lettered in basketball and baseball and was named the academy's outstanding athlete three straight years. Chosen by the Dallas Cowboys as a future selection, Staubach spent four years in the service, one as the Middies' backfield coach and one in Vietnam. Staubach joined the Cowboys in 1969 as a 27-year-old rookie and spent two years as backup to Craig Morton. Taking over in 1971, Staubach led Dallas to a 24–3 win over Miami in the Super Bowl, earning game MVP honors. He again led Dallas to a win in the 1978 Super Bowl. Known as a scrambler, Staubach rushed 410 times for 2,264 yards and 20 TDs. He retired after the 1979 season.

## Pat Sullivan, QB (b. 1-18-50)
**COLLEGE:** Auburn **YEAR:** 1971
**HEISMAN STATS:** 162 comp.; 281 att.; 2,012 yds.; 20 TDs.
The 1971 Heisman race was controversial: Just how good was Ed Marinaro, who rushed for several NCAA records (including a career average of 174.6 rushing yards per game that still stands), but who played for Cornell in the Ivy League? Not good enough, answered the Heisman voters, who picked Auburn quarterback Pat Sullivan over Marinaro. Sullivan, who led the Tigers to a 25–5 record in his three years at the helm, connected with Terry Beasley to set many SEC passing marks. Only twice in his career did Sullivan throw for less than 100 yards in a game. After a brief pro career, Sullivan retired to the bench and is now head coach at Texas Christian.

## Vinny Testaverde, QB (b. 11-13-63)
**COLLEGE:** Miami **YEAR:** 1986
**HEISMAN STATS:** 175 comp.; 276 att.; 2,557 yds.; 26 TDs.
Winning by the second-largest margin in Heisman history, Testaverde established himself as the favorite when he finished fifth in the voting as a junior. He underscored his claim in the third game of the season when he completed 21 of 28 passes—including 14 in a row—for 261 yards and four TDs in Miami's defeat of top-ranked Oklahoma. Testaverde's career passing yardage of 6,058 yards broke Bernie Kosar's school record by 87 yards. Testaverde was taken by the Tampa Bay Buccaneers in the 1987 draft and started in a majority of Tampa Bay's games until 1992, when he was signed as a free agent by Cleveland.

## Gino Torretta, QB (b. 8-10-70)
**COLLEGE:** Miami **YEAR:** 1992
**HEISMAN STATS:** 228 comp.; 402 att.; 3,060 yds.; 19 TDs.
Torretta's brother Geoff had been the backup quarterback to 1986 Heisman winner Vinny Testaverde. Asked why he so enjoyed wearing the Heisman souvenirs Geoff had brought back from Testaverde's ceremony, little Gino answered, presciently, "I'm going to win that trophy." In his Heisman-winning senior year, Torretta threw for 19 TDs and only seven interceptions; over one stretch he threw 123 passes without an interception. But more signifcant than Torretta's individual marks was the Hurricanes' 26–1 record in the games he started. The great blemish on Torretta's career was his disappointing performance in Miami's 34–13 loss to Alabama in the Sugar Bowl, a loss that cost the Hurricanes the national title. Torretta threw three interceptions, all of which went for TDs. He was chosen in the seventh round (192nd overall) in the 1993 NFL draft by the Minnesota Vikings.

## Billy Vessels, HB (b. 3-22-31)
**COLLEGE:** Oklahoma **YEAR:** 1952
**HEISMAN STATS:** 167 att.; 1,072 yds.; 17 TDs.
Distracted early in his Oklahoma career by academic difficulties and then injured most of his junior year, Vessels had a superb senior season. His best game probably came in the Sooners' loss to Notre Dame, when he rushed for 195 yards and scored three TDs. The six-foot, 185-pound halfback scored 35 TDs in his 24-game career and rushed for 2,085 yards. The first Heisman winner to sign with the Canadian Football League, Vessels won the Schenley Award as the CFL's best back as a rookie.

## Doak Walker, HB (b. 1-1-27)
**COLLEGE:** Southern Methodist **YEAR:** 1948
**HEISMAN STATS:** 108 att.; 532 yds.; 8 TDs.
Walker's heroics made him a folk hero in football-mad Texas. Some weeks he received 300 fan letters. And no wonder: In his career he accounted for 52 TDs, 38 of them rushing and 14 passing. He also averaged over 20 yards per kickoff return and nearly 40 per punt. In SMU's 19–19 tie with TCU, he amassed 471 yards in total offense and ran 80, 61 and 56 yards for TDs, the final run giving SMU a last-minute tie. Walker played four brilliant seasons for the Detroit Lions, making All-Pro in four of them, and leading the Lions to NFL titles in 1952 and '53. He retired at 28.

## Herschel Walker, HB (b. 3-3-62)
**COLLEGE:** Georgia **YEAR:** 1982
**HEISMAN STATS:** 335 att.; 1,752 yds.; 17 TDs.
Walker had quite a reputation to live up to when he arrived at Georgia. At Johnson County High in Georgia, he scored 45 TDs in his senior year and 86 in his career, both national records. He combined size (6'2", 222 pounds) and speed (a wind-aided 10.10 for 100 meters) as no back before him. He broke Tony Dorsett's freshman rushing record, with 1,616 yards, and finished third in the Heisman voting, highest ever by a freshman. In the Sugar Bowl he rushed for 150 yards and two TDs, leading the Bulldogs to the national title with a 17–10 win over Notre Dame. Named SEC Player of the Year and consensus All-America three straight years, Walker passed up his senior year to play for the New Jersey Generals in the new USFL. In 1985 Walker rushed for 2,411 yards, the most ever in a single pro season. Signed by the Dallas Cowboys in 1986, Walker has played with Dallas, Minnesota and Philadelphia in the NFL.

## Andre Ware, QB (b. 7-31-68)
**COLLEGE:** Houston **YEAR:** 1989
**HEISMAN STATS:** 365 comp.; 578 att.; 4,699 yds.; 46 TDs.
Ware became the first black quarterback to win the Heisman. Because Houston was on probation, Ware's exploits were not once carried on national TV nor was he able to play in a bowl game. Operating out of Houston's run-and-shoot offense, the 6'2", 205-pound junior broke virtually every NCAA passing record, including season marks for completions (365) and passing yardage (4,699). Against Baylor, which at the time had the nation's top-rated pass defense, Ware threw for six TDs in Houston's 66–10 victory. Taken in the first round of the 1990 draft by the Detroit Lions, Ware has occasionally started but has more frequently been the Lions' backup quarterback.

## Charles White, HB (b. 1-22-58)
**COLLEGE:** Southern Cal **YEAR:** 1979
**HEISMAN STATS:** 332 att.; 1,803 yds.; 19 TDs.
White became a Trojan starter midway through his freshman year and led Southern Cal to four straight bowls (three Rose Bowls). As a senior he gained 1,803 yards in 10 games, averaging 214 per game over the last six. Against Notre Dame he gained 261 yards, and he rushed for 247 in the 1980 Rose Bowl, scoring the winning TD in USC's 17–16 win over Ohio State. Deemed too small at 5'10", 183 pounds to be a pro back, White was nonetheless taken by Cleveland late in the first round. He played eight seasons with the Browns and LA Rams before retiring in 1989.

## National Football League

Address:  410 Park Avenue
New York, New York 10022
Telephone: (212) 758-1500
Commissioner: Paul Tagliabue
Director of Communications: Greg Aiello

## National Football League Players Association

Address:  2021 L Street, N.W.
Washington, D.C. 20036
Telephone: (202) 463-2200
Executive Director: Gene Upshaw
Public Relations Director: Frank Woschitz

## National Football Conference

### Atlanta Falcons

Address:  2745 Burnette Road
Suwanee, GA 30174
Telephone: (404) 945-1111
Stadium (Capacity): Georgia Dome (71,500)
Chairman of the Board: Rankin M. Smith
President: Taylor W. Smith
Director of Player Personnel: Ken Herock
Coach: Jerry Glanville
Publicity Director: Charlie Taylor

### Chicago Bears

Address:  250 N. Washington Road
Lake Forest, IL 60045
Telephone: (708) 295-6600
Stadium (Capacity): Soldier Field (66,946)
President: Michael McCaskey
Coach: Dave Wannstedt
Director of Public Relations: Bryan Harlan

### Dallas Cowboys

Address:  One Cowboys Parkway
Irving, TX 75063
Telephone: (214) 556-9900
Stadium (Capacity): Texas Stadium (65,024)
Owner, President and General Manager: Jerry Jones
Coach: Jimmy Johnson
Public Relations Director: Rich Dalrymple

### Detroit Lions

Address:  1200 Featherstone Road
Pontiac, MI 48342
Telephone: (313) 335-4131
Stadium (Capacity): Pontiac Silverdome (80,500)
President and Owner: William Clay Ford
Executive Vice President: Chuck Schmidt
Coach: Wayne Fontes
Media Relations Director: Mike Murray

### Green Bay Packers

Address:  1265 Lombardi Avenue
Green Bay, WI 54304
Telephone: (414) 496-5700
Stadium (Capacity): Lambeau Field (59,543),
Milwaukee County Stadium (56,051)
President: Bob Harlan
General Manager: Ron Wolf
Coach: Mike Holmgren
Public Relations Director: Lee Remmel

### Los Angeles Rams

Address:  2327 W. Lincoln Avenue
Anaheim, CA 92801
Telephone: (714) 535-7267
Stadium (Capacity): Anaheim Stadium (69,008)
President: Georgia Frontiere
Executive Vice President: John Shaw
Vice President and Coach: Chuck Knox
Director of Public Relations: Rick Smith

### Minnesota Vikings

Address:  9520 Viking Drive
Eden Prairie, MN 55344
Telephone: (612) 828-6500
Stadium (Capacity): HHH Metrodome (63,000)
President: Roger L. Headrick
Vice President of Administrative and Team
Operations: Jeff Diamond
Coach: Dennis Green
Public Relations Director: David Pelletier

### New Orleans Saints

Address:  1500 Poydras Street
New Orleans, LA 70112
Telephone: (504) 733-0255
Stadium (Capacity): Louisiana Superdome (69,065)
Owner: Tom Benson
President and General Manager: Jim Finks
Coach: Jim Mora
Director of Media Relations: Rusty Kasmiersky

### New York Giants

Address:  Giants Stadium
East Rutherford, NJ 07073
Telephone: (201) 935-8111
Stadium (Capacity): Giants Stadium (77,311)
President and Co-CEO: Wellington T. Mara
Chairman and Co-CEO: Preston Robert Tisch
General Manager: George Young
Coach: Dan Reeves
Director of Public Relations: Pat Hanlon

### Philadelphia Eagles

Address:  Veterans Stadium
Broad Street and Pattison Avenue
Philadelphia, PA 19148
Telephone: (215) 463-2500
Stadium (Capacity): Veterans Stadium (65,356)
Owner: Norman Braman
President and Chief Operating Officer: Harry Gamble
Coach: Rich Kotite
Director of Public Relations: Ron Howard

### Phoenix Cardinals
Address:    P.O. Box 888
             Phoenix, AZ 85001
Telephone: (602) 379-0101
Stadium (Capacity): Sun Devil Stadium (73,473)
President: Bill Bidwill
General Manager: Larry Wilson
Coach: Joe Bugel
Director of Public Relations: Paul Jensen

### San Francisco 49ers
Address:    4949 Centennial Boulevard
             Santa Clara, CA 95054
Telephone: (408) 562-4949
Stadium (Capacity): Candlestick Park (66,455)
Owner: Edward J. DeBartolo Jr.
General Manager: John McVay
Coach: George Seifert
Public Relations Director: Rodney Knox

### Tampa Bay Buccaneers
Address:    One Buccaneer Place
             Tampa, FL 33607
Telephone: (813) 870-2700
Stadium (Capacity): Tampa Stadium (74,296)
Owner: Hugh F. Culverhouse
Director of Football Operations and Coach: Sam Wyche
Director of Public Relations: Rick Odioso

### Washington Redskins
Address:    Redskin Park Drive
             Ashburn, VA 22011
Telephone: (703) 478-8900
Stadium (Capacity): RFK Memorial Stadium (55,683)
Owner: Jack Kent Cooke
General Manager: Charley Casserly
Coach: Richie Petitbon
Vice President of Communications: Charlie Dayton

## American Football Conference

### Buffalo Bills
Address:    One Bills Drive
             Orchard Park, NY 14127
Telephone: (716) 648-1800
Stadium (Capacity): Rich Stadium (80,290)
President: Ralph C. Wilson Jr.
General Manager:John Butler
Coach: Marv Levy
Manager of Media Relations: Scott Berchtold

### Cincinnati Bengals
Address:    200 Riverfront Stadium
             Cincinnati, OH 45202
Telephone: (513) 621-3550
Stadium (Capacity): Riverfront Stadium (60,389)
President: John Sawyer
General Manager: Mike Brown
Coach: Dave Shula
Director of Public Relations: Allan Heim

### Cleveland Browns
Address:    80 First Avenue
             Berea, OH 44017
Telephone: (216) 891-5000
Stadium (Capacity): Cleveland Stadium (78,512)
President: Art Modell
Coach: Bill Belichick
Vice President and Director of Public Relations: Kevin Byrne

### Denver Broncos
Address:    13665 Broncos Parkway
             Englewood, CO 80112
Telephone: (303) 649-9000
Stadium (Capacity): Mile High Stadium (76,273)
President: Pat Bowlen
General Manager: John Beake
Coach: Wade Phillips
Director of Media Relations: Jim Saccomano

### Houston Oilers
Address:    6910 Fannin
             Houston, TX 77030
Telephone: (713) 797-9111
Stadium (Capacity): Astrodome (62,021)
President: K. S. "Bud" Adams Jr.
General Manager: Mike Holovak
Coach: Jack Pardee
Director of Media Relations: Chip Namias

### Indianapolis Colts
Address:    P.O. Box 535000
             Indianapolis, IN 46253
Telephone: (317) 297-2658
Stadium (Capacity): Hoosier Dome (60,129)
Owner: Robert Irsay
Vice President and General Manager: Jim Irsay
Coach: Ted Marchibroda
Public Relations Director: Craig Kelley

### Kansas City Chiefs
Address:    One Arrowhead Drive
             Kansas City, MO 64129
Telephone: (816) 924-9300
Stadium (Capacity): Arrowhead Stadium (77,622)
Founder: Lamar Hunt
President and General Manager: Carl Peterson
Coach: Marty Schottenheimer
Public Relations Director: Bob Moore

### Los Angeles Raiders
Address:    332 Center Street
             El Segundo, CA 90245
Telephone: (310) 322-3451
Stadium (Capacity): Los Angeles Memorial Coliseum (92,516)
Managing General Partner: Al Davis
Coach: Art Shell
Executive Assistant: Al LoCasale

## Miami Dolphins
Address:    Joe Robbie Stadium
        2269 N.W. 199 Street
        Miami, FL 33056
Telephone: (305) 620-5000
Stadium (Capacity): Joe Robbie Stadium (74,916)
President: Timothy J. Robbie
Coach: Don Shula
Director of Publicity: Harvey Greene

## New England Patriots
Address:    Foxboro Stadium
        Route 1
        Foxboro, MA 02035
Telephone: (508) 543-8200
Stadium (Capacity): Foxboro Stadium (60,794)
Owner: James Busch Orthwein
President: Francis Murray
Executive VP of Football Operations: Patrick Forté
Coach: Bill Parcells
Director of Public Relations: Mike Hanson

## New York Jets
Address:    1000 Fulton Avenue
        Hempstead, NY 11550
Telephone: (516) 538-6600
Stadium (Capacity): Giants Stadium (76,891)
Chairman of the Board: Leon Hess
General Manager: Dick Steinberg
Coach: Bruce Coslet
Director of Public Relations: Frank Ramos

## Pittsburgh Steelers
Address:    Three Rivers Stadium
        300 Stadium Circle
        Pittsburgh, PA 15212
Telephone: (412) 323-1200
Stadium (Capacity): Three Rivers Stadium (59,600)
President: Dan Rooney
Director of Football Operations: Tom Donahoe
Coach: Bill Cowher
Public Relations Coordinator: Dan Edwards

## San Diego Chargers
Address:    San Diego Jack Murphy Stadium
        P.O. Box 609609
        San Diego, CA 92160
Telephone: (619) 280-2111
Stadium (Capacity): San Diego Jack Murphy Stadium (61,863)
President: Alex G. Spanos
General Manager: Bobby Beathard
Coach: Bobby Ross
Director of Public Relations: Bill Johnston

## Seattle Seahawks
Address:    11220 N.E. 53rd Street
        Kirkland, WA 98033
Telephone: (206) 827-9777
Stadium (Capacity): The Kingdome (66,400)
Owner: Ken Behring
President: Dave Behring
General Manager and Coach: Tom Flores
VP of Admin. and Public Relations: Gary Wright

## Other Leagues

## Canadian Football League
Address:    110 Eglinton Avenue West, 5th floor
        Toronto, Ontario M4R 1A3, Canada
Telephone: (416) 322-9650
Commissioner: Larry Smith
Communications Director: Michael Murray

## World League of American Football
Address:    540 Madison Avenue
        New York, NY 10022
Telephone: (212) 758-1500
Chief Operating Officer: Tom Spock

# College Football Directory

## NATIONAL COLLEGIATE ATHLETIC ASSOCIATION (NCAA)
Address:    6201 College Boulevard
        Overland Park, KS 66211
Telephone: (913) 339-1906
Executive Director: TBA
Director of Communications: Jim Marchiony

## NATIONAL ASSOCIATION OF INTERCOLLEGIATE ATHLETICS (NAIA)
Address:    1221 Baltimore, Suite 1100
        Kansas City, MO 64105
Telephone: (816) 842-5050
Executive Director: James Chasteen
Director of Sports Information: Duane DaPron

## ATLANTIC COAST CONFERENCE
Address:    P.O. Drawer ACC
        Greensboro, NC 27419-6949
Telephone: (919) 854-8787
Commissioner: Eugene F. Corrigan
Director of Media Relations: Brian Morrison

## Clemson University
Address: Clemson, SC 29633
Nickname: Tigers
Telephone: (803) 656-2114
Football Stadium (Capacity): Clemson Memorial Stadium (81,473)
President: Dr. Max Lennon
Athletic Director: Bobby Robinson
Football Coach: Ken Hatfield
Sports Information Director: Tim Bourret

**Duke University**
Address: Durham, NC 27706
Nickname: Blue Devils
Telephone: (919) 684-2833
Football Stadium (Capacity): Wallace Wade Stadium (33,941)
President: Nan Keohane
Athletic Director: Tom Butters
Football Coach: Barry Wilson
Sports Information Director: Mike Cragg

**Florida State University**
Address: Tallahassee, FL 32316
Nickname: Seminoles
Telephone: (904) 644-1402
Football Stadium (Capacity): Doak S. Campbell Stadium (76,000)
President: Dr. Dale W. Lick
Athletic Director: Bob Goin
Football Coach: Bobby Bowden
Football Information Director: Donna Turner

**Georgia Tech**
Address:    150 Bobby Dodd Way
            Atlanta, GA 30332-0455
Nickname: Yellow Jackets
Telephone: (404) 894-2000
Football Stadium (Capacity): Bobby Dodd Stadium/Grant Field (46,000)
President: Dr. John P. Crecine
Athletic Director: Dr. Homer Rice
Football Coach: Bill Lewis
Sports Information Director: Mike Finn

**University of Maryland**
Address:    P.O. Box 295
            College Park, MD 20740
Nickname: Terrapins
Telephone: (301) 314-7064
Football Stadium (Capacity): Byrd Stadium (45,000)
President: William E. Kirwan
Athletic Director: Andy Geiger
Football Coach: Mark Duffner
Sports Information Director: Herb Hartnett

**University of North Carolina**
Address:    P.O. Box 2126
            Chapel Hill, NC 27514
Nickname: Tar Heels
Telephone: (919) 962-2211
Football Stadium (Capacity): Kenan Memorial Stadium (52,000)
Chancellor: Paul Hardin
Athletic Director: John Swofford
Football Coach: Mack Brown
Sports Information Director: Rick Brewer

**North Carolina State University**
Address:    P.O. Box 8501
            Raleigh, NC 27695
Nickname: Wolfpack
Telephone: (919) 515-2102
Football Stadium (Capacity): Carter-Finley Stadium (47,000)
Chancellor: Dr. Larry K. Monteith
Athletic Director: Todd Turner
Football Coach: Dick Sheridan
Sports Information Director: Mark Bockelman

**University of Virginia**
Address:    P.O. Box 3785
            Charlottesville, VA 22903
Nickname: Cavaliers
Telephone: (804) 982-5500
Football Stadium (Capacity): Scott Stadium (42,000)
President: John Casteen III
Athletic Director: Jim Copeland
Football Coach: George Welsh
Sports Information Director: Rich Murray

**Wake Forest University**
Address:    P.O. Box 7265
            Winston-Salem, NC 27109
Nickname: Demon Deacons
Telephone: (919) 759-5640
Football Stadium (Capacity): Groves Stadium (31,500)
President: Dr. Thomas K. Hearn Jr.
Athletic Director: Ron Wellman
Football Coach: Jim Caldwell
Sports Information Director: John Justus

**BIG EAST CONFERENCE**
Address:    56 Exchange Terrace
            Providence, RI 02903
Telephone: (401) 272-9108
Commissioner: Michael A. Tranghese
Asst. Comm. and Publicity Director: John Paquette

**Boston College**
Address: Chestnut Hill, MA 02167
Nickname: Eagles
Telephone: (617) 552-3004
Football Stadium (Capacity): Alumni Stadium (32,000)
President: J. Donald Monan, S.J.
Athletic Director: Chet Gladchuk
Football Coach: Tom Coughlin
Sports Information Director: Reid Oslin

**University of Miami**
Address:    5821 San Amaro Drive
            Coral Gables, FL 33146
Nickname: Hurricanes
Telephone: (305) 284-3244
Football Stadium (Capacity): Orange Bowl (74,712)
President: Edward Foote
Athletic Director: TBA
Football Coach: Dennis Erickson
Sports Information Director: Linda Venzon

# College Football Directory (Cont.)

**University of Pittsburgh**
Address:   Dept. of Athletics, P.O. Box 7436
             Pittsburgh, PA 15213
Nickname: Panthers
Telephone: (412) 648-8240
Football Stadium (Capacity): Pitt Stadium (56,500)
Chancellor: J. Dennis O'Connor
Athletic Director: Oval Jaynes
Football Coach: Johnny Majors
Sports Information Director: Ron Wahl

**Rutgers University**
Address: Piscataway, NJ 08855
Nickname: Scarlet Knights
Telephone: (908) 932-4200
Football Stadium (Capacity): Giants Stadium (76,000)
President: Dr. Francis L. Lawrence
Athletic Director: Frederick Gruninger
Football Coach: Doug Graber
Sports Media Relations Director: Bob Smith

**Syracuse University**
Address:   Manley Field House
             Syracuse, NY 13244
Nickname: Orangemen
Telephone: (315) 443-2608
Football Stadium (Capacity): Carrier Dome (50,000)
Chancellor: Dr. Kenneth A. Shaw
Athletic Director: Jake Crouthamel
Football Coach: Paul Pasqualoni
Sports Information Director: Larry Kimball

**Temple University**
Address:   McGonigle Hall
             Philadelphia, PA 19122
Nickname: Owls
Telephone: (215) 204-7445
Football Stadium (Capacity): Veterans Stadium
(66,592)
President: Peter Liacouras
Athletic Director: Charles Theokas
Football Coach: Ron Dickerson
Sports Information Director: Al Shrier

**Virginia Tech**
Address:   Jamerson Athletic Center
             Blacksburg, VA 24063-0158
Nickname: Hokies
Telephone: (703) 231-6726
Football Stadium (Capacity): Lane Stadium-Worsham
Field (51,000)
President: Dr. James McComas
Athletic Director: David Braine
Football Coach: Frank Beamer
Sports Information Director: Dave Smith

**West Virginia University**
Address:   P.O. Box 0877
             Morgantown, WV 26507
Nickname: Mountaineers
Telephone: (304) 293-2821
Football Stadium (Capacity): Mountaineer Field
(63,500)
President: Neil Bucklew
Athletic Director: Ed Pastilong
Football Coach: Don Nehlen
Sports Information Director: Shelly Poe

**BIG EIGHT CONFERENCE**
Address:   104 West Ninth Street
             Kansas City, MO 64105
Telephone: (816) 471-5088
Commissioner: Carl C. James
Publicity Director: Jeff Bollig

**University of Colorado**
Address:   Campus Box 368
             Boulder, CO 80309
Nickname: Buffaloes
Telephone: (303) 492-5626
Football Stadium (Capacity): Folsom Field (51,748)
President: Dr. Judith Albino
Athletic Director: Bill Marolt
Football Coach: Bill McCartney
Sports Information Director: David Plati

**Iowa State University**
Address:   Olsen Building
             Ames, IA 50011
Nickname: Cyclones
Telephone: (515) 294-3372
Football Stadium (Capacity): Cyclone Stadium-Jack
Trice Field (50,000)
President: Dr. Martin C. Jischke
Athletic Director: TBA
Football Coach: Jim Walden
Director of Media Relations: Dave Starr

**University of Kansas**
Address:   Allen Field House
             Lawrence, KS 66045
Nickname: Jayhawks
Telephone: (913) 864-3417
Football Stadium (Capacity): Memorial Stadium (50,250)
Chancellor: Dr. Gene Budig
Athletic Director: Dr. Bob Fredrick
Football Coach: Glen Mason
Sports Information Director: Doug Vance

**Kansas State University**
Address: Manhattan, KS 66502-3355
Nickname: Wildcats
Telephone: (913) 532-6735
Football Stadium (Capacity): KSU Stadium (42,000)
President: Dr. John Wefald
Athletic Director: TBA
Football Coach: Bill Snyder
Sports Information Director: Ben Boyle

# College Football Directory (Cont.)

**University of Missouri**
Address: P.O. Box 677
Columbia, MO 65205
Nickname: Tigers
Telephone: (314) 882-2121
Football Stadium (Capacity): Faurot Field (62,000)
Chancellor: Charles Kiesler
Athletic Director: Dan Devine
Football Coach: Bob Stull
Sports Information Director: Bob Brendel

**University of Nebraska**
Address: 116 South Stadium
Lincoln, NE 68588
Nickname: Cornhuskers
Telephone: (402) 472-7211
Football Stadium (Capacity): Memorial Stadium (73,650)
President: Dr. Martin Massengale
Athletic Director: Bill Byrne
Football Coach: Tom Osborne
Sports Information Director: Don Bryant

**University of Oklahoma**
Address: 180 W. Brooks
Norman, OK 73019
Nickname: Sooners
Telephone: (405) 325-8231
Football Stadium (Capacity): Oklahoma Memorial Stadium-Owen Field (75,004)
President: Richard Van Horn
Athletic Director: Donnie Duncan
Football Coach: Gary Gibbs
Sports Information Director: Mike Prusinski

**Oklahoma State University**
Address: 202 Gallagher-Iba Arena
Stillwater, OK 74078
Nickname: Cowboys
Telephone: (405) 744-5749
Football Stadium (Capacity): Lewis Field (50,440)
President: Dr. John R. Campbell
Athletic Director: TBA
Football Coach: Pat Jones
Sports Information Director: Steve Buzzard

**BIG TEN CONFERENCE**
Address: 1500 West Higgins Road
Park Ridge, IL 60068
Telephone: (708) 696-1010
Commissioner: James E. Delany
Assistant Commissioner: Mark Rudner

**University of Illinois**
Address: 115 Assembly Hall
1800 S. First Street
Champaign, IL 61820
Nickname: Fighting Illini
Telephone: (217) 333-1390
Football Stadium (Capacity): Memorial Stadium (69,000)
President: Dr. Stanley O. Ikenberry
Athletic Director: Ron Guenther
Football Coach: Lou Tepper
Sports Information Director: Mike Pearson

**Indiana University**
Address: 17th Street and Fee Lane/Assembly Hall
Bloomington, IN 47405
Nickname: Hoosiers
Telephone: (812) 855-2421
Football Stadium (Capacity): Memorial Stadium (52,354)
President: Thomas Ehrlich
Athletic Director: Clarence Doninger
Football Coach: Bill Mallory
Sports Information Director: Kit Klingelhoffer

**University of Iowa**
Address: 205 Carver-Hawkeye Arena
Iowa City, IA 52242
Nickname: Hawkeyes
Telephone: (319) 335-9411
Football Stadium (Capacity): Kinnick Stadium (70,311)
President: Hunter Rawlings III
Athletic Director: Robert Bowlsby
Football Coach: Hayden Fry
Sports Information Director: TBA

**University of Michigan**
Address: 1000 S. State Street
Ann Arbor, MI 48109-2201
Nickname: Wolverines
Telephone: (313) 763-4423
Football Stadium (Capacity): Michigan Stadium (102,501)
President: James Duderstadt
Athletic Director: TBA
Football Coach: Gary Moeller
Sports Information Director: Bruce Madej

**Michigan State University**
Address: East Lansing, MI 48824
Nickname: Spartans
Telephone: (517) 355-2271
Football Stadium (Capacity): Spartan Stadium (76,000)
President: Dr. Gordon Guyer
Athletic Director: Merrily Dean Baker
Football Coach: George Perles
Sports Information Director: Ken Hoffman

## University of Minnesota

Address:   516 15th Avenue S.E.
           Minneapolis, MN 55455
Nickname: Golden Gophers
Telephone: (612) 625-5000
Football Stadium (Capacity): Hubert H. Humphrey
Metrodome (63,699)
President: Dr. Nils Hasselmo
Athletic Director: McKinley Boston
Football Coach: Jim Wacker
Sports Information Director: Bob Peterson

## Northwestern University

Address:   1501 Central Street
           Evanston, IL 60208
Nickname: Wildcats
Telephone: (708) 491-7503
Football Stadium (Capacity): Dyche Stadium (49,256)
President: Dr. Arnold Weber
Athletic Director: Bill Foster (interim)
Football Coach: Gary Barnett
Director of Media Services: TBA

## Ohio State University

Address:   410 Woody Hayes Drive
           Columbus, OH 43210
Nickname: Buckeyes
Telephone: (614) 292-6861
Football Stadium (Capacity): Ohio Stadium (91,470)
President: Dr. E. Gordon Gee
Athletic Director: Jim Jones
Football Coach: John Cooper
Sports Information Director: Steve Snapp

## Penn State University

Address:   Recreation Building
           University Park, PA 16802
Nickname: Nittany Lions
Telephone: (814) 865-1757
Football Stadium (Capacity): Beaver Stadium
(93,000)
President: Joab Thomas
Athletic Director: Jim Tarman
Football Coach: Joe Paterno
Sports Information Director: Budd Thalman

## Purdue University

Address:   Mackey Arena
           West Lafayette, IN 47907
Nickname: Boilermakers
Telephone: (317) 494-4600
Football Stadium (Capacity): Ross-Ade Stadium
(67,861)
President: Dr. Steven C. Beering
Athletic Director: Morgan J. Burke
Football Coach: Jim Colletto
Sports Information Director: Mark Adams

## University of Wisconsin

Address:   1440 Monroe Street
           Madison, WI 53711
Nickname: Badgers
Telephone: (608) 262-1811
Football Stadium (Capacity): Camp Randall Stadium
(77,745)
Chancellor: David Ward (interim)
Athletic Director: Pat Richter
Football Coach: Barry Alvarez
Sports Information Director: Steve Malchow

## PACIFIC-10 CONFERENCE

Address:   800 S. Broadway, Suite 400
           Walnut Creek, CA 94596
Telephone: (510) 932-4411
Commissioner: Thomas C. Hansen
Publicity Director: Jim Muldoon

## University of Arizona

Address:   McKale Center
           Tucson, AZ 85721
Nickname: Wildcats
Telephone: (602) 621-4163
Football Stadium (Capacity): Arizona Stadium (56,197)
President: Manuel Pacheco
Athletic Director: Dr. Cedric Dempsey
Football Coach: Dick Tomey
Sports Information Director: Butch Henry

## Arizona State University

Address: Tempe, AZ 85287-2505
Nickname: Sun Devils
Telephone: (602) 965-6592
Football Stadium (Capacity): Sun Devil Stadium
(73,656)
President: Dr. Lattie F. Coor
Athletic Director: Charles Harris
Football Coach: Bruce Snyder
Sports Information Director: Mark Brand

## University of California

Address: Berkeley, CA 94720
Nickname: Golden Bears
Telephone: (510) 642-5363
Football Stadium (Capacity): Memorial Stadium (75,662)
Chancellor: Chang-Lin Tien
Athletic Director: Robert L. Bockrath
Football Coach: Keith Gilbertson
Sports Information Director: Kevin Reneau

## University of California at Los Angeles

Address:   405 Hilgard Avenue
           Los Angeles, CA 90024
Nickname: Bruins
Telephone: (310) 206-6831
Football Stadium (Capacity): Rose Bowl (102,083)
Chancellor: Dr. Charles Young
Athletic Director: Peter T. Dalis
Football Coach: Terry Donahue
Sports Information Director: Marc Dellins

## University of Oregon
Address:   Casanova Athletic Center
           2727 Leo Harris Parkway
           Eugene, OR 97401
Nickname: Ducks
Telephone: (503) 346-4481
Football Stadium (Capacity): Autzen Stadium
(41,698)
President: Myles Brand
Athletic Director: Rich Brooks
Football Coach: Rich Brooks
Sports Information Director: Steve Hellyer

## Oregon State University
Address:   Gill Coliseum
           Corvallis, OR 97331
Nickname: Beavers
Telephone: (503) 737-3720
Football Stadium (Capacity): Parker Stadium (35,362)
President: Dr. John V. Bryne
Athletic Director: Dutch Baughman
Football Coach: Jerry Pettibone
Sports Information Director: Hal Cowan

## University of Southern California
Address: Los Angeles, CA 90089
Nickname: Trojans
Telephone: (213) 740-8480
Football Stadium (Capacity): Los Angeles Memorial
Coliseum (92,516)
President: Dr. Steven Sample
Athletic Director: Mike Garrett
Football Coach: John Robinson
Sports Information Director: Tim Tessalone

## Stanford University
Address: Stanford, CA 94305
Nickname: Cardinal
Telephone: (415) 723-4418
Football Stadium (Capacity): Stanford Stadium
(86,019)
President: Gerhard Casper
Athletic Director: Dr. Ted Leland
Football Coach: Bill Walsh
Sports Information Director: Gary Migdol

## University of Washington
Address:   202 Graves, GC-20
           Seattle, WA 98195
Nickname: Huskies
Telephone: (206) 543-2230
Football Stadium (Capacity): Husky Stadium (72,500)
President: Dr. William P. Gerberding
Athletic Director: Barbara Hedges
Football Coach: Don James
Sports Information Director: Jim Daves

## Washington State University
Address:   107 Bohler Gym
           Pullman, WA 99164
Nickname: Cougars
Telephone: (509) 335-0270
Football Stadium (Capacity): Martin Stadium (40,000)
President: Samuel Smith
Athletic Director: Jim Livengood
Football Coach: Mike Price
Sports Information Director: Rod Commons

## SOUTHEASTERN CONFERENCE
Address:   2201 Civic Center Boulevard
           Birmingham, AL 35203
Telephone: (205) 458-3000
Commissioner: Roy Kramer
Publicity Director: Mark Whitworth

## University of Alabama
Address:   P.O. Box 870391
           Paul Bryant Drive
           Tuscaloosa, AL 35487
Nickname: Crimson Tide
Telephone: (205) 348-6084
Football Stadium (Capacity): Bryant-Denny Stadium
(70,123)
President: Dr. Roger Sayers
Athletic Director: Cecil "Hootie" Ingram
Football Coach: Gene Stallings
Sports Information Director: Larry White

## University of Arkansas
Address:   Broyles Athletic Complex
           P.O. Box 7777
           Fayetteville, AR 72702
Nickname: Razorbacks
Telephone: (501) 575-2751
Football Stadium (Capacity): Razorback Stadium
(52,968)
Chancellor: Dr. Dan Ferritor
Athletic Director: Frank Broyles
Football Coach: Danny Ford
Sports Information Director: Rick Schaeffer

## Auburn University
Address:   P.O. Box 351
           Auburn, AL 36831-0351
Nickname: Tigers
Telephone: (205) 844-9800
Football Stadium (Capacity): Jordan Hare Stadium
(85,214)
President: Dr. William V. Muse
Athletic Director: Mike Lude
Football Coach: Terry Bowden
Sports Information Director: David Housel

## University of Florida

Address:     P.O. Box 14485
               Gainesville, FL 32604
Nickname: Gators
Telephone: (904) 375-4683 ext. 6100
Football Stadium (Capacity): Ben Hill Griffin Stadium (83,000)
President: Dr. John Lombardi
Athletic Director: Jeremy Foley
Football Coach: Steve Spurrier
Sports Information Director: John Humenik

## University of Georgia

Address:     P.O. Box 1472
               Athens, GA 30613
Nickname: Bulldogs
Telephone: (706) 542-1621
Football Stadium (Capacity): Sanford Stadium (85,434)
President: Dr. Charles Knapp
Athletic Director: Vince Dooley
Football Coach: Ray Goff
Sports Information Director: Claude Felton

## University of Kentucky

Address:     Commonwealth Stadium
               Lexington, KY 40506
Nickname: Wildcats
Telephone: (606) 257-3838
Football Stadium (Capacity): Commonwealth Stadium (57,800)
President: Dr. Charles Wethington Jr.
Athletic Director: C. M. Newton
Football Coach: Bill Curry
Football Information Director: Joey Howard

## Louisiana State University

Address: Baton Rouge, LA 70894
Nickname: Fighting Tigers
Telephone: (504) 388-8226
Football Stadium (Capacity): Tiger Stadium (80,140)
Chancellor: Dr. William (Bud) Davis
Athletic Director: Joe Dean
Football Coach: Curley Hallman
Sports Information Director: Herb Vincent

## University of Mississippi

Address:     P.O. Box 217
               University, MS 38677
Nickname: Rebels
Telephone: (601) 232-7522
Football Stadium (Capacity): Vaught-Hemingway Stadium (42,577)
Chancellor: Dr. R. Gerald Turner
Athletic Director: Warner Alford
Football Coach: Billy Brewer
Sports Information Director: Langston Rogers

## Mississippi State University

Address:     P.O. Drawer 5308
               Mississippi St., MS 39762
Nickname: Bulldogs
Telephone: (601) 325-2703
Football Stadium (Capacity): Scott Field (41,200)
President: Dr. Donald Zacharias
Athletic Director: Larry Templeton
Football Coach: Jackie Sherrill
Assistant Athletic Director and Media Relations Director: Mike Nemeth

## University of South Carolina

Address:     Rex Enright Athletic Center
               1300 Rosewood Drive
               Columbia, SC 29208
Nickname: Gamecocks
Telephone: (803) 777-5204
Football Stadium (Capacity): Williams-Brice Stadium (72,400)
President: Dr. John Palms
Athletic Director: Dr. Mike McGee
Football Coach: Sparky Woods
Sports Information Director: Kerry Tharp

## University of Tennessee

Address:     P.O. Box 15016
               Knoxville, TN 37901
Nickname: Volunteers
Telephone: (615) 974-1212
Football Stadium (Capacity): Neyland Stadium (91,110)
President: Dr. Joseph E. Johnson
Athletic Director: Doug Dickey
Football Coach: Phil Fulmer
Sports Information Director: Bud Ford

## Vanderbilt University

Address:     P.O. Box 120158
               Nashville, TN 37212
Nickname: Commodores
Telephone: (615) 322-4121
Football Stadium (Capacity): Vanderbilt Stadium (41,000)
Chancellor: Joe B. Wyatt
Athletic Director: Paul Hoolahan
Football Coach: Gerry DiNardo
Sports Information Director: Tony Neely

## SOUTHWEST ATHLETIC CONFERENCE

Address:     P.O. Box 569420
               Dallas, TX 75356
Telephone: (214) 634-7353
Commissioner: Steven J. Hatchell
Publicity Director: Bo Carter

## Baylor University
Address:    3031 Dutton
            Waco, TX 76711
Nickname: Bears
Telephone: (817) 755-1234
Football Stadium (Capacity): Floyd Casey Stadium
(48,500)
President: Dr. Herbert H. Reynolds
Athletic Director: Grant Teaff
Football Coach: Chuck Reedy
Sports Information Director: Maxey Parrish

## University of Houston
Address:    3855 Holman
            Houston, TX 77204-5121
Nickname: Cougars
Telephone: (713) 743-9404
Football Stadium (Capacity): Astrodome (60,000)
President: Dr. James H. Pickering
Athletic Director: Bill Carr
Football Coach: TBA
Sports Information Director: Ted Nance

## Rice University
Address:    P.O. Box 1892
            Houston, TX 77251
Nickname: Owls
Telephone: (713) 527-4034
Football Stadium (Capacity): Rice Stadium (70,000)
President: TBA
Athletic Director: Bobby May
Football Coach: Fred Goldsmith
Sports Information Director: Bill Cousins

## Southern Methodist University
Address:    SMU Box 216
            Dallas, TX 75275
Nickname: Mustangs
Telephone: (214) 768-2883
Football Stadium (Capacity): Ownby Stadium
(23,783)
President: A. Kenneth Pye
Athletic Director: Forrest Gregg
Football Coach: Tom Rossley
Sports Information Director: Ed Wisneski

## University of Texas
Address:    P.O. Box 7399
            Austin, TX 78713
Nickname: Longhorns
Telephone: (512) 471-7437
Football Stadium (Capacity): Memorial Stadium
(77,809)
President: Dr. Robert Berdahl
Athletic Director: DeLoss Dodds
Football Coach: John Mackovic
Sports Information Director: Bill Little

## Texas A&M University
Address:    Joe Routt Boulevard
            College Station, TX 77843-1228
Nickname: Aggies
Telephone: (409) 845-3218
Football Stadium (Capacity): Kyle Field (70,210)
President: Dr. William H. Mobley
Athletic Director: Wally Groff (interim)
Football Coach: R. C. Slocum
Sports Information Director: Alan Cannon

## Texas Christian University
Address:    P.O. Box 32924
            Fort Worth, TX 76129
Nickname: Horned Frogs
Telephone: (817) 921-7969
Football Stadium (Capacity): Amon G. Carter Stadium
(46,000)
Chancellor: Dr. William E. Tucker
Athletic Director: Frank Windegger
Football Coach: Pat Sullivan
Sports Information Director: Glen Stone

## Texas Tech University
Address:    Box 43021
            Lubbock, TX 79409
Nickname: Red Raiders
Telephone: (806) 742-2770
Football Stadium (Capacity): Jones Stadium (50,500)
President: Dr. Robert Lawless
Athletic Director: T. Jones
Football Coach: Spike Dykes
Sports Information Director: Joe Hornaday

## WESTERN ATHLETIC CONFERENCE
Address:    14 West Dry Creek Circle
            Littleton, CO 80120
Telephone: (303) 795-1962
Commissioner: Dr. Joe Kearney
Publicity Director: Jeff Hurd

## Air Force
Address: Colorado Springs, CO 80840-9500
Nickname: Falcons
Telephone: (719) 472-2313
Football Stadium (Capacity): Falcon Stadium (53,000)
Superintendent: Lt. Gen. Bradley C. Hosmer
Athletic Director: Col. Kenneth L. Schweitzer
Football Coach: Fisher DeBerry
Sports Information Director: Dave Kellogg

## Brigham Young University
Address:    60 Smith Field House
            Provo, UT 84602
Nickname: Cougars
Telephone: (801) 378-4910
Football Stadium (Capacity): Cougar Stadium (65,000)
President: Rex Lee
Athletic Director: Dr. Glen Tuckett
Football Coach: LaVell Edwards
Sports Information Director: Ralph Zobell

# College Football Directory (Cont.)

**Colorado State University**
Address:    Moby Arena
            Fort Collins, CO 80523
Nickname: Rams
Telephone: (303) 491-5067
Football Stadium (Capacity): Hughes Stadium (30,000)
President: Dr. Albert C. Yates
Athletic Director: Corey Johnson
Football Coach: Sonny Lubick
Sports Information Director: Gary Ozzello

**Fresno State University**
Address:    5305 N. Campus Drive Rm. 153
            Fresno, CA 93740
Nickname: Bulldogs
Telephone: (209) 278-2509
Football Stadium (Capacity): Bulldog Stadium (41,041)
President: Dr. John D. Welty
Athletic Director: Dr. Gary Cunningham
Football Coach: Jim Sweeney
Sports Information Director: Scott Johnson

**University of Hawaii**
Address:    1337 Lower Campus Road
            Honolulu, HI 96822-2370
Nickname: Rainbow Warriors
Telephone: (808) 956-7523
Football Stadium (Capacity): Aloha Stadium (50,000)
President: Kenneth P. Mortimer
Athletic Director: TBA
Football Coach: Bob Wagner
Sports Information Director: Ed Inouye

**University of New Mexico**
Address:    1414 University S.E.
            Albuquerque, NM 87131
Nickname: Lobos
Telephone: (505) 277-2026
Football Stadium (Capacity): University Stadium (30,646)
President: Dr. Richard Peck
Athletic Director: Rudy Davalos
Football Coach: Dennis Franchione
Sports Information Director: Greg Remington

**San Diego State University**
Address: San Diego, CA 92182
Nickname: Aztecs
Telephone: (619) 594-5547
Football Stadium (Capacity): San Diego Jack Murphy Stadium (60,409)
President: Dr. Thomas B. Day
Athletic Director: Dr. Fred Miller
Football Coach: Al Luginbill
Sports Information Director: John Rosenthal

**University of Texas at El Paso**
Address:    500 West University Avenue
            El Paso, TX 79968
Nickname: Miners
Telephone: (915) 747-5330
Football Stadium (Capacity): Sun Bowl (52,000)
President: Dr. Diana Natalicio
Athletic Director: TBA
Football Coach: David Lee
Sports Information Director: Eddie Mullens

**University of Utah**
Address:    Huntsman Center
            Salt Lake City, UT 84112
Nickname: Utes
Telephone: (801) 581-3510
Football Stadium (Capacity): Rice Stadium (32,500)
President: Dr. Arthur K. Smith
Athletic Director: Dr. Chris Hill
Football Coach: Ron McBride
Sports Information Director: Liz Abel

**University of Wyoming**
Address:    P.O. Box 3414
            Laramie, WY 82071-3414
Nickname: Cowboys
Telephone: (307) 766-2292
Football Stadium (Capacity): War Memorial Stadium (33,500)
President: Terry Roark
Athletic Director: Paul Roach
Football Coach: Joe Tiller
Sports Information Director: Kevin McKinney

## Independents

**Army**
Address: West Point, NY 10996
Nickname: Cadets/Black Knights
Telephone: (914) 938-3303
Football Stadium (Capacity): Michie Stadium (39,929)
Superintendent: Lt. Gen. Howard D. Graves
Athletic Director: Col. Al Vanderbush
Football Coach: Bob Sutton
Sports Information Director: Bob Kinney

**University of Cincinnati**
Address: Cincinnati, OH 45221
Nickname: Bearcats
Telephone: (513) 556-5191
Football Stadium (Capacity): Nippert Stadium (35,000)
President: Joseph Steger
Athletic Director: Rick Taylor
Football Coach: Tim Murphy
Sports Information Director: Tom Hathaway

## East Carolina University
Address: Greenville, NC 27858
Nickname: Pirates
Telephone: (919) 757-4522
Football Stadium (Capacity): Ficklen Stadium (35,000)
Chancellor: Dr. Richard R. Eakin
Athletic Director: Dave Hart, Jr.
Football Coach: Steve Logan
Sports Information Director: Charles Bloom

## University of Louisville
Address: Louisville, KY 40292
Nickname: Cardinals
Telephone: (502) 588-6581
Football Stadium (Capacity): Cardinal Stadium (35,500)
President: Dr. Donald Swain
Athletic Director: William Olsen
Football Coach: Howard Schnellenberger
Sports Information Director: Kenny Klein

## Memphis State University
Address: Memphis, TN 38152
Nickname: Tigers
Telephone: (901) 678-2337
Football Stadium (Capacity): Liberty Bowl (62,380)
President: Dr. V. Lane Rawlins
Athletic Director: Charles Cavagnaro
Football Coach: Chuck Stobart
Assistant Athletic Director for Communication: Bob Winn

## Navy
Address: Annapolis, MD 21402
Nickname: Midshipmen
Telephone: (410) 268-6226
Football Stadium (Capacity): Navy-Marine Corps Memorial Stadium (30,000)
Superintendent: Rear Adm. Thomas C. Lynch
Athletic Director: Jack Lengyel
Football Coach: George Chaump
Sports Information Director: Thomas Bates

## University of Notre Dame
Address: Notre Dame, IN 46556
Nickname: Fighting Irish
Telephone: (219) 631-7516
Football Stadium (Capacity): Notre Dame Stadium (59,075)
President: Rev. Edward A. Malloy, C.S.C.
Athletic Director: Dick Rosenthal
Football Coach: Lou Holtz
Sports Information Director: John Heisler

## University of Southern Mississippi
Address:   Box 5161
           Hattiesburg, MS 39406
Nickname: Golden Eagles
Telephone: (601) 266-4503
Football Stadium (Capacity): M. M. Roberts Stadium (33,000)
President: Dr. Aubrey K. Lucas
Athletic Director: Bill McLellan
Football Coach: Jeff Bower
Sports Information Director: Regiel Napier

## Tulane University
Address: New Orleans, LA 70118
Nickname: Green Wave
Telephone: (504) 865-5506
Football Stadium (Cap.): Louisiana Superdome (69,065)
President: Dr. Eamon Kelly
Athletic Director: Dr. Kevin White
Football Coach: Buddy Teevens
Sports Information Director: Lenny Vangilder

## University of Tulsa
Address:   600 S. College
           Tulsa, OK 74104-3189
Nickname: Golden Hurricane
Telephone: (918) 631-2395
Football Stadium (Capacity): Skelley Stadium (40,385)
President: Dr. Robert H. Donaldson
Athletic Director: Rick Dickson
Football Coach: Dave Rader
Sports Information Director: Don Tomkalski

## Down and Out

After three tumultuous seasons, University of Houston football coach John Jenkins resigned in April amid allegations of NCAA rules infractions. Several Cougar players and two former assistant coaches, both of whom had been fired by Jenkins, alleged that he violated rules on the limits on practice time. One of the assistants also accused Jenkins of making an improper payment to a recruit. After his resignation Jenkins continued to deny the charges, but he did confirm reports that he had spliced footage of topless women into videotapes of his team's practices. Jenkins called this practice an "innocent attention-getter."

Bad taste came easily to Jenkins, whose wins at Houston included two in which the Cougars ran up scores of 84–21 and 73–3. But his departure was no doubt hastened by the fact that his record fell from 10–1 his first season to 4–7 in each of the last two years.

Jenkins penchant for secrecy contributed to his downfall as well. He refused to share details of his run-and-shoot offense with high school coaches, who responded by sending their players elsewhere. When the talent recruited by his predecessor, Jack Pardee, dried up, Jenkins's Cougars suffered the consequences.

This episode is another black eye for the Southwest Conference. Its new commisssioner, Steve Hatchell, has vowed to revive a league that has been bufeted by cheating scandals, poor attendance and rumors that Texas and Texas A&M will follow Arkansas's lead and leave for other conferences. Hatchell's task will be made a bit easier by the departure of an operator like Jenkins.